WELL MAY WE SAY ...

WELL
MAY
WE SAY ...
THE
SPEECHES
THAT
MADE
AUSTRALIA

Edited by
Sally Warhaft

Published by Black Inc.,
an imprint of Schwartz Publishing Pty Ltd

Level 5, 289 Flinders Lane
Melbourne Victoria 3000 Australia
email: enquiries@blackincbooks.com
http://www.blackincbooks.com

The National Library of Australia Cataloguing-in-Publication entry:

Well may we say: the speeches that made Australia.

ISBN 1 86395 277 2.

1. Speeches, addresses, etc., Australian. I. Warhaft, Sally.

A825.0108

Book design: Thomas Deverall

Printed in Australia by Griffin Press.

Contents

OPENINGS AND COMMENCEMENTS

LAST WORDS AND FAREWELLS

Introduction

Sally Warhaft

A man has died. In the bush, his friend digs a grave and murmurs to himself, 'Theer oughter be somethin' sed ... tain't right to put 'im under like a dog. There oughter be some sort o' sarmin.'

Henry Lawson's classic tale *The Bush Undertaker* catches an abiding tension in Australian life: the need to say things, the sensation that it's not quite in us to do so. As he fills the grave to the brim and solicitously shapes the mound with his spade, the undertaker strains to find a suitable gravity:

> Once or twice he muttered the words: 'I am the rassaraction.' As he laid the tools quietly aside, and stood at the head of the grave, he was evidently trying to remember the something that ought to be said. He removed his hat, placed it carefully on the grass, held his hands out from his sides and a little to the front, drew a long deep breath, and said with a solemnity that greatly disturbed Five Bob: 'Hashes ter hashes, dus ter dus, Brummy – an' – an' in hopes of a great an' gerlorious rassaraction!'

Australians do not consider theirs an oral culture. Talk, we believe, is a substitute for action rather than a catalyst for it. The expression 'fine words' is usually meant ironically; 'rhetoric' is almost always preceded by the adjective 'empty'. Classically, the Australian is economical in speech, and minimal in elocution. As Hector Dinning put it: 'The Australian often speaks without opening his lips at all, through an immobile slit, and in extreme cases through closed teeth,' thus accounting for the nasal inflection – 'the sound has to emerge from somewhere.' We lose our way in words; we jumble and fumble them. Native laconicism, a kind of objection to formality, sits uneasily with the idea of splendid oratory, at least as it is usually imagined. Where we must speak in public at all, it is considered best to be low-key, sometimes to the point of dreary monotony. 'For its small population,' Ross Campbell once complained, 'this country produces a remarkable number of speakers whose tediousness is of world class.' Of one notoriously leaden parliamentary performer, Mungo MacCallum wrote, 'No one ever seems to listen to what he says; and even after a few minutes, he gives the impression that, since he started speaking, amoebas have evolved into vertebrates, crawled out of the ocean, stood upright, and invented the wheel and the atomic bomb.'

Yet, associated with almost every significant twist and turn of Australian history, there have been speeches, some of them great. Perhaps, in a country where the majority prefer to be thrifty with their expression, to be listeners, there are more opportunities for those with rhetorical talent. Perhaps, in a culture that tends to be energetically critical of the big-noting and the high-falutin', when something does touch us, we are genuinely moved, rather than simply thinking that we should be. This collection traces that tradition, telling Australia's story through the speeches that mattered; some from the moment they were delivered, and others that in hindsight reveal their cultural importance, representing essential styles of rhetoric and significant markers of Australian history. Paul Hasluck described Thomas Carlyle's quotation 'Speech is of time' – used by Sir Robert Menzies as the title for his own book of speeches – as putting 'speech-making in its place as the product of a day against the background of eternity'. Great speeches stand the test of time and can tell us in a relatively simple way the stories of our past and present. They are surprisingly intimate, relying as they do on the voice of a single person.

A book of this kind faces a besetting difficulty. Speeches are supposed to be seen and heard rather than read. As one prime minister, Billy Hughes, remarked:

But words are not sufficient in themselves: so much depends upon the manner of delivery. 'Delivery!' said Demosthenes. 'Delivery!' said Danton. Without this delivery all speech is dead – the words are but as sounding brass and a tinkling cymbal. Speech, gesture, everything – even the very blood that suffuses the face of the man who seeks to warm and inspire his audience – nothing but the whole man suffices.

Yet the same might be said of Shakespeare. Like great theatre, powerful and persuasive oratory can also come to the ears through the eyes – the mind's eye of the reader – and this is not an experience to be dismissed. In some respects speeches repay quiet contemplation as much as eager listening. Imagination and curiosity can conquer the lapse of time: picture Sydney's Baptist Chapel – a Grecian-style specimen of colonial architecture built in 1838 – where the congregation of Christian colonists took in 'an assault on their conscience' delivered from the pulpit to the pews by Reverend John Saunders; or the sumptuous banquet in Queen's Hall – the grand building which filled the space between Victoria's political chambers and the parliamentary library – where seventy-five-year-old Sir Henry Parkes in 1890 sold to his audience the prospect of a continent nation; or the dimly lit, lavishly appointed chamber of the first federal legislative assembly where Alfred Deakin delivered his *magnum opus* on the judiciary bill to the earnest attention of both sides of the House.

We can recall more recent scenes ourselves – perhaps we were there, or were witness thanks to the sciences of amplification and communications. Modern speakers enjoy numerous advantages over their predecessors. A booming voice – whether endowed by nature or learned by tuition – has ceased to be a prerequisite. The radio studio allows carefully composed speeches to be broadcast to audiences of millions; television enlists imagery in the service of words. Political speech-writer Graham Freudenberg argued that television 'reduced to a total fiction the idea of a policy speech being a speech which is actually delivered ... the speech is reduced to the barest outline of the proposed program with a few rhetorical flourishes; the effect – the entrance of the leader, the cheers, the contrived enthusiasm – is everything.' When Gough Whitlam said 'It's time' in the 1972 federal election campaign, he 'carried the practice to its highest pitch'.

Modern communications technology revolutionised another dimension of speechmaking. The first speech of Governor Arthur Phillip at Sydney Cove was made at 11 a.m. on 7 February 1788. An officer recorded that 'the soldiers marched with music, playing drums and fifes, and formed a circle round the whole of the convict men and women who were collected together.' A camp table was set up and two red leather cases containing the sealed commissions investing Phillip as governor and commander-in-chief of the settlement were read aloud by the judge advocate, Captain Collins. Following the proclamations and formalities, the governor addressed his audience. It was not a pompous sermon but a stern haranguing: after a night of drink and debauchery at the arrival of the women, the governor was wresting back discipline and order. The convicts were 'incorrigible' and 'idle', and would now be set to work; attempts 'to get into the women's tents of a night' would be met with gunfire. Phillip gave himself no airs – his words were 'extremely well adapted to the people he had to govern' – and he had the advantage of what was literally a captive audience. Yet his words, as distinct from their tone, went largely unrecorded, like speeches beyond number since.

By contrast, when Whitlam emerged on the steps of Canberra's old Parliament House on Remembrance Day, 1975 and uttered his famous retort to the Governor-General's proclamation of his dismissal, the cameras were history's witness. Once the most perishable of items, the speech can now achieve a startling permanence. Perhaps politicians have always had an unfair advantage in this respect, because the formal apparatus constituted for chronicling their addresses – Hansard – has long spared them even the labour of listening to one another (one of the first cartoons of federal parliament in session, in Melbourne *Punch*, captured this exquisitely, showing Hugh Mahon reading the Sydney *Referee*, Austin Chapman devouring a local paper, George Reid snoozing contentedly on the Opposition front bench and King O'Malley stretched out on the backbench polishing off a novel). Radio, television and recording devices have since become a sort of Hansard of the everyday.

Because words are their stock in trade, and because these words have tended to be documented, politicians occupy a fair proportion of *Well May We Say*. We have Alfred Deakin's historic 1898 address to the Australian Natives' Association, delivered without text or notes, thanks to the accurate record of a shorthand writer – who compelled the board of the association to pay three guineas for the transcript. Journalists were present to hear the young Daniel Denihey's acerbic assault on W.C. Wentworth's 'bunyip aristocracy', delivered in 1854, in a voice 'low and sweet … magical in making its way to the hearts and sympathies of his listeners'. When the radical Irishman Hugh Mahon – 'whose snobbish coldness of demeanour would make a snake shudder' – caused a sensation in 1920 with his protest against 'British tyranny', the transcript reached parliament and led to his subsequent expulsion. Sometimes records remain that describe how speeches were delivered as well as giving us the words themselves. When Dame Enid Lyons rose to give her maiden speech to the federal parliament in 1943 – the first Australian woman to do so – she held six small cards of handwritten notes, now held in the National Library. The three or four phrases on each card were her only prompts for this historic address.

Several Australian leaders of the twentieth century have achieved international renown for their public speaking, each in a different way. Alfred Deakin was one of several delegates appointed to travel to England in 1900 to see through the passing of Australia's constitution in the imperial parliament. He defended it 'to the last comma' in a series of addresses to the British public. Deakin was a masterful orator, who recommended 'working the crowd'. At one public meeting he waited quietly for his turn at the podium while a political opponent delivered 'his scanty store and a great deal of pomposity contrived … trembling, tongue-tied, a picture of helpless imbecility'. According to the age-old tradition of *kategoria* (accusation) and *apologia* (defence), Deakin knew he had his man. On another occasion, at the Barry's Reef Mechanics' Institute, Deakin had a lesson in the power of speech that he would never forget. To a crowd of sturdy miners, he had attacked his political adversary – 'as usual speaking with great impetuosity and fire'. The mood changed:

I was quivering with excitement myself, and the whole crowd appeared to be quivering too … Then my breath almost stopped. Scores of gleaming eyes and vengeful faces were fixed upon mine and turning angrily towards the man in the midst who crouched lower and lower before the approaching storm evidently about to burst upon his devoted head … It needed only a few more words and a gesture and what would have been left of him when he escaped from those sinewy arms would probably have been unrecognisable. When my heart beat again … I realised for the first time what I was doing, that I must not stop but must lead the lightning generated to strike elsewhere.

The target of this tirade 'melted into the night' at the first opportunity, then appeared at Deakin's hotel some hours later: 'Sir, you saved my life tonight and I know it. By God, Sir! You saved my life and I shall never forget it. I will never act against you again.' He never did, and Deakin never repeated his 'dangerous experiment'.

Billy Hughes made his speaking debut as a street-corner orator and later honed his skills on the Sydney docks. When he visited London during World War I, his rhetoric 'swept his hearers off their feet'. Women protested when he departed, marching with placards pleading for his return. The former British prime minister Lloyd George – with battle still clearly on his mind – wrote in the preface to Hughes' collection of war-time speeches that:

No public speeches of modern times have made such an impression on the British public as the series in this book … In public life there are many men who have trained themselves to speak well. But how many are there amongst them who can interest, persuade and move multitudes? Speeches are like shells. You may have a shell perfect in form and polish, but, through inadequate or defective propellant, failing to reach the object at which it is aimed, or, owing to some imperfection in its detonating arrangements, failing to explode if it gets there. Read these speeches and you will find that the sentences get home and that their detonating quality is of the highest order.

If Hughes spoke to arouse passions, Sir Robert Menzies often spoke to cool them, with a calm majesty that seemed to brook no argument, each address a homage to the 'rules of rhetoric – invention, arrangement, elocution, memory and delivery'. His time in the public realm straddled two periods of oratory – that of the old-fashioned statesman who spoke directly to his audience, and that of the modern communications era. Menzies was forced to become proficient not only as an after-dinner speaker, political performer and radio broadcaster, but also, towards the end of his career – and to his loathing – as a politician in the age of television. He flew in the face, in fact, of every habit of modern political speech. He expressed contempt for the practice of employing speechwriters, claiming 'an obstinate objection to having other people's words put in my mouth'. He opposed the recitation of speeches: 'People are roused and stimulated not by the reading of an essay, but by the passion and persuasion of a human being.' And he advised speakers always to omit the best line of a speech – an objection to the evolving genre of the sound-bite.

Paul Keating was of a different school. Renowned for his 'formidable mouth', he was a master of the one-liner, whose forte was taking on disputants from the podium with raw, unscripted offerings. Yet Keating was also, perhaps, the last Australian politician to deliver crafted, thoughtful and truly memorable orations. He had the advantage of a thoughtful speechwriter, Don Watson, attuned to his needs, but there was never a sense of his being a ventriloquist's tool, so thoroughly did he impress his personality on his subjects. The Redfern Park speech, given in 1992 to launch the Year of the World's Indigenous People, combined old and new traditions of oratory in incongruous ways. It was delivered in a park to a disgruntled crowd where persuasion took time; catcalls changed to murmurs of consent, then ultimately applause. And, because the cameras were present, it could strike its intended target – white Australians – while being delivered to a mainly black audience.

Many voices have been raised as a challenge to the general voicelessness of Australia's Indigenous peoples. A century and a half before Redfern Park, a scholar named Robert Lyon delivered an 'inflated, rhetorical and strangely archaic' address to a public meeting in

Guildford that uncannily anticipated Keating's. Lyon told the gathering, 'When your doom is passed, your own children, for whose sakes ye have invaded the country, will join with the disinherited offspring of those ye have slain to pour a flood of curses on your memory.' Anthropologist William Stanner dared to frame his 1968 Boyer lecture as a paradox: his speech was entitled 'The great Australian silence', and concerned the relegation of Aboriginals to 'a melancholy footnote' in our history. Three years later, Senator Neville Bonner stood up in parliament and declared, 'For far too long we have been crying out and far too few have heard us.'

The art of speechmaking is always perceived as being in decline. As long ago as 1930, Keith Hancock wrote: 'Oratory is dying; a calculating age has stabbed it to the heart with innumerable dagger-thrusts of statistics.' The truth is that it faces recurrent threats. The present obsession with communication strangely coincides with a waning in time spent reading and writing. There is less care for how we inspire, explain or persuade with the spoken word. Even in places where words are the currency, there is less speech than talk; universities, for example, have all but given up emphasising verbal presentation in their classes. Most Australian undergraduates cannot recite the second verse of the national anthem, let alone name an important speech; their American counterparts would all know something of the Gettysburg Address, at a minimum.

It is little wonder, then, that the political speech has been eclipsed as a genre. Gough Whitlam's 'It's time' lit the path for others to follow, inaugurating in Australia the era of the pre-digested 'sound-bite' designed to slip neatly into news broadcasts. Nowadays it is usually the 'doorstop' chat, rather than a speech, that produces the outstanding one-liner; calculated to seem spontaneous, but as choreographed as any policy announcement. Talkback radio then allows leaders to flaunt their common touch – while ceaselessly repeating the key phrase – by appearing to speak 'directly' to the people and eschewing the risks of a lengthy address. While speeches have always produced memorable one-liners – 'The crimson thread of kinship', 'The light on the hill', 'Life wasn't meant to be easy' – these were not in the past designed to stand alone. The content of the spoken message is today often assumed to be less important than the impression created.

Journalists review speeches like films, rarely reproducing them, and focusing on reaction over substance.

Yet it is still possible to find words knitted together with care, words that interpret our times and define our problems, that say simply and elegantly what others are thinking but are unable to express themselves. Robert Manne's Deakin Lecture in 2001, 'My country – a personal journey', was a timeless example of speech as offering, inviting listeners into the speaker's innermost thoughts. Even when we know that words are not enough, sometimes, offered humbly and humanely, they are all we have. When Sir William Deane delivered his ecumenical address and leant over the railings to place fourteen sprigs of wattle in the river at Interlaken, Switzerland, his words and actions honouring young Australians who died in a canyoning tragedy said everything that could be said; in the quiet of a dawn service a hushed crowd stood by an eternal flame, reflecting on Clive James' eloquent words on the 'bitter harvest' of war during an Anzac Day address; and in front of tens of thousands at the Telstra Dome, Jason McCartney's retirement from football put a game increasingly ruled by professionalism and populism briefly back in perspective.

Sport, in fact, while it privileges deeds over words, also feasts on rhetoric. Sporting events are characterised by opening and closing ceremonies, welcomes and farewells, while no model of Australian speechmaking is so deliberately designed to inflame passions as the coach's address. When Hawthorn's John Kennedy exhorted his charges to 'Fight for the ball!' at half-time in the 1975 VFL grand final, it did not work; the team was unable to find the performance to match its coach's stirring words. But the tradition of the coach's exhortation is eternal. One of Kennedy's audience that afternoon was his champion rover Leigh Matthews, who never stopped fighting for the ball, and went on to become one of the most successful coaches in Australian Rules Football. Likewise, when Richmond coach Tom Hafey sought to inspire his men at that season's preliminary final, he focused much of his attention on another great coach of the future, Kevin Sheedy: 'Fair dinkum mate, you've got to put your boot into the ball, you're too slow to do all this finessin'.'

While such addresses implore their hearers to action, others belong to a sub-genre of speechmaking that is particularly rich – what historian Ken Inglis describes as 'speech *as* action': Peter Lalor leaping on a stump and declaring 'Liberty!' on the eve of the Eureka Stockade – the shortest speech in this collection; Captain Francis De Groot slicing a decorative ribbon with a sword as he unofficially declares open the Sydney Harbour Bridge; and Sir Frederick Holder, slumping in the Speaker's chair, crying out 'Dreadful! Dreadful!' before collapsing insensible to the floor and becoming the only member of either house to die in the Australian parliament.

For all the well-worn distinctions drawn between 'talking' and 'doing', in fact, Australians appreciate that the best speeches are a kind of act, and that certain deeds and occasions are not simply enriched by words but need their ennobling power. Even if he could not recall the 'right words', and his straining for grandeur disturbed Five Bob, his dog, who appeared to be thinking 'enough o' that talk!', Henry Lawson's bush undertaker understood that the act of burying his mate demanded 'some sort o' sarmin'. Perhaps, then, it is not suspicion of words and rhetoric, but a cautious yearning for them. Certainly, given a significant issue, a suitable forum and a stirring speaker, Australians will take words to heart: like Five Bob the dog, they are 'all ears'.

NATION

'The crimson thread of kinship runs through us all'

Sir Henry Parkes

Speech at the Grand Federal Banquet on the occasion of the Federation Conference in Queen's Hall, Parliament House, Melbourne

6 FEBRUARY 1890

Politicians proclaiming the humbleness of their origins meet their match in Sir Henry Parkes (1815–1896), who laboured in a road gang and in a brick pit before emigrating to New South Wales from Birmingham in 1839 'seeking his fortune', and setting up as an importer of toys and other 'fancy goods' – without much success. Public life proved his forte. Parkes became active in the anti-transportation movement, and in 1848 joined other radicals in the Constitutional Association. Abandoning his failed business in favour of politics and journalism, he won his first parliamentary seat in Sydney in 1854, being destined over the next four decades to serve five terms as NSW Premier and represent nine different constituencies. It was after a well-received trip to England and America in 1881 that he began to talk seriously about federating the colonies, an idea he had considered for more than thirty years. At the age of seventy, Parkes wrote to a friend that he was retiring from politics to improve his finances: he had been bankrupt three times. Yet the drive to bind the colonies in a nation rejuvenated him. He fathered the last of his seventeen children, with his third

wife, aged seventy-seven; he is still considered 'the father of federation'. Alfred Deakin said of Parkes: 'He had always in his mind's
eye his own portrait as that of a great man, and … there was in
him the substance of the man he dressed himself to appear …'
Self-imagined or not, his persona in the series of speeches he delivered on the subject of federation was the highly effective one of
grand old man, rising above temporary exigencies and sectional
interests. There were 400 guests present at the Grand Banquet of
the Federation Conference in 1890. Henry Parkes was greeted
with sustained cheering, a standing ovation and the jubilant waving of handkerchiefs upon rising to give this reply to the toast 'A
United Australasia'.

*

Mr Gillies, my Lord, and Gentlemen:
I feel in a peculiar manner the honour of being asked to respond
to this toast. Your Prime Minister can tell you it certainly was not
of my seeking. I raised such reasonable objections as occurred to me
against taking this prominent part in our gathering tonight; but on
his representations I consented to take the responsibility of responding to the toast, which has been proposed in a speech so conciliatory,
so forcible, in certain respects so telling, and in all respects so worthy
of the honourable gentleman who submitted it for your acceptance.
[*Cheers.*] Mr Service is a citizen of whom any country in the world
might be proud. [*Hear, hear.*] He has on many occasions, under
remarkably trying circumstances, displayed that robustness of character, that clear foresight and decision, which distinguish a brave citizen.
On all occasions, so far as my knowledge enables me to form an opinion, he has been a worthy citizen of this great colony of Victoria. His
speech is one against which no complaint can be fairly raised. He has
made it under circumstances which might have awakened in some
minds an acerbity of feeling, but he has displayed none. [*Cheers.*] It
has been made under circumstances which might in some men have
produced irritation and induced them to show uncharitableness. But
none has been shown. On the whole the speech was worthy of him –
worthy of the country and worthy of our cause. [*Cheers.*] But, sir,

there was one feature in his speech which, under suggestions of friends near me, seems to be capable of humorous treatment. He has told you that certain gentlemen provided water, and the horses would not come to drink. [*Laughter.*] It was suggested by friends near me that unanimity might have been secured if something such as Sir James MacBain might have supplied – [*laughter*] – if that had been added to the water all of them would have come to drink. [*Laughter.*] Be that as it may, we are all here tonight – [*cheers*] – not only to drink of this water of national life, but to do the most we can – and I can answer for the great colony I represent – at some sacrifice to bring about the grand event which is foreshadowed in this gathering. [*Loud cheers.*]

In this human world of ours, so full of wise designs, mixed with so much failure and error, nothing is more noticeable than the delusions which lead men on to great crises. On the eve of that terrible convulsion which shattered France to atoms and startled the world, the ruling people and fashionable life went on as ever. There was marrying and giving in marriage, there were merry-makings and festivals, until the hidden elements burst out from under them and around them, and all the world wondered. No one supposed that they were standing on the brink of a terrible precipice. Without going to such examples as that, many and many is the occasion where men go on with their eyes closed, when only the few far-seeing students of philosophy and history can see. And it may be at this moment that the people of these Australian colonies are going on with their bartering, rejoicing and merrymaking – of which we know they are so fond – without being aware that they are standing on the imminence of an event that can only occur once in the whole world's history – the creation of a nation. [*Cheers.*] The creation of a nation is an event which never can recur. There cannot be two birthdays of national existence. And in this country of Australia, with such ample space, with such inviting varieties of soil and climate, with such vast stores in the hidden wealth under the soil, with such unrivalled richness on all hands, and with a people occupying that soil unequalled in all the whole range of the human race in nation-creating properties, what is there that should be impossible to those people? By the closest calculation that I have been able to make, we, including New Zealand, want 200,000 souls to make four millions of a population. If four millions of a population cannot be the basis for national life, then there never will be a national life. [*Cheers.*] Four millions of population, all of British origin, many and many thousands united to the soil by ties of birth, by ties of parentage, by ties of friendship and love, as well as by ties of marriage and ties of children, if they are not capable of making a nation – a united Australasia, why we are not fit hardly to occupy this bounteous country. [*Applause.*]

But if anyone supposes those are mere flights of imagination, let us come down to the barest possible calculation of facts. A hundred years ago the continent was occupied by a despairing group of outcast persons of British origin, and that British origin speaks volumes in every step of our calculation. Forty years ago the colony of Victoria had no existence. I had been an inhabitant of Australia ten years before Victoria was born; I was an inhabitant of Australia, and had a seat in a Legislature before the colony of Queensland was born. There is, however, no man in Victoria or Queensland who more rejoiced in their prosperous career, and in the grand results that followed, than I did. [*Cheers.*] These two colonies, the great and splendid, if at all less splendid, on our north, are truly daughters of New South Wales. [*Cheers.*] Those colonies sprung as it were from our loins. But there is a difference between us and Adam; for they took a rib from each side of us. [*Laughter.*] However, we rejoice in the fortunes of those colonies, and if my friend Mr Gillies, or our friend Mr Samuel Griffith, doubts that we take a pride and feel a becoming glory in the advance of Victoria and Queensland, let me tell them they are greatly mistaken. [*Loud cheers.*] The mother colony knows too well – of course I don't include some two or three carpers, whatever they do or say just now – New South Wales knows too well that the prosperity of her two daughters means her own. [*Cheers.*] We know that it is a wise dispensation that these large colonies sprang into existence, and we admired them when they were fighting their own battles and working out their own prosperity independently of New South Wales, but the time has now arrived when we are no longer isolated. [*Cheers.*] The crimson thread of kinship runs through us all. Even the native-born Australians are Britons, as much as the men born within the cities of London and Glasgow. We know the value of their British origin. We know that we represent a race – but time, of course, does not permit me to glance even at its composition – but we know we represent a race for the purposes of settling new colonies, which never had its equal on the face of the earth. [*Loud cheers.*] We know, too, that conquering wild territory, and planting civilised communities therein, is a far nobler, a far more immortalising achievement than conquest by feats of arms. We as separate communities have had to fight our way. We have had that which at times, I dare say, has degenerated into antagonism, naturally enough; but on the whole I do not believe that the thoughtful men of Victoria have ever lost sight of the good qualities of the men of New South Wales. [*Cheers.*] I do not believe that the people of the mother colony – and we have many men and women in the second and third generation born on the soil – have ever lost their admiration of the legitimate enterprise and fine emulation of the people of Victoria. What may be said of Victoria may be said of Queensland, South Australia, Tasmania, and may be said of our sister New Zealand, if she will condescend to permit us to call her sister. Is there a man living in any part of Australasia who will say that it would be to the advantage of the whole that we should remain disunited – [*'No, no,' and cheers.*] – with our animosities, border Customs and all the friction which our border Customs tend to produce, until the end of time. [*Cheers.*] I do not believe there is a sane man in the whole population of Australasia who will say such a daringly absurd thing. [*Cheers.*] If this is admitted, the question is reduced to very narrow limits, and it follows that at some time or other, we must unite as one great Australian people. [*Cheers.*]

Let those who are opposed to the union now point out the advantage that would arise from one, five or ten years' delay. It is impossible for the human intellect to conceive that any advantage could arise. Do we not all see that the difficulties would be greater as years go on. If that reasoning is correct, we have now arrived at a time when we are fully justified by all the laws that regulate the growth of free communities in uniting under one government and one flag. [*Cheers.*] The flag of United Australasia means to me no separation from the Empire. [*Prolonged cheering.*] It means to me no attempt to create a foreign political organisation. Admitting, as I do, that the interests of the Australian people ought to be the first object of concern, still I say that our interests cannot be promoted by any rash, thoughtless and crude separation from the grand old country of which we are all so proud. [*Cheers*.] All free communities must have a political head, and I should like to ask any thoughtful student of history what supreme head we could have more attractive, more ennobling, more consonant with the true principles of liberty than our august Sovereign, who, during her beneficent reign, has seen more improvement for the amelioration of the human race than ever any sovereign saw before in the history of the world. There is no reign of emperor, king or potentate, which has included such tremendous changes for the improvement of the world, for the spread of Christian civilisation, and for increasing the happiness of the mass of the human family as that of Queen Victoria. [*Cheers*.] Let it not go forth a moment – and I think I may speak for my colleagues in the conference – that in seeking complete authority over our own affairs in this fair land of Australia we are seeking any separation from the great Empire. [*Cheers*.]

Now what stands in the way of a federated Australasia? A common tariff. National life is a broad river of living water. Your fiscal notions – and I am a free-trader remember – [*hear, hear*] – your fiscal notions on one side or the other, are as planting a few stones or piling up a sandbank to divert the stream for a little, in order to serve some local interest. This question of a common tariff is a mere trifle compared with the great overshadowing question of a living and eternal national existence. Free trade or protection, all must admit, is to a large extent but a device for carrying out a human notion; but there is no human notion at all about the eternal life of a free nation. I say then that what I understand by the sentiment of a united Australasia is a sinking of all subordinate questions. I speak for my colony, which is as great as the rest of you. [*Cheers*.] We are prepared, and I will answer for the Parliament and the people of the country I represent, to go into this national union without making any bargain whatsoever – [*cheers*] – without stipulating for any advantage whatever for ourselves, but trusting to the good faith and justice of a Federal Parliament. [*Cheers*.] We are praying that God will give us power to rise above these secondary considerations, and that we may be able to come to an agreement to create this united Australia which you are as much in favour of as I am. These smaller questions ought not to be considered at the present time, and they ought not to deter us from reaching the great consummation which we have in view. [*Hear, hear.*]

Although I had no wish to speak tonight of the conference, I may say that my colleague and myself have come to Melbourne with no preconceived notion, with no binding instruction, but to enter into unreserved consultation with the delegates from the rest of the colonies. Gentlemen, that is all that I shall say on the subject. If the gentlemen representing the other colonies rise to the dignity of the question which challenges our attention there can be no doubt as to the result. [*Hear, hear.*] But after all, my lord and gentlemen, the determination of this question rests with the populations of the colonies – [*hear, hear*] – and whatever may be done by Cabinets or conferences, depend upon it, the question having been opened will be expanded wider and wider. Light has been thrown upon it, volumes of new light will be cast upon it as days roll on, and believing, as I firmly do, that the people of this country have already made up their minds to be united, I consider that no hand on the face of the earth is strong enough to keep them asunder. [*Cheers.*] But supposing there should be a United Australia, what would be the benefit to us? Well, with one leap we should appear before the world as a nation. [*Hear, hear.*] As separate colonies we are of little consequence, but the potentate does not exist – the ruling authority in human affairs does not exist – who would lightly consider the decision of a United Australasia. [*Cheers.*] We should grow at once – in a day, as it were – from a group of disunited communities into one solid, powerful, rich and widely respected power. [*Cheers.*] Believing, then, as I do, that every man in these colonies would be the better off by this union, and that no injury could result to any honest interest in consequence, I am altogether in favour of no time being lost in carrying out the sublime object. [*Cheers.*] Time would not permit, and I do not think that it would be very appropriate if time did, to refer to examples, but if we look to what other states have done we should find that all the examples were in our favour. We are here a great people united by natural ties, and with all the capacities that civilised communities can possess. We are as capable of managing our own affairs as our countrymen in any other part of the Empire. We are in a fruitful land, separated by the will of Providence from the rest of the world. [*Hear, hear.*] What has been difficult in other parts of the world ought not to be difficult with us, and the only obstacles that stand in the way of a united Australasia are those which arise from our own unfortunate separation. Every conceivable difficulty is based upon the separation which we all deplore. Well, these are difficulties which it is to the benefit of all to get rid of. Remember, gentlemen, that no work worthy of achievement was ever attained without surmounting difficulties. Supposing ours were tenfold greater than they are, they ought not to turn us from our object, for it is sound and good. But seeing that they are similar to those difficulties which occur amongst any other large body of men, seeing that they are not difficulties at all if once looked steadily in the face, why should we delay in bringing about that union, which thoughtful men, not only here but in other parts of the world, who take an interest in the progress of the British race, believe will redound to our lasting and eternal good? [*Cheers.*] I do not think there can be any doubt of the interest which our countrymen in the motherland take in the movement. I do not know, but I venture to say that our proceedings here today will form the keenest topic of attention to the London press. I do know, from sources of information in my possession, that our countrymen in the United States are looking at this movement with the keenest interest. If, then, thoughtful men in the motherland, and thoughtful men in that great offshoot of which we are still proud, and thoughtful men in these colonies are interested in this question, can we have a better guarantee that we are right? [*Cheers.*] It cannot be shown that at some other period we shall be in a better position to bring about a united Australasia. [*Cheers.*] Gentlemen, I have tried to express my individual sentiments on this question. I shall endeavour, in friendly agreement with my colleagues, to do my best towards the same end. I wish to make it known to the world that, so long as I have power, I shall not cease to strive to bring about this glorious consummation. [*Cheers.*] I thank you, gentlemen, for the manner in which you have received this toast, I thank Mr Service for the wise, discriminating, and gratifying remarks which he made in submitting it. I do hope that this meeting tonight – this great representative meeting which does you, Mr Gillies, so much honour – reflects the sentiments of the great colony of Victoria, and that the time is coming when we shall all appear before the world as a United Australia. [*Loud and prolonged cheers.*]

'These are the times that try men's souls'

Alfred Deakin

Speech at the banquet of the annual Australian Natives'
Association (ANA) Conference, Bendigo

15 MARCH 1898

Alfred Deakin (1856–1919) worked as a lawyer and journalist before entering politics as a liberal protectionist candidate for West Bourke in 1879, with the help of his close friend and employer at the Melbourne *Age*, David Syme. Socially progressive but an instinctive moderate and capable mediator, 'Affable Alfred' was known as a 'tactful smoother of ruffled feathers'. He needed all his talents when, following his visit to London for the Colonial Conference in 1887, he became the Victorian leader of the federation movement.

The main item on the agenda of the Australian Natives Association (ANA) Conference in 1898 was consideration of the Constitution Bill – later to be submitted to the public as a referendum on federation. The conference delegates had pledged their support for the bill earlier in the day, and Deakin arrived later to address the banquet. His speech was given without notes or text, and the ANA board were forced to pay three guineas for the transcript to the shorthand writer who had accurately recorded it. The journal of the ANA describes this conference as 'being like the "new baptism" when the disciples of Jesus were filled with the holy spirit', and Deakin's speech became the symbol of this fervour.

Deakin spoke quickly – 'at fever pitch he was capable of 200 words a minute' – in a sonorous, baritone voice, 'which, he claimed, bore no trace of provincial accent'. He had been fascinated as a school boy with the oratory of his headmaster at Melbourne Grammar, Dr J.E. Bromby, and Deakin's own style of speech is said to have been similar. He had ample opportunity to hone his skills as the youngest member of the first federal cabinet, and in three terms as the prime minister of Australia, from 1903–04, 1905–08 and 1909–10.

*

Members of the ANA:

We have heard much tonight of politicians and a good deal from them. We have also heard something of the Federal Convention and addresses from some of my fellow-members; but it is in neither capacity that I propose to speak, because I recognise that the united Australia yet to be can only come to be with the consent of and by the efforts of the Australian-born. I propose to speak to Australians simply as an Australian.

You are entitled to reckon among the greatest of all your achievements the Federal Convention just closing. The idea of such a Convention may be said to have sprung up among you, and it is by your efforts that it must be brought to fruition. One-half of the representatives constituting that Convention are Australian-born. The President of the Convention, the Leader of the Convention, the Chairman of Committees and the whole of the drafting committee are Australians. It remains for their fellow-countrymen to secure the adoption of their work.

We should find no difficulty in apprehending the somewhat dubious mood of many of our critics. A federal constitution is the last and final product of political intellect and constructive ingenuity; it represents the highest development of the possibilities of self-government among peoples scattered over a large area. To frame such a constitution is a great task for any body of men. Yet I venture to submit that among all the federal constitutions of the world you will look in vain for one as broad in its popular base, as liberal in its working principles, as generous in its aim, as this measure. So far as I am concerned, that suffices me. Like my friends, I would if I could have secured something still nearer to my own ideals. But for the present, as we must choose, let us gladly accept it.

I fail to share the optimistic views of those to whom the early adoption of union is a matter of indifference. Our work is not that of an individual artist aiming at his life's achievement, which he would rather destroy than accept while it seemed imperfect. What we have to ask ourselves is whether we can afford indefinite delay. Do we lose nothing by a continuance of the separation between state and state? Do not every year and every month exact from us the toll of severance? Do not we find ourselves hampered in commerce, restricted in influence, weakened in prestige, because we are jarring atoms instead of a united organism? Is it because we are so supremely satisfied with our local constitutions and present powers of development that we hesitate to make any change? …

At a time like the present this association cannot forget its watchword – federation – or its character, which has never been provincial. It has never been a Victorian, but always an Australian Association. Its hour has now come. Still, recognising the quarter from which attacks have already begun, and other quarters from which they are threatening, we must admit that the prospects of union are gloomier now in Victoria than for years past. The number actually against us is probably greater than ever; the timorous and passive will be induced to fall away; the forces against us are arrayed under capable chiefs. But few as we may be, and weak by comparison, it will be the greater glory, whether we succeed or fail. 'These are the times that try men's souls.' The classes may resist us; the masses may be inert; politicians may falter; our leaders may sound the retreat. But it is not a time to surrender. Let us nail our standard to the mast. Let us stand shoulder to shoulder in defence of the enlightened liberalism of the constitution. Let us recognise that we live in an unstable era, and that, if we fail in the hour of crisis, we may never be able to recall our lost national opportunities. At no period during the past hundred years has the situation of the great empire to which we belong been more serious. From the far east and the far west alike we behold the menaces and antagonisms. We cannot evade, we must meet them. Hypercriticism cannot help us to outface the future, nor can we hope to if we remain disunited. Happily, your voice is for immediate and absolute union.

One word more. This after all is only the beginning of our labours. The 150 delegates who leave this Conference, returning to their homes in all parts of this colony to report its proceedings, will, I trust, go back each of them filled with zeal and bearing the fiery cross of federation. Every branch should be stimulated into action, until, without resorting to any but legitimate means, without any attempt at intimidation, without taking advantage of sectionalism, but in the purest and broadest spirit of Australian unity, all your members unite to awaken this colony to its duty. You must realise that upon you, and perhaps upon you alone, will rest the responsibility of organising and carrying on this campaign. The greater the odds the greater the honour. This cause dignifies every one of its servants and all efforts that are made in its behalf. The contest in which you are about to engage is one in which it is a privilege to be enrolled. It lifts your labours to the loftiest political levels, where they must be inspired with the purest patriotic passion for national life and being. Remember the stirring appeal of the young poet of genius [William Gay], so recently lost to us in Bendigo, and whose grave is not yet green in your midst. His dying lips warned us of our present need and future duty, and pointed us to the true Australian goal –

Our country's garment
With hands unfilial we have basely rent,
With petty variance our souls are spent,
And ancient kinship under foot is trod:
O let us rise, united, penitent,
And be one people, – mighty, serving God!

'A monument of legislative competency'

Joseph Chamberlain

'The Commonwealth of Australia': speech on the introduction
of the Constitution Bill in the House of Commons, London

14 MAY 1900

The consummation of federation was staged in London. Joseph
Chamberlain (1836–1914) had been Colonial Secretary of the
British Government for five years – responsible for one-fifth of the
world's land surface – when he invited delegates from the colonies
to attend the passing of the Constitution Bill through the Imperial
Parliament. He was evidently impressed with the Australians and
thought some items in the Constitution 'might be wisely imitated
by ourselves'.

The passions of Chamberlain's political life were democracy,
radical social reform and Empire. He believed that Great Britain's
patriotism would be 'warped and stunted' if it failed to embrace
'the young and vigorous nations carrying everywhere a knowledge of the English tongue and English love of liberty and law'.
With his gold-rimmed monocle popping in and out of his right
eye, a fresh orchid pinned daily to his lapel and a 'cool smile',
Chamberlain was a formidable figure in the House of Commons.
'A man of obvious mystery with rather frightening qualities held
in leash … his voice was fascinating, but it had a dangerous quality to it, and a sentence begun in a low tone, would come to a
trenchant conclusion with something like a hiss.'

Alfred Deakin, C.C. Kingston and Edmund Barton were
among those chosen 'to defend the Constitution to the last
Comma'. In this they enjoyed great success. The only bone of contention was clause 74, which forbade appeals to the Privy Council
on issues relating to interpretation of the Constitution. After considerable debate, the clause was altered in a spirit of compromise
– appeals concerning constitutional issues would require leave of
the High Court, otherwise the right of appeal remained. As the

Australian delegation sailed home in July, dancing 'hand in hand' in celebration, the royal assent was granted to an 'Act to constitute the Commonwealth of Australia'.

*

I have no doubt there are many members of the House who will be inclined to envy me the privilege that has fallen to my lot in introducing this Bill for the federation of some of our greatest colonies – a Bill which marks an era in the history of Australia, and is a great and important step towards the organisation of the British Empire. This Bill, which is the result of the careful and prolonged labours of the ablest statesmen in Australia, enables that great island continent to enter at once the widening circle of English-speaking nations. No longer will she be a congeries of States, each of them separate from and entirely independent of the others, a position which anyone will see might possibly in the future, through the natural consequences of competition, become a source of danger or lead, at any rate, to friction and to weakness. But, if this Bill passes, in future Australia will be, in the words of the preamble of the Bill which I am about to introduce, 'an indissoluble federal Commonwealth firmly united for many of the most important functions of government'. ...

Now, this is a consummation long expected and earnestly hoped for by the people of this country. We believe that it is in the interest of Australia, and that has always been with us the first consideration. But we recognise that it is also in our interest as well; we believe the relations between ourselves and these colonies will be simplified, will be more frequent and unrestricted, and if it be possible, though I hardly think it is, will be more cordial when we have to deal with a single central authority instead of having severally to consult six independent Governments. Whatever is good for Australia is good for the whole British Empire. Therefore, we all of us – independently altogether of party, whether at home or in any other portion of the Empire – rejoice at this proposal, welcome the new birth of which we are witnesses, and anticipate for these great, free and progressive communities a future even more prosperous than their past, and an honourable and important position in the history of the Anglo-Saxon race ...

It will be seen that Earl Grey foresaw that in the future, at any rate, this necessity would arise. He was a little before his time, for when in 1850 he introduced proposals for constituting such central authority, his proposals met with no general support, and the Bill, when it became an Act, was confined to the establishment of the colony of Victoria, separating it from the colony of New South Wales. But from this time, and continuously down to the present day, the subject of some closer union between the separate Australian provinces or States has attracted the attention of all far-seeing and patriotic statesmen, especially in Australia. And among those who laboured in this movement I think it would be ungrateful not to mention the name of Sir Henry Parkes. Sir Henry Parkes was certainly a most remarkable individuality; he had his peculiarities, as most of us have, but no one would deny that he was a man of great capacity, of great power of work, of great resource and of intense local patriotism; and I think that today, when the consummation of the work for which he laboured so long is clearly within sight, we may well bear his memory in respectful regard ...

And so the Bill is presented to us. It comes with the authority behind it of five federating colonies, and it is this Bill, with a few alterations, but substantially this Bill, with 128 clauses, and dealing with a vast number, probably with hundreds or even thousands, of separate propositions of the greatest importance, which I have to ask leave to introduce. I think it will be admitted that this Bill is a Bill worthy of all the care and the labour which has been bestowed upon it. I think I may describe it as, and it certainly is, a monument of legislative competency ... and considering the magnitude and the variety of the interests that we are to deal with, the intricacy and the importance of the subjects with which the Bill has to deal, I think that no praise can be too high for those whose moderation, patience, skill, mutual consideration and patriotism have been able to produce so great a result ...

The Bill has been prepared without reference to us. It represents substantially and in most of its features the general opinion of the Australian people ... On the one hand, we have accepted without demur, and we shall ask the House of Commons to accept every point in this Bill, every word, every line, every clause, which deals exclusively with the interests of Australia. We may be vain enough to think that we might have made improvements for the advantage of Australia, but we recognise that they are the best judges of their own case, and we are quite content that the views of their representatives should be in these matters accepted as final; and the result of that is that the Bill which I hope to present to the House tonight is, so far as ninety-nine hundredths of it, I think I might almost say 999-thousandths of it is concerned ... exactly the same as that which passed the referendum of the Australian people ...

I have now only to ask the House to consent to the introduction of this Bill. I hope they will be content subsequently to pass it exactly as it has been introduced. I am quite certain that no more important measure of legislation has ever been presented to Parliament, and that nothing throughout the whole course of the Queen's reign will be a more beneficent feature in that long and glorious history.

Motion made, and Question proposed, 'That leave be given to introduce a Bill to constitute the Commonwealth of Australia.'

'Unite yourselves and preserve the union'

Sir Edmund Barton

Banquet address in reply to the toast of 'The Commonwealth' at the Sydney Town Hall

1 JANUARY 1901

In the four years leading up to federation and assumption of the office of Australia's first prime minister, Edmund Barton (1849–1920) addressed no fewer than 300 public meetings, evolving the catchcry 'a nation for a continent and a continent for a nation'. With his 'rich and beautifully modulated' voice, he could hardly have been better placed to reply to the toast of the Commonwealth on the very first evening that Australia was one. In some respects, however, his whole life had prepared him for such a moment. Barton studied classics and graduated MA at Sydney University – he retained sufficient Latin as Prime Minister to converse in it with Pope Pius X at the Vatican. He developed his debating skills at the Sydney Mechanics School of Arts and while working as a lawyer, and displayed 'quickness of perception, tact, courtesy and firmness' when promoted to Speaker of the NSW Legislative Assembly four years after entering politics.

An omnivorous reader, an avid angler and a lover of cricket, Barton was tested by a parliament of competing egos, some of whom nursed an abiding antagonism to the federal cause even after its consummation. Yet, as historian J.A. La Nauze remarked, 'he led them all, with an authority never questioned, and sustained by the visible and irrefutable example of plain hard work and conscientious devotion to a task.'

*

My right honourable friend [Sir Samuel Griffith], who is dignified by that title on the same day that I am, and who was my leader in the convention of 1891 and in the framing of the Bill of the year which is the groundwork of the Act of today, has not, I think, been properly received, and has not been properly listened to. [*Hear, hear.*] As one of the framers of the Bill to which I refer, I heartily condemn those who prefer to listen to ordinary conversation rather than to the elevating words of that distinguished man.

In response to the toast of the Commonwealth I may say that we have had an enormously successful gathering today in inaugurating the Commonwealth. Few cities outside of London could have furnished the magnificent demonstration which Sydney furnished this very day. [*Hear, hear.*] New South Wales has today opened her arms to the Australian Commonwealth. We must note that the centre of that demonstration was the people, who may well be complimented for the order and enthusiasm which characterised the proceedings. For myself, I own to a personal indebtedness – to the people for a reception which, in its enthusiasm, I have never experienced before. But I appropriate it to the cause of union, and am not vain enough to attribute this great result to any personal merit of my own. [*Applause.*]

Sydney today had a great right to exult. There were many in Sydney who, on the question of the terms of union, were divided, but who were not opposed to union itself. I find throughout the colony today tens of thousands of good men and women who do not believe in the Constitution in the form in which it is framed, but who nevertheless believe in giving it a fair trial, and accepting it as a measure dictated by the majority of the people, and framed by gentlemen who had the confidence of the people. The chief benefits of the union will, I believe, fall to New South Wales, and the chief place in the Commonwealth – capital or not capital – will, I believe, always be in Sydney, for nowhere else in the whole inhabitable world would you find such facilities as exist here, and which enable Sydney to offer such a splendid spectacle as was presented today. [*Cheers.*] Nowhere else could you find such a combination, such natural resources of wealth and such wonderful resources of beauty as exist in New South Wales. Here our future position is absolutely assured, but I believe it will not be at the expense of the Commonwealth, or at the expense of any other State. [*Applause.*] We shall have to put aside the jealousies and rancorous feelings which once existed, and while New South Wales may prove more prosperous and progressive as a State in the Commonwealth, she will be glad to know that the same benefits will accrue to Australia generally.

If divided we cannot reap the whole benefit of the union; but with union the benefits which we desire to achieve will be accomplished. It is certain that these benefits cannot be attained without union. [*Applause.*] Unite yourselves and preserve the union, and the benefits of the union will follow. It will require honest, earnest and patient effort, as well as tact and mutual consideration, and without these we shall not fulfil the promise of today. [*Applause.*]

The father of the constitution of New South Wales was Wentworth, whose name is honoured with others in the Australian colonies who founded the various constitutions which exist in the other States today. But it was Sir Henry Parkes – [*cheers*] – who, from the very beginning recognised the potentialities of the great union. The work in which he was engaged, and the accomplishment of which we are celebrating by the proceedings of today, was only interrupted by his death. It was a work in which I was content to serve with him as my leader and as one of the rank and file. To Sir Henry Parkes is due the fruition of the struggle to unite the colonies, and which has been today so happily brought about; and it was to me a great privilege to be enabled to continue the great man's work. [*Cheers.*] I ask you to drink in solemn silence to the memory of Sir Henry Parkes.

'Cold climates have produced the greatest geniuses'

King O'Malley

Speech on proposed parliamentary site, House of Representatives, Parliament House, Melbourne

8 OCTOBER 1903

Whimsical, wily King O'Malley (?1858–1953) remains one of the most colourful characters to fill a parliamentary bench. He claimed to be Canadian, but may well have been American, and there is considerable confusion over the year of his birth. Christened 'King' after his mother's maiden name, the young O'Malley emigrated to Australia and became a successful land-lord and businessman. He was elected to the Parliament in 1901 as an independent from Tasmania, and later joined the Labor Party. Melbourne *Punch* described him as 'this weird graft of Western American extravagance upon Australian socialism … his rough and coarse humour, his unexpected quips of phrase and invective "go down" like fresh oysters with a crowd of miners …'

The selection of a site for the national capital caused bitter debate in the federal parliament. O'Malley, as the minister for home affairs, had endured a journey of more than 2700 miles on trains, coaches and traps while inspecting potential sites for the seat of government, and settled in his own mind on Bombala. His speech in favour of the inland town in south-eastern New South

Wales, not far from the coastal town of Eden, was ultimately rejected by the House.

*

I have listened to honourable members for the last forty-eight hours, and I object to being told that I cannot speak because others declare themselves to be ready to vote. I am here, not as a subordinate, but as the peer of every member in this House; and, therefore, I shall talk when it suits me to talk. We have listened to some extraordinary speeches; and it appears to me as though honourable members are suddenly prepared to vote now that Bombala is apparently 'out of the running'. There is collusion somewhere, but I cannot get on to its track. If ever there was a spot set apart by the Creator to be the Capital of this great Australia – the pivot around which Australian civilisation should revolve – it is Bombala. The Americans, in fixing upon Washington, selected a site close to the eastern seas. The result is that today members of Congress have to travel 4000 miles from Oregon, and they are paid 10 cents, or 6d. per mile, as expenses. It is a selfish, if ungodly state of things when men arrive at the stage of thinking only of themselves; the curse of the world today is selfishness. We are legislating now for countless millions still unborn, we are legislating for centuries hence, and posterity will rise in its might and curse us if we select the wrong site. It will be a black crime against posterity if we select any place but Bombala. A number of honourable members, including the honourable and learned member for Indi, have asked how honourable members will reach the seat of government, if it be fixed at Bombala. Why, the leader of the Opposition, for instance, could step on a steamer in Melbourne and next morning be at Twofold Bay, whence he might be wafted to the scene of his legislative labours in the buckets of an aerial railway. It is not two years since I met the leader of the Opposition fishing in the Snowy River, and it is that stream and not the Murray which is the national river of Australia. The Snowy River is fed by Heaven from the eternal snows of the mountains. In the very beginning the Garden of Eden was laid to the eastward; and when I reached the hills, after having climbed Black Jack and entered Monaro, I thought of the story of Adam and

Eve. I looked back over 6000 years, and, in fancy, I could almost see the Garden of Eden at Bombala. I could see Adam and Eve leaving after they had eaten of the tree of life – for the tree of life is growing there today.

[An Honourable Member: 'They must have been starved out at Bombala.']

They were not, because Eden was an irrigation colony, with the Euphrates at hand.

[Mr Higgins: 'Did the honourable member see any snakes at Bombala?']

I saw fat snakes fit to eat, but every snake I saw at Tumut was dead. The Royal Commission seems to me to have been like some bulldozed Commission from South Carolina or Georgia. The result is sometimes peculiar when pressure is put on a man; the pressure may not be from without but from within, and yet it has the same effect. It is extraordinary that Mr Oliver should have given such a splendid report of Bombala. The history of the world shows that cold climates have produced the greatest geniuses, all of whom were born north of a certain degree. I have heard some remarks about a 'toy State,' but how big is Scotland, whose sons are all over the earth? How big is Rhode Island, whose sons can make wooden nutmegs? How big is the State of Maine? That State is not as big as Bombala, and yet it gave birth to Longfellow. How big was Greece or Sparta? There are more people today around Bombala than there were in Greece and Sparta when Miltiades won the liberty of mankind on the field of Marathon. There are more people round Eden and Bombala today than were gathered on all the seven hills of Rome when she commenced a sway which afterwards embraced the whole earth. It is all nonsense to talk about population and size; the history of the world shows that small territories and small republics have produced the greatest men. It will be the same today. This is the first opportunity we have had of establishing a great city of our own, where we can experiment with our socialism, as it is called. Socialism is going to rule this earth, and to destroy the selfishness and the misery that has come into the world through the greed and avarice of humanity. In conclusion, let me say this: look where we like, it will be found that wherever a hot climate prevails, the country is revolutionary. Take the sons of some of the greatest men in the world, and put them into a hot climate like Tumut or Albury, and in three generations their lineal descendants will be degenerate. I found them in San Domingo on a Sabbath morning going to a cock-fight with a rooster under each arm, and a sombrero on their heads. I want to have a cold climate chosen for the capital of this Commonwealth. I am glad that the Minister for Defence has put that point before us. I want to have a climate where men can hope. We cannot have hope in hot countries. When I go down the streets of this city on a hot summer's day and see the people in a melting condition, I look upon them with sorrow and wish I were away in healthy Tasmania. I hope that the site selected will be Bombala, and that the children of our children will see an Australian Federal city that will rival London in population, Paris in beauty, Athens in culture and Chicago in enterprise.

'The hardy pioneer in Australian literature'

Miles Franklin

'Novels of the bush': speech at the close of Authors' Week at the Blaxland Galleries, Sydney

12 APRIL 1935

The grandiloquence of the title of Miles Franklin's (1879–1954) debut novel, *My Brilliant Career*, was always ironical: the author was only nineteen. Her English publishers kept it that way, grudging her just £24 in royalties and pocketing the rest themselves. The great-great-granddaughter of a convict of the First Fleet was undismayed, and never ceased championing the case of Australian writing. Introduced to the precepts of feminism by her mentor, Rose Scott, she travelled to the United States in 1906 where she was politically active in the National Women's Trade Union League of America. On returning to Australia in 1932, after also living in England, she began promoting local literature through the Fellowship of Australian Writers, speaking regularly at literary events and on radio. This address, broadcast on 2BL, illustrates the commitment to indigenous culture that would motivate her to endow by the terms of her will the annual Miles Franklin Award for Australian Literature.

*

The bush novel has been an inevitable and indispensable factor in our national development. The literature of Australia, which is truly indigenous, which really captures the essence of our country, so far has largely depended upon the bush novel. Not only has this kind of novel been the kingpin of our literary output, but it is a heartening institution on its own account.

When the ballad-writing which went before the present boom in novels was at its height, one of our most famous balladists, when he was asked about his health, used to say that he was well, except for the blight of 'Little Things of my Own.' This was his way of describing the prevalence of verses or doggerel, which almost snowed him under. In those days verses grew on trees! A disqualified jockey 'on the make' would edge up to him with a 'pome'; a cast-iron business man, admired and reverenced for his money-making, nevertheless would take the successful poet aside and coyly produce a little poem of his own.

This kind of popularity has now fallen upon the novel, which has become a game – or a gamble – almost as popular as cricket, though not so sociable. The most unsuspected people write novels. Age or sex, poverty or wealth, education or no education, overwork or leisure, place of residence, or class of occupation – regardless of any of these things, all kinds of people try. So widespread is the sport of writing novels in Australia that I'm sure that not only the half-dozen people intentionally listening to me, but also every single, simple, Solomon Simon one of us, including the six thousand tuned-in in readiness for the racing results, if he hasn't already written a novel, has the intention of doing so at any moment. In any case we will all be so gaily unaware of and unafraid of consequences that we wouldn't mind 'giving it a fly'. That probably is because pioneering trains people to make light of hardship and to overcome impossibilities.

Even I, in my seething adolescence, seized some foolscap and tried to plough new ground in a novel; and to my intense surprise and confusion was warmly applauded and encouraged by my fellow Australians. Since then I have been suspected of writing many more novels, which I didn't.

I shall not deal here with the shortcomings of our novels, but have time to mention only some of those which I feel have done service in crystallising reality – that spiritual and national reality which, complexly, must be reflected in our art before it becomes part of our consciousness.

Away down the bullock-track were half-a-dozen novels, which have weathered time and remain with us like the red-gum cornerposts that our grandfathers put up about the old station homesteads. There is *Geoffrey Hamlyn*, which enjoys the prominence of an only child of its period. It has overshadowed Catherine Spence's *Clara Morison*, a much better novel, the product of a more soundly furnished mind and a soul valiantly awake to the destiny open to Australians. This novel by the Grand Old Woman of Australia should be republished. *For the Term of His Natural Life* (so magnificently named) moved me eight years ago, on re-reading, just as deeply as it did when I was in my teens, so that I cannot tackle it again just yet. Then came *Robbery Under Arms* – another splendid title – and a story of the bush, bushy. These two books embalm early phases of Australian life which cannot be ignored.

Then intervened, or supervened, the Australians, our inimitable and dearly-loved balladists – the era of Lawson and Paterson and a cloud of others, developed and delimited by the school of J.F. Archibald. In this school's heyday, and outside of rules and regulations, came that masterpiece, *Such is Life*, by Tom Collins. Those were the days of *On Our Selection*, a book as solitary as *Such is Life*, though so different in character and quality. Steele Rudd's novel, or cluster of stories, has as many lives as a cat, and has been expanded by stage and film production; and the broad farce and slapstick applied have not quite defeated the drama. Steele Rudd's story remains a hardy and wholesome folk tale which can provoke laughter even in those who are cross about its inconsistencies. Those inconsistencies are the result of its being a preposterous play, in the purist's meaning of this word. There is national life and there is the parodying, the burlesquing, the caricaturing of the special peculiarities of that life. Steele Rudd did not wait for national life to be pigeonholed here, but pioneered a burlesque of it in advance. But only partly. There was pathos under his humour, and those who knew and loved Australia from the bone outward, and who had suffered from the deprivation and hardships of the life presented, sighed or wept as often as they smiled or laughed.

Then we fell on lean days. *On the Wool Track*, by C.E.W. Bean, had to shoulder the work of a novel in the gap. D.H. Lawrence came, and saw Australia through a stranger's eyes, but they were inspired eyes, and the consequent illumination a valuable gift to Australians. When *Working Bullocks*, by Katherine Prichard, appeared in the middle of the '20s, it stood alone for several years as a well-rounded embodiment of the Australian scene. More recently, perhaps because the competition inaugurated in 1928 brought effort to a head, and the exchange operated in favour of local production, we have had so many novels, bush and otherwise, that it is difficult to remember them all. Lack of time prevents discussion of a dozen with worthy points, among them prize winners and circumspect literary efforts; and there others I have not yet read. Some open arrestingly, but do not sustain their promise to the fulfilment of rounded works of art. They are patchy. This may be partly due to the working of a new environment – making our ore malleable – and also to the conditions under which we have to work. Some women have produced their novels hurriedly, without peace or repose; some men have written theirs by the light of a hurricane lantern in camp after the day's work. When the author's body is weary from physical toil, his or her novel is likely to be uneven and mediocre. Producing literature, in the most favourable circumstances, means hard work. To take one well-known example, compare the conditions under which a *Forsyte Saga* was produced with those of the writers of the bush novel, and it will be conceded that to tackle a novel under the usual bush conditions is heroic.

Since *Working Bullocks*, Katherine Prichard has given us *Coonardoo*, an original contribution to the study of miscegenation and the tragedy of our vanishing Aborigines. The chronicles of Brent of Bin Bin end – or shall we say pause – in *Back to Bool Bool*, which a visiting foreigner recently termed a splendidly thoughtful and lyrical book. The two first of this series deal with past days; the third, *Back to Bool Bool*, much the cleverest of the three, and a striking performance, deals with new days of the bush and the city, and in the modern manner. This writer – or team of writers, according to A.G. Stephens – is one of the most humorous of Australian writers. London *Punch* said: 'Deep drama and laughter our author can mix, an hour with him's worth three of the "flicks".' He is certainly in love with his background and nails a great many of the 'possum pelts of Australian life to the bookshelf.

Singing Gold was triumphant in its bush atmosphere. *No Escape* had notable chapters. *Burnt Sugar* hurriedly broke new ground and indicated the power of its author to make characters come alive – an uncommon power which I wish he would take time to develop. Bernard Cronin and F.S. Hibble, in *The Sow's Ear* and *Karangi* respectively, have contributed two studies of communities, one in Tasmania, the other in New South Wales, which demand attention because they depict girls in our land leading dreary lives and being thrust into sordid marriages in the style of Irish and New England dramas.

In considering bush novels deserving of the high classification because they have extracted the essence of the land, we must include the balladists and short-story writers, who through ten or fifteen years performed the services of novelists, the biggest and most popular figure being Henry Lawson. There are two later books on my special Australian shelf. These are a collection of sketches entitled *Bark House Days*, by Mary Fullerton, which breathe the magic of bush ways of the last generation in Gippsland; and *Manshy*, by F.D. Davison, which charms from the first page to the last, because of its indelible Australianism as much as its literary merit.

Strangely enough, there are not so many town novels which capture anything essentially and distinctively Australian. It would be interesting to discover why. Are the cities less productive of interesting characters and background than the bush? Many of our novelists, who would have been town novelists, depart to succeed magnificently in well-worked fields overseas. Some of our city novelists who have remained, nevertheless have not tackled the city and suburban scene, but have flown in imagination to distant and hoary arenas.

One novel which has caught the special atmosphere of the city as successfully as those I have named that caught the bush is *Jonah*, by Louis Stone. This writer has pickled for all time the Australian hoodlum, who used to be known as the larrikin. He has painted his portrait in his slums as unmistakably as Tom Collins has portrayed the bullocky on the tracks of Riverina – two contrasting but equally definite Australian types, and now bygone products of Australian life.

The bush novel has been the hardy pioneer in Australian literature; it has ridden the boundaries and built the huts. To progress beyond it and be worthy of our great English classical tradition in the novel is an adventure awaiting all Australian novelists today in town or bush, city or country; and that adventure will be furthered, I believe, not by imitation, but by the release of originality in keeping with this continent which for the present we hold in trust.

And so I'll say 'Good afternoon,' or, as the old bushmen used to say, 'So long, mates!'

'Lawson was as Lawson wrote'

Miles Franklin

Speech at the Henry Lawson statue, Outer Domain, Sydney

5 SEPTEMBER 1942

Miles Franklin's fascination with Australian writing inevitably led her to the work of Henry Lawson (1867–1922), the balladist and short-story writer described as an 'acute observer of bush life with an almost intuitive grasp of the forces transforming his own society'. The statue of Lawson erected in Sydney's Domain after his death became the meeting place for an annual ceremony and commemorative address, arranged by the Fellowship of Australian Writers. Franklin's personal recollections of Lawson evoke the esteem in which he was held by younger writers twenty years after his death.

*

… When I was in my tens and teens, Henry Lawson was a hero glamorous with success. He had all of sympathy, all of glory that youthful adoration could bestow. In that wonderland that was opening to us we were unaware of the struggles of literary geniuses. We could judge only by the literary product, and that enchanted us. We were sure that if we could see Henry Lawson he would understand our every delight, our every aspiration, our every growing pain of discontent. He was a superman – the perfect big brother of our dreams.

With this conception of Henry Lawson it was inevitable that I should reach him with my literary growing pains. The result is part of the Lawson legend. With your indulgence I should like to add my recollection of Henry Lawson in the flesh.

What is so rare to critical, exacting, over-sensitive youth, he fulfilled my expectations of him, and more. I remember my first sight of him. He was beautifully dressed. His linen was irreproachable. He was tall and slim, with exceptional physical beauty. The beauty of his eyes is also part of his legend. His manner – it had that sensitive warmth, that winning gentleness, that understanding – well, Lawson was as Lawson wrote. You had not to work up to friendliness with him: he was spontaneously a mate. He called on me, alone, he said, with a humorous smile skimming across his features, to find out what sort of an animal I was – whether a mate or a mere miss. He would come next day to take me to his wife. The Lawsons were then living in a most delightful cottage with its garden paths embowered in shrubs. Mrs Lawson was equally up to expectation in her friendliness, her youthfulness, her beauty.

Henry Lawson was then at the height of his powers. He was preparing for the inevitable hegira to London. This lent additional romance to his doings. He was rising to increasing renown and surely it must be accompanied by prosperity. He went to London.

I came down from the bush and saw him again on his return. I recall the last time I saw him. He and his family were waving good-bye to me from the wharf as I boarded a ferry. No family group could have excelled it in charm: the beauty of the parents was repeated in the two children.

No other portrait of Henry Lawson has for me ever overlaid my own. Nothing blurs it nor detracts from it. It was etched indelibly by the clear-cutting mind of youth.

I never saw Henry Lawson again. I too left Australia. When I returned, the earth – that Australian earth cleansed of history by an oblivion of fallowhood, lay kind upon him who had helped to give it national significance.

I had no more than settled in the house after the bustle of arrival before my mother said, 'You must see where they have laid your friend, Henry Lawson. I'll take you tomorrow.'

No one can estimate what Henry Lawson may mean to the future of this country: what will be the fate of small national groups in the post-war order no prophet can say. But having succeeded in our military struggle, if we shall be able to retain here in this isolated paradise of the Pacific our continuing Australian identity, then Lawson's fame will be sure with the years.

Our indebtedness to him will increase because he has rendered this continent. He has helped to make Australia ours in a way that no system of land exploitation nor even droughts and floods and pests can take it from us – a great gift from a greatly gifted man – Henry Lawson!

'There are sinister elements in our midst'

Bessie Rischbieth

'The British way of life – is it challenged?': speech at the state
conference of the Women's Service Guild, Perth

28 July 1949

A strong, stylish woman of 'indomitable spirit' who devoted
her life to the work of social reform and the rights of women,
Bessie Rischbieth (1874–1967) was associated with campaigns
ranging from female suffrage and equal pay to the conditions of
women's prisons and female representation in parliament. Her
belief that women's rights would be achieved through legislation,
not revolution, caused friction with other leading feminists of
her age, with one opponent describing her as 'a real rotter'. But
her ability to couch sometimes radical sentiment in conservative language won her many admirers and made her one of the
most important figures in the Australian women's movement. In
the following speech, delivered at the state conference of the
Women's Service Guild, a Perth feminist organisation established
in 1909, Rischbieth defends democratic institutions against the
threat of communism and warns members of the guild to
beware the peace movements emerging in response to the Cold
War.

*

Under the protection of the British flag, Australia has grown in a
little over 160 years from a Crown Colony to a full blown nation
with full self-determination. But this fact of Nationhood makes us
no less a child of Britain and we still speak of the 'Mother Country'.
We also pride ourselves that we are ninety-eight per cent British
people and we cherish the traditions and customs of the British way
of life.

Now, what are these traditions?

The greatest tradition is the spirit of liberty, a vital seed of continuing life. The British nation lives today because its institutions are free institutions and its task is to survive as one of the world's guardians of human liberty. As British people our responsibility to posterity is therefore to preserve this nucleus of human freedom. It is vital to progress that the human mind should be free from controls of fear and uniformity.

Our State Annual Conference has already declared its belief that by a democracy we mean a system where impartial justice protects the individual against arbitrary action by any public or private institution – which arrives at its conclusion by free discussion without an artificial unity based on suppression of opinion; which gives equal rights to all citizens where there is a free press, freedom of speech, freedom of worship.

These things belong to the Australian way of life because of our British heritage, and long may we cherish them as of vital concern, not only to ourselves, but to the whole world. We cannot deny, however, that there are sinister elements in our midst, and Australia is facing a dangerous and far-reaching challenge. This nationwide strike and the Royal Commission sitting in Victoria to examine communist activities are clear evidence of this challenge. But, is it not a fact, that all nations are facing a similar challenge?

The world is dividing into two groups and nations and peoples are called upon to make a choice between two ideologies. This, in my humble opinion, is unavoidable under present circumstances and indeed even hopeful.

As I see it, these two groups – The Western Democracies (under the Atlantic Pact) on the one hand – and Russia and the satellite countries on the other hand – will be in a more advantageous position to exchange ideas by conferring and bargaining. This may have the effect of modifying any new world social pattern which is slowly and painfully evolving. The alternate choice is 'Sovietisation' of the world into one uniformity of pattern by domination.

As far as Australia is concerned and according to the evidence placed before the Royal Commission sitting in Victoria the plan is in hand to establish an 'Australian Soviet Republic'.

These are among the many conflicting elements to be met with in our Guild today and which have required and will require an amount of discrimination on our part to pick our way through the difficulties and retain our freedom. They must be faced, we dare not at our peril pretend they do not exist.

We cannot escape responsibility of choice and it is therefore necessary to examine carefully the possible motive behind new movements before joining them. This applies especially to peace movements. This desire for world peace is a very natural yearning in the heart of women which may be open to exploitation.

Indeed I am informed of a 'Peace Action Group' which was formed in Perth of quite recent date. This group is opposed to the Atlantic Pact recently entered into by the Western Democracies and which the Western Democracies claim 'marks a great stride towards the consolidation of the free world for self-defence'.

My motive in placing these remarks before you is to suggest that we confer with one another more intimately in regard to new movements before we commit ourselves.

Quite an amount of information comes into the office in regard to these matters which it is impossible to deal with from the platform, but which would place our members in a better position to judge for themselves. I would also suggest that our Guilds inform themselves about the Atlantic Pact, by inviting a qualified speaker to address them.

On March 18th the Foreign Secretary, Mr Ernest Bevin, announced in the House of Commons 'that full agreement had been reached among the negotiating countries in what he describes, as one of the greatest steps towards world peace and world security, which has been taken since the end of the first World War.' This announcement met with the overwhelming assent of the House of Commons by all parties.

I would like also to see the United Nations Association (WA Division) become more responsible for a popular peace movement, rather than allow less responsible groups to take the initiative. This association could popularise the structure on which the United Nations is built – what it is doing to bring about social justice – better education facilities – better health conditions and it is doing good work in these important directions. To do this a popular fee for membership would help.

In placing these few ideas before you I am impressed with the change that has taken place in our work and outlook since the inception of the first W.S. Guild in 1909. Possibly we were happier then because our interests were localised whereas today we live in the midst not only of Australia-wide conflict but world-wide conflict. It is impossible therefore to avoid the responsibility of wise choice.

Our Australian forebears were pioneers in the realm of physical things, they had to conquer the great bush, clear the lands for closer settlement. In doing this they laid the foundation of a free country which we inherit today. Our task today is in the realm of mind and we are called upon to help clear the mental fog and to preserve intact those values which involve human freedom. This is our pathway to the future and we must add our humble contribution to the glorious legacy of freedom our pioneers have left in our hand.

The coming generations expect this of us and we must not disappoint them. The lamp of human freedom must be handed on or we are unworthy of our British heritage.

We ask Divine Guidance for help in the coming years of work and if our task proves difficult, it will be at least worthwhile in support of wise change.

'To me it means ...'

Sir Robert Menzies

'The British Commonwealth of Nations in international affairs':
the Roy Milne Memorial Lecture, Adelaide

26 JUNE 1950

No individual looms larger than Robert Menzies (1894–1978) in the political life of twentieth century Australia. An exceptional scholar and prominent King's Counsel, he won the United

Australia Party seat of Kooyong in 1934 and went on to serve as attorney-general and minister for industry before his first term as prime minister between 1939 and 1941. His second period of leadership lasted for sixteen years, benefiting from post-war prosperity and optimism, and Menzies' complete command of the Liberal Party in whose 1944 foundation he had been a prime mover.

Menzies was born into a period of intense loyalty to England and Empire – he remembered the death of Queen Victoria when he was six years old – and his unfeigned love for the 'Mother Country' never left him. Although Australia's security interests after World War II were increasingly aligned with the United States, Menzies' loyalty to the Commonwealth was unflagging; to him, allegiance to the crown went beyond external association and ought encompass 'an inner feeling'. The depth of this feeling was expressed in the following section of the speech where Menzies outlines what England 'means to me' – not merely in the content, but in the famous voice, once described as 'well-modulated … with its full vowels and clearly enunciated consonants, the sort of voice which conveyed education, confidence and respect for England'.

*

… I would like to be able to say to all the British people of the world, if they cared to listen to so small a voice, that our true brotherhood must be a matter of feeling and not merely a matter of thought; no vain glory, no arrogant sense of power, no jingoism, but an unquenchable sense of common destiny and common duty and common instinct. To many people the British Commonwealth is a curious machine that has worked; looking to the outsider rather like a Heath Robinson invention; but relied upon by mankind twice during this century, to their great deliverance. But what does it mean to you? I think I know what it means to me. May I break through our usual polite reticences and tell you?

To me it means (and here you will find a curious jumble in both time and place) a cottage in the wheat lands of the north-west of the State of Victoria, with the Bible and Henry Drummond and Jerome K. Jerome and *The Scottish Chiefs* and Burns on the shelves. It means the cool green waters of the Coln as they glide past the church at

Fairford; the long sweep of the Wye Valley above Tintern, with a Wordsworth in my pocket; looking north across the dim Northumbrian moors from the Roman Wall, with the rowan trees on the slope before me, and two thousand years of history behind; old colour and light and soaring stone in York Minster. It means King George and Queen Mary coming to their Jubilee in Westminster Hall as Big Ben chimed out and Lords and Commons bowed, and, as they bowed, saw beyond the form of things to a man and a woman greatly loved. It means Chequers, and, from the crest beyond, that microcosm of history in which you may, with one sweeping glance, see the marks of British trenches, the 'Roman Road to Wendover', the broad Oxford plains, and (by the merest twist) the plumed figure of John Hampden walking through the fields to the church whose spire is just to be seen, at Great Kimble, to address the gentlemen of Buckinghamshire on Shipmoney. It means, at Chequers, Winston Churchill, courage and confidence radiating from him, the authentic note of the British lion in his voice, the listening world marvelling at how such triumph could be built upon such disaster. It means the Royal Mile at Edinburgh, and a toast from kilted clansmen in the Valley of the Tay, and a sudden cold wind as I came one day up from a Yorkshire dale. It means laughter in Lancashire, Jack Hulbert and Cicely Courtneidge. It means Australian boys in tired but triumphant groups at Tobruk and Benghazi; Cunningham at Alexandria, with his flashing blue eyes, talking to me of the Australian, Waller; Australian airmen in Canada, in Great Britain, all over the world. It means, at Canberra, at Wellington, at Ottawa, at Cape Town, the men of Parliament meeting as those met at Westminster 700 years ago; at Melbourne the lawyers practising the common Law first forged at Westminster. It means Hammond at Sydney, and Bradman at Lords, and McCabe at Trent Bridge, with the ghosts of Grace and Trumble looking on. It means a tang in the air; a touch of salt on the lips; a little pulse that beats and shall beat; a decent pride; the sense of a continuing city. It means the past ever rising in its strength to forge the future.

Is all this madness? Should I have said, as clever, modern men are wont to do, that the British Commonwealth means an integral association of free and equal nations, whose mutual rights and obligations you will find set out in the Balfour Formula, the Statute of

Westminster, and later documents? Or should I have watered it down, as some would have us do and define it in terms of friendship, or alliance, or pact, as if we were discussing an Anglo-Portuguese treaty?

A plague take such notions. Unless the Commonwealth is to British people all over the world a spirit, a proud memory, a confident prayer, courage for the future, it is nothing.

> It may be that the gulfs will wash us down:
> It may be we shall touch the Happy Isles,
> And see the great Achilles, whom we knew.
> Tho' much is taken, much abides; and tho'
> We are not now that strength which in old days
> Moved earth and heaven; that which we are, we are;
> One equal temper of heroic hearts,
> Made weak by time and fate, but strong in will
> To strive, to seek, to find, and not to yield.

'For in the last analysis it is ideas that count'

Sir Howard Florey

Australia Day address, London

26 JANUARY 1963

Howard Florey (1898–1968) was working as a researcher for the Pathological Institute at Oxford University when he began devoting his attention to the human body's innate protective powers against infectious disease. His work pioneered the development of penicillin and the use of antibiotics, an achievement acknowledged when he was awarded the 1945 Nobel Prize for medicine.

Sir Robert Menzies said in praise of Florey that 'it was a matter of gratitude that in terms of talent, all humans were not equal. Because then you get peaks of greatness, peaks in the graph of ability ... here today we have a man, famous all over the world, who has been having a fit of misery for the last half hour listening to the words of praise heaped on him. Yet he is entitled to praise and gratitude, because ultimately when things in the world get sorted out and settled down, his name will be regarded absolutely as one of the greatest names in Australian history.'

After growing up in Adelaide, Florey spent most of his working life overseas, but retained strong links to his country of birth. Although he spoke infrequently to the public on science and medicine – once saying in an interview that his time was limited and he would prefer to devote it to lecturing doctors on the correct use of penicillin – Florey did make occasional speeches on more general topics. In the following Australia Day address, delivered in London, Florey speaks frankly about attenuating links between Australia and Great Britain, urging increased intellectual collaboration to match the two nations' sporting rivalry.

*

My Lord President, Lord Mountbatten, Your Excellencies, Your Graces, My Lords, Ladies and Gentlemen:

I think I'd better take you into my confidence at once and tell you about a President of the Royal Society who was in office about the middle of the eighteenth century – that is not long after Newton. He used to go to sleep in the Chair during meetings and somebody produced a couplet which went in this way:

Should e'er he chance to wake in Newton's chair,
He wonders how the devil he got there.

These words have had a profound effect on me, for although I do not go to sleep in the Chair ostentatiously, the other thought enshrined in the couplet frequently passes through my mind. It did when I was given the honour of replying to the Toast of Australia tonight, but I took courage and convinced myself at least that, because I had spent more than half my life in this country, I might be regarded as a reasonable choice, for I may be some sort of symbol of the very close relationship which exists between two countries at the extreme ends of the earth. It's true that probably the only reply from

Australia that many natives of this country present tonight want to hear is something like 'Australia all out for twenty-seven'.

It's probably no exaggeration to say that if most people were asked to answer immediately the question, what image does the word Australia conjure up, they would say 'cricket'. This is very remarkable, for there have been times when I could have made out a good case that cricket is merely a game invented by schoolmasters to keep twenty-two boys quiet for a whole afternoon. And perhaps to indicate that I am not unduly biased, I may say that like a number of people here tonight I have actually played on the Adelaide Oval. Not with much success, I can add. But be that as it may, cricket is only one link among many which join our countries together.

That many Australians are permitted to live here is no doubt due to the fact that you are highly intelligent; but you are more than that, for above all you are very kind and patient. As you know, most Australians are potentially, if not actually, rather irritating. We air our views in vigorous and unrestrained language, and, indeed, we are not considered true to type if we don't stamp unnecessarily hard on the feet of unwary persons from time to time. I am assured by my colleagues that I am true to type, and therefore it is no routine gesture for me to say how grateful the Australians here tonight are to Lord Mountbatten for the felicitous and witty way in which you have proposed this toast and for a glimpse of your activities while a young man which has given us all hope.

The friendliness and toleration of which I have spoken become of greater importance in the world in which we are living today. For we are witnessing the increasing grip that nationalistic forces are gaining in many parts of the world. There is national pride in race, political institutions, past history, intellectual prowess, skill in sport and so on. We are indulging in the inborn combativeness of man, the desire to excel and the desire to impose our point of view. In a civilisation now more obviously than ever before dominated by technological achievements, every country appears to be trying to maintain an export surplus. Though how all countries are to manage this is not at all clear to me. With this necessity constantly in view, nations are becoming more exclusive and less cooperative because they must be more competitive. The fact that this country is considered by some to be an off-shore island is perhaps symptomatic of this. Indeed it did occur to me that it might now be possible to refer to the inhabitants as the 'islanders' to avoid any difficulties with the word 'British'.

Fortunately there are forces acting to bring people together. And between no two countries should they be stronger than between Australia and Great Britain. No doubt it's a good thing that both countries play cricket, but it's not on games alone that lasting cohesion will be based. In my opinion the intellectual compatibility that exists between our two countries is of the greatest importance. Over a long period of time this compatibility was fairly obvious, for although when Australians come to Great Britain and when the Islanders go to Australia unpleasant mutual criticisms are sometimes uttered, there is underlying our relationship a very great area of understanding which never needs expression in words. There are, of course, many reasons for this, and into these I needn't go, but with the passage of time these may become less compelling unless appropriate steps are taken, and taken in time. This country has in the past been a great magnet for Australians, but this will not necessarily continue to be so, for other countries now exert a powerful influence. As I am a scientist perhaps I may be permitted to mention scientists specifically. The reasons for Australian scientists to seek experience in the United States rather than here are increasing. And this means that the draw of this country is diminishing. I deplore this, not because I am anti-American, far from it, but because like so many Australians I wish to see this country playing a noble part in the rapidly changing modern world. There is at present perhaps a certain lack of fire in the belly here. At least there hasn't been enough heat to keep the cold weather away. The time has come for bold projects and not least in the intellectual field. Both Australia and this country could be doing a great deal more to see that a real community based on fundamental ideas is fostered, for in the last analysis it is ideas that count. It is universal experience that many notions that at the time they are propounded seem to be nonsense later become accepted as doctrine on which decisions of far-reaching importance are taken. Great heart would be put into the relations of our two countries if we could more consciously pursue intellectual collaboration as well as sporting rivalry. Perhaps we are waiting for a modern Cecil Rhodes, or even a government who would think it worthwhile to see that conditions are created for some of the intellectual cream of this country to find it possible and profitable to visit Australia, not just for a fleeting week or two but for at least one or two years. I venture to suggest that this might benefit our countries a great deal more than some of the expensive and perhaps phoney projects to which we seem to be committed.

I've spoken tonight as an Australian, but as I've been treated so generously in this country I feel myself an Islander; perhaps therefore I may be favourably placed to see some of the similarities between Australians and Texans. We are both, it is said, boastful. You are probably aware that Texans are kind, hospitable people, so it would not surprise you to know that when a stranger arrived in a remote town in Texas and promptly died, the townsfolk saw to it that he was properly buried. At the graveside, according to local custom, the clergyman asked if anyone would like to say a few words about the deceased. There was a silence, but then a man stepped forward and said 'If no one wants to say anything about the deceased, I should like to say a few words about Texas'. I should like to say a few words about Australia, but I've learnt the lesson that the greatest satisfaction given by an after-dinner speaker is at the moment of his sitting down.

Thank you again, Lord Mountbatten, and for the way you have drunk the Toast.

'I would rather a first-hand Australian failure than another second-hand success'

Robin Boyd

'Creative man in a frontier society': Boyer Lecture, broadcast nationally on ABC radio

17 OCTOBER 1967

Robin Boyd (1919–1971) never shied from expressing his vision of Australia as he saw it or as he thought it ought to be. A member of the well-known artistic family – he was the grandson of painter Arthur – Boyd became the best known architect of his generation and an astringent critic of 'Australian Ugliness'. He believed Australia's adoption of other countries' ideas reflected a lack of cultural confidence and original thinking; the amateur copying of modern American architecture ran 'like a caramel sauce over the cities and the bushland'. Boyd advocated a more creative civil consciousness and more imaginative design deriving from indigenous inspirations.

Boyd served in Australia and Papua New Guinea during World War II before entering the public domain as director of the *Age* Small Homes Service between 1947 and 1953. While he designed many notable Australian homes, it is for his ideas that he is mostly renowned. Historian Geoffrey Blainey said of Boyd: 'He would pick up a theory as if it were a knife and fork and quickly eat with it instead of exalting it into an ornamental box of Sheffield cutlery.' In this broadcast Boyd discusses what he views as a cultural split in Australian thinking.

*

Everyone is a mixture of doer and dreamer. The proportions vary greatly, however, so one person turns out to be a practical man of action and another a creative man of vision. Thus two kinds of people, respectively eclectic and creative by nature, have existed throughout our history, carrying down their two different views of what Australia should be: something borrowed, or something new. The creators were here from the start, most unexpectedly, in the unlikeliest of conditions. Imagine that painfully temperamental, redheaded, visionary convict, Francis Greenway, fighting on matters of artistic principle with his Governor Macquarie, not to mention lesser officers. Imagine that sensitive young creative surveyor, Robert Russell, in the unpleasant Melbourne of 1836, painting, carving cameos, writing a novel, in his hut across the river from where a city was being born in the mud. What a marvellous misfit! In fact, there was always a higher than average spirit of creativity in this country, more than the official histories ever recognised. Details keep coming out now in the more introspective close-ups of history that we have been writing and reading in the two decades since the Second World War.

Think of the creative excitement in literature and illustration when politics were put aside at the old *Bulletin* office in Sydney, and the pure adventure at Heidelberg near Melbourne of those first Australian Impressionists. With all this, and so much more, happening even before the present century began, it is always a little disarming to remember that the impression of the characteristic Australian held by the world outside is inclined to be quite the opposite of a cultured and creative man. And really the most self-satisfied of us has to admit that those historic creative figures were small and spare in our history and that this land was in truth the original Diggerdom where all men were of equal mental mediocrity. The archetype Australian, who made life hard for the creative minority, was the frontierman: lean and leathery, with mouth almost permanently closed against the dust and flies – which was just as well, since when it opened it was found to contain only a few bad teeth and fewer, worse words. Against this rock-bodied and rock-headed man the wings of Australia's creative people were smashed again and again, and there were never enough of them for the cries of anguish and frustration to be heard above the roar of the racetrack crowd.

Yet a country cannot become largely urbanised, cannot contain at least two big cities, cannot send a continuous flow of young people through university, cannot grow older, with all the emphasis and interest so heavily weighted on one side. And so now, in the late years of the 1960s, about 180 years after the foundation, it is not really surprising that a new social phenomenon has been forced into being by the sheer weight of numbers on the smaller side. For the first time in Australia there begins to exist now an articulate intellectual opposition.

Its challenge to the established Australian values is not yet dramatic. This also is characteristic of Australia, which is a closely knit country, as countries go. Indeed, one of the things which most Australians will place high on their list of justifications for national pride is the comparative absence of bitter sectional hatreds and violent political confrontations. We are not used to race riots or to fistfights in Parliament or other colourful explosions of mass emotion, because we are fortunate enough not to have many mass emotions outside the football arena. There are few other countries in the world where the extremists at either ends of the spectrum in politics, in religion, or most of the other social segregators, are able to meet and be matey at the pub bar level. And even fewer other countries where one is likely to encounter such consistency in the subjects of conversation at most social gatherings on Saturday night, whether these take place in the poorest or in the richest houses in the land. Moreover, although in those two houses the standard of wellbeing is distinctly different, the contrast between average poor and average rich is still less pronounced here than in most competitive societies.

However, this apparently homogeneous, easy-going, sports-loving and even classless country, where a knighted stockbroker will drive in the front seat of a taxi – not for fear of offending the driver but because he really wants to talk – actually harbours, as we all know, numberless conflicts of opinion and interest, and divisions into different categories: old and new Australians, white and non-white, conservative and progressive, more and less educated. Yet on such grounds as these all countries of the world are divided, whereas we have, in addition, this other division, the cultural division, that I have mentioned. And it is rather unique. Australia is divided – not into halves, but into two uneven sections – by a jagged, vertical crack near the left end. Facing each other across it are two Australians who are as different and wary of each other in some ways as the Aborigine and Captain Cook.

On the larger side is the modern Australian who believes in the long-established, still popular, anti-intellectual Australian values, who is convinced that the Australian state and rate of progress are satisfactory. On the other is the modern Australian who sees so many shortcomings in Australian social development that he is on the point of despair. I am not referring to the dissent over our overseas involvements. I am speaking of much less dangerous and immediate problems, of attitudes with perhaps much greater long-term consequences, and of the climate that determines where a country stands, or progresses, or backslides, on the road to a desirable civilisation where people may enjoy satisfying and expanding lives.

I must admit that all countries are split somewhere into the haves and have-nots of ideas and the appreciation of others' ideas, but here various qualities in this familiar vertical social split make our version of it characteristically Australian. For instance, when the Englishman or the American dissents, his complaint is lodged against the world. He does not imagine a better place to which he might with luck escape one day. But when the Australian dissents, his complaint is directed squarely against Australia; and he is not in total despair because he always holds the secret thought that ultimately he can escape, if things get too bad, to more enlightened areas of the world.

Another characteristic is the curious nature of the relationship between those on opposite sides of this split. They regard each other with genuinely amused antagonism; each thinks the other is not a permanent menace so much as a temporary laughing-stock.

What I am talking about is not the simple difference between creatively-sensitive people and philistines, which again may be found anywhere in the world. Australia's is a special kind of philistinism, an immovable materialism which puts art and ideas of any kind deliberately and firmly to one side to let the serious business of living proceed without distraction.

Many Americans regard Australia with nostalgia as some sort of reincarnation of their own nation in its youth, when it was driving the frontier out west. Some who so believe are rash enough to migrate here in search of freedom, promise and adventure; and some of these soon return home again, disillusioned. They found here a frontier but it was already pegged out with red tape.

Australia is, in fact, an old man's bureaucracy. We who were born here always have known that, and most of us oldies accept it. But some young people on both sides of the cultural split are perhaps just as bitterly disappointed with this aspect as an American migrant. To understand this cultural split it must be accepted that those on the materialist side are not all doddering conservatives. There can be a progressive attitude as well as the conservative one on both sides of the split, indeed even a pioneering attitude. The young eclectic materialist may be as conscious as the creative man of the immaturity of this country and of the great load of unfinished business lying between it and a wholly desirable civilisation. However, he is convinced that Australia at this stage of its development should still be concerned virtually exclusively with physical, economic, organisational and political problems of the land and its industrial production. He has no time for people with ideas, only for the physical outcome of practical ideas. He is, as indeed we have often heard, a supreme pragmatist, an empiricist. He is the frontierman gone indoors, believing only in what he can borrow successfully from older sources or what he learns from his own experience. And he contends that any other approach to life, any pretensions to original thinking or theorising, are positively out of place and unbecoming in a young country.

The man on the other side must admit the physical problems of Australia; yet he thinks that in their different way these are not much worse than the physical problems of other countries and not sufficient excuse for neglecting all parts of the human anatomy above the nostrils. He denies the need for Australia to continue a life overbalanced on the materialist side. He refuses to believe in an infinite projection of economic security and physical comfort and spectator sports as the goal of living. In optimistic moments he sees Australia already as a comparatively mature country, at least for the moment mature in Western ways compared with some of its Eastern neighbours; he sees the promise of a new Australia actively creating or intelligently receptive to ideas expressive of this country's special condition. Art, science, industry, commerce, politics and international relations are all seen by him as potential channels for this creativity.

This new Australian is a delayed and different type of angry (and sometimes ageing) young man. Among the things which raise his anger are the shortage of money for research, our industry's habitual copying of all kinds of processes and patterns from abroad, the worship of the Overseas Expert – until he has been here for a time, the poverty and conservatism of the everyday arts, the unenlightened design of so much of the artificial side of Australia, the censorship, the loss overseas of so many talented young men and women. All these are symptoms of the ultimate fear of any bold, original, new steps. Most of all, the new Australian is impatient with the old Australian who takes these things for granted, as if all countries were like this. You remember how we used to laugh at Japan for its practice of copying. In proportion to population Japan now registers for patent twice as many new industrial inventions as Australia does. The new Australian feels that the greatest loss suffered in Australia, which is otherwise so good, so generous, so free with meat, beer and sugar, so young and yet so old, is the idea of the idea. He yearns for the excitement of 'the tradition of the new' which has always sparked America.

The minority movement of this new Australian is still young and still small, but there is no scope for reasonable doubt about its future. We can all understand that for the first century and a half of Australian history there could be little or no time for the thought that original Australian ideas could be taken seriously. Too many other demands tugged at the colonial sleeve. In the country some degree of physical mastery of the hostile land was the first consideration; while in the adolescent cities the only goal which entered the colonists' heads was to make a passable reproduction of the comforts of Home. Until about half a century ago, in the drowsy days before the First World War, Australia felt no suggestion of a cultural split, and recognised no dissentient body worth considering. The frontier society faced so much physical work that even the artists and philosophers who managed to exist were apt to agree that they were superfluous.

On the other hand, if we can be optimistic enough to assume the passage of another 150 years without furious war, who can doubt that by then Australia will be a relatively educated, even cultivated country, dominated economically no doubt by another much larger one but pulling its own weight in the world of ideas, contributing to civilisation?

The evolution from a sponge-like culture, absorbing anything useful that floats by, to a crawling and finally free-ranging active culture happens spontaneously and quite suddenly in a society, but only when enough individuals consciously revolt against being sponges. It is interesting to speculate about the moment when the present movement will be strong enough to topple Australia into its own little Renaissance. We live now in the region of possibility of a dramatic change; that is one of the fascinating things about Australia at this time. It could happen any year in the next two decades. If you insist on a finer estimate, I would forecast the revolutionary change of attitude to happen between twelve and fifteen years from now. I base this on the evidence of Canada, which has just this year entered the world cultural club as a fully paid-up member. This event was preceded by a long preparatory period when French Canada came out in open internal cultural revolt, while the external pressure of American influence on all Canada forced the introspection which culminated in the now-famous Massey report. Gradually Canada acquired a new confidence which led to the positive swagger of Montreal at Expo '67.

Australia is not, of course, entirely comparable with Canada. We started after the Second World War almost the equal of her in terms of self-respect and self-confidence. Then in relation to her we fell back. We lack the stimulating irritation of two languages. Yet we have followed closely the Canadian pattern, largely by coincidence, at the respectful distance of about fifteen years. We are not yet at the stage of essential introspection that promoted the Massey Commission and launched the new deal for Canadian arts eighteen years ago. The change may take longer than I estimate, or, of course, it may come sooner. But if we may assume no violent or catastrophic fluctuation in our fortunes, one day in the foreseeable future Australia must arrive at a state of maturity sufficient to qualify it for contributing membership of world civilisation.

Even then this country will still be split vertically between the satisfied materialists and the restless creators, the sponges and the explorers, for all groups of men are so divided. But the split will be nearer the centre. There will be a state of cultural equilibrium, an acceptable balance.

Then the creators – artists, inventors and creative thinkers in all walks of life – will be appreciated. I do not mean to suggest a cultural millennium, or a welfare state dedicated to pampering any earnest, humourless and boring pursuer of art. I mean only that the creative people will be appreciated for what they are worth – little or much, as best the auditors can judge – just as they are now in any civilised country. They will not first have to justify their very existence in a hostile region.

You may think that I make too much of all this. You may contend that Australia is not hostile to creators. Look at the new national acknowledgement of the artists: for instance, men like Dobell, Drysdale and Nolan, not to mention the younger men. Why, one of them even has a knighthood! Indeed, I admit there is some artistic appreciation in the community; otherwise there would be no split at all. Yet the great mass on one side of the split still needs to be convinced that any man of imagination is worth his keep in this tough land of droughts and bushfires. A fairly recent book of biographies of artists spent most of its time explaining that the artists described were, in fact, underneath their art, good, ordinary people. One of our best-known art critics, describing a new sculptor a month or two ago in one of the few daily newspapers in Australia which might be called intellectual, felt obliged to ingratiate his subject to his readers by saying: 'He is big, has a lot of blond hair and looks as if he could throw a punch in the pub if anybody went crook at it.'

I don't want to suggest that all artists in all fields are misunderstood people in Australia. Some of them are as lacking in originality and as reliant on outside ideas as anyone else. Yet, generally speaking, those are not the ones to suffer. The misunderstood, neglected or unhonoured ones are the men with something new of their own to show.

For so long as the man of ideas and imagination is made to feel obliged to justify his very existence – by being able to throw a punch in a pub, for instance – the drain off the top of promising young men will continue and the split in society will keep growing. The smugness with which many Australians regard the development of their country will be countered by a growing fierce reactionary distaste, almost a rejection, by others.

I suppose the split is noticed most keenly by people of my age, in the late forties, for we grew up in an Australia entirely ruled by the frontier philosophy, and any of our friends who had the smallest imaginative inclinations were made to feel in some way subversive. The very fact of living in the city – not being out there smashing down the bush with one's bare fists – was in some way suggested by our elders and betters to indicate a frivolous, perhaps cowardly, certainly contemptible streak. Yet as we grew older we met more and more young contemptibles, and today the movement of which I speak is perceptible even to the conservatives.

It is a movement of Australians who cannot share the old faith that Australia must drift inexorably towards Utopia, no matter what we don't do. Its members have, I think, a strange sort of love-impatience with their country. The love is still there, sure enough, behind the impatience. The fascination of the background myths and the Australian saga, still seep through the irritation and captivate a part of the emotions of anyone who grew up here. It is largely this love that keeps the rebel here, but a part of the myth he does not love is the anti-intellectualism. His aim is to push Australia into the world. He knows that the missing quality necessary to bring this about is the official and popular encouragement of Australian ideas. He realises that this goes against the grain of Australian life up to now, but still he protests. He may not always be intellectual but he is anti-anti-intellectual.

In the ever more crowded and competitive world of the last third of the twentieth century the product that the whole world is craving, and will reward most highly wherever it finds it, is not our wool, and not even our iron or bauxite or natural gas that lay here so long waiting to be discovered. It is brains – and not just acquisitive brains and not just academic brains, but creative brains, imaginative brains exercised to the edge of their capacity – which is the sort of exercise that has been least respected in our 180 years of development. The one precious new thing in this old world is the new idea.

In a later lecture in this series I will try to explain in detail what I mean by ideas in relation to my own field of buildings and cities. In the meantime, I should explain in general terms that I mean by ideas not, of course, half-baked notions and gimmicks, but the real stuff of creative progression which will give us eventually a real Australian civilisation – instead of a second-hand British, or second-hand American, or second-hand second-rate, second-best anything else. At this stage of our development, I would rather a first-hand Australian failure than another second-hand success, but let us hope we can achieve now a few more first-hand, first-rate Australian successes in ideas. I cannot accept that this is impossible simply because our world is dominated by the USA. We need only look at Sweden and Switzerland and Canada to realise that a small nation can still be individual and creative. I cannot accept that we should lie down resignedly under the flood of foreign mass-produced culture. This country is not the USA, nor the UK, nor Scandinavia. It is not European and not Asian. And the details of life's realities here are not the same as the details in any other place. And we have no real civilisation unless we express somehow the realities of our own life in this unique place.

I am not talking of a chauvinistic, nationalistic, Jindyworobak kind of Australianism. I am simply saying that we live in a corner of the globe which is different from other corners for various reasons, and it cannot be completely served at this stage of the world's development by almost total reliance on ideas born elsewhere. For ideas to prosper here, a certain reverse of attitude is necessary. Nothing much can happen while nearly everyone is intent simply on doing.

Yet, this is not a pessimistic time. Admittedly no one at present should expect a strange Australian idea, however good, to be warmly received by every Australian. But at least now it can survive; the climate is just a little more encouraging. The big hope is that the social transmutation is inevitable. The big fear is that it may be delayed by extraneous pressures. But one day this country could quite suddenly start to emphasise creativity, and Australia then would be in her secondary pioneering era, in the field of creative ideas, and we would be on the way to join the world.

'So it was acceptance by me and of me'

Sir Ninian Stephen

'What it means to be an Australian': speech at the National Press Club, Canberra

25 JANUARY 1989

Sir Ninian Stephen (1923–), Australia's twentieth governor-general, was perhaps the outstanding constitutional lawyer of his generation. Taking silk after fourteen years at the Victorian bar, he became a High Court justice in 1970, noted for his voluminous memory and crisp expression. Stephen was born in Oxfordshire, England, and migrated to Australia in 1940, serving with the AIF in the Pacific from 1941 to 1946 before establishing his commercial legal practice. Since his retirement, Stephen has had numerous postings in Australia and overseas, most notably as a judge on the

United Nations Criminal Tribunal for the Former Yugoslavia, Chairman of the United Nations Expert Group on Cambodia and Chairman of the Constitutional Centenary Foundation. In the following Australia Day address, near the end of his seven-year term as governor-general, Stephen speaks about what it means to be an Australian from the perspective of a British immigrant.

*

I was honoured, yet a little alarmed, to receive your invitation, or should I say summons, to address this National Press Club in these dying days of my term as Governor-General.

Long ago the summons of a Byzantine emperor had much the same effect; to disobey it meant extinction, to obey might lead to no happier an end, a wet and painful one, sent up in a bag and cast into the Bosphorus. Lake Burley Griffin, as yet, has not acquired quite that reputation; but to address Press Club Luncheons may involve other, more subtle sanctions. One is surely seeing the media critically reading your speech before you give it. However, I was consoled that my predecessor, Sir Zelman Cowen, spoke here at the club just before his retirement, almost seven years ago – and survived; though one wonders whether it was that experience which then drove him to accept, perhaps in search of revenge, the role of Chairman of the British Press Council.

In any event, a pre-retirement appearance of this sort seems now to be becoming something of a tradition. National Press Club lunches have, of course, over the years and imperceptibly, themselves become a great Canberra tradition just as the Club itself has become one of our National Treasures, a fact which any Government with an ounce of discernment would long since have recognised in some appropriate way; perhaps, at the very least, by listing the more notorious of your members in the ranks of the Bicentennial's 200 Great Australians or even by nominating one or more of you as ACT Fathers or Mothers of the Year. That this has not been done can no doubt properly be added to those lists of shameful Australian acts and omissions which, as a nation, we seem to delight in compiling and then publicly brooding over.

I have been told that my speech should be on that most dreaded of all subjects, a topic of one's own choice, but that it might be appropriate, as a run up to Australia Day, to reflect on Australia and what it has meant to me to be an Australian, especially over the past more than six and a half years as Governor-General, and what I foresee for Australia's future.

As luncheon topics all this sounds pretty indigestible. Of course, a particular difficulty I face is how to say anything remotely interesting yet, while I am still in office, wholly uncontroversial. I can think of perhaps two things that I would like to say today. The first concerns that totally uncontroversial topic – multiculturalism.

There is one aspect of that much abused and overused word that I think *is* worth special mention. We hear, and read, a great deal about what governments, state and federal, should be doing in the area. The thing that distresses me is how *little* most children and grandchildren of overseas-born Australians seem to be retaining of the culture and especially of the language of their lands of origin.

Over the years I've spoken to countless Australians whose mother tongue was other than English and who confess that their children, brought up in Australia, can't speak that mother tongue. And language is so important; it is the key to the understanding of cultures and peoples. To lose an ancestral tongue is to lose a whole heritage. Its loss seems to me to be grievous, both for the individual and for the nation. We should be a nation of great linguists; we boast of being a nation of peoples from many lands, speaking many more than a hundred different tongues. Yet thirty years down the track, with a new, Australian-born generation, that mother tongue so often is lost forever, and this in households where the older generation still speak it.

The trouble is that our Australian culture and lifestyle, while it may not be so startlingly superior to others, is enormously seductive; that, combined with conformist pressure on the young, threatens a monolingual future for a country which should remain *alive* with the languages and cultures of the world.

In a sense I am an example of the very process of which I complain, though I can't blame Australia for it; it happened before I arrived here. My grandparents spoke the Gaelic as fluently as they spoke English, but in one generation it and all the richness of culture it involved, was lost.

Though no Highland Scot would admit it, many would say that that was a special case, the case of a dying language. True or false in the case of Gaelic, it has no application at all to Italian, Greek, German, Russian, Chinese, Vietnamese, the languages of Yugoslavia and of the Baltic states and all the many others that are spoken by first generation Australians today. The retention of these in subsequent generations is what we should be encouraging and preserving. Teach English as a second language by all means, in the second generation it will become the first language; but encourage and applaud in that second and on into later generations bilingual skills that do not have to be hard learned in school but can be absorbed at home, in child-hood, and nurtured there.

It goes without saying that in all this I see no threat to our national identity as Australians or to our sense of being members of one united Australian community. Nor am I saying anything about what should be our future immigration policy; that is a matter for those who from time to time hold elective office in this nation. So, regardless of that policy, even, for instance, in the unlikely event, urged by no one, that all immigration were to cease and we be left with the rapidly shrink-ing population which our own negative-growth birth rate would give us, my hope would still be that as many young Australians as possible grew up at least bilingual.

Which does, I suppose, bring me, in a roundabout way, to the mandated topic – What it Means to be an Australian. Let me turn that around a little and give you my own description of what it meant to *become* an Australian, something of which, our Aboriginal peoples excepted, all of us, or our ancestors before us, have had experience.

My own experience must have been typical of countless other migrants. I arrived in Melbourne, in my teens, knowing no one, with no family or friends already settled here. One great advantage I had, of course: I spoke the language – or thought I did – when my mother and I, in 1940, boarded the ship that was to take us through the Suez Canal and on to Australia. I met my first Australian males on board and four of us got off at Port Said, took a hire car to see the pyramids and were going to rejoin the ship at the other end of the Canal, at Suez. Halfway across the desert the car stopped, the Australians got out and one turned to me and asked whether I wanted what, as a British schoolboy, I knew only as a rather tasteless vegetable to which, as their national emblem, the Welsh were curiously devoted. That was my first introduction to the new language of Australia!

Arriving as a sixteen-year-old in Easter 1940, when the war still seemed a distant, European thing, two terms of school here and then a year as, first, office boy and then articled clerk with a firm of lawyers, certainly didn't make me an Australian. What did was, I think, the four and a bit years in the Army that followed, especially the first of those years, in Australia, mainly in the west, north of Geraldton, living in the bush, six to a tent, with a couple of hundred other, late teenage, Australians.

What's the process? I'd say it is very much a two-way affair: both a sense of feeling that your home is here, that this is your country and Australians your people, and also it is being accepted by Australians as one of *them*. So it was both acceptance by me and of me. And, typically of things Australian, it was a process as undramatic and imperceptible as it was absolute, so that by 1946, when I was discharged, there was no question in the world about what I was, an Australian, although back in the civilian world I still knew almost no one in Melbourne and had only the vaguest idea of what the immediate future might hold.

There are, I think, some fundamental beliefs involved in this business of being an Australian. I necessarily speak for my own generation because no one can speak with assurance of generations earlier or later that one's own.

Central to those beliefs seems to me to be unity of identity, that we are one nation, superficially regional in a state-loyalty sense but wholly without separatist tendencies. This regionalism is pervasive, we all tend to carry stereotypes in our minds of the people of each state and the opening gambit in conversation so often is, 'which state are you from?' so that the particular stereotype can be fitted into place. But this regionalism is really a perverse manifestation of our unity, of the total absence of any inclination towards secession from the Federal union.

Then, closely linked to this unity of identity, is a unity of belief in the form of Government we want: unhesitatingly a democratic one, however much we complain about too frequent elections and too many politicians. Incidentally, I don't sense the same national certainty about our mode of federalism as I do about unity and democracy; despite our regional loyalties, one could *conceive* of a single, central government, combined with a local government system with greater powers than at present, as something acceptable to many, though of course not all, Australians, especially if marketed on a 'fewer politicians and more grass roots democracy' basis.

Another pretty fundamental belief, and much stronger now than a hundred or even fifty years ago, is social egalitarianism, which we have come to so accept that we don't even notice it until, after being overseas, one arrives back home, at Mascot or Tullamarine, and plunges into it again. This isn't to deny the existence of a class structure of a kind, made up of wealth, power and education, but it is to emphasise not just the absence of, but the conscious rejection of anything approaching rigid and discernible caste marks, coupled with a deep-rooted belief in, and satisfaction with, a high degree of social mobility.

A further Australian characteristic is a cheerful cynicism, a refusal to be, or at least to appear to be, reverential about what other nations regard as solemn and sacrosanct; things like the office of Governor-General! And I suppose that of all Australians the journalist members of the Press Club best represent that particular characteristic – which makes this invitation to lunch with you all the more noteworthy.

What has made the past six-and-a-half years or more such fascinating ones for my wife and me in this curious vice-regal role has been the interaction of these four qualities and all the other traits and tendencies that go to make up the social environment of the nation. For those years, made easy for us by the warmth of friendship that we have everywhere encountered, we are deeply grateful, our gratitude so far-reaching that it even encompasses that most unlikely of all subjects of gratitude, the Australian media.

Thank you for inviting us here, to your Club, on this, our last Australia Day in Canberra.

'Neither column in this moral ledger will cancel the other out'

Robert Manne

'My country – a personal journey': the Alfred Deakin Lectures,
Capitol Theatre, Melbourne

20 MAY 2001

Robert Manne (1947–) is Professor of Politics at La Trobe University and one of Australia's most prominent public intellectuals. His ability to translate complex political problems into intelligent and simple language has made him one of the most widely read social critics of our times. A student at Melbourne University of the ardent anti-communist Frank Knopfelmacher, Manne became editor of the conservative journal *Quadrant*. But his political trajectory since has been of a conspicuously independent mind: he has identified with causes traditionally the preserve of the left, criticising government policies in Aboriginal affairs and immigration. His autobiographical Deakin Lecture at Melbourne's Capitol Theatre, delivered in a gentle, measured tone that belied the passion of its sentiments, brought together some of the people and events that have informed Manne's thinking about Australia and his place in it.

*

A strange thought came to me recently. I was born in Australia. I have lived here for almost one-quarter of the time since European settlement and for more than half of the time since federation. And yet, if I am completely honest with myself, I must admit that I still feel in Australia something of an outsider, that is to say, that I feel I do not belong to this country in the way that those of what is called Anglo-Celtic background do. Why?

The answer is not complicated. Both my parents were Jewish

refugees from Central Europe who were among those fortunate enough to make their escape from Europe and to be accepted by Australia before the German government decided upon the policy of the extermination of the entire Jewish people. The circumstances of my parents' flight shaped both my political identity and my sense of Australia. I was never able to overcome the soul-shock I experienced as a child when I came to realise that, only a few years before I was born, the Nazi regime had systematically set upon a policy of removing my people from the face of the earth. I have always felt gratitude to Australia and Australians for their willingness to offer my parents sanctuary and, thus, spare them from the fate that awaited the millions of Jews who were trapped in Europe at the outbreak of the Second World War. My sense of Australia began with the complex feelings associated with being the child of refugees.

Shortly after the war ended my father established a small furniture-making business, of the kind his family had been involved with in pre-Nazi Vienna. He designed very distinctive, elegant and quite beautiful individual pieces of furniture in a half-Bauhaus, half-baroque Viennese style. The chairs and tables and wardrobes were produced in a small workshop in Lygon Street by two or three highly skilled craftsmen, all of whom, as far as I can remember, were also European migrants, recently arrived. My father's clients were all Jewish refugees from Central Europe. In the long term the business was doomed, hopelessly old-fashioned, altogether unable to compete with the high-quality mass-produced furniture that was coming onto the market at this time. In the short term, however, it gave my parents – after the darkness that had descended in Europe and before death and illness caught up with them here – some precious moments of reprieve.

In that decade of happiness my father designed and had built a house on the boulevard in East Ivanhoe, where, at the time, a number of young Australian families, mainly of the professional or business middle class, were also building and settling. Apart from us the boulevard at East Ivanhoe was completely Anglo-Celtic. My parents had a number of Jewish and German friends. But when they visited us, they came from many miles away. None of my closest friends at this time were the children of migrants, let alone Jewish. It was through these Australian boys and their parents that I gained my early understanding of the country where I happened to be born.

My first truly political experience occurred in 1953 shortly after I arrived at the East Ivanhoe State School. I do not think that I realised at the time that Australia was part of something called the British Empire. One morning we were, as was our custom, listening to a broadcast of 'Kindergarten Playtime' on the ABC. The broadcast was interrupted by a solemn voice announcing that King George VI had died. My teacher wept in front of us. I was not at all affected by the rather abstract news about the death of the King, of whose existence I was, at most, dimly aware. But I was profoundly affected by the tears my teacher shed. I learnt at that moment something about the nature of allegiance and also about the very British nature of Australia at that time. These lessons were soon underwritten by the Royal Tour of 1954, when we were, like so many school children, taken to a point where we could observe the Queen pass by, each one of us hoping that she might glance at us. When I became a Republican in later years it was, in part, because of my recognition of how feeble, in comparison with 1954, the symbolic power of the British Crown in Australian life had gradually become.

Because I was the son of Jewish refugees and because our home was filled with Central European food and friends and memories and nightmares and because beyond the home my world was so thoroughly a part of British Australia I always felt myself divided in identity – an Australian at home; an outsider in the neighbourhood and school. As a kind of emblem of that outsiderness a tiny incident stuck in my mind. I was at a friend's birthday party. In the evening his mother summoned us inside, to get away, as she said, from the 'mozzies'. Everyone, apart from me, knew precisely what she meant. Was there laughter when I later asked a friend what a mozzie was?

I do not know what our young Australian neighbours privately made of the fact that a Jewish family had settled in amongst them. I only know that throughout my entire childhood – in both my neighbourhood and school – I did not encounter a single remark or gesture with an anti-Jewish edge or anti-Semitic undertone.

I am sure that, for many reasons, my experience was not typical.

My parents, in particular my mother, who came from an old Berlin Jewish family, were expert in the art of assimilation. Very many Polish Jews who arrived in Australia at the end of the war, often in even more traumatic circumstances than my parents, were not. Almost certainly they found the powerful expectation of assimilation to the behaviour and manners of old Australia more confusing and difficult to accommodate than we did and thus, probably, experienced in their daily lives more tension and unpleasantness than did my family. There was a time when I was more uncritical of the assimilation era than I am now. The underlying assumption of assimilation was that non-British migrants and their families could not be truly 'Australian' until they shed the ways of behaving and thinking they had brought with them from their homelands. For some the expectation of assimilation to the norms of British Australia was relatively painless. If I can speak of my own situation it amounted to little more than an awareness of being an outsider; a mild shame about my parents' manners; the loss of the language of my parents, who decided that if I spoke English with even a hint of a German accent I would suffer disadvantage. For others the expectation of assimilation asked too much, consigning those migrants and even their children to an altogether unnecessary cultural marginality for far too long. It was when, eventually, I came to this view that I became an enthusiast for the prospect of multiculturalism, which Gough Whitlam's government pioneered and Malcolm Fraser's made bi-partisan and secured.

In my early years, then, as I have said, I experienced no anti-Semitism in my daily life. What I knew about it came from books and from the silences in my home about the Holocaust. I did, however, encounter a mild but real religious bigotry of a more authentically home-grown variety, anti-Catholic sectarianism. My primary school was almost entirely Protestant. I remember one day a group of my school friends encountering a group of Catholic students on our way home. I remember the tension between them; the insults hurled, which included the abusive suggestion, that at the time I did not understand, that Catholics were the kind of people who drank human blood and ate human flesh – a reference, as I later understood, to the Catholic sacrament of transubstantiation. Another early sectarian memory is even more vivid. My best friend had a television in his house years before I did. One day I recall his mother launching herself at the television set in a genuine fury and turning it off. A film was being screened. Its name was 'It's a Great Day for the Irish'. This was obviously too much for my friend's mother to bear. She was a very strong-minded woman of Scots Presbyterian background who had, as I discovered at this moment, a visceral hatred of Irish Catholics. In her passion she taught me something about Australia I would never forget, the difficulty of establishing civility in Australia between the Protestant and Catholic immigrants at a time when the Irish question remained unsettled. I am certain that the later success of multicultural Australia in managing the conflicts of warring ethnicities from the Balkans or the Middle East or Indo-China is connected with what the Australian political culture had learned about how peace between Scottish Presbyterians and Irish Catholics could be maintained. I discovered at that moment why Australians still asked of each other at their places of work not to discuss religion or politics. Had I been born a decade later I would have known nothing about this. In the late 1950s or early 1960s the Protestant-Catholic tension suddenly and rather mysteriously disappeared. The strange death of Australian sectarianism still awaits its historian.

Awareness of the sectarian dimension of our history was not the lesson my friend's mother hoped to teach. I think, rather, she aspired to turn me into an ally of the Scots, even going so far as to invite me – a little Jewish boy in short pants – to participate in the Scottish dancing which took place on a regular basis in her suburban home. I enjoyed the highland fling. Alas, I never learned to dislike Irish-Australian Catholics, several of whom became very close friends when I finally encountered this part of Australia during my university days.

My friend's mother taught me another lesson about Australia I would never forget. She was connected with farming families from the Western District of Victoria. Because of her I once spent a week on a sheep farm there. I gained an admiration for the toughness of the farming life. I also learned, by accident, something else. Late one night I overheard a conversation I was not meant to hear. It concerned general agreement, recently predicted, about the imminent end of the world. In the short term I waited, with an open mind, to see whether or not the prediction was true. In the longer term I think I intuited on that night, in seeing how readily a group of intelligent country Australians could accept warnings about an impending apocalypse, the potential force of irrationalism in politics, the openness of rural Australia to the conspiratorial theories of the extreme right. Hansonism in this country did not come altogether as a surprise.

As I look back I can only wonder at the gulf between the world of unspeakable horror which had overtaken my people in Europe and the safety and security of the Australian middle-class milieu of the 1950s in which I grew up. In my childhood I knew, at first hand, almost nothing even about the condition of the Australian working class. When I went from Ivanhoe to the city I stared, almost in disbelief, at the ugly, cramped and rubbish-strewn backyards of the slums of Richmond and Collingwood through which the train passed. Only once did a genuinely working-class boy arrive at our school, very short and wiry with a mean pair of fists. Having seen those fists at work, out of purest opportunism, I decided to befriend Billy and then discovered that I actually liked him as well. In the world I grew up in class divisions were perhaps not as stark as in Britain. They were, however, notwithstanding the official egalitarianism ethos, very real.

It almost goes without saying that for someone from the neighbourhood in which I grew up that I did not encounter a single Aboriginal child in my primary or high school years – and can recall only two lessons where we learnt something about the Aborigines. In one lesson we were required to copy down the words of, I think, William Dampier about the Aborigines being the most miserable people in the world. I would like to think that intuitively I grasped their racism, but I doubt this was so. Another lesson was even more memorable. My grade three teacher, on one occasion, wrote on the blackboard the words 'Segregation or Assimilation?' These were the words of the Aboriginal policy debate of the early 1950s. Again, to be perfectly honest, I am sure I recall this lesson not because of the issues we were invited to explore but because I was almost entranced by the invitation to think about concepts as abstract as assimilation and segregation, words which, as a nine year old, I had never previously heard. How strange that today we are being invited by newspaper articles and right-wing magazines once again to discuss Aboriginal policy in the absence of Aboriginal people and in almost identical terms to the 1950s, the only difference being that those who believe in land rights and self-determination are being accused of being segregationists by the conservatives who have become the champions of a neo-assimilationism.

My childhood political education about Australia was still not quite complete. Two experiences, in particular, stayed with me. When I was eleven or so my father, whose furniture business had, predictably, collapsed, died suddenly of a cerebral haemorrhage. Shortly after my mother became very ill as multiple sclerosis took hold. The minor prosperity which my family had once enjoyed was no more. Not only could my mother not work. She was crippled and required a permanent nurse/housekeeper while my sister and I were at school. If we survived these years in a reasonable financial state it was because my mother received an invalid pension from the Commonwealth government and small reparations payment, on account of the acts of the Nazis, from the government of West Germany. Without these pensions we would have been ruined. These were the days before Medibank. My mother relied for her medical care, in part at least, on a doctor whose fees were paid by the local council. As a child it was not so much the provision of the government pensions that stirred my political imagination but the regular visits of the council-funded doctor. There seemed no obvious reason why the society into which my parents had fled, should take any interest in us or the problems we now faced. And yet it did seem to care. I was grateful that that doctor visited my mother. I did not take these visits for granted. And in later years, when I spoke in defence of the maintenance of the 'welfare state' – that complex of pensions and service provisions for those in different kinds of need – I am sure that my family's own experiences informed my convictions. I am, of course, aware that beyond a certain point welfare provisions can overstretch budgets and unbalance economies. I am also, of course, aware that, in certain circumstances, reliance on welfare can do harm to economic initiative and self-esteem. Nevertheless the attempted transformation of the welfare state into the nanny state in the public imagination was one of the many reasons why I was opposed to the New Right when it emerged throughout the English-speaking world in the 1980s. I still regard the

creation of the welfare state as one of the great humanising achievements of the twentieth century. Of all the things that turned me into
a democratic socialist this is the one that still survives.

In my early childhood there was one final political experience
that affected me quite deeply but which lay dormant for many
years. When I was nine years old the Olympic Games were held in
Melbourne. I was an enthusiastic seeker of autographs. On one occasion I spotted a group of East German athletes who were training on
the golf links very near to where I lived. After training the athletes
returned to their mini-bus. I went there too. Could I have their autographs? The first one signed with a grin on his face. He passed the
book to a second who burst into hearty and fierce laughter. He passed
the book to a third. The same thing occurred. And so on. Eventually
the whole mini-bus was filled with laughter. I was completely non-
plussed. That night I told my mother about the incident. She asked
if she could look at the autograph book. The first East German run-
ner, she explained, had written down, as his name, Joseph Stalin.

The tense Stalin laughter in the mini-bus interested me as deeply
as the tears of my teacher on hearing of the death of King George.
Although at the time I knew about the slaughter of the Hungarians
by Russian troops, it was not really until I went to study at the
University of Melbourne a decade later that the laughter in the mini-
bus became comprehensible to me.

I was a teenage leftist. In part this was because I hoped for human
equality and in part because in the Europe from which my parents
had fled, the threat to Jewish existence had come from the murderous
intentions of the extreme right. My father was a small businessman
who had once been tempted to vote for Mr Menzies, through normal
motives of self-interest, I suppose. My mother, a Weimar German,
who knew considerably less about politics and history than my father,
forbade him from doing so. My political prejudices were unambigu-
ously on my mother's side.

At university ambiguity set in. The reason, again, was straight-
forward. Under the influence of two brilliant but very different
teachers, the Catholic poet and critic, Vincent Buckley and the Jewish
anti-communist social scientist, Frank Knopfelmacher, I became
convinced that the crimes committed by the communist regimes of

Stalin and Mao Xedong were comparable in their evil with the crimes of Nazi Germany. Most of my generation was radicalised in the great antinomian revolution of the late 1960s. My political trajectory was counter-cyclical. 1968 was the critical year. In that year I read and reviewed Robert Conquest's book about Stalin's 'great terror'. It was clear now that massive criminality was not the monopoly of the extreme racist right. In the same year the Soviet Union led an invasion of Czechoslovakia because the orthodox regime there was attempting to liberalise and democratise its ways. This confirmed the direction in which my reading on Stalin and Mao was taking me. Buckley and Knopfelmacher were right.

The most important issue of my student days was the Vietnam War. Concerning this war I was hopelessly divided. I could not support the hideous means which the Americans were using to fight their war and the obscene inequality of suffering which was a consequence of both their technological superiority and their cultural arrogance. On the other hand I believed that if North Vietnam was victorious the people in the south would fall under a brutal, neo-Stalinist regime. When I marched in the moratorium of 1970 I gravitated towards a banner which read 'Neither Washington Nor Hanoi'.

When I returned from Oxford University at the end of the Indo-China wars my ambivalence about Vietnam was expressed in two main ways – in an argument with that part of the left which was at the time in denial about the crimes of the Khmer Rouge and through an involvement in a small lobby group urging the admission of large numbers of refugees from the new communist regimes of South Vietnam, Cambodia and Laos. It has always seemed to me that the admission of large numbers of refugees from Indo-China marked the definitive end of the white Australian dream. These refugees were not handpicked professionals from Singapore or India but ordinary people from across the social classes. I am pleased to be able, on this occasion, to call attention to the very honourable role played by the government of Malcolm Fraser on the matter of the Indo-China refugees.

For today's students the intellectual struggles between left and right in the Cold War must now seem almost as antiquated and unfathomable as the issues which divided cavaliers and roundheads in the English Civil War. For a very long time it seemed to me as if the Cold War and its very predictable lines of divide would never come to an end and that those who were involved in these arguments would be condemned to go on repeating the well-rehearsed moves and counter-moves for the remainder of our lives.

There were many different responses to the end of the Cold War. My own was, at first, a certain disorientation and, then, an immense relief, a feeling of being released from a prison of the mind.

During these years I had been preoccupied by the crimes of the communist regimes in Europe and Asia, because, I am sure, my political identity had been shaped by the knowledge of the Holocaust. Liberated from the preoccupations of the Cold War, I now saw, as if for the first time, something about my own country, of which I had always been vaguely familiar but on which I had never really focused – the catastrophe that had befallen the indigenous people following the arrival of the British on Australian shores. Having belatedly discovered something which Charles Rowley, Bill Stanner and Henry Reynolds could have taught me twenty years before, the historical questions concerning the dispossession and the political questions concerning reconciliation have become dominant preoccupations over the past few years.

Strangely enough it was a remark that I heard on the ABC television documentary series, *Frontier*, with which, I believe, Marcia Langton was involved, which plunged me into serious study. The remark came from the Chief Protector of Aborigines in Western Australia in the inter-war years, A.O. Neville. It was made at the first-ever national conference of the principal administrators of Aborigines who met in Canberra in April 1937. 'Are we going', Neville had asked, 'to have a population of one million blacks in the Commonwealth or are we going to merge them into our white community and eventually forget that there were any aborigines in Australia?'

Neville's rhetorical question struck me with the force of lightning. Was he really advocating a policy for the disappearance of the Aboriginal people? Was this not a clearly genocidal thought? I decided to read the proceedings of the conference where the remark was made. I discovered that Neville's idea of merging or absorbing the so-called 'half-caste' Aborigines into the European population by a process of encouraged inter-breeding had won the approval of all the delegates to the conference – who were, more or less universally alarmed by what they thought of as 'the problem of the half-caste'. I had stumbled upon an aspect of my country's history to which I had previously been blind. As I began to read about the dispossession and its aftermath my sense of Australia became unstable; the ground on which I stood began to shift.

Concerning the country which had offered my parents refuge and where I was born and which I loved, I had now two main thoughts, not one. For the immigrants to this country – from Britain and Ireland, from Europe, the Middle East and Asia, Australia had always been and still remained, despite the problems at the age of globalisation, one of the most attractive societies in human history – well-governed, liberal, law-drenched, tolerant, civil, democratic, spacious, prosperous, egalitarian in its ethos and so on. However for its indigenous inhabitants, from the arrival of the British until the 1960s or beyond – it has been a site of real tragedy – of dispossession, loss of land, culture and language; of murder, disease and demoralisation; of incarceration on missions and reserves, of racial condescension and contempt.

At present, on the Aboriginal question, Australians are polarised between what we have come to call the black armband and the white blindfold points of view. If I can put this division in Cold War terms – while the left is churlish about the great achievements of Australian history but clearsighted about the Aboriginal tragedy, the Right understands the genuine accomplishments of Australian civilisation but is incapable of acknowledging, without equivocation, the self-evident truths about the terrible wrongs inflicted on the Aborigines in the building of the nation.

In Australian history very great achievements and very great injustices occurred. Neither column in this moral ledger will cancel the other out. It is my hope that one day the large majority of Australians will be able to accept the ambiguity at the heart of our history without the need to flinch and turn away.

Like many, although not most Australians, I had hoped that we might have celebrated the centenary of federation in a mood of optimism, by making our transition to the republic and with a consensual declaration of reconciliation. Instead we are celebrating it in the shadow of the failure of the republican referendum, with the rejection of the declaration on reconciliation and with plans, sixty years after the arrival here of my parents, for the construction of two new prison-like detention centres for refugees. At the centenary of federation, deepening divisions between winners and losers, elites and ordinary people, prosperous capital cities and declining country towns, have led, in my opinion, to a peculiar national mood – uncertain, pessimistic, in part, even sour.

There is, of course, great cause to celebrate. There is also, in my country, if I can call Australia that, a great deal we must still achieve.

AUSTRALIA AT WAR

'Our last man and our last shilling'

Andrew Fisher

Speech at an election meeting, Colac, Victoria

31 JULY 1914

In June 1914, a double dissolution of parliament was granted and an election called for 5 September. The Scottish-born leader of the Labor Party and former prime minister Andrew Fisher (1862–1928), campaigned against the Liberal prime minister of the day, Joseph Cook. In response to Cook's commitment of full support for Britain in the war, Fisher responded with his now famous pledge, thereby neutralising Australia's war commitment as an election issue. Fisher routed the government on polling day, and became responsible for overseeing the first dispatch of troops overseas and the financial management of World War I. His legacy in government also includes the creation of the Commonwealth Bank, the Australian Navy and maternity allowances.

There were around 1000 people crammed into the Victoria Hall in Colac – many more strained to hear from the street outside – when Fisher rose to speak, following an address by the local candidate, T.W. Bourke. This was a campaign meeting, and the substance of Fisher's speech was on domestic issues including tariffs, the 'rights of parliament', and financial management. His promise on the war effort was the only part of his speech reported in the first person, but it is widely quoted to this day.

*

... Turn your eyes to the European situation, and give the kindest feelings towards the mother country at this time. I sincerely hope that international arbitration will avail before Europe is convulsed in the greatest war of any time. All, I am sure, will regret the critical position existing at the present time, and pray that a disastrous war may be averted. But should the worst happen after everything has been done that honour will permit, Australians will stand beside our own to help and defend her to our last man and our last shilling. [*Loud applause.*] ...

'We turned our backs on the purifying waters of self-sacrifice'

William 'Billy' Hughes

'On the issues at stake': speech at the Savoy Hotel, London

17 MARCH 1916

No Australian politician viewed the issues of World War I in such extreme terms as William 'Billy' Hughes (1862–1952), who became prime minister in October 1915. When he visited London the following year, war had been raging twenty months, but his rhetoric startled Britons with its intensity. In a series of speeches pressing for increased pressure on Germany and more cooperation between the dominions, he 'swept his hearers off their feet'. Women marched with placards saying 'We want Hughes back' and a popular cartoon depicted 'the Billiwog': 'No war is complete without one'. Later, at the Versailles Peace Conference, Hughes would fight 'like a weasel' and quibble over every point. Most people found him impossible – 'something of an *enfant terrible* to the more dignified delegates' – but particularly American president Woodrow Wilson, who thought him 'a pestiferous varmint'.

Hughes' skills had been honed on the Sydney docks after migrating to Australia from London at the age of twenty-two, where he soon aligned himself with the trade union movement and the Socialist League, winning his first parliamentary seat by 105 votes as a NSW Labor candidate in 1894. In 1901 he was elected into the first federal parliament as a free-trader, becoming minister of external affairs three years later and subsequently serving several terms as attorney-general. Scrawny, hot-tempered and deaf – literally, and to arguments he did not want to hear – Hughes' voice was 'harsh and monotonous, but he trained himself to use it effectively'. He was always controversial: to some, a great statesman, whose contribution to the early Labor movement and wartime leadership would never be matched; to others, a renegade leader who bitterly divided the country over conscription and became Labor's greatest 'rat'.

*

I am glad of the opportunity of stating again what is at present the very inspiration of our life and the burden of all our immediate hopes, activities and desires – our determination to save our civilisation and our liberties from the onslaught of barbarous Prussia.

Many of the members of this society are Americans. I do not think this is the time to judge America's attitude towards this war. For the help that has been given we are, of course, most grateful. As an Australian I may be permitted to say to the American members of this society two things.

The first is that we in Australia face the United States across the Pacific, and so have, with her, common interests and should have closer friendship. The second is that we are winning – we shall win. I speak as one from the frontier of Anglo-Saxonism when I say that, to those who know the British Empire, and the resolute men and women who inhabit it, there is not a shadow of doubt that the vast might of our empire, and of our race, as it can and must be organised, will be invincible and completely victorious.

This dreadful war was forced upon us. By no act of ours did we provoke it. No people desired war less than those who make up that congeries of nations which we designate by the term 'British Empire'. We were, and are by instinct, a peaceful people and we may be, indeed, best described as a civilised people. No better and clearer distinction can be drawn between us and that great nation with which we are now locked in deadly struggle than the fact that the British nation stands for the highest ideals of civilisation. What the other stands for, let all their dreadful deeds since war began, and the vile doctrines upon which their nation for forty years has battened, say.

It may be said with certainty that there is not an ideal cherished by us that finds an answering echo in the minds of the enemy. With them Might is Right. There is between the ideals of Britain and Germany a gulf as wide as divides heaven from hell, right from wrong.

The issues at stake are vital, and the fate of the world hangs upon them. And the people of the earth – although some may look on with an air of indifference and hold themselves aloof – are being enveloped against their will in this struggle, which, like some great tidal wave, sweeps resistlessly over the whole earth and cannot be dammed here or there by the act of any man or any nation. The destiny of the world today is trembling in the balance, and every nation, as every man, must make up its mind on which side it shall take its stand.

This war will leave the world very different from what it found it. There were many of us drifting along pleasant, profitable channels. The call of duty fell dully on our ears. We turned our backs on the purifying waters of self-sacrifice. We thought only of pleasures, or, at best, of privileges rather than duties.

This war has come as a mighty incentive to urge us on – a spur needed perhaps by our race for its salvation. In any case, it has come, and it will profoundly affect the destiny of the whole world.

If by any malign stroke of fate the issue should turn against us, the clock of civilisation would be set back a hundred years. The outlook of mankind would be profoundly changed. Evil would have overcome good. Force would have trampled upon right. We should fall back into what, although it might be disguised under the thin veneer of Kultur, would nevertheless be a real state of barbarism, for barbarism does not differ from civilisation in appearance, but in reality; not by their garments alone do civilised men differ from barbarians, but in their thoughts, in their outlook upon life, in their conduct and by the acceptance of the standard of Right not Might.

We have gone out to do battle with the enemy. Out of evil cometh good. The war fell upon an empire menaced with turmoil. But at the first rattling of the sabre turmoil died down, dissensions ceased, we were a united people. There is not from Dan to Beersheba, from one end of this mighty empire to the other, a place where the people do not stand four-square against their common enemy. This war has welded together, by bonds that time will not dissolve, that nothing but our own incredible folly can wholly break asunder, the loose federation known as the British Empire into one homogeneous nation.

I have come here, after some eighteen months of war, as the representative of a great dominion. During this time the dominions – Canadians and South Africans and Australians – have, on the field of battle, proved that the ancient valour of their sires still burns in their veins. They have all proved themselves worthy of their breeding. They have realised clearly that this war is not one that concerns Britain only, nor even the empire as such, but is one which affects the very foundations upon which civilisation rests. I have come here as the chosen representative of the most democratic government in the world. I stand here as a representative of Labor and all the ideals that you and I jointly cherish and the ideals of organised Labor. And all these, I say, rest upon the foundations of liberty, and must fall if we lose this battle.

We in Australia have fought, are fighting, and shall continue to fight to the end for those institutions which to free men are dearer than life itself. We fight not for material wealth, not for aggrandisement of empire, but for the right of every nation, small as well as large, to live its own life in its own way. We fight for those free institutions upon which democratic government rests. In Australia what the people say goes; whatever they choose to make law is law; they are the rulers of their own destiny. But in the country against which we are fighting today the will of the German proletariat, though 10 millions, though 50 millions stand behind it, is as nothing beside the will of the Kaiser.

Liberty does not dare to venture into that cold and chilling atmosphere – I do not speak of that poor, pallid cadaver of liberty that slinks through the land surrounded by the Prussian Guards. Our ancestors have fought and died for liberty, and shall we, if needs be, do less?

We fight, therefore, in this war for liberty. We fight for those free democratic institutions without which life as we know it would lose its savour. We could have purchased for the passing hour an ignoble peace had we but consented to bend the knee to Baal. If we had but abased ourselves before this mighty Moloch all would have been well. The Germans were prepared to hold out the hand of friendship to Australia. But we, like Belgium, knowing that their friendship was even more fatal than their enmity, chose rather to die as free men than live as the creatures of despotism. And it is in this spirit that the British race faces this great crisis today.

Although we are a peace-loving people, although we have slumbered in a lotus land for many years, we have shown to the world that we have not lost the valour of our forefathers. The dominions have proved themselves worthy to stand alongside the men from the Motherland. Today, whatever Germany may not know, she does know that when she fights Britain, she fights not merely the 45 million people in the United Kingdom, but also those millions of free men scattered throughout the world who look to Britain as the cradle of their race – men of adventure, men of resolution, who will fight to the bitter end alongside those from the land of their sires, to whom they owe their liberties and institutions of free government.

And here, on St Patrick's Day, let us pay a tribute to the loyalty of the Irish people and the valour of the Irish troops. And when I, as an Australian, express my elation at the glorious deeds of those thousands of young Irish-Australians in the Australian Forces, who have put the cause of liberty above life itself, is there one of you who does not share my feelings?

I feel that I stand here today in the reflected glory of the Australian soldier. I never speak, I cannot speak, of their bravery but I choke with emotion. We speak with pride, and rightly, of the glorious charge of Balaclava. There men went out in the broad light of day, with pulses leaping under the stimulus that a knee-to-knee charge on swift-galloping horses gives to men. They raced, side by side, into the jaws of death, and their glory lives after them. But the story of how the men of the 8th Light Horse of Australia went out to die in the dark hour before the dawn, when the tides of life are at their ebb, is one by which even that of the Charge of the Light Brigade must pale its fires.

There were some 500 of them, and they were to attack in three waves. They were given their orders six, eight, ten hours before. Every man believed that he was going out to almost certain death. Yet they did not hesitate. They made their preparations. They handed to those who were to remain in the trench their poor brief messages of farewell, and waited calmly for the order.

In the dark hour when night is yielding doggedly to day, these young soldiers of Australia went out to die. As the blast of the whistle sounded, the first wave leaped from the trench, but nearly all fell back dead upon their fellows who were waiting their turn in the trench. None got more than a few yards before being shot down. In the face of this awful sight the second line, undaunted, leaped out. Of these only five or six remained on their feet after they had gone ten or twelve yards. The third wave followed in their turn and met the same fate. The wounded lay exposed to the pitiless machine-gun fire of the Turks, which poured a veritable hail of death into their poor, bleeding bodies. The colonel was killed at the head of his men fifty yards from the trench. Eighteen officers went out – two only returned. Of the men the merest handful survived.

We must look back into the grey dawn of history before we find a deed parallel with this. The Spartans of Thermopylæ have left an imperishable name, whose glory has shone through the ages with a lustre which time has not dimmed and which will burn brightly when the pyramids have crumbled to dust and the proudest monuments of kings are no more. But surely what these young Australian soldiers did that day – these men of a new nation, the last but one in the family of the great British Empire – what these men did, too, will live for ever!

We have fought, and we are fighting, this battle as if it were a battle of life and death. We did not enter it lightly, nor shall we quit it while life remains in us. Australia has sent out of the country, to the European or Asiatic battlefields, up to the first week in March, 150,000 men. We shall have enlisted, by the beginning of June, 300,000 men. The Australian is coming out to do battle for the country that made him what he is. Australia is a great country; indeed, it is a continent

— a country of tremendous distances, a country in which men imbibe the spirit of liberty with every pore, and in which men, of necessity, take a wider outlook than those whose environment is more cramped. It is a country in which men would rather die than lose liberty.

They are coming out, these men nurtured in the free air of a great land, with bodies magnificently developed and spirits unbroken and unbreakable; they are coming out to do battle for the country that made them. They are showing today the mettle of their pasture. They are fighting for everything they hold dear by land or sea. They are fighting this battle in deadly earnest, knowing it to be a battle to the death. For it is a battle from which we are to emerge triumphant, with our great empire welded indissolubly together, or in which we must go down with all prospects of achieving our destiny forever damned.

Germany's barbarous practices — her submarines, her gases, her devilish cruelties — are with us still; but the policy of frightfulness, though it horrifies the world, cannot daunt the men of our race. And it has been powerless to affect more than a very small percentage of the mighty mercantile marine of Britain. From the most distant shores her argosies cleave their way undismayed. To her shores they are going from distant Australia and the Canadian shore, carrying grain, provisions, ammunition — everything necessary for the successful prosecution of this war. The German navy, built for our destruction, is locked within the narrow waters of its home.

True, Britain was unprepared in a military sense. Yet she has done wonders. One can hardly forbear to ask what she would have done *had* she been prepared.

I only know that Australia has been able to do what she has, because we adopted as the cornerstone of our democratic edifices the system of compulsory military training. We believe that there is but one way by which a nation, being free, can remain free, and that is that every man shall be willing not only to defend his country, his home and his liberties, but be trained to do so.

The defence of one's country is the primary duty of citizenship; it is the first duty of free men. Two years before the outbreak of war we had established in Australia a system of universal military training. To this we owe that complex and widespread organisation for training officers and non-commissioned officers, for manufacturing small arms, ammunition, clothing and so on, without which we should have been almost helpless in this great struggle.

A small community of under 5 million people, we have been able to train, to equip from head to foot, a great army of men. It is a great thing, and one which we may mention with pride and satisfaction, that Canada and Australia together have put into the field nearly twice the number of the original British Expeditionary Force.

I have no doubt, nor has any citizen of our empire any doubt, of what the result will be. Britain and her allies at the outset of this fight were caught at a disadvantage. We were like peaceful citizens taken unaware by bandits. But we are gradually mustering our tremendous resources. We are turning our men of peace into men of war. We are gathering against our great opponent – and I pay every tribute to the bravery of the great German nation – the tremendous resources of a free people who will die to the last man rather than be defeated.

And we shall win. We have encircled this tremendous and ferocious foe with a wall of steel which, despite her most frantic efforts, she cannot break.

'Feed your troops on Victory'

Sir John Monash

'Leadership in war': address to the Beefsteak Club, Melbourne

30 MARCH 1926

In hindsight, Sir John Monash (1865–1931) was overendowed with all the attributes necessary for success as a military leader: he was a meticulous administrator with a compendious memory, an engineer with a scientific detachment, but a sensitive man with a comprehension of the toll in human suffering inherent in battle. While prepared to court unpopularity, he wrestled with the 'appalling strain' of having to throw his men again and again into the 'blood tub'. Billy Hughes remarked that Monash 'was the only general with whom I came in close contact who seemed to me to give due weight to the cost of victory'. His command of troops in the battle of Hamel in July 1918 was acclaimed by military historians as 'the perfect battle'.

After the war, when he was the first chief executive of the Victorian State Electricity Commission, Monash became a member of the Melbourne Beefsteak Club, an association of twenty or so gentlemen who met monthly to enjoy an evening of 'Beef and Brotherhood'. The members assembled 'to partake of the Monthly Dish of Steaks' on Saturday evenings. A speaker was often engaged to address the Brotherhood, for 'The sauce to meat is ceremony,' and – like his attention to detail in the battlefield – Monash considered his topic and prepared his speech with care.

*

… War does not lend itself greatly to philosophic thought; it rests more upon considerations of expediency than of principle. The application of principle, even where possible, is generally subconscious. Time and circumstance rarely permit of ordered reasoning or deliberately formed judgements. The successful exercise of leadership must, therefore, in the end, rest upon the degree of success with which a man is able to make his decisions, and make them soundly, without that detailed review of the relevant data, and that process of deliberate reasoning which are the customary mental processes applied to most other human affairs.

The capacity to form judgements, rapidly and soundly, is, I believe, more temperamental than intellectual. I grant that a well-stored mind, a well-exercised mentality and a fund of varied experiences in the affairs of life are a necessary stock-in-trade. But these would avail a man little in war if he had not the right temperament for that environment.

A successful leader must be unemotional to the extent of being callous to the external influences which evoke joy or sorrow, elation or despondency; he must be indifferent to praise or blame; he must have the capacity to persevere calmly and dispassionately with the business in hand, undisturbed either by the menace of imminent calamity, or by the exultation of success. He must be patient to a degree. He must have determination and steadfastness of purpose of a very high order. He must have an exalted confidence in himself and in the correctness of his judgement, amounting to an intellectual arrogance. His capacity to appreciate the working of the minds of others must be automatic and swift. His personality must be of a kind which inspires confidence in others, and which dominates their instinct to exercise independent judgement.

He should be, in short, temperamentally, a paragon of excellence, which, I fear, none of us, in spite of earnest aspirations, ever completely reached. Yet, the AIF did produce a number of competent and successful war leaders, each in his respective sphere. This was very definitely the result of the elimination of the unfit, more than of training and adaptation to environment – I am thinking mainly of that phase of the war during which (and not until which) we achieved real success in the sense of definitely accelerating the consummation of final victory, that is, the 1918 campaign in France. ...

By that time, everyone had naturally gained some years' experience in the technology of tactics, of weapons and munitions, and of the many and varied problems of the maintenance of armies in the field. But that was not enough to make successful leaders. It was this technical experience, only when superimposed upon inherent temperamental qualities, which did so in the case of those leaders who survived until the stage of victory was reached. Those who possessed no high technical knowledge of the art of war were not necessarily failures, provided that their personality was otherwise of the right kind. But, on the other hand, many men, who had during peace time won high reputations as text writers and authorities on the technicalities of war and war machinery, failed to achieve successful leadership. ...

It may be thought – indeed it seems to be generally considered – that personal popularity among the troops is essential to successful leadership. This is so far from being true that the contrary proposition can be argued. Besides, the popularity of a war leader is, in the last resort, gauged, by the rank and file, not from his personal contact with them and their impressions of his personality, but by the success of his organisation and command. A force which finds itself well-equipped, well-fed and well-quartered, and which is able to achieve victories in battle without serious losses, will speedily elevate its leaders in its regard and esteem even if it has but rare personal contact with them.

Perhaps the highest and most critical of all the tasks of a leader are the creation and maintenance of the morale of his men, the practical task of which is their collective readiness to allow themselves to be used as the instruments in his hands for the execution of his plans. The larger the military formation, the more difficult is such a task; because the leader is more and more removed from personal contact with the rank and file, and must therefore more and more rely upon the cooperation of intermediate commanders and staffs. The measure of his success in this rests, therefore, upon his power of inspiration.

It is one of the commonplaces of military training and adminis-tration which says that a platoon is the mirror – the reflex – of the personality and temperament of its platoon commander. This small group of some twenty men is a faithful embodiment of his own characteristics. My experience is that this is, in practice, literally true. An unpunctual, untidy, unenterprising and discontented platoon becomes an infallible criterion of the character of its commander, and a wise exercise of supervision by higher authority should lead to his speedy elimination.

In the same but wider sense, it is the inspiration of the supreme commander of the whole formation which permeates through all its detailed ramifications. This is a process which is partly active and conscious, but in greater part automatic. It must be remembered that, in its essentials, the organisation of an army is intensely autocratic. A commander, of whatever grade, holds his subordinates in the hollow of his hand. He has the power to make and to break men at his whim and pleasure. It is a power which is but rarely curbed, even if it may sometimes be exercised unjustly and wantonly. It is more expedient that the authority of a commander in his treatment of his subordi-nates should be upheld under all circumstances, than that occasional wrongs and petty tyrannies should go unredressed. And that is why it happened but rarely and only in aggravated and sustained cases that acts of arbitrary and unjust treatment of subordinates were ever vis-ited upon a senior commander. ...

It is this very authority also which places in his hands the means for exercising a beneficent inspiration throughout his entire command. A corps commander is in daily, indeed hourly, contact with his divisional generals, his staff, his artillery, aircraft and tank commanders, each one of whom has been schooled, by experience, to submit himself to the will of his leader. All the greater, therefore, is the responsibility of that leader to infuse, by his example, by his methods and by his self-expression, that spirit of just and humane exercise of his absolute powers, that devotion to the cause, that will to victory, that high sense of duty and that application of his utmost intellectual and physical powers, which together make up *morale* and are the essential ingredients of successful leadership.

Just in the ratio that he does succeed in doing so, will his senior subordinate commanders, if they are men of the right calibre, absorb and disseminate those same influences in their respective spheres; and so, in the broad result, the army, as a whole, becomes the true reflex of the character of its commander, just as does the platoon.

I have said already that character is of more importance than technical knowledge or skill in its application to the problems in hand. A leader can, if he must, lean for technical detail upon his expert staff; and, if he be wise, he will see to it that he has at his elbow a trustworthy expert in each branch of the war-like art. But that is not to say that he will not be all the better a leader, and all the more competent exponent of his plans and policies, if he has himself a good working knowledge of the minutiae of the various services and branches of his command.

It is just at this point that a number of the so-called 'amateur' generals of Australia and Canada were at a distinct advantage in contrast with many of the professionally trained soldiers of the Imperial Divisions; and the same applies to quite a number of British officers who achieved senior rank during the war, but who were 'amateurs' in the same sense, in that they had had no previous war or army experience. This advantage rested upon a wide civilian training as engineers or architects or as captains of industry, a training far more useful for general application to new problems than the comparatively narrower training of the professional soldier. In the regular army one knows all about one or two applied arts very thoroughly – horsemastership, or gunnery, or musketry, or chemical warfare, or military law, or military engineering, and very little about anything else. It was indeed characteristic of the senior army officer of the best type that he could talk well and informatively of his particular arm of the service, and of polo or fox hunting, and of the traditions of the army, but that he was dilettante, if not entirely uninterested, in every other subject of science, art or philosophy.

Now, although the basic principles of strategy are unchangeable throughout the centuries, and although, even in tactics, the late war produced no fundamental changes or wide departures from previously established doctrines – yet there arose many new problems associated with improvements in the mechanism of fighting material. The use of aircraft, in their multitude of widely differing types, the automatic machine guns, the numerous types of grenade, both manually and mechanically propelled, the gradual evolution of the tank as a thoroughly mobile and largely self-protective means for concentrated attack upon otherwise invulnerable objectives, the employment of camouflage (which, by the way, means disguise, and not concealment – a crucial distinction), the use of smoke, poison gas and new forms of high explosive all presented entirely new problems with which the regular army was just as unfamiliar as were the comparatively untrained auxiliary forces of Great Britain and the dominions. In the mastery of these problems, in the acquisition of the new technique involved and in the employment of these new agencies to the best advantage, it is my contention that commanders and staff officers who had, before the war, had adequate scientific or technical training and experience, were actually at a definite advantage over the average regular army officer with his stereotyped but narrow training.

I well remember one incident which bore in upon my mind the conviction that some, at least, of the very senior army leaders, of whom we colonial divisional generals stood in such awe, did not possess the type of mind which would permit of their adapting themselves very readily to the use of new ideas. It was at the first lecture and demonstration of the use of poison gas, in the form known as 'cloud' gas, carried out by one Colonel Fookes (not, by the way, a regular soldier, but an industrial chemist of high pre-war standing) which I attended early in 1917, at which there was a considerable gathering of corps, divisional and brigade generals who happened to be free from other obsessions on that day. I thought it a very fine and able demonstration, carrying conviction as to the value of this means of offence under suitable conditions. After the lecture and when questions were invited, one very senior and physically strikingly picturesque corps commander, carefully adjusting his monocle, spoke up thus: 'What do you say would happen, Colonel, if the wind were blowing from the direction of the enemy's trenches towards our own?' Fookes looked bewildered, and stammered that under such conditions, the cloud of poison gas would probably be very damaging to our own men. Then said the great man with much impressement and with a triumphant look around, speaking very deliberately 'Ah, indeed. I knew quite well there was a catch in this thing somewhere!'

Now that story illustrates an attitude of mind responsible for a condition of things which will probably rather surprise you. The best brains of the empire were constantly at work on the invention and perfecting of new means of offence and defence, both on land, at sea and in the air. But in very many cases it did not follow at all that a new appliance, or method, or substance, even after ample demonstration of its utility, became universally adopted, say, by the Army Council, or generally used by the fighting troops on a mandate from above. Far from it. ...

Don't forget that, in substance, this is only another manifestation of the doctrine which dominates all military organisation and training, which is that you have to legislate for the average or sub-average man in every branch and department of military work. Any military structure built upon the supposition that the personnel of an army, of whatever rank, is of more than average intellectual capacity would be doomed to failure, in view of the inevitably low average quality of the human material of which an army must necessarily be composed. That is the reason – and the good reason – for the red-tape and stereotyped routine of army procedure, for the adoption of 'rule-of-thumb' methods and the universal empiricism of treatment of army problems. ...

The popular impression is that war consists mainly of fighting. The truth is that fighting is but an occasional interlude in a dreary routine of work, both mental and physical. The mere maintenance of an army absorbs fully one-half of the total available man-power; and the fighting half is occupied incessantly in the tasks of training, of perfecting its defensive dispositions or of detailed preparations for occasional offensive action, and often in all of these tasks simultaneously. Maintenance implies much more than the mere feeding and clothing and quartering of the personnel. It involves also the organisation, administration and normal operation of the entire territory occupied, for the time being, by each formation. It includes the construction and maintenance of roads and waterways, the upkeep and operation in all details of railways leading back to the base port and often the construction of new railways to prolong the line of supply, the creation of works of water supply and sanitation, the control of the civilian population, and the continuance, as far as practicable, of civilian life and industry, the salvaging of derelict stores and material, the supply of munitions and warlike stores to all the fighting units, the custody, handling and evacuation of prisoners of war, the medical, surgical and dental care of the whole personnel with its elaborate system of preventive and curative treatment of the healthy, the sick and the wounded, similar services for the riding, draught and pack animals, the collection and dissemination of intelligence and information bearing upon the campaign both in general and in relation to the particular situation of the moment. Even front-line units, when not 'resting', which is a euphemism for intensive training and for the compliance with constant demands for the supply of 'working parties' to supplement the man-power of the maintenance services, are continuously employed in field fortification, bridging, draining, and fetching and carrying of every sort and kind.

The number of individuals and the proportion of their waking hours which have to be devoted to the mere clerical work of regulating and supervising such a mass of varied activities may be imagined – especially when it is remembered that the whole machine must be made to work smoothly in the face of the constant daily and hourly efforts of the enemy to impair or totally destroy the organisation. ...

You will appreciate, therefore, that a corps commander, even during times of comparative inactivity so far as field operations are concerned, has, if he takes his work seriously, a pretty handful of anxieties and perplexities; for, even if he is so fortunate as to have an experienced administrative staff (as distinct from his fighting staff) the mere administration of his command involves an amount of supervision, a degree of personal handling of a multitude of troublesome and difficult questions, and a continuous preoccupation with problems of improving efficiency and economising man-power which are, to say the least, of formidable proportions. Upon these duties, which never abate, even during fighting periods, you must superimpose the rarer, but stupendously more important, task of attempting to plan and direct victorious operations against the enemy.

As this is the real objective and consummation of successful leadership in war, it may be of interest to dwell a little upon that phase of a commander's work. In this, more than in any other phase, will his personal disposition be reflected, ranging from reckless audacity to cautious timidity. As in most human affairs, it is the happy mean between such extremes which will, in the long run, prove most fruitful of sustained success. One principle is, however, fundamental. No form of passive defence can lead to a decision. Even when the prescribed role is defensive in policy, it is still true that offence is the best defence. ...

A commander must, therefore, have sufficient enterprise and daring to keep his troops 'tuned up' in fighting morale by frequent excursions into offensive tactics, yet be sufficiently calculating and conservative to make certain that his enterprises are uniformly successful. Nothing was so stimulating to all as success, however small, so long as it was tangible and definite. The capture of a handful of prisoners and machine guns in a petty raid, or the capture of enemy artillery in a larger set-piece operation, such as Messines, was always enough to thrill and embolden the multitude. But failure, or heavy losses without overbalancing results would have been equally depressing and discouraging. 'Feed your troops on Victory' is the maxim which is the touchstone of the successful leader. ...

These notes have reached the limit of my time, and, I greatly fear, the limit of your patience. They have been jotted down in a scrappy manner, in odd moments, in an all-too-rare leisure. They partake, by turns, of scraps of personal memoirs, of didactic and dogmatic expressions of opinion. They make no claim either to an adequate or a consecutive treatment of the theme on which I embarked, namely to describe some of the problems and phases of leadership in war which it fell to my lot to experience. But I console myself with the thought that, if these notes were worth writing at all, the Beefsteak Brotherhood is the only audience before whom I could have dared to speak with so little reserve, such complete freedom from restraint, and such confidence that the obtrusively but unavoidably personal tone of this paper will not be misunderstood.

'It is an occasion for elevating the public spirit'

Sir John Monash

Speech at a reunion of ex-service men, Melbourne

26 April 1930

Even before it became a popular date of commemoration, Sir John Monash was never in doubt about the significance of Anzac Day. Beginning a speech at his alma mater Scotch College on Anzac Day in 1922, he emphasised: 'It was on this day, seven years ago, just as day was breaking, that the soldiers of Australia and New Zealand stormed the beetling cliffs of Gallipoli, and in so doing, founded the tradition of the Australian nation.' As the tradition of the march was established, the 'natural spokesman for returned soldiers' emerged at its forefront: from 1925 until his death, Monash led Melbourne's Anzac Day march, and was instrumental in the construction of the Shrine of Remembrance.

The following extract, from a handwritten collection, is all that remains of a speech Monash delivered the day after Anzac Day in 1930. Even though it is incomplete, the words suggest that the 'deeper significance' of the commemoration of Anzac Day – beyond a march and an act of remembering – has always been tangible.

*

I want to point out that a public celebration like we had yesterday (Anzac Day), is very much wider, and has a deeper significance than appears on the surface. It is true that it is intended as an act of remembrance of our comrades who have gone, as an act of homage to their memory, and an act of pride in the achievements of Australia, but it is something more than that. It is an occasion for elevating the public spirit and public sentiment. We are gathering together our citizens in hundreds of thousands, who have presented to them noble ideals and noble thoughts, and they are animated by common ideals of worthy purpose. Heaven knows we need such stimulation today. That is why I have tried to throw myself whole-heartedly into another project – the great memorial known as the Shrine of Remembrance. I think that, too, when it is completed in all its glory and grandeur, will become an object of reverence to the community, and will have an influence which will be uplifting, and will band the community together in elevated thought and common national purpose.

'It is in this outlook that danger lies for Europe'

Sir Thomas Blamey

'The Sentinel', broadcast no. 6, 3UZ

1 May 1938

Few military commanders have inspired such loyalty and loathing as Sir Thomas Blamey (1884–1951), commander-in-chief of the Australian Military Forces between 1942 and 1945, under the overall command of the American military patrician General Douglas MacArthur. A veteran of Gallipoli, he was described by the British General Birdwood as 'an exceedingly able little man' who was 'by no means a pleasing personality'. This emerged clearly in a controversial eleven-year term as chief commissioner of the Victorian Police which ended in 1936 with him destroying the Police Association and alienating both the press and the Labor Party. Monash, nonetheless, praised his 'infinite capacity for taking pains', and this emerged when, during the eighteen months before the outbreak of World War II, he broadcast an anonymous weekly radio program for station 3UZ on the situation in Europe. The program was known only as 'The Sentinel', and the identity of the broadcaster was not revealed until after his final program, entitled, 'The Tragedy of Poland is Approaching'. The following extract of the sixth 'Sentinel' broadcast, which went to air shortly after Hitler's annexation of Czechoslovakia, shows a sophisticated grasp of the dynamics of the German Reich, and casts prophetic doubts on the 'peace in our time' that British prime minister Neville Chamberlain thought he had obtained in Munich.

*

… The German coup in Austria is still fresh in our mind. The key of recent German activity in Europe is to be found in the teachings of Hitler in his book *Mein Kampf*, widely, almost compulsorily read in Germany and without doubt expressing the German attitude today. The first part of this book was written in prison, but the second volume was written with the help of the German General Staff. So that when it proclaims a method it should be carefully weighed. Hitler's method has followed the book rather consistently so I would draw your attention to this when he says:

> However much we recognise the necessity of a reckoning with France this would yet remain ineffective if it were to become the only goal of foreign policy. It can only have sense if it acts as a cover for an enlargement of the living room of our people in Europe. It is not to colonial acquisition that we must look for a solution of this question, but exclusively to the acquisition of territory for settlement which will increase the area of the Motherland.

And again:

Do not look upon the Reich as secure if it cannot give for centuries to come its own piece of land and soil to every branch of our people.

It is in this outlook that danger lies for Europe. The method is to stir up by propaganda the border Germans as in Austria and to make demands by the Nazi Party leader to be followed by the menace of the national sword. Germany will not find it nearly so easy a task in Czechoslovakia as she found in Austria, but the pressure on Eduard Beneš [Czechoslovak president] and Milan Hodza [Czechoslovak prime minister] may be so great as to force them to give away much that they would not give except under the menace of their geographical isolation and weak strategical position.

'It is my melancholy duty to inform you'

Sir Robert Menzies

'Australia is at war': national radio broadcast

3 SEPTEMBER 1939

As a British dominion, Australia was committed to World War II from the moment Britain declared war on Germany, two days after the Wehrmacht stormed across the Polish frontier. On 23 August 1939, after the surprise announcement of a pact between Germany and Russia, Britain had announced its solidarity with Poland if that country's territorial integrity was threatened; Robert Menzies (1894–1978), Australia's prime minister for five months, announced that if Britain was 'forced into war it will not go alone'. His speech from a Melbourne radio studio on the Sunday evening, therefore, was not unexpected; it has power, nonetheless, in its sadness and solemnity in the foreshadowing of an undertaking that would take six years to discharge.

*

Fellow Australians. It is my melancholy duty to inform you officially that, in consequence of a persistence by Germany in her invasion of Poland, Great Britain has declared war upon her, and that, as a result, Australia is also at war.

No harder task can fall to the lot of a democratic leader than to make such an announcement. Great Britain and France, with the co-operation of the British dominions, have struggled to avoid this tragedy. They have, as I firmly believe, been patient; they have kept the door of negotiations open; they have given no cause for aggression. But, in the result, their efforts have failed, and we are therefore, as a great family of nations, involved in a struggle which we must at all costs win, and which we believe in our hearts we will win.

What I want to do tonight is just to put before you honestly and as clearly as I can a short account of how this crisis has developed. The history of recent months in Europe has been an eventful one. It will exhibit to the eyes of the future student some of the most remarkable instances of a ruthlessness and indifference to common humanity which the darkest centuries of European history can scarcely parallel. Moreover, it will, I believe, demonstrate that the leader of Germany has for a long time steadily pursued a policy which was deliberately designed to produce either war or a subjugation of one non-German country after another by the threat of war. We all have vivid recollections of September of last year. Speaking in Berlin on September 26, 1938, Herr Hitler said, referring to the Sudeten–German problem, which was then approaching its acutest stage: 'And now the last problem which must be solved, and which will be solved, concerns us. It is the last territorial claim which I have to make in Europe.'

Four days later, at Munich, when the problem had been settled on terms which provided for the absorption of the Sudeten country into Germany, and which otherwise professed to respect the integrity of the remainder of the Czechoslovak state, Hitler participated with the Prime Minister of Great Britain in a statement which went out to all the world. Its most important sentence was this:

> We are resolved that the method of consultation shall be the
> method adopted to deal with any other question that may

concern our two countries, and we are determined to continue our efforts to remove possible causes of difference and thus to contribute to assure the peace of Europe.

What a strange piece of irony that seems today, only twelve months later. In those twelve months, what has happened? In cold-blooded breach of the solemn obligations implied in both the statements I have quoted, Herr Hitler has annexed the whole of the Czechoslovak state; has, without flickering an eyelid, made a pact with Russia, a country the denouncing and reviling of which has been his chief stock-in-trade ever since he became Chancellor; and has now, in circumstances which I shall describe to you, invaded with armed force, and in defiance of civilised opinion, the independent nation of Poland. Your own comments on this dreadful history will need no re-enforcement by me. All I need say is that whatever the inflamed ambitions of the German Fuhrer may be, he will undoubtably learn, as other great enemies of freedom have learned before, that no empire, no dominion can be soundly established upon a basis of broken promises or dishonoured agreements.

Let me say something about the events of the last few days. The facts are not really in dispute, they are for the most part contained in documents which are now a matter of record. On Friday, August 25 – that is, nine days ago – Herr Hitler asked the British ambassador to call on him, and had a long interview with him. Herr Hitler said he wished to make a move towards England as decisive as his recent Russian move, but that first, the problem of Danzig and the Corridor must be solved. He went on to indicate that he was looking forward to a general European settlement, and that if this could be achieved he would be willing to accept a reasonable limitation of armaments. On Saturday, August 26, the British ambassador flew to London to give a detailed account of his conversation to the British government. On Sunday, August 27, the British cabinet fully considered the whole matter, and incidentally, was appraised by me of the views of the Australian Government. On Monday, August 28, the British reply – which I may say was entirely in line with our own views – was taken back to Berlin, and was delivered to Herr Hitler in the evening. That reply stated that the British government desired a complete and lasting understanding between the two countries, and agreed that a prerequisite to such a state of affairs was a settlement of German–Polish differences. It emphasised the obligations which Great Britain had to Poland, and made it clear that Great Britain could not acquiesce in a settlement which would put in jeopardy the independence of a state to which it had given its guarantee. The government said, however, that it would be prepared to participate in an international guarantee of any settlement reached by direct negotiation between Germany and Poland which did not prejudice Poland's essential interests.

The note pointed out that the Polish government was ready to enter into discussions, and that it was hoped that the German government would do the same. On the night of Tuesday, August 29, Herr Hitler communicated to Sir Nevile Henderson his reply to the British note. In it he reiterated his demands, but agreed to accept the British government's offer of its good offices in securing the dispatch to Berlin of a Polish emissary. In the meantime, it was stated, the German government would draw up proposals acceptable to itself, and would, if possible, place these at the disposal of the British government before the arrival of the Polish negotiator. Astonishingly enough – for the German proposals were not then even drafted – the note went on to say that the German government counted on the arrival of the Polish emissary on Wednesday, August 30, which was the very next day. Sir Nevile Henderson pointed out at once that this was an impossible condition, but Herr Hitler assured him that it was only intended to stress the urgency of the matter. On the Wednesday Herr Hitler's communication was received by the British government, and their reply was handed by Sir Nevile Henderson to von Ribbentrop, the German Foreign Minister, at midnight. At the same time the British ambassador asked whether the German proposals which were to be drawn up were ready, and suggested that von Ribbentrop should invite the Polish ambassador to call, and should hand to him the proposals for transmission to his government. I would have thought this was a very sensible suggestion, but von Ribbentrop rejected it in violent terms. Von Ribbentrop then produced a lengthy document containing the German proposals, which you subsequently saw in the newspapers, and read it aloud in German at top speed. Sir Nevile Henderson naturally asked for a copy of the document, but the reply was that it was now too late as the Polish representative had not arrived in Berlin by midnight.

You see what a travesty the whole thing was. The German government was treating Poland as in default, because she had not by Wednesday night offered an opinion upon or discussed with Germany a set of proposals of which, in fact, she had at that time never heard. Indeed, apart from the hurried reading to which I have referred, the British government had no proper account of these proposals until they were broadcast from Germany on Thursday, August 31.

On the night of August 31 the Polish ambassador at Berlin saw von Ribbentrop, and told him that the Polish government was willing to negotiate with Germany about their disputes on an equal basis. The only reply was that German troops passed the Polish frontier and began war upon the Poles on the morning of Friday, September 1.

One further fact should be mentioned and it is this: in the British government's communication of August 30 it informed the German Chancellor that it recognised the need for speed and that it also recognised the dangers which arose from the fact that two mobilised armies were facing each other on opposite sides of the Polish frontier, and that accordingly, it strongly urged that both Germany and Poland should undertake that during the negotiations no aggressive military movements would take place. That being communicated to Poland, the Polish government on Thursday, August 31, categorically stated that it was prepared to give a formal guarantee that, during negotiations, Polish troops would not violate the frontiers, provided a corresponding guarantee was given by Germany. The German government made no reply whatever.

My comments on these events need not be very long. The matter was admirably stated by the British Prime Minister to the House of Commons in these words:

> It is plain, therefore, that Germany claims to treat Poland as in the wrong because she had not by Wednesday night entered upon discussions with Germany about a set of proposals of which she had never heard.

Let me elaborate this a little. You can make an offer of settlement for two entirely different purposes. You may make your offer genuinely and hoping to have it accepted or discussed with a view to avoiding war. On the other hand, you may make it hoping to use it as 'window dressing' and with no intention or desire to have it accepted. If I were to make an offer to my neighbour about a piece of land in dispute between us and before he had had the faintest opportunity of dealing with my offer I violently assaulted him, my offer would stand revealed as a fraud. If Germany had really desired a peaceful settlement of questions relating to Danzig and the Corridor she would have taken every step to see that her proposals were adequately considered by Poland and that there was proper opportunity for discussion. In other words, if Germany had wanted peace, does anybody believe that there would be today fighting on the Polish frontier, or that Europe would be plunged into war? Who wanted war? Poland? Great Britain? France?

A review of all these circumstances makes it clear that the German Chancellor has, throughout this week of tension, been set upon war, and that the publication of his proposals for settlement was destined merely as a bid for world opinion before he set his armies on the move.

We have, of course, been deluged with propaganda from Berlin. We have been told harrowing stories of the oppression of Germans; we have been told that Poland invaded Germany; we have even been told – somewhat contradictorily – that Germany was forced to invade Poland to defend herself against aggression. The technique of German propaganda, of carefully fomented agitations in neighbouring countries; the constant talk of persecution and injustice; these are all nauseatingly familiar to us. We made the acquaintance of all of them during the dispute over Czechoslovakia and we may well ask what has become of the Czech minority and the Slovak minority since the forced absorption of their country into the German state.

It is plain – indeed it is brutally plain – that the Herr Hitler ambition has been, not as he once said, to unite the German peoples under one rule, but to bring under that rule as many European countries, even of alien race, as can be subdued by force. If such a policy were allowed to go unchecked, there could be no just peace for the world.

A halt has been called. Force has had to be resorted to to check the march of force. Honest dealing, the peaceful adjustment of differences, the rights of independent peoples to live their own lives, the honouring of international obligations and promises – all these things are at stake.

There never was any doubt as to where Great Britain stood in relation to them. There can be no doubt that where Great Britain stands, there stand the people of the entire British world. Bitter as we all feel at this wanton crime, this is not a moment for rhetoric, prompt as the action of many thousands must be, it is for the rest a moment for quiet thinking, for that calm fortitude, which rests not upon the beating of drums, but upon the unconquerable spirit of man created by God in His own image.

What may be before us, we do not know; nor how long the journey. But this we do know; that Truth is our companion on that journey, that Truth is with us in the battle and that Truth must win.

Before I end may I say this to you? In the bitter months that are to come, calmness, resoluteness, confidence and hard work will be required as never before. This war will involve not only soldiers and sailors and airmen, but supplies, foodstuffs, money.

Our staying power, and particularly the staying power of the Mother Country, will be best assisted by keeping our production going; by continuing our avocations and our business as fully as we can; by maintaining employment, and with it, our strength. I know that in spite of the emotions that we are all feeling, you will show that Australia is ready to see it through.

May God in His mercy and compassion grant that the world may soon be delivered from this agony.

'The hands of the democracies are clean'

John Curtin

Australia announces war on Japan: national radio broadcast

8 DECEMBER 1941

John Curtin (1885–1945) – like Ben Chifley – has attained heroic, even martyred, status in the annals of the Australian Labor Party. Self-taught after leaving school at thirteen, Curtin joined the Victorian Socialist Party in 1910 before entering federal politics and eventually winning the Labor leadership in 1935. Curtin mastered his alcoholism in order to fulfil his political ambitions, but lived every moment of Australia's war effort, struggling to reconcile the sometimes competing needs of Australian and imperial security. After his death in office just a month before World War II was over, James Scullin, an earlier Labor prime minister, remarked that 'his end teaches us that it is not hard work, either mental or physical, that kills a man; it is anxiety and worry'.

Curtin declared war on Japan one hour after Japanese bombers struck at Pearl Harbor on the morning of 7 December 1941 – again on the radio from a studio in Melbourne. He had been in office for exactly two months following the disintegration of the Menzies administration, and this was his worst nightmare: Australia had been geared for imperial defence in the northern hemisphere and was underprepared for the opening of a new theatre of war in the Pacific. This was, he felt, 'the gravest hour of Australia's history'.

*

The Australian Government and its representatives abroad have struggled hard to prevent a breakdown of this kind. We did not want war in the Pacific. The Australian Government has repeatedly made it clear, as have the governments of the United Kingdom, the United States of America and the Netherlands East Indies, that if war came to the Pacific it would be of Japan's making. Japan has now made war.

The hands of the democracies are clean. The discussions and negotiations between Japan and the democracies were no mere bandying of words on the democracies' part. Since last February it has been the aim of the democracies to keep the peace in the Pacific. The best brains of the democracies were brought to bear for this end. It is on record that the President of the United States and Secretary of State, Cordell Hull, and the British and Dominions governments worked untiringly and unceasingly. Yet when the President of the United States decided to communicate direct with the Japanese Emperor in support of an appeal for imperial intervention on the side of peace, the war government of Japan struck. That war government, bent on aggression, and lusting for power, and acting in the fashion of its Axis partners, anticipated the undoubted weight of the President's message and shattered the century-old friendship of the two countries.

For the first time in the history of the Pacific, armed conflict stalks abroad. No other country than Japan desired war in the Pacific. The responsibility for this actual resort to war is therefore upon Japan … Australia goes to its battle stations in defence of its very way of living.

'We are fighting mad'

John Curtin

Speech to the people of America, broadcast on Radio Australia

20 MARCH 1942

Following a request from the Melbourne *Herald* for a New Year Message, John Curtin wrote a statement to the nation entitled 'The task ahead', in which he predicted 'a year of immense change in Australian life': 'Without any inhibitions of any kind, I make it quite clear that Australia looks to America, free of any pangs as to our traditional links or kinship with the United Kingdom.'

He amplified the statement several times in the coming months, including in an address to the American people broadcast on Radio Australia. This period of Curtin's leadership marks a shift towards a more independent Australian foreign policy; away from the weakening British Empire and towards a new alliance.

*

Men and women of the United States: I speak to you from Australia. I speak from a united people to a united people, and my speech is aimed to serve all the people of the nations united in the struggle to save mankind. On the great waters of the Pacific Ocean war now breathes its bloody steam. From the skies of the Pacific pours down a deadly hail. In the countless islands of the Pacific the tide of war flows badly for you in America. For us in Australia it is flowing badly.

Let me, then, address you as comrades in this war, and tell you a little of Australia and Australians.

I am not speaking to your government. We have long been admirers of Mr Roosevelt, and have the greatest confidence that he understands fully the critical situation in the Pacific and that America will go right out to meet it. For all that America has done, both before and after entering the war, we have the greatest admiration and gratitude.

It is to the people of America I am now speaking, to you who are or will be fighting, to you who are sweating in factories and workshops to turn out the vital munitions of war, to all of you who are making sacrifices in one way or another to provide the enormous resources required of our great task.

I speak to you at a time when the loss of Java and the splendid resistance of the gallant Dutch together give us a feeling of both sadness and pride. Japan has moved one step farther in her speedy march south, but the fight of the Dutch and Indonesians in Java has shown that a brave, freedom-loving people are more than a match for the yellow aggressor, given even a shade below equality in striking and fighting weapons.

But facts are stern things. We, the allied nations, were unready. Japan behind her wall of secrecy, had prepared for war on a scale of which neither we nor you had knowledge.

We have all made mistakes. We have all been too slow. We have all shown weakness, all the allied nations. This is not the time to wrangle about who had been most to blame. Now our eyes are open.

The Australian Government has fought for its people. We never regarded the Pacific as a segment of the great struggle. We did not insist that it was the primary theatre of war; but we did say, and events have so far unhappily proved us right, that the loss of the Pacific can be disastrous.

Who among us, contemplating the future that day in December last when Japan struck the assassin at Pearl Harbor, at Manila, Wake and Guam, would have hazarded a guess that by March the enemy would be astride the south-west Pacific, except General MacArthur's gallant men and Australia and New Zealand?

But that is the case, and, realising very swiftly that it would be the case, the Australian Government sought a full and proper recognition of the part the Pacific was playing in the general strategic disposition of the world's warring forces.

It was, therefore, but natural that within twenty days after Japan's first treacherous blow I said on behalf of the Australian Government that we looked to America as the paramount factor on the democracies' side in the Pacific.

There is no belittling of the old country in this outlook. Britain has fought and won in the air the tremendous Battle of Britain. Britain has fought, and with your help has won the equally vital battle of the Atlantic. She has a paramount obligation to supply all possible help to Russia. She cannot at the same time go all out in the Pacific.

We Australians represent Great Britain here in the Pacific. We are her sons, and on us the responsibility falls. I pledge you my word we will not fail. You, as I have said, must be our leader. We will pull knee to knee with you for every ounce of our weight.

We looked to America, among other things, for counsel and advice, and therefore it was our wish that the Pacific War Council should be located at Washington. It is a matter of some regret to us that even now, after ninety-five days of Japan's staggering advance south, ever south, we have not obtained first-hand contact with America.

Therefore we propose sending to you our Minister for External Affairs, Dr Herbert V. Evatt, who is no stranger to your country, so that we may benefit from discussions with your authorities. Dr Evatt's wife, who will accompany him, was born in the United States.

Dr Evatt will not go to you as a mendicant. He will go to you as the representative of a people as firmly determined to hold and hit back at the enemy as courageously as those people from whose loins we spring, those people who withstood the disaster of Dunkerque, the fury of Goering's Blitz, the shattering blows of the Battle of the Atlantic.

He will go to tell you that we are fighting mad, that our people have a government that is governing with orders and not with weak-kneed suggestions, that we Australians are a people who, while somewhat inexperienced and uncertain as to what war on their soil may mean, are nevertheless ready for anything, and will trade punches, giving odds if need be until we rock the enemy back on his heels.

We are then, committed heart and soul to total warfare. How far, you may ask me, have we progressed along the road?

I may answer you in this way. Out of every ten men in Australia, four are now wholly engaged in war as members of the fighting force or making the munitions and equipment to fight with. The other six, besides feeding and clothing the whole ten and their families, have to produce the food and wool and metals which Britain needs for her very existence.

We are not, of course, stopping at four out of ten. We had over three when Japan challenged our life and liberty. The proportion is now growing every day. On the one hand, we are ruthlessly cutting out unessential expenditure, so as to free men and women for war work; and, on the other, mobilising woman power to the utmost to supplement the men. From four out of ten devoted to war, we shall pass to five and six out of ten. We have no limits. We have no qualms here. There is no fifth column in this country. We are all the one race, the English-speaking race. We will not yield easily a yard of our soil. We have great space here, and tree by tree, village by village, and town by town we will fall back if we must.

That will occur only if we lack the means of meeting the enemy with parity in materials and machines.

For, remember, we are the Anzac breed. Our men stormed Gallipoli. They swept through the Libyan desert. They were the 'Rats of Tobruk'. They were the men who fought under bitter, sarcastic, pugnacious Gordon Bennett down Malaya, and were still fighting when the surrender of Singapore came.

These men gave of their best in Greece and Crete. They will give more than their best on their own soil, where their hearts and homes lie under enemy threat.

Our air force is in the Kingsford-Smith tradition. You have no doubt met quite a lot of them in Canada. The Nazis have come to know them at Hamburg and Berlin, and in paratroop landings in France.

Our naval forces silently do their share on the seven seas.

I am not boasting to you, but were I to say less I would not be paying proper due to a band of men who have been tested in the crucible of world wars and hall-marked as pure metal.

Our fighting forces are born attackers. We will hit the enemy wherever we can, as often as we can, and the extent of it will be measured only by the weapons to our hands.

Dr Evatt will tell you that Australia is a nation stripped for war. Our minds are set on attack rather than defence. We believe, in fact, that attack is the best defence. Here in the Pacific it is the only defence we know. It means risks, but safety first is the devil's watchword today.

Business interests in Australia are submitting with a good grace to iron control and drastic elimination of profits. Our great labour unions are accepting the suspension of rights and privileges which have been sacred for two generations and are submitting to an equally iron control of the activities of their members. It is now work or fight for everyone in Australia.

The Australian Government has so shaped its policy that there will be a place for every citizen in the country. There are three means of service: in the fighting forces, in the labour forces, in the essential industries. For the first time in the history of this country a complete call-up, or draft as you refer to it in America, has been made.

I say to you, as a comfort to our friends and a stiff warning to our enemies, that only the infirm remain outside the compass of our war plans.

We fight with what we have, and what we have is our all. We fight for the same free institutions that you enjoy. We fight so that in the words of Lincoln, 'Government of the people, for the people, by the people, shall not perish from the earth.' Our legislature is elected the same as yours, and we will fight for it and for the right to have it, just as you will fight to keep the Capitol at Washington the meeting place of freely elected men and women, representatives of a free people.

But I give you this warning: Australia is the last bastion between the west coast of America and the Japanese. If Australia goes, the Americas are wide open.

It is said that the Japanese will bypass Australia, and that they can be met and routed in India. I say to you that the saving of Australia is the saving of America's west coast. If you believe anything to the contrary, then you delude yourselves.

Be assured of the calibre of our national character. This war may see the end of much that we have painfully and slowly built in our 150 years of existence, but even though all of it may go there will still be Australians fighting on Australian soil until the turning point be reached, and we will advance over blackened ruins, through blasted and fireswept cities, across scorched plains until we drive the enemy into the sea.

I give you the pledge of my country. There will always be an Australian Government, and there will always be an Australian people. We are too strong in our hearts, our spirit is too high, the justice of our cause throbs too deeply in our being, for that high purpose to be overcome.

I may be looking down a vista of weary months of soul-shaking reverses, of grim struggle, of back-breaking work, but as surely as I sit here talking to you across the war-tossed Pacific Ocean, I see our flag, I see Old Glory, I see the proud banner of the heroic Chinese, I see the standard of the valiant Dutch.

And I see them flying high in the wind of liberty, over a Pacific from which aggression has been wiped out, over peoples restored to freedom and flying triumphant as the glorified symbols of United Nations strong in will and in power to achieve decency and dignity, unyielding to evil in any form. Good luck to you all.

'We shall win, or we shall die'

General Douglas MacArthur

Speech at a parliamentary dinner, Canberra

26 MARCH 1942

On 19 March 1942 it was announced that General Douglas MacArthur (1880–1964) had arrived in Australia, following his appointment as Supreme Commander of the Allied Forces in the south-west Pacific – it was a month since the bombing of Darwin had shattered Australian complacency. MacArthur was at the time beating a retreat, having fled the Japanese assault in the Philippines, though he had already sworn his famous oath, 'I came through, and I shall return'.

This speech at a parliamentary dinner was part of a strategy of rebuilding the MacArthur aura. He had that same day been awarded the Congressional Medal for Honour, the highest decoration for valour in the American Army, and been praised by President Roosevelt for his 'utter disregard for personal danger' and his 'gallantry and intrepidity above and beyond the call of duty in action against the invading Japanese forces'. Australian willingness to fall in step behind the great general was evinced by the lavish praise for this address, described by those present as 'the finest speech in their memory'.

*

I am deeply moved by the warmth of greeting extended to me by all of Australia. The hospitality of your country is proverbial throughout the world, but your reception has far exceeded anything I could have anticipated.

Although this is my first trip to Australia, I already feel at home. There is a link that binds our countries together which does not depend upon written protocol, upon treaties of alliance or upon diplomatic doctrine. It goes deeper than that. It is that indescribable consanguinity of race which causes us to have the same aspirations, the same hopes and desires, the same ideals and the same dreams of future industry.

My presence here is tangible evidence of our unity. I have come as a soldier in a great crusade of personal liberty as opposed to perpetual slavery. My faith in our ultimate victory is invincible, and I bring you tonight the unbreakable spirit of the free man's military code in support of our just cause.

It embraces the things that are right, and condemns the things that are wrong. Under its banner the free men of the world are united today. There can be no compromise. We shall win, or we shall die, and to this end I pledge you the full resources of my country, and all the blood of my countrymen.

Mr Prime Minister, tonight will be an unforgettable memory for me. Your inspiring words and those of your compatriots will be emblazoned always in my memory as though they had been carved on stone or bronze. Under their inspiration I am taking the liberty of assuming the high honour of raising my glass in salute to your great country and its great leaders.

'My faith in victory never wavers. Does yours?'

Bessie Rischbieth

'A talk by an Australian to Australians': broadcast by BBC radio, empire-wide, from London

LATE 1942

Bessie Rischbieth (1874–1967) spent World War II in London working for the Australian Women's Voluntary Service, and despite the privations and terrors of successive German bombing campaigns was 'never afraid'. After journeys to the countryside as part of her volunteer work Rischbieth said she was 'always glad to return to London, bombs and all ... aptly described as battered a little, yes, bothered a little, but quite unbowed'. This spirit infected her regular broadcasts over the BBC to Australia giving up-to-date accounts of the atmosphere in the war-torn city. In this address, late in 1942, Rischbieth describes the work of the volunteers and the state of the Australian servicemen they were assisting at that time.

*

It is well over two years since I left Australia. I never imagined that I should be absent for more than six or seven months. The war forcing me to remain here has been worthwhile, for it has provided me with a strange new experience. To be in the midst of danger has had a stimulating effect on me. During the bombing periods and the continuous black-outs I've thought often of sunny Australia ten thousand miles away from the danger zone. It seemed like a paradise on earth, far removed from the madding crowd.

But alas now the unexpected has happened! Many of us are exiles in this island fortress; while our country is suddenly faced with the grave peril of invasion. My intense and general feeling of cut-offness is shared to the full by many Australians in London. Especially by the men of the war services, whom I meet at the Australian Forces Centre at Australia House.

We are deeply concerned for you all by the threat of this Japanese menace. Our hearts go out to you, our people; and to our country, and we want you to know this.

The canteen at Australia House is a hive of activity and goodfellowship. It would thrill you all at home, could you but catch a glimpse of the facilities and comforts provided for our men. What is always so evident is the happy home atmosphere which prevails. The men of the naval, army, air and merchant services on leave make for this centre. All feel that it's a bit of home from home. The things done for them range from mending their socks to mending their hearts, with refreshments thrown in. Some stay for hours of recreation, playing games, reading, writing or just talking.

The large voluntary staff of helpers are all Australians. Under the direction of a most capable committee of women, the organisation and development of this work is successfully carried out by the Australian Women's Voluntary Services. Our airmen tell us that because of danger shared in common they experience a sense of comradeship which is never the same in ordinary life. Whatever their rank we make no difference, nor do the men among themselves.

The other day in the canteen it made my heart rejoice to hear a hefty, bearded able seaman say, 'You're as good to me as me Mother is. And that's saying something.'

We have our tragic moments as well as our amusing ones, for we hear of many different experiences.

Recently I noticed a rather dejected sailor with a plastered face come hesitatingly up to the snack-bar. I smiled at him and asked, 'Were you here for the celebration of Australian Foundation day? We had a splendid party.'

'No,' he said. 'My party was a very different character. I am one of twenty survivors of 140 bombed at sea. All I have now is what I stand up in.'

He was feeling very much the loss of his pals. Although he appeared outwardly composed, I noticed how tense and over-wrought he really was. We began talking to him about things Australian and about Australia and his family. In no time he was happier and in a quieter frame of mind.

Arrangements were then made by the hospitality section (a most important branch of the work) for him to visit some of his own Australian friends now living in the north of England. Before he left he was much recovered. He was given a large parcel of woollies and a small hamper which he intended to share with his friends.

Our men here sometimes feel very cut off from their home surroundings. England makes up for this by extending a warm welcome, and they enjoy the hospitality of some of the most charming English homes. Those who've had the most harrowing experiences usually have the first choice.

Some of the lads have such fun on their sight-seeing tours around London. One very young sailor came in with a beaming face, chuckling and laughing. With his fair hair, clear skin, blue eyes and cap on the back of his head, he looked carefree. With a twinkle in his eye he said, 'You don't know what's happened to me.'

He was so excited about it we all thought that at least he had been received at Buckingham Palace, and asked him if he had. 'Not quite that. But nearly as good. I was looking over the law courts, when a group of barristers in their wigs and gowns and white ties passed through the corridor. They stopped and questioned me. Then they took me off to lunch. There was I sitting in the middle of them. And didn't they give me a jolly good feed.'

The men who have married over here bring along their young brides to receive a welcome.

Even under war conditions and wholesale destruction, romance still plays its part. We know of several cases of lovers who actually met last war. Through unforeseen circumstances they were parted and now have met again, after twenty-five years. This time they have had the opportunity to marry each other.

Girl friends as guests are allowed provided they are in uniform. A charming English girl in the WRNS came along with a young naval cadet. On her cap was 'HMS *Mercury*'. She was a high-upped motor-cycle dispatch-rider, sometimes doing a hundred miles on one journey. She was proud to be working with the Aussies, as she says they are always first on the spot when things go wrong.

I'm sure I need not ask you whether you listen in to the session 'Anzacs Calling Home,' when the messages by your absent men are made possible by the close collaboration of the Forces Centre and the BBC. We help them write their messages, which are then recorded in their own voices. Although they are far away from home they feel they are actually brought very near to you by the microphone. One man wondered if maybe his baby or his dog were 'listening in', in the hope that his voice may be remembered.

An Aussie airman, whose brother had been killed in Greece, wanted to speak to his home folk to give them a word of sympathy and cheer. He asked them not to grieve as his brother did well and he died well. 'Cheerio, chins up,' were his parting words.

The Queen's visit to Australia House created a sensation. The men loved meeting her. Their story to you over the microphone 'I met the Queen' lost nothing in the telling. One merchant serviceman reminded her of a previous meeting in Australia and said quite spontaneously, 'We've met before. I met you in Australia, and you haven't altered a bit.' Much to the amusement of the Queen.

By this time you are all familiar with the voice of the announcer Mr H.H. Stewart of Sydney, who is most popular with the men. We hope you enjoy the listening in as much as we do the transmitting.

I have told you something of the work done for our men and women of the War Services in London. Now let me talk to you about another side of the women's voluntary work. Your 'Parcels for Britain' containing many valuable gifts are carefully distributed among the blitzed women and children of London. At one of our sewing and knitting centres, a tea-party was arranged for bombed children and their mothers. I can assure you it was a red-letter day for both mothers and children who came from the East End. Some of the mothers had not left their district for seventeen years.

The helpers dressed a small girl aged three in a complete hand-knitted set of bright red woollies. Another small boy in blue and another in lemon and so on. The children strutted round the room for inspection and were obviously very proud of their new clothes. You can guess the extraordinary good effect of getting new clothes – a most refreshing experience when one is all dusty and done in. It was a great consolation and joy that those so far away had thought of them.

You have done much to contribute to all this activity in London, and our sincere thanks go out to you. We feel now that this is your hour of need and all our thoughts are with you. Australians over here fully appreciate the magnificent stand made by our men to stem the tide of the advancing Japanese in Malaya and Dutch East Indies. Here among us, we feel greatly relieved that General MacArthur is with you. A man of outstanding ability and courage. It thrilled us all when we read of the interview between him and the accredited war correspondents. These men admitted that, although a hard-boiled lot, each came away with faith revived and with inspired words ringing in their ears – the words of a man who means to conquer, who will conquer. And that is how we Australians in London also feel about it.

The spot-light is now on Australia. Under the present challenge, I feel on this side of the globe a deeper public interest in the future of

Greater Britain overseas. A desire to understand the real attachment between us 'Down Under' and this dear old country. Our men in the Services are frequently asked this question, 'Why did you volunteer to come over here to fight?' A Yorkshire friend of mine sent me a press cutting of an interview with an Aussie in the ranks. Pressed for an answer as to why he had volunteered he said, 'Well, we were told that someone was trying to down the old lady. So we came along to help square up.' This was the answer of a man three generations removed from the original British stock.

On another occasion I was at a small social gathering. A Polish countess, who by the way was a refugee in this country and had lost all her possessions, took me aside and in a confidential manner said, 'As a writer, I am most curious to understand the reason why your men volunteer to come ten thousand miles to fight a war so far removed from their own shores.' She seemed struck with the fact that men who were not conscripted from cradle to grave as in Europe should want to fight.

My reply was, 'Ninety-seven per cent of our people are British stock. Blood is thicker than water. These blood ties will never be broken so long as human hearts continue to beat. You see, our men live in a country under a free government. They therefore value human freedom. The choice before all nations today is freedom or enslavement. To keep their own freedom, the Aussies at the outset were eager to throw in their lot with the liberty-loving peoples of the earth.' What I had said interested her greatly.

As a result of this conflict, to my mind, the people over here will eventually get a clearer conception of what a greater Britain really means. My faith in Victory never wavers. Does yours? A new world will gradually issue from this ruined heap. This is no ordinary war but the end of an old age and the beginning of a new era. We know that under all circumstances you will carry through with calm courage and resolution. Just as the people of old England are doing. And the Russians and the Chinese.

As I see it, world focus is passing to the New World in the Pacific. I firmly believe, that in spite of the dark shadow which threatens our country at this hour, Australia is destined eventually to be the nucleus of a Great Tomorrow.

'The rabbit that runs is always in more danger than the rabbit that sits'

Padre Fred Burt

Speech to the Returned Services League, Perth

MARCH 1943

In November 1942, commander-in-chief of the Australian Military Forces, Thomas Blamey (1884–1951), made a speech in New Guinea to the men of the 21st Brigade during a troop review that left the entire parade 'almost molten with rage and indignation'. The soldiers had been looking forward to their commander's review, following the congratulations of Major-General Arthur Allen, and expected words of praise for their fine work on the Kokoda Trail. Instead, the men were subject to an aggressive and uncontrolled outburst from their leader, who, they felt, had accused them of cowardice. Blamey was under a great deal of pressure at the time; organising an assault on the Japanese with General MacArthur, and nettled about proposed changes in the army administration.

While the speech was never recorded, the substance of it 'spread like a grass-fire borne on a summer gale' and 'sped along the signal lines to forward troops and scattered outposts'. One man who was witness to the outburst was Padre Fred Burt (1904–?), a priest and officer of the 2/16 Australian Infantry Battalion; he related the story in an address to the Perth RSL five weeks after he returned from New Guinea. His address was recorded and submitted to Perth's *Daily News*. The newspaper forwarded it to the Chief Publicity Censor, E.G. Bonney, who 'killed' the story and reported the matter to the Defence Secretary, Frederick Shedden, where it was 'read with interest'.

Burt's speech describes the hardships of Kokoda and ends with a short account of Blamey's outburst – a story which has been confirmed over the years by numerous other officers and soldiers. It is a moving and harrowing first-hand description of the war in New Guinea, and the stresses and tests of leadership.

*

I don't know what you read in the newspapers, but this is the truth. If you can't get the truth in the newspapers you get a sort of fear at the back of your mind that you can't believe anything you read. War correspondent Chester Wilmot wrote the true story and lost his job. I hope for the sake of the men I saw killed, and their children who are left, that the true story of the campaign will not be published.

We came from the Middle East and Syria to New Guinea. From Port Moresby we went up the Pass in a sort of lift, and jumped straight into a different climate. We went from forty-five inches of rain a year to 165 inches. After four or five days' camp, the brigadier told us that we were going up the Kokoda track ... that one battalion would take Kokoda, another Buna.

We got to Owens Corner and came out onto the track. It was a ten-day trek, up and down all the time. The natives had no idea of going round to take off the height. Heavy rains had fallen, and tree roots were about six feet out of the ground. The soldiers were carrying sixty to one hundred pounds, with their guns and packs, over the rough stony track.

We came to Myola, an open clearing where planes were to drop stores. But there were no stores, and we had to stay there for three days, waiting. The brigadier stirred things up, and five planes came over to drop our stuff.

We got to the Gap. We were told that we could hold the Japs with a machine gun and a platoon – it would have taken a Division to hold it. Militia troops had been sent to reinforce the 39th Battalion there. They had been in the army for twelve months. They were taken to Port Moresby about two weeks after joining up, and quite a large proportion were between eighteen and nineteen years of age. They'd had no training. We were told that on the way up they were shown parts of a Bren gun they had never seen before. They were taught to use it along the track.

The Japs had pushed back one battalion which had done a good job, and another which never got into position when it was sent back. They were untrained, too.

When we arrived, the Japs had got five transports of troops in – fresh men from Malaya, huge fellows full of fight. Then the two battalions were left to hold it. The thing was hopeless from the start. We couldn't hold them, we hadn't the men. We were told to get out. I saw men who were supposed to be stretcher cases crawling back on their hands and knees. They had broken legs and arms, and they had to climb over rocks.

We fought for two days. Then came Euro Creek. We could see the Japs over on Alola Ridge holding 'corroborees'. Our morale was the highest, and after twenty-four hours' fighting our men had the game by the throat. If we'd had more men we could have pushed the Jap back as he pushed us back. In the middle of his corroborees he got a few grenades in his middle, and didn't like it. He came in that night, but we held him. We were told to move off at dawn. We went so quietly that six of our chaps didn't know we had gone. They woke up and saw soldiers they thought were ours. A sergeant strolled over to one and asked him for a light from his cigarette. They took a look at each other and ran.

We withdrew off the track and made a detour. There was only one battalion of about 250 men left out of the remnants of the two battalions. I saw some wonderful exploits, but it would not be fair to mention anyone in particular.

Then another battalion came up to meet us. We had been asking for them all the time, but they wouldn't send them. They said they were needed for the defence of Port Moresby. The brigadier had sent them a message: 'Send the battalion or send my successor.' Those behind could not appreciate the position.

This battalion fought at Butcher's Corner, and lost some very fine men. We tried to cut our way through the Japs, but had to make another detour. What was left of the other battalion was cut off in the bush. They wandered there for three weeks without food.

We got back to Ioribiwa Ridge, and were reinforced by a brigade and a battalion. With the remnants of the other battalion and these four battalions we still had to retire. But the Jap never came on. He just walked back. He had had enough, what with casualties we had inflicted, dysentery, disease, malaria and the difficulties of communication. He got back to Kokoda, and we were pulled out for a rest.

I never saw better morale than our fathers showed. Fellows half-dead with dysentery, who should never have been there. Ninety per cent got malaria. They were pulled out, but as soon as their temperatures went down they were sent back into it. A lot died of wounds simply because they didn't have the resistance to fight them.

When it was over we had 120 men left, and another battalion only eighty. If we'd had men to replace the sick everything would have been alright. If they had got a Division of men around the coast to Buna we could have stopped the Jap the same as he was stopped at Milne Bay, cleaned them out.

And when we got back, a general thanked us for saving Port Moresby.

Blamey got the rap, because apparently this show and the Solomons show were supposed to synchronise. There was an investigation. Blamey told the men: 'The rabbit that runs is always in more danger than the rabbit that sits.' He said he supposed we realised we had been beaten by an inferior force, that the Japs had more casualties than we had. Half a dozen of the men said then that they would like to meet some of the bowler hats, and find out the truth. It's time we had a clean-up in the army.

'We have reduced ourselves to impotence in the field of diplomacy'

Arthur Calwell

Speech to the House of Representatives on Vietnam

4 MAY 1965

According to his press secretary Graham Freudenberg, the three great loves of the life of Arthur Calwell (1896–1973) were 'his country, his party and his [Catholic] church.' He never fulfilled his ambitions with either of the first two. An ALP branch secretary at the age of nineteen, he entered federal politics in 1940 and became leader of the Labor Party twenty years later, but lost three elections before standing aside for his deputy, Gough Whitlam, in 1967. A faltering speaker, often numbingly dull, he was usually bested in parliament by prime minister Robert Menzies. But he found a cause in the Vietnam War on which he was cogent and persuasive – and, unfortunately for him, far ahead of public opinion. Called upon to respond to Menzies' decision, on 29 April 1965, to commit a battalion of troops to fight in Vietnam, he gave what was widely felt to be his finest performance. An isolationist who believed that the defence of Australia ended at its shoreline, he cited the lessons of history with utter conviction. Calwell remains the only leader of an Australian federal political party to have been the target of an attempted assassination, during the 1966 election campaign.

*

The government's decision to send the 1st Battalion of the Australian Regular Army to Vietnam is, without question, one of the most significant events in the history of this Commonwealth ...

The overriding issue which this parliament has to deal with at all times is the nation's security. All our words, all our policies, all our actions, must be judged ultimately by this one crucial test: what best promotes our national security, what best guarantees our national survival? It is this test which the Labor Party has applied to the government's decision. We have, of course, asked ourselves other related questions, but basically the issue remains one of Australia's security. Therefore, on behalf of all my colleagues of Her Majesty's Opposition, I say that we oppose the government's decision to send 800 men to fight in Vietnam. We oppose it firmly and completely.

We regret the necessity that has come about. We regret that as a result of the government's action it has come about. It is not our desire, when servicemen are about to be sent to distant battlefields, and when war, cruel, costly and interminable, stares us in the face, that the nation should be divided. But it is the government which has brought this tragic situation about and we will not shirk our responsibilities in stating the views we think serve Australia best.

Our responsibility, like that of the government, is great but, come what may, we will do our duty as we see it and know it to be towards the people of Australia and our children's children. Therefore, I say, we oppose this decision firmly and completely.

We do not think it is a wise decision. We do not think it is a timely decision. We do not think it is a right decision. We do not think it will help the fight against communism. On the contrary, we believe it will harm that fight in the long term. We do not believe it will promote the welfare of the people of Vietnam. On the contrary, we believe it will prolong and deepen the suffering of that unhappy people so that Australia's very name may become a term of reproach among them. We do not believe that it represents a wise or even intelligent response to the challenge of Chinese power. On the contrary, we believe it mistakes entirely the nature of that power, and that it materially assists China in her subversive aims. Indeed, we cannot conceive a decision by this government more likely to promote the long-term interests of China in Asia and the Pacific. We of the Labor Party do not believe that this decision serves, or is consistent with, the immediate strategic interests of Australia. On the contrary, we believe that by sending one quarter of our pitifully small effective military strength to distant Vietnam, this government dangerously denudes Australia and its immediate strategic environs of effective defence power. Thus, for all these and other reasons, we believe we have no choice but to oppose this decision in the name of Australia and of Australia's security ...

The government will try, indeed it has already tried, to project a picture in which once the aggressive invaders from the north are halted, our men will be engaged in the exercise of picking off the Vietcong, themselves invaders from the north and stranded from their bases and isolated from their supplies. But it will not be like that at all. Our men will be fighting the largely indigenous Vietcong in their own home territory. They will be fighting in the midst of a largely indifferent, if not resentful, and frightened population. They will be fighting at the request of, and in support, and presumably, under the direction of an unstable, inefficient, partially corrupt military regime which lacks even the semblance of being, or becoming, democratically based. But, it will be said, even if this is true, that there are far larger considerations – China must be stopped, the United States must not be humiliated in Asia. I agree wholeheartedly with both these propositions.

But this also I must say: our present course is playing right into China's hands, and our present policy will, if not changed, surely and inexorably lead to American humiliation in Asia. Communist China will use every means at her disposal to increase her power and influence. But her existing military machine is not well adapted to that objective. It is not so at this moment and it may not be so for the next ten years. Therefore, she chooses other means. Yet we have preferred to look at China mainly in terms of a military threat and thus have neglected to use other, far more effective weapons at our disposal, or, because of our preoccupation with the military threat, we have used those weapons badly and clumsily. We talk about the lesson of Munich as if we had never learnt a single lesson since 1938.

Preoccupied with the fear of a military Munich, we have suffered a score of moral Dunkirks. Preoccupied with the military threat of Chinese communism, we have channelled the great bulk of our aid to Asia towards military expenditure. Preoccupied with the idea of monolithic, imperialistic communism, we have channelled our support to those military regimes which were loudest in their professions of anti-communism, no matter how reactionary, unpopular or corrupt they may have been. Preoccupied with fear of communist revolution, we have supported and sought to support those who would prevent any sort of revolution, even when inevitable; and even when most needful. Preoccupied with so-called western interests, we have never successfully supported nationalism as the mighty force it is against communism. We have supported nationalism only when it supported the west, and we have thereby pushed nationalism towards communism. Preoccupied with the universality of our own Christian beliefs, we have never tried to understand the power of the other great world religions against communism.

Each of those preoccupations has worked for our defeat in Vietnam, and is working for our defeat in Asia, Africa and South America. And herein lies one of the greatest dangers of the government's decision on large-scale military commitments. It blinds and obscures the real nature of the problem of communist expansion. It lends support and encouragement to those who see the problem in purely military terms, and whose policies would, if ever adopted, lead to disaster …

We are not impotent in the fight against communism. We are not powerless against China, if we realise that the true nature of the threat from China is not military invasion but political subversion. And that threat, if we believe for one moment in our own professions, and in our own principles, we can fight and beat. But to exhaust our resources in the bottomless pit of jungle warfare, in a war in which we have not even defined our purpose honestly, or explained what we would accept as victory, is the very height of folly and the very depths of despair …

By its decision, the Australian Government has withdrawn unilaterally from the ranks of the negotiators, if indeed it was ever concerned about them. Our contribution will be negligible, militarily. But we have reduced ourselves to impotence in the field of diplomacy. We should have been active in the field of diplomacy for a long time. But we have done nothing in that field of affairs …

Australia's aim should have been to help end the war, not to extend it. We have now lost all power to help end it. Instead we have declared our intention to extend it, insofar as lies in our power. We have committed ourselves to the propositions that communism can be defeated by military means alone and that it is the function of European troops to impose the will of the west upon Asia. These are dangerous, delusive and disastrous propositions. The Prime Minister pays lip service to President Johnson's call for a massive aid program, financed by all the industrialised nations, including the Union of Soviet Socialist Republics. But it is clear that the right honourable gentleman's real thinking, and that of his government, run only along the narrow groove of a military response …

How long will it be before we are drawing upon our conscript youth to service these growing and endless requirements? Does the government now say that conscripts will not be sent? If so, has it completely forgotten what it said about conscription last year? The basis of that decision was that the new conscripts would be completely integrated in the Regular Army. The voluntary system was brought abruptly to an end. If the government now says that conscripts will not be sent, this means that the 1st Battalion is never to be reinforced, replaced or replenished. If this is not so, then the government must have a new policy on the use of conscripts – a policy not yet announced. Or, if it has not changed its policy, the government means that the 1st Battalion is not to be reinforced, replaced or replenished from the resources of the regular army. Which is it to be? There is now a commitment of 800. As the war drags on, who is to say that this will not rise to 8000, and that these will not be drawn from our voteless, conscripted twenty-year-olds? And where are the troops from America's other allies? It is plain that Britain, Canada, France, Germany and Japan, for example, do not see things with the clear-cut precision of the Australian Government.

I cannot close without addressing a word directly to our fighting men who are now by this decision, committed to the chances of war: our hearts and prayers are with you. Our minds and reason cannot support those who have made this decision to send you to this war, and we shall do our best to have that decision reversed. But we shall do our duty to the utmost in supporting you to do your duty. In terms of everything that an army in the field requires, we shall never deny you the aid and support that it is your right to expect in the service of your country. To the members of the government, I say only this: if, by the process of misrepresentation of our motives, in which you are so expert, you try to further divide this nation for political purposes, yours will be a dreadful responsibility, and you will have taken a course which you will live to regret.

And may I, through you, Mr Speaker, address this message to the members of my own Party – my colleagues here in this parliament, and that vast band of Labor men and women outside: the course we have agreed to take today is fraught with difficulty. I cannot promise you that easy popularity can be bought in times like these; nor are we looking for it. We are doing our duty as we see it. When the drums beat and the trumpets sound, the voice of reason and right can be heard in the land only with difficulty. But if we are to have the courage of our convictions, then we must do our best to make that voice heard. I offer you the probability that you will be traduced, that your motives will be misrepresented, that your patriotism will be impugned, that your courage will be called into question. But I also offer you the sure and certain knowledge that we will be vindicated;

that generations to come will record with gratitude that when a reckless government wilfully endangered the security of this nation, the voice of the Australian Labor Party was heard, strong and clear, on the side of sanity and in the cause of humanity, and in the interests of Australia's security.

Let me sum up. We believe that America must not be humiliated and must not be forced to withdraw. But we are convinced that sooner or later the dispute in Vietnam must be settled through the councils of the United Nations. If it is necessary to back with a peace-force the authority of the United Nations, we would support Australian participation to the hilt. But we believe that the military involvement in the present form decided on by the Australian Government represents a threat to Australia's standing in Asia, to our power for good in Asia and above all to the security of this nation.

'All the way with LBJ'

Harold Holt

Speech at a state reception, the White House, Washington D.C.

30 JUNE 1966

When Harold Holt (1908–1967) met United States president Lyndon Baines Johnson in Washington in 1966, the visit was upgraded from a small luncheon to a state reception with an honour guard and a seventeen-gun salute on the south lawns of the White House. The United States president received the Australian leader 'with an outpouring of hospitality and honours which almost inundated the new prime minister'. And Johnson, at the time in need of a friend, found one.

A solicitor for a brief time, Holt entered politics in 1935 as a protégé of Robert Menzies and served as minister of labour and national service, immigration, and as treasurer before taking over as prime minister on Menzies' retirement in 1966. His popularity after a landslide victory in the national election on 26 November the same year was short lived, largely due to growing pressure from the public anxious about the nation's involvement in the Vietnam War. His famous promise to go 'all the way with LBJ' alienated and angered many Australians.

After waiting so long in the shadows, and climbing 'over nobody's dead body' to gain the highest political office, Holt served as prime minister for less than two years.

'I know this beach like the back of my hand,' Holt told friends of the Portsea surf in which he was presumed drowned while swimming on 17 December 1967; his body was never found.

*

The outcome of this struggle is critical for the hopes that you and we share for a better and more secure way of life for the free people of Asia.

But it does not take a war to bring Americans and Australians close together.

We like each other. Friendships form quickly between us.

We have many mutually beneficial links. Our trade with each other, the investment that you make with us with your capital ...

You know that in Australia you have an understanding friend.

I am here, sir, not asking for anything – an experience which I am sure you value at times when it is not so frequent as it might be.

You have in us not merely an understanding friend but one staunch in the belief of the need for our presence with you in Vietnam.

We are not there because of our friendship, we are there because, like you, we believe it is right to be there and, like you, we shall stay there as long as seems necessary to achieve the purposes of the South Vietnamese government and the purposes that we join in formulating and progressing together.

And so, sir, in the lonelier and perhaps even more disheartening moments which come to any national leader, I hope there will be a corner of your mind and heart which takes cheer from the fact that you have an admiring friend, a staunch friend that will be all the way with LBJ.

'And the world needs Australia at this critical hour – all the way'

Lyndon Baines Johnson

Speech at a parliamentary lunch, Canberra

21 OCTOBER 1966

The 750,000 people who lined Melbourne's St Kilda Road to catch a glimpse of the United States president Lyndon Johnson (1908–1973) during his lightning 1966 tour to Australia were as divided as the rest of the nation over his role in the Vietnam War. While most issued a warm welcome, others demonstrated their objection by throwing paint bombs at his limousine and chanting: 'Hey hey LBJ – how many kids did you kill today?'

The president was reciprocating the support of prime minister Harold Holt after his visit to America earlier in the year, and to ensure that Australia's military involvement in the war continued. At a wreath-laying ceremony at the Canberra War Memorial Johnson whispered in the ear of an Australian Vietnam veteran, 'We are grateful to you, son.'

*

The foundations of the friendship between our two peoples are deep, and they are increasing.

We live at a time when foreign affairs go beyond their traditional scope. They now have strong new ties with the domestic life of all our countries.

Since 1945, the United States has been found where freedom was under attack, or where world peace was threatened. The stage has shifted many times. The stakes have grown as man's capacity for destruction increased.

Of course, our policies are shaped with a proper regard for our security and welfare, but much of the energy of our efforts has come because we believe it is right that the strong should help the weak defend their freedom; that the wealthy should help the poor overcome their hunger; that nations, no matter how small or fragile, or young, should be free from the coercion of others.

We have steadily resisted communist efforts to bring about by force and intrigue a world dominated by a single ideology.

Our convictions, our interests, our life as a nation demand that we oppose, with all of our strength, any effort to put the world in a straitjacket.

On continent after continent, in dozens of countries, hundreds of millions of people struggle to exist on incomes of scarcely more than a dollar a week. Many people have less to spend each day on food and on shelter and on clothing, on medicine, on all of their needs, than the average Australian spends for a package of cigarettes.

They live in shacks hardly worth the name. They live without heat or water or sanitation, or promise ...

So we must deal today with these urgent drives, the drive for security, for the defence of freedom, for the preservation of independence; and the drive for satisfaction, for self-respect, for equality of justice and opportunity.

This is what is happening today in Vietnam, where the demands of security and the urge for satisfaction mingle in a single crucible.

There our men stand together – as they have stood before – to check aggression. And there they serve – as they have served before – to help build and preserve and protect freedom.

The raw conflict of one, and the elusive attainments of the other, make their duty more difficult – and more essential.

I would like every Aussie who stands in the rice paddies of Vietnam on this sunny day to know that every American and LBJ is with Australia all the way.

I believe there is light at the end of what has been a long and lonely tunnel. I say this not just because our men are proving successful on the battlefield.

I believe it is for this reason: there is a widening community of people who feel responsible for what is happening in Vietnam.

This is the Asia to which I journey ...

The challenge of the new Asia comes to Australia at a conspicuous time in your history. You have already shown that your commitment is a matter of policy and action – not rhetoric.

You have played a leading role in the Colombo Plan.

You have brought tens of thousands of Asian students to your universities.

You have contributed generously and patiently to planning the future of the Mekong Valley.

You have been among the leaders in creating the Asian Development Bank.

You have joined eight other nations who, on their own initiative, have formed the Asian and Pacific Council …

The man who sent me to Australia – Franklin Delano Roosevelt – once prophesied that 'one day a generation may possess this land, blessed beyond anything we now know, blessed with those things – material and spiritual – that make man's life abundant. If that is the fashion of your dreaming, then I say: Hold fast to your dream. America needs it.'

Well, I would amend his vision somewhat.

For Franklin Roosevelt belongs to the world, and so does his faith in what lies ahead.

I would say, therefore, to the people of the Pacific and of Asia: 'If that is the fashion of your dreaming then I say: Hold fast to your dream. The world needs it.'

And the world needs Australia at this critical hour – all the way.

'Our work will not be done till we have eradicated the habit of war'

Patrick White

'A letter to humanity': Hyde Park, Sydney

PALM SUNDAY 1982

Australia's most distinguished twentieth-century novelist, Patrick White (1912–1990), had an ambivalent relationship with his country, where he saw an 'exaltation of the average', and his century, overshadowed as it was by the threat of nuclear apocalypse.

White began drafting novels prior to university, publishing his first two books in the early years of World War II before joining the RAF as an intelligence officer and being posted to the Middle East. As his canon and literary reputation grew, he became an outspoken critic of the despoliation of the environment, the dismissal of the Whitlam government and nuclear proliferation. White read his 'letter to humanity' in Sydney's Hyde Park in front of 40,000 people.

*

Fellow human beings …

My addressing you in this way could sound a bit whimsical. I do so – with good reason, I think – because an outrage against humanity has brought us here today. Nuclear war is undoubtedly the most serious issue the global family has ever had to face. After Hiroshima it should appear the most hideous to any but thoughtless minds. Fortunately, increasing numbers of human beings are becoming aware of the implications of nuclear warfare. The people of the world are disturbed by the direction in which their political mentors are leading them. There is a gathering anger. Just as the earth too, is angry. For it seems to me that the earth's erupting volcanoes and repeated earthquakes are more than coincidental in these days of nuclear tests.

Australians must – a lot of us do accept the fact that the nuclear situation affects us as much as those living in the northern hemisphere. We are united by the polluted skies and oceans as well as by the earth's crust. The French nuclear tests in the Pacific should bring the future very close indeed to those Australians who would like to think their island inviolable. Many of those who have been alerted and who have come here today, either in quandary or out of conviction, see the nuclear issue as transcending party politics, class, race. It involves people of whatever religious faith or philosophical persuasion. I like to think that all of us at this demonstration are people of faith – faith in humanity – and continuing life on this abused planet. In Europe, Britain and the United States intellectuals, churchmen, scientists (in particular medical authorities) are uniting with the man in the street to question what they see as foolhardiness on the part of their political leaders. Draft avoidance by millions of young Americans is one of the most striking symptoms of unrest, the biggest act of civil disobedience since the end of the Vietnam War, an expressive sign of the rapidly expanding peace movement. In June, one million are expected to demonstrate while the UN special session on disarmament is taking place. In many cases the reaction of these draft resisters is moral rather than political. Nuclear disarmament is humanity's answer to the paranoiacs and megalomaniacs, whether American or Soviet, and our own lilliputian leaders intent on supplying the giants with the material for global destruction.

More than half the uranium used in West European power plants is enriched in the Soviet Union. The first Australian uranium destined for the Soviet Union will reach the Latvian port of Riga later this year, be taken by train to a Soviet enrichment plant, not yet identified by our officials, then leave Leningrad for its final destination, a Swedish-built nuclear power plant in Finland. Australia has signed uranium deals with four countries which use Soviet enrichment: Finland, West Germany, Sweden and France. All contracts written since 1977 are held by the only two companies now producing in Australia: Queensland Mines, which owns the Nabarlek Reserve, and has signed sales with Japan, Finland and South Korea; and Energy Resources of Australia, operator of the Ranger Deposit, which has contracts with

Japan, West Germany, South Korea, the US, Sweden and Belgium. So the governments of the world are linked by the cross-threads of a monstrous web, spun from the motives of material gain, fear and suspicion, and in the case of the two superpowers, determination to dominate the world at whatever cost.

We talk of *safeguards* – when obsolete nuclear submarines are to be dumped in the ocean – when American Tridents and their Soviet counterparts will be cruising through our waters – when the South American rivals Brazil and Argentina are flat out to control the nuclear cycle and build a bomb. In the present circumstances it isn't any wonder that countries like India and Pakistan, courted by the US and the Soviet Union, indulge in political juggling, and Israel is reduced to hijacking shiploads of material to conduct its nuclear experiments. Australia's future as uranium exporter depends on two nations in particular – Japan, the samurai turned merchant – and France, whose materialist techniques in economic matters, whichever the political party in power, are far more sophisticated than our own crude game of grab. France, with unabashed cynicism, continues to explode its nuclear devices not so far distant from our Pacific seaboard. At least our government, with comparable cynicism, has asked for it. The most innocent victims of the universal swindle are those to be pitied most – the Australian Aborigines who, after the original invasion of their land, are now invaded by uranium miners who drive bulldozers across their burial grounds and sacred sites and smash or steal their sacred emblems. The Ranger Agreement was signed between our former Aboriginal Affairs Minister, Mr Viner, and four of the traditional owners of the land that was to be mined. The four who signed were bullied into it by a government which told them all the Aboriginal communities had been consulted – which later proved to be untrue.

Not surprisingly, when the virtues of nuclear power are out-weighed by its capacity for evil, the history of the product in Australia and its diplomatic concomitants is one of lies, hypocrisy, naivety and ignorance. Over the years, those who governed us seem to have been at their most naive in allowing the Americans to estab-lish their bases at North West Cape, Nurrungar, the Omega Station in Gippsland, and most important, the CIA-controlled monitoring and information complex at Pine Gap, which those who have seen the Gil Scrine film, *Home on the Range*, will realise has played a significant part in Australia's political history – not least the episode of Sir John Kerr, claimed by the CIA as one of their so-called 'assets'. Under the spell of their American ally's advances our government appeared unaware of what they might be letting us in for. Some of the negotiations were positively light-headed. Take for instance the film-clip in which Harold Holt, in true music-hall style goes into a little soft-shoe shuffle as he and the American ambassador quip about peppercorn rentals. And what of the agreement by which American B52s may land at Darwin without any active concern about knowing whether they are bombed up? By now Australia has become an important nuclear target, not just the American installations, but even our cities.

The Australian people, who have been kept in the dark, will bear the brunt of a nuclear attack. *They* will be the incidental target, not the politicians in their well-planned shelters. *Nowhere* have the *people* been consulted, whether in Britain, where women have been camped all through the recent severe winter round sites prepared to receive American Cruise nuclear missiles, nor in the Unites States, where the Frankenstein consortium of millionaires who launched their monster Reagan – a figure from one of his own B films – listened with apparent equanimity to his suggestion that the aged should be the first out to test the effects of nuclear ash. I'd have thought the creaking monster himself might have qualified to dip his toe before anybody.

But from being the suckers of the world, the people have begun to act. Individuals who are prepared to accept their fate say to me: But what can you or I do to resist the policies of governments? I reply there are millions of you and me. Small-scale passive resistance can work wonders, as some of you will have found out in your domestic lives. On a larger scale it worked in India, where the great Mahatma Gandhi won independence for his country. Let me quote you some of this great human being's own words:

I am a Christian and a Hindu and a Moslem and a Jew. The politician in me has never dominated a single decision of mine, and if I seem to take part in politics, it is only because politics encircles us today like the coil of a snake, from which one cannot get out, no matter how much one tries. I wish therefore to wrestle with the snake, as I have been doing with more or less success consciously since 1894, unconsciously, as I have now discovered, ever since reaching years of discretion. I have been experimenting with myself and my friends by introducing religion into politics. Let me explain what I mean by religion. It is not the Hindu religion, which I certainly prize above all other religions, but the religion which transcends Hinduism, which changes one's very nature, which binds one indissolubly to the truth within and which ever purifies. It is the permanent element in human nature which counts no cost too great in order to find full expression and which leaves the soul utterly restless until it has found itself, known its Maker and appreciated the true correspondence between the Maker and itself.

Gandhi's words are pretty hard to live up to. But through his faith he achieved what he set out to do. In these days of advanced nuclear development, *we* shall have to call on all our reserves of faith. Ah yes, some of my friends say, but what about the Russians? … Perhaps it isn't generally known what the Russian Orthodox Church still means to a large percentage of Soviet citizens and that they still attend its services. You may not know of the peace movement in East Germany, where a large demo was recently organised in Dresden to commemorate the thirty-seventh anniversary of that city's destruction by British and American bombers and the deaths of 35,000 people. The gathering was sponsored by the regional head of the Protestant Church, Bishop Hempel, who proposed that East Germany should unilaterally renounce the stationing of Soviet-built nuclear missiles in its territory, and called for compulsory 'peace education' in East German schools. As the protest had an anti-western undertone, the party has been in two minds how to proceed. At least man's conscience is still alive – men of faith – whether Russian Orthodox – East German Protestant – the Dutch, whose churches are conducting a very methodical anti-nuclear campaign – we know about the Roman Catholics of Poland

– and in Australia, and throughout the world, we have the support of numbers of staunch rationalists.

Passive resistance is of course fraught with danger. (Gandhi was referred to by the scientist-philosopher Albert Einstein as '… the only truly great figure of our age. Generations to come will scarcely believe that such a one as this ever walked on this earth in flesh and blood …') Gandhi was assassinated in 1948. I personally feel that the dangers and suffering those who choose to practise passive resistance are bound to encounter are preferable to the moral seepage and contaminating ashes which will overwhelm those who passively accept the nuclear holocaust their political leaders are preparing for them. Though I don't go along with President Reagan's practical suggestion, the aged are of less importance. I am old, childless. I've led a full life. You're the ones the issue concerns most deeply – the parents, the children, the grandchildren – the youth of the world – and particularly the youth of Australia, because Australia is ours, and you are the ones on whom this *potentially* great country depends. I know many of you young people have been badly done by in recent times. But my hope is that you will not let yourselves be ground down by despair – that you will rise above present social and economic injustices – that you will not hold *life* responsible for these – and that you will carry a banner into the kind of future we all want. One more point – if the powers were to see the light, halt the nuclear build-up, and return to settling their differences by conventional means, we must remember that since the end of World War II nearly 40 million people have been killed by conventional weapons. So our work will not be done till we have eradicated the *habit* of war. But let it be understood – the battle we must win before all others is that of nuclear disarmament. However perilous the non-violent risks run by those who espouse this cause, I – and I hope, you too – would rather contribute to the *life* force than collaborate in the death of the world.

'There was a harvest of our tallest poppies. A bitter harvest'

Clive James

Anzac Day address, Battersea Park, London

25 APRIL 1988

An alumnus of Sydney University, Clive James (1939–) left Australia for London in 1962 after working for a short time as a journalist for the *Sydney Morning Herald*. He joined the crowd of expatriate Australian artists and writers who had made London their home and obtained a degree at Cambridge University where he was president of the theatrical society. In 1972 he was appointed as the television critic for the London *Observer*, a position he held for ten years. As a writer, critic and broadcaster, James has been both prolific and protean, producing volumes of literary criticism, novels, satirical verse and essays. While never returning permanently to the land of his birth, James has always maintained a watchful eye on Australia, wickedly funny and intensely serious by turns. In this Anzac Day address, James brings his serious side to bear, reflecting on a topic which changed forever both his native and adopted lands.

*

It's said that whenever Winston Churchill fell prey to the fits of intense depression he called Black Dog, he would dream about Gallipoli and the Dardanelles, of the dead soldiers in the water and on the cliffs. The Dardanelles campaign had been his idea, and it was a brilliant idea: if it had been successful it would have altered the course of the war, breaking the murderous stalemate of trench warfare on the Western Front. It would have stemmed the slaughter. But it wasn't successful, the enemy was waiting, and all that was altered was the course of many young lives – and of those, too many belonged to us, to Australia and New Zealand, little dominions with not much population, and certainly none of it to spare.

There was a harvest of our tallest poppies. A bitter harvest. Recently – by commentators with their own, no doubt heartfelt and even admirable purposes – the notion has been encouraged that the Anzacs were fed into the battle to save British lives, as imperial cannon-fodder. The cruel fact was that three times as many British troops as Anzacs went into that cauldron and never came out. But the British were counting their troops in millions anyway, and soon they would be counting their dead by the same measure. For us, young men dead by the thousand was a lot, an awful lot, and the same was still true in the second war, and always will be true if it happens again.

But nothing quite like those wars, not even Vietnam, ever has happened again, or is likely to, and that consideration, perhaps, is nearer the heart of this ceremony than we might easily realise. The memory is fading, even as the myth grows, and it is fading precisely *because* we have got the world our parents dreamed of. In our generation and probably for all the generations to come, the privileged nations no longer fight each other, or will fight each other. It is, and will be, the sad fate of the underprivileged nations to do all that. In the meanwhile the way is open for our children to misinterpret history, and believe that a ceremony like this honours militarism. Except by our participation in this moment of solemnity – the solemnity that always courts pomposity, unless we can forget ourselves and remember those who never lived to stand on ceremony – how can we convince our children that the opposite is true?

Militarism, in both the great wars, *was* the enemy. It was why the enemy had to be fought. Almost all our dead were civilians in peacetime, and the aching gaps they left were not in the barracks but on the farms and in the factories, in the suburbs and the little towns with one pub. The thousands of Australian aircrew who died over Europe, and are commemorated here by this stone, would, had they lived, have made an important contribution to Australia's burgeoning creative energy after World War Two. We might have found our full confidence much sooner. But without their valour and generosity we might never have found it at all. Had Hitler prevailed, and Britain gone under, nowhere in the world, not even America, would have remained free of his virulent influence. Those of us who are very properly concerned with what the Aborigines suffered at the hands of Anglo-Saxon culture should at least consider what they might have suffered at the hands of a Nazi culture, as it would undoubtably have been transmitted by the occupying army of Hitler's admiring ally. They would have been regarded as a problem with only one solution – a final solution.

Where we say that the lives of any of our young men and women under arms were wasted we should be very careful what we mean. We who are lucky enough to live in the world they helped to make safe from institutionalised evil can't expect any prizes for pronouncing that war is not glorious. They knew that. They fought the wars anyway, and that *was* their glory. It's obviously true that the world would have been a better place if the wars had never happened, but it's profoundly true that it would have been an infinitely worse place if they had not been fought and won.

All our dead would rather have lived in peace. But there was no peace. Now there is, and perhaps, in our protected, cushioned and lulling circumstances, one of the best ways to realise what life is really worth is to try to imagine the intensity with which they must have felt its value just before they lost it. Sacrifice is a large word, but no word can be large enough for that small moment. The only eloquence that fits is silence – which I will ask you to observe with me as I fulfil my gladly accepted duty and unveil this plaque.

'We gather here in sorrow, in anguish, in disbelief and in pain'

John Howard

Address to memorial service, Australian Consulate, Bali

17 OCTOBER 2002

When Jemaah Islamiyah terrorists detonated bombs in Paddy's Bar and the Sari Nightclub in Bali's Kuta Beach tourist precinct on 12 October 2002, Australians awoke to a horror unique in their existence. Of 202 fatalities, eighty-eight Australians – mostly young tourists – were killed in the inferno. National grief merged with the sudden and real evidence of post-September 11 'insecurity'. In the days following the attack a massive evacuation effort took place and the hunt for the perpetrators began. Prime Minister John Howard (1939–) led a united delegation of Australian parliamentarians to Bali, where he witnessed the commitment and despair among those still searching for the missing and the agony of the injured. His address to the memorial service took place just five days after the bombings, when around 114 Australians and many other nations' citizens were still unaccounted for.

*

As the sun sets over this beautiful island, we gather here in sorrow, in anguish, in disbelief and in pain. There are no words that I can summon to solve in any way the hurt and the suffering and the pain being felt by so many of my fellow countrymen and women and by so many of the citizens of other nations. I can say though to my Australian countrymen and women that there are nineteen and a half million Australians who are trying, however inadequately, to feel for you and to support you at this time of unbearable grief and pain.

The wanton, cruel, barbaric character of what occurred here last Saturday night has shocked our nation to the core. I know the anguish that so many are feeling, the painful process of identification which has prolonged the agony for so many, the sense of bewilderment and disbelief that so many young lives with so much before them should have been taken away in such blind fury, hatred and violence. I can on behalf of all of the people of Australia declare to you that we will do everything in our power to bring to justice those who were responsible for this foul deed. We will work with our friends in Indonesia to do that and we will work with others to achieve an outcome of justice.

Can I say to our Balinese friends, the lovely people of Bali, who have been befriended over the decades and the generations by so many Australians who have come here, we grieve with you, we feel for you, we thank you from the bottom of our hearts for the love and support that you have extended to our fellow countrymen and women over these past days.

As the Chaplain said, there will be scars left on people for the rest of their life, both physical and emotional. Our nation has been changed by this event. Perhaps we may not be so carefree as we have been in the past, but we will never lose our openness, our sense of adventure. The young of Australia will always travel. They will always seek fun in distant parts. They will always reach out to the young of other nations. They will always be open, fun-loving, decent men and women.

And so as we grapple inadequately and in despair to try to comprehend what has happened, let us gather ourselves around each other, let us wrap our arms around not only our fellow Australians but also around the people of Indonesia, of Bali, let us wrap our arms around the people of other nations and the friends and relatives of the nationals of other countries who have died in this horrible event. It will take a long time for these foul deeds to be seen in any kind of context. They can never be excused. Australia has been affected very deeply, but the Australian spirit has not been broken. The Australian spirit will remain strong and free and open and tolerant. I know that is what all of those who lost their lives would have wanted and I know it is what all of those who grieve for them would want.

POLITICS

'The keystone of the federal arch'

Alfred Deakin

Second reading of the Judiciary Bill, House of Representatives

18 MARCH 1902

The federal seat of Ballarat came easily to Alfred Deakin (1856–1919) in the first national election, and he held on to it until his retirement in 1913. But there were daunting issues to be addressed in the inaugural parliament, particularly for Deakin, the newly appointed attorney-general. The making of a nation did not stop with the act of federation.

The Commonwealth of Australia Constitution provided for the establishment of a High Court, and it was Deakin's job to create it. The High Court's sphere of duty was defined by the constitution; it was to be a federal Supreme Court whose role was to interpret the constitution and hear all cases arising from it. It was also the highest court of appeal in the nation. The Judiciary Bill demanded all of Deakin's masterful skills in advocating its functions and importance. His celebrated second reading speech focused on matters of principle over detail, and Deakin emerged triumphant. It was reported to be Deakins's most 'cherished' measure.

*

The Bill must be legal, because of the subject matter with which it deals, because it springs from a constitution which, in one of its aspects, is simply a legal instrument, and depends on legal construction. But in its substance, in its influence, in its true character, this is not merely a legal measure. It is a fundamental proposition for a structural creation which is the necessary and essential complement of a federal constitution. As such it affects every calling. Indeed, although it relates to legal machinery, the purposes to be served by that machinery are but in a fractional sense legal, are in the main general, and in a very particular sense political – affecting directly not only the businesses and bosoms of our population, but also the representatives of the people in both chambers of this parliament; affecting directly the executive of this country; affecting, in fact, every portion of that constitution of which this court is created to be the guardian.

This Bill will be followed by another almost wholly mechanical in character – the Bill for procedure which honourable members see on the notice paper, supplying the necessary setting for the courts now proposed to be created, and suitably providing for the transaction of their business, that is if the House should see fit to give its assent to this Bill. These two measures, no doubt, will be found capable of improvement, and any suggestions for their improvement will receive most favourable consideration. But this Bill requires to be dealt with as a whole, to be considered as practically embodying a single proposition, for the creation of a national court. To put this view, forced upon me, in a sense, by the apparent attitude of public opinion, it may be necessary to repeat many of the truisms of our federal debates, to recall those constitutional doctrines upon which great stress was laid at the Convention, and in the referendum campaigns throughout Australia. It was not then, any more than it is now, truly a question of details. What was submitted to the public of Australia then was the establishment of a High Court as an integral part of a federal constitution. Though there are other considerations and other functions of this court of the highest importance with the most far-reaching influence, yet after all it is in that respect it must still be regarded, in order that the criticisms offered both upon the creation of the court, and upon the scale on which it is sought to be established, are to be understood. In its other relations – that is to say, apart from those constitutional operations – the Bill is of the utmost importance. It will complete so radical a reform of the legal relations of the people of these states to each other that it might fairly be termed a revolution. At the same time it is a revolution accomplished not by destruction, but by construction, not by the taking away to any considerable extent of powers that exist, but by their being focused in a new centre from which they may be radiated to the greater advantage of the whole of this community. ... The High Court, in its sphere, and the parliament, in its sphere, are both expressions of the union of the Australian people. That union cannot be completed on the judicial side without the establishment of this court, any more than on the political side it could have been completed, or even commenced, without this parliament. ...

Its first and highest function as an Australian court – not its first in point of time, but its first in point of importance – will be exercised in unfolding the constitution itself. That constitution was drawn, and inevitably so, on large and simple lines, and its provisions were embodied in general language, because it was felt to be an instrument not to be lightly altered, and indeed incapable of being readily altered; and, at the same time, was designed to remain in force for more years than any of us can foretell, and to apply under circumstances probably differing most widely from the expectations now cherished by any of us. Consequently, drawn as it of necessity was on simple and large lines, it opens an immense field for exact definition and interpretation. Our constitution must depend largely for the exact form and shape which it will hereafter take upon the interpretations according to its various provisions. This court is created to undertake that interpretation. ...

What are the three fundamental conditions to any federation authoritatively laid down? The first is the existence of a supreme constitution; the next is a distribution of powers under that constitution; and the third is an authority reposed in a judiciary to interpret that supreme constitution and to decide as to the precise distribution of powers. These are the three acknowledged characteristics and fundamental principles of every federation, and if honorable members look at them for a moment, they will see that the first and second absolutely depend for their effect upon the third. The constitution is to be the supreme law, but it is the High Court which is to determine how far and between what boundaries it is supreme. The federation is constituted by distribution of powers, and it is this court which decides the orbit and boundary of every power. Consequently, when we say that there are three fundamental conditions involved in federation, we really mean that there is one which is more essential than the others – the competent tribunal which is able to protect the constitution, and to oversee its agencies. That body is the High Court. It is properly termed the 'keystone of the federal arch'. 'The legislature,' as Marshall puts it, 'makes, the executive executes, and the judiciary declares the law.' What the legislature may make, and what the executive may make, and what the executive may do, the judiciary in the last resort declares; so that the ties which unite the judiciary to the legislature – the Australian High Court to the Australian parliament – are those of mutual association and dependence in the accomplishment of a common task. The High Court exists to protect the constitution against assaults. It exists because our constitution, although an imperial Act, has a dual parentage. It proceeds from the people of the whole continent. It is one of the institutions which the people of Australia, when they accepted the constitution, required to be established for the purpose of insuring that there should not be a departure from the bond into which they thereby entered for themselves and for posterity. This constitution is not the creation of our state parliaments only, neither is it the creation of the imperial parliament only. It draws its authority directly from the electors of the Commonwealth, and it is as their chosen and declared agent that the High Court finds its place in the constitution which they accepted. ...

The people did not err in giving the High Court the prominence which it has in the constitution. May I quote the words of the greatest political philosopher of our nation – Burke – who, with marvellous prescience and foresight into constitutional principle, said that: 'Whatever is supreme in the state ... ought to give a security to its justice against its power. It ought to make its judicature, as it were, something exterior to the state.'

If those words apply, as he applied them, to a unitary system of government, how much more do they apply to the federal governments which have grown up since his day? ...

Of course we speak lightly, and oftentimes severely, of individual members of the legal profession. We recognise the abuses that have grown around our various institutions for the administration of justice. But admitting all these inevitable perversions, it is impossible for us to forget our debt to similar institutions. It is not for men of knowledge, or of our country, to look with a slighting and indifferent regard upon proposals to extend the area within which law operates. The fundamental choice still remains between war and law, between violence and reason, between force and justice. My honourable friends, the members of the Labor Party, are of late years proving their appreciation of its possibilities in their own sphere by seeking as a substitute for industrial wars, or strikes, a tribunal of arbitration before which the differences which exist between employers and employed may come up for judgement. We do not now see the old tendency of doubt and suspicion towards such extensions of the realm of law. The Liberal Party all the world over are being helped to a better realisation of the possibilities of a peaceful advance, which are afforded by the statute-book, and the necessary concomitant of the statute-book – courts capable of interpreting it – and seeing that its behests are enforced.

The marvellous empire of imperial Rome has passed away, leaving its treasures and achievements merely dust or records, but it also left behind it that imperishable system of Roman law, which today lives in continental as well as to a large degree in Scotch law. Today the British Empire is at the meridian of its splendour, and not at its decline, but even its territories are not large enough to contain its system of jurisprudence. This has overflowed across the Atlantic. It is firmly established in these southern seas. Whatever may be the fortunes of the British Empire as a political entity, the fate of its jurisprudence is as stable, and its future will be as permanent as that of Roman law. It will be the task of the High Court to administer and expand that law in accordance with the necessities of these young states and their union. Behind it lies what is more important even than the law itself – that which was its seed and fruit – the law-abiding instincts of our people. A greater demand than ever is now to be made upon this essential quality of good citizenship in Australia. The federal government, with all its complex interrelations and cooperations, demands a law-abiding people. No other can make it a success.

'Cricket ... if there were three elevens in the field'

Alfred Deakin

Speech at a luncheon of the Australian Natives' Association, Melbourne Exhibition Buildings

1 FEBRUARY 1904

The first two federal elections did not produce a workable political system. There were three parties: prime minister Alfred Deakin's protectionists who wanted high tariffs, George Reid's free-traders, and the nascent Labor Party. Each of these groups gained almost equal representation in the lower house, forcing Deakin to depend on the Labor Party to remain in office. Allegiances were constantly being created then collapsing. The precariousness of political power in Australia finally called forth a colourful summer metaphor from Deakin, who had not long before attended the Adelaide Test match – where, incidentally, Australia lost the Ashes. Deakin was not himself a great cricket lover, but understood how to harness the Australian devotion to sport in making a political point. But he would be compelled to operate in this uncomfortable environment until the Fusion Ministry of 1909 when free-traders and protectionists united to remove a team from the field.

*

It is not for me to inflict on you a political program. That depends on parliament. Everything depends on parliament. I should like someone to tell me what the new federal parliament is going to do. [*Laughter.*] Our parliaments, as we have them, and all our traditions, are based upon the existence of two great parties, and two great parties alone, interchanging responsibility at the will of the people in accordance with a definite program submitted to them. The whole machinery of our constitution is derived from the fact that it has been built up in the mother of parliaments. The problem of how to conduct that parliament when, instead of a majority and a minority, you have three practically equal parties taking part in the proceedings, has not yet been solved in any other part of the world. [*Laughter.*] If we were citizens of the United States or Switzerland we might look upon this condition of affairs with apparent equanimity. It might paralyse legislation, but the administration would not be touched in the slightest degree, as the administration in those places stands outside, but in this country the administration also comes directly within the purview of parliament. Administration, as well as legislation, has been shaped on the principle of one majority with a minority of critics opposing. They can never be shaped with practically three equal parties. The position is unstable; it is absolutely impossible. It cannot continue, it ought not to continue. [*Hear, hear.*] Ask yourselves the question in machinery with which you are acquainted. What a game of cricket you would have if there were three elevens in the field instead of two, and one of those elevens sometimes playing on one side, sometimes on the other, and sometimes for itself. [*Laughter.*] I think that homely illustration best describes the difficulty. That is the difficulty which the new parliament has to face, and it is a task the difficulty of which has never been exceeded.

[A voice: It is simply 'cut-throat euchre'. (*Laughter.*)]

If the interjector has found that a simple game it is not my experience. [*Laughter.*] It is a game in which the 'joker' plays too large a part. [*Laughter.*] It is absolutely essential that, somehow or other, the existing three parties resolve themselves into two, either as parties or parts of parties, in order that constitutional government may be carried on. I have not the slightest idea as yet which two are going to endeavour to unite, but unite they must, and there are only two questions to be asked. The first of those is, what terms? I don't mean personal terms. [*Laughter.*] I mean what terms as to policy, although, as your laugh suggests, I am afraid personal considerations may not be entirely absent. [*Laughter.*] However personal the interest is, someone or other must give way for the benefit of the commonwealth. Which will give way is a delicate issue, and it is illustrated in the immortal 'Bab Ballads', when the last two survivors of the shipwrecked crew regard each other with expectation as to which is to remain:

I loved that cook as a brother, I did,
And that cook he worshipped me,
But we would both be blowed if we'd stowed,
In the other fellow's hold, you see.

[*Laughter.*] That may describe the sentiments with which some political leaders viewed the outlook. From the public point of view only
one thing is important, and that is that there should be no secret
compact. The terms should be published. There should be a treaty of
alliance, however it could best be drawn, on questions of policy and
principle known to the whole world. [*Applause.*] Until that happens
the ministry of the day has but one duty, and that is a plain one,
namely, to go straight on with the program submitted and with the
business of the country, in the hope that the good sense and judgement of the whole of the members would enable the situation to
be solved with the least delay possible, so that the business of the
country may be proceeded with. [*Applause.*]

'The forgotten people'

Sir Robert Menzies

Speech broadcast on 2UE in Sydney and 3AW in Melbourne

22 MAY 1942

With the government wracked by disunity between his United
Australia Party, the Country Party and independents, Robert
Menzies (1894–1978) resigned as prime minister in August 1941,
saying that he would 'lie down and bleed awhile'. He described
it as 'the stroke of doom; everything was at an end'. But this consummate politician remained a force even from the backbenches,
beginning in early 1942 a series of radio broadcasts on international affairs which aired each Friday night for over two years.

The most resonant speech in the series addressed the Australian middle class, reflecting a change in emphasis since his

political demise; from big business and labour to home values and the identification of a class of individuals linked not simply by their economic status, but through shared values, morals, attitudes and aspirations. Seven and a half years later, it was these 'forgotten people' who would return Menzies to office, keeping him there until he retired from public life in 1966.

*

Quite recently, a bishop wrote a letter to a great daily newspaper. His theme was the importance of doing justice to the workers. His belief apparently was that the workers are those who work with their hands. He sought to divide the people of Australia into classes. He was obviously suffering from what has for years seemed to me to be our greatest political disease; the disease of thinking that the community is divided into the rich and relatively idle, and the laborious poor, and that every social and political controversy can be resolved into the question: what side are you on?

Now, the last thing that I want to do is to commence or take part in a false war of this kind. In a country like Australia the class war must always be a false war.

But if we are to talk of classes, then the time has come to say something of the forgotten class – *the middle class* – those people who are constantly in danger of being ground between the upper and the nether millstones of the false class war; the middle class who, properly regarded, represent the backbone of this country.

We don't have classes here as in England, and therefore the terms don't mean the same. It is necessary, therefore, that I should define what I mean when I use the expression 'the middle class'.

Let me first define it by exclusion: I exclude at one end of the scale the rich and powerful; those who control great funds and enterprises, and are as a rule able to protect themselves – though it must be said that in a political sense they have as a rule shown neither comprehension nor competence. But I exclude them because in most material difficulties the rich can look after themselves.

I exclude at the other end of the scale the mass of unskilled people, almost invariably well-organised, and with their wages and conditions safeguarded by popular law. What I am excluding them from is my definition of the middle class. We cannot exclude them from the problem of social progress, for one of the prime objects of modern social and political policy is to give to them a proper measure of security, and provide the conditions which will enable them to acquire skill and knowledge and individuality.

These exclusions being made, I include the intervening range, the kind of people I myself represent in parliament -- salary-earners, shopkeepers, skilled artisans, professional men and women, farmers and so on. These are, in the political and economic sense, the middle class. They are for the most part unorganised and unselfconscious. They are envied by those whose social benefits are largely obtained by taxing them. They are not rich enough to have individual power. They are taken for granted by each political party in turn. They are not sufficiently lacking in individualism to be organised for what in these days we call 'pressure politics'. And yet, as I have said, they are the backbone of the nation.

The communist has always hated what he calls 'the bourgeoisie' because he sees clearly that the existence of one has kept British countries from revolution, while the substantial absence of one in feudal France at the end of the eighteenth century and in tsarist Russia at the end of the last war made revolution easy and indeed inevitable.

You may say to me: 'Why bring this matter up at this stage when we are fighting a war, in the result of which we are all equally concerned?'

My answer is that I am bringing it up because under the pressures of war we may, if we are not careful, if we are not as thoughtful as the times will permit us to be, inflict a fatal injury upon our own backbone.

In point of political, industrial and social theory and practice there are great delays in time of war. But there are also great accelerations. We must watch each, remembering always that whether we know it or not, and whether we like it or not, the foundations of whatever new order is to come after the war are inevitably being laid down now. We cannot go wrong right up to the peace treaty and expect suddenly thereafter to go right.

Now, what is the value of this middle class, so defined and described?

First: It has 'a stake in the country'. It has responsibility for homes – homes material, homes human, homes spiritual.

I do not believe that the real life of this nation is to be found either in great luxury hotels and the petty gossip of so-called fashionable suburbs, or in the officialdom of organised masses.

It is to be found in the homes of people who are nameless and unadvertised, and who, whatever their individual religious conviction or dogma, see in their children their greatest contribution to the immortality of their race. The home is the foundation of sanity and sobriety; it is the indispensable condition of continuity; its health determines the health of society as a whole.

I have mentioned homes material, homes human and homes spiritual.

Let me take them in their order: what do I mean by 'homes material'?

The 'material home' represents the concrete expression of the habits of frugality and saving 'for a home of our own'. Your advanced socialist may rage against private property even whilst he acquires it; but one of the best instincts in us is that which induces us to have one little piece of earth with a house and a garden which is ours, to which we can withdraw, in which we can be among our friends, into which no stranger can come against our will.

If you consider it, you will see that if, as in the old saying, 'The Englishman's home is his castle,' it is this very fact that leads on to the conclusion that he who seeks to violate that law by violating the soil of England must be repelled and defeated.

National patriotism, in other words, inevitably springs from the instinct to defend and preserve our own homes.

Then we have 'homes human': A great house, full of loneliness, is not a home. 'Stone walls do not a prison make' nor do they make a house; they may equally make a stable or a piggery. Brick walls, dormer windows and central heating need not make more than a hotel.

My home is where my wife and children are; the instinct to be with them is the great instinct of civilised man; the instinct to give them a chance in life is a noble instinct, not to make them leaners but lifters.

If Scotland has made a great contribution to the theory and practice of education, it is because of the tradition of Scottish homes. The Scottish ploughman, walking behind his team, cons ways and means of making his son a farmer, and so he sends him to the village school. The Scottish farmer ponders upon the future of his son, and sees it most assured not by the inheritance of money but by the acquisition of that knowledge which will give him power, and so the sons of many Scottish farmers find their way to Edinburgh and a university degree.

The great question is: 'How can I qualify my son to help society?' and not, as we have so frequently thought: 'How can I qualify society to help my son?' If human homes are to fulfil their destiny, then we must have frugality and saving for education and progress.

And, finally, we have 'homes spiritual': this is a notion which finds its simplest and most moving expression in 'The Cotter's Saturday Night' of Burns. Human nature is at its greatest when it combines dependence upon God with independence of man.

We offer no affront, on the contrary we have nothing but the warmest human compassion, for those whom fate has compelled to live upon the bounty of the state, when we say that the greatest element in a strong people is a fierce independence of spirit.

This is the only *real* freedom and it has as its corollary a brave acceptance of unclouded individual responsibility.

The moment a man seeks moral and intellectual refuge in the emotions of a crowd, he ceases to be a human being and becomes a cypher.

The home spiritual so understood is not produced by lassitude or by dependence; it is produced by self-sacrifice, by frugality and saving.

In a war, as indeed at most times, we become the ready victims of phrases. We speak glibly of many things without pausing to consider what they signify. We speak of 'financial power', forgetting that the financial power of 1942 is based upon the savings of generations which have preceded it.

We speak of 'morale' as if it were a quality induced from without,

created by others for our benefit, when in truth there can be no
national morale which is not based upon the individual courage of
men and women. We speak of 'man power' as if it were a mere matter of arithmetic, as if it were made up of a multiplication of men and
muscles without spirit.

Second: the middle class, more than any other, provides the intelligent ambition which is the motive power of human progress. The
idea entertained by many people that in a well-constituted world we
shall all live on the state is the quintessence of madness, for what is
the state but *us* – we collectively must provide what we individually
receive.

The great vice of democracy, a vice which is exacting a bitter retribution from it at this moment, is that for a generation we have been
busy getting ourselves onto the list of beneficiaries and removing ourselves from the list of contributors, as if somewhere there was somebody else's effort on which we could thrive.

To discourage ambition, to envy success, to hate achieved superiority, to distrust independent thought, to sneer at and impute
false motives to public service, these are the maladies of modern
democracy, and of Australian democracy in particular. Yet ambition,
effort, thinking and readiness to serve are not only the design and
objectives of self-government but are the essential conditions of its
success.

If this is not so, then we had better put back the clock and search
for a benevolent autocracy once more.

Where do we find these great elements most commonly?

Among the defensive and comfortable rich?

Among the unthinking and unskilled mass?

Or among what I have called 'the middle class'?

Third: The middle class provides more than perhaps any other
the intellectual life which marks us off from the beast; the life which
finds room for literature, for the arts, for science, for medicine and
the law.

Consider the case of literature and art. Could these survive as a
department of state? Are we to publish our poets according to their
political colour? Is the state to decree surrealism because surrealism
gets a heavy vote in a key electorate? The truth is that no great book

was ever written and no great picture ever painted by the clock or according to civil service rules. These things are done by *man*, not men. You cannot regiment them. They require opportunity, and sometimes leisure. The artist, if he is to live, must have a buyer; the writer, an audience. He finds them among frugal people to whom the margin above bare living means a chance to reach out a little towards that heaven which is just beyond our grasp.

It has always seemed to me, for example, that an artist is better helped by the man who sacrifices something to buy a picture he loves than by a rich patron who follows the fashion.

Fourth: This middle class maintains and fills the higher schools and universities and so feeds the lamp of learning.

What are schools for?

To train people for examinations?

To enable people to comply with the law?

Or to produce developed men and women?

Are the universities mere technical schools, or have they, as one of their functions, the preservation of pure learning, bringing in its train not merely riches for the imagination but a comparative sense for the mind, and leading to what we need so badly – the recognition of values which are other than pecuniary?

One of the great blots on our modern living is the cult of false values, a repeated application of the test of money, of notoriety, of applause.

A world in which a comedian or a beautiful half-wit on the screen can be paid fabulous sums, whilst scientific researchers and discoverers can suffer neglect and starvation, is a world which needs to have its sense of values violently set right.

Now, have we realised and recognised these things, or is most of our policy designed to discourage or penalise thrift, to encourage dependence on the state, to bring about a dull equality on the fantastic idea that all men are equal in mind and needs and desires, to level down by taking the mountains out of the landscape; to weigh men according to their political organisations and power, as votes and not as human beings?

These are formidable questions and we cannot escape from answering them if there is really to be a new order for the world.

I have been actively engaged in politics for fourteen years in the State of Victoria and in the Commonwealth of Australia. In that period I cannot readily recall many occasions upon which any policy was pursued which was designed to help the thrifty, to encourage independence, to recognise the divine and valuable variations of men's minds. On the contrary, there have been many instances in which the votes of the thriftless have been used to defeat the thrifty. On occasions of emergency, as in the depression and during the present war, we have hastened to make it clear that the provision made by a man for his own retirement and old age is not half as sacrosanct as the provision which the state would have made for him had he never saved at all.

We have talked of income from savings as if it possessed a somewhat discreditable character. We have taxed it more and more heavily. We have spoken slightingly of the earnings of interest at the very moment when we have advocated new pensions and social schemes. I have myself heard a minister of power and influence declare that no deprivation is suffered by a man if he still has the means to fill his stomach, to clothe his body and to keep a roof over his head!

And yet the truth is, as I have endeavoured to show, that frugal people who strive for and obtain the margin above these materially necessary things are the whole foundation of a really active and developing national life.

The case for the middle class is the case for a dynamic democracy as against a stagnant one. Stagnant waters are level and in them the scum rises. Active waters are never level; they toss and tumble and have crests and troughs, but the scientists tell us that they purify themselves in a few hundred yards.

That we are all, as human souls, of like value cannot be denied; that each of us should have his chance is and must be the great objective of political and social policy.

But to say that the industrious and intelligent son of self-sacrificing and saving and forward-looking parents has the same social desires and even material needs as the dull offspring of stupid and improvident parents is absurd.

If the motto is to be: 'Eat, drink and be merry for tomorrow you will die, and if it chances you don't die, the state will look after you;

but if you don't eat, drink and be merry, and save, we shall take your savings from you' – then the whole business of life will become foundationless.

Are you looking forward to a breed of men after the war who will have become boneless wonders? Leaners grow flabby; lifters grow muscles. Men without ambition readily become slaves. Indeed there is much more slavery in Australia than most people imagine.

How many hundreds of thousands of us are slaves to greed, to fear, to newspapers, to public opinion – represented by the accumulated views of our neighbours? Landless men smell the vapours of the street corner. Landed men smell the brown earth and plant their feet upon it and know that it is good.

To all of this many of my friends will retort: 'Ah, that's all very well, but when this war is over the levellers will have won the day.'

My answer is that, on the contrary, men will come out of this war as gloriously unequal in many things as when they entered it. Much wealth will have been destroyed; inherited riches will be suspect; a fellowship of suffering, if we really experience it, will have opened many hearts and perhaps closed many mouths. Many great edifices will have fallen, and we will be able to study foundations as never before, because war will have exposed them.

But I don't believe that we shall come out into the overlordship of an all-powerful state on whose benevolence we shall live, spineless and effortless; a state which will dole out bread and ideas with neatly regulated accuracy; where we shall all have our dividend without subscribing our capital; where the government – that almost deity – will nurse us and pension us and bury us; where we shall all be civil servants, and all presumably, since we are equal, head of departments!

If the new world is to be a world of men we must be not pallid and bloodless ghosts, but a community of people whose motto shall be '*to strive, to seek, to find and not to yield*'.

Individual enterprise must drive us forward. That doesn't mean that we are to return to the old and selfish notions of laissez faire. The functions of the state will be much more than merely keeping the ring within which the competitors will fight. Our social and industrial obligations will be increased. There will be more law, not less; more control, not less.

But what really happens to us will depend on how many people we have who are of the great and sober and dynamic middle class – the strivers, the planners, the ambitious ones.

We shall destroy them at our peril.

'The dignity and worth of the family'

Dame Enid Lyons

Maiden speech, House of Representatives

29 SEPTEMBER 1943

A federal election was held on 21 August 1943 and Labor won a resounding victory, gaining a majority in both houses of the parliament, but one of the key developments was on the conservative side of politics: Dame Enid Lyons (1897–1981) was elected as the United Australia Party's candidate for the seat of Darwin in Tasmania, and became the first woman to represent a constituency in the House of Representatives. She was the widow of Joseph Lyons, the former prime minister, who had died in 1939. Their marriage was regarded as 'a political love story'. Joseph described his wife as 'a wonderful woman, a good mother of twelve, and no mean politician'; Enid dedicated her memoir *So We Give Thanks* to 'the men and women who made this story possible by their faith in the man whose life I shared'.

The newspaper reports on 30 September 1943 described the maiden speech of the maiden parliamentarian as 'one of the most notable since Federation'. The prime minister, John Curtin, responded generously to the 'historic episode', saying in reply that 'the struggle for the enfranchisement of women, and for women to sit in legislative assemblies, belongs indeed to the great struggle for freedom and free institutions which have marked the evolution of our race.'

*

It would be strange indeed were I not tonight deeply conscious of the fact, if not a little awed by the knowledge, that on my shoulders rests a great weight of responsibility; because this is the first occasion upon which a woman has addressed this House. For that reason, it is an occasion which, for every woman in the Commonwealth, marks in some degree a turning point in history. I am well aware that, as I acquit myself in the work that I have undertaken for the next three years, so shall I either prejudice or enhance the prospects of those who wish to follow me in public service in the years to come. I know that many honourable members have viewed the advent of women to the legislative halls with something approaching alarm; they have feared, I have no doubt, the somewhat too vigorous use of a new broom. I wish to reassure them. I hold very sound views on brooms, and sweeping. Although I quite realise that a new broom is a very useful adjunct to the work of the housewife, I also know that it undoubtably is very unpopular in the broom cupboard; and this particular new broom knows that she has a very great deal to learn from the occupants of – I dare not say this particular cupboard. At all events, she hopes to conduct herself with sufficient modesty and sufficient sense of her lack of knowledge at least to earn the desire of honourable members to give her whatever help they may be able to give. I believe, very sincerely, that any woman entering the public arena must be prepared to work as men work; she must justify herself not as a woman, but as a citizen; she must attack the same problems, and be prepared to shoulder the same burdens. But because I am a woman, and cannot divest myself of those qualities that are inherent in my sex, and because every one of us speaks broadly in the terms of one's own experience, honourable members will have to become accustomed to the application of the homely metaphors of the kitchen rather than those of the operating theatre, the workshop or the farm. They must also become accustomed to the application to all kinds of measures of the touchstone of their effect upon the home and the family life. I hope that no one will imagine that that implies in any way a limitation of my political interests. Rather, it implies an ever-widening outlook on every problem that faces the world today. Every subject, from high finance to international relations, from social security to the winning of the war, touches very closely the home and the family. The late

King George V, as he neared the end of a great reign and a good life, made a statement upon which any one may base the whole of one's political philosophy when he said, 'The foundation of a nation's greatness is in the homes of its people.' Therefore, honourable members will not, I know, be surprised when I say that I am likely to be even more concerned with national character than with national effort.

Somewhere about the year 1830 there began a period in Australian history which for me has always held a peculiar fascination. I should like to have been born at about that time. I should like to have been alive in the days when bushrangers flourished, when life was hard and even raw, when gold was discovered, when the colonies became states, and when all of the great social and political movements were born which so coloured the fabric of Australian life; because, during all those years very much of what we now know as the Australian character was formed. It was during those years that we learned those things which still characterise the great bulk of our people – hatred of oppression, love of 'a fair go', a passion for justice. It was in those years that we developed those qualities of initiative and daring that have marked our men in every war in which they have fought – qualities which, I hope, will never be allowed to die. We are not on the threshold of such another era, when further formative measures will have to be taken; because we are today an organised community which no longer exists purely upon the initiative of its individual members, and if we would serve Australia well we must preserve those characteristics that were formed during that early period of our history.

I have been delighted, since I came here, to find the almost unanimity that exists in respect of the need for social service and in respect of many of the other problems that have been discussed in this chamber. In the matter of social security one thing stands out clearly in my mind. Such things are necessary in order that the weak shall not go to the wall, that the strong may be supported, that all may have justice. But we must never so blanket ourselves that those fine national qualities of which I have spoken shall no longer have play. I know so well that fear, want and idleness can kill the spirit of any people. But I know, too, that security can be bought at too great a cost – the cost of spiritual freedom. How, then, may we strike a balance? That, it seems to me, is the big question for us to decide today. There is one answer. We know perfectly well that any system of social security devised today must be financed largely from general taxation. Yet I would insist that every person in the community in receipt of any income whatsoever must make some contribution to the fund for social security. I want it to be an act of conscious citizenship. I want every child to be taught that when he begins to earn, then, for the first time, he will have the first privilege and right of citizenship – to begin to contribute to the great scheme that has been designed to serve him when he is no longer able to work and to help all of those who at any period of their lives may meet with distress or trouble. In such a scheme, I believe, there should be pensions for all; there should be no means test; those who have should contribute according to their means. But every one, however little he or she earns, should contribute something, be it only a three-penny stamp, as a sort of token payment for the advantage of being of Australian citizenship …

I am delighted that the honorable member for Denison (Dr Gaha) should have secured the honour of having introduced to this chamber, in this debate, the subject of population … I, like him, have pondered on this subject – not with my feet upon the mantlepiece, but knee-deep in shawls and feeding bottles … I believe that something more than decentralisation is necessary if the population of Australia is to be increased. It would be well to go back a little while and look for the reasons for the decline of population during the last fifty or sixty years. Two main reasons are ascribed, the first the growth of industrialism and the changed conditions resulting therefrom. Population became urban instead of rural, and the conditions in which children were brought up became less and less suitable. People were crowded. Housing was inadequate, and the large families went to the wall … At the other end of the social scale other reasons can be found for the declining birthrate. New inventions, and the provision of luxuries, provided new ways of spending incomes and leisure. There was less domestic help to be had. Finally, people began to think that the woman who became the mother of a family was something of a lunatic. About thirty years later she began to be regarded as something of a criminal lunatic. In the end the belief developed that it was a social virtue to produce fewer and fewer children. Where such a state of affairs exists, it is a matter of courage, even of hardihood, to have a family of more than two or three ...

Certain things are necessary to be done in order to ease the burden on families, but they must be looked upon only as measures of justice to those who are prepared to face their responsibilities. We need maternity and nursing services; we need some kind of domestic help service; we need better houses. But those things cannot in themselves revive the falling birthrate. We must look to the basic wage, which at present provides for the needs of three children for every man who receives it; yet how many thousands of men in this country have no children at all? How many have fewer than three – yet the three notional children of the man who has not any militate against the success in life of the children in other families of six and seven and eight. The basic wage is meagre enough in all conscience – too meagre – but it should be estimated upon the needs of a man and his wife, or of a man who must provide later for a wife, and the children should be provided for by an extension of the child endowment system. Let the man's wages be a direct charge upon industry, but the children should be a charge on the whole community. If we hope to increase the birthrate we must look to a resurgence of the national spirit, a resurgence of national vitality. We must look to a new concept of the dignity and worth of the family in the social order.

Let us pause for a moment and think of the time when the war shall end. Many speakers in the course of this debate have said that they believe that the war will end during the life of this parliament, and all too many people hope and believe that by the attainment of victory we shall step straight into the golden age. Nothing could be more foolish, because the golden age will arrive only when you and I and everyone else have made some contribution towards it. We shall have to plan for it, and work for it and sacrifice ourselves for it ...

I, too, believe in a scheme of national housing. I believe that it will help in the reabsorption of discharged men, but I believe also that we face a grave danger that the housing scheme will be overloaded with unnecessary costs. We have in Australia what I call a bricks-and-mortar complex. We cannot carry out any activity without housing it in a palace. We want in the homes that are to be built something less than is provided in some of the houses that I have seen designed. We want good walls and strong foundations; we want good fittings; but we do not want something that will cost more than is necessary. Permanency in a cathedral is a wonderful thing, but no one wants a house to last for 300 years ...

There was a reference in the Governor-General's speech to an overhaul of the manpower situation ... At the present time, there are thousands of women in the services and in the munition factories. By a slight readjustment of hours, it should be possible for them to receive some training that would fit them for civilian life, particularly in the domestic sphere where I hope most of them will eventually find their place ... so that when the men come home, torn, worn and wrecked, as many of them will be by their war experiences, they will have women to meet and greet them who will not be immediately harassed by a lack of knowledge of domestic work, and the running of happy homes.

Now let me turn just for a moment to the international sphere ... Because of what has happened to me in this war I have become disillusioned. For years I went about the world preaching peace and friendship and cooperation. I believed with all my heart in disarmament, but I can never again advocate such a policy. I believe that we must arm ourselves to meet whatever danger may threaten us, but I also believe that we must cooperate with all those forces of good that are working for peace, and with all those people who have a will for peace, so that we may do whatever lies in our power to preserve peace in our time. However, it is not sufficient merely to cooperate, nor should we limit the sphere of goodwill. Surely we can see that if Germany should rise again in Europe, Japan will rise again in the east as surely as the sun itself rises. The other evening I ... saw a film dealing with the war in Europe. There was one scene which portrayed the evacuation from Dunkirk. We saw how the German army flowed across the low countries and over northern France, and how the small British army was squeezed into an ever-decreasing compass, until finally it was compressed into the small area immediately around Dunkirk. Then the picture showed a mist on the water, and the voice of the announcer said this: 'And then out of the mist there came a strange flotilla – warships and fishing smacks, and craft of all kinds filled the sea. It was the seagoing English come to rescue their own.' And I felt, as I believe every other person felt who saw the picture, that this indeed was one of the greatest moments in the history of our race. I thought then, as I think now, that we should not fail occasionally to pause and look back upon the great moments of our past. We go along, thinking always that we progress, but sometimes we have to pause and take stock. I think that every Australian should pause now and again and say to himself, 'Only 150 years ago this land was wilderness. Now we have great cities, wonderful feats of engineering and beautiful buildings everywhere. And this is still a land of promise.' We cannot afford to neglect some recognition of our past, even though we gaze into the future.

Now, honourable members will forgive me, I know, when I say that I bear the name of one of whom it was said in this chamber that to him the problems of government were not problems of blue books, not problems of statistics, but problems of human values and human hearts and human feelings. That, it seems to me, is a concept of government that we might well cherish. It is certainly one that I hold very dear. I hope that I shall never forget that everything that takes place in this chamber goes out somewhere to strike a human heart, to influence the life of some fellow being, and I believe this, too, with all my heart, that the duty of every government, whether in this country or any other, is to see that no man, because of the condition of his life, shall ever need lose his vision of the city of God.

'Freedom from fear can never be separated from freedom from want'

Herbert Vere Evatt

'Australia and the United Nations Charter': national radio broadcast by the ABC

28 APRIL 1945

Dr Herbert 'Bert' Vere Evatt (1894–1965) entered federal politics as a Labor Party member in 1940 with impressive academic credentials including a BA, MA, LLB, LLD and D. Litt, two University Medals and triple first-class honours. He was a brilliant scholar and became the youngest justice of the High Court of Australia at the age of thirty-six. When Arthur Calwell once remarked, 'Doc, you are bordering on being a genius,' Evatt replied, 'What's this "bordering on"?' In 1941, 'The Doc' was appointed attorney-general in John Curtin's government, and from 1946 to 1949 was Ben Chifley's deputy prime minister. Two years after Labor lost office in the 1949 election, Evatt took over the leadership of the Opposition, and both the party and the leader went into a spiral of decline, culminating in the 'split' of the party in 1955. Evatt was 'captain of a rather unseaworthy vessel' and never fulfilled his ambition for prime ministerial office.

The zenith of Evatt's career was his chairmanship of the United Nations General Assembly from 1948 to 1949, a position he termed – 'with insufficient irony', as one observer put it – as 'president of the world'. Evatt had led the Australian delegation to the United Nations in 1946, 1947 and 1948, and won international admiration for his efforts. His historic fight against the conditions of the veto for the great powers 'was the most spectacular episode of the conference' and although he received little support for his arguments in 1945 there is now more widespread acceptance of their wisdom.

*

You can take it that the policy of the Australian delegation at the San Francisco Conference will be clear and definite. Australia, as a nation that has taken part in two world wars, has a deep and permanent interest in the establishment of an international organisation which will secure peace. Therefore, we gladly accept the Dumbarton Oaks proposals in principle. But, in our considered view, these proposals are capable of clarification, improvement and expansion in important respects. Therefore, we are taking steps to propose a number of important amendments.

I shall not attempt in this talk to state Australia's policy in detail. I want rather to try to indicate the basic reasons for Australia's attitude.

While people are still suffering all the pains and sacrifices of war it is easy to regard peace as an end in itself. We would insist on the other hand that peace is not a featureless negative, the mere absence of military hostilities. We certainly want peace, but we want peace with social justice – a peace that shall afford to the peoples of all countries positive opportunities to lead full and happy lives. That is why we are especially anxious to expand the statement of the purpose of the new organisation so as to include the moral and political principles on which the United Nations will act. We believe that the Charter should make it plain that the purpose of the new organisation is not merely to preserve peace but to protect and foster those principles of right conduct which must govern the actions of all civilised nations.

Again, we think express provision should be made in the Charter to give better recognition to the 'want' of preserving the political independence and territorial integrity of every nation. Unless this basic national right is respected, the sovereign equality of nations becomes meaningless.

Again, freedom from fear can never be separated from freedom from want. Since political security must be built on social justice, we believe it is important that these social and economic aims should be clearly set forth in the Charter. Australia, therefore, wants the Charter to include an undertaking by which all members of the organisation will pledge themselves to take appropriate action, both national and international, to secure for all peoples, including their own, improved labour standards, economic advancement and social security. We believe in particular that the achievement of *full employment* is not merely a domestic responsibility which each government owes to its own people, but should also be a fundamental international obligation. To provide effective machinery for the realisation of these great aims, we desire the Economic and Social Council to be made one of the principal organs of the world organisation. We feel that in the Dumbarton Oaks proposals this council is given only a minor role. Economic welfare is no less important than political security. We therefore believe that the Economic and Social Council should, like the Security Council, remain in permanent session with the continuous representation of those nations elected to it. We also propose to urge amendments to the Dumbarton Oaks proposals that are designed to produce a better balance between the powers and responsibility of the great powers on the one hand and the middle and smaller powers on the other. We recognise and accept the right of veto by each of the five great powers, in so far as this applies to the use of economic or military sanctions. But we cannot agree that the veto power is justified at the preliminary stage when an effort is being made to settle a dispute by conciliation, arbitration or other pacific means.

Again, we do not agree that the veto can be properly exercised in order to prevent the future amendment of the Charter. We fully recognise that responsibility for maintaining peace must rest mainly on the great powers and that they must enjoy an authority commensurate with their economic and military resources. We distinguish, however, between leadership and domination. We support leadership; we reject domination.

We feel very strongly that, in the selection of the non-permanent members of the Security Council, the fullest consideration should be given to the claims of what we in Australia call 'security powers'. If the Security Council is to work successfully, it must be made up of members who have the proved will and capacity to make practical contributions to security. We think it should be recognised that outside the great powers there are certain nations who, by reason of their resources and geographical position, will prove to be of key importance for the maintenance of security in different parts of the world. Moreover, there are certain of these powers, and Australia is obviously one of them, who have proved by their record in two world wars that they have not only the capacity and the resources but the determined will to put everything they have into the struggle against aggressors who threaten the world with tyranny. Surely these powers have a claim to special recognition in any security organisation. In urging this claim, we are not trying to push any purely selfish national interest. We believe that the new organisation can work effectively only if it is based on the wholehearted support of these security powers. We are not arguing a case for Australia alone, although Australia is greatly concerned. We are arguing a case which we believe must be accepted if the welfare and security of all peace-loving nations are to be preserved.

'The light on the hill'

Joseph 'Ben' Chifley

Address to the State Conference of the Australian Labor Party, New South Wales

12 JUNE 1949

Ben Chifley (1885–1951) has an undiminished status as a legend of the Australian Labor Party, usually represented as the humble, patient, pipe-smoking servant of the nation. A former engine driver turned union official, he entered federal parliament in 1940 – after a short stint a decade earlier – and became treasurer in John Curtin's wartime cabinet. When Curtin died in office in 1945, Chifley was his party's choice as successor, to implement its vision of post-war reconstruction.

His 'simple tastes and homespun manner' won the hearts of his supporters and the respect of many of his opponents. Every day at lunchtime he would lock his parliamentary office door, 'have some toast and his own blended tea and take a twenty minute nap', as he always had done as an engine driver. He articulated his party's philosophy most famously as a gathering of the faithful, and in so doing made the words of inspiration – 'the light on the hill' – 'the most powerful of Labor catchcries'. But the vision was out of step with the aspirations of Australians after decades of economic and wartime austerity, and Labor would lose office six months later and not regain it for twenty-three years. Chifley's death in his room at the Hotel Kurrajong while dignitaries and ministers were attending a state ball to celebrate fifty years of federation, stopped the music and cast a pall over the national celebrations.

*

I have had the privilege of leading the Labor Party for nearly four years. They have not been easy times and it has not been an easy job. It is a man-killing job and would be impossible if it were not for the help of my colleagues and members of the movement.

No Labor minister or leader ever has an easy job. The urgency that rests behind the Labor movement, pushing it on to do things, to create new conditions, to reorganise the economy of the country, always means that the people who work within the Labor movement, people who lead, can never have an easy job. The job of the evangelist is never easy.

Because of the turn of fortune's wheel your Premier (Mr McGirr) and I have gained some prominence in the Labor movement. But the strength of the movement cannot come from us. We make plans and pass legislation to help and direct the economy of the country. But the job of getting the things the people of this country want comes from the roots of the Labor movement – the people who support it.

When I sat at a Labor meeting in the country with only ten or fifteen men there, I found a man sitting beside me who had been working in the Labor movement for fifty-four years. I have no doubt that many of you have been doing the same, not hoping for any advantage from the movement, not hoping for any personal gain, but because you believe in a movement that has been built up to bring better conditions to the people. Therefore, the success of the Labor Party at the next elections depends entirely, as it always has done, on the people who work.

I try to think of the Labor movement, not as putting an extra sixpence into somebody's pocket, or making somebody prime minister or premier, but as a movement bringing something better to the people, better standards of living, greater happiness to the mass of the people. We have a great objective – the light on the hill – which we aim to reach by working the betterment of mankind not only here but anywhere we may give a helping hand. If it were not for that, the Labor movement would not be worth fighting for.

If the movement can make someone more comfortable, give to some father or mother a greater feeling of security for their children, a feeling that if a depression comes there will be work, that the government is striving its hardest to do its best, then the Labor movement will be completely justified.

It does not matter about persons like me who have our limitations. I only hope that the generosity, kindliness and friendliness shown to me by thousands of my colleagues in the Labor movement will continue to be given to the movement and add zest to its work.

'The minnow among the thirty-six tritons'

Sir Robert Menzies

Speech in the House of Representatives

3 APRIL 1963

When Arthur Calwell and Gough Whitlam were photographed by the *Daily Telegraph* in the early hours of the morning, standing under a street light waiting for a decision by the federal executive conference of the Labor Party regarding a proposal for the United States to build a naval communications base in Western Australia, they made a rod for their political backs. Robert Menzies denounced the Labor Party as the tool of an unelected 'outside parliament' of thirty-six 'faceless men', and enjoyed reminding voters of the exquisite imagery. Menzies used the following parliamentary speech – following the Cuban missile crisis – to thwart a want-of-confidence motion in his government, before a trip abroad that encompassed his investiture as Knight of the Thistle and delivering the Jefferson Memorial Oration at Monticello.

*

Mr Speaker, the honourable member for Batman (Mr Benson) is a very experienced pilot, but he will forgive me when I say that during his speech I was very much struck by the fact that he was steering a course that gave the impression that he was sheering about in a five-knot ebb tide in the rip off Point Lonsdale. He will understand exactly what that means. I think he has fallen into the common error of thinking that to refer a matter to the United Nations is in itself a constructive policy. Time after time it has become necessary to say that it is not. To go to the United Nations with a policy is one thing, but to say that Cuba, for example, should have gone to the United Nations, or that something else should have gone to the United Nations, is not a policy at all. It is a mere evasion of national responsibility and of national decision.

The honourable member permitted himself to comment adversely – he is not the only one on the Opposition side to have done so – about President Kennedy's handling of the Cuba incident and about this government's instant declaration that we agreed with what President Kennedy had done. What do honourable members opposite want us to do? This was one of the really significant events in post-war history – a critical event which, if it had not been dealt with promptly and strongly by the President of the United States, might have altered the balance of power in the world. The President of the United States took in splendid terms a strong and definite attitude on these matters, but honourable members opposite say: 'Oh, it should have gone to the United Nations.' I wonder whether honourable members know what they mean. Do they mean that the matter should have gone to the Security Council so that it could have been neatly vetoed by the Soviet Union? That would have occupied a certain amount of time. In the meantime, the Soviet Union would have continued to put its weapons – its missiles – into Cuba, building a base close to the United States which could alter the entire balance of power in the world. Is that what honourable members opposite mean? No doubt it is. Then they say, 'Now that you come to mention it, of course the Soviet Union would use its veto so that a reference to the Council would come to nothing; but then you could go to the General Assembly.' That would involve a fortnight's debate. You would have all of the communist satellites lined up and speech after speech made. All the time the communist position in Cuba would be being built up until ultimately the balance of power in the world was upset.

Mr Speaker, these are very serious matters. If the Opposition's attitude is that the President of the United States was wrong and that we were wrong to be the first people to give our approval to the United States action, then the people of Australia should know about this. I think they will, and they might think about it. They might wonder whether they should entrust not only their economic affairs but also their security and their entire future to the people on the other side of this parliament. Now, sir, I speak as some sort of an expert on this matter. There are two objectives in a no-confidence motion – I know: I have been at the giving end and at the receiving end. One objective is to put the government out. That is an admirable attitude for an Opposition to have, but it has taken an awful long time for this Opposition to decide on that attitude. The other objective of a censure motion is, of course, to put the Opposition in. This would not be an unfair analysis of the aims – to put us out and to put the Opposition in.

For the purposes of simplicity, therefore, I propose to divide my own contribution tonight between these two aspects. I do not need to say as much as I otherwise would, because later on in this debate my colleagues, the Minister for Trade (Mr McEwen) and the Treasurer (Mr Harold Holt), will have admirable opportunities to deal in detail with some of these matters. But I will not let them go by entirely. I, therefore, start by saying something about the aim of putting the government out, and the reasons for that.

My distinguished friend, the Leader of the Opposition (Mr Calwell) has, of course, a professional gloom about the Australian economy. It is his duty to be depressed and, if possible, to depress other people. Therefore he gave us a professionally gloomy account of Australia's present economic condition, which was so much at variance with the facts as to be almost ludicrous. I hear it was read by people in other countries. They would, of course, burst into hilarious laughter, on looking at their own countries, to be told about this one which is in a state of economic despair and depression!

[Mr O'Brien: That is not true.]

Of course that is not true. After all, the Leader of the Opposition was careful to omit from his attack – I will call it an attack – all the material facts in the economic position. I do not recall him saying anything about the remarkable success of the government's policy against inflation. Members of the Opposition laugh on both sides of their faces. I am familiar with all those chaps. On one hand they laugh because they have always said that inflation is silly talk and that it is a bogy, and on the other side they laugh because they are not very pleased to have to admit, in their hearts, that the consumer price index has been stable now for years.

[Mr Ward: How does it compare with 1949?]

I always know I am scoring when some of you yelp. But I do not worry myself about that. I am not addressing myself to East Sydney. Whenever I have addressed myself to East Sydney I have needed police protection. I repeat that we have a stable consumer price index. In other words, the inflationary pressures in this country, which were desperately dangerous a few years ago, have been brought under control. But the Leader of the Opposition said not a word about that! Not a word about the remarkable increase in employment in Australia. Not a word about the remarkable increase in production in Australia!

[Mr O'Brien: And shortened wages!]

It is all right. Some of the new boys will learn in due course that a few facts are much more important than some of the arguments they present.

[Mr Cross: Give us the facts.]

Even you cannot deny that there has been a most remarkable increase in production in this country in the last few years and a most remarkable increase in savings. I can go back a little while and remember –

[Mr Pollard: Back to the eighteenth century!]

And it was a very good century, too. Do you know why, sir? Because it was a century of good sense.

[Mr Allan Fraser: Yes, it was the century of the rich. You are an eighteenth-century prime minister.]

The honourable member for Eden-Monaro says 'an eighteenth-century prime minister'. All I can say is that at the tail-end of the eighteenth century they had some jolly good prime ministers and he might have been proud to be one of them. But he has forgotten his history. As I was saying, there have been increased savings. I can remember the time when my distinguished opponent, the Leader of the Opposition, used to say: 'Look at the way savings have fallen away. This is a sign that the government is ineffective.' Now, when he sees that there are record savings – another £200 million in the savings banks – he says 'That is no good. This is a sign that people have no confidence in the future.' You cannot satisfy some honourable members. The Leader of the Opposition did not say a word about the development works program, except in one respect that I will come to in a minute. He did not say a word about the record home-building in Australia – an undoubted and undeniable fact. He did not say a word about the record activity in commercial building in the cities. He did not say a word about the public credit being high both here and overseas. He did not say a word about interest rates falling. He did not say a word – except a hostile word – about investment in this country from overseas. He did not say a word about the remarkable and increasing growth in the export of manufactures from Australia. He said nothing about all these matters, yet the fact is, and wherever you go you can encounter it, that there is an increasing feeling in this country, even among those who were critical, that the government's policy has been right. Confidence is building up every week and every month. However, I do not want to take up too much of my time on these matters. Other speakers who will follow me can deal with the details.

[Mr Cope: Put a tiger in your tank. You have gone a bit flat!]

I have always noticed that when the honorable member is afraid to listen he makes a noise. No, sir, the Leader of the Opposition was kind enough to make a glancing reference or two to me in the course of his speech. At one stage he said that I was reported to have told my federal executive something. All I can say is that I have never heard of the report until he mentioned it last night. It was quite untrue and I am sorry that he should retail things from the gossip columns. He also referred to me – and this fascinated me because I do not know whether it was a compliment or a subdued attack – as the sole triton of post-war Liberalism.

[Mr Cross: That was a compliment.]

I suppose he meant to convey the impression that I was a triton among the minnows. That, I think, was overdoing it. It was supposed to be a compliment to me and an offence to those who for so many years have been with me in the problems of this country. All I want to say to the Leader of the Opposition – he has exposed his flank a little on this – is that to be a triton among the minnows is not half so bad as being a minnow among the thirty-six tritons who run the Labor Party and that is what, by confession, he is. He is the minnow swimming around the tritons, coming up occasionally, listening – if a fish can listen – and then diving down again. The minnow among the thirty-six tritons!

... If Labor is to go in, I think it is essential that the people of Australia should know where the members of the Labor Party stand on the great issues confronting this country. I have already explained that they do not quite know where they stand even on matters on which they attack us. But where do they stand on the matters on which I propose to attack them? They are putting themselves forward as the alternative government. Apparently they do so very confidently – more confident today than they will be in a month's time; more confident in a month's time than they will be in a year's time. They know that; they are not so silly as not to know. However, they are putting themselves forward as the new government. Now, sir, what kind of a government would this Labor government be?

[Mr Costa: A good one.]

Eric, if you are in it, I will be delighted. But what kind of a government would it be? The government, of course, would be the tied spokesman of thirty-six outsiders, none of them elected by the Australian people and any nineteen of them able to control the minds and the voices of a Labor government. As the honourable member for Higinbotham (Mr Chipp) said this afternoon, this is what is called democracy. It may have been different in the days when Labor had strong leaders, but it is not good today when Labor has leaders who bow in the corridors, who wait for their orders and who then proceed as best they can to carry out their orders. In other words, the country is not being offered by Labor a government of people who will attack problems, exercise their own judgement and stand by their judgement, but people who will look around the corner and say to these obscure nonentities who give them their orders, 'Please, what is it we are allowed to do.' That is as clear as a pikestaff, and if it needed to be made clear, my honourable friend with his deputy leader made it clear at the last federal conference of the Australian Labor Party. A more humiliating spectacle could hardly be imagined!

[Mr Pollard: That is not what you said to Bury. You said, 'Do it or else.']

That was a prime minister; he was the leader. He was not a prime minister who had to go away to thirty-six people and say, 'Please oblige me by telling me.'

[Mr Allan Fraser: You are a one-man government.]

The honourable member for Eden-Monaro keeps muttering about a one-man government. I am the Prime Minister because the people have elected my supporters, who have chosen me. There is no parallel on my side of politics to this outside control by a group of thirty-six, or any other number you care to choose, completely irresponsible people to whom the so-called leaders of the country would have to make their obeisance.

'It is jolly decent of the Prime Minister to let us know officially'

Gough Whitlam

Response to the announcement of the election date, House of Representatives

10 OCTOBER 1972

Speculation over the date of an impending federal election is something of a national sport in Australia. When prime minister William McMahon announced the date for the 1972 election to the House of Representatives on 10 October, his opponent, Gough Whitlam (1916–), was delighted. Whitlam had entered parliament in 1952 after serving in the war and working in a legal practice. He had been leader of the Opposition since 1967, modernising the Labor Party and wresting control of policy from the federal executive. Whitlam towered over McMahon physically and intellectually, and had memorably dubbed him 'Tiberius with a telephone' for his taste for political intrigues. Whitlam's response to the election announcement oozes confidence, contempt and the expectation of vindication.

*

The Prime Minister has steadfastly adhered to the principle he announced for himself on this subject last March: 'What I have never done is to fix a date until I have made up my mind what the date is likely to be.' We have not only had speculation on the election date; we have even had just as much speculation about the day that the date would be announced. Whoever will be able to say that the right honourable gentleman cannot keep a secret? Who will ever say again that he cannot grasp the nettle? The date announced places the Deputy Prime Minister (Mr Anthony) in a quite extraordinary position. He appeared to intend to hold his own election on 25 November – the ultimate gesture of Country Party independence. Certainly one now has a magnificent example of the trust, the confidence, the comradeship between the two leaders of the coalition. As the Deputy Prime Minister said: 'He (McMahon) told me he would not tell me the date so I did not ask him.' So now we have the date, and I must say I think it is jolly decent of the Prime Minister to let us know officially. The second of December is a memorable day. It is the anniversary of Austerlitz. Far be it from me to wish, or appear to wish, to assume the mantle of Napoleon, but I cannot forget that the second of December was a date on which a crushing defeat was administered to a coalition – another ramshackle, reactionary coalition.

'It's time'

Gough Whitlam

Labor Party policy speech, Blacktown Civic Centre

13 November 1972

In twenty-three years, the Australian Labor Party had suffered nine successive election defeats. At the Blacktown Civic Centre on 13 November 1972 – in one of the suburban electorates whose aspirations Whitlam hoped to tap – the atmosphere was 'not so much a public meeting as an act of communion and a celebration of hope and love'. Whitlam's speech writer Graham Freudenberg recalled that Whitlam touched him 'lightly on the shoulder' as he moved to address the audience, 'a curious ritual that had developed between us before major speeches on which we had collaborated, an act not of superstition but of remembrance of things past. Whitlam said, "It's been a long road, comrade, but we're there."' He then began the speech with the evocative words used by John Curtin in his wartime radio broadcasts.

*

Men and women of Australia!

The decision we will make for our country on 2 December is a choice between the past and the future, between the habits and fears of the past, and the demands and opportunities of the future. There are moments in history when the whole fate and future of nations can be decided by a single decision. For Australia, this is such a time. It's time for a new team, a new program, a new drive for equality of opportunities; it's time to create new opportunities for Australians, time for a new vision of what we can achieve in this generation for our nation and the region in which we live.

It's time for a new government – a Labor government.

My fellow citizens, I put these questions to you:

Do you believe that Australia can afford another three years like the last twenty months? Are you prepared to maintain at the head of your affairs a coalition which has lurched into crisis after crisis, embarrassment piled on embarrassment week after week? Will you accept another three years of waiting for next week's crisis, next week's blunder? Will you again entrust the nation's economy to the men who deliberately, but needlessly, created Australia's worst unemployment for ten years? Or to the same men who have presided over the worst inflation for twenty years?

Can you trust the last-minute promises of men who stood against these very same proposals for twenty-three years? Would you trust your international affairs again to the men who gave you Vietnam? Will you trust your defences to the men who haven't even yet given you the F-III?

We have a new chance for our nation. We can recreate this nation. We have a new chance for our region. We can help recreate this region.

The war of intervention in Vietnam is ending. The great powers are rethinking and remoulding their relationships and their obligations. Australia cannot stand still at such a time. We cannot afford to limp along with men whose attitudes are rooted in the slogans of the 1950s – the slogans of fear and hate. If we made such a mistake, we would make Australia a backwater in our region and a back number in history. The Australian Labor Party – vindicated as we have been on all the great issues of the past – stands ready to take Australia forward to her rightful, proud, secure and independent place in the future of our region.

Our program has three great aims. They are:

- to promote equality
- to involve the people of Australia in the decision-making processes of our land
- and to liberate the talents and uplift the horizons of the Australian people.

We want to give a new life and a new meaning in this new nation to the touchstone of modern democracy – to liberty, equality, fraternity.

'Dressed in safari suit and wearing dark glasses'

Fred Daly

Speech on the 'Khemlani affair', House of Representatives

28 October 1975

After growing up in rural NSW, Fred Daly (1913–1995) left school at fourteen and gained employment as a bicycle messenger in Sydney during the Depression – the perfect apprenticeship for the future federal Labor Party whip. He entered politics after serving on the executive of the NSW branch of the Federated Clerk's Union, winning his first seat in 1943. By the time Daly retired in 1975, he was known as the 'Father of the House', widely admired on both sides of the assembly and appreciated as a salty raconteur.

Daly's career spanned ten prime ministers but he did not gain a ministerial portfolio until he was elected minister for services and property and leader of the House in the Whitlam government. He thought himself 'made for that', with a thorough knowledge of the Standing Orders 'from twenty-nine years experience breaking them'. His tenure, however, would be brief. The 'loans affair' – the name given to the unorthodox methods of the government's overseas fundraising – was about to precipitate the dismissal of the Labor government. Tirath Khemlani, a shady intermediary employed by the minister for minerals and energy, Rex O'Connor, to raise petro-dollars for the government's ambitious plans for resource developments, was brought to Australia by the Liberal Party to help expose the government scandal. Daly describes Khemlani's arrival in Australia – and subsequent interview by two Opposition frontbenchers, including John Howard – with the wit for which he was renowned. A fortnight later the government was dismissed and Daly retired.

*

I understand that yesterday afternoon a Commonwealth ministerial car was booked by the Deputy Leader of the Opposition to meet Ansett flight 361, 2.10 p.m. from Sydney, and that of course commenced a drama in Canberra yesterday that has rarely been equalled. The car was to meet a person named Mr Khemlani. I understand that the gentleman approached the Commonwealth car dressed in safari suit and wearing dark glasses. He was met by bearded investigators who hustled him into the VIP room while the Commonwealth car backed into the normally restricted luggage area and his eight bulging briefcases were loaded into it.

Mr Khemlani was then pushed into the Commonwealth car along with two sinister bearded staff members and taken on a high-speed chase through the back streets of Fyshwick reaching speeds of one hundred kilometres per hour, turning down side streets and doing sudden U-turns before coming to a sudden stop at his destination – a $23-a-night room at the Hotel Wellington. Mr Khemlani, still using the car, and the men then disappeared into room forty-nine – the room adjoining the motel shoe-shine box. Lemonade, potato chips and two Sydney afternoon papers were pushed through the breakfast hatch. He stayed locked in his room while the staff members stayed huddled in a corner sifting through his eight suitcases of documents.

Later in the afternoon Mr Khemlani was taken on another high-speed car chase. This time, as a taxi pulled up at the front of the motel, Mr Khemlani disappeared out the back door and sped off in a late-model gold Torana with the manager of the Wellington Hotel at the wheel. That is service. It raced through the peak-hour traffic, went one and a half times around State Circle, and reached speeds of up to 120 kilometres along Commonwealth Avenue before swinging around and returning to the hotel. Then Mr Khemlani disappeared.

An hour later his briefcases were lugged into a lift at the $33-a-night Lakeside Hotel where Mr Khemlani usually stays. But he was not booked in there last night. Last night Mr Khemlani was locked up with two Opposition frontbenchers, Mr Bob Ellicott and Mr John Howard, going through suitcases full of documents. As if he were not in enough trouble without being locked up with them! I come back again to the Commonwealth car. Poor Mr Khemlani: he had come all the way from Singapore at his own cost and without a visa, to clear his name and he had all that excess baggage with him. What must he think of Australia – his life was endangered by high-speed car chases in Commonwealth cars; his bags were searched by bearded investigators, and as far as we know they were not false beards; he was booked into a $23-a-night room next to a shoe-shine box yet his bags were booked into a $33-a-night international hotel; he was locked up all afternoon with bearded men and then all night with two members of the Opposition.

[Mr Whitlam: And fed with peanuts.]

And then fed with peanuts. He must also be wondering why the Opposition would pay out all that money for his bags but was too lousy to pay for a taxi fare for him to go from the airport to the hotel.

'Fishes on bicycles'

Susan Ryan

Speech to the Department of the Senate, Canberra

23 March 1992

A founding member of the Women's Electoral Lobby in the early 1970s and the architect of the Sex Discrimination Act, Senator Susan Ryan (1942–) became the first woman in the Labor Party to hold a cabinet portfolio when she was appointed minister for education in the Hawke government in 1983. It was no sinecure. Ryan saw 'second-wave' feminism in Australia not as 'one big breaker rolling smoothly to the shore but a myriad currents, rips and dumpers', and after leaving politics Ryan admitted: 'Many women did not feel represented by me and did not wish to be.' She served as a federal politician from 1975 to 1988, pushing through the anti-discrimination and equal opportunity legislation and assisting the prime minister on the status of women before venturing into publishing and later taking executive directorships of several business associations.

*

A woman without a man is like a fish without a bicycle. Did the slogan that adorned many of the doors and walls of women's liberationists in the 1970s imply anything about women and politics? Women in parliament are not women without men, they are women surrounded by them. But in making their way through the congestion of legislation, policy, scrutiny, representation, electioneering and leadership, are women as unnatural and unlikely as fishes on bicycles? Do a few fishes on bicycles change our perception of fish?

According to which social commentator you favour, social change is either excruciatingly slow or frighteningly rapid. It depends on your viewpoint and the issues. In the history of the human race, or even the history of the Australian parliament, seventeen years is not a long time. It will be seventeen years this December since I was elected to the Senate. The changes to the parliamentary program, to policies and legislation, to the media's expectation of what happens in parliament and to the community's expectations about who their political leaders will be and what they should look like, have changed in that time.

When I first went into parliament women parliamentarians were not quite as rare a sight as a fish on a bicycle: they actually did exist.

After being elected in 1975, I joined four women who had already been in the Senate for a short period, Liberal Senators Guilfoyle and Martin, and Labor Senators Coleman and Melzer. Senator Walters from Tasmania was also elected in 1975. So there were six: a small but noticeable number. Across King's Hall in the House of Representatives there were no women. Four women had been elected to sit in the House of Representatives since Enid Lyons broke that barrier in 1943, but in 1975 there was none. There was no woman leader or minister in any state parliament. The memory of Enid Lyons had faded. Margaret Guilfoyle became the first, and sole, female cabinet minister in the Fraser government.

I was the first Labor senator for the Australian Capital Territory, along with John Knight who was the first Liberal senator for the Australian Capital Territory. My election was greeted with many media comments and profiles emphasising my gender, age, hair colour, marital status, physical size and motherhood. About my political agenda they were less informative. Being female evoked comment, but even more remarkable than my female presence in the Senate, I was a feminist. Most people, including senators and members of my own caucus room, did not quite know what that meant. I did. I had formed my political aspirations and drawn my political energy from feminism, that movement for gender equality beginning at the end of the 1960s, called, in retrospect, second-wave feminism and at the time, women's liberation. It was my first political involvement and I did not linger very long. I was interested in the questions being explored within women's liberation: the nature of the female; the operation of oppression; defining the patriarchy; the possibility of a 'women's culture'. But there were more urgent and important questions for me. Along with other activists I moved straight from the basic assumption of feminism, that women were treated unfairly by society (all societies), to the conclusion that the remedy for this unfairness was in the hands of women themselves. This was a political solution – one that required the exercise of political power.

As I conducted my analysis of the obstacles to equality and fairness to women, I was drawn again and again to the political system. External obstacles to equality for women abounded. Many of them were rooted in legislation and public policy created in the parliaments of Australia: practices such as denying permanency of employment to married women; limited women's education; restricting them to a narrow range of training and employment; wages policies that refused to accept the reality of female economic independence and failed to note that many women supported dependents; refusal to acknowledge the consequences for women of women's fertility.

Considering these policy failures, and examining the way in which parliament made laws and budgets, I came to believe that not only was a woman's place in the House and in the Senate, as my first campaign slogan proclaimed, but a feminist's place was in politics.

In our kind of democracy, particular groups seek to impact on political decision-makers through the formation of lobbies. This method had traditionally been pursued with success in Australia by farmers and miners. More recently, the ethnic and green lobbies have achieved many victories. It occurred to some of us very early on that a women's lobby should be established to influence the content of laws and the performance of politicians. We formed the Women's Electoral Lobby in the year leading up to the election of the Whitlam government in December 1972. WEL utilised shock tactics, the media, persuasion and a bit of psychological terrorism, to get issues like child care, equal pay, reproductive control, and access to education and training, onto the agenda of the newly elected Whitlam government.

From my feminist perspective, this lobbying was necessary but not sufficient. It left women on the outside of political power, waiting, persuading, threatening, but not acting directly to achieve change.

That short and intense period where the Women's Electoral Lobby became an effective part of the 1972 election campaign determined my parliamentary career. How much more efficient, I thought, how much more effective, if we were in there making the decisions, instead of knocking on doors trying to attract support. Debate on the ill-fated Lamb–McKenzie Abortion Reform Bill in 1973 exemplified the problem: the debate was conducted in an all-male chamber; the women were outside rallying, organising, shouting through loud hailers, preparing for disappointment. I decided that next time we should be in there making the laws.

I set about organising a preselection base throughout the Labor Party branches in the ACT. I worked with other Labor Party feminists and progressive male members to try to ensure that the branches reflected this new and dynamic commitment to gender equality. This strategy, to the amazement and annoyance of seasoned political commentators, succeeded: I was endorsed and won a Senate seat in 1975.

I was often asked at this time, and subsequently, what I expected, what misgivings I had. It is hard to say whether my expectations were too modest or totally extravagant. I did expect that I would be able to make changes. It was both better and worse than I anticipated. I found many supporters, but so much that seemed to me to be logical, sensible, fair and of general benefit to the community, seemed to others to be radical, eccentric and impractical.

My central objective in parliament was economic independence for all, including women. Economic independence means the capacity to provide for your own needs and for the needs of those for whom you are directly responsible. Although the Whitlam government had persuaded the Conciliation and Arbitration Commission to accept the principle of equal pay, it would be decades before that principle became reality for all workers. How were women to achieve economic independence? The answer involved a logical series of policy initiatives. Women needed to be able to compete on merit for permanent and rewarding jobs. I never believed that such jobs should simply be handed out according to some numerical concept of fairness, nor that others, in this case men, should be deprived of their economic independence in order to make way for women.

So, the next logical step involved education and training. If women were to compete on merit for good jobs, then they had to have access to the fullest and widest range of education. That meant reforming schools, changing the universities, and giving women access to apprenticeships and technical training. Further, I never expected that as a result of the reforms I was advocating, women as a group would lose interest in bearing children. While I respected individual choice in these matters I thought it likely that the majority of women would, like myself, have children and seek employment. The logical consequence of that prediction was better provision by society for support and assistance in the rearing of children, particularly very young children, hence the policy of child care.

In developing a logical policy framework, it had to be acknowledged that contraception and family-planning techniques were, to sum up in one word, unreliable. That is they did not work for all of the people all of the time. While the unplanned pregnancy often became the wanted and much-loved child, there were cases in which it could be a personal catastrophe. The choice of termination should be available to women.

This was the policy framework that provided the direction for my parliamentary career and explains to a large extent its successes and failures.

I still find it hard to believe that the objectives that I had at that time – equal opportunity in employment; access to education and training; child care services; fertility control – were radical enough to upset and destabilise the parliamentary system and the community it represented. But enormous resistance was organised to these objectives. There was resistance within the Labor Party and inside the federal caucus. My advocacy for child care, reproductive control or equal pay was often met by my own colleagues expressing fear at the electoral danger I was creating with such views. Some notable Labor figures complained that I was taking up the cause of a tiny majority of over-educated women, a cause that would be unsettling and unwelcome to the vast majority of Australian women who (I could only infer from the comments of my colleagues) were totally satisfied with their lot.

That resistance was overcome. The Labor Party, despite being in many respects a reflection of the conservative society it inhabits, does have a central core of commitment to equality, and therefore to change that will create better opportunities. Slowly the Labor Party started to build policies to address the inequalities suffered by women.

In my early attempts at women's policy there were times when I felt like a fish on a bicycle. But the work of a parliamentarian, even one with special commitments, can never relate to one set of issues only. I had two broad objectives when I entered parliament. One was to bring into consideration matters of vital importance to women which had been neglected; the other was to establish, through my work and by supporting the work of other women in the parliament, recognition that women were capable parliamentary performers. I wanted to demonstrate that the neglect of female candidates by the major political parties had been an error, and had deprived the nation of a great deal of capacity.

A summary of my early speeches, questions and Senate committee work reveals an extraordinary array of topics from ASIO to environmentalism to Aboriginal issues to telecommunications, media monopoly, taxation reform and urban planning. This diversity characterises the work of many energetic backbenchers. In my case, it reflected a concern to ensure that no one could justly accuse me of being a single-issue politician.

I spent seven years in opposition and five and a half years as a cabinet minister. We have heard of the double burden of the working mother. I suggest the double burden concept also applies to the woman member of parliament, the female minister, because she has two jobs. The jobs have synergy and reinforce each other, but there are two jobs nonetheless. You need to respond to, take up, defend and advocate the special interests of women; and you need to demonstrate that in fulfilling this role you are not taking away from your capacity to contribute to other vital areas of policy; you are not engaging in special pleading, and you are not asking someone else to shoulder your burden. This is a complicated message and media and other commentators often get it wrong.

I have been concerned in the four years since I resigned from parliament, to detect a theme emerging in what is written and said by some journalists, women parliamentarians and feminist academics, about the burdens. The comments are often too negative, and do not reflect the reality as I saw and experienced it. This negativism has a discouraging effect on women who are contemplating a parliamentary career. When one runs into difficulties, loses crucial support of a faction, or fails to persuade the expenditure review committee of a budgetary submission, it is too easy to say 'the boys stopped me; I experienced this failure because I am a woman.' I am not decrying the personal experience of women who say that is how they felt; I am not saying that I have never been the victim of sexism or the double standard. But I am loath to support the thesis that life in parliament is really too hard for women. It must be remembered that men have their policy failures, experience factional treacheries and lose cabinet debates. When I and my colleagues who had worked hard to rebuild Labor's electoral fortunes after the terrible defeats of 1975 and 1977 came into office in 1983, each and every one of us in cabinet was sometimes overwhelmed by the enormity of the task. I was not the only minister who felt torn between the ideals in our platform and the reality of government, who felt miserable at failing to persuade my colleagues to a particular policy. These were experiences we shared. Look at prime ministers and Opposition leaders. At the pinnacle of parliamentary power, there is no ivory tower, no shelter from the storm, and ultimately no buffer against ambition, disaffection, treachery or failure. Everyone in parliament has to endure such experiences, women included. It is important to acknowledge the difficulties that are universal in order to deal with those that do arise from discriminatory attitudes to women.

Looking back on my time in parliament, I can identify issues and actions that typify the parliamentarian anxious to achieve social change. All who have embarked on such a course, the many men and the few women, have had turbulent times. My involvement with reforms for women made my parliamentary work even more turbulent and controversial. The presence of a newcomer in the citadels of power is always a challenge, whether the novelty is to do with a person's gender or as in the case of Senator Neville Bonner, the person's race. There is no avoiding that extra dimension of controversy. Only when a critical mass of women parliamentarians is achieved, will gender cease to be an issue.

I would like to conclude this lecture with two main points. First, I will answer the questions I am most often asked – what were your greatest achievements and what was your greatest failure?

The achievements which give me greatest satisfaction come from the two areas with which I was most closely associated in government.

In terms of policy, I was pleased to be able to maintain an extensive commitment to public education from the beginning of school through to the funding of universities for undergraduate and post-graduate studies and research. Even more rewarding is the fact that the objective I advanced at the Economic Summit in 1983 of lifting the school retention rate from one third to two thirds before 1990 has been easily achieved, thus improving opportunities for an entire generation.

In terms of the legislative role of the parliament, I am enduringly grateful that I had the opportunity to initiate and implement laws against discrimination against women in the workplace and other areas. I monitor, with continuing pride, the success of the Affirmative Action legislation with its careful, evolutionary strategy to desegregate the Australian workforce and increase both the range of job opportunities available to women, and the pool of talent available to industry and higher education.

The failure that continues to distress me is the failure of Aboriginal policy. In the three years I spent as Shadow Minister for Aboriginal Affairs I worked closely with Aboriginal people in cities, towns and tiny communities in remote areas. I pursued their concerns in parliament on a daily basis. The two ministers I shadowed, Fred Chaney and Peter Baume, were capable and committed. Our collective efforts at that time have not been productive. Good intentions abound, resources are increasing, new administrative and representative structures have been put in place, but the injustices experienced by Aboriginal Australians continue. I failed to make significant change.

My second concluding point involves the diminishing credibility of parliaments throughout Australia. Failures of economic policy and administration have resulted in a deepening cynicism about the parliamentary system and those who work in it. This is a problem for all of us but perhaps women parliamentarians, especially those with feminist values, can make a special contribution. It seems to have been the case that women parliamentarians, both federally and at the state level, have been able to establish more credibility with the electorate than their male colleagues. In the case of our two women premiers, reflecting their feminist values they have deliberately sought to be more consultative, more flexible, more cooperative and more reasonable in their demeanour inside and outside of parliament. At the same time, they have demonstrated decision-making capacities at the highest level. Perhaps this is a signal pointing the way to reform of parliamentary conventions and procedures. If women parliamentarians can make a contribution to regenerating the authority of parliament, then for that reason as for many others, I hope in the next decade we see many more fishes on bicycles.

'This is the sweetest victory of all'

Paul Keating

Election victory speech, Bankstown Sports Club

13 MARCH 1993

Paul Keating (1944–) had been elected to his first cabinet portfolio – minister for the Northern Territory – for only a few weeks when Gough Whitlam walked past him on 11 November 1975 and said, 'You're sacked.' 'What have I done?' Keating replied, but received no answer. The dismissal was a formative initiation in the hurly-burly of politics for one who would lead an aggressive period of Labor Party reform that began eight years later with his next ministerial appointment – as treasurer under prime minister Bob Hawke. Largely self-educated in economics, he presided over the most ambitious program of economic reform in the nation's history, exposing to the rigours of the market sections of the economy that had hitherto been spared them.

When Keating displaced Hawke as prime minister in December 1991, the reforming zeal of his years in treasury was turned on Australian culture. Keating advocated a republic, closer engagement with Asia and a new approach to Australia's indigenous people. But his 'big picture' politics proved divisive, and by the time an election was called for March 1993, few commentators gave him any chance of re-election. They were mistaken. At 11.24 p.m. on the night of the election, as his supporters maintained the chant 'We want Paul,' Keating made his way to a microphone at the Bankstown Sports Club and announced, 'You've got me.'

*

Well, this is the sweetest victory of all – this is the sweetest. This is the victory for the true believers, the people who in difficult times have kept the faith and to the Australian people going through hard times – it makes their act of faith all that much greater.

It will be a long time before an Opposition party tries to divide this country again. It will be a long time before somebody tries to put one group of Australians over here and another group over there.

The public of Australia are too decent and they are too conscientious and they are too interested in their country to wear those sorts of things.

This I think has been very much a victory of Australian values, because it was Australian values on the line and the Liberal Party wanted to change Australia from the country it has become, a cooperative, decent, nice place to live where people have regard for one another.

And could I just say that this has been a hard campaign and I can assure every member of the public out there, when they think we don't know in the political system how tough it is, I can assure you I can tell you how tough it was in those last few weeks.

But I can say to you that I wanted to win again, to be there in the 1990s to see Australia prosper as it will.

The thing is, I said to the Australian people, 'We've turned the corner'. Can I say now, after the election, let me repeat it: we have turned the corner. The growth is coming through. We will see ourselves as a sophisticated trading country in Asia and we've got to do it in a way where everybody's got a part in it, where everybody's in it.

There's always cause for concern but never pessimism and Australia, wherein for the first time in our history, located in the region of the fastest growth in the world, and we've been set up now, we are set up now as we've never been set up before to be in it, to exploit it, to be part of it.

It offers tremendous opportunities for Australians and now we have to do it, and we have to do it compassionately.

I give an assurance to the people that this victory won't go to the heads of the government of the Labor Party. We'll take it seriously, we'll take it thankfully, and we'll do a great deal with it.

The people of Australia have taken us on trust and we'll return that trust and we'll care about those people out there, particularly the unemployed – we want to get them back to work.

If we can't get them back to work immediately, as sure as hell we are going to look after them. We are not going to leave them in the lurch. We are not going to leave them in the lurch and we are going to put our hand out and we are going to pull them up behind us.

And we are going to move along, this country is going to move along together. We have such enormous opportunity. This world recession is now starting to dissipate, we've made the break out of it, America's starting to turn, it won't be that long before the Japanese economy starts to turn, and hopefully we'll be away and running in the '90s in a low-inflationary period of prosperity.

I can assure you the government will now be redoubling its efforts to be as good a government as you hope and expect we can be. To be as conscientious with this mandate as we possibly can be, to give it our every effort, our every shot, to see that we recover quickly and we get going and we put this recessionary period behind us and we get this country of opportunity off and running.

But keeping the opportunity for everybody – keeping those great … keeping those great nostrums of access and equity. Getting people into the game. The policies of inclusion. The policies of one nation. And that's what it has got to be about.

So can I say again, this is a tremendous victory. It's a tremendous victory for all those who have got imagination and faith. The people who believe in things, who are not going to let good beliefs be put aside for essentially miserable ideas to divide the place up.

I mean, I think the Australian people have always had such remarkable sense to spot the value and to cut their way through it.

Now part of this victory is ours … part of it is them spotting what they think were the dangers in the Liberal Party's policies. What I hope is that the next election the victory is one hundred per cent due to the good government of Labor.

Now, I'd like to start thanking some people and the first person I'd like to start with is my wife, Annita, who has helped me right through the campaign. Thank you.

And can I also say, can I give an extra special note of thanks to the women of Australia, who voted for us believing in the policies of this government.

I want to pay a particular thanks also to – good on you, mate – I want to pay a particular thanks to the architects of this victory, my personal staff. Don Russell, Mark Ryan, Don Watson, my press secretaries and the rest.

And most particularly to those people in the Labor Party who've never lost faith, never lost heart, and are there at the polling booths to work and to fight for good things. Thank you. The people who never give up but always keep on believing and are always there no matter how heavy the travails may be, to you I say thank you very, very much indeed.

Thank you again and thank you for believing.

But could I most particularly, and again finally, thank the Australian people without whose faith and decency and commitment to what's fair and what's reasonable and what is decent in this country, without those conscientious judgements this victory could not have been consummated and put together. Thank you.

And I conclude on this note, to say we thank you, we appreciate it, we won't let you down. Thank you.

'Why would they go to the photocopiers?'

Paul Keating

Last speech as prime minister, National Press Club, Canberra

29 FEBRUARY 1996

The ABC's Fran Kelly thought the National Press Club luncheon where Paul Keating gave his last speech as prime minister had 'a bit of a feel ... of a last supper'. When journalist Bruce Juddery asked whether he should double a $50 bet on the Labor Party winning another term, Keating advised him to 'follow your nose, follow your instinct'. Keating's own instinct probably told him – like the polls – that a second victory was highly improbable; that his time had run out. So the address he gave was an off-the-cuff summary of why that should not be so, reiterating his government's vision and achievements with the aggression and relish for which he was known.

*

Thank you. Thank you very much. Well ... I've had bouts of popularity in the press gallery, but I never knew it was quite this strong. I'm overwhelmed. Can I say that I'm glad to be back? I think I've been here more often – well, I know I have actually, it's just a statistical fact – more often than anyone in public life – partly because I've been doing things for a long time. It's also because I regard the process as important, and I came here at this time in the last election campaign – when I was the only party leader to come here – when some said that it was quite a clever tactic not to come. I've always believed that there's been a position of importance between the government and the media, and I'd like to think that over the years I've been able to work with the press gallery and the media, to talk about Australia – to tell people about the need for changes, to tell them why, to try and describe the sort of country we want – and I think that together we've been able to see something larger and to work towards it. I'd like to think that rather than looking at the stories that were written when the government came to office, which were in descending order of importance – leadership challenges, tax cuts, election speculation and the occasional espionage scandal – that we've opened and risen up to the really deep and fundamental issues facing Australia.

The fact that we were an industrial graveyard with smokestack industries with no future. The fact that we were ring-fenced by tariffs. That we were insular, without confidence, and introspective. That we didn't see the world and the opportunities around us as they truly are. That Australia had no premium on education, with only three young people in ten completing secondary school. That it had no real premium on manufacturing industry or product innovation. That we knew by handing out tariff protection we had companies dozing away, and sleeping in a sort of fog of uncompetitiveness – and we knew also that the terms of trade were moving inexorably against us. We knew that from the high point of the Korean wool boom and the post-war commodity prices, that there had been an inexorable decline in our national income – and we knew that a succession of governments had done nothing about it – that it suited them to look the other way. And that while the media wanted to get into the stories, when governments were run by the bureaucracy – because bureaucrats do not have political authority – all the changes were incremental. It was incrementalism. In fact, bureaucracy was very happy to get just the most modest of movements, and that modesty of movement became the norm in public comment – and so it became the standard. The big leaps and the big boundary jumping and the big changes had not yet arrived, and they hadn't arrived because ministers were not running the government. Cabinet was not running Australia. We'd had, in the main, a quarter of a century of Coalition government where ministers were happy to have the ministerial cars and all the badges of office, but were not prepared to wear the responsibility for change – and a bureaucracy would settle into what they thought was their only forte – for millimetre-at-a-time movements, and hence Australia was left in jeopardy.

The story of all these years since, is that Australia has changed inexorably and for the better – it's changed at the hands of a conscientious government. It's changed at the hands of a government that was determined to give the country an even break. It was determined not to treat the public cynically – not to hand them mush – as Coalitions had handed them for years and years and years, and that the hollow men of the Liberal Party should take their proper places in the parliament on the Opposition side. ...

The government built a market economy and grafted onto it an equitable social policy – the likes of which Australia had never seen – and the compact together is now unique in the Western world. It's given us quite phenomenally high rates of economic growth, spectacular rates of employment growth and low inflation. It's given us a complete change in our industrial culture. That compact has with the Australian community, come by way of the Wages Accord – the good sense in setting wages and conditions. That compact has come in trying to build a better country, and the community's interest in change and their preparedness to take it on – always believing that the turbulence and the living with it was a good thing for them, and that together we're going places. And they've been right, because together we've gone many places and as a consequence – the Australia today compared to a decade or so ago is almost unimaginably different. It's an interesting, vibrant, lively, competitive, outward-looking country. It's confident, it's exciting. It's got a future which I think has no parallel for us. I've said before in this campaign and I think it's worth repeating – what nation has been given an inheritance like we have? Eighteen million of us, a continent of our own, a border with no one – and the chance to actually live in a beautiful country, rather than one simply spoiled by the careless commitment of industrial resources. And on top of that, living in the fastest growing part of the world – in the region of the world where there's an economic revolution taking place without precedence in history. An economic revolution that will make the industrial revolution look like a Sunday afternoon picnic – 2.5 billion people, economies growing at eight to ten per cent a year, and we're right in the middle of it – and we're out there, competitive and ready to embrace it. But we know that you have to go there together, we have to go there as a united country. We have to declare that we are unique. We have to be assertive about ourselves, and that confidence and assertion can only come with confidence in who we are and what we are – that we're not a derivative place. That we're out there as a society which we built here, and we're out there, I believe also as you know, saying that our Head of State is one of us – and that we don't need to borrow the monarch of another country – that there's nothing derivative about us, and that we're out there as a unique society.

All countries need a break in their history. The great break for us was the post-war migration program. It made us more diverse, more interesting, more vibrant and gave us more critical mass. I think the next break was the market economy's social graft which Labor has put into place, because then we've got the best of all worlds – vitality, diversity, strength, critical mass and a good economy with the right bases to it, and a cohesive social fabric that makes every Australian feel as though they matter and that they are important. These are the things that I think have happened, and I think with you – and I say this, with you in the media – we've tried to create a new standard for Australia. New standards in public policy, new standards in accountability, in the articulation of change – and as well as that, new standards in energy – keeping the change going, keeping the fire burning. This election puts all that to the test. Did we build a new standard? Have we created a change? Or are we going to slide back into the old comfort station of someone who says he feels relaxed and comfortable about the past, the present and the future? Do we just nod gently off, back to sleep again, like we did in the Rip van Winkle years of Menzies and his successive governments? Or will the new standard of energy, of drive, of ministers actually running the policy, of accountability, of truth – will all these things be simply a remnant of a decade of change – which then finishes or closes were a Coalition government to be elected? Because I think this is what the election is boiling down to.

The Coalition have laid out no philosophical basis for their election. At Mr Howard's policy speech there was no philosophy, there was no structure, there was no thoughtfulness – just a grab bag of promises driven by a polling agency and an advertising agency. In other words, he thinks that if he puts a few baubles in the right places on the basis of rote and rotation – that it's his turn, the fact that he's just stuck around so long – government will just fall into his lap. I believe there's always got to be a road-map for Australia, there's always got to be philosophy, there's always got to be belief, and there's always got to be passion. Because if the ministers and the prime minister are not passionate, they don't believe, and they haven't that thing which is not at any place in the Liberal campaign manual – imagination – Australia would have remained just a modest country with very modest prospects. Now, Mr Howard has listened well to his advertising agency and his polling stations, his poll-driven campaigners and those who've directed the campaign. He's always marketed himself to all of us as a conviction politician. Right now he stands for nothing. He stands for convenience. He stands for only putting out those things which he thinks will help. Even the things he's nominated in the course of the campaign, they've just unravelled. ...

Let's not kid ourselves – we've had an unreality debate here – an unreal debate. And the debate has been reported within the capsule of what the parties have been saying, and not the reality, because the reality is that there's no way that John Howard is going to keep Medicare. He's philosophically opposed to it – he always has been. When people ask me why do I want to keep Medicare, what's my first answer? We believe that the health of any one of us is important to all of us – that's why we have Medicare. Universal access and coverage in a public hospital is an Australian right. ... And an eighty-five per cent rebate from a doctor. Ask John Howard why he says he'll keep Medicare – he says: oh, because I think Australians have come to believe in it, and we think we can do some other things in private health. Not one dollar of his commitments went to public health – not one dollar. Nothing to help the main system that holds that promise of health protection out for Australians – the public health system – not one dollar. Only money kicked upstairs for private hospitals and specialists – as always, as always. Always run by the lowest common denominator of the Liberal Party.

So when he says we'll keep Medicare, he will destroy it. He can destroy it in one of a thousand ways, and they'll do what they did in the 1970s – and remember it was John Howard's first Budget in 1978 that dismantled Medibank – the exact same scheme as Medicare. He was the person who actually did it, after his leader and he committed himself to keeping it. And what did we end up with? Medibank Private – a private health fund bearing its name – that's what we ended up with. They'll just put a co-payment on it, or they'll take the bulk-billing off, or they'll just take the money out of the public hospitals. Are they going on about the fact that Jeff Kennett and the rest of the state premiers have pulled $700 million out of public hospitals in three years? Have you heard one comment in defence of the public hospital system? Not on your nelly. John Howard will pull Medicare apart as sure as I'm standing here, if he gets a chance.

Take industrial relations – they're running their cheap little ads on radio over the weekend. Well, isn't it nice to go into an election where both parties agree on Medicare – both parties agree on industrial relations, both parties agree on the environment – authorised by A. Robb for the Liberal Party. Now why would they authorise a decent thing like that? Because they want to pretend that they'll keep Medicare and a decent industrial relations system, and support for the environment. …

The fact of the matter is, that John Howard has gone through this election campaign believing in none of those things. Left to his own devices he'd rip Medicare apart, he would go to the wages system he's always wanted. Even in this campaign, in February, he said that industrial relations had always been the area of great challenge for him. He'd go to that. There wouldn't be a consensual wages policy, on the environment the same, and on superannuation. So, the things we won't have – we won't have an Accord, we won't have universal health insurance, we won't have universal superannuation, and we won't have the drive into Asia – all of that would stop. This is from people who say I'm obsessed with Asia – to which I say: too right I am, because I'm obsessed with Australian prosperity, Australian jobs and Australian incomes. They say that they want to keep their traditional alliances with our Western allies – that means Britain and the United States – and that's fine with me, but not to the exclusion of the area in which we live – which is what they really mean. So we won't have that continuing drive – the elements of the social wage, the support for families, the family allowance supplement, fee relief in child care, the funding of TAFE, the growth funding of TAFE where we put $1.5 billion since *One Nation* into TAFE – will go.

We will not have a government which believes in these things, because the Opposition is not a social democratic party – it's a deeply conservative party. And John Howard correctly has described himself as the most conservative leader the Liberal Party's ever had, and that's why these policies are the way they are. The other thing about it is, you can't have a little bit of them. You can't have three months of John Howard, or six months, and find the government is not basically able to govern Australia. After all, they have been a hopeless, incompetent Opposition for years and years. Yet government is ten times harder, so why does anyone think that a hopeless, incompetent Opposition can actually take on the task of government which is ten times harder? In other words, when you've got them, you're stuck with them – and there's no turning it out until another election. And then will the fire keep burning? Will the fire go out? Will the drive be lost? I think it will, because I don't think you could just pick these threads up again.

There's no doubt, that if you wake up on March the 3rd with John Howard, you'll have a cabinet of very doubtful competence. Alexander Downer, who doesn't have the respect of his own party or the Australian people, will now be seeking to earn respect for Australia abroad. The person who would be out there seeking to garner respect for Australia, would be the person who doesn't have it in his own party – who was removed as leader because of his incompetence. Then Tim Fischer, whether you think him nice or nasty, the real question would be: would he be a competent Minister for Trade? And I don't think you need a pol-science degree to give us the answer. Bronwyn Bishop, she would seal Telstra's fate – the largest company in the country, $30 billion of market capitalisation – she'd be the one standing between value for the people of Australia and the people out there in the international broking industry. Peter Costello, who would be Treasurer – and I put this rhetorical question in the policy speech, and I think it's worth repeating. Have you ever heard him say anything interesting or creative about Australia's future? Just one thing? Never have I heard him say it. So that would be the cabinet. …

A government with no philosophy or direction, or sense of urgency – no commitment to our *Native Title Act*, no commitment to the fundamentals of reconciliation, no commitment to the Republic. A government with a National Party rump which will always be its bottom line, which will always be dragging it back to the meanest and most regressive philosophy that we've ever seen.

So this is 'the time for a change' proposal. Mr Howard says – the subliminal message is, 'it's time for a change', to which we say: a change to what, Mr Howard? He says: oh, we want to change, we want to change, but we think that Labor's got it pretty right on Medicare, the environment and IR – we're even advertising the fact we have similar policies. We want to change to look just like you. We want a change of government, so we can be just like you. To which I say: well, if that's what the Australian people want, why wouldn't they take the architects of the policy, the authors of the policy – the believers who put the structure into place? Why would they go to the photocopiers? So I'll finish on these two points. We should never start the new century on the back foot. We shouldn't elect to office a prime minister who will not lead us into that century – understanding its future, having enough imagination to grasp it, and the leadership and the courage to actually go and do it – to actually make it work. We shouldn't do that. Because, were that to happen we would be giving up the opportunity of our history – the most strongest growing part of the world, the most exciting time, and us never more able to participate in it.

When the government changes, the country changes. When the government changed from McMahon to Whitlam, the country changed. When it changed from Whitlam to Fraser, the country changed. When it changed from Fraser to Hawke, the country changed. But what we've built in these years is I think so valuable – to change it and to lose it, is just a straight appalling loss for Australia. So, this election is going to boil down to two things – philosophy and competence. Whether each of the parties has a philosophy for government and is competent? Whether it can actually do the job? Whether it can cut the mustard of the hard policy and the discipline and the accountability and the calibration, and the belief of it all and the truth of it all? Or whether we're going to go back really, to the dismal old days of the '70s – with a group of ministers who just can't make it all work, can't bring the public with them – and where we slide back into that morass of uncompetitiveness, and where we look backwards and not forwards?

GREAT DEBATES

'The United Provinces of Australia'

John Dunmore Lang

'The coming event': speech at the Theatre of the School of Arts, Sydney

16 APRIL 1850

John Dunmore Lang (1799–1878) emigrated to New South Wales from Scotland at the age of twenty-four to establish a Presbyterian ministry in the young colony, where for more than forty years he would attract attention and notoriety with his 'vituperative and vindictive' tongue. Jailed three times, once for debt and twice for libel, Lang was ousted from his ministry in 1842, but formed his own synod and commenced a political career the following year. The loudest and most radical democrat in the NSW Legislative Assembly, Lang campaigned tirelessly against the renewal of convict transportation, and was among the first to actively promote a detailed plan for a federated Australian republic, free of all formal ties with Britain: a 'representative democracy under the universal government of God'.

Following a journey to England to recruit 'respectable Presbyterian immigrants', Lang delivered three public lectures concerning his proposed republic entitled 'The coming event'. The second lecture includes an attack on transportation, formally discontinued just a few days before, and Lang's proposal for 'The Australian League', formed ten days after the speech but ultimately unsuccessful.

*

In my former lecture I stated and illustrated what may be styled the *a priori* reasons for the immediate concession of entire freedom and independence to the Australian colonies. [*Applause.*] Antecedently to every instance of bad government that can be urged against the mother country, these reasons establish the strongest possible case for us colonists – even taking into consideration the interests of the mother country exclusively. But the colonists have a long list of positive grievances to complain of, the existence of which strengthens their case inconceivably, and aggravates exceedingly the irksomeness and the bitterness of their bondage. [*Strong expressions of assent.*] ...

Now there is no principle of the British constitution so generally admitted as that the taxes of any country are the property of the people, and can only be appropriated by the people through their acknowledged representatives. [*Applause.*] But this palladium of British freedom has been withheld from these colonies in the most offensive manner – mere nominees of the Crown being foisted into our provincial legislature, without the sanction and concurrence of the people in any way, and large amounts being abstracted from our colonial revenue, for a variety of purposes, without even asking the opinion of the people or their representatives. [*Shouts of indignation.*] It was a grievance of this particular character – taxation without their own previous consent – that roused the spirit and nerved the arm of the American colonists for their great and successful struggle for entire freedom and independence in the year 1776; [*applause*] and it is mortifying to reflect that British despotism should have become no wiser from the lesson it was then taught, notwithstanding the lapse of a full seventy years. Does Great Britain require that instructive lesson to be taught her in the southern hemisphere, as it was in the northern? It would appear that she does ...

Had this lecture been delivered a few days ago, I should have had one colonial grievance more – the greatest of all – to denounce: I mean the recently contemplated renewal of the transportation system, and the proposed degradation of this colony into a mere receptacle for the convicted felons of Great Britain and Ireland. But the recent

dispatches from Downing Street, announcing the entire discontinuance of transportation to this territory, will render this portion of
my lecture unnecessary. To use the expression of a playwright, when
accusing one of his fellow workmen in a theatrical row, Earl Grey has
'stolen my thunder'. [*Much laughter.*] There is nothing, however, that
more strongly exhibits the miserable state of vassalage to which these
colonies are subjected under Downing Street domination, than this
atrocious attempt from first to last. And let me add, gentlemen, as a
word of comfort and encouragement, there is nothing that more
strongly evinces our own complete power to ensure the redress of all
our political grievances, provided only that the dormant energies of
our community were brought out into life and action, than the result
in this instance. [*Cheers.*] Do not suppose that there was any change
of opinion in our favour at Downing Street, to bring about the gratifying change of practice that has just been announced. It was the formidable demonstrations of public opinion both at the Cape and here
that produced the change, combined with the belief and conviction,
on the part of the whole corps of incapables, that unless that change
was effected immediately, these demonstrations would assuredly be
followed up by others of a far more serious and formidable character.
[*Much cheering.*] It is somewhat singular that my friend and brother,
the Rev. Dr Adamson, minister of the Scots Church, Cape Town,
should have been singled out by the government press of England as
the principal offender in connection with the convict question in that
colony, and that I should be deemed worthy of the same distinction
for this colony in consequence of my parting letter to Earl Grey.
[*Renewed cheering.*] Dr Adamson had stated, it seems, that the Cape
Colony had already a military organisation throughout, and was quite
able, from the physical character of the country, to resist any attempt
on the part of Great Britain to coerce it into unwilling obedience; and
my offence consisted in telling his Lordship that if he persisted in
sending convicts to this colony, in defiance of the repeated remon-
strances and protests of the colonists, the colonists would very soon
take another method of redressing their grievances – one that might
not prove quite so palatable to his Lordship. [*Cheering.*] It is worthy
of particular observation that this letter of mine was received by Earl
Grey on the 14th of November, for I posted it at Gravesend that

morning, and that the famous dispatch, announcing the entire discontinuance of transportation to this colony, was written on the 18th – only four days thereafter. [*Renewed cheering.*]

The only light in which I can regard the attempted resumption of transportation to this territory, is that of a conspiracy on the part of the government and a few of the principal squatters, against the rights and interests of the colonists generally [*expressions of assent*]; the government having virtually sold the country to the squatters by their notorious Act of 1846, and the squatters, at least certain of their number, having volunteered to repay the compliment by assisting the government to degrade the colony into a mere convict settlement. Happily, however, the virtuous portion of the colonists have proved too strong in the end for both government and squatters together. [*Cheers.*] Earl Grey has been compelled most unwillingly to beat a retreat – an inglorious retreat – on this question; and let me add that the victory we have thus gained for the colony, instead of inducing us to sit down and be thankful – I mean to Earl Grey – should only induce us to persevere in a course of vigorous and manly effort till we obtain our entire freedom and national independence. [*Great cheering.*] …

In the circumstances in which we are thus placed it is vain to look either for help or for sympathy from England. Of the three great moral powers of the mother country, the parliament, the public and the press, there is not even one that cares a rush for us, and they would all have been but too glad if we had only consented on the late occasion to become a great moral cesspool for their national convenience. [*Expressions of indignation.*] The *Times*, the leading journal of Europe and the virtual organ of the government, repeatedly asked, in express terms, within the last few months, 'Of what use are colonies to the mother country, if they cannot be turned to such purposes as these?' And the parliament and the public re-echoed the sentiment by giving it their silent and willing assent.

In such a conjuncture there is one course that remains for us, as the friends and advocates of peace, and it is one for which we can fortunately plead the precedent and example of the earliest and best times of British colonisation. In the year 1643, the scattered settlements of New England, consisting exclusively of men who had been driven into exile for conscience's sake, formed a league for their mutual protection and defence, under the designation of 'The United Colonies of New England'. And in the year 1690, that is eighty-six years before the declaration of independence – when it was found that the colonies had common grievances to complain of and common interests to promote – this league was extended to the whole of the American colonies, delegates being appointed by each of these colonies to meet together periodically, to deliberate on their common affairs, and to form a National Congress in the city of Philadelphia. It was this Congress, existing as it did in colonial times and for colonial objects exclusively, that issued the famous Declaration of Independence in the year 1776, and that thereby gave freedom and nationality to their country. [*Cheers.*] ...

Guided and stimulated by these precedents and examples, I took the liberty before leaving England to consult certain parties of the highest standing in the political world, and well known to be well-affected towards the colonies, as to the propriety of mooting the formation of a great political league, for the accomplishment of certain great objects of common interest for the Australian colonies, on my return to this country. And I am happy to state that the idea was cordially received and approved of; as the course which it indicated was, in the opinion of the gentlemen alluded to, the only course that was fitting for the colonies in the present momentous crisis. [*Applause.*] And in regard to the ultimate object which such a league ought to propose, I did not hesitate to declare it as my own private opinion that, under existing circumstances, it would be ridiculous and absurd to propose as the ultimate object of such a league anything less than the entire freedom and independence of the Australian colonies, and their erection into a great federal republic, under the style and title of 'The United Provinces of Australia'. [*Vehement and continued cheering.*] This idea, I am happy to state, was also entirely approved of by the gentlemen to whom I have referred; and as an encouragement to proceed in such a course, I was assured that England was now fully prepared for such a movement on the part of her colonies generally, those of them especially that were able and willing to govern themselves, and to offer her proper terms for the future; that the day for sending forth British troops to put down insurgent colonies, and to hold them against their will, was past for ever [*renewed cheers*]; and that for example there was now no man of commonsense in England who would hesitate for one moment to concede entire freedom and independence to the North American colonies, although annexation to the United States, which the Canadians proposed, was too bitter a pill for England to swallow without making many wry faces on the occasion. [*Much laughter.*] One of the gentlemen I refer to gave me a copy of a Quebec paper, of the 15th October last, which he had just received from Canada, containing the annexation manifesto, with a list of the names appended to it from the city of Montreal; recommending that I should publish it by way of a guide and stimulus in New South Wales, as he conceived the case of our Australian colonies was beyond all comparison stronger than that of Canada. [*Great applause.*]

I would propose, therefore, that a great political league, to be designated 'The Australian League', should be formed in each of the five colonies of New South Wales, Van Diemen's Land, South Australia, Port Phillip and Cooksland, or the Moreton Bay Country [*applause*]; that this league should, in the colony of New South Wales with which alone we can have anything to do, comprise a president, a vice-president, a treasurer and one or more secretaries, with a council of fifteen including these functionaries; all colonists being admissible as members on the payment of an entrance fee of five shillings each, with a yearly subscription of not less than ten shillings, payable either yearly, half-yearly or quarterly, at the option of the member; and that the objects of such a league be:

First – To unite in one grand political league, for mutual protection and defence, and for general advancement, the five Australian colonies of New South Wales, Van Diemen's Land, South Australia, Port Phillip and Cooksland, or the Moreton Bay Country; that the inhabitants of these colonies may henceforth feel and know that they are no longer isolated and detached communities – to be governed and oppressed separately and independently by Ukases from Downing Street, with none to interfere for them from without – but one people, having common interests and common objects, the nucleus and elements of *one great Australian nation.* [*Great cheering.*]

Second – To prevent the degradation of any one of these colonies into a mere receptacle for the convicted felons of Great Britain and Ireland; and to remedy, as far as may be practicable, the enormous evils that have already resulted from the prevalence and abuse of the transportation system in certain of these colonies.

Third – To encourage and promote, by every legitimate means, the influx of an industrious, virtuous and thoroughly British population into these colonies; that their vast and inexhaustible resources may be duly and fully developed, and that they may be fitted, as speedily as possible, for taking the high and influential place which they are evidently destined to hold in the civilised world, as the great leading power of the southern hemisphere. [*Great applause.*]

Fourth – To achieve, by moral means exclusively, and with the full approbation and concurrence of Britain, the entire freedom and independence of these colonies and their erection into sovereign and independent states; to be incorporated into one great political federation, like the Swiss Cantons of Europe or the United States of America, under the style and title of 'The United Provinces of Australia'. [*Prolonged cheers.*]

I would propose, moreover, that the management or directory of the league should be merely provisional, until it shall comprise at least a thousand members, and that permanent officers should then be elected by the members in the usual way: the funds accruing both from entrance-money and from subscriptions and donations to be appropriated for the following purposes, viz.

First – For the erection of a suitable hall in Sydney, for the public meetings of the league, and of a range of offices for the transaction of its business. [*Applause.*]

Second – For publication and circulation of tracts and pamphlets, explanatory of its views and objects and in defence of its proceedings.

Third – For the payment of the salaries of its paid officers, including suitable persons to hold meetings and to deliver addresses on its behalf in the different towns and villages of the colony, to indoctrinate the colonists in the knowledge of their political rights, interests and duties. [*Cheers.*]

Fourth – For bearing the expenses of a delegate to proceed to England, along with delegates from the other four colonies, as soon as it shall be deemed expedient and necessary, to promote the great objects of the league, both with the government and the public at home. [*Renewed applause.*]

The example of New South Wales in forming such a league would doubtless be followed spontaneously by all the other four colonies which it is proposed to comprise, although it would probably be desirable to forward a suitable address on the subject to each of these colonies, and to employ some fit and proper person or persons to visit them successively to encourage and stimulate the general movement. In the event of the successful establishment of a league, of a corresponding character, in each of these colonies, it would be desirable to hold a congress of delegates from each in the city of Sydney to deliberate on their common interests and objects, and to arrange for some future course of combined and energetic action …

In endeavouring to accelerate a consummation so devoutly to be wished for all parties and interests concerned, I would beg for my own part, as well as for those with whom I may cooperate, solemnly to disclaim all desire or intention to have recourse in any way to physical force [*cheers*]; being resolved to confine our efforts to a course of peaceful but earnest and energetic agitation, but determined at the same time not to intermit these efforts until the United Provinces of Australia shall be recognised by Great Britain, as well as by the whole civilised world, as a sovereign and independent power. [*Continued cheering.*]

It would perhaps be a waste of time to enquire what form of government should be established in these provinces in such an event as I have supposed. Great Britain and her colonies may, in this respect, be compared to a hen that has hatched duck's eggs – the young brood will infallibly take the water as staunch republicans, although the old hen should continue to cackle on the brink to the end of the chapter about the superior advantages of monarchy and its appendages. [*Shouts of laughter mingled with strong expressions of assent.*] A republican form of government is the only form that is practicable in British colonies, in the event of their being left to themselves. We have neither the requisite material nor the requisite traditions for any other. [*Applause.*]

It would seem, indeed, that Earl Grey has had serious intentions, since he came into office, of instituting an order of colonial nobility, forsooth [*ironical cheers and laughter*], to perpetuate the old system of the mother country in this territory in a reduced and colonial form; and Sir Henry Young, the present Governor of South Australia, appears, from a speech he delivered on his arrival in that colony, to have been authorised to feel the pulse of the colonists on the subject. For my own part, I think his Lordship ought to send out a consignment of bibs and tuckers, with some old staid gentlewoman as dry nurse, along with his intended colonial titles [*renewed laughter of an ironical character*]; for I am much mistaken if he has not greatly misapprehended the character and spirit of full-grown Australian men of the nineteenth century, when he takes it for granted that, like mere children, they would be: 'Pleased with a rattle, tickled with a straw.' [*Much ironical laughter.*] ...

Fellow colonists of New South Wales, is it necessary after these explanations that I should now call upon you to join the Australian League, to give freedom and independence to your adopted country? There is clearly nothing else worth agitating for in our present circumstances, and be assured that if you do agitate for this great boon with earnestness and determination, you will certainly obtain it. So long as we continue a dependency of England, our condition will be that of a mere football, kicked about at pleasure by every underling in Downing Street, and condemned to utter insignificance as a community. [*Strong expressions of assent.*] But as a sovereign and independent state, our noble city would be the flourishing capital of a great and powerful confederation – a confederation whose representatives would be respected and honoured in every nation in Christendom, and which would ere long give the law to the boundless Pacific. [*Much cheering.*] As a mere colony we shall descend rapidly, as we are now actually doing, into insignificance and poverty, and be pointed at with the finger of scorn by all free nations; but as a sovereign and independent state, capital and emigration, enterprise and moral worth would again flow to our shores, the vast resources of our noble country would be rapidly developed, and prosperity would again revisit and cheer our land. [*Loud and protracted cheering.*]

Natives of New South Wales, it cannot surely be needful to call upon you to join a league for the achievement of the freedom and independence of your native land. You have hitherto, even in the estimation of Great Britain herself, been the tail of the world, and every brainless creature of blighted prospects and broken fortunes from England, with no personal merit but servility, and no intellectual qualification but toadyism, has been systematically placed above you even in this the land of your birth. Why, it is a rule of the service under the present *regime* that no native of the colony, however able, talented and meritorious he may have proved himself, can be appointed by the Governor to any office under government with a salary above £100 a year. [*Loud and indignant cries of 'shame'.*] You have all heard, I doubt not, of our public educational institutions going down and proving an utter failure one after another: but is there not a sufficient reason for such a calamity in this systematic exclusion of the native youth from all such offices and employments under government, as would create a demand for a superior education, and call forth the talents and energies of an ingenious mind? [*Loud and indignant expressions of assent from all quarters.*] In fact there is no career open for the native youth in this their own country, under that vile system of government under which it is our calamity to live. [*Continued expressions of approbation.*] Unless they can get into a draper's shop or into a merchant's office as a junior clerk, which it is generally very difficult for them to do, or into a solicitor's office – in which case they will have to prowl about the Supreme Court for years together, no very safe situation for a young man of unfixed principles – they must either go as shepherds and stockmen into the interior, or open a butcher's shop, or get a publican's license for one or other of our colonial towns, expending their energies thenceforth in such trivial and contemptible pursuits as horse-racing, boat-racing and cricketing. And what sort of cattle are those that are sent out as heads of departments here, with the Secretary of State's own brand upon them, to live at our expense and to eat the fat of the land? Why, as I told Lord Stanley once, the treasury benches of the late Legislative Council might, with only one or at the utmost two exceptions, have been styled with the greatest propriety the 'Refuge for the Destitute'. [*Great laughter and cheers of assent.*] But as a sovereign and independent state, some native youth would in all probability rise to be one of the heads of the civilised world, instead of being the very tail of it as at present, and our country would forthwith assume one of the proudest and most influential positions on the face of the earth. [*Great cheering.*] Indeed there can scarcely be a limit set to the wealth and resources, the power and the grandeur of the future Australian nation. From the South Cape of Van Diemen's Land to Cape York, it will one day comprise a whole series of powerful states, and its influence will be beneficially felt over the multitude of the isles of the western Pacific. In short, taking into account the vast galaxy of isles to the eastward and northward of Australia, in addition to the extensive coasts of the great continental island itself, I question whether even the United States of America will have a more extensive field of political power and of moral influence to expatiate over than will one day acknowledge the sovereignty of the United Provinces of Australia. [*Renewed and continued cheering.*]

> Sons of the soil! The die is cast!
> And your brothers are nailing their flag to the mast;
> And their shout on the land, and their voice on the sea,
> Is 'The land of our birth is a land of the Free.' – [*Loud cheering.*]

To conclude, the past history of the world sufficiently proves that the birth of a nation has hitherto been a process somewhat similar, in regard to the parties directly concerned, to that of an individual – exhibiting violent throes on the part of the parent, and desperate struggles into life on the part of the child. Look at the case of Great Britain and the United States of America – at the vast expenditure of human life and treasure, of pain and sorrow and national degradation, which it cost Great Britain to give birth to that first-born of her strength; insomuch that the child, vigorous and healthy as it speedily proved, was notwithstanding its utmost efforts almost strangled in the process of coming into life. But as medical men tell us that the corporeal system is so relaxed in these southern regions that events of the kind I have mentioned take place with far less pain and agony to the parent than in the old world, I am in great hopes it will prove so also in the birth of our Australian nation. [*Great cheering.*] I wish not a man from England to be shot on the occasion, nor a single sixpence of English money to be lost. [*Cheers.*] I wish the interesting event to take place without a single cry on the part of the parent, or the slightest struggle on the part of the child. [*Renewed cheers.*] And when the healthy and vigorous bantling [*much laughter*] walks alone, without support of any kind from his parent, I hope to see that parent patting him on the head and clasping him to her bosom with all the conscious pride of a mother, while the darling boy returns her caresses with the tear of joy in his eye, saying, in the fullness of his heart, 'Though all other nations should disown and forsake thee, yet will not I. I will treasure up thy much-loved image in my grateful remembrance: I will engrave thy honoured and venerable name on the palms of my hands and the tablet of my heart.' [*Cheering loud and long.*]

'The Commonwealth of Australia shall mean a "white Australia"'

Alfred Deakin

'For a white Australia': speech in the House of Representatives

12 SEPTEMBER 1901

The debate about who should be allowed to settle in Australia – and who should not – is an abiding one. In the decades following settlement, immigration was linked closely to necessity; the ending of convict transportation and the need for cheap labour led to the importation of indentured Asian migrants to south-eastern Australia. This was followed by the gold rush and the entry of large numbers of Chinese. From 1855, restrictions began to be introduced by the colonies. The debate was shaped by imperial loyalty, isolation and fear – of jobs being taken, of 'difference', of invasion – culminating in universal support for the *Immigration Restriction Act 1901*, whose nature was adumbrated by attorney-general Alfred Deakin (1856–1919) in this second reading speech on the Bill in the first session of the new nation's federal parliament.

*

At this early period of our history we find ourselves confronted with difficulties which have not been occasioned by union, but to deal with which this union was established. No motive power operated more universally on this continent, or in the beautiful island of Tasmania, and certainly no motive operated more powerfully in dissolving the technical and arbitrary political divisions which previously separated us than the desire that we should be one people and remain one people without the admixture of other races. It is not necessary to reflect upon them even by implication. It is only necessary to say that they do not and cannot blend with us; that we do not, cannot and ought not to blend with them. This was the motive power which swayed tens of thousands who take little interest in contemporary politics – this was the note that touched particularly the Australian-born who felt their selves endowed with a heritage not only of political freedom, but of an ample area within which the race might expand, and an obligation consequent upon such an endowment – the obligation to pass on to their children and the generations after them that territory undiminished and uninvaded.

A coloured occupation would make a practical diminution of its extent of the most serious kind. It was this aspiration which nerved them to undertake the great labour of conquering the sectional differences that divided us. We, therefore, find ourselves today confronted with the possibility of dealing in a practical way, and for the first time in the history of our union, with the question which assisted so largely to unite us. We are fortunate, since at the very outset of our career, and indeed when the foundations of the Commonwealth of Australia were being laid, that the Convention which drafted the constitution was alive to the vital character of this problem. Fortunately we are better equipped than our cousins across the Atlantic. Our constitution marks a distinct advance upon and difference from that of the United States, in that it contains within itself the amplest powers to deal with this difficulty in all its respects. It is not merely a question of invasion from the exterior. It may be a question of difficulties within our borders, already created, or a question of possible contamination of another kind. I doubt if there can be found in the list of powers of legislation – a cluster more important and more far-reaching in their prospect than the provisions contained in subsections (26) to (30) of section 51, in which the bold outline of the authority of the people of Australia for their self-protection is laid down. We have power to deal with people of any and every race within our borders, except the Aboriginal inhabitants of the continent, who remain under the custody of the states. There is that single exception of a dying race; and if they be a dying race, let us hope that in their last hours they will be able to recognise not simply the justice, but the generosity of the treatment which the white race, who are dispossessing them and entering into their heritage, are according them.

In regard to the people of every other race within our midst we have special power to legislate. We have power over emigration and immigration, of which this measure proposes to take advantage. We have the power of dealing with the influx of criminals, without restriction of race or colour. We have the undefined powers relating to external affairs and the connexion of the Commonwealth with the islands in the Pacific, the exact meaning of which no one today can exactly define, and very happily so. I undertake to say that those provisions, like certain sections of the American constitution, may slumber for a certain time – in our own case, perhaps, not a long time – but they can be interpreted, and will be interpreted, to meet whatever may be the necessities of any situation that arises outside the boundaries of the Commonwealth affecting the future of this country, or of the multitudinous islands of the Pacific.

So we enter on the consideration of this great matter fully equipped in our constitution. The responsibility of dealing with it rests directly on our shoulders. It is that burden we are now endeavouring to lift. We inherit a legacy in the shape of the aliens which have been already admitted within our borders. The program of a 'white Australia' means not merely its preservation for the future – it means the consideration of those who cannot be classed within the category of whites, but who have found their way into our midst. Unfortunately the statistics of the last census are not sufficiently advanced in this regard to enable one to say definitely the number of those within our territory who are capable of being dealt with under subsection (26) of section 51 of the Constitution. But I should say that at a very moderate estimate, based on reference to the last census, there are from 70,000 to 80,000 aliens already in Australia. A certain number of these may be naturalised, and a certain number may have been British subjects before they came here.

I should say there are about 80,000 coloured aliens in Australia. Of these, probably somewhat less than one-half are Chinese, and apparently about 9000 are Polynesians. The remainder are recruited from a variety of people, mainly those of the neighbouring countries of Asia. We find on our hands this not inconsiderable number of aliens who have found admission to these states, either before there was the protection such as several of the states now enjoy, or who are still able to find their way into states which, like Victoria, are unhappily not protected to the same degree. It has to be remembered in connexion with this question that so long as any of the states of the union remain without their doors closed as much as other states, the protection which those other states enjoy is absolutely defeated and rendered of no effect. From the states which have no restrictions immigration is sure to flow, and is flowing overland into those which have certain restrictions.

What we have to face, therefore, is not an Australia protected to the full extent of state powers, but an Australia which, being only in part protected, is scarcely protected at all – excepting in regard to the Chinese. Even in regard to these, there are considerable differences between the restrictions imposed in the various states. We find ourselves today, it may be said, with at all events a half-open door for all Asiatics and African peoples, through which, as the experience of the honourable member for Southern Melbourne proves, there is still entry from time to time. It was with a full recognition of those facts that the first plank in the government platform, as submitted at Maitland and emphasised at every opportunity since, was the plank which for ease of reference was called the declaration for a 'White Australia'. It was for this reason that so much stress was laid on this issue, and it is for this reason that since the government took office, no question has more frequently or more seriously occupied their attention, not only because of this one proposal now before the House, but with regard to executive acts that have been and will be necessary. There have been determinations which hereafter may have important consequences arising out of our administration, as well as other measures which will be submitted to parliament, all having in view the accomplishment of the same end. That end, put in plain and unequivocal terms, as the House and the country are entitled to have it put, means the prohibition of all alien coloured immigration, and more, it means at the earliest time, by reasonable and just means, the deportation or reduction of the number of aliens now in our midst. The two things go hand in hand and are the necessary complement of a single policy – the policy of securing a 'White Australia'. ...

The origin – the source of our action – requires some little exposition to those who look at us with old-world eyes. One can well understand the attitude of the statesmen of Europe, absorbed in their own affairs and in the control of large populations within comparatively narrow areas, approaching amazement when they regard what appears to be the arrogance of a handful of white men, most of them clustered on the eastern littoral of this immense continent, adopted before they have effectively occupied a quarter of the continent, and with the great bulk of its immense extent little more than explored, or with a sparse settlement. Those European statesmen may well view with surprise the anxiety exhibited here in this respect. There are those who mock at the demand of a white Australia, and who point to what they consider our boundless opportunities for absorbing a far greater population than we at present possess, who dwell, if commercially-minded, on the opportunities for business we are neglecting by failing to import the cheapest labour to develop portions of our continent which have not as yet been put to use. But the apprehensions of those abroad, even when cursorily examined, are soon seen to proceed from a far narrower outlook than that which belongs to those who feel themselves charged with the future of this country. We should be false to the lessons taught us in the great republic of the West; we should be false to the never-to-be-forgotten teachings from the experience of the United States, of difficulties only partially conquered by the blood of their best and bravest; we should be absolutely blind to and unpardonably neglectful of our obligations, if we fail to lay those lessons to heart. Cost what it may, we are compelled at the very earliest hour of our national existence – at the very first opportunity when united action becomes possible – to make it positively clear that as far as in us lies, however limited we may be for a time by self-imposed restrictions upon settlement – however much we may sacrifice in the way of immediate monetary gain – however much we may retard the development of the remote and tropical portions of our territory – those sacrifices for the future of Australia are little, and are indeed nothing when compared with a compensating freedom from the trials, sufferings and losses that nearly wrecked the great republic of the West, still left with the heritage in their midst of a population which, no matter how splendid it may be in many qualities, is not being assimilated and apparently is never to be assimilated in the nation of which they are politically and nominally a part. It is we, and not our critics, who in this matter are adopting the broader and more serious view – the view which the future will approve. It is a view which, when explained, will, even by critical statesmen, be necessarily admitted to be sound – one in which a democracy in some respects impatient, is imposing itself as a restraint in the interests of the future generations who are to enter into and possess the country of which we at present only hold the border.

This note of nationality is that which gives dignity and importance to this debate. The unity of Australia is nothing, if that does not imply a united race. A united race means not only that its members can intermix, intermarry and associate without degradation on either side, but implies one inspired by the same ideas, and an aspiration towards the same ideals, of a people possessing the same general cast of character, tone of thought – the same constitutional training and traditions – a people qualified to live under this constitution, the broadest and most liberal perhaps the world has yet seen reduced to writing – a people qualified to use without abusing it, and to develop themselves under it to the full height and extent of their capacity.

Unity of race is an absolute essential to the unity of Australia. It is more, actually more in the last resort, than any other unity. After all, when the period of confused local policies and temporary political divisions was swept aside it was this real unity that made the Commonwealth possible. It prevented us from repeating the ridiculous spectacles unhappily witnessed in South America between communities called republics, the same in blood and origin, but unable to develop together or live side by side in peace. ...

If we exclude all coloured peoples we go a long way towards obtaining a white Australia. While the educational standard may exclude a great many, it will not exclude all of these, as there are races whom it is desired to exclude who are quite capable of fulfilling all the conditions imposed in the Bill. I shall not take advantage of the objection that the persons who annoy us most – the Syrians and Afghans, who seek to make a living by peddling; the Polynesians, from whom there is little danger once the state legislation has been dealt with, and ninety-nine per cent of the Chinese who come here – would fail to pass the test imposed by the Bill. The Chinese and Japanese who arrive belong to poorly-paid classes, and are the least educated and least informed of their countrymen. It is not the highly-cultured who come here. The number of such people who come here in any one year could be counted upon the fingers of both hands. ...

When it becomes necessary for us to exclude people like the Japanese it is reasonable that we should exclude them in the most considerate manner possible, and without conveying any idea that we have confused them with the many uneducated races of Asia and untutored savages who visit our shores. To lump all these peoples together as Asiatics and undesirables would naturally be offensive to a high-spirited people like the Japanese, and surely without any request from the British government or without any representations from the Japanese mere considerations of courtesy, such as should exist between one civilised people and another, should lead us to make this distinction. Considerations of simple politeness, such as honourable members extend to each other in this House, should at least govern the actions of civilised nations in their dealings with one another.

I say that the Japanese require to be absolutely excluded. I contend that the Japanese require to be excluded because of their high abilities. I quite agree with the honourable member for Moreton that the Japanese are the most dangerous because they most nearly approach us, and would, therefore, be our most formidable competitors. It is not the bad qualities, but the good qualities of these alien races that make them dangerous to us. It is their inexhaustible energy, their power of applying themselves to new tasks, their endurance and low standard of living that make them such competitors. I quite agree with the honourable member for Bland that the difference that separates them from us is as much in their standard of living as anything else. At all events, the faculties that make them dangerous to us are those which make their labour so cheap and their wants so few. The effect of the contact of two peoples, such as our own and those constituting the alien races, is not to lift them up to our standard, but to drag our labouring population down to theirs. It is the business qualities, the business aptitude and general capacity of these peoples that make them dangerous, and the fact that while they remain an element in our population, they are incapable of being assimilated, makes them all the more to be feared. The Japanese represent the highest class of those who seek to come here, and they are people who are capable of being dealt with on the same footing as any other civilised power. The government of Queensland met Japan by means of a treaty, and succeeded in a great measure in preventing the introduction of more Japanese into that state. This was a graceful recognition by Queensland of the position of Japan amongst civilised nations, and has enabled that state to check the influx of Japanese without giving any offence to a friendly power.

It has not been absolutely stopped, but it should be stopped; and it remains for us to provide for the absolute prohibition of this and every other class of coloured alien immigration by such means as shall not be unnecessarily offensive to the peoples to whom they belong. We ought to accomplish our ends with their goodwill, and probably in the case of Japan and of India, with the assistance of the government concerned. ...

We have received an express assurance to which we can if necessary hold the imperial authorities, but to which it is not necessary to hold them, that they will in this matter lend us every possible assistance in their power. They approve of our object. All they ask is that we shall adopt such means to gain our ends as will avoid giving offence to other nations, although it is plainly indicated that they would in the last stage accept the course proposed if Australia absolutely believes that no other course is possible. Any other suggestion misrepresents their attitude, and it is an attitude which should not be misrepresented in this chamber, where they have no representatives who are under any obligation to speak for or defend them. Evidently what is sought is to put those who are sensible of what we owe to the mother country in the apparent position of being prepared on that account to sacrifice some Australian right or some Australian privilege.

The government, of which I am a member, and myself also, are under no obligation whatever to this or any other British government that every citizen of Australia is not under. But I did think that in the earliest days of the Commonwealth, when we looked at the charter so recently gained with the unanimous approbation of both Houses of the British parliament and of the whole British people – an endowment of freedom such as has never been paralleled in the history of the world, conceded to us in the most cordial manner possible and without any question of bargaining or exchange – that we should have recollected at least sufficient of our origin to have prevented the expression of such opinions. We should ill begin our career by repudiating our incalculable obligations to the mother country. Until we are challenged by some act of the British government which calls for resentment, it is in the highest degree unstatesmanlike and mischievous to set up such a bogy to obscure the issue with which we are confronted.

I have freely expressed all that I think upon this matter, but have said it without being personal. That is the whole position. The difficulties with which we are confronted are not difficulties of our own creation. Charges have been levelled against the government measure, and tirades and torrents of meaningless epithets have been employed. It has been said that the Bill is a fraud, that it is underhanded, that it is an hypocrisy and in some sense a deceit. These charges are made in regard to a measure that is drawn expressly in view of the published and printed declarations of the British government. When the British government ask that a particular course shall be adopted and this government adopts it, we are told that we are adopting an underhand, fraudulent course, and that our object is to deceive the British government. The only charge which can be laid against us is that this Bill proposes to ask the House to put a large trust in the administration of the day, whoever that administration may consist of.

This measure imposes an educational qualification without distinction of race or colour. It can be applied to white as well as to black and to black as well as to brown. It can be applied to all. Then having drawn the Bill so as to place in the hands of the administration power to apply it to all, the Prime Minister couples it with a declaration that it is not and never was intended to be applied to those white residents of European countries who come here to make their homes with us and many of whom are among our worthiest citizens and most prosperous settlers. When he indicates that the measure is not intended to apply to Germans, Scandinavians, etcetera, that they will be welcome to come and make their homes with us, and to assist in building up the nation of which they would soon become a part, we are charged with bringing down a hypocritical measure. I do not say that there are not classes of white-skinned people against whom it may be necessary to protect ourselves. The power placed in the hands of the administration of the day is the power to specially discriminate between white and white. Between white and brown there is no difficulty in discriminating. We hold that the test should exclude alien Asiatics as well as the people of Japan, against whom the measure is primarily aimed. But while it is primarily so aimed it is not to be construed that the power in the hands of the executive will not be used to exclude certain persons who are white-skinned. …

This Bill incidentally may exclude, in some few cases, white-skinned people, but it is not intended to exclude qualified European immigrants who come here to make their homes amongst us, and who, whether they pass the test or not, we shall be glad to welcome. Whether they can write fifty words in English or not we are anxious to have such immigrants here, because they are men of enterprise and courage, who strengthen every country into which they enter. When the House is told by the head of the government exactly what the intention of the Bill is, I confess that I do not understand the charge that we are pursuing an underhand course. If any declaration could be plainer or more explicit and unequivocal, I should like to hear it. I submit, in conclusion, that the Bill is drawn in the best interests of Australia, and is so drawn because similar tests, though not so stringent, have proved effective in all the states in which they have been applied. If so desired to make the Bill more stringent on the same lines, that can be done later without the slightest prospect of the passage of the measure being delayed at all. Any other course will involve delay – not defeat, but delay.

It might be a few months, but who can say? I have no information as to its being delayed at all, except what is contained in the printed and published documents read today, which show that nations have to be considered, their susceptibilities studied and communication addressed to them. They show, also, that if we insist on what is considered unnecessarily discourteous action, and to make the burdens of British statesmen heavier instead of lighter, we can follow our own course, and, like spoilt children, get our own way.

But when we have the frank assurance this continent will be reserved for the people of the white race by any means not offensive to other portions of the Empire or foreign powers, we may safely rely on that assurance. No one will insinuate that the British government may not be relied on to fulfill its pledges. We have the opportunity of immediately securing this continent against the influx of aliens, which is already taking place day by day, an influx which is not so large, but yet is too large. It is an influx which we can absolutely prohibit at the instant. The men who came today, and were seen riding on a lorry, would, I have no doubt, not be able to write fifty words of English, even if they could speak them; and to prevent such immigration would be a great gain. In addition, when this Bill goes elsewhere it goes explained by this debate.

No one welcomes more than the government the frankness and freedom of speech which have been properly used in the House in regard to this great issue. There will be no mistake as to our meaning when these speeches are read, and when our votes are seen.

Members on both sides of the House, and of all sections of all parties – those in office and those out of office – with the people behind them, are all united in the unalterable resolve that the Commonwealth of Australia shall mean a 'white Australia', and that from now henceforward all alien elements within it shall be diminished. We are united in the resolve that this Commonwealth shall be established on the firm foundation of unity of race, so as to enable it to fulfill the promise of its founders, and enjoy to the fullest extent the charter of liberty under the Crown which we now cherish.

'If the Allies are defeated, we go down'

William 'Billy' Hughes

'What Australia must do': speech on the National Referendum,
Sydney

18 SEPTEMBER 1916

The issue of conscription was the most bitter and divisive
debate in Australian history. The prime minister, Billy Hughes
(1862–1952), had worried about the size of the national army since
entering politics, and for five years before the outbreak of World
War I had pushed for compulsory universal military training
based on the Swiss model. Hughes believed 'men that cry peace
when there is no peace are enemies of peace.' Having persuaded
the Labor Party to adopt compulsory training for home defence
Hughes then turned his sights to conscription for overseas military service during the war; with a determination that produced
mounting hysteria as hundreds, sometimes thousands of young
Australian men were laid waste on European battlefields.

Hughes initiated a referendum on the issue and travelled
the country vehemently arguing his case. The results proved the
nation to be almost equally divided, with the 'No' vote gaining a
majority of just under fifty-two per cent. Hughes would try again
fourteen months later with a slightly more clear-cut result, leading
to his expulsion from the Labor Party. He retained the prime ministership by forming a coalition Nationalist Party with the conservative Opposition, inaugurating the rich tradition of treachery to
the Labor cause. The following speech, delivered at the Sydney
Town Hall to a packed house, illustrates the mood of the 'Yes'
campaign leading up to the first referendum.

*

I speak to you tonight in the greatest crisis in the history of the
Australian Commonwealth. I speak, indeed, in the gravest crisis not

only in our history, but in the history of the world – at a point when the civilised world is locked in death grips with the most formidable power that despotism has ever raised in its eternal attacks against liberty. It needs no words of mine – or it should need none – to bring home to every man and woman what this means to the world, to democracy and to us. But there is reason to believe that very many people in this country do not yet realise that this is our war. Very many do not realise that this life and death struggle in Europe and Asia is a struggle in which our lives and our liberties are being determined. They must be made to face the great realities of life; they must be made to face the fact that in this great struggle in Europe defeat writes our national epitaph. We citizens of this free and favoured land have gone on these two years during which Europe has been drenched in blood and ravaged by fire and sword – we have gone peaceably on our way as though no war raged at all. Many mourn those who will return no more, and many scan every day those ever-lengthening lists which tell the price – the eternal price – of war. But in the main we have gone on as though no war existed. To many Australians this war has merely brought a new thrill and glamour into their lives. They have often looked on the bloody spectacle as though it were only a bioscope view of distant events. But the inexorable finger of fate has brought it nearer, and it is now under our very eyes.

This is our struggle – our war. And we must win it, or lose everything that we value dearer than life. [*Cheers.*] Victory must be ours, and it is in order that we may achieve that victory – in order that Australia may do her part in achieving that victory – that I desire to place the proposals of the government before you tonight. What is the position? We have an army in the field now, as you know, hitherto maintained by voluntary enlistment. There are five divisions – in round numbers, 100,000 men. This is a much smaller army in proportion to that raised by Great Britain. Britain has raised one-tenth of her whole population, and these are now under arms. She has raised, in addition to that, one-twelfth of her male population, and these are engaged in making munitions and work incidental to war. She has raised also a great army of women – [*applause*] – who are working in the munition factories of Britain. Britain has raised, I say, an army, or army and navy, of over 5 million men. She has raised more than one-tenth of her total population. We have raised, at the outside, about one-twentieth. These are the facts, and they cannot be gainsaid.

I am a man who in this country and out of it has eulogised Australia, and has said, as I always shall say, that Australia has done well. [*Applause.*] But the time has come when she must do better. [*Applause.*] We have those 100,000 men in the battleline. Our task is to maintain these five divisions at their full fighting strength. That is the task allotted to us. That is the task we must perform. The government recognises it as its duty, and in pursuance of that duty has put these proposals before you and the country. I want to set forth these proposals, not carried with the glamour of rhetoric, not by way of appeal to sentiment or passion, but by an appeal to reason – for patriotism, rightly understood, rests upon reason. It is the soundest reason in the world, for every nation that is not patriotic must perish. [*Applause.*] Let me set out the position. Let me say that the British government has asked us for the first time in the history of responsible government to supply a given number of men.

Hitherto, for these two years the Allies have been on the defensive. Now the time has come when the mighty resources of the Empire and the Allies, having been marshalled, it is necessary to assume the offensive. It is not by being on the defensive that one achieves victory. It is by attack, and ever by attack. The time has come for us to pay back in kind that which we have suffered at the hands of Germany. Our way to liberty, to peace, to freedom, lies through the legions of Germany, and in no other way can we achieve it. The great offensive now being, by general consent, carried on on all the allied fronts, has been crowned with great success, but there is still a long way to go before Germany is defeated. The price of the offensive has been heavy. Our divisions have suffered not less than others, and because of this we are called upon to make a supreme effort. We are called upon to make this supreme effort in order to shorten the war – to lessen the toll of human life – in order to lessen the appalling outpouring of money and treasure from this country.

Now, what are we called upon to do? In September we have to supply 32,500 men, and in the succeeding months 16,500 men. We have now, of men available here and in England, 103,500 men. These will supply all the requirements of the British government's demands until the end of January, and then our trained troops now in reserve will be gone. The government's proposal is to recruit each month the same number of troops as are taken out of our reserves, so that there will be always as many coming in as going out. We have to fight these people with trained troops, and not with untrained men. The proposals will enable us to meet the requirements of the British Army Council, and to supply each month the number asked for.

On 1st October, if there are not 32,500 men in camp or on their way there, the provisions of the Defence Act of Australia will be put into operation, and 32,500 men will be called to the colours.

Thereafter we will call up 16,500 per month to the colours. [*Cheers.*] On 28th October a referendum of the people will be taken and authority will be asked for to send these men so recruited overseas. The government proposals are adequate to the circumstances; they are immediately effective, and they are democratic in nature. They rest upon the broad foundation of government of the people by the people for the people. [*Cheers.*] And let those who impugn them no longer call themselves democrats, whatever else they may call themselves. [*Cheers.*]

Now, let me deal with one or two misrepresentations, to call them by a mild term, that have been industriously circulated in reference to the government's proposals. Many who wish to defeat our policy are trying to influence the minds of the people of Australia by filling them with misrepresentation and with deliberate falsehood. [*Cheers.*] I want to warn you again to beware lest they include the agents of our enemies, of that treacherous Germany, who has her mouth in every ready ear and her finger in every open palm.

When the policy of the government is carried, as I believe it will be – [*cheers*] – we shall not forget the necessity of maintaining the national as well as the family life. The government is alive to the fact that for the sake of the family and industry there must be a careful scheme of exemptions. The government does not consider it will be necessary to draw upon married men. [*Cheers.*] We have examined the war census returns and have brought them up-to-date, and we believe that, supplemented by volunteers – voluntaryism will still run side by side with compulsion – the supply of single men will be sufficient for our purposes.

Leaving aside married men, the government proposes exemptions among single men, as follows: it will not compel men under twenty-one years of age. [*Cheers.*] They may volunteer if they like, but we shall not compel them to go. [*Hear, hear.*] We shall not take the only sons of families. Where a single man is the sole support of dependents he, too, will be excused. And where there are one or more members of a family who have gone to the war, the remaining members up to one-half of the family will be excused. [*Cheers.*] In addition to these exemptions, which will be granted without recourse to exemption tribunals, other exemptions, based on the necessity for carrying on the industry of the country, will be made. The wheels of industry must be kept moving in order that we may be able effectively to carry on the war. Any person who thinks he ought not to go, and is called upon to go, may appeal to exemption tribunals of a non-military character. These tribunals will be presided over in the locality by a magistrate. There will be an appeal to the state court, presided over by a state judge, and there will be a final court of appeal, presided over by Justices of the High Court of Australia. These exemption courts will be civil courts. Every man will be able to have his case heard and fairly decided on its merits.

There is one more point. An insidious and lying statement has been circulated most industriously. It is that directly compulsion comes into force for overseas service, the pay of soldiers will be cut down. Let me speak plainly. There is not one word of foundation for such a statement. [*Applause.*] The only alteration in pay will be that for married men. The maximum separation allowance will be increased from 8s. to 10s. Otherwise, those who are compelled to serve, and those who volunteer, will be paid exactly the same. All will be paid alike.

Now that I have dealt with that misrepresentation, and set out in plain terms what the proposals of the government are, let us look at the basic principles that underlie this great question of compulsory military service. What is the position? The state is at war. The state is fighting for its life. Unless it be victorious it will cease to exist as a free state. That is the position. Does anyone who loves his country; does anyone who is not an enemy of Britain and Australia, doubt that if Germany wins in this war she will lay her predatory hands on this country of ours? What was the avowed purpose of Germany when she went into war? It was world power; a place in the sun; to extend her power over the whole world.

Is there in the world a greater prize than Australia? Consider the position. We have five millions peopling a great and rich continent, while Germany, fourteen times as small as Australia, has 70 million people. Do you doubt that Germany will claim this land as one of the greatest of her spoils if she should win? The state, then, is at war, fighting for her life. It is written that if Germany wins and the Allies are defeated, Australia, free Australia, exists no more. Yes, there are men who hesitate. Think of that all you that hesitate; that babble about your rights, as if rights were things of which you had some sacred title. Some title that exists apart from the state to whom you owe all your rights. What is there that you value – liberty, political power, high wages, the possibilities of the future – that will remain if the Allies lose?

Men speak as though this war was something distant, something incredibly remote from them, which would pass over this nation and leave it practically the same. This war is a dark cloud which, if it come and rest over this fair land, will leave us very different from what it found us. How are the political powers, these liberties, and improved labour conditions that the Australians possess going to be maintained by them – by babbling about their rights, or drawing the sword to fight for them? [*Applause.*] I want to tell you plainly that if the Allies are defeated we go down. If Germany pierced the legions of the Allies, if she were victorious in France, if she were able to pierce the hitherto impregnable line of the British navy, then if every man in Australia rushed to the standard they could not for one moment avert the triumphant march of the enemy. For in modern war neither numbers nor valour prevail unless there be disciplined armies, great guns and an abundance of ammunition. Will any man say we have these things? I tell you, and I am armed with knowledge, that our position is hopeless. What is the position? We may say what we like, but once the Allies' line is broken in France – which, please God, it shall never be – [*applause*] – there is an end of us. Get that into your minds. Let every man who hesitates, who talks about liberty, who sees in this some dreadful menace to democracy, know that it is on the battlefields of France his fate is being decided. But for the allied armies and the British navy we are doomed men. We may bleat and we may struggle, but we are like sheep before the butcher, and nothing can save us.

Do you say that the state has no right to call on its citizens to defend it? By what right do they claim citizenship other than that they have, as you, my Lord Mayor, said, obligations equal to their privileges? It is the duty of every citizen to defend his country, and it is upon his country that he depends for the protection of what he is pleased to call his rights. Without the state those rights of his would not endure for an hour, yet they say that the state has no right to compel men to fight. We are, in fact, told that the state has no right to compel men to do anything against their will. That would be to make states as we know them impossible. It is a law which applies to democratic states where the whole of the people determine the laws, as well as to those states which are under the domination of a monarchy or oligarchy. The principle that the state has the right to compel men to obey the law is an axiom that no one denies. Let me tell you some of the things the state can do. It has the power to tax men, and take away their property. It has power, and it has exercised it, to take property and pay what it will. It has power to take a man's wheat and pay what it pleases, and has done so. It has power to compel employers to pay certain wages, whether they like it or not. The state has power to take away the liberty of those who break its laws – it has power to take away life itself.

As to those men who have enmeshed themselves in umbrage, who are struggling with some horrid monster they have conjured up, do not they know we have the power they speak of? I can, in as little time as it takes me to get two other members of my government together, call upon and put every man in this building under arms. [*Applause.*]

Do you know that for fifteen years it has been the law of this country that every man from eighteen to sixty could be summoned to the colours, drilled and sent to any part of the Commonwealth, perhaps 2000 or 3000 miles from home, and be made subject to military law under all circumstances whatever, to meet an enemy within our own gates? Do you know that? Why, you have lain for fifteen years calmly and peacefully under this monstrous thing conscription, and it has done you no harm. What man amongst you these two last years that war has waged fiercely, when we have had that power to the fullest extent, has had his liberties lessened or who has been treated oppressively because of that power? Not one. Those people who talk about conscription with stuff that passes current for argument do not think for themselves and have no reason at their backs.

Now let me say something about this industrial conscription that is being talked about. We have had the power to compel to work at any work we chose for them, and for any wages we chose to pay them. But we have not used it, and we do not propose to use it. The power we wish for is the power to send men away to fight in France. [*Cheers.*] The question to be asked at the referendum is:

> Are you in favour of the government having, in this grave emergency, the same compulsory powers over citizens in regard to requiring their military service, for the term of the war, outside the Commonwealth, as it now has in regard to military service within the Commonwealth?

There are two points here. First: it is for the time of the war, and that only; and secondly, it is only an extension of the powers we already have for home service that we are asking. [*Cheers.*] I say to those who concede the right of the state to use compulsion to make men fight an enemy inside Australia, and who deny it to the government to send men to fight the enemy outside Australia, that they have no ground to stand on, because their argument turns on the inviolability of human life. They say human life is sacred. Very well them, why has the government power to take it when the enemy is in Australia, at say the Gulf of Carpentaria, and none when he is in German New Guinea, not so far away?

Duty and national honour alike beckon us on. What Australian will consent to partial withdrawal from this life and death struggle? Who among us will support a base abandonment of our fellow citizens who are fighting for us to the death with deathless heroism? Tens of thousands of our kinsmen in Britain have died that we might live free and unmolested. [*Cheers.*] Is there one man who will say that we ought not to pay the debt we owe to Britain, with our lives if need be, for shielding our country with the bodies of her glorious soldiers and sailors from the scorching blast of war? [*Cheers.*] In this great hour, when our country and all we hold dear are in deadly peril, who among us will not rise greatly, and putting aside all other things, prove himself by his deeds worthy of these great sacrifices, and prove himself worthy of the great privileges of citizenship in a free democracy?

Australians! This is no time for party strife. The nation is in peril, and it calls for her citizens to defend her. Our duty is clear. Let us rise like men, gird up our loins and do that which honour, duty and self-interests alike dictate.

'Wait and see what they have ready for you'

Archbishop Daniel Mannix

Speech on the second conscription referendum at the Stadium, Melbourne

OCTOBER 1917

Like his arch-rival prime minister Billy Hughes, Catholic archbishop Daniel Mannix (1864–1963) was either loved or loathed for his Irish-Australian nationalism and his controversial teachings in the church. Pushed by an ambitious mother, Mannix obtained his doctorate of divinity in 1895 and was an outstanding theological scholar. He was consecrated titular bishop of Pharsalus in 1912 and appointed coadjutor archbishop to Melbourne's St Patrick Cathedral, arriving in Australia on Easter Saturday 1913. He became archbishop in 1917.

Mannix was outspoken on many issues including the funding of Catholic schools, his support of Ireland's Sinn Fein leader Eamon de Valera, and his hatred of communism – alongside his political adviser B.A. Santamaria, he founded a secret branch of the National Secretariat of Catholic Action, otherwise known as 'The Movement'. Mannix is probably best known, however, for his bitter denunciations of conscription. He put 'Australia above the Empire' and contributed to the failure of both referendum campaigns. Hughes accused him of 'preaching sedition'. A 'scathing, laconic' orator who commanded the devotion of hundreds of thousands over the term of his long reign, Mannix died aged ninety-nine with Arthur Calwell and Santamaria at his bedside. The bells of St Patrick's Cathedral tolled ninety-nine times. The following speech was delivered to 6000 people two months before the second conscription referendum in 1917.

*

Of course, you read the Melbourne morning papers, and, like myself, you were more or less surprised this morning – less surprised, probably, some of you – to find that the ministers had at last plucked up courage to do what some of them were itching to do all along, and that we were to have another referendum on conscription. [*'They will be beaten!'*] I hope so. [*Applause.*] It is only twelve months since the people of Australia pronounced their emphatic verdict – not only the people here in Australia, but even the soldiers at the front – [*cheers*] – that Australia is a democratic country, and that there is no room here for slavery and conscription. [*Sustained cheering.*] Now you are asked to pronounce on the same question again. [*'We will vote "No" again.' Cheers.*] I would put to you this question to begin with: if the answer in October 1916 had been the other way, would you have got another opportunity now of reversing it? [*'No.'*] Certainly not. But, now that another opportunity is given to you, I hope that your answer will be the same as before, but more emphatic and decisive.

This question of conscription here is not a Catholic question, nor an Irish nor an English question; it is purely and simply an Australian question. [*Cheers.*] When I speak from this platform on public questions – on this question of conscription or any other question – I do not speak as a priest or as an archbishop, but simply as an honest, straight and loyal citizen of Australia. [*Great cheering.*] I do not question the right of others – Catholics or non-Catholics – to differ from me. Why should I? I may regard their views as opposed to the best interests of Australia, but I do not think of charging them with disloyalty. [*Applause.*] Catholics are likely to differ among themselves, as do non-Catholics, on this question of conscription, and they have a perfect right to do so. [*Applause.*] But I hope that the majority of Catholics, and of non-Catholics also, will be on the side of freedom and liberty for Australia. [*Sustained cheers.*] We are quite ready to hear anything that the conscriptionists have to add to what they said on the previous occasion. [*Loud laughter.*] Many things said then have since been unsaid, because they were untrue. [*Applause.*] This time, I hope that, even at the cost of some effort, they will stick as closely as they can to the truth. [*Laughter and applause.*]

We were told a year ago that we should vote for conscription because there was some great secret locked up in the bosom of the Prime Minister. [*Ironical laughter.*] I hope there is no secret there now. Let us hear the worst. [*Renewed laughter.*] Indeed, we are likely to get very gloomy news from this to the taking of the referendum. We always get the news that fits the occasion. At other times, all our battles are victorious and our losses are very light. [*Laughter.*] But now the Allies will suffer one defeat after another – and all for the lack of conscription in Australia and of a few more Australians in the trenches. [*Laughter.*] Do not take my word for this. Just watch the papers. Wait and see what they have ready for you during the next few weeks. [*Great laughter.*]

You will be appealed to as if everything depended on what Australia does or leaves undone. [*Laughter.*] Now, Australians are – have proved themselves to be – the bravest of the brave. [*Applause.*] But, if every man of them was as brave as Hector – [*'They are!'*] – a hundred thousand of them, more or less, would not count for much when 15 million of men are said to be engaged. [*Hear, hear.*]

But, though they could do very little at the front, it would cost a great deal to do that little, and that fact, no doubt, would for the present be kept in the background by our conscriptionist friends. Every Australian soldier will cost this country five to ten times as much as a European soldier sent into the firing line, and who will pay our huge war bill? Very often it will be those least able to bear the burden. [*Applause.*] Of course, the imperialists will pour out their wrath upon anyone who talks of finance while, as they say, the Empire is in danger. Next moment, they will tell us there is no danger, because England is never stronger than when she has her 'back to the wall'.

[*Laughter.*] However, let that pass. They talk loudly enough about the 'last man'. They talk in a more subdued key about the 'last shilling'. But when it comes to raising the taxes, these people and their press are ready enough to pass the burden to others and to talk about spoliation. [*Cheers.*]

Now, we know these gentlemen well. [*Applause.*] When it comes to providing for the soldiers, many of whom had returned maimed and broken, these gentlemen who talk so loudly do not show much anxiety to pay their last or second last shilling. [*Cheers.*] They are – some of them – content to send poor little state school children into the streets to pick up pennies to pay for the maimed Australian soldier. [*'Shame!'*] You are not likely to be cajoled by those who ask you to put finance out of the question. [*Applause.*] With or without conscription, an undue share of the cost of the war will be borne in the end by the people, who are already paying more than their fair share, because those who should be made to pay, those who are responsible, perhaps, for the making and for the continuance of the war, often succeed in passing on the burden of taxation to people who, in reality, have no taxable income at all. [*Applause.*]

This is my first opportunity of referring to conscription, and I wish to say I stand exactly where I stood before. [*Great cheering.*] On the last occasion I offended a great many people, and I fear that I should have to offend every one of them again. [*Applause.*] I hope the Australian people will not waver – [*applause*] – and that there will be still a larger majority in favour of maintaining the liberties which we enjoy, and against conscription in Australia. [*Applause.*]

'Is it to be back to the kitchen?'

Jessie Street

Broadcast on ABC radio's National Program

17 APRIL 1944

Jessie Street (1889–1970) was one of the most energetic and important feminist activists in Australian history. Born in India and migrating to Australia at the age of seven, she completed an arts degree at Sydney University in 1910 before commencing her activities to improve the status and rights of women and Aborigines. Street joined the League of Nations Union in 1918 and was appointed secretary to the National Council of Women in 1920, before playing a leading role in the formation of the United Associations of Women, Australia's first umbrella feminist organisation, in 1929. She was the only woman on the Australian delegation to found the United Nations in 1945.

Before the outbreak of World War II, Street joined the Australian Labor Party and almost won the blue-ribbon Liberal seat of Wentworth in the 1943 election. She lost again in a second attempt in 1946. Accused of being a communist sympathiser and earning the nickname 'Red Jessie' for her pro-Soviet stance in the Cold War, Street attracted criticism for her radical and idealist vision. She was under surveillance by ASIO for decades although there is no evidence she was ever a member of the Communist Party.

As a little girl, Street had spent many hours with the local Aboriginal stockmen and their families, while riding horses on the family farm. But her provocation by the injustices and inequities of the life of Aborigines, curiously, grew most pronounced when she was living overseas in the 1950s. Her efforts to bring together Aboriginal and non-Aboriginal activists were considered by many to be her 'crowning achievement', resulting in the formation of the Federal Council for Aboriginal Advancement. She helped initiate the campaign for the 1967 referendum on the status of Aborigines, one of very few to have been successful.

Street was a polished public speaker – in radio broadcasts, election campaigns and campaign meetings. The following address is on a theme close to her heart throughout her life – the insistence on economic independence for all women.

*

There is a good deal of talk just now about what they are going to do after the war with the women: Must they be made to return to the home? Are they going to take them out of the factory, the office, off the land?

To me, this sort of discussion is very disquieting. It makes me think we've already forgotten the reasons why we're fighting this war. Aren't we fighting for liberty, for democracy and to eradicate fascism and Nazism in every form? Surely we don't mean liberty and democracy for men only? Indeed, I hope women will enjoy the liberty which they have helped to win and be permitted to choose what they want to do. Do you remember that one of the first things the Nazis did when they came to power was to put women out of the professions, out of the factories? They barred the doors of the universities to all but a few women and they severely limited women's opportunities for any kind of higher education; by these methods the Nazis forced women back to the home – back to the kitchen. I can't help thinking that if any attempt is made here after the war to force women back to the home, it will be proof that fascism still has strong roots in Australia.

Women should not be forced to return to the home, but they should be free to return there if they wish to. I don't like what's implied in the suggestion that women will have to be forced back into the home – that's a slight not only on home life, but also on the work of bearing and rearing children, don't you agree? The greatest happiness for many women is to care for a home and to raise a family. The trouble in the past has been that society has failed to make it possible for all the women who wanted to have homes and raise families to do so.

And while we're on the subject of women in the home, I think that this life could be made attractive to many more women by developing amenities and customs that render home less of a prison than it is to many women with young families. Just think of the prospects of family life, as lived under present conditions, to a clever, energetic, bright young girl. Soon after marriage there will be a baby, and from then on she cannot move unencumbered. The more babies, the harder she has to work and the greater her restrictions. If we want more women to choose home life, we must make home life less hard. But how can we do this? Well, we can have crèches and kindergartens and supervised playgrounds where children can be left in safe sur-roundings. Then we must change many of our conventions. Why should a woman do all the work in the home? Why can't we, for example, have community kitchens and laundries? If a woman wants to work outside the home, why shouldn't she? Let her be free to choose. There's just as much and more reason to believe that the best interests of her family and of society will be served by giving a woman a free choice than by expecting her to adhere to a lot of worn-out conventions.

Anyway, the contribution that women can make to public life through the professions or in industry is important. Women in the past have been very much hampered by their inexperience in these spheres. They haven't had the opportunity to qualify for representa-tive positions or positions of control and direction. In other words, because of the lack of opportunity to gain experience they're denied the opportunity of exerting any influence in framing policies or directing public affairs.

I am pretty sure that many women will remain in industry after the war, for we shall be in need of more skilled hands rather than less. Remember, we couldn't exert a full war effort until women were absorbed into industry; therefore, how can we exert a full peace pro-gram without making use of their services? Everyone knows how short we are of houses and hospitals and offices, of furniture, of bathroom and kitchen fittings, of curtains, wallpaper, clothing, food-stuffs, in fact, hundreds of commodities. Can you imagine the tremendous amount of work that will be required? Not only have we to make up the deficiency of the war years, but we must provide all these amenities on a much larger scale after the war. There were large numbers of people before the war who had no homes, not even enough to eat; hospital accommodation was inadequate, and so on. Although all these could have been provided for a few million pounds, we believed we could not afford to better these conditions. It took a total war to show us what we could do with our own resources. If we can raise money for war we can raise it for peace, surely. It would be inexcusable in the future to condemn people to live under the conditions so many endured before the war.

Why is there so much opposition to women remaining in industry? The secret isn't far to seek. It's simply that they got paid less – they are cheap labour, certainly not, as so many have alleged, because they're weaker or less efficient. Unfortunately, because their labour is cheaper, women not only threaten the wage standards of men workers, but they also threaten the standard of living of all workers. The obvious and just way to avoid this is to give equal pay to men and women.

To put this in a nutshell, I believe that in a democratic, free society women should be at liberty to choose whether they will take up home life or work outside the home; that men and women should receive equal pay and equal opportunity; that home life should be made less of a tie and the burden of raising a family be lightened. If we can face these peacetime problems with the spirit of determination and conciliation with which we're facing our war problems, we may hope to solve them.

'It is a portrait within the meaning of the words in the will'

Ernest David Roper

Finding on the Dobell portrait of Joshua Smith, NSW Supreme Court

8 NOVEMBER 1944

Upon his death in 1919, the founder of the *Bulletin*, J.F. Archibald, left shares worth ten per cent of his £89,061 estate to establish a portrait prize in his name. Controversy, criticism and debate have ensued ever since; the terms of the will, the size of the works and the worthiness of the sitters have all come under scrutiny. Yet nothing has compared to the outcry and debate following the announcement of the winner by the Trustees of the National Gallery in Sydney in January 1944. William Dobell's painting of his friend and fellow artist Joshua Smith bitterly divided the art community and was contested in the NSW Supreme Court by two losing contestants. One Sydney critic said, 'When you look at a portrait you should feel that what you see is human – not that you should send for the ambulance.' Bernard Smith, by contrast, saw in it 'a symbol of the twentieth-century artist living on in the last days of a dying culture'. Others found it a welcome challenge 'to the hegemony of the gloomy academic style'. Supreme Court Justice Ernest David Roper (1901–1958) refrained from giving his personal opinion of the painting in his judgement, but found in favour of the artist. Dobell recalled that his 'nerves went to the pack' after the furore, and he left his flat in Kings Cross for the countryside, where he produced two more Archibald winners, in 1948 and 1959.

*

… The picture in question is characterised by some startling exaggeration and distortion, clearly intended by the artist, his technique being too brilliant to admit of any other conclusion. It bears, nevertheless, a strong degree of likeness to the subject, and is, I think, undoubtedly a pictorial representation of him. I find it a fact that it is a portrait within the meaning of the words in the will, and consequently the trustees did not err in admitting it to the competition.

Whether as a work of art or a portrait it be good or bad, and whether limits of good taste imposed by the relationship of the artist and sitter have been exceeded are questions which I am not called upon to decide, and as the expression of my opinion upon them could serve no useful purpose I refrain from expressing it.

I mention those matters, however, because I think that the witnesses for the informant and relators, whose competency to express opinions in the realm of art is very great, were led into expressing the opinion that the work was not a portrait because they held strong views upon those questions. They excluded the work from portraiture, in my opinion, because they have come to regard as essential to a portrait characteristics which, on a proper analysis of their opinions, are really only essential to what they consider to be good portraiture. …

'Two Wongs do not make a White'

Arthur Calwell

Speech on Australia's immigration policy in the House of
Representatives

2 December 1947

Re-appointed the minister for immigration in the Chifley Labor government after the 1946 federal elections, Arthur Calwell (1896–1973) was responsible for overseeing an extensive new policy of European immigration: 'New Australians' would help ensure an annual population increase of two per cent. Politicians were unanimously in favour of bolstering Australia's dwindling birthrate and agreed to take new migrants from Europe's refugee camps following the upheavals and displacement of World War II. Calwell, however, was an adamant supporter of the White Australia policy, and while able to defend protests of an 'olive peril' was apt to harp on fears and prejudices of Australians towards the Chinese. The numbers of Chinese in Australia had declined from 38,000 in 1880, to around 7000 by the year Calwell made this unforgettable speech.

*

The government has decided that all persons who came to Australia as evacuees or refugees during the war and who, under our immigration laws, are not eligible to become permanent residents of this country, must leave. We have been very tolerant of these people. We could have asked them all to go immediately the war ended, but we have allowed them to stay for a certain period, in some cases so that they might wind up their affairs here and in other cases so that they might get decent shipping facilities to take them back to their own countries. In all, 15,000 evacuees of all nationalities came to Australia during the war. Of that number, 4400 were Asiatics. Most of the evacuees, including the Asiatics, have gone. There are about 500 Chinese, mostly seamen, and about fifty Malays left. All of these people will have to leave Australia. There have been protests from a number of very reputable people, particularly in Sydney, on emotional and sentimental grounds, about the repatriation of the fourteen Malays mentioned by the honourable member. I have advice that, of those fourteen Malays who married Australian women, two of them had wives in Malaya at the time of 'marrying' in Australia. A photograph of one of them with his two children and his Australian 'wife', who is expecting another child shortly, was published recently in the Sydney *Sun*. He already has a wife and two other children in Malaya. That, of course, is the reason why he does not want to go back to Malaya. Probably that, too, is the reason why he has persuaded his Australian *de facto* wife that our immigration laws and policy ought to be waived so that he might be permitted to remain in Australia. What this government proposes to do is not unusual. I am carrying out the policy that has been carried out by every Australian government since federation, and, as far as I am concerned, it will not be altered. In that regard, I think I have the support of a great majority of the Australian people. The honourable member's question also referred to a Chinese, who, according to today's press, has been resident in Australia for twenty years and has been told that he must go. The policy which I have just mentioned relates to evacuees who came to Australia during the war. This Chinese is said to have been here for twenty years, and obviously, therefore, is not a wartime evacuee. Speaking generally, I think that there is some claim for him to be regarded as a resident of Australia, and I have no doubt that his certificate can be extended from time to time as it has been extended in the past. An error may have been made in his case. The gentleman's name is Wong. There are many Wongs in the Chinese community, but I have to say – and I am sure that the honourable member for Balaclava will not mind me doing so – that 'two Wongs do not make a White'.

'The power of money'

Dame Dorothy Tangney

'Women and banking': broadcast on 6PM in Perth

23 NOVEMBER 1949

The most contentious political debate in the late 1940s was the Chifley government's proposal to nationalise Australian banks – an ambition of the party since the austerities of the Great Depression. The bid to bring private banking under full government control opened a stark divide in Australian politics, which Opposition leader Robert Menzies characterised as being a question of 'whether the government was the master of the people, or the people the master of government'. Menzies alleged that a single public bank would 'create in the hands of the ruling political party a financial monopoly, with unchecked power to grant or withhold banking facilities ... in the case of every individual citizen'.

Senator Dorothy Tangney (1911–1985) was the first woman to sit in the Upper House of the federal parliament. Elected on the same day as her political opponent, Liberal MP Enid Lyons, Tangney came from a staunch Labor background, leaving a teaching post to successfully contest the 1943 election. In this radio broadcast, delivered three weeks before the 1949 election, Tangney aimed to quell the fears of women over the banking issue. The issue ended up being the main contributor to Chifley's defeat, although Labor continued to control the numbers in the Senate, where Tangney remained until her retirement in 1968.

*

Good morning, listeners.

This morning I am going to discuss the question of banking. Prior to 1910 there was no Commonwealth Bank – all banking was in the hands of private trading concerns which failed to avert such terrific disasters as the 1893 bank smash, when thousands of persons lost their life-savings. When the Labor prime minister in 1910, Andrew Fisher, introduced legislation to set up the Commonwealth Bank there was a similar outcry to that raised today against Labor's financial policy. 'Fisher's Flimsies', as the Commonwealth Bank pound notes were called, were stated to be worthless, and yet time has proved their stability as our chief medium of exchange. To show how important is the part played by money and banking in your everyday life may I give you the statement of the Honourable R. McKenna, ex-Chancellor of the Exchequer of the British government and chairman of the Midlands Bank, the largest trading bank in England, who when addressing the shareholders of the bank in 1924 said, 'They who control the credit of the nations, direct the policy of government and hold in the hollow of their hands the destiny of the people.'

So great is this power then that the Labor movement believes that it should not rest in the hands of a few private individuals responsible

Well May We Say

to no one but themselves, but should be the sacred trust of the duly elected representatives of the people in the national parliament. No thinking woman will deny the commonsense of this. Many of you will remember the misery and starvation of the Depression. True there was a Labor government in office only in Canberra at that time, but it had no power. First because it had an anti-Labor Senate and secondly, it had no power to compel the banks to lend money for full-time employment of the 250,000 men who could not work. Mr Scullin, who was then prime minister, submitted a plan to obtain finance from the private banks in conjunction with the Commonwealth Bank, whereby the miseries of the million people on the dole would have been alleviated. But this was refused him, and while bank deposits remained idle, thousands went homeless and hungry. I know the Depression in Australia was part of a worldwide financial crisis, but the part played in it by private banking institutions is summed up by Sir Herbert Holden, an eminent banking authority in Britain who states:

> What brought about the Depression? Everybody knows that the Depression was caused by the bankers the world over in following up their time-old policy in calling up their overdrafts and advances.

Therefore I ask you most earnestly not to be misled by all this propaganda being issued by our opponents regarding the Labor Party's banking proposals. There is nothing sinister or furtive about them. All that the government intends to do, and what it is constitutionally permitted to do, is to give back to the people of Australia the right to control that very important factor in their lives, the power of money.

'This is a bill to outlaw and dissolve the Australian Communist Party'

Sir Robert Menzies

Second reading of the Communist Party Dissolution Bill, House of Representatives

27 APRIL 1950

The Communist Party of Australia was formed in 1920 three years after the Russian revolution. The activities of the Communist International caused acute anxiety among Western governments throughout the twentieth century, but at no time more than during the Cold War, after the descent of the Iron Curtain, the rise of the Berlin Wall, war in Korea, and evidence, real and imagined, of the infiltration of political, military and cultural institutions by communist subversives.

In 1950 prime minister Robert Menzies (1894–1978) launched a campaign to ban the Communist Party in Australia. His Second Reading Speech focused on the deceptive methods the communists employed in their attempts to achieve their aims. This was an important and carefully prepared speech for Menzies; a draft and notes are in his papers at the National Library. Passed through parliament, the legislation was overturned by the High Court as unconstitutional, and a referendum held in 1951 was narrowly defeated. But turning back the communist tide became a leitmotiv of successive Menzies administrations.

*

This is a Bill to outlaw and dissolve the Australian Communist Party, to pursue it into any new or associated forms and to deal with the employment of communists in certain offices and under certain circumstances. The Bill is admittedly novel, and it is far-reaching. It is not an industrial law. It is not a law made under the conciliation and arbitration power. We are, therefore, not seeking by this Bill to make any amendments to the *Commonwealth Conciliation and Arbitration Act*. This proposed law is, in a most special and important sense, a law relating to the safety and defence of Australia. It is designed to deal with, and, in certain cases, to give the government power to deal with, the King's enemies in this country. If it touches certain communists in their industrial office, as it certainly does, that is merely an inevitable consequence of a self-defending attack upon treason and fifth-columnism wherever they may be found. Let me say at the outset that ... for some years I and other persons resisted the idea of a communist ban on the ground that, in time of peace, doubts ought to be resolved in favour of free speech. True, that was my view after the war, and it was the view of many others. But events have moved. We are not at peace today, except in a technical sense. The Soviet Union – and I say this with profound regret – has made perfect the technique of the 'cold war'. It has accompanied it by the organisation of peace demonstrations – peace demonstrations, save the mark! – designed, not to promote true peace, but to prevent or impair defence preparations in the democracies. We in this House and in this country, and people all over the British world, have witnessed the most threatening events in eastern Europe, in Germany, in East Asia and in South-East Asia. If we have learned nothing from all these things then, in the famous phrase, there is no health in us.

The real and active communists in Australia present us with our immediate problem – not the woolly-headed dupes, not the people who are pushed to the front in order to present respectable appearance, but the real and active communists. We have a clear choice, and we must make it clearly. We can attack these communists frontally, or we can adopt inaction and justify it by accepting one or all of the arguments that are used currently to justify inaction. Let me examine one or two of them before I go any further. I have selected merely those that have the greatest currency. The first argument that is put is, 'Well, the communists are wrong, but we must not impair liberty, because liberty is democracy's cause.' Why, then, did we fight the Germans? Because they sought to overthrow liberty! Can we recognise and deal with the enemies of liberty only when they actually take up arms? Are we to treat deliberate frustration of national recovery, of economic stability and of proper defence preparations as a mere exercise of normal civil rights? In any event, what is liberty? Liberty is not an abstraction. It must be related in this world and in these days to the recognition of the state and, in a democracy, to the recognition of self-governing institutions. Unless that is true there can be no such thing as treason, no such thing as subversive activity. After all, what liberty should there be for the enemies of liberty under the law? It is a curious and dangerous error of thoughts to be prepared to deal with individual sedition but to give immunity to sedition in the mass.

The second argument that is advanced is, 'You cannot suppress ideas.' That is quite true. Ideas may be the most powerful things in the world. But if ideas give rise to overt action, and that action is against the safety and defence of the realm, we are not only entitled but bound to suppress it. Nothing nauseates me more than to discover the skill with which these communists can put into their vanguard some deluded minister of the Christian religion. I should like to say to all of them that I have no hostility to minority movements. Christianity itself is the greatest minority movement of history, but they should remember the words of its founder. Christianity from the beginning was never the enemy of law or order. 'Render unto Caesar the things that are Caesar's, and unto God the things that are God's.'

The third argument is, 'You must not touch a communist if he is a union official.' That is an arrogant claim, because it seeks to put the trade unions above the law, and most unionists, as good democrats, will reject it. A brief analysis will demonstrate its want of substance. If communism is just a peaceful political philosophy, then the communists should go free whether they be unionists or non-unionists. If communism in action is just militant unionism, opposed to arbitration but determined to alter the law by lawful means, no punitive action against communism can be justified. But if communism is an international conspiracy against the democracies, organised as a prelude to war and operating as a fifth column in advance of hostilities and if it is a subversive movement challenging law, self-government and domestic peace, then the alleged immunity of the official of a union or any other body is utter fantasy. For, once you establish that the communist is our enemy, the fact that he occupies a key industrial position with power to hold up work, so far from being a ground of immunity, is the best reason in the world for removing him from that position.

At the last general election, 87,958 persons, a small fraction of the total number of electors, voted for communist candidates. The importance of the Australian communist is, therefore, not numerical but positional. It is the position he occupies that counts ...

I hope that it will be well observed in this country that these communists are not to be ignored as if they were a mere handful. They occupy key positions in key organisations in the industries upon which this country would have to depend if tomorrow it were fighting for its life. The choice before us is a grim but a simple one. We can do nothing, and let a traitorous minority destroy us, as they most assuredly intend to do; we can leave the communist free to do his work so long as he is a union official, but deal with him in any other capacity; or – and this is the answer to the choice – we can fight him wherever we find him, leaving him no immunity and no sanctuary at all. It is an insult to the Australian unionist to treat him as a man incapable of reason, or as a citizen indifferent to the march of communism in the world or to the safety of his own land.

So far I have dealt with three arguments that have been raised. I turn now to the fourth. That argument is that by banning the communists we shall merely drive them underground. In the light of what we now know of the international and domestic activities of communism, that argument is not to be taken seriously. Some of the deeds of the communists see the daylight, but their planning is done by stealth and in secrecy. In short, they are underground already. One thing that we can be certain about, and that I am grateful for, is that once the taint of illegality is placed on this organisation of conspiracy its capacity to delude well-meaning people into providing it with a respectable 'front' will be sensibly diminished ...

Honourable members are familiar, of course, with the jargon of the Marxist writers. They talk about the bourgeoisie and the proletariat. Indeed, they seem incapable of saying things in what we would regard as a simple way, although their meaning, I am afraid, is all too clear and their actions are even clearer. A 'bourgeois', wretched creature, began life in France as what we call a 'burgess' – that is to say, the citizen of a city or a burgh as distinct from a country dweller. But as Marx and Engels and their successors use the term, it describes what would be called in other countries the middle classes, the capitalists, great or small, the people with money saved, the shop-keepers, the farmers and all those who are not wage-earners and not those who, in the words of Engels: 'having no means of production of their own, are reduced to selling their labour power in order to live'. The latter are the proletariat. I pause to make that short explanation because, clearly, we in this parliament, whether we like it or not, belong to the bourgeoisie, and so, thank heaven, do many hundreds of thousands of other Australians dwelling peacefully in their homes and among their children ...

The security and defence of Australia are dependent not only upon the valour of our troops in time of war and upon the industry with which they are supported in the factory and on the farm, but also upon the continuity of those great industries that are vital to a national effort should war come. It is a childish idea that the fifth column springs miraculously into existence when a war is on. It is carefully prepared and organised in advance. By strike and sabotage, it conducts its own Cold War and the success of that war depends upon the strength, or weakness, of the community in which it operates. We would not have tolerated a fifth column in Australia from 1939 to 1945. We certainly do not propose to tolerate one in 1950, at a time when militant communism, checked for the time being in western Europe, is moving east and south-east to carry out its plans to put down democracy and to usher in the revolution. Coal-mining, iron and steel, engineering, transport, building and power are key industries. There may well be others which under this legislation the Governor-General may from time to time proclaim. In the considered judgement of His Majesty's government in Australia it would be an act of criminal folly to leave revolutionary communists in key positions in those industries so that with all their smallness of numbers they may achieve destructive results which five army corps could hardly hope to achieve ...

'What is the upshot of this Petrov affair?'

Herbert Vere Evatt

Speech to parliament on the Royal Commission on Espionage

19 OCTOBER 1955

In April 1954, Vladimir Petrov, a colonel in the Soviet intelligence service and Third Secretary of the Soviet Embassy in Canberra, defected to Australia with his wife Evdokia, setting prime minister Robert Menzies and Opposition leader Herbert 'Doc' Evatt (1894–1965) on a collision course. A royal commission into Soviet espionage activities in Australia concluded that no prosecutions need be launched. But Evatt's self-devouring determination to prove a political conspiracy theory would end his career and leave his party riven.

Evatt was allotted two hours for his parliamentary speech on the royal commission although he would have liked 'twelve days'. An ASIO staffer 'sensing that this speech might prove of some significance in Australian history' recorded the address, in which Evatt reiterated his arguments – by this time all old and familiar – amidst bursts of merciless laughter and taunting interjections.

*

What is the upshot of this Petrov affair? Two foreigners, the Petrovs, and one foreign-born Australian spy, Bialoguski, have made a lot of money. The forum in which they appeared cost the taxpayers £140,000, plus unlimited security service expenses. The nation has suffered heavy loss in trade, and the breaking of diplomatic relations with a great power. There has been the attempted smearing of many innocent Australians, and grave inroads have been made into Australian freedoms by attacks on political non-conformity.

[*Honourable members interjecting.*]

[Mr Deputy Speaker (Mr C.F. Adermann): Order! I ask honourable members to maintain silence. These interjections must not continue.]

But after eighteen months of inquiry, at this great cost to the nation, no spies have been discovered. Not a single prosecution is recommended.

It is now clear that the Prime Minister (Mr Menzies) must have known, when appointing the commission, that there would be no legal evidence fit to warrant the prosecution of any person, that there was in fact no security ground for the inquiry itself. Indeed the inquiry has in many ways been destructive of the national security of Australia. Furthermore, it is now abundantly clear that the Prime Minister knew many months before the 13th April 1954, when he made his melodramatic and coldly calculated announcement to the House, that Petrov's defection was being deliberately organised by security agents under his ministerial control. He waited, and sprang the announcement on the House on the very last sitting night of the parliament prior to the May general elections. He completely deceived the House into rushing through legislation to appoint a commission. In the apparent emergency, there was no opportunity of examining any of the basic facts. His statements should be re-read in the cold light of the facts which have since been established during the last eighteen months since the 13th April, 1954. Let it all be read. ...

Determined to ascertain the truth of these grave matters, I took two steps, as follows: first of all, I communicated with His Excellency the Foreign Minister of the Soviet Union. I pointed out that most of the Russian language documents in the Petrov case were said to be communications from the MVD, Moscow, to Petrov, MVD resident in Australia. I pointed out that the Soviet government or its officers were undoubtedly in a position to reveal the truth as to the genuineness of the Petrov document.

I duly received a reply, sent on behalf of the Minister of Foreign Affairs of the Union of Soviet Socialist Republics, Mr Molotov.

[*Honourable members interjecting.*]

Honourable members can laugh and clown but they've got to face up to some facts tonight. They will not put me off by their organised opposition. They have to listen to this because this is the truth of the affair. The letter to which I have referred informed me that the documents given to the Australian authorities by Petrov can only be, as it had been made clear, at that time and as it was confirmed later, falsifications fabricated on the instructions of persons interested in the deterioration of the Soviet–Australian relations and in discrediting their political opponents.

I attach grave importance to this letter which shows clearly that the Soviet government denies the authenticity of the Petrov documents. It seems to me that in these circumstances the matter cannot be left where it is, and that, if possible, some form of international commission should be established by agreement with the Union of Soviet Socialist Republics to settle the dispute once and for all. The Soviet Union was not represented at the hearing. It will be in a position to prove clearly, definitely and unequivocally that the letters were fabricated.

I subsequently took a second step to check the authenticity of one document at least produced by Petrov as part of exhibit G and alleged by the Petrovs to have been written by Sadovnikov. The photostat of one of the G documents was made available to me by the solicitor for one of the witnesses called before the royal commission. At the same time, two other persons who had both been witnesses before the royal commission, courteously made available for inspection undoubtedly authentic specimens of Sadovnikov's handwriting.

An official photostat of the alleged Sadovnikov document, exhibit G, and photographs of two specimens of Sadovnikov's genuine handwriting were submitted to Dr Charles Monticone, an outstanding New South Wales expert on handwriting. Early in this month Dr Monticone certified that the result of his analysis of the handwritings was as follows: documents A on one side, that is, the alleged Sadovnikov handwriting in exhibit G, and documents B and C on the other side, that is, the authenticated specimens of Sadovnikov's real handwriting, 'have been written by two entirely different persons'. This opinion, if correct, as I most certainly believe it is, means that the Sadovnikov document produced by Petrov and now included as part of the vital G series was not written by Sadovnikov at all and was an undoubted fabrication. If so, of course, the foundation of the case built up in relation to the G documents is broken and it collapses. These two separate matters provide overwhelming ground for my demanding – and I do now demand – that all the documents in the Russian language produced by Petrov should be immediately tabled in the House and made available for inspection by honourable members. These are vital matters. Nobody can deny their importance to the relationship between this country and other countries and also to the internal affairs of this country.

Let us now look at the real origin of this sensational episode. The fact is that early in 1954, shortly before Petrov's defection, the Menzies government faced an uncertain position in relation to the forthcoming elections.

A Gallup poll on the 7th March predicted a majority against the government. The government had done its best, of course, to keep the communist issue alive, having snatched electoral victory on that false electoral issue in 1949 and again in 1951. But it had been defeated in the referendum of September 1951, and overwhelmed in the Senate vote of 1953. I think that government supporters frankly admitted the desperate need to produce a rabbit out of a hat if they were to succeed at the general elections, and there was undisguised glee on the part of government supporters after the announcement in the House on the 13th April, and the insinuations of misconduct against unnamed Australians. The 'red' bogy was to be exhumed again in a slightly different form. ...

Let me turn now to the speech of the Prime Minister on that night. He said that 'some days ago' Petrov had applied for asylum in Australia. He further referred – and I quote his words – to the 'comparatively few days' that had elapsed since Petrov 'came to our security people'. These carefully worded phrases are now shown by the established facts to be untrue and deliberately misleading. 'Some days ago' was, in fact, nearly two weeks, and the phrase 'comparatively few days' was also deliberately misleading, even if it was meant to refer to the mere fact that Petrov had formally – and quite unnecessarily – signed a document asking for asylum. On the most conservative estimate, Petrov had come to security and was under the control of Bialoguski, the security agent, at least seven months previously. Bialoguski had been working towards Petrov's defection since the middle of 1951, a period of three years. Moreover, Petrov never came to security! Security came to Petrov! ...

Remember the Prime Minister's statement that 'a few days ago Petrov came to our security service'. But the security service had been after Petrov for three years! They 'had him in the net'. That is the phrase used. The wire recording was taken under circumstances which were indescribable and disgusting from the point of view of ordinary decent Australians. The plan for Petrov's reception was communicated to the heads of Commonwealth departments on the 17th February 1954. Did the Prime Minister not know that? It went to the head of his department. Did he not know of the instruction that if Petrov came to any of their offices he was to be given protection if he wanted it? That was fifty days before the Prime Minister's announcement to the House. On the 4th March 1954, Richards received from Spry, forty days before the announcement in the House, the sum of £5000 for the very purpose of paying it to Petrov. That is the position. It was dangled before Petrov just as a sign of good faith that if and when he did what was required of him he would get the cash. Is anyone in the House or the country prepared to believe that the Prime Minister knew nothing of this great and elaborate coup; of the careful government planning involved in organising 'Operation Petrov', and the use of £5000 of Commonwealth money? I say that if Spry used money like that for such a purpose, without informing the responsible minister, he does not deserve to stay another moment in his job. ...

In the published account of his part in the Petrov affair, Bialoguski reveals that he made a special visit to Canberra to see the Prime Minister. His only job was to secure the defection of Petrov. He had no other security job and he was discontented with his status. He had had trouble with security. He said he was going to appeal to the Prime Minister and he came to Canberra. Of course, no one would accept Bialoguski's account of anything unless it was independently corroborated, but the facts and the date of his visit to Canberra are set down in the sealed letter to the Prime Minister which was handed on his behalf, by Mr Yeend, his private secretary. With the letter open in front of them, the matter was discussed by Bialoguski and Mr Yeend. ...

It is clear now, and I submit it to the judgement of the House and the people, that the Petrov affair was saved up for the 1954 elections. The wire recordings show that Richards and Bialoguski were using his chicken farm as bait for Petrov. That is the very phrase that Bialoguski used in his *Saturday Evening Post* articles. It was bait to catch Petrov. In their conversations the date was fixed on which Petrov, who was then in the position that he had to do what he was told, should defect. The date was fixed as the 5th April. It was two days out, because the date of his actual defection was the 3rd April. Her Majesty was due to leave Australia a couple of days before, and that was the date which was fixed, when the election date had been practically fixed for May.

Once that conclusion is reached – and it is inescapable – the Petrov case, as I said in August of last year, will rank in history as far worse than that of the notorious Zinoviev letter which was produced from anti-Labor sources on the eve of the 1924 elections for the purpose of defeating the British Labour government. The only difference is that the Petrov case was on a bigger scale.

The main impression of the report is that some of its findings bear little relation to the published evidence. The commissioners' findings imply attempted espionage in one or two cases, yet they recommend against prosecution. They insinuate the inadequacy of the laws that prevents prosecution, but a study of the evidence shows that it is not the inadequacy of the laws that prevents prosecution, but the complete absence of any legal evidence of espionage or criminality that makes prosecution impossible. Indeed, some of the findings of the commissioners are in absolute conflict with the published evidence and with certain well-established rules of British legal procedure. ...

The absence of any sound evidential support ... raises the question whether there was any evidence to justify the inquiry, and what was its real purpose. There was nobody to be prosecuted. There was no breach of law. The law is quite sound. It is very clear. Had there been evidence, a prosecution could have been launched. The ordinary security way of attacking a problem like the Petrov case, in order to decide whether there is a possibility of a breach of the law, is to let security in the first instance act, search and see whether it can find evidence on which to prosecute. That would have been the normal thing. We pointed out that fact in the House at the time. But that was not done, and, of course, there was no evidence, as I have said. It is a clear feature of the report.

I want honourable members, if they will – it is not possible for me to do it in the short time available – to look at the opening address of counsel, no doubt prepared after consultation with the Prime Minister who gave the instruction that the £5000 was not to be mentioned in the opening address.

[Mr Gullett: Ah!]

It is no good ah-ing about it. The people of Australia would say 'Oh,' not 'Ah.' When we have a man like this who has £5000 – 5000 good reasons for doing this – is it not relevant to tell the jury? Why is that information kept back on the eve of an election? It is a perfectly scandalous thing, and it has never happened before –

[Mr Deputy Speaker: Order! There is whistling in the House. If I find out who is whistling, he will be named.]

I ask the House and the country to compare that opening address with the sworn evidence. In his opening address, counsel forecast the finding of spies. He referred to 'traitorous activities', 'a spy-ring', and 'a systematic and organised group'. That was a dramatic opening, conducted dramatically. It was melodramatic. No expense was spared, as we know. The old Albert Hall was converted into a great film house for the time being, and public servants in certain degrees were told they should go down and show their loyalty. The press was there, and the broadcasters were there. Never was there such a sensational opening.

[Mr Ward: The Hollywood touch.]

The Hollywood touch! We have had it before here. We had it on the night the Prime Minster introduced the Communist Party Dissolution Bill, which the people subsequently rejected. The Australian people were told to expect that there would be evidence of widespread espionage. Window-dressing statements were made referring to the Soviet government in such terms as a 'tyrannical government' and 'despotic' and to certain Australians as persons 'not troubled by conscience or by scruple' and 'who have no firmly anchored religious faith'. Just imagine it, coming into a cold inquiry into espionage! It had nothing whatever to do with the case if facts only were to be presented. I wonder who was the draftsman of this last phrase?

'Human beings can be much more than we have allowed ourselves to be'

Dennis Altman

Speech at a forum on sexual liberation, Sydney University

19 JANUARY 1972

For most of Australia's history, homosexuality has been condemned as deviant and its sexual expression deemed illegal, forcing gay men and women into a sinful underworld. Dennis Altman (1943–) was a Fulbright scholar at Cornell University in the 1960s when he met and began working with leading gay activists in the United States. Returning to Australia in 1969, he taught politics at Sydney University, and in 1971, published his book *Homosexual: Oppression and Liberation* – considered an important intellectual contribution to the ideas that shaped Australia's gay movement. In 1985, Altman accepted an appointment at La Trobe University, where he is now Professor of Politics; he was recently appointed the visiting Chair of Australian Studies at Harvard University. When Altman gave the following speech in 1972 – at a time male homosexual activity was 'shadowy and ill-understood', and still illegal – it was regarded as groundbreaking. He remained active in organisations dedicated to the amelioration of life for homosexuals, serving on the Australian National Council on AIDS and other international AIDS organisations including the AIDS Society of Asia and the Pacific, of which he is president.

*

Sisters and brothers. This is a rather special moment for me and for a number of people in the audience. Because, as some of you have noticed when you came in tonight, this is the first appearance at Sydney University, in Sydney, indeed in Australia, of a Gay Liberation group. [*Loud cheers from the audience.*] As they have now identified themselves by the process of exhibitionism, which, as we all know is the hallmark of homosexuals, you will of course be aware that gay liberation has come out not only in Sydney but also in Australia. And I want to suggest to you, under the general topic of sexual liberation, that gay liberation has in fact ramifications and importance – not only for those of us who are homosexuals, who are finding the courage and self-assurance to come out in public, but indeed has importance and ramifications for everyone else. For what I wish to suggest is that the repression of homosexuality is one of the major forms that the repression of sexuality takes in our society.

Being an academic, I am allowed at least one quote, and as the topic is sexual liberation I shall quote from Freud. Writing in his autobiography he said:

> The most important of the perversions, homosexuality, scarcely deserves the name. It can be traced back to the constitutional bisexuality of all human beings. Psychoanalysis enables us to point to some trace or other of a homosexual object choice in everyone.

It seems to me that our society denies the inherent bisexuality of all humans in two ways. The first is that among most people who identify themselves as heterosexual there is a very determined and calculated attempt to deny their homosexual component, and this leads to quite grotesque cults of masculinity and femininity that are so much a part of our society, and against which both women's liberation and gay liberation are aiming their attack. It is of course common to attack women's liberationists as lesbians, thinking thereby somehow to deny the rightness of their cause. Equally, men are constantly being asked to uphold a standard of aggressiveness that somehow makes for masculinity. And this, it seems to me, is shown up best in that great Australian institution, the gang rape. I well remember a local TV program in which a guy who'd been up on a charge of pack rape said, 'The real fun is doing it with your mates.' While I obviously would subscribe to that, I would subscribe to it in a somewhat different manner. And it seems to me that if one wants a classic statement of oppressed homosexuality and its very sad and severe consequences for this society, that's it.

Further, we have this very peculiar situation whereby we live in a society in which chastity is upheld at least for some as not only natural but in fact admirable, whereas homosexuality or loving a member of your own sex is considered a perversion. I am tempted to use one of my other quotes and remind you of a statement by the Frenchman, Rémy de Gourmont, who said that among all sexual aberrations, chastity remains the most astonishing.

There are of course a number of us whose self-identification is homosexual. We face persecution and discrimination of all sorts and all kinds. And it's about this that I want to say something tonight. It is common knowledge that homosexuality or, at least, that homosexual acts among men (women being excluded for various reasons that I shall not attempt to explain), are illegal. It is also common knowledge that homosexuals are fair game – not only for the police but for large numbers of men who somehow feel that you prove your masculinity in beating up 'poofters'. And there is of course among certain sections of the psychiatric profession a more sophisticated version of beating up 'poofters' which is known as aversion therapy, wherein you give people shock treatment to teach them that loving somebody of your own sex is infinitely inferior to feeling aggressive towards them. Second, there is that large amount of discrimination which exists against homosexuals in our society and which takes the form of social ostracism of all kinds, and is exemplified in the fact that even in societies where homosexual acts are not illegal, there are no provisions for homosexual marriages, homosexuals find great difficulty in getting jobs, homosexuals find difficulties in finding housing, and I could go on and on with examples like these. The reason I don't do so is that I want to point to two less often noticed forms of discrimination that homosexuals face – the first being denial and the second being tolerance.

If you have a look at the TV commercials that intersperse the American programs that our TV channels show, you will find that they are in all cases directed at happy, smiling, young and even now occasionally middle-aged couples. But the couples are in all cases heterosexual. There is apparently no place for a homosexual in a TV advertisement, although from what one knows of people who work in television, one would imagine that the phenomenon is not unknown to them. Equally you will find, if you read the social columns of the Sydney papers (which I strongly recommend to you for entertainment), that even though social columnists may be, and in some cases are or have been, homosexual, they may under no circumstances report their social activities in any way that might lead the reader to suggest this. Which means, and here I refrain from detail for fear of the laws of libel, that we in fact get a very distorted version of what is going on in the upper echelons of Sydney society. If I might make my one mandatory chiding (I won't call it attack) on Germaine Greer, it is to say that I think, in part anyway, her book exemplified some of this denial, a refusal to recognise that homosexuals form an important section, not only of men in our society but also of women. Where is the lesbian in *The Female Eunuch*?

I do want to note, because I know there are a number of people from the press here tonight, although they're pretty well disguised, that the press seems to regard gay liberation as a taboo subject. I know in fact that the New York correspondents of one of our metropolitan newspapers have been instructed not to report gay liberation activities. And it occurs to me that perhaps one of the few advantages of being a gay liberationist as opposed to being a women's liberationist is that one avoids the danger of being treated as a sex object, because those reporters who might feel inclined to do so are far too terrified of their editors to write as they'd like.

The last sort of persecution or discrimination, and I think perhaps the worst, is the liberal tolerance, the 'boys in the band' syndrome, the 'well, they can't help it, poor dears, and we feel terribly sorry for them in jail, because after all that doesn't really help, does it,' and all the rest of it. And as an example of liberal tolerance at its best, I quote from that magazine of impeccable, indeed liberal credentials, the *Australian Humanist*, where a woman known as Helen Gurley Brown, whom I name as female chauvinist of the month, if we had such things, is quoted as saying that homosexuals have several uses for the life of a single girl: flat decorating; giving fashion advice; and providing a disinterested escort when the social occasion is so conventional that a girl cannot go alone.

Now of course sexual liberation, to return to the main topic of tonight's forum, involves more than merely overcoming the enormous amount of repression of bisexuality that is part of our whole social fabric. And unfortunately I don't have much time to dwell on what I see as two other very important components – the first being the rediscovery of what Freud referred to as polymorphous perversity, or to put it simply, the ability to take sensual pleasure and enjoyment from each others' bodies. The ability in fact to do more than just fuck. The ability to make love. And the ability to make love with people to whom you feel close, no matter their sex or age, not just with one person at a time, and without this necessarily leading to some sort of heavy possessive relationship. Because it seems to me that particularly in Western Anglo-Saxon societies, and God knows we're screwed up badly enough as it is sexually in this sort of society, the loss of this ability to naturally touch and feel each other is one of the greatest damages that has been done to us by the Protestant ethic. And secondly, any discussion of sexual liberation has to take into account the whole question of relationships and has to get away from the idea that sexual relationships are some form of possession. Norman Mailer wrote once that politics is property, but I would suggest that it would have been much more apt for Norman Mailer to have said that sex is property. It is, I think, a very sad feature of our society that sexual relationships are regarded in proprietal terms. The worst example I know of, and one that Germaine referred to today in her lunchtime talk in Canberra, is the rejection of two hundred thousand women by their husbands in Bangladesh because they'd been raped by Pakistani soldiers. You see, the property had been soiled, and therefore there was no further use for it. And I think that in a much less dramatic way the same attitude towards lovers, wives, husbands is very much a part of our society.

I said at the beginning, and I want to reiterate, that gay liberation is more than the liberation of homosexuals – it is in fact the liberation of us all. It is not a particularly original thought for me to put forward the idea that the homosexual within our society is a potential revolutionary. Jean Paul Sartre explores that idea in his study of Genet; Marcuse touches on the idea in *Eros and Civilisation*, although interestingly enough most of the left-wing activists who have followed Marcuse have tended to completely ignore this fact; and perhaps most surprisingly of all, Huey Newton, the leader of one faction of the Black Panther party, in a statement in August 1970 referred to the potential of the homosexual as a revolutionary within modern American society. And this, I should hasten to add, is something that petrifies most homosexuals. Most homosexuals, who of course aren't here tonight but are trying to make it in one of the numerous bars around Sydney (which, because they pay enough protection to be allowed to do so, cater to the homosexual trade), are in fact trying desperately to live, outwardly at least, respectable lives. But it is almost impossible, ultimately, for the homosexual to live a respectable life as our society defines this. And it is this fact that makes the homosexual into a revolutionary within the body of Western affluent societies. For, in the end, the homosexual stands outside the basic unit of our society, which is the nuclear family, and challenges by her or his very existence, the views of sexuality and of sex roles that are so much a part of our society. That is, they challenge the idea that sexuality can only be justified by procreation, and indeed I think that one of the real reasons that homosexuality is so stigmatised in our society is because it cannot be justified for any reason other than a purely hedonistic one. As you don't make babies by it, you can't persuade the Catholic Church that it's a good thing.

Secondly, homosexuality challenges the idea that men and women are somehow doomed or destined to move along narrowly predefined channels – channels which are defined in reference to each other, so that ultimately a man or woman is measured by the woman or man that he or she finds as a partner. And this is symbolised in the fact that a woman in our society is still told that her ultimate achievement is to lose her name and become Mrs somebody else.

Now liberation too involves a total concept much more than sexuality. And obviously I don't have time to develop a full discussion of the concept of liberation within the sort of society that Australia or America or Great Britain is today. But it seems to me that ultimately any vision of liberation is one that sees us breaking out of the quite unnecessary narrow limits on the human potential that exists within our society; that recognises that human beings can be much more than we have allowed ourselves to be; that recognises that humans have a right to diversity; that diversity is not a threat to a society as our so-called moral leaders would have us believe, but is rather something that strengthens that society. And that we needn't and we shouldn't be imprisoned by antiquated ideas of what is natural and what is normal. This, it seems to me, is ultimately what liberation is all about.

'There is a rival view, which I call the "black armband" view'

Geoffrey Blainey

The John Latham Memorial Lecture, Sydney

28 APRIL 1993

Once described as 'the lone prospector in Australian history', Professor Geoffrey Blainey (1930–) has been the most wide-ranging and independent historian of our times. His teacher at Melbourne University, Manning Clark, remembered his former student as 'a shy boy, wise beyond his years, sitting attentively at the back of the class'. Avoiding the conventional paths of historians of his generation, newly-graduated Blainey accepted a commission to write the history of Tasmania's Mount Lyell Mining Company. In his early years, writing ground-breaking histories of institutions including Melbourne University and the National Bank of Australasia, he honed an approach that was both unorthodox and practical. Blainey returned to Melbourne University in 1961, where he worked for the next twenty-seven years, writing and speaking on topics ranging from the development of Broken Hill to the emergence of Australian Rules football with unvarying acuity and an uncanny ear for the resonant phrase, reflected in titles like *The Rush That Never Ended*, *The Tyranny of Distance* and *A Land Half-Won*. In the 1980s, his views attracted criticism, particularly those concerning immigration and Australia's Aboriginal and Torres Strait Islander peoples. What he described as 'historical realism' was subject to unprecedented attack, although his 1993 speech on 'The black armband view of history' attracted little attention until Prime Minister John Howard borrowed the phrase three years later. Then it 'took off like a rocket' and entered the vernacular, although its originator contends that most of its critics 'had no idea what it signified'.

*

What has been good and what has been bad in the history of Australia? I selected this topic because it raises several difficult and dovetailed issues. Moreover, these issues are central in Australian politics and indeed in the nation's own sense of itself and where it is going.

Everyone will draw up a different balance sheet. It will depend partly on the historian's own experience and assumptions and bias. The exact balance sheet depends partly on the year when they happen to draw up the credits and debits, for some years are more buoyant than others. In this short time I will not attempt to draw up a full balance sheet but concentrate on several vital facets of European and also Aboriginal history.

To some extent my generation was reared on the 'three cheers' view of history. This patriotic view of our past had a long run. It saw Australian history as largely a success. While the convict era was a source of shame or unease, nearly everything that came after was believed to be pretty good. Now the very opposite is widely preached, especially in the social sciences.

If you first went to school in the 1930s you learned little Australian history but you accepted that the pioneers were at least as worthy as their inheritors. This was the view handed down to the young through school lessons or papers or radio. A nation fighting for its life usually sees that life, present and past, as very much worth defending by persuasion as well as arms. The left wing and the right wing were alike in their congratulations, though they rarely congratulated the same events.

There is a rival view, which I call the 'black armband' view of history. In recent years it has assailed the generally optimistic view of Australian history. The black armbands were quietly worn in official circles in 1988, the bicentennial year. Until late in that year

Mr Hawke rarely gave a speech that awarded much praise to Australia's history.

Even notable Labor leaders from the past – Fisher, Hughes, Scullin, Curtin and Chifley – if listening in their graves in 1988, would have heard virtually no mention of their names and their contributions to the nation they faithfully served. Indeed the Hawke government excised the earlier official slogan, 'The Australian achievement', replacing it with 'Living together' – a slogan that belongs less to national affairs than to personal affairs. The multicultural folk busily preached their message that until they arrived much of Australian history was a disgrace. The past treatment of Aborigines, of Chinese, of Kanakas, of non-British migrants, of women, the very old, the very young and the poor was singled out, sometimes legitimately, sometimes not. These condemnations of Australia's past treatment of various categories of people were so sweeping that at times close to eighty per cent of the population was in the 'hit list' – a suspiciously high percentage, you must admit, when this really was one of the world's most vigorous democracies.

My friend and undergraduate teacher Manning Clark, who was almost the official historian in 1988, had done much to spread the gloomy view and also the compassionate view with his powerful prose and his Old Testament phrases. For Manning Clark, Australia was the land where the money-changers had recaptured the temple – a biblical takeover in reverse. Clark spoke of 'the sickness of society at large,' and the perpetual rule of the tough and the ruthless. Australia, he wrote, is a nation which throughout its history had equated 'material achievement with public virtue'. These are powerful views, and some evidence can be found to back them, but I do not think, with all respect, that the evidence is strong enough.

Even Australia's material achievements of the past are under the hammer; and some recent books by historians see mainly injustice in the present, and poverty and inequality in the past. Why a million people a year were clamouring to enter such an unattractive society, and why so many people had been eager to come across the world in the majority of past decades, was a point not quite explained. Now schoolchildren are often the target for these views. In contrast, the general public for the most part remains proud of the nation's history, or what they know of it – their affection stood out in Sydney on Australia Day, 1988.

To some extent the black armband view of history might well represent the swing of the pendulum from a position that had been too favourable, too self-congratulatory, to an opposite extreme that is even more unreal and decidedly jaundiced.

Australia – until, say, the last quarter century – was one of the great success stories in the economic history of the world. In the economic realm Australia was more successful one hundred years ago than it is today; but it still must be classed as successful. It is in the top twenty-five, using virtually every definition, and by some economic observers it stands in the top fifteen. Whether such high places will be retained on the world's ladder is difficult to forecast. Australia is likely, on present evidence, to decline further in the next ten years.

We should measure economic success partly by the steepness of the mountain that had to be climbed. This was a tough country to colonise. I'm sure the Aboriginal pioneers found it difficult and in many ways they succeeded. The British also found it difficult. It was far from their homeland. The return voyage was hazardous: the sea route past Cape Horn was the main route from Australia for about ninety years. Australia was probably the finest triumph of long-distance colonisation the world so far had seen.

The newcomers found that the various climates of this continent were strange. The climates remained a riddle. The first settlement at Sydney was made on the basis, understandably, of a blunder about climate. An additional shock was to discover that so much of the continent was arid. This shock was still being felt by explorers in the 1870s. We still do not know what is a normal run of seasons.

Australia is the world's largest museum of soil deficiencies. Farming here, compared to North America, was a lottery because the soil, so deficient in phosphate and other minerals, seemed exhausted after only a few crops. Of course the land had natural advantages – sweeping grasslands in which the natural predators were not prolific and a winter climate that did not require the penning of livestock under a roof.

All in all it was a great achievement to turn Australia into one of the world's great producers of foods and fibres. The natural fibres are costlier and less in favour in this era of synthetic fibres but in the cold winters of the northern hemisphere, how many hundreds of millions of lives were made more liveable or even prolonged by Australian wool? Likewise Australian-grown food is not so urgently needed at present but its era will probably come again. Meanwhile, in a reasonably favourable year of the last decade Australia was probably producing enough food to sustain – on a modest intake of calories – close to 100 million people here and overseas. That is a remarkable achievement in a continent where probably fewer than one million people could feed themselves in Aboriginal times.

The story of mineral production in Australia needs no comment, except to say that it depends more on effort, imagination and efficiency than on luck. If luck really is all-important, why did the Aborigines have so little luck as miners? The phrase 'lucky country' is plainly misleading when applied unthinkingly to any primary industry, let alone to the whole economy.

When you place the obstacles on one side and the economic achievements on the other, you have to give three cheers – or if you are mean, two and a half. It is true, as many critics point out, that the wealth produced has not been evenly spread. At the same time those regimes which, like the Soviet Union, claim to have been successful in spreading wealth have failed dismally to produce enough wealth to spread. For most of the last one hundred years it was better to be a poor Australian than a middle-income member of most other nations.

The heyday of Australia's economic success was in the period from the end of the first gold boom to about the eve of the First World War. The late Professor N.G. Butlin of the Australian National University placed Australia's living standards at the top of the world at about the start of this century, and this verdict is proudly passing into Australian folklore. It is difficult to know whether this verdict is valid: international comparisons are so hazardous. I myself would call it a powerfully argued guess. Moreover, his calculations excluded the Aborigines. At the same time, Australians almost certainly stood on one of the top four rungs of the world's ladder of prosperity in most years from 1870 to 1914.

Why has Australia, while still standing high on the world's economic ladder, been forced to step down so many rungs? A significant part of the descent took place in the last decade, and can be explained by poor economic management, more in Canberra but also in the tall glasshouses of Melbourne, Sydney, Adelaide, Perth and Brisbane. But the major descent from the top rungs of the ladder began even earlier. Two reasons for the relative decline between 1914 and 1950 were geographical. In a period when the world moved steadily from firewood and coal towards oil, we lacked our own supply of oil: so an energy-rich country lost its advantage. Moreover, the climate in south-eastern Australia, so important to the rural economy, was relatively dry.

Over a longer period, our economic decline owes much to cultural factors reinforced by political decisions: a reluctance to save money, partly because of the increase in social security; a high preference for leisure; and a work culture which is more laid-back than our powerful and vigorous sports culture. The difference between our Friday and our Saturday values is almost a cultural iron curtain.

Beyond dispute, the colonising of Australia since 1788 has done great damage to the environment, mostly in the areas of urban and agricultural settlement. What we call economic progress took place with such speed and with such scant knowledge of the environment. There was a heavy toll, including the destruction of rare species of plants and animals, the increasing salinity of irrigated lands, the clearing of forests and the deliberate introduction of new animals – rabbit, cat, fox and many others – that displaced or preyed on native species. On the basis of damage for each one hundred square kilometres, we cannot feel sure whether greater alteration was made to Australia than to Europe in the last 200 years, though in the last 2000 years Europe has probably been altered the more, simply because of the sheer density of its human settlement.

There are various ways of measuring comparative ecological damage just as there are of defining democracy. Do you apportion the blame for ecological damage partly by counting the damage done in relation to the number of lives lived in the region, or the damage done for each 1000 square kilometres of a nation's territory, or the relative vulnerability of the environment to damage of certain kinds? For example, a small population occupying a large area that is not very vulnerable does not necessarily deserve high marks for inflicting less harm on the species and landscape. No doubt the settled regions of south-eastern Australia are one of the world's areas damaged the most in a short space of time. Admittedly, it was one of the more vulnerable areas, even before the First Fleet arrived. The Aboriginal record of damage was also high, when one considers their simple technology and the fact that so few new species were introduced in addition to human beings and dingoes.

I count democracy as one of the major credits on the national balance sheet. Australia was an early convert. By 1860, the overwhelming majority of Australia's population lived in democratic territory – Western Australia and most of the Aboriginal people were the exception. I guess I'm the originator of the statement, now creeping into wider usage, that Australia is one of the five or six oldest continuous democracies in the world, but I am only too aware that it is one of those statements that passes muster so long as it is not inspected too closely. After all, what is a democracy? What was called a democracy in the time of Disraeli or Bismarck might not be called one today. What proportion of adults must possess the right to vote if their land is to be called a democracy? If fifty per cent is required, then there was no democracy in the history of the world even as late as 1890.

Even when nearly all the adult men had the right to vote in the election of representatives to a lower house – and Australia had reached that stage by the 1860s – their ultimate power, and their legitimate title to the word democracy, was in effect limited by a variety of countervailing powers. The checks and limits included the monarchy and its colonial representative who was the governor. They included the power to conduct foreign policy (a power largely residing in Westminster), the courts, a restrictive upper house and uneven electorates. Even allowing for the variety of such checks which operated in virtually all European or colonial democracies as late as 1890, and even allowing for the different checks operating in the republic of the United States (including the fact of slavery), Australia is by any reasonable definition one of the oldest continuous democracies in the world. The word *continuous* is important because many European democracies were crushed by Hitler.

There is a valid case for arguing that Australia is the oldest continuous democracy in the world, for in 1903 it became the first national parliament to permit women both to vote and to stand for election. I did not hear in the bicentennial year of 1988 our national leaders refer even once to this long and remarkable democratic achievement of the country they were allegedly celebrating.

In Australia democracy is less in favour in intellectual circles today than thirty years ago. The more emphasis that is placed on the rights of minorities, and the need for affirmative action to enhance those rights, the more is the concept of democracy – and the rights of the majority – in danger of being weakened. Likewise, the High Court in recent years might be seen as a quiet challenger to democracy. At times it is beginning to see itself as a third and very powerful house in the federal system of government. The 1988 referendum, fortunately rejected, was a subtle attempt by the federal government to increase those powers.

Australia won democracy with relative ease in a series of blood-less steps. We tend to take it for granted and to think that it is an easy system to operate. It is not, however, so easily operated. In fact it depends partly on a society which emphasises individual responsibility as much as individual rights. We became a rights-mad society in the 1970s and 1980s, forgetting that there will never be enough rights to go around. A firm right granted to one person or group is often a loss of a right to another person or group. The Bill of Rights that nearly passed through the federal parliament in 1986 was a traffic jam of competing rights. It would be unwise, indeed complacent, to see democracy as a permanent victory for Australia.

Many Australians see the treatment of Aborigines, since 1788, as the blot on Australian history. Fifty years ago, fewer than 50,000 Australians probably saw this as the blot. Now maybe several million are convinced that it is the main blot and maybe half of the population, or even more, would see it as highly regrettable. Irrespective of whether deep shame or wide regret is the more appropriate response, this question will be here to vex or torment the nation for a long time to come.

My own view on this question is much influenced by my own particular interpretation of Australian history. My starting point you might disagree with, but I have held it for some twenty years, have often reconsidered it, and will hold on to it until contrary evidence arrives.

The meeting of the incoming British with the Aborigines, at a thousand different parts of Australia spread over more than a century, was possibly a unique confrontation in recorded history. No doubt a version of the episode happened somewhere else, hundreds of years earlier, on a smaller scale. But there is probably no other historical parallel of a confrontation so strange, so puzzling to both sides, and embracing such a huge area of the world's surface. If we accept this fact we begin to understand the magnitude of the problem that appeared in 1788, puzzled Governor Arthur Phillip, a man of good-will, and is still with us. It will probably remain with us for the foreseeable future, defying the variety of quick-fix formulas that sometimes attract the federal government, tempt the High Court, and tantalise thoughtful Aboriginal leaders.

In 1788, the world was becoming one world. Europe's sailing ships had entered nearly every navigable sea and strait on the globe, and the ships' crews were alert for anything that was tradable, and so they were sure to return to any place of promise. In 1788, the industrial revolution was also beginning. Here landed representatives of the nation which had just developed the steam engine, the most powerful machine the world had known, and also the semi-mechanised cotton mill. On the other hand Australia represented the way of life that almost certainly prevailed over the whole habitable globe some 10,000 years earlier. The Aborigines had no domesticated plants and animals and therefore a very different attitude to the land – this is part of the long painful background to the Mabo case. They had no pottery, they had implements of wood and bone and stone but none of metals, they had no paper and no writing, though they were skilled at a variety of other signs. They had no organisation embracing more than say 3000 people, and probably no organisation capable of putting more than 200 people into a battlefield at the one time. They had few, if any, permanent villages, and only a token ability to hoard food. They believed in a living, intervening god – here was a close resemblance – but not the God seen as the correct one. It was a society with many distinctive merits, often overlooked, but it was startlingly different to the one that supplanted it.

In 1788, Aboriginal Australia was a world almost as remote, as different as outer space. We now think of Aboriginal Australia as having a unity, but it had even less unity than Europe possesses today. There were countless economic and social differences, and an amazing variety of languages. Accordingly the idea, widely voiced now, that the incoming British could have – and should have – signed a treaty with *the* Aborigines, and so worked out rights and compensations, rests on a faith in the impossible. Any treaty would have been one-sided, with the Aborigines as losers.

Even if the First Fleet had brought out not the dross but the wisest and most humane women and men in England, and even if the Aborigines whom they met at Sydney Harbour were the wisest of all their people, how conceivably could a treaty have been signed – given the differences in language and understanding? And if a treaty were signed, how far inland and along the coast would it have extended? The north and south sides of Sydney Harbour, then as now, had different languages and tribal arrangements. (I do not use this argument, incidentally, to comment on the question of whether there should or should not be a treaty today.) There was a huge contrast between the two cultures, the incoming and the resident. Every Australian still inherits the difficult consequence of that contrast.

How can we fairly summarise this complex and delicate question: was the treatment of Aborigines an ineradicable stain on Australian history? There are many answers, each of them a part answer.

The Aborigines probably enjoyed a very high standard of living, so long as their population remained low. My belief – I have set it out elsewhere – is that they were a highly successful society in the economic sphere, and that the typical Aborigines in 1788 had a more varied and more secure diet than the typical Europeans. This kind of semi-nomadic society once existed everywhere in the inhabitable world, but in the years of the neolithic revolution it had vanished from every large landmass except Australia. A highly skilled system, it was extravagant – and we are too – in the use of space and land and resources. A huge area was needed to support few people. Such were the land needs that the whole globe in the time of the hunters and gatherers perhaps supported only one per cent of its present population.

Such a form of land use was bound to be overthrown or under-mined. The world's history has depended heavily on the eclipse of this old and wasteful economic way of life – wasteful in terms of human potential though not wasteful in terms, modern terms, of the whole range of living things. There is no way it could be preserved. The mir-acle is that it survived until 1788 and later. It was tragic for the gener-ation that had to lose it. Any idea that the Aboriginal way of life of 1788 could have been retained for centuries more is a daydream. It is strange that the Australian version of land rights almost tries to restore this archaic and untenable way of life.

After the British arrived, the treatment of Aborigines was often lamentable: the frequent contempt for their culture, sometimes the contempt for the colour of their skin, the removal of their freedoms and usually the breaking of their precious link with their tribal home-lands. And also the killing of them, in ones and tens and even occa-sionally in the hundred. In 150 years it may be that as many as 20,000 Aborigines were killed, predominantly by Europeans but sometimes by Aborigines enrolled as troopers.

After many attempts to help Aborigines, it came to be widely believed by about 1850 that nothing effective could be done to pre-serve or rescue them. So dramatically were their numbers declining that they were expected by learned opinion in Europe and the Americas to die out. Learned opinion was mistaken. Interestingly, this mistaken view was in part self-serving but it was the considered view of science at a time when science was being enthroned as king. Charles Darwin, the greatest biological scientist of his day, believed that the Aborigines were doomed. It is ironical that science, which transformed Australia and made it so productive, was so astray on a matter so vital to the Aborigines.

Oddly, the vilification of Aborigines by Europeans who lived in the nineteenth century is now almost matched by the vilification of those same Europeans at the hands of the present-day moralists, scholars, journalists and film-makers. Again and again we see and hear the mischievous statements that the Aborigines' numbers were drasti-cally reduced by slaughter. In fact, diseases were the great killer by a very large margin.

It is also timely to recall that the loss of life in traditional

Aboriginal society – whether through infanticide or through warfare and other kinds of violence – was probably on a large scale. There is a tendency today to treat traditional Aboriginal society as especially peace-loving, a view to which I do not at present subscribe, though the evidence is sparse. The Aborigines were and are human beings with the same capacity as Europeans to live in peace or to make war. At present there is a tendency, maybe a welcome tendency, not to look too closely at traditional Aboriginal society. Certainly it was grossly over-criticised in the past. At the same time, it is unwise and unfair if the temporary drawing of the blinds over that society is accompanied by crude propaganda directed at the equally vulnerable European society which pushed aside the Aborigines.

Even on recent issues the accounts of the treatment of Aborigines have little relation to fact. How often, for example, do we now hear it said that the Aborigines had no vote until 1967? Credit should be given for attempts to redress past wrongs.

It is not easy to draw rules for the handling of such explosive questions. We have to try, however, to be fair to both sides – the early Australians and the Europeans who arrived later. Understanding is needed on all sides, and neither I, nor anybody else, can claim an adequate understanding of such a complicated and unusual question. Nothing does less to promote discussion than the constant use of the word racist. It is often a correct word but it is also becoming the favourite word of the prejudiced, the ignorant and often the intellectually unscrupulous.

Anyone who tries to range over the last 200 years of Australia's history, surveying the successes and failures, and trying to understand the obstacles that stood in the way, cannot easily accept the gloomier summaries of that history. Some episodes in the past were regrettable, there were many flaws and failures, and yet on the whole it stands out as one of the world's success stories. It is ironical that many of the political and intellectual leaders of the last decade, one of the most complacent and disappointing decades in our history, are so eager to denounce earlier generations and discount their hard-won successes.

Many young Australians, irrespective of their background, are quietly proud to be Australian. We deprive them of their inheritance if we claim that they have inherited little to be proud of.

'I'm inviting these young idealists to get real'

Helen Garner

'The fate of *The First Stone*': Larry Adler Lecture, Sydney
Institute

8 AUGUST 1995

Helen Garner (1942–) was a high school teacher in Melbourne
until classroom discussions about sexuality and use of 'bad language' led to her controversial dismissal in 1972. Garner turned
to writing and five years later published her first novel – *Monkey
Grip*. Following this remarkably successful literary debut – the
book was a bestseller and was made into a film – Garner took up
full-time writing, producing novels, screenplays, reviews and
feature articles. In March 1995, her first extended foray into non-
fiction led to one of Australia's biggest cultural controversies. *The
First Stone,* which examined the politics of sex and power behind
a sexual harassment case at Melbourne University's Ormond
College, was described by some as 'an ideological assault on feminism' and praised by others as 'an important literary contribution'. The book provoked at times vicious public comment;
Garner gave her first detailed response to the critics in a speech at
the Sydney Institute.

*

Many years ago I came across a remark made by the poet A.D. Hope.
He said, 'With hostile critics of my work, I am always scrupulously
and cheerfully polite.' Professor Hope's subtle resolution came back to
me last March, when *The First Stone* finally appeared, and I had to
stand up and defend it ad nauseam. I hung on like mad to the poet's
tactic, and I'm happy to report that it's possible, in the face of the
most intense provocation, to keep your temper for as long as four
whole months. One of the things that enabled me to perform this feat

of self-control was the knowledge that I was to deliver the Larry Adler Lecture. I bit my lip and gnawed my fist and went on taking deep breaths and counting to ten – partly because I wonder if, when the chips are down, courtesy is all we have left; but mostly because I knew that, thanks to the invitation of the Sydney Institute, I would be able to stand up here tonight, to put forward calmly some thoughts about the way this book has been received, and to tell you some of the things I've learnt from the strange experience of publishing *The First Stone*.

Our culture at large is obsessed, at the moment, with matters of sex and power in the relations between women and men. Given this, and given the attempts by the women complainants to get access to the book in the courts before its publication, I shouldn't have been surprised by the *extent* of the response to the book. But what did astonish me, and still does, is the *nature* of the response – its primal quality. People in the grip of a primal response to the very existence of a book like this will read it – if they consent to read it at all – between the narrow blinkers of anger and fear.

I realise now, having had it forced on me by this experience, that there are as many versions of *The First Stone* as there are readers of it. And yet there *are* certain words and sentences on its pages, put there on purpose in a certain order by the hand of a certain person – namely, me. So I'd like to take the liberty, here, of briefly and firmly listing a few of the things I did *not* say.

I did *not* say that the two young women who brought allegations of assault against the Master of their college *ought* to have agreed to be interviewed by me. I was terribly frustrated that they wouldn't, and in the book I often expressed this frustration, but right up to the end of the book I continue to respect their right not to speak to me.

I did *not* say that women should 'go back to wearing ankle-length sacks'.

I did *not* say that the correct way to deal with sexual assault or harassment is to knee a man in the balls.

I did *not* say that women are responsible for the way men behave towards them.

And I most emphatically did *not* say that women who get raped are asking for it.

I know it's the fate of all writers to feel themselves misread. But it's dispiriting to learn what rotten readers a lot of journalists and academics and so-called prominent feminists are. I hoped I was writing in such a way as to invite people to lay down their guns for a moment and think again – and not only think, but *feel* again. Naively, perhaps, I wanted people to read in an alert way – alert to things between the lines, things that the law prevents me from saying outright.

The book is subtitled not 'an argument about sex and power', but 'some questions about sex and power'. There are more questions in it than there are answers. Because it declines – or is unable – to present itself as one big clonking armour-clad monolithic certainty, it's not the kind of book that it's easy to review briskly. Because it's a series of shifting speculations, with an open structure, it's hard to pull out single quotes without distorting it. What the book invites from a reader is openness – an answering spark.

But I found that many people, specially those who locate their sense of worth in holding on to an already worked-out political position, are not prepared to take the risk of reading like that. Perhaps they can't, any more. What is not made explicit, for readers like these, is simply not there. Being permanently primed for battle, they read like tanks. They roll right over the little conjunctions and juxtapositions that slither in the undergrowth of the text. It's a scorched-earth style of reading. It refuses to notice the side paths, the little emotional and psychological byroads that you can't get into unless you climb down from your juggernaut, and take off your helmet and your camouflage gear and your combat boots. It's a poor sort of reading that refuses the invitation to stop reading and lay down the page and turn the attention inwards. And it's always easier, or more comfortable, to misread something, to keep it at arm's length, than to respond to it openly.

Thus, several prominent feminists have used the word 'sentimental' to dismiss the scene in the book where the ex-Master's wife speaks, through inconsolable tears, of the devastation these events have brought to her and her family. Less doctrinaire critics have been able to recognise, in this scene, a terrible example of the human cost of political action which narrows its focus to the purely legal, and thus divorces thought from feeling.

Certain feminists, even – incredibly – some who teach in universities, have declared it correct line not to buy *The First Stone* or to read it at all. This position is apparently quite widespread, judging by countless reports that have reached me of bitter arguments around dinner tables, in women's reading groups and at bookshop cash registers. This sort of feminist, while refusing to sully her party credentials by reading the book, also knows, however, or has absorbed from the ether by some osmotic process, exactly what the book 'says', so she is able to pontificate freely on how I have 'betrayed the feminist cause', and 'set feminism back twenty years'. One woman, representing the student body of an institution in the town where I was born, wrote to let me know that, the minute she heard I was going to write the book, she had got rid of all my other books off her shelves. She rebuked me for having 'profiteered' off other people's misfortunes, and suggested in a challenging tone that I should donate my ill-gotten gains to a worthwhile feminist organisation. Here I permitted myself the luxury of a coarse laugh.

The question of money in this context is fascinating. The accusation of 'profiteering' is the last refuge of one's enemy. I've watched one so-called prominent feminist down in Melbourne step back and back, in her public pronouncements about the book, from engaging with what it's trying to say. Before I even wrote it, Dr Jenna Mead tried to block my attempts to research the story. Then, when it *was* published, it wasn't theoretical enough to be taken seriously: I didn't understand contemporary theories of feminism, and had failed to engage with these. Most recently she too has retreated on to the money turf: she writes, 'I have only one question about this book – why should Helen Garner be making any money out of our lives?' Another Melbournian – and only a tenure-hungry academic would utter such a perverse and idiotic opinion – stated confidently to a friend of mine, 'Of course, Helen's motivation was purely commercial.' Yet another one said, 'It's all right for *her* – *she* lives in Elizabeth Bay.'

No doubt this person imagined me wallowing about in a fabulous penthouse with harbour views and a big fat Merc throbbing downstairs in security parking. The reproach is densely packed with psychic content. If *The First Stone* had been a jargon-clogged pamphlet bristling with footnotes, if it had sold a comfortably obscure, say, 3000 copies over a couple of years, the response to it from feminism's grimmer tribes would have been much less poisonous. But among those who maintain a victim posture vis-à-vis the big world, where one can earn an honourable living by writing in a language that the person in the street can understand, nothing is more suspicious than a book which appears to have succeeded.

Crudely, there are two possible attitudes that a hostile feminist might take towards the annoying fact that a lot of people, including feminists of broader sympathy, have defied the girlcott and responded favourably to *The First Stone*. The first one is easy: Garner is a sell-out, a traitor to her sex. She's caved in to the patriarchy. This leaves the grim tribes feeling and looking – to each other, at least – squeaky clean.

The other alternative is to wonder whether something might have happened to feminism. Maybe something's gone wrong. Maybe something good and important has been hijacked. Maybe the public debate about women and men has been commandeered by a bullying orthodoxy.

I'm not here to bash feminism. How could I, after what it's meant to me? After what its force and truth have made possible? But I hate this disingenuousness, this determination to cling to victimhood at any cost, which seems to have become one of the loudest voices of feminism today.

Why do the members of this orthodoxy insist that our young women are victims? Why do they insist on focusing the debate on only one sort of power – the institutional?

Why do they refuse to acknowledge what experience teaches every girl and woman: that men's unacceptable behaviour towards us extends over a very broad spectrum – that to telescope this and label it all 'violence against women' is to distort both language and experience?

The hysteria that this book has provoked in some quarters reveals clearly and sadly that feminism, once so fresh and full of sparkle, is no different in its habits from any other political theory. Like all belief systems and religions and art forms – like any idea that has the misfortune to have an '-ism' tacked on to it – feminism has a tendency to calcify, to narrow and harden into fundamentalism. The life spark slips out of it and whisks away, leaving behind an empty con-crete bunker.

To disagree with a fundamentalist feminist, I've learnt, to question acts carried out in the name of women's rights, is not to challenge her, but to 'betray' her, to turn her into more of a victim than she was already.

Cassandra Pybus wrote a three-page review of *The First Stone*, which was published in the monthly *Australian Book Review*. Alongside her review was a four-page transcript of the Radio National program on which she expressed in her carpet-bombing style, to me and to the nation, her criticisms of the book and her belief that it should never have been written. Shortly after these seven pages of her views appeared, I got a call from the editor of the *Sydney Morning Herald*, a man I have never met and have never spoken to since. He asked me to write a piece for the *Herald* about the response to the book.

I told him I was saving it all up for this lecture, but I drew his attention to Pybus's long article in the *Australian Book Review*. Off he went to read it. Two days later, the *Sydney Morning Herald*, surely one of Australia's major newspapers, ran Pybus's attack on *The First Stone*, slightly edited, on its opinion page. Great – this was debate. A month passes – and lo and behold, Pybus is complaining now, in the letters pages of the *Australian Book Review*, that she has been denied, by me, what she calls her 'position from which to speak'.

Next we come to the question of the so-called stolen stories. Lucy Frost is a feminist academic in Victoria. In her criticisms of *The First Stone*, she invokes a cosy entity she calls 'the community of women who are feminists in Australia'. She puts forward the idea that in telling the Ormond story against the will of the young women involved, I had committed a treachery in the same league as the betrayal of the tribal secrets of the Hindmarsh Island Aboriginal women. The Ormond women, she wrote in the *Australian Book Review*, 'did not want their story told by Helen Garner, writer of fic-tion making a guest appearance as a journalist. She told their story anyway, has stolen the story that they did not want her to have.'

I find this a piece of the most breathtaking intellectual dishonesty. Firstly, it lends to the Ormond women's complaints a sacred hue, which with all the goodwill in the world I can't see they deserve. Secondly, in what sense *is* it 'their' story? It is distorting and deeply wrong to bestow on the Ormond complainants the ownership of this story. It could be truthfully called *their* story only if they had decided to keep it to themselves, to hold it to themselves as a private trauma. I don't suggest for a single second that they should have done this. And they didn't. They took their complaints to the police. And the police took them to the courts.

Now the law covering sexual assault may still be seriously skewed against women's interests: it plainly is, and I strongly support the correction of this; but a court in a democratic country like Australia is an open forum. Painful as this might be, *a court is open*. It is open to the scrutiny of the citizens *in whose names* justice is being aimed at. So, once the complaints reached the courts, the story ceased *of necessity* to belong to the young women, or to the college, or to the man against whom the allegations were made. It stopped being 'their' story, and it became 'our' story – a new chapter in the endless saga of how we, as a community, try to regulate the power struggle between women and men.

I want now to speak briefly about something called eros.

I used the word rather loosely, perhaps, in the book. You could define eros – if it would stay still long enough for you to get a grip on it – as something lofty and mythological like 'the gods' messenger', or 'the life spirit'. You could call it the need of things to keep changing and moving on. The Jungians call it 'the spark that ignites and connects'. Eros, most famously, comes bounding into the room when two people fall in love at first sight. But it's also in the excitement that flashes through you when a teacher explains an intellectual proposition *and you grasp it* – or when someone tells a joke *and you get it*.

Eros is the quick spirit that moves between people – *quick* as in the distinction between 'the quick and the dead'. It's the moving force that won't be subdued by habit or law. Its function is to keep cracking open what is becoming rigid and closed off. Eros explodes the forbidden. Great stand-up comics thrill us by trying to ride its surge. It's at the heart of every heresy – and remember that feminism itself is a heresy against a monolith. Eros mocks our fantasy that we can nail life down and control it. It's as far beyond our attempts to regulate it as sunshine is – or a cyclone.

But Vivienne Porzsolt, criticising *The First Stone* in the *Australian*, wants us to accept that 'the dynamics of eros', as she puts it, 'are historically produced'. 'We need,' she says, 'to reconstruct eros between men and women *on an equal basis*.'

There will always be these moments, I know, when people who think politically and types like me with a metaphysical bent end up staring at each other in helpless silence, with our mouths hanging open. Vivienne Porzsolt thinks I'm airyfairy and blithe and irresponsible. I think she's possessed by hubris.

The whole point of eros, its very usefulness as a concept, is that it's *not* reconstructable. Eros doesn't give a damn about morals or equality. Though eros moves through the intellect, eros is not intellectual. It moves through politics, but it's not political. It moves between men and women, but it's not in itself sexual. When I talk in the book about eros, I'm trying to talk about that very thing – the thing that's beyond us – the dancing force that we *can't* control or legislate or make fair.

It's an article of faith among some young feminists that a woman 'has the right' to go about the world dressed in any way she pleases. They think that for a man to respond to – and note, please, that I don't mean to threaten or touch or attack – for a man to respond to what he sees as a statement of her sexuality and of her own attitude to it, is some sort of outrage – and an outrage that the law should deal with. I find the talk of rights in this context quite peculiar. What right are you invoking here? You can only talk about rights, in this context, by pretending that it *means nothing at all* to wear, say, a low-necked dress in a bar at 2 a.m., or a pair of shorts that your bum's hanging out of on a public beach. To invoke rights, here, you have to fly in the face of the evidence of the senses. It's as if such feminists believed that each person moves round the world enclosed in a transparent bubble of rights.

And who's going to protect these notional rights? Which regime will provide a line of armed police to make sure that no bloke looks at a woman's breasts with the wrong expression on his face? I'm inviting these young idealists to get real – to grow up – better still, to *get conscious*. Know what you're doing, what its likely effect is, and decide whether that's what you want. Sexy clothes are part of the wonderful game of life. But to dress to display your body, and then to project all the sexuality of the situation on to men and blame them for it, just so you can continue to feel innocent and put-upon, is dishonest and irresponsible. Worse, it's a relinquishing of power. If a woman dresses to captivate, she'd better learn to keep her wits about her, for when the wrong fish swims into her net.

A woman of my age knows – and it's her responsibility to point this out to younger women – that the world is full of different sorts of men. Many are decent. Some are decent until they start drinking. Many have grown up enough to have learnt manners. Some have taken seriously *their* responsibility to get conscious. Many men like women, and want to be around them. Some men *hate* women, and want to be around them. Many have been taught by imagination, or by reason, or by painful or happy experience, that a woman is a person and not just a clump of sexual characteristics put there for him to plunder.

Some men have learnt to recognise and respect the boundary between their fantasy and what is real. Others, trapped in instinct, have not, and never will – and it's a sad fact that we can't depend on the law to *make* them. Nor will laws alone save us from their depredations, whether trivial or serious. Society makes laws. I am strongly in favour of tough legislation that will give women redress against assault – but around and above and below the laws, for good or ill, there is this fluid element, life. And what I'm proposing is that there's a large area for manoeuvre, for the practical exercise of women's individual power, before it's necessary or appropriate to call in the law.

In the book I describe a photograph. It's a black and white shot of a young woman dressed in an elegant and revealing gown. I wrote, 'It is impossible not to be moved by her daring beauty. She is a woman in the full glory of her youth, as joyful as a goddess, elated by her own careless authority and power.' In response to this page of the book there emerged a grotesque mutation of feminist thought. Cassandra Pybus, for whom perhaps all gods are vengeful, wrote that my admiring description of this lovely, rather wild young woman was in actual fact an invocation, in modern dress, of that monstrous, punitive, man-hating figure of myth, what Pybus calls 'vagina dentata in her full glory'.

Other feminists have told me that by 'sexualising' young women, I had 'disempowered' them. Leaving aside the hideousness of the language, you don't have to be Camille Paglia to see that this is sick, and mad.

There's been a lot of talk, triggered by the book, about symbolic mothers and daughters. Cassandra Pybus has a doom-laden approach to giving maternal advice. The young woman in the beautiful dress is not, she insists, in possession of any power whatsoever, potential or actual, and it is wicked of me to suggest that she might be. For Pybus, only one sort of power is admissible to a discussion of events like these, and that is *institutional* power. This splendid young woman, then, so clever and lovely and full of life, is nothing but a sad victim. These traumatic events, Pybus solemnly assures her, 'will blight her life'.

What sort of a mother, literal or symbolic, would insist to her daughter that an early experience in the rough adult world, no matter how painful or public, would blight the rest of her life? That is not good mothering. That is pathetic mothering. That is the kind of mothering that doubles the damage. A decent mother, when the dust has settled, would say to her daughter: 'Right. It's over. Now we can look at what's happened. Let's try to *analyse* what's happened. See how much of what's happened was other people's responsibility, and then try to see how much of it, if any, was yours. Take responsibility for your contribution, be it small or large. You are not responsible for men's behaviour towards you, but you *are* responsible for your own. Pick yourself up now. Wipe your tears. Spit out the bitterness and the blame before they poison you. You're young and clever and strong. Shake the dust of this off your feet. Learn from it, and then move on.'

If all I had to go on, as responses to *The First Stone*, were the critiques of these prominent feminists, I'd be feeling pretty sick by now. But I'll finish tonight with the good bit. I've had letters, hundreds and hundreds of long, frank letters from strangers. I estimate the male/female ratio of the letters at about thirty-five/sixty-five. I was surprised at how few of them were from cranks or nutcases. By no means did all of these letters – and they're still coming – express blanket approval of the book. But almost all of them were from people who had been prepared to respond to the book in the way I'd hoped: with the defences down – with an answering spark. They're prepared to lay out and re-examine examples, from their own lives, of encounters big and small with the opposite sex, which at the time had bewildered them, or hurt them, or made them angry. I lost count of the people who said, 'I'd like to tell you something that happened to me – of something that I did – many years ago; something that until I read the book I had forgotten – that I'd buried.'

Some of the letters were hilarious. You might recall an incident I relate in the book, about a masseur at a particular Fitzroy gym who kissed me when I was naked on the table. One woman wrote to me, 'I shrieked when I read about that masseur.' She said the same bloke had kissed *her*, and that furthermore *she'd* paid him too, so I wasn't to feel I was the only mug. A man wrote and suggested to me very disapprovingly that I must have led the masseur on. 'Why did you take your clothes off in the massage room,' he sternly asked, 'instead of in the change rooms? What you did was tantamount to striptease.' A masseur who could see as striptease a middle-aged woman scrambling hastily out of a sweaty old tracksuit in a corner gets my prize for sexualising against overwhelming odds.

Some letters, from both men and women, are full of pain, and anger, and shame. Others tell stories of the patient unravelling of interpersonal and institutional knots, and of happy resolutions.

But the word that crops up most frequently is *relief*. Again and again people speak of the relief they feel that it might be possible to acknowledge that the world of daily work and social life isn't as horrible and destructive and ghastly as punitive feminists insist. People are relieved that it might be possible to admit sympathy in human terms with people on the opposite side of a power divide. They're relieved that ambiguity might be readmitted to the analysis of thought and action. And especially they're relieved that to admit gradations of offence is not to let the side down or to let chaos come flooding in.

A lot of people have asked if I regret having written this book – and more particularly, if I regret the letter of ignorant sympathy that

I wrote to the Master when I first became aware of the case – the letter that got me into so much trouble, and caused so many doors to be slammed in my face. The answer is no, and no.

I accept that this book has caused pain. I know it's no comfort – that it's almost a cheek – for me to say that I regret this. But sometimes a set of events erupts that seems to encapsulate, in complex and important ways, the spirit of its time. These are the stories that need to be *told*, not swept away like so much debris, or hidden from sight. My attempt to understand this story was frustrated. My version of it is full of holes. But I hope that these holes might, after all, have a use; that through them might pass air and light; that they might even provide a path for the passage of eros; and that they might leave, for women and men who want to think generously about these things, room to move.

'I consider myself just an ordinary Australian'

Pauline Hanson

Maiden speech to the House of Representatives

10 September 1996

Most maiden speeches in federal parliament leave no trace. The maiden speech of the disendorsed Liberal member for the seat of Oxley, Pauline Hanson (1954–), is an arresting, perhaps unique, exception. Expressing a discontent about Asian immigration and welfare policies for Indigenous people, it launched Hanson on a heady career as an 'anti-politician' leading the One Nation Party which two years later gained nine per cent of the national vote. Hanson's own career, however, was short, and her influence was neutralised by a shift to the right in government policies which many believe stole much of her ground, by internal disputes within the One Nation Party, and by conviction for electoral fraud in 2003 – since quashed – after which Hanson spent almost three months in jail.

*

Mr Acting Speaker, in making my first speech in this place, I congratulate you on your election and wish to say how proud I am to be here as the independent member for Oxley. I come here not as a polished politician but as a woman who has had her fair share of life's knocks.

My view on issues is based on commonsense, and my experience as a mother of four children, as a sole parent and as a businesswoman running a fish and chip shop. I won the seat of Oxley largely on an issue that has resulted in me being called a racist. That issue related to my comment that Aboriginals received more benefits than non-Aboriginals.

We now have a situation where a type of reverse racism is applied to mainstream Australians by those who promote political correctness and those who control the various taxpayer funded 'industries' that flourish in our society servicing Aboriginals, multiculturalists and a host of other minority groups. In response to my call for equality for all Australians, the most noisy criticism came from the fat cats, bureaucrats and the do-gooders. They screamed the loudest because they stand to lose the most – their power, money and position, all funded by ordinary Australian taxpayers.

Present governments are encouraging separatism in Australia by providing opportunities, land, moneys and facilities available only to Aboriginals. Along with millions of Australians, I am fed up to the back teeth with the inequalities that are being promoted by the government and paid for by the taxpayer under the assumption that Aboriginals are the most disadvantaged people in Australia. I do not believe that the colour of one's skin determines whether you are disadvantaged. As Paul Hasluck said in parliament in October 1955 when he was Minister for Territories:

The distinction I make is this. A social problem is one that concerns the way in which people live together in one society.

A racial problem is a problem which confronts two different races who live in two separate societies, even if those societies are side by side. We do not want a society in Australia in which one group enjoy one set of privileges and another group enjoy another set of privileges.

Hasluck's vision was of a single society in which racial emphases were rejected and social issues addressed. I totally agree with him, and so would the majority of Australians.

But, remember, when he gave his speech he was talking about the privileges that white Australians were seen to be enjoying over Aboriginals. Today, forty-one years later, I talk about the exact opposite – the privileges Aboriginals enjoy over other Australians. I have done research on benefits available only to Aboriginals and challenge anyone to tell me how Aboriginals are disadvantaged when they can obtain three per cent and five per cent housing loans denied to non-Aboriginals.

This nation is being divided into black and white, and the present system encourages this. I am fed up with being told, 'This is our land.' Well, where the hell do I go? I was born here, and so were my parents and children. I will work beside anyone and they will be my equal but I draw the line when told I must pay and continue paying for something that happened over 200 years ago. Like most Australians, I worked for my land; no one gave it to me.

Apart from the $40 million spent so far since Mabo on native title claims, the government has made available $1 billion for Aboriginals and Torres Strait Islanders as compensation for land they cannot claim under native title. Bear in mind that the $40 million spent so far in native title has gone into the pockets of grateful lawyers and consultants. Not one native title has been granted as I speak.

The majority of Aboriginals do not want handouts because they realise that welfare is killing them. This quote says it all: 'If you give a man a fish you feed him for a day. If you teach him how to fish you feed him for a lifetime.'

Those who feed off the Aboriginal industry do not want to see things changed. Look at the Council for Aboriginal Reconciliation. Members receive a $290-a-day sitting allowance and a $320-a-day travelling allowance, and most of these people also hold other very well-paid positions. No wonder they did not want to resign recently!

Reconciliation is everyone recognising and treating each other as equals, and everyone must be responsible for their own actions. This is why I am calling for ATSIC to be abolished. It is a failed, hypocritical and discriminatory organisation that has failed dismally the people it was meant to serve. It will take more than Senator Herron's surgical skills to correct the terminal mess it is in. Anyone with a criminal record can, and does, hold a position with ATSIC. I cannot hold my position as a politician if I have a criminal record – once again, two sets of rules.

If politicians continue to promote separatism in Australia, they should not continue to hold their seats in this parliament. They are not truly representing all Australians, and I call on the people to throw them out. To survive in peace and harmony, united and strong, we must have one people, one nation, one flag.

The greatest cause of family breakdown is unemployment. This country of ours has the richest mineral deposits in the world and vast rich lands for agriculture and is surrounded by oceans that provide a wealth of seafood, and yet we are $190 billion in debt with an interest bill that is strangling us.

Youth unemployment between the ages of fifteen to twenty-four runs at twenty-five per cent and is even higher in my electorate of Oxley. Statistics, by cooking the books, say that Australia's unemployment is at 8.6 per cent, or just under one million people. If we disregard that one hour's work a week classifies a person as employed, then the figure is really between 1.5 million and 1.9 million unemployed. This is a crisis that recent governments have ignored because of a lack of will. We are regarded as a Third World country with First World living conditions. We have one of the highest interest rates in the world, and we owe more money per capita than any other country. All we need is a nail hole in the bottom of the boat and we're sunk.

In real dollar terms, our standard of living has dropped over the past ten years. In the 1960s, our wages increase ran at three per cent and unemployment at two per cent. Today, not only is there no wage increase, we have gone backwards and unemployment is officially 8.6 per cent. The real figure must be close to twelve to thirteen per cent.

I wish to comment briefly on some social and legal problems encountered by many of my constituents – problems not restricted to just my electorate of Oxley. I refer to the social and family upheaval created by the *Family Law Act* and the ramifications of that Act embodied in the child support scheme. The *Family Law Act*, which was the child of the disgraceful Senator Lionel Murphy, should be repealed. It has brought death, misery and heartache to countless thousands of Australians. Children are treated like pawns in some crazy game of chess.

The child support scheme has become unworkable, very unfair and one sided. Custodial parents can often profit handsomely at the expense of a parent paying child support, and in many cases the non-custodial parent simply gives up employment to escape the, in many cases, heavy and punitive financial demands. Governments must give to all those who have hit life's hurdles the chance to rebuild and have a future.

We have lost all our big Australian industries and icons, including Qantas when it sold twenty-five per cent of its shares and a controlling interest to British Airways. Now this government wants to sell Telstra, a company that made a $1.2 billion profit last year and will make a $2 billion profit this year. But, first, they want to sack 54,000 employees to show better profits and share prices. Anyone with business sense knows that you do not sell off your assets especially when they are making money. I may only be 'a fish and chip shop lady', but some of these economists need to get their heads out of the textbooks and get a job in the real world. I would not even let one of them handle my grocery shopping.

Immigration and multiculturalism are issues that this government is trying to address, but for far too long ordinary Australians have been kept out of any debate by the major parties. I and most Australians want our immigration policy radically reviewed and that of multiculturalism abolished. I believe we are in danger of being swamped by Asians. Between 1984 and 1995, forty per cent of all migrants coming into this country were of Asian origin. They have their own culture and religion, form ghettos and do not assimilate. Of course, I will be called racist but, if I can invite whom I want into my home, then I should have the right to have a say in who comes into my country. A truly multicultural country can never be strong or united. The world is full of failed and tragic examples, ranging from Ireland to Bosnia to Africa and, closer to home, Papua New Guinea. America and Great Britain are currently paying the price.

Arthur Calwell was a great Australian and Labor leader, and it is a pity that there are not men of his stature sitting on the Opposition benches today. Arthur Calwell said:

> Japan, India, Burma, Ceylon and every new African nation are fiercely anti-white and anti-one another. Do we want or need any of these people here? I am one red-blooded Australian who says no and who speaks for ninety per cent of Australians.

I have no hesitation in echoing the words of Arthur Calwell.

There is light at the end of the tunnel and there are solutions. If this government wants to be fair dinkum, then it must stop kowtowing to financial markets, international organisations, world bankers, investment companies and big business people. The Howard government must become visionary and be prepared to act, even at the risk of making mistakes.

In this financial year we will be spending at least $1.5 billion on foreign aid and we cannot be sure that this money will be properly spent, as corruption and mismanagement in many of the recipient countries are legend. Australia must review its membership and funding of the UN, as it is a little like ATSIC on a grander scale, with huge tax-free American dollar salaries, duty-free luxury cars and diplomatic status.

The World Health Organisation has a lot of its medical experts sitting in Geneva while hospitals in Africa have no drugs and desperate patients are forced to seek medication on the black market. I am going to find out how many treaties we have signed with the UN, have them exposed and then call for their repudiation. The government should cease all foreign aid immediately and apply the savings to generate employment here at home.

Abolishing the policy of multiculturalism will save billions of dollars and allow those from ethnic backgrounds to join mainstream Australia, paving the way to a strong, united country. Immigration must be halted in the short-term so that our dole queues are not added to by, in many cases, unskilled migrants not fluent in the English language. This would be one positive step to rescue many young and older Australians from a predicament which has become a national disgrace and crisis. I must stress at this stage that I do not consider those people from ethnic backgrounds currently living in Australia anything but first-class citizens, provided of course that they give this country their full, undivided loyalty.

The government must be imaginative enough to become involved, in the short-term at least, in job-creating projects that will help establish the foundation for a resurgence of national development and enterprise. Such schemes would be the building of the Alice Springs to Darwin railway line, new roads and ports, water conservation, reafforestation and other sensible and practical environmental projects.

Therefore I call for the introduction of national service for a period of twelve months, compulsory for males and females upon finishing year twelve or reaching eighteen years of age. This could be a civil service with a touch of military training, because I do not feel we can go on living in a dream world forever and a day believing that war will never touch our lives again.

The government must do all it can to help reduce the interest rates for business. How can we compete with Japan, Germany and Singapore, who enjoy rates of 2 per cent, 5.5 per cent and 3.5 per cent respectively? Reduced tariffs on foreign goods that compete with local products seem only to cost Australians their jobs. We must look after our own before lining the pockets of overseas countries and investors at the expense of our living standards and future.

Mr Acting Speaker, time is running out. We may have only ten to fifteen years left to turn things around. Because of our resources and our position in the world, we will not have a say because neighbouring countries such as Japan, with 125 million people; China, with 1.2 billion people; India, with 846 million people; Indonesia, with 178 million people; and Malaysia, with 20 million people are well aware of our resources and potential. Wake up, Australia, before it is too late. Australians need and want leaders who can inspire and give hope in difficult times. Now is the time for the Howard government to accept the challenge.

Mr Acting Speaker, everything I have said is relevant to my electorate at Oxley, which is typical of mainstream Australia. I do have concerns for my country and I am going to do my best to speak my mind and stand up for what I believe in. As an independent I am confident that I can look after the needs of the people of Oxley and I will always be guided by their advice. It is refreshing to be able to express my views without having to toe a party line. It has got me into trouble on the odd occasion, but I am not going to stop saying what I think. I consider myself just an ordinary Australian who wants to keep this great country strong and independent, and my greatest desire is to see all Australians treat each other as equals as we travel together towards the new century.

I will fight hard to keep my seat in this place, but that will depend on the people who sent me here. Mr Acting Speaker, I thank you for your attention and trust that you will not think me presumptuous if I dedicate this speech to the people of Oxley and those Australians who have supported me. I salute them all.

'I felt a terrible sense of personal responsibility for Ronald Ryan's death'

Barry Jones

Speech at the launch of *The Hanged Man*, Grand Ballroom, Windsor Hotel, Melbourne

12 FEBRUARY 2002

On the morning that Ronald Ryan (1925–1967) was hanged at Melbourne's Pentridge Prison on 3 February 1967 many of the city's trams and cars pulled to a halt in the streets and the church bells across the city pealed in unison. His execution by the state would be the last in Australia. None who were opposed to it could counter the singular determination of Liberal premier Sir Henry Bolte that the execution be carried out. Many of those associated with the hanging – including Justice John Starke, defence counsel Philip Opas, Father John Brosnan and Pentridge governor Ian Grindlay – would suffer grievously for their involvement.

The secretary of the Victorian Anti-Hanging Council from 1962 to 1975 was history teacher and ALP member, Barry Jones (1932–). At the time of Ryan's execution, when he was otherwise known to the public as the remarkable champion of television's quiz show 'Pick a Box', Jones went to extraordinary lengths in his efforts to win a reprieve for Ryan. An unsuccessful appeal to the Privy Council in London, and the ultimate failure of the Anti-Hanging Council's efforts in the case left Jones deeply affected.

The following speech, at the launch of Mike Richards' biography, *The Hanged Man*, was the first time Jones had spoken in public about the Ryan hanging since the execution. Although ultimately successful in having the death penalty abolished – in 1975 – Jones' speech demonstrates the depth of feeling that the case aroused and the personal cost of its outcome. He had by this time led a long political career, most prominently as minister for science in the Hawke government and as national president of the ALP in 1992, but no issue in that career had taken such a toll.

*

Of all the causes I have been involved in, the abolition of the death penalty has been the one with the longest commitment and the deepest feeling. I was passionately opposed to hanging from the age of six, and I remember reading of two executions in Victoria in 1939 as if it was yesterday.

The hanging of Ronald Ryan, thirty-five years ago this month, left a scar in my mind which will never heal. He was the 186th person to hang in Victoria and the last in Australia.

As Secretary of the Victorian Anti-Hanging Committee from 1962 until the death penalty was abolished in 1975, I took great personal satisfaction in having helped to secure the reprieve of Robert Tait.

But I felt a terrible sense of personal responsibility for Ronald Ryan's death. If I had only worked harder, networked more effectively, thought more strategically, would the outcome have been different?

I think there is much to be said for the 'Tait substitute' theory.

If Tait had hanged in 1962 and Henry Bolte had not suffered such a humiliation due to a forced reprieve after what was really an appalling crime, his manic determination to hang someone would have been satiated and Ryan would not have been chosen.

I doubt if Ryan had an intention to kill but I am certain that Bolte did.

On the morning of Ryan's hanging, I could not bring myself to go out to the vigil outside Pentridge but stood with another crowd standing in silent protest under the clocks at Flinders Street Station.

After the deed was done I went home and lay on the bed all day, just staring at the ceiling. I could hardly bear to imagine the feelings of Ryan's mother, his wife, his children, his lawyers Phil Opas and Ralph Freadman, Father John Brosnan, the witnesses and participants at the execution, let alone Ryan himself.

I was traumatised and it took some weeks to recover fully. I remain deeply grateful for all the loving support I had at that time.

I was a member of the Victorian parliament in 1975 when Dick Hamer introduced the Crimes (Capital Offences) Bill providing for the abolition of hanging, and persuaded his party to allow a free vote on the issue. I thought that my Second Reading Speech, on 19 March 1975, was probably the most passionately argued of my whole political career and it had a role in converting some Liberals, Lindsay Thompson among them. Helping to end hanging gave me a greater sense of satisfaction than anything else I was ever involved in.

I felt such acute sensitivity about the Ryan hanging that until today I have never spoken about it in public, and I have refused all interviews on the subject. When I spoke at length in the Victorian parliament, I mentioned Ryan's name only twice, just in passing.

The Milanese economist Cesare Beccaria (1738–1794), writing in the eighteenth century, argued for the abolition of the death penalty with a classic simplicity – that there is no demonstrable correlation between the severity of punishment and the crime rate: all punishment deters but there is no statistical evidence that execution, or torture, deters uniquely. The aims of punishment, he insisted, are reformation and deterrence, and certainty of apprehension and conviction are the major determinants of the crime rate. The appropriate penalty is the lowest penalty consistent with public safety.

Beccaria was very much opposed to the power of pardon – which indicated a deficiency in the law. 'Clemency,' he wrote, 'ought to shine in the code and not in private judgement.' He insisted, 'If I can prove that the death penalty is neither necessary nor useful, I shall have achieved the triumph of mankind.'

Leo Tolstoy once saw an execution in France and it haunted him all his life:

> I witnessed many atrocities in the war and in the Caucasus, but I should have been less sickened to see a man torn to pieces before my eyes than I was by this perfected, elegant machine by means of which a strong, clean, healthy man was killed in an instant. In the first case, there is no reasoning will, but a paroxysm of human passion; in the second, coolness to the point of refinement, homicide-with-comfort, nothing big.
>
> When I saw the head part from the body and each of them fall separately into a box with a thud, I understood – not in my mind, but with my whole being – that no rational doctrine of progress could justify that act, and that if every man now living in the world and every man who had lived since the beginning of time were to maintain, in the name of some theory or other, that this execution was indispensable, I should still know that it was not indispensable, that it was wrong.

I told the House, 'This is not really a debate about hanging,' because in 1975 nobody in the parliament believed there would ever be another execution in Australia. It was really a debate which gave MPs:

> ... an opportunity to declare, not on party lines, just what manner of men and women we are.
>
> The free vote will enable us to say, 'Here I stand: I can do no other.' This free vote will enable me to cast my vote for abolition, but only incidentally for abolition. Essentially I cast it against darkness, against obscurantism, against instinct, against pessimism about society and about man's capacity for moral regeneration.

I congratulate Mike Richards on a wonderful book. It is a very rare case of a Ph.D thesis converted into something written with passion and precision. We have waited for it a long time – but it is worth the wait.

The story is a parable about power and its misuse, differing concepts of justice and confusion between justice and retribution.

Forgive if I leave the last word not with Mike Richards, but with Pascal, number 200 of the *Pensées*, where he reflects on the fragility of human existence, and insists that morality is inextricably linked with thinking:

> Man is but a reed, the feeblest in nature, but he is a thinking reed. There is no need for the whole universe to take up arms to crush him. A vapour or a drop of water is enough to kill him. But even if the universe were to crush him, man would still be nobler than his killer, for he knows that he is dying and that the universe has the advantage over him. The universe knows nothing of this.
>
> Thus all our dignity consists in thought. It is on thought that we must depend for our recovery, not on space or time, which we could never fill. Let us then strive to think well; that is the basic principle of morality.

'The question is: are we up to it?'

Hugh Mackay

'The three hurdles republicans face': speech at NSW Parliament House

4 JULY 2003

Australia has a history of republican sentiments dating back to the nineteenth century, although their emphases have varied. Opposition to tyranny rather than monarchy was the focus of earlier movements, while colonial republicanism was often used as a bluff to gain demands from the British government. In recent years republicanism has focused on a single aim; to have an Australian elected head of state. The Australian Republican Movement (ARM) was formed in 1991, emerging out of a commitment from the Labor government for a republic by 1 January 2001. A constitutional convention held in 1998 determined that an Australian head of state should be elected by a joint sitting of parliament, and this model was put to the public in a 1999 national referendum. The proposal was narrowly defeated and the Queen remained as Australia's head of state. Since the referendum defeat, the ARM has continued promoting its cause while evaluating the reasons behind the public's decision. Hugh Mackay (1938–), a prominent social researcher, psychologist and writer, has been an outspoken advocate for constitutional change. Described 'as a conduit for public opinion', Mackay's concerns about political disengagement and a lack of vision and inspiration in 'explaining us to ourselves' are the themes of his speech for the ARM.

*

It would be very easy to become pessimistic about the republican movement. We lost the 1999 referendum and we have been off the community's radar ever since.

Even the recent fracas over the resignation of Peter Hollingworth didn't really help our cause. When the dust had settled, the Prime Minister was able to say, with some plausibility, 'See how smoothly the system works!'

There are three big hurdles that seem to stand in our way, and they are easy to identify. But although I want to acknowledge them and describe them, my main message is that we face, right now, a golden opportunity to tap into a yearning in this community that is not yet recognised as a 'republican yearning', but easily could be.

First, the hurdles.

1 John Howard

As long as we have a staunch monarchist as prime minister, Australia won't become a republic. It's as simple as that.

Since federation, no referendum has ever been passed without the wholehearted endorsement of the prime minister of the day. So it doesn't matter what republicans say or do, and it doesn't matter what the Labor Party says or does on this issue: the Prime Minister is a huge roadblock.

Of course, we don't have this problem on our own. He is also a roadblock in the path of Aboriginal reconciliation. He is a roadblock in the path of those who are hoping for a more just, equitable and humane society.

John Howard won't be prime minister forever. When he goes, there is likely to be a sudden and dramatic change in our national mood. At present, his very high popularity is actually quite fragile, because it depends on a paradox: he must both keep us scared and make us feel safe. But the price he pays for maintaining this balancing act is that we know he is diminishing us; he is bringing out the worst in us; he is reinforcing our fears and prejudices; he is narrowing our focus.

But he's there, he's a hurdle, and the problem for us is compounded by his determination to run a presidential-style prime ministership (thus blurring the distinction between head of government and head of state).

2 A disengaged electorate
Australians have been destabilised by too much change, and by a growing sense of uncertainty and threat. In the past twenty-five years, we have lived through too many revolutions at once – the gender revolution, the economic revolution, the IT revolution and even a revolution in our sense of what it means to be an Australian.

Worn out by the rate of social change and by the demands of too many issues and challenges, we have shifted our gaze from the big picture to the miniatures of our personal lives and our local circumstances.

We can't get enough TV programs about backyards, cooking and interior decorating.

We're obsessed with 'the village', even calling high-rise apartment blocks 'vertical villages'.

The soundtrack of our lives is not the national anthem, but the hiss of the ubiquitous espresso machine.

Our focus has turned relentlessly inward as an antidote to our anxiety. We are cocooning ourselves in self-indulgence. (Even in the case of Iraq, we have already moved on: we don't want to know about the aftermath of our invasion.)

Too much change! Too many issues! Too many challenges! No wonder the message coming from the community is 'Give us a break … leave us alone.' This is not good news for the republican movement.

3 *The wrong language*

As committed republicans, we keep using two words that the community-at-large doesn't like: 'republic' and 'president'. Many Australians find these words rather spooky: they have frightening associations with assorted 'banana republics' and tin-pot dictator-ships. Some of us have come here from republics and presidents we didn't like, and all of us can quote nasty examples of republics in South America, Africa or Central and Eastern Europe.

Certainly, we don't mind Ireland, France or even the USA (though we don't like the association of the US presidency with so much power and money).

What we do feel comfortable with is a word we know and trust: Commonwealth.

But let's not dwell on these difficulties or on the details of why we might have failed in the past. The practicalities – even the language – are easy to sort out.

Let's look at the big opportunity that is staring us in the face, and consider whether we have the courage to seize it.

The golden opportunity

In the last election of the twentieth century – a time when we were yearning for a new sense of ourselves as a nation bursting with poten-tial and brimful of millennial confidence – what did we get? A goods and services tax.

In the first federal election of the new century, what did we get? Flagrant manipulation of our fears and insecurities – via the *Tampa* episode – and an almost hysterical obsession with border protection.

Both of these election themes were a huge disappointment to those Australians who were hoping for something more visionary and inspirational. And yet, in a way, those two elections were symbolic of a significant culture shift. The GST was the last gasp of the economic era, and *Tampa* was a potent symbol of the dawning of the security era.

The question for the republican movement is this: are we going to shrug our shoulders, accept that Australians are only really interested in security, and simply wait for a more propitious time – for some distant turning of the tide in our favour? It's true that when John Howard goes, a republican will replace him (from either side of politics), and the republic will gradually drift back onto the political agenda. Are we simply going to wait for that to happen, or are we going to seize the agenda and promote our cause in a bold and more engaging way?

There's not much point in wringing our hands about John Howard. He won't go away in a hurry, so there won't be a winnable referendum coming our way for the foreseeable future.

And endless suggestions for alternative methods of appointment of a head of state are unlikely to capture the public imagination when the electorate is in its present mood. Too many republicans have fallen for the 'magic model' trap – as if we only have to crack the formula (public nominations/parliamentary election; parliamentary nomination/popular election; electoral college; advisory council; etc.) ... all we have to do is find the right model and this will strike such a responsive chord that the citizens will rise up and say, that's it! Let's do it! (I don't think so.)

Abandoning the words 'republic' and 'president' would help, but there will be no inherent magic in whatever words we might choose to replace them.

The real opportunity is for us to fill the vacuum where debate about the very character of this precious Commonwealth should be.

What we're lacking – and neither side of federal politics is going to give it to us any time soon – is a guiding story: a presentation of coherent ideals, values, beliefs that define where we've come from, where we are now and where we are going. Imaginatively couched, such a presentation could give us a framework for making sense of our national life and it could encourage us to take bolder, more confident and more independent steps towards our future. We need the present to be clearly set within the sweep of our history, so that we can see the inexorable process of national independence unfolding.

But we need much more than that. Someone needs to be telling us our own story – explaining us to ourselves – interpreting that history – enabling us to weave some meaning and purpose into our lives as citizens.

Listen to how the American social analyst, Walter Truett Anderson, explained the popularity of Adolf Hitler in pre-war Germany:

> He made his mark on the world, not as a political theorist, certainly not as a military tactician, but as a dramatist. He was a story-maker.

Other story-makers were in business in Germany at the time: Freudians, existentialists, theologians, scientists and ideologues of all kinds were offering their own versions of what was happening. Hitler outdid them all – at least for a while – because he was able to place the German people in an awesome story that thundered through their blood and bones.

And so did Winston Churchill for the British. And so did Franklin D. Roosevelt for the Americans – and so, to a lesser extent, did John F. Kennedy. Gough Whitlam did it for Australians in the 1970s.

Inspirational story-telling – explaining us to ourselves – is not enough, of course. We will always need workmanlike politicians, managers, bureaucrats, business and professional people and others to do the hard work of policy development and implementation. But we are in urgent need of leaders – or even one leader – who can tell us the story of who we are, where we are going, how to get there and why the journey should be undertaken at all.

The ARM's challenge is not to perfect some model; not to lay out a timetable for a series of referenda. It is to inspire Australians with a new sense of pride in themselves as the citizens of an increasingly independent nation. It is to start painting the big picture – beyond politics. It is to restore our confidence and optimism, to enlarge our vision, and to nurture our faith in this unique and wonderful Commonwealth.

The voice of republicanism will be heard when we recognise it as a voice that is talking about us – a voice with the power not to cajole or plead or persuade, but to encourage and inspire.

The question is: are we up to it?

INDIGENOUS AFFAIRS

'Reflect. You have seized upon a land that is not yours'

Robert Lyon

Speech at a public meeting, Guildford

JUNE 1833

Confident, sophisticated and a highly educated scholar, Robert Lyon was one of the most prominent humanitarians of the 1830s. Lyon arrived in Western Australia in 1829 as an English settler, but did not put down roots. Instead, he travelled extensively around the colony, becoming increasingly moved by the plight of the Indigenous people. Like other humanitarians, Lyon studied the language and customs of local clans, and came to believe that they were 'harmless, liberal and kind-hearted', and in numerous ways superior to Europeans. He believed the vilification of Indigenous Australians was a means of justifying colonial invasion of their land.

An outsider among the settlers, Lyon made public his views, writing books and letters and speaking at meetings. 'Are your hearts made of adamant?' he asked colonists. Mostly they were. Lyon returned to England for several years to take an appointment as professor of Greek and English at Royal College, returning permanently to New South Wales in 1839. His speech at Guildford at a meeting of 'magistrates, gentlemen and yeomen' is described by historian Henry Reynolds as 'inflated, rhetorical and strangely archaic in manner', but also 'one of the most distinguished humanitarian speeches delivered in colonial Australia.'

*

But if ye have taken their country from them, and they refuse to acknowledge your title to it, ye are at war with them; and, having never allowed your right to call them British subjects, they are justified by the usages of war in taking your property wherever they find it, and in killing you whenever they have an opportunity. Ye are the aggressors. The law of nations will bear them out in repelling force by force. They did not go to the British isles to make war upon you; but ye came from the British isles to make war upon them. Ye are the invaders of their country – ye destroy the natural productions of the soil on which they live – ye devour their fish and their game – and ye drive them from the abodes of their ancestors ...

Think not, then, that the Aboriginal inhabitants of Australia, offspring of the same great parent with yourselves, and partakers of all the kindred feelings of a common humanity, can resign the mountains and seas, the rivers and lakes, the plains and the wilds of their uncradled infancy, and the habitation of their fathers for generations immemorial, to a foreign foe, without the bitterness of grief. What, though the grass be their couch and the tree of the forest their only shelter, their blue mountains and the country where they first beheld the sun, the moon and the starry heavens are as dear to them as your native land with all its natural and artificial beauties, its gilded towers and magnificent spires, is to you ...

But what shall we say to the barbarous practice of firing upon them wherever they are seen – a practice unconfined to the lower orders, and common to some from whom better things might be expected! Apart from the fiend-like wickedness of thus wantonly destroying human life, what will such a course of proceeding profit you in the end? They have tendered their services to you as hewers of wood and drawers of water; could the most despotic conqueror – the most iron-hearted tyrant – require more? The very powder and ball ye expend in shooting them would *purchase* their lands ...

They may stand to be slaughtered; but they must not throw a

spear in their own defence, or attempt to bring their enemies to a sense of justice by the only means in their power – that of returning like for like. If they do – if they dare to be guilty of an act which in other nations would be eulogised as the noblest of a patriot's deeds – they are outlawed; a reward is set upon their heads; and they are ordered to be shot, as if they were so many mad dogs! Thus, in the barbarous manner, ye practise what in them ye condemn, the law of retaliation ....

Remember, too, that ye have never attempted to make peace with them. Every cessation of arms has only been a tacit truce – a calm that preceded a storm. And while ye act upon a wavering uncertain policy, the war will assume a more sanguinary character on every recurrence of hostilities, till it becomes interminable, and, staining your title deeds with blood, involves the destruction of one of the most interesting races of Aboriginal inhabitants now to be found on the face of the globe.

There are still two courses open for you to pursue – either a decidedly pacific one, or a decidedly hostile. To the adoption of the former, I know of no obstacle that may not yet be easily surmounted. They have all along shown themselves ready to be reconciled, desirous to live in peace and amity with you, and even willing to be taught your manners, laws and polity. It remains for you to consider the consequences of adopting hostile measures. A bad name to the colony, a stop to emigration and a depreciated property are but minor evils. An exterminating war, the flames of which, spreading with increasing fury among the surrounding tribes as the settlement extends itself, must be the consequence. An exterminating war over a continent as large as Europe, and abounding with tribes unknown and innumerable! The very thought is appalling ...

Taking advantage of your distance from the mother country, ye may flatter yourselves with the idea that it is possible either to commit the infamous deed of extermination clandestinely, or that ye can persuade the world that ye were not the aggressors. Vain thought! ... The fate of Cain will be yours. Ye may enjoy the blood-stained spoils of an innocent, unoffending people; but ye cannot bury the crime ye perpetrate in the graves of your victims, nor escape the eyes of Him who has drawn the lines of demarcation around the inheritance of every nation. Your fallen countenances will betray you. The voice of your brother's blood will cry from the ground where it is shed. The land of your fathers will abhor you; and the page of history will brand you to the latest posterity with the guilt of the unparalleled deed.

Choose for yourselves. If ye determine upon a war of extermination, civilised nations will be mute with astonishment at the madness of a policy so uncalled for, so demoniacal … When your doom is passed, your own children, for whose sakes ye have invaded the country, will join with the disinherited offspring of those ye have slain to pour a flood of curses on your memory.

If ye have any feelings of compunction, before the die be cast, let the Aboriginal inhabitants of Australia live. Ye have taken from them all they had on earth. Be content with this, and do not add to the crime of plundering them that of taking their lives. Let them live that they may be put in possession of a title to a better country – a country where the invading foe dare not enter.

'I do not select individual delinquents, but impeach the nation'

Reverend John Saunders

'Claims of the Aborigines': sermon at the Baptist Chapel, Sydney

14 OCTOBER 1838

Originally trained as a solicitor, John Saunders (1806–1859) was considering missionary service in India when he received an invitation from the Baptist Missionary Society to leave his home city of London and take up a vacancy for a Baptist pastor in Sydney. He arrived in 1834 and ministered in the Bathurst Street chapel for thirteen years. Known as 'the Apostle of Temperance' for his opposition to rum traffic, and equally vehement in his opposition to transportation, Saunders crusaded tirelessly for his causes.

Among them was his concern for the treatment of Indigenous Australians. In a celebrated sermon before his congregation, Saunders used verse 21 from chapter 26 of the Prophecy of Isaiah – 'Behold the Lord cometh out of his place to punish the inhabitants of the earth for their iniquity: the earth also shall disclose her blood, and shall no more cover her slain' – to expound the dangers of divine retribution, arguing that crimes against Indigenous people were crimes against God. Saunders' sermon – believed by some to be the first of its kind – argued that Indigenous people were entitled 'to the full rights and privileges of humanity'. The Aborigines Protection Society was established a few days after it was delivered. Saunders returned to England in 1847 suffering ill health and continued his ministry in London's suburban churches for another twelve years.

*

The duty of the colonists toward the Aboriginal natives of this territory is the important subject of discourse this evening. It is a topic which naturally falls within the scope of the Christian ministry, for it constitutes a part of Christian doctrine. It is a part of morals, for kindness to the unfortunate is involved in this precept, 'Whatever ye would that men should do to you do ye even so to them,' and it gains great importance from the doctrine that 'God our Saviour will have all men to be saved, and come to the knowledge of the truth.' This topic has therefore come under the notice of my ministry at different times in an incidental manner, but now it behoves us to give it a serious consideration, for it occupies both public and private attention and it is a matter of no small importance, that Christians should think rightly, speak rightly and act rightly in this respect. The conduct of the colonists towards the original proprietors of the soil is a theme of the highest interest, and upon our benevolent intention and righteous principles depends the happiness of a portion of the human race. Hence arises the duty of serious reflection, and hence the propriety of taking the word of God as an unerring guide, and hence the obligation of implicit obedience to that word whatsoever its dictates may be.

In pursuit of this object, I might present the case of the Aborigines in various ways; I might appeal to your pity, your love or your justice. If the native black be but an inferior animal, he is at least entitled to brotherly love, and as a fellow creature he is entitled to justice. These suggestions ought to awaken a prejudice in his favour in every well-disposed mind, but it is not my intention so much to awaken your compassion, as to appeal to your sense of justice, and to try the question by the evidence of the conscience, and before the tribunal of God.

If we have not committed injustice, and do not premeditate it, we have nothing to fear … Not only is it said that 'God will render to *every man* according to his deed,' which involves the whole of man's existence, and the retribution of a future state; but it is evident that even on earth a man is frequently visited according to his own doings … It is not for us to state in what degree this principle shall be applied to any particular people, nor to predict the precise moment of its application, but we may be sure that the unchanging word of God has been fulfilled, and is still accomplished toward every one of the tribes of Adam. The measure of forbearance, the weight of visitation and the time of indignation are in the hands of the Eternal, but the certainty of a righteous retribution towards all is clearly established. An additional point is also obvious, that if there be anything which calls for a swifter and a more severer punishment than another, it is the shedding of human blood. For this the nations receive a prompt and condign visitation. Oppression, cruelty and blood gather the clouds of vengeance, and provoke the threatening thunder of the Omnipotent, and attract the bolt of wrath …

The tenor of this discourse will lead me to select the sin in which the whole colony has been engaged, and for which, therefore, the whole colony is answerable – our injustice to the Aborigines. I do not select individual delinquents, but impeach the nation; for whether in ignorance or with a guilty knowledge, we certainly have been culpable in our neglect and oppression of this despised and degraded tribe of our fellow men.

The whole charge, however, rests upon their being *men*, which some are disposed to question, and which some even dare to deny. It becomes my duty, therefore, to assert the title of the Aboriginal native to a place in the family of man ... There may be differences in cerebral development; but until the ignorance of the serf and the idiocy of the European can exclude them from the human family, the rudeness of the savage and his frontal deficiency can never banish him from the same household.

The whole difference between the savage and the civilised is that one is cultivated and the other an uncultivated being ... There is no fundamental discrepancy. Does man laugh at the wit of his neighbour, or join in mirthful glee? The black man does the same. Does man mourn over departed friends, and drop the tear of sympathy? The New Hollander does the same. Are there stirring emotions of pride, anger, pity, love, indignation and benevolence in the heart of the white? The same emotions are found lodged in the bosom of the black. Does the civilised being feel a secret monitor within which we term conscience? The same agent whispers monitions to the savage. Does man pour forth an intellectual existence through the breathing of articulate sounds? The New Hollander has his fountain of thought, and can spontaneously pour forth its living water in a stream of intelligible words. Above all, I believe that black and white, barbarian and civilised, are alike capable of forming the notion of a God ... With these considerations I cannot fail to conclude that the Aboriginal native is a man; and being a man, with what sublimity does he rise before us; he is the august possessor of a moral and intellectual nature, the owner of an immortal soul. Then he is our fellow creature – the descendent of a common ancestor – our brother upon earth, and possessed of a joint title to the mercy of God in Christ Jesus, and to an inheritance in heaven. He then becomes invested with all the natural rights which belong to humanity, and is entitled to all the charities which man is bound to show to man.

These inferences usher in the solemn enquiry whether we have fully discharged our duty towards our brother, or whether we have wronged him? The answer will be painful but the truth must be told. Our influence has been deeply fatal to the black. It might have been supposed that a Christian nation colonising the Australian wilderness would have sought to bless the original possessor of the wild; but so far from this, we have inflicted a series of wrongs ... First we have robbed him without any sanction that I can find either in natural or revealed law; we descended as invaders upon his territory and took possession of the soil ... Surely we are guilty here.

Secondly, we have brutalised them. We brought the art of intoxication to them – we taught them new lessons in fraud, dishonesty and theft – we bribed them to shed the blood of each other in our public streets; and we encouraged them to licentiousness and self-destroying profligacy ... We came to eclipse what little they had of happiness – we came to draw deep night over the barbarian gloom. I am precluded from illustration by the painful character of the details; but the fact is notorious. Verily we are guilty here.

Thirdly, we have shed their blood ... I speak not of the broils and murders which might find a parallel in the conduct of the white towards the white, but of those extra murders in which so many have fallen. We have not been fighting with a natural enemy, but have been eradicating the possessors of the soil, and why, forsooth? Because they were troublesome, because some few had resented the injuries they had received, and then how were they destroyed? By wholesale, in cold blood ... The spot of blood is upon us, the blood of the poor and the defenceless, the blood of the men we wronged before we slew, and too, too often, a hundred times too often, *innocent* blood. We are guilty here.

'Shall not I visit for these things, saith the Lord; and shall not my soul be avenged on such a nation as this.' When he maketh 'inquisition for blood', will he not find it here? And finding it, surely we have reason to dread his visitation. In what way he may chasten us it is not for me to suggest; he is a sovereign, and acteth according to the counsels of his own will; but it is only to glance at his resources, and we can at once discern abundant reason to fear; he could parch us with drought, scatter our commerce, pinch us with penury and lower us with disease; the plague, the tornado and famine are at his back; above all, he could weary us with civil dissension, with the misery of an overflowing wickedness or with the power of a hostile sword. These things God in his infinite mercy has restrained, but how soon could he let loose their malignant influence upon us! We have, therefore, reason to dread the approach of the Lord when he cometh out of his place to punish the inhabitants of the earth for their iniquity ...

It may be difficult to restrain the lawless aggressions of some on the borders of the colony, but if we are faithful to our principles, and work with these upon public opinion, even the distant stockman will be influenced by it, and be held in check … It is our duty to recompense the Aborigines to the extent we have injured them … We are required to protect the natives from further aggression, and shed upon them every blessing within our power …

'We wish to make you happy'

George Gawler

Speech to Aboriginals, South Australia

1 NOVEMBER 1838

Soldier George Gawler (1795–1869), the second governor of South Australia, arrived in Adelaide with his wife and five children aboard the *Pestonjee Bomanjee* on 12 October 1838. Three weeks later he gave this speech, which was translated to his audience by Dr William Wyatt, the official protector of Aborigines. The address reflects some of the qualities for which Gawler would become known – his naivety, authoritarianism and overzealous religious evangelism.

Gawler was accused by his critics of 'paternal benevolence' towards Indigenous peoples, and of obstructing efforts to discipline them. He was also found to be an accessory to murder after two Ngarrindjeri Aboriginals were hanged and two were shot dead by a detachment of police sent to administer justice following the murders of survivors of the shipwrecked *Maria* in 1840 – but the matter was passed over.

*

Black men:

We wish to make you happy. But you cannot be happy unless you imitate good white men. Build huts, wear clothes, work and be useful. Above all you cannot be happy unless you love God who made heaven and earth and men and all things.

Love white men. Love other tribes of black men. Do not quarrel together. Tell other tribes to love white men, and to build good huts and wear clothes. Learn to speak English. If any white men injure you now, tell the Protector and he will do you justice.

'No matter what we do, they will die out'

Auber Octavius Neville

Address to the Conference of Commonwealth and State Aboriginal Authorities, Canberra

21 APRIL 1937

As the chief protector of Aborigines in Western Australia between 1915 and 1936, Auber Octavius Neville (1875–1954), advocated 'breeding out the coloured population'. Born in England, Neville arrived in Victoria aged twelve, and ten years later moved to Western Australia where he worked as a clerk and an immigration officer before joining the Department of the North-West and commencing his career shaping the official policy towards Indigenous Australians. Neville promoted segregating Indigenous people of 'full descent' – whom he believed were near extinction – and training those of 'part descent' to be absorbed into the white population. Known as 'Mister Neville', he was seen as the main adversary and 'one of the worst enemies' of many – particularly educated – Indigenous people. Neville was the most prominent participant in the first Conference of Commonwealth and State Aboriginal Authorities. Professor Robert Manne has argued:

'If there exists a more terrible moment in the history of the twentieth-century Australian state ... I for one do not know where it is to be discovered.'

*

The opinion held by Western Australian authorities is that the problem of the native race, including half-castes, should be dealt with on a long-range plan. We should ask ourselves what will be the position, say, fifty years hence; it is not so much the position today that has to be considered. Western Australia has gone further in the development of such a long-range policy than has any other state, by accepting the view that ultimately the natives must be absorbed into the white population of Australia ...

In Western Australia the problem of the Aborigines has three phases. In the far north there are between 7000 and 8000 pure-blooded Aborigines; in the middle north the number of half-castes is increasing, and the full-blooded Aborigines are becoming detribalised; and in the south-west there are about 5000 coloured people. We have dropped the use of the term 'half-caste'. As a matter of fact, in the legislation passed last session the term 'Aborigines' has been discarded altogether; we refer to them as natives whether they be full-blooded or half-caste. Quadroons over the age of twenty-one years are, however, excluded. From childhood quadroons are to be as whites. In my state there are several institutions for the treatment of the natives, including eleven missions and a number of departmental establishments ...

If the coloured people of this country are to be absorbed into the general community they must be thoroughly fit and educated at least to the extent of the three R's. If they can read, write and count, and know what wages they should get and how to enter into an agreement with an employer, that is all that should be necessary. Once that is accomplished there is no reason in the world why these coloured people should not be absorbed into the community. To achieve this end, however, we must have charge of the children at the age of six years; it is useless to wait until they are twelve or thirteen years of age. In Western Australia we have power under the Act to take any child from its mother at any stage of its life, no matter whether the mother be legally married or not. It is, however, our intention to establish sufficient settlements to undertake the training and education of these children so that they may become absorbed into the general community ...

The different states are creating institutions for the welfare of the native race, and as the result of this policy, the native population is increasing. What is to be the limit? Are we going to have a population of one million blacks in the Commonwealth, or are we going to merge them into our white community and eventually forget that there were any Aborigines in Australia? ...

I see no objection to the ultimate absorption into our own race of the whole of the existing Australian native race. In order to do this we must guard the health of the natives in every possible way so that they may be, physically, as fit as is possible. The children must be trained as we would train our own children. The stigma at present attaching to half-castes must be banished. In Western Australia half-caste boys and men take part in football, cricket and other games on a footing equal to that of their white clubmates, but are excluded from the social life of the community. They feel this deeply, as do their white companions in sport. This state of affairs will have to disappear ...

There are a great many full-blooded Aborigines in Western Australia living their own natural lives. They are not, for the most part, getting enough food, and they are, in fact, being decimated by their own tribal practices. In my opinion, no matter what we do, they will die out. It is interesting to note that on the departmental cattle stations established in the far north for the preservation of these people, the number of full-blooded children is increasing, because of the care the people get. The establishment of these stations has also had the effect of putting to an end the cattle killing which formerly prevailed. At the present time, however, there are in Western Australia about 10,000 full-blooded Aborigines who are detribalised, but among them there are only 1932 children. On the other hand, among the 2559 half-castes there are approximately 2000 children. It will be seen, therefore, that the problem of the future will be not with the full-bloods, but with the coloured people of various degrees. The full-bloods may be looked after on the cattle stations for the time being, but their number is decreasing rapidly as the result of tribal practices. In a bad season in the north practically no children are reared, while in a good season the number may be fairly considerable. Infanticide and abortion are extensively practised amongst the bush people. They follow their own customs, and no attempt to influence them has much result. We have to consider whether we should allow any race living amongst us to practise the abominations which are prevalent among these people ...

Reference has been made to institutionalism as applied to the Aborigines. It is well known that coloured races all over the world detest institutionalism. They have a tremendous affection for their children. In Western Australia, we have only a few institutions for the reception of half-caste illegitimate children, but there are hundreds living in camps close to the country towns under revolting conditions. It is infinitely better to take a child from its mother, and put it in an institution, where it will be looked after, than to allow it to be brought up subject to the influence of such camps. We allow the mothers to go to the institutions also, though they are separated from the children. The mothers are camped some distance away, while the children live in dormitories. The parents may go out to work, and return to see their children are well and properly looked after. We generally find that, after a few months, they are quite content to leave their children there ...

When they enter the institution, the children are removed from the parents, who are allowed to see them occasionally in order to satisfy themselves that they are being properly looked after. At first the mothers tried to entice the children back to the camps, but that difficulty is now being overcome ...

'Inattention on such a scale cannot possibly be explained by absentmindedness'

William Stanner

'The great Australian silence': Boyer Lecture broadcast nationally on ABC radio

7 NOVEMBER 1968

The 1968 Boyer Lectures, entitled 'After the Dreaming', helped break what Professor William Stanner (1905–1981) described as 'the great Australian silence'. An anthropologist who worked with the Indigenous people of the Daly River region in the Northern Territory, Stanner was appointed Professor of Anthropology at the Australian National University between 1964 and 1970, having worked on research projects at the London School of Economics, the Australian National Research Council and Oxford University. Stanner's anthropological studies in the south-west Pacific, Uganda and Kenya gave him a unique comparative perspective from which to view the relationship between Indigenous and white Australia; his 'seriousness, clarity and respectability' enabled him to make a difference in Australian attitudes and policy towards Indigenous peoples. Described as an 'irrepressibly radical thinker with a common touch', Stanner's second Boyer Lecture was a groundbreaking reading of Australia's past.

*

In my first lecture I spoke about a structure of racial relations that had come about between us and the Aborigines in the early days and had stayed more or less unchanged for 150 years. I tried to sketch something of the frame of mind and vision we had when we saw the skeleton beginning to walk in the early 1930s.

Why it began to walk then, and not earlier or later, is a question to which I cannot give a very satisfactory answer. There was scarcely any interest in the Aborigines of the settled areas of the east and south. Concern over them is a very recent development indeed. What had aroused public feeling in 1926 and afterward were reports of atrocities in the outback and the subsequent disclosure of many bad practices. But I do not think that pastoralists, miners and other employers had suddenly become harder on their Aborigines than in the past. I doubt if authority had suddenly become more observant or active; indeed, one of the great difficulties of the time was to get the executive, administrative and legal arms of authority to notice what was afoot, let alone to move. The people whom W.K. Hancock acknowledged in his book *Australia* (1930) as ever-present – 'the enthusiastic friends' of the Aborigines – were active but I doubt if their ranks were any stronger. Perhaps there had been a true rise in public sensibility but I find it hard to pin down any changes of conditions that may have brought it about. The explanation may simply be that just as in earlier times the view from Exeter Hall had been clearer than the view from Sydney, so now it was clearer from Sydney than from a town like Alice: and there was now much more to see. The road, the motor car, the aeroplane and the radio had put an end to the old isolation of the bush. It was a humdrum affair to drive from Sydney and Melbourne to Cape York and the Kimberleys. There was a piling up of evidence or near-evidence into a presumption that intolerable things were happening in the lonely places, and a certain taint of hugger-mugger about some of the official disclaimers did nothing to allay suspicion. What I am suggesting then is simply that people heard more, and heard more quickly, about a pattern of outback life that probably had not changed greatly for the worse.

Some people consider that 1934 was the main 'turning point' of Aboriginal policy. I cannot say that I recall anything about that year that suggests a sudden access of public virtue or a new vision at all widely shared. It seems to have been just another year on the old plateau of complacence.

In 1931 the prime minister of the day, Mr Scullin, still showed little inclination to credit that much could be amiss in Commonwealth territory and seemed not ill-content to plead the constitutional limit on his responsibility for events in the states. In 1932 the federal Minister for Home Affairs, Mr Parkhill, went very close to giving the

Northern Territory a coat of whitewash. Even after the Arnhem Land affair of 1933 and 1934 the prime minister of that time, Mr Lyons, thought it appropriate to continue substantially with existing policy. There was, perhaps, a certain softening of official attitudes and if so I do not think we can altogether dissociate the fact from enquiries which had been made by the Dominions Office through the High Commissioner in London. But we are hardly justified in placing the 'turning point' before 1938 when Mr McEwen, the then Minister for the Interior, placed before the Commonwealth parliament the proposals which later became known as 'the New Deal for the Aborigines in the Northern Territory'. It was then that the new concept of 'assimilation' came into use, although another ten years had to pass before its effects became at all noticeable.

It is an interesting question whether we should connect the change with another 'turning point' which is supposed to have taken place at that time. I refer to R.M. Crawford's theory that a 'New Australia' – the phrase is Peter Coleman's, not Crawford's – came into being in the second half of the 1930s, and that from then on the whole stream of Australian life and thought, in public policy, social and economic attitudes, culture and letters, took a new course. The new and the stretched ideas and activities that have been cited in evidence do make an impressive list. The writers who have discussed the matter would include the great expansion of CSIRO, the recruitment of graduates to the Commonwealth public service, the generous patronage of culture, art and letters by the ABC and the Commonwealth Literary Fund, the formation of the Literature Censorship Board and the Contemporary Arts Society, the welcoming of Jewish refugees from Europe and the new liberalism towards immigration in general, the new confidence in industry and trade, and even such developments as the penetration of key unions by the Communist Party and the establishment of the National Secretariat of Catholic Action. These are perhaps the leading items from a catalogue which could of course grow to almost any size by the same principle of selection, that is, to take a handful of roughly contemporary things and regard them as a collected bundle.

As far as I am aware, no one yet has put the new Aboriginal policy into the bundle. The omission is surely significant. But of what?

Part at least of the answer, I suggest, can be given by extending the examination into the war years. So far as domestic affairs were concerned the main powerhouse of progressive social thought was the Department of Post-War Reconstruction. I have good authority for saying that the idea of taking the Aboriginal situation as a challenge simply never occurred to the collective mind of that exciting and vital department. That more than anything else confirms me in my view that for all the quickening and deepening of the national stream only a trickle of new thought ran towards the Aboriginal field, and it ran around the edges, not through the middle. The only natives we were prepared to think about at all seriously at this time were those of New Guinea. The Aborigines came a bad second. This is not to say that the war years were a blank. There was some progressive thinking in the Northern Territory, where some excellent men found themselves too far ahead of government to make their ideas felt, and the new Commonwealth Department of Social Services also made some useful advances in association with federal and state Aboriginal agencies and with missionary bodies. But Aboriginal Australia simply could not compete with New Guinea either for public resources or for public interest. What with one thing and another the new policy of assimilation hung fire for more than a decade. I know that even in 1952, when I returned to the Northern Territory after a long absence, I could start to work very much where I had left off without any acute sense of change in the Aboriginal life around me or in their relations with white Australia. There were some changes but they were more the effect of war and the new price-inflation than of policy.

I am therefore inclined to argue that the two 'turning points' had precious little to do with each other. I suspect that the achievement of the new policy of assimilation was the product of a compartment of Australian thought and experience quite separate from and much weaker than that which led to the great energising of the rest of Australian society and culture. The 'feedback' from the greater into the lesser movement – the 'trickle' I spoke of – was entirely minimal. There is small doubt in my mind that that continues to be the case, and that it is one of the main reasons for the slowness with which we are mastering our Aboriginal problems. It is absurd that so small a part of the talent and ingenuity that exist in our departments of state, our great private industries, our universities and our research organisations should be turned toward these problems.

I will not pursue that theme further for the moment, although I will come back to it. I want instead to pick up a dropped thread. It seems clear to me now that the change of attitude and policy towards the Aborigines which we trace back to the 1930s was confined very largely to a rather small group of people who had special associations with their care, administration or study. Outside that group the changes made very little impact for a long time and, within the group, it was a case of the faithful preaching to the converted about a 'revolution' which in fact had arrived only for them. The situation has altered very considerably in the last five or six years – witness, for example, the referendum of 1967 – but has a very long way to go before we are justified in using words which, like 'revolution', suggest a total change of heart and mind.

Turning this thought over in my mind the other day I asked myself whether it could be tested for truth-value even if only in part. If, for example, the two 'turning points' were not as I suggested distinct and separate, but were connected in some vital way; that is to say, if more than a very few people had been aware of a struggle waged and won in the Aboriginal field, surely (or so I argued) there should have been a marked response from the 'New Australia' that was coming into being in the late 1930s; surely the serious literature from that time on should show some evidence of a consciousness that here was another old, cluttered field to renovate by the new progressive thought. I put to one side the large array of technical papers and books expressly concerned with the Aborigines, such as Paul Hasluck's *Our Southern Half Castes* (1938) and *Black Australians* (1941) and E.J.B. Foxcroft's *Australian Native Policy* (1941), and looked instead at a mixed lot of histories and commentaries dealing with Australian affairs in a more general way. They seemed to me the sort of books that probably expressed well enough, and may even have helped to form, the outlook of socially conscious people between say, 1939 and 1955, by which time some objections of a serious kind were beginning to be made to the idea of assimilation.

The first book I looked at was M. Barnard Eldershaw's *My Australia* (1939). The Aborigines feature quite prominently in it; their affairs, indeed, make up nearly one-tenth of the book; but it is only too clear that they are marginal, and in a deeper sense, irrelevant to the author's story. Hardly a word on the other 280 pages would have to be changed if they were dropped from the prologue ('A mask of Australia for inaudible voices') and if one chapter ('The Dispossessed') were snipped out.

The writers take over from W.K. Hancock his thesis that 'in truth, a hunting and pastoral economy cannot coexist within the same bounds', but they do not like his plain language, and they prefer to say that 'the twentieth century and the Stone Age cannot live together'. They also have it that the white man did the black man 'very little willful harm' and that the rest was 'inevitable'. The revolution of attitudes had certainly not arrived for these writers. In the next book, Hartley Grattan's *Introducing Australia* (1942), we are given a good thumbnail sketch of old, familiar facts. I could not deny that Grattan has a sense of change: he mentions it in one sentence on one of his 300 pages. But Brian Fitzpatrick's *The Australian People* (1946) does not show even this degree of awareness. Only one or two of his 260 pages makes any mention of the Aborigines and, although it says well what it has to say, it is all backward-turned.

Much the same is the case with H.L. Harris's *Australia in the Making: A History* (1948). There are some fragments about Dampier, Banks, Cook and Sturt, but there it ends. The next book, Geoffrey Rawson's *Australia* (1948), has a chapter entitled 'Aborigines' which also deals with wildlife, so the title could as well have been 'Aborigines and other fauna', after the style of John Henderson, who in 1832 wrote some 'Observations on zoology, from the order Insecta to that of Mammalia; the latter including the natives of New Holland'.

I then turned to the 1950s hoping for rather better things. My hand fell first on R.M. Crawford's splendid little book *Australia* (1952). There is a chapter on the Aborigines; not the shortest chapter, and not a tailpiece, but one full of good information and well-moulded general statements, and – a great novelty, this – a lively awareness of questions which historians ought to have but apparently had not, asked; for example, what were the relations between the squatters and the Aborigines? But there is little that bears on either of the 'turning points'. The next was George Caiger's *The Australian Way of Life* (1953), in which the word 'Aboriginal' is not to be found; no, I am wrong; it does occur – once, in a caption under the photograph that displays two of Australia's scenic attractions, the Aborigines and Coogee Beach. To the next book, W.V. Aughterson's *Taking Stock: Aspects of Mid-Century Life in Australia* (1953), there were ten contributors. Only one of them, Alan McCulloch, the art critic, has anything to say about the Aborigines, some passing but perceptive observation on their art. Incidentally, the book opens with a chapter entitled 'The Australian way of life', written by W.E.H. Stanner, who can safely be presumed never to have heard of the Aborigines, because he does not refer to them and even maintains that Australia has 'no racial divisions like America'. (At this point in my reading I could hardly resist feeling that all the authors so far mentioned should surely have used M. Barnard Eldershaw's title '*My* Australia'; that, clearly, was what they were writing about.) The intense concentration on ourselves and our affairs continues in Gordon Greenwood's *Australia: A Social and Political History* (1955). The other books by comparison are in the light or middleweight divisions; this one is nearly a heavyweight. It sets out to give a broad but comparatively detailed study of our history; to discover significant elements and the organic relations between them; to reveal the essential spirit and the dominant characteristics of each stage; and, more, to show 'what gathering forces transmuted the existing society into another, different in outlook and constitution'. It is written by six eminent scholars and has been reprinted half a dozen times, so it seems to have been influential. How does it deal with the Aborigines? It mentions them five times – twice, quite briefly, for the period 1788 to 1821; twice again, as briefly, for the period 1820 to 1850; once, in sidelong fashion, for the period 1851 to 1892; and thereafter not at all.

Here I was, then, seventeen years after the 'turning point' in Aboriginal policy, only to find that some of our most perceptive thinkers seemed to be unaware of it, or if they were, had nothing to say about it. Perhaps they were right; perhaps in 1955 there were still no 'gathering forces' seeking to 'transmute' Aboriginal–European relations; perhaps my theory of two unrelated compartments of Australian life and thought could have something in it. By picking and choosing a little I went on to persuade myself that for a number of writers the lack of interest ran on even into the 1960s. For example, Peter Coleman's *Australian Civilization* (1962) leaves little of our life and thought unexamined, but by its total silence on all matters Aboriginal seems to argue that the racial structure which is part of our anatomy of life has no connection with our civilisation past, present or future.

I need not extend the list. A partial survey is enough to let me make the point that inattention on such a scale cannot possibly be explained by absentmindedness. It is a structural matter, a view from a window which has been carefully placed to exclude a whole quadrant of the landscape. What may well have begun as a simple forgetting of other possible views turned under habit and over time into something like a cult of forgetfulness practised on a national scale. We have been able for so long to disremember the Aborigines that we are now hard put to keep them in mind even when we most want to do so. It might help to break the cult of disremembering if someone made a searching study of the moral, intellectual and social transitions noticeable in Aboriginal affairs from the 1930s to the 1960s. It seems to me to beg to be written.

I am no historian and I should stick to my task, but the history I would like to see written would bring into the main flow of its narrative the life and times of men like David Unaipon, Albert Namatjira, Robert Tudawali, Durmugam, Douglas Nicholls, Dexter Daniels and many others. Not to scrape up significance for them but because they typify so vividly the other side of a story over which the great Australian silence reigns; the story of the things we were unconsciously resolved not to discuss with them or treat with them about; the story, in short, of the unacknowledged relations between two racial groups within a single field of life supposedly unified by the principle of assimilation, which has been the marker of the transition. The telling of it would have to be a world – perhaps I should say an underworld – away from the conventional histories of the coming and development of British civilisation. I hardly see that it could afford two assumptions. One is that it satisfies the canons of human relevance and social influence to allow men of the kind I have mentioned to flit across the pages as if they were the Benelongs and Colbys of the day. The other is that the several hundred thousand Aborigines who lived and died between 1788 and 1938 were but negative facts of history and, having been negative, were in no way consequential for the modern period. In Aboriginal Australia there is an oral history which is providing these people with a coherent principle of explanation of which I will speak later. It has a directness and a candour which cut like a knife through most of what we say and write. We would have to bring this material – let me be fashionable and call it 'ethno history' – into the sweep of our story.

One consequence of having given the Aborigines no place in our past except that of 'a melancholy footnote' is both comical and serious. Comical, because one of the larger facts of the day is the Aboriginal emergence into contemporary affairs, but about all we can say, on the received version of our history, is the rising twin of that immortal observation, 'from this time on the native question sank into unimportance.' Serious, because the surfacing of problems which are in places six or seven generations deep confront us with problems of decision, but we are badly under-equipped to judge whether policies towards the problems are slogans, panaceas or sovereign remedies, or none of them.

In one sense, of course, the historians have been right. It is incontestable that few of the great affairs of the past took any sort of account of the continued Aboriginal presence. It is also the case that some great affairs of the present – the plans for the development of sub-tropical Australia – take all too little account of the continued Aboriginal presence there. But it is precisely this situation which calls for a less shallow, less ethnocentric social history. Fish swim in water, and what we do with our fin, gills and tails is not unrelated to the permissive-resistant medium in which we move. For example, it occurred a long time ago to W.G. Spence, that father-figure of trade unionism, that the weakness of our system of local government was connected with the rapid decimation of local native populations. As he saw it we did not devolve protective and other powers locally because there was no need to do so. The medium was in that respect permissive. But a poorly working parish pump is at one end of a scale. Let me go to the other end. All land in Australia is held in consequence of an assumption so grand and remote from actuality that it had best be called royal, which is exactly what it was. The continent at occupation was held to be disposable because it was assumed to be 'waste and desert'. The truth was that identifiable Aboriginal groups held identifiable parcels of land by unbroken occupancy from a time beyond which, quite literally, 'the memory of man runneth not to the contrary.' The titles which they claimed were conceded by all their fellows. There are still some parts of Australia, including some of the regions within which development is planned or actually taking place, in which living Aborigines occupy and use lands that have never been 'waste and desert' and to which their titles could be demonstrated, in my opinion beyond cavil, to a court of fact if there were such a court. In such areas if the Crown title were paraded by, and if the Aborigines understood what was happening, every child would say, like the child in the fairytale, 'but the Emperor is naked'. The medium, in this matter once permissive, is now turning resistant, and the fact is one of the barely acknowledged elements of the real structure of Australia which is working its way towards a more overt expression. Like many other facts overlooked, or forgotten, or reduced to an anachronism and thus consigned to the supposedly inconsequential past, it requires only a suitable set of conditions to come to the surface, and be very consequential indeed.

I hardly think that what I have called 'the great Australian silence' will survive the research that is now in course. Our universities and research institutes are full of young people who are working actively to end it. The Australian Institute of Aboriginal Studies and the Social Science Research Council of Australia have both promoted studies which will bring the historical and the contemporary dimensions together and will assuredly persuade scholars to renovate their categories of understanding. If we could have done this in the 1920s and 1930s, perhaps we would not have had to wait until the middle of the 1950s to see any real product of the new 'positive' policy. For example, the effort to preserve the Aborigines within inviolable reserves was the last ditch of an older policy, and we were then beyond the last ditch. I do not recall that we asked ourselves at all clearly: what comes *after* a policy which *by definition* is one of *last* resort? The inability to ask the question in that way left us, not rebels without cause, but doctors without a diagnosis, and it is interesting to recall how few people then thought in terms of some of the notable advantages that have in fact come about – the grant of equal political status, the suffrage, the extension of civil liberties, the ending of legal discrimination, the right to social services and other things of the kind. One wonders what equivalent astigmatisms may affect our contemporary vision. I will suggest later that one of them is a certain inability to grasp that on the evidence the Aborigines have always been looking for two things: a decent union of their lives with ours on terms that let them preserve their own identity, not their inclusion willy-nilly in our scheme of things and a fake identity, but development within a new way of life that has the imprint of their own ideas. But that is a topic for another lecture, and I want now to round out what I have been saying.

The impulse to make radical changes in the Aboriginal situation had little force or product until the last decade. Twenty years of the 'revolution' were thus years of the locust. The ideal of assimilation took shape when no one dreamed that galloping development would overrun all of Aboriginal Australia, and no one devised a very convincing human strategy or technical method even for the older circumstances. We thus enter on a new time with a heavy backlog of unsolved older problems. A glance at the human map of Australia still shows one of the worst of them. The map is disfigured by hundreds of miserable camps which are the social costs of old-style development that would not let any consideration of Aboriginal interest stand in its way. Development over the next fifty years will need to change its style and its philosophy if the outcome is to be very different. I have begun to allow myself to believe that there is now a credible prospect of that happening. A kind of beneficial multiplier could be starting to have effect. One notices the coming together of things from different starting points. The private industries which use and in some measure may depend on Aboriginal labour do not all resist as they once did the idea that it is in their interest to rehabilitate this broken society. We may see a market take shape in private industry for workable proposals. The public instrumentalities concerned with Aboriginal affairs have a head of steam towards their tasks which was not the common rule a few years ago. The flow of public funds specifically earmarked for Aboriginal advancement is relatively generous. Some very worthwhile ideas are starting to come forward from some sectors of the Aboriginal population. Perhaps the one thing now needed to increase the power of the multiplier is a projection of the costs, monetary and social, that will be a charge on the national pocket in default of a rapid advance of the Aboriginal people to self-support. A native population which promises to double itself well within twenty years will otherwise become a fiscal problem of magnitude.

One cannot talk of everything, even in a generous series of lectures of this kind, and I must now narrow my span to one of the things that interfere with our judgement of a scene that is being transformed under our eyes. That is to say, our folklore about the Aborigines. It had a lot to do with the making of our racial difficulties and it still has a lot to do with maintaining them.

'For far too long we have been crying out and far too few have heard us'

Neville Bonner

Maiden speech to the Senate

8 September 1971

The Queensland Liberal Party's selection of Neville Bonner (1922–1999) to fill a casual vacancy in the federal Senate in 1971 drew interest worldwide. Bonner was the first Aboriginal to fill an Australian parliamentary bench and his was a classic 'rags to riches' story. With only a third-grade education, Bonner had endured a poverty-stricken childhood, working as a carpenter, labourer and stockman before finding his political voice as president of the One People of Australia League in 1963. He remained in the Senate, promoting Aboriginal and Torres Strait Islander rights and the environment, for twelve years, before his criticism of the Queensland National-Liberal Party eventually cost him preselection. Out of parliament, Bonner spent his remaining years serving as an adviser, a director of the ABC and a senior official visitor to Queensland prisons.

Bonner described giving his maiden parliamentary speech as 'one of the most traumatic experiences I have been through'. He arranged to give his address on a Wednesday evening – when the Senate proceedings were broadcast – and stood nervously in the chamber. 'This was the first time an Aborigine was going to be speaking in the federal parliament, in any Australian parliament,' he recalled. 'It seemed so much depended on my being able to speak well in there.' At 8.26 p.m. Bonner began, 'his fingers tightly entwined behind his back'. At the completion, senators from both sides of the House cheered 'Hear, Hear' and got up to shake his hand. The *Sydney Morning Herald* editorial the next day said: 'His cry should cut deeply into the consciousness of white Australians.' Bonner was pleased: 'Ah, today the white man stood still and allowed me to be an Aborigine.'

*

It is with very deep and mixed emotions that I participate in the debates of this parliament for the first time. I feel overawed by the obvious education of honourable senators within this august chamber. I assure honourable senators that I have not attended a university or a high school and, for that matter, I do not know that I can say that I have spent very much time at a primary school. But this does not mean that as a senator from Queensland I am not able to cope. I have graduated through the university of hard knocks. My teacher was experience. However, I shall play the role which my state of Queensland, my race, my background, my political beliefs, my knowledge of men and circumstances dictate. This I shall do, through the grace of God, to the benefit of all Australians. For more than 20,000 years my people have loved this country. They have appreciated its beauty and its capacity to provide for human needs. Throughout that long period my race developed many traditions and one generation has passed on to another a respect for these traditions. Traditions are preserved and honoured in the Australian parliament also. The awareness of these traditions and the long and illustrious line of people who have upheld them in the interests of freedom and democracy makes me humble because I realise the privilege and the double responsibility which has been bestowed on me. At the same time I am sure that honourable senators will agree that I could hardly be blamed if I confessed to a feeling of pride at this time.

First and foremost I participate here as an Australian citizen. Through the valour of its fighting men in two world wars and by the vigour and skill of its leaders, Australia has earned an honoured place in the world. As an Australian, I am concerned for the future of my country, for the welfare of its people and for the quality of life that they enjoy. However, I am conscious of the fact that I am the first member of my race to participate in parliamentary proceedings. I am proud that, however long it has taken, this form of participation has been achieved. To those who took the decisions which resulted in my being here today, I proffer my thanks ...

I turn now to the business before the Senate, which is, in part, consideration of the government's Budget proposals for the 1971–72 financial year. As I understand it, the Budget is the most important business to come before the parliament each year. It involves huge sums of money and has far-reaching effects on every Australian – from the pensioner hoping for an increase in his or her fortnightly cheque to the manufacturer worrying about the impact of the Budget on his undertaking ...

Item number seven refers to the expenditure on territories, excluding Papua New Guinea, and shows an increase of $40 million. Item number ten shows an increase of $41 million for other expenditures. Both items are of special interest to me because they include considerable sums for Aboriginal advancement, mainly for special programs of housing, health and education. These three items are of supreme importance to the welfare and quality of life of all Australians, none more so than Aborigines. Mr President, I crave your indulgence and the indulgence of honourable senators in that for a very short time all within me that is Aboriginal yearns to be heard as the voice of the Indigenous people of Australia. For far too long we have been crying out and far too few have heard us. I stand humbly in the presence of honourable senators to bring to their attention what I believe to be the lot of those of my race in 1971. It would be an understatement to say that the lot of my fellow Aboriginals is not a particularly happy one. We bear emotional scars – the young no less than the older.

By and large we are unskilled with, here and there, a breakthrough. In early days we were a very simple people. My people had simple needs. We saw no need for agriculture or industry because nature provided our needs for over 20,000 years.

Less than 200 years ago the white man came. I say now in all sincerity that my people were shot, poisoned, hanged and broken in spirit until they became refugees in their own land. But that is history and we take care now of the present while, I should hope, we look to the future. Following the advent of the white man came a transitional period which still exists today. Then began to appear the emotional scars; the psychological wounds became a torment from which by and large we have still not recovered. The Aborigines today find themselves drifting between two worlds, accepting some of the white man's virtues, but alas, also many of his vices, subconsciously retaining to some extent the intricate pattern of relationship, the wonderful gift of sharing one with the other to such an extent that it infringes on the laws of white society, or Australian society as we know it today.

Whilst I commend the government for its awareness of the need for improved programs of housing, health and education, I want to take this opportunity to point out that in common with all citizens, Aborigines of Australia are most certainly not looking for handouts. They have suffered enough from the stigma of paternalism, however well-intentioned it may have been. I am sure that they will respond to efforts being made to enhance their self-esteem, particularly through the programs of social development and vocational and general education.

I want to emphasise the urgency of greater Aboriginal participation particularly in the areas of social development and vocational and general education. I believe there is need for a program wherein Aborigines, and not necessarily academically qualified or young Aborigines, but those armed with understanding and compassion plus the ability to communicate, can be fielded to liaise with Aborigines and all relevant government departments and organisations working in the field today.

I wish to make only two more points. Firstly I express my appreciation of what the government is already doing to make preschool education facilities available for my people. I appeal for even greater efforts to be made in this area, particularly by state governments as well as the Commonwealth Government. In case I appear to be biased on this subject I shall quote from a recent book by Mrs Lorna Lippmann. She wrote:

> One normally expects a deprived minority, living in poverty in a degraded physical environment, to have a low educational standard. Obligingly, Aborigines live up to that expectation in every part of Australia.

Professor D.W. McElwain, whose research into the cognitive ability or intelligence of Aborigines in Queensland is well known, has concluded as a result of a study of 1000 subjects: 'There are no inborn or genetic limitations on the basic intelligence of Aborigines.' Mrs Lippmann also wrote:

> Preschools are all-important to ensure that Aboriginal children do not begin school impoverished as to language and background. Instruction within the school needs to be individualised and ungraded (so that the child will go at his own pace in each subject). Extra-curricular activities should be encouraged so that the student can excel in some field of his own choosing and know the joy of learning, of creativity and of success.

I turn now to consider Aboriginal enterprises. As Mrs Lippmann has pointed out, every able-bodied person wants to succeed in some field of his own choosing and to know the satisfactions which come from creativity and success. Economically viable Aboriginal enterprises offer just these satisfactions. I congratulate the government on the policy decision to further these enterprises and I appeal to those who are responsible for developing further policies and implementing them to use every means available to help them along. Australians are noted for their willingness to take a risk. I ask for a greater degree of gambling on Australia's Indigenous population who, since the arrival of the white man, have to a degree gambled just on existing.

It is to be regretted that artefacts which have been identified with Aborigines should now be mass-produced overseas and imported into Australia at such prices and in such quantities that the Indigenous manufacture of such artefacts as boomerangs is no longer economically feasible. I wonder whether it would be possible for some sort of tariff protection to be applied to boomerangs at least, so that cheap imitations from overseas would not undercut the authentic Aboriginal article in such a way that, as has occurred, it would be difficult to find anything but an imported imitation in retail stores and shops which cater for tourists.

It may also be possible to bring down legislation to restrict the manufacture of boomerangs within Australia to those people who own it as their special heritage – the Aboriginal race. I have made enquiries about the possibilities of a patent over the boomerang and have been advised that as it is by no means a recent scientific invention it would not be possible for anyone to take out a patent for it. Likewise, I understand, the law of copyright would apply only to individual designs on an artefact. I have been told that the word 'boomerang' cannot even be registered as a trademark as the term is probably too deeply entrenched in the English language to be legally registered now as distinguishing the goods of particular manufacturers or traders. If some solution to this problem can be found it may be one small way of fostering an Aboriginal enterprise which I know surely has considerable potential.

Mr President and honourable senators, although my entering the Senate was a unique event in Australian history in that apart from being a senator for Queensland, I am also an Australian Aborigine, I was not at all surprised to find that there is absolute equality. I thank you, Sir, and honourable senators for this, not on my own behalf but as a representative of the Indigenous people throughout Australia. In conclusion I desire to clarify one point. From this year onwards, who are to be termed the Indigenous people of Australia? In my experienced opinion, all persons who desire to be so classified, regardless of hue of skin, and who have flowing in their veins any portion, however small, of Aboriginal or Torres Strait Island blood, are Indigenous people. It does not necessarily follow that the degree of one's emotional scars matches the darkness of personal pigmentation or that the lightness of one's skin necessarily indicates a lessening of knowledge of and belief in Aboriginal or Torres Strait Island culture and tradition.

I have listened earnestly to the debate on the Budget. I have heard criticism of the government and I have heard favourable comment. I say sincerely that I am proud to have an opportunity to stand in the Senate. Perhaps it is a little too early for me to really play a very great part in the debate on the Budget. But I am proud to be here and I am proud of the fact that I have been accepted in the Senate as an equal by all other senators. That is what I want to see achieved in our wonderful country. We live in a wonderful country. Recently I gave an address, the title of which was 'This is a grand country'. It will be a grand country only while those who sit in this chamber and in another place really and truly believe in this aim and work towards achieving it. I believe that we should forget our petty differences and really work for those who have put us here and have entrusted the nation to our hands. I thank you, Mr President, for the courtesy with which you have listened to me. I look forward to my association with my fellow senators. I trust that our deliberations will be, in fact, for the true welfare of all Australians.

'These lands belong to the Gurindji people'
'We will be mates, white and black'

Gough Whitlam and Vincent Lingiari

Speeches at the handover of lease to the Muramulla Gurindji Company

16 AUGUST 1975

A week after taking office in December 1972, prime minister Gough Whitlam (1916–) announced that there would be a royal commission to advise his new government on the granting of Indigenous land rights. At the same time, negotiations began on the issuing of a lease to the Gurindji people of the Victoria River district in the Northern Territory, whose land had been occupied since the 1850s by the Wave Hill pastoral station, and later, by the British pastoral company, Vestey Ltd. In 1966, Aboriginal elder Vincent Lingiari (1908–1988) had led his people off the station to a nearby riverbed. The strike began over the station owner's refusal to pay the Indigenous stockmen $25 a week in wages, but soon transformed into a greater demand for their ancestral lands.

In 1975 the Gurindji people were granted a land lease to 3250 square kilometres of the old Wave Hill station, including significant sacred sites. On 16 August, prime minister Whitlam – known to the Gurindji as 'Jungarni', meaning 'that big man' – and other prominent guests took part in a ceremony to return the land to the Gurindji people. At the conclusion of his speech, Whitlam picked up a handful of soil from the ground and poured it into Lingiari's outstretched hand, symbolising the handover of the Crown lease, which he had also given to Lingiari moments before. The Gurindji people renamed their land Daguragu Station, and by 1977 were running over 5000 head of cattle, installing new bores and fencing new paddocks. In 1986 the lease was converted to freehold. Lingiari was awarded an Order of Australia in 1976 and he is remembered as an important and widely respected tribal leader. His speech in reply to prime minister Gough Whitlam at the handover ceremony was translated from the original Gurindji language by Patrick McConvell.

*

Prime Minister Gough Whitlam

On this great day, I, Prime Minister of Australia, speak to you on behalf of the people of Australia – all Australians who honour and love this land we live in.

For them I want:

- First, to congratulate you, and those who have shared your struggle, on the victory you have won in that fight for justice begun nine years ago when in protest you walked off Wave Hill Station;
- Secondly, to acknowledge that we Australians have still much to do to redress the injustice and oppression that has for so long been the lot of black Australians;

- Thirdly, to promise you that this act of restitution which we perform today will not stand alone – your fight was not for yourselves alone and we are determined that Aboriginal Australians everywhere will be helped by it;
- Fourthly, to promise that, through their government, the people of Australia will help you in your plans to use this place fruitfully for the Gurindji;
- Finally, to give back to you formally in Aboriginal and Australian law ownership of this land of your fathers.

Vincent Lingiari, I solemnly hand to you these deeds as proof, in Australian law, that these lands belong to the Gurindji people and I put into your hands this piece of the earth itself as a sign that we restore them to you and your children forever.

Vincent Lingiari

1 The important white men are giving us this land ceremonially, ceremonially they are giving it to us.
2 It belonged to the whites, but today it is in the hands of us Aboriginals all around here.
3 Let us live happily together as mates, let us not make it hard for each other.
4 The important white men have come here, and they are giving our country back to us now.
5 They will give us cattle, they will give us horses, then we will be happy.
6 They came from different places away, we do not know them, but they are glad for us.
7 We want to live in a better way together, Aboriginals and white men, let us not fight over anything, let us be mates.
8 He [the Prime Minister] will give us cattle and horses ceremonially; we have not seen them yet; they will give us bores, axes, wire, all that sort of thing.
9 These important white men have come here to our ceremonial ground and they are welcome, because they have not come for any other reason, just for this [handover].
10 We will be mates. White and black, you [Gurindji] must keep

this land safe for yourselves, it does not belong to any different 'welfare' man.

11 They took our country away from us, now they have brought it back ceremonially.

'The time has come for you to take on new courage and new hope'

Pope John Paul II

Speech in Alice Springs

29 NOVEMBER 1986

When Pope John Paul II (1920–) addressed his audience in Alice Springs during the 1986 Australian Papal tour it was widely expected that he would comment on Indigenous affairs. He had been entertained before the speech with Aboriginal translations of the gospels and enjoyed a ceremonial welcome. The Pontiff's explicit call for land rights for Indigenous Australians was, however, a much stronger and more political comment than was expected. Drawing applause from some and criticism from others – historian Geoffrey Blainey described it as 'an act of political meddling that has few parallels in Australian history' – the speech was among the most contentious ever given by a visitor.

*

Dear brothers and sisters,

It is a great joy to me to be here today in Alice Springs and to meet so many of you, the Aboriginals and Torres Strait Islanders of Australia. I want to tell you right away how much the Church esteems and loves you, and how much she wishes to assist you in your spiritual and material needs.

At the beginning of time, as God's Spirit moved over the waters, he began to communicate something of his goodness and beauty to all creation. When God created man and woman, he gave them the good things of the earth for their use and benefit; and he put into their hearts abilities and powers, which were his gifts. And to all human beings throughout the ages God has given a desire for himself, a desire which different cultures have tried to express in their own ways.

As the human family spread over the face of the earth, your people settled and lived in this big country that stood apart from all the others. Other people did not even know this land was here; they only knew that somewhere in the southern oceans of the world there was 'The Great South Land of the Holy Spirit.' But for thousands of years you have lived in this land and fashioned a culture that endures to this day. And during all this time, the Spirit of God has been with you. Your Dreaming, which influences your lives so strongly that, no matter what happens, you remain forever people of your culture, is your own way of touching the mystery of God's Spirit in you and in creation. You must keep your striving for God and hold on to it in your lives.

The rock paintings and the discovered evidence of your ancient tools and implements indicate the presence of your age-old culture and prove your ancient occupancy of this land. Your culture, which shows the lasting genius and dignity of your race, must not be allowed to disappear. Do not think that your gifts are worth so little that you should no longer bother to maintain them. Share them with each other and teach them to your children. Your songs, your stories, your paintings, your dances, your languages, must never be lost. Do you perhaps remember those words that Paul VI spoke to the Aboriginal people during his last visit to them in 1970? On that occasion he said:

> We know that you have a lifestyle proper to your own ethnic genius or culture – a culture which the Church respects and which she does not in any way ask you to renounce ...
>
> Society itself is enriched by the presence of different cultural and ethnic elements. For us, you and the values you represent are precious. We deeply respect your dignity and reiterate our deep affection for you. (Sydney, 2 December 1970.)

For thousands of years this culture of yours was free to grow without interference by people from other places. You lived your lives in spiritual closeness to the land, with its animals, birds, fishes, waterholes, rivers, hills and mountains. Through your closeness to the land you touched the sacredness of man's relationship with God, for the land was the proof of a power in life greater than yourselves. You did not spoil the land, use it up, exhaust it and then walk away from it ... The silence of the bush taught you a quietness of soul that put you in touch with another world, the world of God's Spirit.

Your careful attention to the details of kinship spoke of your reverence for birth, life and human generation. You knew that children need to be loved, to be full of joy. They need a time to grow in laughter and to play secure in the knowledge that they belong to their people. You had a great respect for the need which people have for law as a guide to living fairly with each other. So you created a legal system – very strict it is true ... but closely adapted to the country in which you lived your lives. It made your society orderly. It was one of the reasons why you survived in this land. You marked the growth of your young men and women with ceremonies of discipline that taught them responsibility as they came to maturity. These achievements are indications of human strivings and in these strivings you showed a dignity open to the message of God's revealed wisdom to all men and women, which is the great truth of the Gospel of Jesus Christ.

Some of the stories from your Dreamtime legends speak powerfully of the great mysteries of human life, its frailty, its need for help, its closeness to spiritual powers and the value of the human person. They are not unlike some of the great inspired lessons from the people among whom Jesus himself was born. It is wonderful to see how people, as they accept the Gospel of Jesus, find points of agreement between their own traditions and those of Jesus and his people.

The culture which this long and careful growth produced was not prepared for the sudden meeting with another people with different customs and traditions, who came to your country nearly 200 years ago. They were different from Aboriginal people. ...

The effects of some of those forces are still active among you today. Many of you have been dispossessed of your traditional lands, and separated from your tribal ways, though some of you still have your traditional culture. Some of you are establishing Aboriginal communities in the towns and cities. For others there is still no real place for camp fires and kinship observances except on the fringes of country towns. There, work is hard to find, and education in a different cultural background is difficult. The discrimination caused by racism is a daily experience.

You have learned how to survive, whether on your own lands, or scattered among the towns and cities. Though your difficulties are not yet over, you must learn to draw on the endurance which your ancient ceremonies have taught you. Endurance brings with it patience; patience helps you to find the way ahead, and gives you courage for your journey. Take heart from the fact that many of your languages are still spoken and that you still possess your ancient culture. You have kept your sense of brotherhood. If you stay closely united, you are like a tree standing in the middle of a bushfire sweeping through the timber. The leaves are scorched and the tough bark is scarred and burned; but inside the tree the sap is still flowing, and under the ground the roots are still strong. Like that tree you have endured the flames, and you still have the power to be reborn. The time for this rebirth is now!

We know that during the last two hundred years certain people tried to understand you, to learn about you, to respect your ways and to honor you as persons. These men and women, as you soon realised, were different from others of their race. They loved and cared for the Indigenous people. They began to share with you their stories of God, helped you cope with sickness, tried to protect you from ill-treatment. They were honest with you, and showed you by their lives how they tried to avoid the bad things in their own culture. These people were not always successful, and there were times when they did not fully understand you. But they showed you goodwill and friendship. They came from many different walks of life. Some were teachers and doctors and other professional people; some were simple folk. History will remember the good example of their charity and fraternal solidarity.

Among those who have loved and cared for the Indigenous people, we especially recall with profound gratitude all the missionaries of the Christian faith. With immense generosity they gave their lives in service to you and to your forebears. They helped to educate the Aboriginal people and offered health and social services. Whatever their human frailty, and whatever mistakes they may have made, nothing can ever minimise the depth of their charity. Nothing can ever cancel out their greatest contribution, which was to proclaim to you Jesus Christ and to establish his Church in your midst.

From the earliest times men like Archbishop Polding of Sydney opposed the legal fiction adopted by European settlers that this land was 'terra nullius' – nobody's country. He strongly pleaded for the rights of the Aboriginal inhabitants to keep the traditional lands on which their whole society depended. The Church still supports you today. Let it not be said that the fair and equitable recognition of Aboriginal rights to land is discrimination. To call for the acknowledgement of the land rights of people who have never surrendered those rights is not discrimination. Certainly, what has been done cannot be undone. But what can now be done to remedy the deeds of yesterday must not be put off till tomorrow.

Christian people of goodwill are saddened to realise – many of them only recently – for how long a time Aboriginal people were transported from their homelands into small areas or reserves where families were broken up, tribes split apart, children orphaned and people forced to live like exiles in a foreign country. The reserves still exist today, and require a just and proper settlement that still lies unachieved. The urban problems resulting from the transportation and separation of people still have to be addressed, so that these people may make a new start in life with each other once again. The establishment of a new society for Aboriginal people cannot go forward without just and mutually recognised agreements with regard to these human problems, even though their causes lie in the past. The greatest value to be achieved by such agreements, which must be implemented without causing new injustices, is respect for the dignity and growth of the human person. And you, the Aboriginal people of this country and its cities, must show that you are actively working for your own dignity of life. On your part, you must show that you, too, can walk tall and command the respect which every human being expects to receive from the rest of the human family.

The Gospel of Our Lord Jesus Christ speaks all languages. It esteems and embraces all cultures. It supports them in everything human and, when necessary, it purifies them. Always and everywhere the Gospel uplifts and enriches cultures with the revealed message of a loving and merciful God. That Gospel now invites you to become through and through Aboriginal Christians. It meets your deepest desires. You do not have to be people divided into two parts, as though an Aboriginal had to borrow the faith and life of Christianity, like a hat or a pair of shoes, from someone else who owns them. Jesus calls you to accept his words and his values into your own culture. To develop in this way will make you more than ever truly Aboriginal. The old ways can draw new life and strength from the Gospel. The message of Jesus Christ can lift up your lives to new heights, reinforce all your positive values and add many others, which only the Gospel in its originality proposes.

Take this Gospel into your own language and way of speaking; let its spirit penetrate your communities and determine your behavior towards each other, let it bring new strength to your stories and your ceremonies. Let the Gospel come into your hearts and renew your personal lives. The Church invites you to express the living word of Jesus in ways that speak to your Aboriginal minds and hearts. All over the world people worship God and read his word in their own language, and color the great signs and symbols of religion with touches of their own traditions. Why should you be different from them in this regard? Why should you not be allowed the happiness of being with God and each other in Aboriginal fashion? As you listen to the Gospel of Our Lord Jesus Christ, seek out the best things of your traditional ways. If you do, you will come to realise more and more your great human and Christian dignity. Let your minds and hearts be strengthened to begin a new life now. Past hurts cannot be healed by violence, nor are present injustices removed by resentment. Your Christian faith calls you to become the best kind of Aboriginal people you can be. This is possible only if reconciliation and forgiveness are part of your lives. Only then will you find happiness. Only then will you make your best contribution to all your brothers and sisters in this great nation. You are part of Australia and Australia is part of you. And the Church itself in Australia will not be fully the

Church that Jesus wants her to be until you have made your contri-bution to her life and until that contribution has been joyfully received by others. In the new world that is emerging for you, you are being called to live fully human and Christian lives, not to die of shame and sorrow. But you know that to fulfil your role you need a new heart. You will already feel courage rise up inside you, when you listen to God speaking to you in these words of the prophets: 'Do not be afraid for I have redeemed you: I have called you by your name, you are mine. Do not be afraid, for I am with you.'

And again:

I am going to gather you together and bring you home to your own land. I shall give you a new heart and put a new spirit in you. You shall by my people and I will be your God.

With you I rejoice in the hope of God's gift of salvation which has its beginnings here and now and which also depends on how we behave towards each other, on what we put up with, on what we do, on how we honour God and love all people.

Dear Aboriginal people, the hour has come for you to take on new courage and new hope. You are called to remember the past, to be faithful to your worthy traditions, and to adapt your living cul-ture whenever this is required by your own needs and those of your fellow man. Above all you are called to open your hearts ever more to the consoling, purifying and uplifting message of Jesus Christ, the Son of God, who died so that we might all have life, and have it to the full.

'It begins, I think, with that act of recognition'

Paul Keating

Speech at Redfern Park

10 DECEMBER 1992

When prime minister Paul Keating (1944–) began his speech to launch the Year of the World's Indigenous People at Redfern Park, there were catcalls from the back of the mainly black audience. An angry Indigenous population from the depressed inner-city Sydney suburb of Redfern felt alienated and abused by mainstream politics, and expected little but platitudes. Yet, as the speech was delivered, with its message of hope and recognition, the atmosphere changed; catcalls turned to murmurs of assent and appreciation. The speech was seen by many as a turning point in communication between black and white Australia, with its simple themes of acknowledgement, responsibility and the need for imagination to resolve deeply rooted and extremely complicated problems. The address at Redfern Park followed the High Court decision in the Mabo case earlier in 1992, which had overturned the doctrine of *terra nullius*, and preceded the Native Title Act introduced by Keating in 1993. The Redfern Park address is probably the best known of Keating's speeches composed with his speech writer Don Watson. Although delivered to an Indigenous audience, it was – in Watson's words – 'an appeal to white Australians'.

*

This will be a year of great significance for Australia. It comes at a time when we have committed ourselves to succeeding in the test which so far we have always failed. Because, in truth, we cannot confidently say that we have succeeded as we would like to have succeeded if we have not managed to extend opportunity and care, dignity and hope, to the Indigenous people of Australia – the Aboriginal and Torres Strait Island people.

This is a fundamental test of our social goals and our national will: our ability to say to ourselves and the rest of the world that Australia is a first-rate social democracy, that we are what we should be – truly the land of the fair go and the better chance. There is no more basic test of how seriously we mean these things. It is a test of our self-knowledge. Of how well we know the land we live in. How well we know our history. How well we recognise the fact that, complex as our contemporary identity is, it cannot be separated from Aboriginal Australia. How well we know what Aboriginal Australians know about Australia.

Redfern is a good place to contemplate these things. Just a mile or two from the place where the first European settlers landed, in too many ways it tells us that their failure to bring much more than devastation and demoralisation to Aboriginal Australia continues to be *our* failure.

More I think than most Australians recognise, the plight of Aboriginal Australians affects us all. In Redfern, it might be tempting to think that the reality Aboriginal Australians face is somehow contained here, and that the rest of us are insulated from it. But, of course, while all the dilemmas may exist here, they are far from contained. We know the same dilemmas and more are faced all over Australia.

This is perhaps the point of this Year of the World's Indigenous People: to bring the dispossessed out of the shadows, to recognise that they are part of us, and that we cannot give Indigenous Australians up without giving up many of our own most deeply held values, much of our own identity – and our own humanity.

Nowhere in the world, I would venture, is the message more stark than it is in Australia. We simply cannot sweep injustice aside. Even if our own conscience allowed us to, I am sure that in due course, the world and the people of our region would not. There should be no mistake about this – our success in resolving these issues will have a significant bearing on our standing in the world.

However intractable the problems seem, we cannot resign ourselves to failure any more than we can hide behind the contemporary version of social Darwinism which says that to reach back for the poor and dispossessed is to risk being dragged down. That seems to me not only morally indefensible but bad history.

We non-Aboriginal Australians should perhaps remind ourselves that Australia once reached out for us. Didn't Australia provide opportunity and care for the dispossessed Irish? The poor of Britain? The refugees from war and famine and persecution in the countries of Europe and Asia? Isn't it reasonable to say that if we can build a prosperous and remarkably harmonious multicultural society in Australia, surely we can find just solutions to the problems which beset the first Australians – the people to whom the most injustice has been done?

And, as I say, the starting point might be to recognise that the problem starts with us non-Aboriginal Australians.

It begins, I think, with that act of recognition. Recognition that it was we who did the dispossessing. We took the traditional lands and smashed the traditional way of life. We brought the diseases. The alcohol. We committed the murders. We took the children from their mothers. We practised discrimination and exclusion. It was our ignorance and our prejudice. And our failure to imagine these things being done to us.

With some noble exceptions, we failed to make the most basic human response and enter into their hearts and minds. We failed to ask, how would I feel if this were done to me? As a consequence, we failed to see that what we were doing degraded all of us.

If we needed a reminder of this, we received it this year. The report of the Royal Commission into Aboriginal Deaths in Custody showed with devastating clarity that the past lives on in inequality, racism and injustice; in the prejudice and ignorance of non-Aboriginal Australians; and in the demoralisation and desperation, the fractured identity, of so many Aborigines and Torres Strait Islanders.

For all this, I do not believe that the report should fill us with guilt. Down the years, there has been no shortage of guilt, but it has not produced the responses we need. Guilt is not a very constructive emotion. I think what we need to do is open our hearts a bit. All of us.

Perhaps when we recognise what we have in common we will see the things which must be done – the practical things. There is something of this in the creation of the Council for Aboriginal Reconciliation. The Council's mission is to forge a new partnership built on justice and equity, and an appreciation of the heritage of Australia's Indigenous people.

In the abstract, those terms are meaningless. We have to give meaning to 'justice' and 'equity' – and, as I have said several times this year, we will only give them meaning when we commit ourselves to achieving concrete results. If we improve the living conditions in one town, they will improve in another. And another. If we raise the standard of health by twenty per cent one year, it will be raised more the next. If we open one door, others will follow.

When we see improvement, when we see more dignity, more confidence, more happiness – we will know we are going to win. We need these practical building blocks of change.

The Mabo judgement should be seen as one of these. By doing away with the bizarre conceit that this continent had no owners prior to the settlement of Europeans, Mabo establishes a fundamental truth and lays the basis for justice. It will be much easier to work from that basis than has ever been the case in the past. For that reason alone, we should ignore the isolated outbreaks of hysteria and hostility of the past few months.

Mabo is a historic decision. We can make it a historic turning point, the basis of a new relationship between Indigenous and non-Aboriginal Australians. The message should be that there is nothing to fear or lose in the recognition of historical truth, or the extension of social justice, or the deepening of Australian social democracy to include Indigenous Australians. There is everything to gain.

Even the unhappy past speaks for this. Where Aboriginal Australians have been included in the life of Australia they have made remarkable contributions. Economic contributions, particularly in the pastoral and agricultural industry. They are there in the frontier and exploration history of Australia. They are there in the wars. In sport, to an extraordinary degree. In literature and art and music. In all these things they have shaped our knowledge of this continent and of ourselves. They have shaped our identity. They are there in the Australian legend. We should never forget – they have helped build this nation.

And if we have a sense of justice, as well as commonsense, we *will* forge a new partnership. As I said, it might help us if we non-Aboriginal Australians imagined ourselves dispossessed of land we had lived on for fifty thousand years – and then imagined ourselves told that it had never been ours. Imagine if ours was the oldest culture in the world and we were told that it was worthless. Imagine if we had resisted this settlement, suffered and died in the defence of our land, and were told in history books that we had given up without a fight. Imagine if non-Aboriginal Australians had served their country in peace and war and were then ignored in history books. Imagine if our feats on sporting fields had inspired admiration and patriotism and yet did nothing to diminish prejudice. Imagine if our spiritual life was denied and ridiculed. Imagine if we had suffered the injustice and then were blamed for it.

It seems to me that if we can imagine the injustice we can imagine its opposite. And we can *have* justice. I say that for two reasons. I say it because I believe that the great things about Australian social democracy reflect a fundamental belief in justice. And I say it because in so many other areas we have proved our capacity over the years to go on extending the realms of participation, opportunity and care.

Just as Australians living in the relatively narrow and insular Australia of the 1960s imagined a culturally diverse, worldly and open Australia, and in a generation turned the idea into reality, so we can turn the goals of reconciliation into reality.

There are very good signs that the process has begun. The creation of the Reconciliation Council is evidence itself. The establishment of the ATSIC – the Aboriginal and Torres Strait Islander Commission – is also evidence. The Council is the product of imagination and good will. ATSIC emerges from the vision of Indigenous self-determination and self-management. The vision has already become the reality of almost eight hundred elected Aboriginal regional councillors and commissioners determining priorities and developing their own programs.

All over Australia, Aboriginal and Torres Strait Islander communities are taking charge of their own lives. And assistance with the problems which chronically beset them is at last being made available in ways developed by the communities themselves.

If these things offer hope, so does the fact that this generation of Australians is better informed about the injustice that has been done, than any generation before. We are beginning to more generally appreciate the depth and the diversity of Aboriginal and Torres Strait Islander cultures. From their music and art and dance we are beginning to recognise how much richer our national life and identity will be for the participation of Aboriginals and Torres Strait Islanders. We are beginning to learn what the Indigenous people have known for many thousands of years – how to live with our physical environment. Ever so gradually, we are learning how to see Australia through Aboriginal eyes, beginning to recognise the wisdom contained in their epic story. I think we are beginning to see how much we owe the Indigenous Australians and how much we have lost by living so apart.

I said we non-Indigenous Australians should try to imagine the Aboriginal view. It can't be too hard. Someone imagined this event today, and it is now a marvellous reality and a great reason for hope.

There is one thing today we cannot imagine. We cannot imagine that the descendants of people whose genius and resilience maintained a culture here through fifty thousand years or more, through cataclysmic changes to the climate and environment, and who then survived two centuries of dispossession and abuse will be denied their place in the modern Australian nation. We cannot imagine that. We cannot imagine that we will fail. And with the spirit that is here today I am confident that we won't.

I am confident that we will succeed in this decade.

'I speak for all Australians in expressing a profound sorrow to the Aboriginal people'

John Howard

Apology on national TV

3 JULY 2000

In an episode of the satirical TV series *The Games* (1998–2000), organisers of the 2000 Olympics decided that a prime ministerial apology to Indigenous Australians should be televised to a national audience, but were unable to extract one from the incumbent. Their solution: have a namesake, the actor John Howard, do the job. Since graduating from NIDA in 1979, John Howard (1952–) has been acclaimed for many of his roles – most notably as Nicholas Nickleby for the Sydney Theatre Company and Bob Jelly in the ABC series *Sea Change*. Here he was in the novel position of playing himself playing a prime minister. Conceived and written by the comedian John Clarke and Ross Stevenson, *The Games* was one of the most successful and popular Australian series of its time. Although satirical, the 'Howard apology' seemed to express sentiments previously regarded as inexpressible.

*

Good evening. My name is John Howard and I'm speaking to you from Sydney, Australia, host city of the year 2000 Olympic Games.

At this important time, and in an atmosphere of international goodwill and national pride, we here in Australia – all of us – would like to make a statement before all nations.

Australia, like many countries in the new world, is intensely proud of what it has achieved in the past 200 years. We are a vibrant and resourceful people. We share a freedom born in the abundance of nature, the richness of the earth, the bounty of the sea. We are the world's biggest island. We have the world's longest coastline. We have more animal species than any other country. Two-thirds of the world's birds are native to Australia. We are one of the few countries on earth with our own sky. We are a fabric woven of many colours and it is this that gives us our strength.

However, these achievements have come at great cost. We have been here for 200 years but before that, there was a people living here. For 40,000 years they lived in a perfect balance with the land. There were many Aboriginal nations, just as there were many Indian nations in North America and across Canada, as there were many Maori tribes in New Zealand and Incan and Mayan peoples in South America. These Indigenous Australians lived in areas as different from one another as Scotland is from Ethiopia. They lived in an area the size of western Europe. They did not even have a common language. Yet they had their own laws, their own beliefs, their own ways of understanding.

We destroyed this world. We often did not mean to do it. Our forebears, fighting to establish themselves in what they saw as a harsh environment, were creating a national economy. But the Aboriginal world was decimated. A pattern of disease and dispossession was established. Alcohol was introduced. Social and racial differences were allowed to become fault-lines. Aboriginal families were broken up. Sadly, Aboriginal health and education are responsibilities we have still yet to address successfully.

I speak for all Australians in expressing a profound sorrow to the Aboriginal people. I am sorry. We are sorry. Let the world know and understand, that it is with this sorrow, that we as a nation will grow and seek a better, a fairer and a wiser future. Thank you.

'Seeking an apology from John Howard is progressivist and is not the main game'

Noel Pearson

Speech at the launch of Don Watson's *Recollections of a Bleeding Heart*, Sydney

7 MAY 2002

Aboriginal leader Noel Pearson (1965–) believes that passive welfare dependency is largely to blame for what he describes as some of 'the most dysfunctional societies on the planet'. He refers specifically to the chronic problems of unemployment, alcohol abuse and violence in Indigenous communities of Cape York, in far north Queensland. Pearson grew up in a two-bedroom fibro house at a former Lutheran mission at Hope Vale, Cape York, in a family he describes as 'terribly poor' but 'socially strong'. He won a scholarship to St Peter's Lutheran Secondary College in Brisbane and later graduated in history and law at Sydney University. But Pearson turned his back on a corporate legal career in favour of returning to his community and becoming an adviser to Indigenous organisations. He was part of the negotiating team during the drafting of the *Native Title Act* in 1993, executive director and later director of the Cape York Land Council, and advocate of Cape York Partnerships, a regionally focused political program that aimed to link up disparate government departments with local Indigenous groups. Pearson's outspoken views on welfare dependency corrupting Indigenous values and attacks on 'the Left' – who, he argued, 'have got to get real' – incurred the ire of previous supporters. But at the launch of Don Watson's biography of Paul Keating, *Recollections of a Bleeding Heart*, Pearson reiterated his views on 'Labor and the Left' and confronted his critics.

*

Paul Keating was correct in his acknowledgement of the truth of Australia's colonial history. His Redfern Park speech of December 1992 was and continues to be the seminal moment and expression of European Australian acknowledgement of grievous inhumanity to the indigenes of this land. The prime minister had spoken on behalf of all Australians and to the extent that he used the rhetorical 'we' in that speech, he had of course not claimed the individual responsibility of Australians for the actions of the past, but rather a collective owning up to the truth of that past, and to its legacies in the present.

The prime minister had explicitly said it was not a question of guilt, but one of open hearts. How could this acknowledgement have been better put?

As much as I could never understand the reactions and campaigns on the part of the right in relation to Paul Keating's Redfern Park speech, I could never understand the subsequent incessant campaign on the part of the Left seeking an apology from John Howard. The truths of the past in relation to the stealing of children and the destruction of families were already the subject of prime ministerial acknowledgement. And that acknowledgement came without prompting and could not have been more sincerely expressed.

As to the pointless campaign for an apology from John Howard, to the extent that it expresses the importance which people attach to reconciliation, I can understand it, but to the extent that it is touted as one of the most important questions in Aboriginal policy, it underlines the distinction between being progressive and progressivist. Paul Keating's Redfern Park speech was progressive. Seeking an apology from John Howard is progressivist and is not the main game in terms of what is important in Aboriginal policy.

Federal Labor is dominated by what I call the progressivist intellectual middle stratum. They have played a role in achieving recognition of Aboriginal property rights, but the prejudice, social theories and thinking habits of Left-leaning, liberally minded people make them unable to do anything further for Aboriginal people by attacking our real disadvantage factors.

The only answer to the epidemics of substance abuse that devastate our communities is organised intolerance of abusive behaviour. The late Professor Nils Bejerot pointed out that historically substance abuse epidemics have been successfully cured without much in the way of research and voluntary rehabilitation. What can still save our communities is that a policy based on absolute intolerance of abuse gains credibility. In this situation, the progressivists tend to support policies that can only waste more precious time: further research, rehabilitation, harm minimisation, improved service delivery and so on.

Let me give just one example of the strange thinking that has gained acceptance among the progressivist middle class. The Australian Council of Social Service and Australians for Native Title and Reconciliation organised a seminar called 'Practical reconciliation or treaty talks? Which way forward for Indigenous social justice?' Two papers were presented. One was titled 'Indigenous disadvantage: Australia's human rights crisis', and even though it contained a section called 'Historical causes of Indigenous disadvantage', did not once mention substance abuse (but had a lot to say about the United Nations and international law). The other paper stated that grog was not the only reason why Aboriginal people live as itinerants in Darwin and Alice Springs – and that was all. Making such grave omissions while discussing justice for the women and children in Aboriginal communities and the historical causes of their disadvantage is absurd.

Age columnist Robert Manne wrote last year that:

> Pearson's contempt for the sentimentality of the pro-reconciliation liberal left has grown rapidly in recent times. In my view the indulgence of this irritation is a political mistake. Pearson is in danger of forgetting ... that in their common struggle for the survival of the Indigenous peoples against the indifference of the mainstream and the assimilationism of the right, the support of the good-hearted, bridge-walking middle-class liberal left remains an asset of inestimable worth.

Though I am a great admirer of Professor Manne – particularly his outstanding defence of the true history of the breaking up of Aboriginal families – I disagree with his political analysis. On the contrary, I would like to take my argument from last year one step further.

I contended that the two most important factors maintaining and worsening Aboriginal disadvantage are the substance abuse epidemics and passive welfare. But these two factors ultimately depend on one single factor: the thinking of the progressive, liberally minded intellectual middle class.

A radical shift here would be the single most beneficial change for Aboriginal people, because the people in the communities who want change cannot effect it if left alone; dysfunction and social disintegration have gone too far. They need support, but it is crucial that this support is based on a new understanding of the real situation.

In recent years there has been a great change in the discussion about Aboriginal affairs. Women have spoken out about what things are really like after several decades of progressivist policies. Federal Labor has been unable to handle this situation.

Labor is confined to passively scrutinising the government's policy. In recent weeks they have pointed to government bungling in Aboriginal education and the large amounts spent on litigation against Indigenous interests that the federal government included in their 'record spending' on 'practical reconciliation'. This is of course good, but I can't discern any tendency to an adequate response from Labor in the face of the real current crisis.

Because the present shift in the debate that reality imposes on us is in conflict with their prejudice and world outlook, federal Labor seems to have abandoned Aboriginal people and simply ceased trying to develop a credible policy. It is not the case that the government has a raft of innovative policies aimed at helping communities to move beyond passive welfare and to confront substance abuse directly – they do not.

The same energy and insight that Labor had in 1983 when it confronted a sclerotic economy – and the same courage to reform its thinking – is needed in this new century if Labor is going to have any solutions to the social predicaments in our nation, not the least the predicaments of those whose social misery is the most egregious.

Federal Labor has a very hard job ahead of them changing this sorry state of affairs. I suggest they look at Paul Keating's break with old thinking and renewal of Labor economic policy for inspiration.

ATTACKS, SCANDALS AND CONTROVERSIES

'I suppose we are to be favoured with a bunyip aristocracy'

Daniel Deniehy

Speech on the Constitution Bill, Victoria Theatre, Sydney

15 AUGUST 1853

When William Charles Wentworth (1790–1872), Legislative Councillor and chairman of the committee appointed to draft a new constitution for NSW, proposed the introduction of an hereditary peerage in the colony, he expected cordial support. His opposition came in the unanticipated form of a twenty-five-year-old 'boy orator' and 'extreme liberal', Daniel Deniehy (1828–1865), whose description of the proposal as a 'bunyip aristocracy' mocked it into oblivion. The son of Irish convicts, Deniehy was a gifted lawyer, politician and journalist – poet Richard Henry Horne described him as the 'brightest spirit of all young Australians' – who seemed to struggle with the harshness of his times, and finally lost a prolonged battle with alcoholism.

*

Why I have been selected to speak to the present resolution I know not, save that as a native of the colony I might naturally be expected to feel something like real interest, and to speak with something like real feeling on a question connected with the political institutions of the colony. I will do my best to respond to that invitation to 'speak up', and will perhaps balance deficiencies flowing from a small volume of voice by in all cases speaking plainly and calling things by their right names.

I protest against the present daring and unheard-of attempt to tamper with a fundamental popular right, that of having a voice in the nomination of men who are to make, or control the making of, laws binding on the community – laws perpetually shifting and changing the nature of the whole social economy of a given state, and frequently operating in the subtlest form on the very dearest interests of the citizen, on his domestic, his moral and perhaps his religious relations.

The name of Mr Wentworth has several times been mentioned here today, and upon one or two occasions with an unwise tenderness, a squeamish reluctance to speak plain English, and call certain shady deeds of Mr Wentworth's by their usual homely appellations, simply because they were Mr Wentworth's.

Now, I for one am not wisely disposed, as preceding speakers have seemed, to tap the vast shoulders of Mr Wentworth's political recreancies – to damn him with faint praise and mistimed eulogy. I have listened from boyhood upwards to grey tradition, to Mr Wentworth's demagogic areopagiticas – his speeches for the liberty of the unlicensed printing regime of Darling; and for these and diverse other deeds of a time when the honourable member for Sydney had to the full his share of the chivalrous pugnacities of five-and-twenty, I was as much inclined to give Mr Wentworth credit as any other man. But with those fantasias, those everlasting varieties on the 'Light of other days' perpetually ringing in my ears, I was fain to inquire by what rule of moral and political appraisal it was sought to throw in a scale directly opposite to that containing the flagrant and shameless political dishonesty of years, the democratic escapades, sins long since repented of, in early youth. The subsequent political conduct, or rather the systematic political principles, of Mr Wentworth had been of a character sufficiently outrageous to cancel the value of a century of service.

The British constitution has been spoken of this afternoon in terms of unbounded laudation. That stately fabric, it is true, deserves to be spoken of in terms of respect; I respect it, and no doubt we all share in that feeling. But mine is a qualified respect at best, and in all presumed assimilations of the political hypothesis of our colonial constitution-makers, I warn you not to be seduced by mere words and phrases, sheer sound and fury. Relatively, the British constitution is only an admirable example of slowly growing and gradually elaborated political experience applied and set in action, but it is also eminent and exemplary as a long history, still evolving of political philosophy.

But, as I have said before, it is, after all, but relatively good for its wonderfully successful fusion of principles the most antagonistic. Circumstances entirely alter cases, and I again warn you not to be led away by vague associations, exhaled from the use of venerable phrases that have what few phrases nowadays seldom could boast, genuine meanings attached to them.

The patrician element exists in the British constitution, as does the regal, for good reasons: it has stood in the way of all later legislational thought and operation as a great fact; as such it is handled, and in a deep and prudential spirit of conservatism it is allowed to stand; but as affecting the basis and foundation of the architecture of a constitution, the elective principles neutralise all detrimental influences, by conversion, practically, into a mere check upon the deliberations of the initiative section of the legislature.

And having the right to frame, to embody, to shape it as we would, with no huge stubborn facts to work upon as in England, there is nothing but the elective principle and the inalienable right and freedom of every colonist upon which to work out the whole organisation and fabric of our political institutions.

But because it is the good pleasure of Mr Wentworth, and the respectable toil of that puissant legislative body whose serpentine windings are so ridiculous, we are not permitted to form our own constitution, but instead we are to have one and an upper chamber cast upon us, built upon a model to suit the taste and propriety of certain political oligarchs who treat the people at large as if they are cattle to be bought and sold in the market, as indeed they were in American slave states, and now in the Australian colonies, where we might find bamboozled Chinese and kidnapped coolies.

And being in figurative humour, I might endeavor to cause some of the proposed nobility to pass before the stage of our imagination as the ghost of Banquo walked in the vision of Macbeth, so that we might have a fair view of those harlequin aristocrats, those Australian magnificos.

We will have them across the stage in all the pomp and circumstance of hereditary titles. First, then, stalks the hoary Wentworth. But I cannot believe that to such a head the strawberry leaves would add any honour. Next comes the full-blooded native aristocrat, Mr James Macarthur, who will, I suppose, aspire to an earldom at least; we would therefore call him Earl of Camden, and suggest for his coat of arms a field vert (the heraldic term for green), and emblazoned on this field should be the rum keg of a New South Wales order of chivalry. There is also the much-starred Terence Aubrey Murray, with more crosses and orders – not orders of merit – than a state of mandarinhood. Another gentleman who claims the proud distinction of a colonial title is George Robert Nichols, the hereditary Grand Chancellor of all the Australias. Behold him in the serene and moody dignity of that picture of Rodiad that smiles on us in all the public-house parlours. This is the gentleman who took Mr Lowe to task for altering his opinions, this conqueror in the lists of jaw, this victor in the realms of the gab. It might be well to ridicule the doings of this miserable clique, yet their doings merit burning indignation; but to speak more seriously of such a project would too much resemble the Irishman 'kicking at nothing, it wrenched one horribly'. But though their weakness is ridiculous, I can assure you that these pygmies might work a great deal of mischief; they will bring contempt upon a country whose best interests I feel sure you all had at heart, until the meanest man that walks the streets would fling his gibe at the aristocrats of Botany Bay.

I confess I find extreme difficulty in the effort to classify this mushroom order of nobility. They could not aspire to the miserable and effete dignity of the worn-out grandees of continental Europe. There, even in rags, they had antiquity of birth to point to; here I will defy the most skilled naturalist to assign them a place in the great human family. But perhaps after all it was only a specimen of the remarkable contrariety which exists at the Antipodes. Here we all know that the common water-mole was transformed into the duck-billed platypus; and in some distant emulation of this degeneracy I suppose we are to be favoured with a bunyip aristocracy.

However, to be serious, I sincerely trust that this is only the beginning of a more extended movement, and from its commencement I see the happiest results. A more orderly, united and consolidated meeting I have never witnessed. I am proud of Botany Bay, even if I have to blush for some of her children. I take the name as no term of reproach when I see such a high, true and manly sensibility on the subject of their political rights; that the instant the liberties of their country are threatened, they could assemble and with one voice declare their determined and undying opposition. But I would remind you that this is not a mere selfish consideration; there are far wider interests at stake.

Looking at the gradually increasing pressure of political parties at home, we must in the not distant future prepare to open our arms to receive the fugitives from England, Ireland and Scotland who would hasten to the offered security and competence that were cruelly denied them in their own land. The interest of those countless thousands are involved in our decision upon this occasion, and they looked, and were justly entitled to look, for a heritage befitting the dignity of free men.

Bring them not here with fleeting visions and delusive hopes. Let them not find a new-fangled Brummagem aristocracy swarming and darkening these fair, free shores. It is yours to offer them a land where man is bountifully rewarded for his labour, and where a just law no more recognises the supremacy of a class than it does the predominance of a creed.

But, fellow citizens, there is an aristocracy worthy of our respect and of our admiration. Wherever human skill and brain are eminent, wherever glorious manhood asserts its elevation, there is an aristocracy that confers eternal honour upon the land that possesses it. That is God's aristocracy, gentlemen; that is an aristocracy that will bloom and expand under free institutions, and forever bless the clime where it takes root.

I hope you will take into consideration the hitherto barren condition of the country we are legislating for. I myself am a native of the soil, and I am proud of my birthplace. It is true its past is not hallowed in history by the achievements of men whose names reflected a light upon the times in which they lived. We have no long lines of poets, or statesmen or warriors; in this country, Art has done nothing, but Nature everything. It is ours, then, alone to inaugurate the future.

In no country has the attempt ever been made to successfully manufacture an aristocracy *pro re nata*. It could not be done; we might as well expect honour to be paid to the dusky nobles of King Kamehamaka, or to the ebony earls of the Emperor Souloque of Haiti.

The stately aristocracy of England was founded on the sword. The men who came over with the conquering Norman were the masters of the Saxons, and so became the aristocracy. The followers of Oliver Cromwell were the masters of the Irish, and so became their aristocracy. But I will inquire by what process Wentworth and his satellites have conquered the people of New South Wales, except by the artful dodgery of cooking up a Franchise Bill.

If we are to be blessed with an Australian aristocracy, I should prefer it to resemble, not that of William the Bastard, but of Jack the Strapper.

But I trespass too long on your time, and will in conclusion only seek to record two things: first my indignant denunciation of any tampering with the freedom and purity of the elective principle, the only basis upon which sound government can be built; and second, I wish you to regard well the future destinies of our country. Let yourself, with prophetic eye, behold the troops of weary pilgrims from foreign despotism which will ere long be flocking to these shores in search of a more congenial home, and let us now give our most earnest and determined assurance that the domineering clique which made up the Wentworth party are not, and should never be, regarded as the representatives of the manliness, the spirit and the intelligence of the free men of New South Wales.

'Liberty'

Peter Lalor

Speech at Bakery Hill, Ballarat

30 November 1854

Lured by gold to Victoria in 1852, Irish-born Peter Lalor (1827–1889) led the protest that culminated in the 1854 Eureka Stockade – the rebellion of miners in the goldfields of Ballarat that resulted in an attack by government troops. Thirty diggers and five police officers died and many more were wounded. The Eureka Stockade became a symbol of Australian identity and democratic protest, and Lalor – who lost an arm in the rebellion – was elected to the Victorian parliament the following year.

At a public meeting on the eve of the stockade, miners had burned their licences and declared: 'We swear by the Southern Cross to stand truly by each other, and fight to defend our rights and liberties.' Lalor looked around and saw no one to respond to the declaration: 'I saw brave and honest men, who had come thousands of miles to labour for independence ... the grievances under which we had long suffered ... flashed across my mind ...' He leapt onto a stump, and in what historian Ken Inglis describes as the most powerful 'speech as action' in Australian history, issued his one word proclamation.

*

Liberty!

'I do not agree with that; it is not fair to Judas'

William 'Billy' Hughes

Speech in the House of Representatives

28 MAY 1909

The month of May 1909 produced scenes in the federal parliament that were unprecedented in the levels of political manipulation, confusion, duplicity and contempt. Late in 1908 Andrew Fisher's Labor government had taken office and Alfred Deakin's liberal protectionist party looked finished; its numbers the smallest in a parliament still composed of the 'Three Elevens' – the Labor Party, the protectionists and the free-traders. Joseph Cook and his free-traders and John Forrest's protectionists refused to work under one another, but Deakin was convinced he could liberalise the conservatives, join them together and steal back the leadership. In May they agreed to amalgamate into a 'fusion' coalition, and a bewildered prime minister Fisher and his minority Labor government were abruptly dismissed.

Billy Hughes (1862–1952) had been attorney-general in the short-lived Fisher ministry, and responded to the fusion with scorn so strong it helped limit the Deakin–Cook ministry to less than a year. He travelled the country denouncing Deakin's treachery, but it was his speeches in parliament on 27 and 28 May which are best remembered as 'masterpieces of political invective'. When the member for Hume, William John Lyne, denounced Deakin as a 'Judas', Hughes famously retorted that this slandered Jesus' disciple.

*

The honourable and learned member for Ballarat has just favoured us for the first time with some excuses for his present action. He has found that which we feared he had lost forever – his facility for explaining and excusing everything – and given us fresh occasion for amazement, and for some little amusement. The honourable gentleman has been endeavouring to elevate political assassination into a fine art, and to place it upon a scientific basis. It appears now that the reason why he assassinated the Watson government was that he was inveigled under specious pretences to draft an amendment which he had not the faintest idea would have the result that followed its adoption.

The honourable member for Ballarat has explained that he was entrapped into drafting the amendment which brought about the defeat of the Watson government. I quoted last night, by way of reply, the words used by the right honourable member for East Sydney to the effect that that was a hollow and specious statement of facts. If the honourable member says it is not true that he drafted that amendment, or that he voted for it under the belief that it was not vital to us, let him still take refuge in what flimsy protection such a denial will give him, for no other man in the country will believe him.

He has explained and justified the assassination of the Watson government which he promised to loyally support. Had De Quincey lived until now he would have been able to include in his delightful essay, 'Murder as a fine art' the methods of the honourable member for Ballarat, for no man has adopted such a variety of methods, and none has contrived to more successfully evade the consequences of his political crimes. His last assassination in some respects out-Herods Herod, but his former achievements ran it hard for first place. Then there was the assassination of the Reid government: he made that government, he pledged himself to support it, he destroyed it by a speech which the right honourable member for East Sydney very properly assumed was not only the beginning of the end, but the end itself. The right honourable member therefore came down with a governor-general's speech of one paragraph; but did that save him from the wrath to come? We go out because our speech contains thirty-two clauses. He went out because his contained only one clause. Was the life of the right honourable member's government cut short because the program put before the House was too long for consideration? Rather it was such as could have been comfortably got through in one sitting day, and the right honourable member had such in contemplation. But it did not save him for a single hour.

The honourable and learned member for Ballarat has told us that the right honourable member for East Sydney was under a complete misapprehension. When at Ballarat he gave the right honourable member notice to quit, he never meant it. At the very moment when the right honourable member's political brains were falling over his shoulders, when his scalp was dangling at the honourable member's belt, the honourable member was really his best friend. God save us from such friends!

Last night the honourable member abandoned the finer resources of political assassination and resorted to the bludgeon of the cannibal. Having perhaps exhausted all the finer possibilities of the art, or desiring to exhibit his versatility in his execrable profession, he came out and bludgeoned us in the open light of day. It was then that I heard from this side of the House some mention of Judas. I do not agree with that; it is not fair – to Judas, for whom there is this to be said, that he did not gag the man whom he betrayed, nor did he fail to hang himself afterwards.

Had the prime minister known that it was the length of our program to which exception was taken, we should have been most happy to cut off the part which offended the honourable member. But since I have been in parliament I have never known the leader of any government to bring down a program – except in the one case that I have already referred too – which the House did not say and know was unlikely to be wholly complete in that session. It is the custom of governments to do so, and it has never been the practice of any House desirous of pushing on with public business to throw out a government because its program was too long, when that program contained those things which were necessary to be done at the time. Now what is to be done? The honourable member says that his program and ours are the same.

His is the Liberal government, and he has allied himself with those Liberals whom we see around him – wolves whose eyes gleam redly through their sheep's-wool covering – in order the more speedily and effectively to carry it out. He says that he slew us quickly in order to

save us from the tortures of a lingering death, and that in order that
there should be no interruption of public business. He declared that
it was this alone that actuated him in committing an act of the basest
ingratitude towards this party, and one without precedent at any rate
in the history of the Commonwealth parliament.

The people of this country, in spite of every effort to the contrary,
will be made acquainted with the true facts of this case. Although the
honourable member has thrown over him the shield of the most powerful organ in this state, if not in Australia, he will find that even that
will not now save him, for the people can never be made to understand how it happens that the honourable member, who was our ally
for the best part of nine years, and who was prepared to be our colleague fifteen months ago.

The honourable member for Ballarat has an excuse and an explanation for everything, but I will put this point in such a way that
neither excuse nor explanation will help him. The honourable member offered at that time two alternatives. At the best, all he can say is
that there were to be four portfolios for each party, and he was to be
prime minister.

There were to be four portfolios allotted to each party. This should
be most interesting to honourable members opposite.

Where we were, the honourable member and his party are now. I
commend to all honourable members opposite these facts. There were
to be four portfolios for each party. Either the present Prime Minister
was to lead, or the honourable member for Ballarat.

The honourable member was willing, as always, to step down for
the good of his country. In the alternative, there were to be five portfolios for the Labor Party.

I was approached personally by a member of the Deakin government, and a distinct offer was made to me that, in case we pushed the
matter, we should have five portfolios.

Nothing is done on the honourable member's behalf, or for which
he will take the responsibility. But the facts are as I have stated, and
the honourable member has only two alternatives. If he did not
propose to go into the ministry, he proposed to desert and assassinate
it as he is doing now; or he was going to sit in a cabinet in which
the Labor Party had an overwhelming predominance, and which,

certainly, as he must have known, would if formed have promoted exactly those measures which it now proposes to do.

This is a program that changes to fit the bewildering circumstances of political warfare. It is the program of those who from time to time are whirled in violence around the honourable member. He still remains the same. Parties change. Circumstances change. He alone remains constant and unshaken. But yesterday he was here. Today he is there. But the day before he offered to stand equal in all things with us.

Indeed, he offered us the superior position. Now he leads the cohorts of the Opposition. Mr Speaker, these are facts that no explanation or excuse from a man even more ingenious and more evasive than the honourable member can get over.

The people of this country will know that here is a man who condemned a party to whose policy even yet he can formulate no objection on political grounds, and who resorts to that contemptible weapon the 'gag' in order to consummate his nefarious purpose; a man who, when the inscrutable Providence which decides the puny affairs of men places him and his new party on this side, will in the fullness of time assassinate them, and bravely declare he did it for their own good.

There is surely some moral obliquity about a nature such as his. No act that he commits, no party that he betrays, no cause that he abandons, affects him at all. He regards himself as the selected and favoured agent of Providence. Everything that he does he does for the very best. He does it because there is nothing else that can be done to conserve the welfare of the people and the interests of the nation. To realise this noble ideal he has assassinated governments and deceived the people. Just now he wishes to fill the empty spaces of Australia; and he gathers about him those gentlemen who are responsible for the monopolisation of the lands of Australia. He proposes to establish a citizen defence force. He has been converted to that policy. I have to declare that he has done much good in his time, for I heard him convert himself on the question of a national defence force when he spoke in London. Up to that time he had been uncertain.

The honourable member may change again, of course. He may come round to the other side once more. But he proposes to establish compulsory military training with the assistance of gentlemen who have declared it to be the most dangerous and infamous expedient to which a British-speaking people could resort.

Ah, yes! The cohorts behind this honourable member for Ballarat declare that we on this side of the House are disloyal; that when we seek to establish an Australian navy we do wrong. And so, the honourable member for Ballarat has allied himself with those who have always upheld what they call the cause of loyalty to the British Empire. Amongst others he has allied himself with the honourable member for Parkes. That honourable member of late has been profoundly moved in reference to the position of imperial affairs. We are given to understand that he has addressed many public meetings in regard to this matter, and that everywhere he has met with the most amazing expressions of approval of his policy – whatever that may be. This is what the honourable member for Parkes says of the honourable member for Ballarat:

> Mr Deakin has told the people of England, through the Colonial Conference in 1907, that the present contribution (to the Naval Subsidy) is 'unpopular in Australia', that 'nobody approves of it'; and in doing so, he has, I have contended, said what is politically untrue, and has libelled the Australian people in regard to their loyalty to the Empire, as well as charged them, inferentially, in the eyes of their kith and kin, and in the hearing of other nations, with national ingratitude.

The honourable member for Parkes said this in a letter addressed to the present Prime Minister, dated 20th May, 1909. He also said:

> Australia has been maligned and discredited unjustly in the eyes of the British people by Mr Deakin; and you and your fellow Labor representatives, who voted against a contribution of any amount in 1903, failed to voice the feelings of the Australian people, but represented only certain labour organisations, by whose mistaken judgement the principle of opposition to a participation in the cost of Empire defence became part of the 'Labor' program.

Formerly the honourable member for Ballarat assumed an attitude of unrelenting hostility towards honourable members opposite, and would never ally himself with them. Then, however, he was still hoping to be taken into the bosom of Father Abraham!

He is the political mercenary of Australia. He will lead any party – he will follow none! He is faithful to only one thing – himself. He is true to only one power and bends the knee to only one principle, and that is that which is at any time the most powerful. To the age he never turns a deaf ear. Of that organisation, the Orange Lodge, a manifestation of whose power in active politics we saw lately, owing to the incredible energy of our friend the honourable member for Dalley, we see him a servile and humble adherent. He has done all these things; he has abandoned his party, and he has applied the gag to those who were his friends and allies, and prevented them from explaining their policy, a policy which he declared – was it five or six or ten days ago – to be a good one for Australia and a policy which even now he is unable to attack successfully.

He sits there now and declares that he is content to leave everything to the cool judgement of the people. He means the refrigerated, the hypnotised judgement of the people. Let him get to the people, whilst the facts and the memory of his latest acts are fresh in their minds. When he says, 'We will sweep the country,' the statement is perfectly true. The honourable gentleman will sweep the country, but we shall be the men who hold the broom and he will be the broom with which we shall sweep it.

'If there is a just God in heaven, those sobs will reach Him'

Hugh Mahon

Speech at Richmond Reserve, Melbourne

7 NOVEMBER 1920

Irish journalist and Catholic patriot Hugh Mahon (1857–1931) fled his home country and migrated to Australia as a paid agent for the Irish National Land League in 1882, having served a jail term in Dublin for his radical political activities. He edited newspapers in NSW and Western Australia before winning the seat of Coolgardie for the Labor Party in the 1901 federal elections. Described by the *Westralian Worker* as 'a democrat whose snobbish coldness of demeanour would make a snake shudder,' Mahon nonetheless enjoyed a twenty-year parliamentary career including a spell as minister for external affairs.

Mahon never modified or mollified his Irish sympathies, which often invited controversy, especially after the Easter uprising. In November 1920 at an open-air meeting in Melbourne organised by the INLL, of which he was now president, Mahon launched a savage attack on British policy and the Empire, after the death of the Lord Mayor of Cork, Terence McSweeney, from a hunger strike in Ireland. The content of the speech and its audience of three thousand caused a sensation. Following demonstrations in Melbourne, Billy Hughes introduced a motion to expel Mahon from the parliament for his 'seditious and disloyal utterances'. After a bitter debate the motion was carried and Mahon thrown out; a unique occurrence in the history of Australian politics and the ultimate payback from Hughes, whose own expulsion from the Labor Party over conscription three years earlier Mahon had supported.

*

There is one whose absence from this meeting will be greatly missed, and that is his Grace the noble Archbishop of Melbourne. [*Cheers.*] I take it that the outrage upon that eminent cleric will never be forgotten by the Irish people of Australia. [*Hear, hear.*] The action taken against him by the British government was one of the most damnable outrages ever committed upon free man in an alleged free country. [*Hear, hear.*] The very hypocrites who pleaded with us to fight for the liberty of small nations are virtually jailing the Archbishop of Melbourne, refusing him the right to visit his native land and his venerable mother. I ask you: Was there ever such black-hearted hypocrisy as this? [*Cries of 'No.'*] Whatever the Germans did in Belgium and Poland, remember that they were at war; but this gang of vile hypocrites, led by George, has in time of peace committed an infinitely greater outrage upon Archbishop Mannix than was ever offered by Germany to the Cardinal Archbishop of Malines. [*Hear, hear.*] And these people have the audacity to rail at and reproach young Australians for not sacrificing themselves to uphold a rule of this kind. I consider it a sacred duty to hand down to your children the memory of the unparalleled indignity on our Archbishop of which this infamous gang has been guilty.

We have met here today to express sympathy with the widow and family of the late Lord Mayor of Cork – a man irreproachable in domestic and private life, trusted and beloved by his fellow citizens, and the chief magistrate of an ancient and important city. What sort of a government is it that has only a felon's cell for a man of his attainments and intellectual gifts, his self-sacrifice and his patriotism? Why there never was in Russian history during the time of the most bloody and cruel tsars a government of a more infamous character – to subject to a lingering and a painful death a man of the type of Terence McSweeney. When we read in the papers that his poor widow sobbed over his coffin, I said: 'If there is a just God in heaven, those sobs will reach Him and will one day swell into a volume that will shake the foundations of this bloody and infamous despotism.'

I was reproached the other day that the police were being shot in the back – if they are being shot in the back they must be running away. But, anyway, there are no police in Ireland; they are spies, informers and bloody cut-throats. It is a satisfaction to know that the rotten Irish government cannot get its uniformed soldiers to do its dirty work, and is forced to import into Ireland the off-scourings of English jails, now known as the 'Black and Tans'. [*Groans.*] Some of these thugs, the murderers of innocent men, women and children, have been sent to their account. Their souls, if they had souls, are probably in hell, so it is fitting that their carcasses should 'go whence they came'. I would not have the sweet pastures of holy Ireland poisoned by their clarion clay. [*Applause.*]

We have a splendid signal from America which is a severe blow to Ireland's enemies. The treacherous and cowardly Democratic Party has gone to the wall and, thank God, the Irish in America rallied to the support of even an indifferent person in the Republican candidate rather than return to the Democrats. [*Cheers.*] The late Democratic president proclaimed self-determination, the rights of small nations and all this sort of cant at the Paris conference, but turned a deaf ear to the representatives of Ireland; and this man who assumed to speak on behalf of the democracy of the world, is now out; and so, thank God, is his bastard League of Nations, which has come to an end with him – [*cheers*] – a spurious international body which took no account of the wrongs of one of the most ancient and honourable countries in the world. Really, when you come to think of it, we have a right to thank God that this rotten gang in America has gone to the wall, and that no more is to be heard of the League of Nations with the hypocritical English politicians sitting in the chief positions.

The other day I moved a motion in the House of Representatives – [*hear, hear*] – a harmless one, to call attention to the infamous murder of the Lord Mayor of Cork, but the renegade rats of the Labor movement and the vinegary-visaged wowsers backing up Hughes put on the gag. They were afraid to hear the truth about Ireland. One impudent and ignorant person said: What is this to do with Australia? My rejoinder is: What the hell did the war have to do with Australia? [*Cheers.*] If these are not proper subjects to debate in a national parliament, in the name of heaven, what is? Have we no soul? But we have a direct and very deep interest in what is going on in Ireland. [*Hear, hear.*] Even those imperialistic bullies, if they had any sense, would know what a danger to the Empire it is to have Ireland in such a state. A discontented Ireland is always a danger, but a free and contented Ireland would try and forget the accumulated wrongs of eight hundred years and not be a menace to England. Thus, those jingoes who pretend to be the best friends of the Empire are really its most damnable enemies. [*Hear, hear.*] The nation which survived Cromwell – a decent man compared with Lloyd George – which out-lived the infamies of 1798, is not the one to go down before this gang of false-hearted hypocrites, who only occupy the treasury benches of the House of Commons by conspiracy and fraud. [*Cheers.*]

'I was compelled to consider the qualifications of the new leader'

Earle Page

Speech in the House of Representatives

20 April 1939

Earle Page (1880–1961) spent forty-two of his eight-one years in parliament – including nineteen days as a caretaker prime minister – much of them defined by his ambivalent relationship with Robert Menzies. In a private conversation in 1938, Menzies sought Page's advice as to whether he should retire from politics, as he felt himself 'out of step in the cabinet'. Page urged him to remain, and suggested that his problem might be that he expected too much, that gaining agreement in cabinet – from those who represented all sections of the community – was the best way to gain acceptance of political decisions by the community. Page said to Menzies, 'If we were to arrange a dinner to which each diner contributed something, it would be a good dinner if Lyons brought the roast beef, I brought the vegetables, someone else brought the pudding, and [you] the champagne. But if everyone brought champagne it might be a bright party but could scarcely be regarded as a sustaining meal.' Menzies admitted 'he had never thought of cabinet in that way' and upon consideration decided to remain in parliament.

The harmony did not last. On 7 April 1939, prime minister Joseph Lyons died in office and Page, leader of the Country Party, became caretaker prime minister until the United Australia Party (UAP) elected a new leader. The votes went to Menzies. Page was committed to resign from the prime ministership upon the UAP's appointment, but he refused to serve in any coalition government under the newly elected Menzies, believing him lacking in the leadership qualities necessary in a country on the brink of war. When parliament resumed, Page launched an attack on Menzies that was reported in the *Sydney Morning Herald* as 'a violation of the decencies of debate'. Menzies, upon commencing his self-defence, described the attack as 'an extraordinary speech, delivered, if I may say so, at a most inappropriate time'. Menzies' wife Pattie, who was in the public gallery that day, left during Page's attack, and never acknowledged him again, although he subsequently resiled from his views and was welcomed back into cabinet.

*

… Honourable members will recall the dramatic onset of the last stage of the illness which brought about Mr Lyons' death. On Tuesday he was present at a meeting of the cabinet in Canberra; that night he travelled to Sydney. On Wednesday, at about 10 a.m., he informed me by telephone that he did not think that he would be well enough to attend the luncheon of the Royal Agricultural Society … and he asked me to take his place. When next day I, in company with the Treasurer (Mr Casey), saw him in hospital he was very much better, and his doctor said that he had a reasonable chance of recovering quickly. I left him at about one o'clock, having promised to interview another minister on his behalf. I had no sooner reached my home, not more than ten minutes' travel by car, when I received a phone call asking me to go back to the hospital. Mr Lyons had suddenly become unconscious, and the authorities at the hospital had broadcast a message to Dame Enid Lyons and myself to return to the hospital immediately …

The position then was that the United Australia Party, which was in partnership with the Country Party in the government of the country, and which being the larger party had always provided the leader of the government, was temporarily without a deputy leader; therefore, no officer of that party could rightly be said to be in the direct line of succession. In those circumstances, and without any advice from me, the Governor-General decided to commission me to form a government to carry on the affairs of this country. As honourable members will agree, it was obvious to all at that time that at any moment Australia might find itself at war, and that it was imperative there should be a government fully clothed with all powers ... to deal with any situation that might arise ... I told my colleagues, without any pressure at all ... that when the United Australia Party elected its leader I would tender my resignation to the Governor-General and give to him whatever advice might be sought. That is the position I am still in. As I have said, as soon as the right honourable member for Kooyong (Mr Menzies) was elected, I indicated my readiness to take immediate action. However, it is beyond question that the change in the leadership of the UAP has resulted in a change in the relationship of the two parties composing the government. The general basis for the successful functioning of a composite government must be the fullest mutual confidence and loyalty between the parties composing it. For twelve years in this parliament, I have sat in composite governments with Mr Bruce and Mr Lyons under such conditions ... Mutual confidence and loyalty are still essential conditions for the existence and proper functioning of a composite government; but at present, unfortunately, there is another consideration which overrides, but does not dislodge, these conditions. Everyone realises that today we are perhaps on the threshold of war ... It seems to me that if a wartime government is to function – and that may be the position at any time, although I hope not – it must function in such a way as to secure the greatest possible measure of cooperation in the community. The Australian Government needs a leader with not merely the qualities I have mentioned, but also the three essential qualities of courage, loyalty and judgement, in such degree as will ensure that the people of Australia will give the last ounce of their energies and resources in a united national effort to ensure our preservation. Therefore, as the leader of the Country Party, which has been associated for so many years with the UAP in the government of this country, I was compelled to consider the qualifications of the new leader of the UAP ... I was entitled to consider whether he possessed the qualifications necessary for his high office. I had to ask myself whether his public record was such as to inspire the people of Australia to the maximum unstinted effort in a time of national emergency. Because of that I was reminded of three incidents in the public career of the newly elected leader of the UAP.

The first of the three happened only twenty-four days previously, when, honourable members will remember, the right honourable gentleman tendered his resignation as Attorney-General in the Lyons administration. This country is spending many millons of pounds in preparations for a defensive war, and we are endeavouring to get every industry to put forward the maximum effort in order that Australia may be prepared for any eventuality. At this time, when all our efforts were being strained to put the defences of this country in order, the right honourable gentleman insisted on resigning from the government because he differed from its attitude towards national insurance ... I shall quote but one sentence from his letter of resignation to the late prime minister. He said:

> I frankly do not think we can expect to be taken seriously if we start off again with conferences and drafting committees at a time when we have already so notoriously failed to go on with an act which represents two years of labour, a vast amount of organisation, and a considerable expenditure of public and private funds.

Now the right honourable gentleman says that that is exactly what he intends to do.

The second incident is this: some twenty-four weeks ago he went to Sydney, where he made a speech on leadership; that pronouncement was regarded by the public and the press of Australia as an attack upon his own leader. I do not say that it was; I merely say that it was construed in that way ...

[Mr Speaker: Order!]

I come now to the third incident: some twenty-four years ago the right honourable member for Kooyong was a member of the Australian Military Forces and held the King's Commission. In 1915, after having been in the military forces for some years, he resigned his commission and did not go overseas.

[Mr James: That is dirt!]

... I am not calling into question the reason for the right honourable gentleman's action, nor would I question the reason for any other individual in similar circumstances. All I say is that the right honourable gentleman has not explained, to the satisfaction of the very great body of people who did participate in the war, his reasons, and because of this I am afraid that he will not be able to get that maximum effort from the people of Australia to which I have referred ...

My position may be shortly stated: the leader of the United Australia party having been elected, I shall see the Governor-General this afternoon and tender the resignation of my commission as prime minister ...

'We must fight to destroy their use of the Chifley legend'

Bartholomew Augustine 'Bob' Santamaria

'The movement of ideas in Australia': speech at the annual Movement Convention, Albury

EARLY 1954

Described as 'the most famous Australian lay-Catholic of the twentieth century', and 'a medieval monk of the anti-communist crusade', Bob Santamaria (1915–1998) dedicated his life to fighting communism. From the age of twenty-two he worked alongside Daniel Mannix for the National Sectariat of Catholic Action and founded the *Catholic Worker*, before forming an effective anti-communist organisation known variously as the Catholic Social Studies Movement, the Catholic Movement and simply the Movement. The Movement was a powerful force in countering attempts by the Communist Party to infiltrate the trade union movement in Australia. It also worked – actively and secretly – against the leadership in the Labor Party and was instrumental in the 1955 split of the ALP. In the following speech, Santamaria discusses the ideology of the anti-communist battle in the unions and addresses his concern about the growing anti-American feeling inside the ALP. His suggested antidote provoked outrage among his detractors. The general secretary of the Australian Workers Union, T. Dougherty, wrote a pamphlet in response to the speech entitled 'Santamaria unmasked: cloak and stiletto methods exposed' to counter Santamaria's denunciation of the 'Chifley legend'.

*

… Ideas can be held in three types of ways. They can be absolutely honest ideas put forward by a group of dedicated men who subordinate themselves and their private interests to that particular idea. Now the real inner nucleus of the Communist Party, I don't mean the careerists – the blokes who wanted communism to get a job and to hold themselves in power in the union movement – but the dedicated Marxist, had that sort of idea. Some of our own people have that sort of idea, an idea honestly held, to which a man subordinates the whole of his life.

There is another type of idea and this is the one which you are going to meet during the next two years; the idea and the argument that a man puts forward, perhaps quite honestly in his own conscience, but which is not the real reason for which he puts the argument forward at all. The idea, for instance, that ALP industrial groups are dangerous to the structure of the Labor Party, that they are going to break up the Labor machine. You find quite a lot of people opposed to us putting that idea forward today and saying that they oppose us because of that. They may honestly believe that themselves, but I think that the priests here in particular would know how a man can argue himself into a false state of conscience over a particular problem. Very many of these people are simply after power. They can't put forward an argument for power nakedly and unashamedly, therefore they find a point of dispute and they build that up until they convince themselves of it. Now the majority of ideas that we are going to contest are that type of idea.

Finally, there is the idea that is put forward in utter cynicism. I remember having a discussion with a most prominent official of the Labor Party – a federal official – a little while ago, and he said that the rearmament program in Australia had to be chopped by £60 million. I put it to him, 'Look, you can't do that, if you do Australia won't be armed properly,' and his answer in effect was that 'I'm not interested in the moral values of the argument, it's what will go down with the people, chop armament by £60 million.'

The same argument on migration. He said, 'You've got to stop migration, there's unemployment.' But I said 'What about our population?' Again the same argument, 'not interested in that, it's what will go down at the elections.'

Now, there is a great danger that any man who puts forward that idea is a man without a soul, but whether he is a man without a soul or not, that sort of idea is cynically held, and you have to meet it and you have to defeat it. Now gentlemen, I don't know if I have diagnosed the three forms of ideas. Are they clear? ...

My thesis is this, that although ideas in the last analysis do determine events, ideas just don't grow out of the ground. The material situation, the actual concrete situation of the fight from time to time, very largely dictates what sort of ideas grow out of it. You know what Marx's idea was; Marx's idea was that the productive process – how men earn their living – absolutely determines the ideas that they hold. Now there is heresy. But we can believe that ideas just don't come out of the air, they do relate to the world in which we are moving.

In 1943 to 1947, what was the situation? It was the period you will remember of our gallant ally the Soviet, fighting on our side. It was the period when the communists in Australia were consolidating their hold on the trade union movement, they were building up their control of the ACTU in the Congress of 1945. Now that was admitted, but nobody worried about it, because it was held that the communists could be trusted with that industrial power. They could be trusted with the military power they had in Europe. They were on our side, and we who were fighting both of those forms of trust, those versions, were very unpopular with non-Catholics and Catholics alike. We were held to be the people who saw communists under every bed, they remember that. Now that idea, leading to our unpopularity, was based largely on the fact that Stalin was fighting with us.

You came then to the period 1947 to 1951. It was a different time. Internationally it was the time when communism marched on its role of aggression. They conquered the Iron Curtain countries, they conquered China, and the whole thing finished in the Berlin Air Lift, and everybody got frightened then of communism internationally. In Australia, if you remember, it was the period of the strikes, the great strikes paralysing the eastern seaboard, and then it was touch and go which way the ACTU would go with those strikes, and at that time because communism was really beginning to use the power that it had accumulated in the earlier years, then people realised the danger and we who had been unpopular suddenly became very popular. You got no arguments at all among either Catholics or non-Catholics about the legitimacy and the justice and the desirability of your action.

From 1951 onwards something new happened. This is the period when internationally after the conquest of China, the communists stopped their aggression and started to mark time. They might be causing little bursts of trouble in Korea and Malaya, but no huge conquests like the conquests of three or four years before. Internally our forces started to win in Australia – you remember the wins culminating in the cleansing of the Ironworkers Federation last year – but the whole series of wins was building up in 1951, and the communists, defeated in one way and having the strength to realise that they had to play a much slower game if they were to rebuild their forces in Australia, started to match their international policy of holding their hands, and as soon as they did that the view arose, 'Communism is defeated in Australia.' I have heard that expressed again and again last year, that the comms are on the run, and as soon as that view began to be accepted a new line of criticism came against our work. I may say among non-Catholics in the Labor movement, and among Catholics. ...

The article of foreign policy is by Allan Fraser, who is MHR, federal member of parliament, representing the Eden-Monaro area. Allan Fraser is writing a series of articles entitled 'When Labor governs'.

The first one is on foreign policy and this is what Fraser says: 'While Australian adherence to the United Nations and to the system of collective security against aggression' (that relates to Korea) 'is an article of unwavering Labor faith, discontent prevailing in the party of some attitudes of the Menzies government justified under the cloak of this policy, has been publicly expressed by certain Labor members. Those attitudes of Menzies, which will certainly be re-examined by a Labor government include' (and here is the vital point) 'the surrender of Australian independence of voice and vote at the United Nations meetings. Whilst Australia's influence in such gatherings may not be powerful, nevertheless the status of Australia in world affairs which this government inherited from the work of Dr Evatt and which it has undermined, was very high, moreover full exercise of the Australian rights described at the United Nations of the cause we believe in, is fundamental to continue Australian popular support for it. Australians will not be led by the nose. Firstly, a demand for independence of Australia's voice at the United Nations – we've got to throw our weight around at the United Nations. Now, what does this mean? Uneasiness at this attitude of the present ministry is underlined by the well evidenced belief that it is based on one overriding concept of foreign policy to tie this country at whatever cost to the powerful United States as our future's sure shield and buckler against the rising Asia.' That is what it says is the Menzies policy, to subordinate ourselves entirely to the United States in order to get military support against Asia.

What did he say of it? 'That the trail implicit in this concept and the inability to guarantee fulfillment of his hopes alike condemn it. It is impossible for the most coarse opponent of the Labor Party to deny its anxiety to promote the closest ties of friendship with America and to make all possible arrangements with her for her aid in resisting attacks upon us, but not at any price. Certainly not at the price of weakening Britain, to which too many signs recently point.' See, down with America, up with Britain, and this concern with Britain I think, is the first time that it has arisen with Labor policy in Australia.

He goes on. 'The ALP is Australian first, but it is deeply British in feeling.' Now, I think that is something very, very new in the ALP and something which has really been discovered by Allan Fraser, but that is the line, down with America, up with Britain, not merely for kinship sake, but because realistically on Britain's survival our own survival depends.

The next point. 'This is a truism which was constantly emphasised by Mr Chifley.' Now there is a Chifley legend, that is the next thing. Down with America, up with Britain, and when these people say on what authority do we base ourselves, it's always on the authority of Mr Chifley. People might not follow Dr Evatt or Mr Calwell, but the Chifley legend is held to be strong enough to make orthodox any policy that they put forward, and to condemn any policy that we put forward.

I think that that is quite sufficient to show the general line on foreign affairs that this particular force in the Labor movement is going to adopt. Australia must throw its weight around at the United Nations, it must not surrender the control of its foreign policy to anybody, but particularly no subservience to the United States, and as everybody realises that we have got to hang on to somebody as we're not powerful enough ourselves, then we raise the old British kinship as the counterbalance to our support of the United States. I think this is clear.

That is the first line of policy that we will meet. The second one relates to the one against communism. Here on page fifteen of the same issue, there is an article: 'Will industrial groups split the Labor machine?' asks J.P. Ormond, who as you know is a Catholic. It is a very clever article, clever in its political implications, not very cleverly expressed; it is a very hard argument to follow, but this is what Ormond and the forces around him, or the forces whose views he represents, say of the ALP industrial groups, which are the essential methods which we use in the fight against communism internally. He says: 'The groups are over-reaching themselves and are endangering the Labor machine. Having defeated the communists they are now in the position of deciding who are the militants. That is the situation which Mr Chifley warned us against.' Again the sacred cow, Mr Chifley's legend rolled in against American policy in one article, and against the industrial groups in the other one. 'It must be clear by now that a great number of workers see no inconsistency in voting for a

392 • *Well May We Say*

communist in a union ballot and for the ALP in parliamentary elections. It is only by education and strong leadership that this condition
of mind can be altered, not by the use of political force.' Of course
the example of the ironworkers, which did use political force, is
conveniently ignored.

He adds: 'The recent ballot in the Miners' Federation showed that
hundreds of miners who voted for the communist Idriess Williams as
their general president, also voted for the ALP members Neilly and
Cotterill, for the district positions. To all our anti-communists' (and
that is us, that is how we are categorised) 'this might seem cock-eyed,
but the workers are sometimes cock-eyed people,' says Mr Ormond.
'After all an ALP miner working underground with the communists,
filling coal for the same pay, taking the same risks, can hardly be
expected to harbour the same hate for a communist as some of our
enthusiastic young groupers, not working under these conditions.
They see the communists as a menace to their religious or national
security.' See the things brought in there, that we hate them, that we
don't know the conditions of miners, that we're animated largely by
religious and not by political or any other interests. All very cleverly
brought into the one sentence. 'The position now is that the Labor
Party is of the fabric of the trade union movement, there is no room
at present between the unions and the Labor Party for another party,
say an industrial Labor Party, in which the communists would pre-
dominate.' And here is the salient point: 'That if the ALP industrial
groups were to drive away any considerable section of the industrial
movement, there would be the beginning of the emergence of another
political force which in time could become a challenge to the political appeal of the Labor Party with large sections of the workers.'

Now there is the line of 'voice' internally, in the internal fight
against communism. You see what it is based on, the threat of a new
Labor Party against the old Labor Party to scare away the people running the Labor machine. The use of sectarianism, calling us a group
entirely motivated by religious objections, and finally an appeal there
for sympathy for the communists, because in the Miners they work
underground with ALP miners.

Finally, how did this all add up, what is it getting to? Are they
isolated objections on foreign policy and on internal policy, or has

this paper, and I'm going to discuss the strength of its ideas in a few moment, has it any overriding idea? The comms have an overriding idea; we have an overriding idea; has this paper an overriding idea? The overriding idea is given in the editorial of the same issue, and the title to me is most revealing 'Must we choose?' 'We have devoted more space than usual in this issue' (and it quotes the pages some of which I have quoted from) 'to a consideration of what we believe to be the twin evils of the present age, Stalinism and McCarthyism.' We are McCarthyites, supporters of Senator Joseph McCarthy of the United States, and you know the public opinion in which he is held. ...

Now, and this is the final culmination. 'If we fight Stalinist methods without at the same time fighting the McCarthyists and their ilk' (us) 'we are laying ourselves open to embracing the attitude of mind and doctrinal reaction as totalitarian and as insidious as that of the Stalinists.' And again I refer to the original title 'Must we choose?' I may sum up the doctrine of 'voice' by saying that it's this. It is a doctrine of political agnosticism, that in the political struggle today there is no absolute truth, that it is to be not that Moscow is better than Rome, but neither Rome nor Moscow. They are both equally bad. One is as bad as the other, and in the whole political fight there are far more important issues than this battle against communism, and hence communism must sink back, the fight against communism must be driven into its 'proper' perspective.

You can sum it all up by saying that this line of 'voice', political agnosticism, no absolutes, anti-Catholic as well as theoretically anti-communist, and therefore again it stifles action, as I will try to indicate. Now, you may say what is the importance of this, it is only a paper? I will put it to you that the paper itself may be of relatively little importance, but what it stands for is fundamentally important, because that policy today is enunciated by that paper, represents the majority view on the federal executive and the federal conference of the ALP. It represents the majority view there. ...

What is the danger of this force? I put it to you this way. In the immediate battle against communism, it does the job that Stalin and Malenkov asked to do at the nineteenth congress of the Communist Party. In other words, it splits the anti-communist front. It says, it splits it with the side issues by saying that those side issues of social services are much more important than the battle against communism. It brings about this degree of political disbelief in any absolute, and in the end what it does is destroys your will to act. You get to ask yourself in the end, I know as I have asked myself, really in the viewpoint of history, are we giving the battle against communism a dignity and importance which it doesn't warrant? In the end it plays on your conscience and if it plays on ours it will play very powerfully among the non-Catholic people who supported it in the past – is communism the major issue? That is the first result, it does the job that the communists want it to do, and it destroys the capacity to act among the anti-communists.

Secondly, I will put this to you. In a post-communist era if communism were to be met and defeated, either peacefully or as a result of war, you would have a future that could be just as dangerous to all that we stand for as at the present. The future that Bevan and those others are building up to is a future of national socialism of the Tito type, and it will be anti-religious, it will be against all civic liberties and it will be against private property and the family. It would be a very unrewarding battle, if Stalinism were to be defeated simply to enable Titoism and Bevanism to be the successor states in the new order, and that is the danger.

I had intended to say something about the way in which this force projects itself into Catholic thinking, but as time has gone on I will leave this aside for the time being, we may deal with that in questions. The question that immediately arises is – how are we going to deal with this third force here in Australia? I would put forward for your consideration that this force does exist, its doctrines and the refutation of its doctrines must be worked clearly and intellectually. We have got to win the argument of ideas. It can be answered alright, but unless you describe it and dispose it and answer it, you won't know what you are fighting, and the people whom you are trying to influence will deny the existence of the very enemy against whom you are coming against today.

Secondly, it must be given a name, we mustn't call it the third force as I have called it for purposes of convenience, because a third force between communism and anti-communism is tremendously attractive to the people who have not got any stomach for fighting. You have to give it another name and so far I certainly haven't thought of the name. It must be given a name so that like any disease it can be isolated and labelled, diagnosed and dealt with.

Thirdly, within the Labor movement we must fight to destroy their use of the Chifley legend. You are always against a disadvantage today when they can say Chifley said this in foreign policy, Chifley said that in bank nationalisation; it's a kind of infallible statement. You have got to destroy the Chifley legend in two ways. In the matter of international relationships you can destroy the Chifley legend by appealing to the now forgotten Curtin legend, and the meaning of Mr Curtin's actions in the field of foreign relationships was to call on America instead of Great Britain. He said that very, very clearly when MacArthur came to Australia. You have therefore got a rallying point; that legend to counterweight the Chifley legend. Then there is a big task of research to be done in Chifley's own speeches, recently obligingly published through the cooperation of the Labor Party, to show that the doctrines of Chifley in the last year of his life were not the doctrines that he held in the previous five or six years. That is the third thing, to destroy the order of infallibility given to these arguments by the Chifley legend.

Next, within the Labor movement we have got to prepare now, and we haven't done it so far, a strongly argued case in favour of the ALP industrial groups; you have got to answer the Ormond argument, that the groups threaten the structure of the Labor Party. Unless that is done and that argument is propagated everywhere, you will find that the groups will be subject to constant attack just as Lloyd Ross has been whittled away from them, so you will find in time the danger of Laurie Shorts and Neillys and others being whittled away. Therefore, the argument against the groups in particular must be answered.

Fifth, within the Labor movement we have got to get our people to develop policies and to speak honestly and straightforwardly in favour of the policies that they support. Can you name half a dozen union leaders who we have supported, or people on the political side of Labor, who would come out strongly in defence of America's action, who would come out strongly in favour of our economic policy? There may be half a dozen who would come out strongly along these lines, but if there are, I haven't seen them, and until they strongly come out and urge the policies which they really support in their hearts, you are always giving the battle away to the enemy by default. I believe above all that our leaders in the trade union movement have got to be pledged this year to show an answer to Lloyd Ross, who said that he stands for the idea of joint consultation for dealing with the employers on a level of statesmanship, whereas our fellows stand for nought, and if we do not do something, instead of talking about joint consultation this year Ross in his next attack will beat Kenny and all that Kenny stands for in New South Wales.

Lastly, and this is the most difficult task of all, so far in the battle against communism it has been the Catholic workers, tradesmen, members of unions who have borne the whole brunt of the struggle. The educated Catholics, the people with secondary and university education have not come into the fight hardly at all, and because they are not in the fight, their actions and their statements today, in argument, in Catholic papers, are very often irresponsible and dangerous. They have got to be brought into the struggle and won to the struggle. Then you not only sidetrack that line of argument, but you bring into the fight all of the intellectual resources which the church in Australia is capable.

'God save the Queen'

David Smith

Proclamation by the Governor-General dismissing the Whitlam government: steps of Parliament House, Canberra

11 November 1975

No day in Australian politics, appropriately, is remembered like Remembrance Day 1975. With the Coalition majority in the Senate blocking supply to the Labor government in the House of

Representatives, the Governor-General, Sir John Kerr, resolved the deadlock by dismissing Gough Whitlam and his government. The dismissal took place during the parliament lunch-break. Malcolm Fraser – sitting in another room at the Governor-General's residence until Whitlam had been and gone – was invited as the leader of the Opposition to form an interim ministry until a double dissolution of both houses would force an election. It was a stunning and bewildering end to a federal administration, and the Australian constitution's gravest test.

Crowds began to gather on the steps of the old Parliament House demanding to hear from Whitlam before a formal announcement had been made. At 4.45 p.m., David Smith (1933–), the official secretary to the Governor-General, read the proclamation dissolving both Houses of parliament before the vociferous crowd. He could hardly be heard. The hostility of the audience left Smith unmoved. He served as the official secretary to five governors-general between 1973 and 1990, before taking up an appointment as a visiting scholar at the Australian National University's Faculty of Law and participating in the 1998 Constitutional Convention as a non-parliamentary appointed delegate.

*

PROCLAMATION

By His Excellency, the Governor-General of Australia

Whereas by section 57 of the constitution it is provided that if the House of Representatives passes any proposed law, and the Senate rejects or fails to pass it, or passes it with amendments to which the House of Representatives will not agree, and if after an interval of three months the House of Representatives, in the same of the next session, again passes the proposed law with or without any amendments which have been made, suggested or agreed to by the Senate and the Senate rejects or fails to pass it, or passes it with amendments to which the House of Representatives will not agree, the Governor-General may dissolve the Senate and the House of Representatives simultaneously.

And whereas the conditions upon which the Governor-General is empowered by that section of the constitution to dissolve the Senate and the House of Representatives simultaneously have been fulfilled in respect of the several proposed laws intitled:

- *Health Insurance Levy Act 1974*
- *Health Insurance Levy Assessment Act 1974*
- *Income Tax (International Agreements) Act 1974*
- *Minerals (Submerged Lands) Act 1974*
- *Minerals (Submerged Lands) (Royalty) Act 1974*
- *National Health Act 1974*
- *Conciliation and Arbitration Act 1974*
- *Conciliation and Arbitration Act (No. 2) 1974*
- *National Investment Fund Act 1974*
- *Electoral Laws Amendment Act 1974*
- *Electoral Act 1975*
- *Privy Council Appeals Abolition Act 1975*
- *Superior Court of Australia Act 1974*
- *Electoral Re-distribution (New South Wales) Act 1975*
- *Electoral Re-distribution (Queensland) Act 1975*
- *Electoral Re-distribution (South Australia) Act 1975*
- *Electoral Re-distribution (Tasmania) Act 1975*
- *Electoral Re-distribution (Victoria) Act 1975*
- *Broadcasting and Television Act (No. 2) 1974*
- *Television and Stations Licence Fees Act 1974*
- *Broadcasting Stations Licence Fees Act 1974*

Now therefore, I Sir John Robert Kerr, the Governor-General of Australia, do by this my Proclamation dissolve the Senate and the House of Representatives.

(L.S.) Given under my Hand and the Great Seal of Australia on 11 November 1975.

By His Excellency's Command,
Malcolm Fraser
Prime Minister
God Save the Queen!

'Well may we say'

Gough Whitlam

Speech on the steps of Parliament House, Canberra

11 NOVEMBER 1975

Until the day he was sacked, Gough Whitlam (1916–) believed the appointment of Sir John Kerr as governor-general was one of the best he had ever made. At the Lodge immediately following the dismissal, Whitlam met with some of his ministers. When the minister for services and property, Fred Daly, walked into a small room on the verandah, Whitlam stood up and said, 'The bastard has done the dirty on us. We've been sacked.' Daly replied, 'Who?' 'All of us,' said Whitlam. In the hours following there was chaos and confusion. At 2.34 p.m. Malcolm Fraser announced to the House that he had been commissioned to form a new government. Two hours later, Whitlam emerged from the front entrance of the old Parliament House and listened as David Smith read out the governor-general's proclamation dismissing his government. With the crowd shouting, 'We want Gough,' Whitlam responded.

*

Ladies and gentlemen [*applause and cheering*], well may we say God save the Queen [*pause*] because nothing will save the Governor-General. [*Applause and cheering.*] The proclamation which you have just heard read by the Governor-General's secretary was counter-signed Malcolm Fraser [*boos and jeering*] who will undoubtedly go down in Australian history from Remembrance Day 1975, as Kerr's cur …

They won't silence the outskirts of Parliament House, even if the inside has been silenced for the next few weeks. [*Cheering.*] The Governor-General's proclamation was signed after he already made an appointment to meet the speaker at a quarter to five. The House of Representatives had requested the Speaker to give the Governor-General its decision that Mr Fraser did not have the confidence of the House [*pause*] and that the Governor-General should call me to form the government … [*Cheers and applause.*] Maintain your rage and enthusiasm through the campaign for the election now to be held and until polling day.

'I am speaking to you from my study in Canberra'

Sir John Kerr

Australia Day address, broadcast nationally on ABC radio and television

26 January 1976

Sir John Kerr (1914–1991) appeared never to understand why his decision to dismiss the Whitlam government aroused such anger and division. A distinguished barrister and judge of the Industrial Court, his actions were rooted in his understanding of the law and the constitution. The hostility and harrassment that followed him ever after had much to do with the way he acted, especially his failure to warn Whitlam about the depth of his misgivings. Kerr appeared to be fearful of his own dismissal and, perhaps seduced by his status, behaved more like the judge he was trained to be rather than a mediator of a crisis. Subject to relentless abuse following his decision, Kerr resigned as governor-general in 1977 and moved to Europe. The following speech was the first Australia Day address after the dismissal, and his second-last as governor-general.

*

This Australia Day message is being broadcast at a time when I am in London. Indeed I shall be today attending an Australia Day reception in that city. As I did not want to break the tradition of an Australia Day message to the people of Australia from the Governor-General, this was prepared in advance just before I left for the United Kingdom.

I am speaking to you from my study in Canberra. When it came to a decision about what I should say to all Australians on this important day, it seemed to me that I should not ignore the fact that towards the end of last year Australia passed through a serious parliamentary and constitutional crisis, one which imposed some strain on our machinery of government.

Over many years governors-general have watched and participated in the passing parade of Australian life, often from and in this study.

As history unfolds, major events and problems occur and a nation has to accommodate itself to the impact upon it of great forces. It has to make big decisions. Within living memory Australia has passed through great wars and encountered grave economic difficulties. We have the advantage of substantial resources in the quality of our people and in wealth, with great opportunities for our country to grow and become greater in its influences in the world.

Every country, from time to time, faces both economic and political challenges and conflicts. Countries which have stable political institutions do so with confidence. Australia is fortunate in this respect.

The events of the past three months have focused our attention on the basis of our system of parliamentary government and on our written constitution. Regrettably, a most difficult and unusual situation developed in the parliament, making it necessary for me to make a difficult decision. These events are now part of our history.

On this Australia Day we have an opportunity to look again at our constitution. Is it appropriate and adequate for our modern needs? Should it or can it be altered? Australia exists as a federation under the constitution and has existed as such for seventy-five years. The bargain made seventy-five years ago, and written down, still controls our political destiny.

Whatever changes one group or another thinks should be made, whatever defects may be apparent to many, the constitution is the instrument of government that we in fact have and we must follow it.

We have grown up within its framework. We cannot change it except in the constitutional way which it specified. With whatever faults it has, it has helped us to become a nation with great creative potential. ...

We have a great heritage; we have a great future. I express the belief that we also have a capacity for originality and the sense of national purpose and of national unity which will enable us to produce great results in the years ahead.

'The consumer is in the saddle'

Rupert Murdoch

Speech on the future of world media, Banqueting Hall, London

2 SEPTEMBER 1993

Rupert Murdoch (1931–) once remarked that 'Monopoly is a bad thing until you have it.' When his father, editor and entrepreneur Sir Keith, died in 1952, the Murdoch family was left with only the poorly performing Adelaide *News* once it had paid death duties. Rupert threw himself into every aspect of the paper's production – applying skills he had learned at England's *Daily Express* – with the determination that would make him one of history's wealthiest and most diverse media tycoons: the News Corporation empire spans newspapers, magazines, film studios, and terrestrial and satellite television networks in Australia, the US, the UK, Europe and Asia. Despite becoming an American citizen in 1985 to overcome US laws restricting foreign ownership, Murdoch remains the world's best-known Australian-born individual.

In 1993, when unveiling a new package of pay-television channels for his company BSkyB, Murdoch gave a remarkable speech that was broadcast via satellite to analysts and investors at various locations around the world. Walking into London's Banqueting Hall, he began by admiring the Rubens paintings among the artwork on the walls: 'I am particularly fond of "Hercules Crushing

Envy", from which we have suffered much,' he said. He proceeded to boast that the spread of his operations – and telecommunications generally – was a new and powerful threat to totalitarian regimes. His vision of the new frontier of communications pleased investors, but a month later, when the Chinese government banned all Murdoch satellite dishes, threatening his $825 million investment in the mainland, totalitarianism did not seem so tractable. The sequel was ignominious. Murdoch's acts of atonement included agreeing to drop the BBC World Service from his satellite operations into China, paying $5.4 million to the central totalitarian media apparatus, the *People's Daily*, and spending the rest of the decade 'attempting to re-establish links with Chinese leaders'.

*

We are on the edge of a new technological revolution. It is confusing, frightening and breathtakingly exciting.

For years man has been both beguiled and frightened by new technologies, and with reason. The motorcar brought with it an enormous increase in personal mobility and a parallel increase in congestion and pollution. Nuclear power gave us a virtually limitless supply of energy, and the means to blow ourselves up. Television created both a new means of entertaining and informing huge numbers of people, and the possibilities of totalitarian control by Big Brother laid out by George Orwell in his frightening *1984*.

We are almost a decade beyond Orwell's fateful date and he has been proved wrong. Advances in the technology of telecommunications have proved an unambiguous threat to totalitarian regimes everywhere. Fax machines enable dissidents to bypass state-controlled print media; direct-dial telephony makes it difficult for a state to control interpersonal voice communications. Satellite broadcasting makes it possible for information-hungry residents of many closed societies to bypass state-controlled television.

The march of telecommunications technology has been a key reason in the enormous spread of freedom that is the main distinguishing characteristic of recent years. The Bosnian Serbs cannot hide their atrocities from the probing eyes of BBC, CNN and Sky News cameras; starvation in Africa can no longer be ignored, because television brings it into our living rooms.

I must add (with maybe a tiny touch of regret) that this technology has also liberated people from the once-powerful media barons. The days when a few newspaper publishers could agree to keep an entire nation ignorant of an important event are long gone.

Technology is racing ahead so rapidly, news and entertainment sources are proliferating at such a rate, that the media mogul has been replaced by a bevy of harassed and sometimes confused media executives, trying to guess at what the public wants. The consumer is in the saddle, driving the telecommunications industry. The technology is galloping over the old regulatory machinery.

Time does actually fly. Not so long ago, as we were preparing to launch Sky Television, it was impossible to switch on the BBC, ITV or Channel 4 – or indeed read a newspaper or go to a media seminar in Europe – without being confronted with predictions that the allegedly golden age of British broadcasting was coming to an end. Instead, we have had an expansion of consumer choice. In addition to – not instead of – the programs offered by traditional broadcasters, we have a variety of news, entertainment and sport that for many marks the start of a real golden age, not its end.

Choice is only one characteristic of the new telecommunications era. The others are equally extraordinary: convergence and interactivity. Convergence is seeing some of the world's largest industries trying to accept a new age in which few of the old rules seem to apply and traditional distinctions are breaking down. Five of the world's biggest industries – computing, communications, consumer electronics, publishing and entertainment – are converging into one dynamic whole.

Here in the UK, the News Corporation is working with British Telecom and Cellnet to explore these critical issues, to develop what President Clinton has called the digital super-highway of the future. This involves combining satellite technology with telephone networks, allowing consumers to access communications, television, movies, sporting events and information services as simply as possible.

It is a striking example of how the consumer will literally drive the new communications era. The new super-highways of communications will lead where consumers decide they want the technology to take them, not where scientists want them to go. The recent acquisition by News Corporation of a majority interest in Star Television, based in Hong Kong, has changed the landscape of this company's broadcasting strategy. Put simply, it represents the most exciting challenge in broadcasting in the world with a reach of more than two-thirds of the entire planet. But if it has enormous potential, it also carries with it enormous responsibilities.

We will introduce a wide range of new programming including an open university and educational channels. Our ambitions include the creation of new channels with worldwide reach. With our partners, we will aim to create and cover global events such as the search for the world's best young opera singer.

I must emphasise that this new technological era does not offer opportunities for News Corporation alone; it is an environment that all media companies can and should participate in. For instance in January, News Corporation and the German broadcaster PRO 7, affiliated with the Kirch Corporation, will introduce one of the most advanced forms of pay television.

Last Friday, we concluded arrangements for a joint venture between Fox Broadcasting and Televisa of Mexico to produce 500 hours of original, multilingual drama.

On October 1, Sky News, already seen and respected in thirty-three countries, will be satellited to southern Africa. Plans are well advanced to take Sky News, or a parallel service, to all the continents of the world. A second Sky Sports Channel will start early in the new year, in time for the English cricket tour of the West Indies.

Looking further ahead, to digital compression, we have been for some time developing the means with which people will access the almost infinite wealth of programming and services this technology will bring.

Yesterday we signed an agreement with some of the best brains in the business to develop, cooperatively, what will be the common digital satellite system throughout Europe, Asia and the Americas. The group consists of the British Research and Telecommunications

Organisation, NTL, an American high-technology company, Comstream, and our own access control and encryption company, News Datacom.

It is easy to be cynical about the wilder concepts of new technology, but I am sharply reminded of a statement by Sir Richard Woolley, the Astronomer Royal, in 1956 who dismissed space travel as 'utter bilge'.

One year later Sputnik was launched, occasioning the futurologist Arthur C. Clarke to observe: 'When a distinguished and elderly scientist states that something is possible, he is almost certainly right. When he states that something is impossible, he is very probably wrong.' To further expand our planned electronic publishing services this week, we have bought Delphi Internet Services, one of the five big recognised on-line data services in the United States. This service will provide endless data and information, even electronic newspapers, to anyone in the world with the necessary equipment to receive it.

We are here tonight to celebrate an event which is very much of the future, the most significant event in satellite television in Britain since the launch of Sky Television in February 1989. Sky Multi-Channels is a package of fourteen television channels, working together to create the future platform for satellite broadcasting in Britain.

The fourteen networks range from general entertainment to three different kinds of music, two channels for children, news, a channel mostly for women, and for the first time, a shopping channel, the very beginning of an interactive relationship between television and its viewers.

British Sky Broadcasting owns only two of the fourteen channels: Sky One and Sky News. Our partners include TCI, Cox Communications and Viacom.

Politicians like to say that the most important twelve-letter word in the English language is 'jobs jobs jobs'. As old industries and large companies contract, those new jobs are coming from industries such as ours which directly employ technicians, actors, writers, production and construction crews, food service people, secretaries and thousands of others, all of whom spend their hard-earned money on groceries, housing and transport.

It is estimated that when the technology convergence is complete, our industry will be the third largest in the world. News Corporation is pleased to be part of this process of economic expansion.

We feel that our company, with its worldwide network of talent, can make an important contribution to this exciting industry and, in the process, enrich the countries in which we and their peoples work.

IDEAS AND INSPIRATION

'A man ought always to be young and careless'

Mark Twain

Speech to the Yorick Club, Collins Street, Melbourne

28 September 1895

Eighty-five gentlemen gathered at Melbourne's Yorick Club in Collins Street to spend an evening with American writer Mark Twain (1835–1910) during his visit to Australia in 1895. Twain had fallen on hard times following a disastrous foray into publishing, and had undertaken an international lecture tour in a successful attempt to restore his financial fortunes; Australians were over-joyed to welcome him.

The night was described as 'the supreme evening in the club's history'. There were a number of distinguished guests in the gathering – Alfred Deakin proposed the toast to 'The Stars and Stripes'– and the party went on until after 3.00 a.m. Twain's after-dinner speech illustrates the writer's famous flair for 'massaging his audience' and his love for the Mississippi River of his youth.

*

It is not worthwhile to try to put into language the delight that you give me when you receive me in this hearty way. Language is for another office. Language is simply to portray the milder emotions of the human heart, but a welcome like this – a welcome that comes out of the heart – deep down – and expressed in a way that one cannot mistake – that is a thing which moves a man all the way through and through. [*Cheers.*] It does seem to me that in order to get such a welcome you've got to come all the way from America to Australia. You Australians seem to deserve the title of 'the cordial nation'. I have seen so much of your kindness, and have been so moved by it, and so charmed with it, that in thinking things over – I sit and think sometimes, and try to make out the characteristics of this nation and the characteristics of that nation – try to fasten a trademark on them, putting down one as frivolous, another as ox-like and stupid, a third as vivacious, and so on – it seems to me that you should be branded and trademarked as 'the cordial nation' – certainly when you meet me. [*Laughter.*] And that is most pleasant, that is most delightful. Now, I have been to a great many places where there were things to eat, where there was a supper, and where there was a chairman [*laughter*], and the distinctive quality of that chairman was always to make a speech that had nothing in it which you could use as a text afterwards. [*Laughter.*] That was the way with all the chairmen I ever saw – except this one. [*Laughter.*] But he has really so loaded me up with texts that it is an embarrassment of riches. [*Laughter.*] I don't know where to begin. If I used all the texts he has furnished me with there would be nothing left of us when I got through. [*Laughter.*]

There is one fact he brought out happily which stupid people who speak the English language all over the world are prone to overlook or to ignore, and that is – let us chaff and jaw and criticise one another as we please, when all is said and done, the Americans, and the English, and their great outflow in Canada and Australia are all one. [*Loud cheers.*] You have not stayed at home all your lives, and you know that sentiment which I have felt so many times. I have been around a good deal here and there in the world, and there is one thing that I have always noticed, and which you must have noticed under similar circumstances. Let one of us be far away from his own country – be it Australia, or England, or America, or Canada – and let him see either the English flag or the American flag, and I defy him not to be stirred by it. [*Cheers.*] Oh yes! Blood is thicker than water, and we are all related. If we do jaw and bawl at each other now and again, that is no matter at all. [*Laughter.*] We do belong together, and we are parts of a great whole – the greatest whole this world has ever seen – a whole that, some day, will spread over this world, and, I hope, annihilate and abolish all other communities. [*Loud cheers and laughter.*] It will be 'the survival of the fittest'. The English is the greatest race that ever was, and will prove itself so before it gets done – and I would like to be there to see it. [*Laughter.*] I am getting old. ['*No.*'] I am getting pretty old – but I don't find it out when I'm around this way. It is when one sits at home, melancholy, perhaps, when nothing is going on. But when I'm around this way with my own kind I don't know that I'm not quite young again – say, fifteen or sixteen – and I feel perfectly comfortable.

My friend on the right [Mr Deakin] and I were talking just now about that very thing. I said I thought that if I had created the human race – [*laughter, and a voice, 'You did some of them'*] – oh! I could have done it. [*Laughter.*] I was asked nothing about it, and I didn't suggest anything. [*Laughter.*] But I thought that if I had created the human race, and had discovered that they were a kind of a failure – [*laughter*] – and had drowned them out – [*loud laughter*] – well, I would recognise that that was a good thing. And then, fortified by experience, I would start the thing on a different plan. [*Laughter.*] I would have no more of that 969 years' business. I wouldn't let people grow that old. I would cut them off at thirty. Because a man's youth is the thing he loves to think about, and it is the thing that he regrets. It is the one part of his life that he most thoroughly enjoys. My friend on the right suggests that we should go as far as forty years, as he doesn't want any of his forty years rubbed out. Well, perhaps you really might go up to forty, because then you get a perspective upon youth, and that has its value. That has its charm. But, oh, dear me! I never would have created age. [*Laughter.*] Age has its own value – but that is to other people, not to those who have it. [*Laughter.*]

The chairman, among other things, touched upon my experience as a Mississippi pilot. That is connected with what I am now talking about. That is one of the things that you engage in when you are young and careless – and a man ought always to be young and careless. [*Cheers.*] Then everything that comes is satisfactory. You don't suppose that I would enjoy being a pilot on a Mississippi steamboat now, and be scared to death every time it came a fog. [*Laughter.*] But at that time fogs and dark nights had a charm for me. I didn't own any stock in that steamboat. [*Laughter.*] And that is one of the very advantages of youth. You don't own any stock in anything. [*Laughter.*] You have a good time, and all the grief and trouble is with the other fellows. [*Laughter.*] Youth is a lovely thing, and certainly never was there a diviner time to me in this world. All the rest of my life is one thing – but my life as a pilot on the Mississippi River when I was young – oh! that was a darling existence. There has been nothing comparable to it in my life since. And, speaking of that, I may tell you a little story.

I had that sort of instinct which anybody would have who had been separated by long years from a life of that kind. He would look back and remember this thing and that thing, and everything that happened to him when he was young; it was all so dear, and so beautiful and so fine – so much finer than anything he had experienced since. Well, I carried out that instinct, and I went out on the Mississippi River about 1880. I had not seen that river for I don't know how long – perhaps for a quarter of a century – and I went there with a sort of longing. One sometimes has a yearning to see again the scenes that were dear to him in his youth, in his prime, in the time when he had the heart to feel, and I thought that I would like to see that river and what was left of that steamboat life exactly as I saw it long, long, long ago. And so I went under a fictitious name. I didn't want to be found out. [*Laughter.*] I wanted to be able to go up into the pilot house, and talk to that pilot just as I used to see passengers talk to him, and I wanted to ask him the same idiotic questions. [*Laughter.*] And I wanted to get myself loaded up with the same misinformation just as they used to do. [*Loud laughter.*] So I went under a fictitious name, and the thing went along very well until, after I had signed my name 'John W. Fletcher' on the register of the Southern Hotel in St Louis, the man behind the counter bowed and said pleasantly – 'Show Mr Clemens to Number 165.' [*Loud laughter.*] Now you can imagine the interest I felt when I really was launched on the steamboat. She was a vile, rusty old steamboat, but she was the only one that was going down the river that day, and I wanted to go. I got on board that boat two hours before she was advertised to sail. I was

so anxious to see again that old steamboat life I had been so familiar with. I knew she wouldn't sail at the time she was advertised
[*laughter*], but I knew she would go some time that week. [*Laughter.*]
I was loafing about the decks just as happy as a man could be, notic-
ing details in the construction of that boat, which I hadn't seen in any
other boat or ship for ever so long. [*Laughter.*] …

When the boat had sailed I was so impatient that I got up in the
morning with the first dawn, to see what I could of that majestic river,
which used to be as familiar to me as the joints of my own fingers –
a river that I knew foot by foot, detail by detail, night or day, for 1300
miles. I was impatient to find if that old river was still familiar to me.
I did hope that I would recognise some parts of it, but when I came
up on that hurricane deck and looked round, I saw that that hope was
blighted. I didn't seem to recognise any part of it at all. At length I saw
a place on the right-hand side where there were some willows growing that I thought I did recognise, but no, I knew those willows were,
so to speak, creatures of a day, and that there must have been hundreds of them since I was there twenty years before. It was a deep disappointment to me. But then I thought – 'Never mind, I can cheer
up the occasion by getting up into that old pilot house, and letting
that man load me up with a lot of lies, as they did the historical
passenger.' [*Laughter.*]

I glanced up three or four times to make sure that I had never seen
that pilot before. No; he was too young for me to know at all. He
must have come into the pilot house after I left the river twenty years
before. I crept up in there, and to my joy I was received exactly like
the passenger of the old times. The pilot, when he heard the latch of
the door, turned round and gave me that sort of indifferent look – a
look that was, oh, so indifferent that if you could just get capital
enough, and collect enough of it, you wouldn't need any of those
refrigerating processes – it would freeze all the sheep in Australia.
[*Loud laughter.*] The old thing exactly. [*Laughter.*] I didn't expect any
more notice, and I didn't want any. I sunk down on the bench in the
pilot house. There was a little boy about seven years old playing
round. I got into conversation with him for a few minutes and then
he went away and we were left alone – I, and that pilot who had no
hospitality, no welcome, for me.

And then I began to ask my questions, just as the old-time passenger did. [*Laughter.*] I said, just in the same timid way – 'Would
you be kind enough to tell me what that thing there is for, that
speaking-tube?' 'Oh,' he said, 'that speakin' tube; that's to call the
chambermaid.' [*Laughter.*] Well, I felt so happy. [*Laughter.*] The thing
was going beautifully. I asked him another question – about another
speaking-tube. He said that was to call the boy who scrubbed the
deck. What was that bell for? You know, the bell that signals 'Go
ahead', and so on. That was to call somebody else. Everything was to
call somebody. That man could not apparently tell the truth, even by
accident. [*Laughter.*] And so I felt perfectly happy. I was getting
loaded up just as I wanted, and I would put it in a book. It was jolly
good stuff, and I was feeling very comfortable.

All of a sudden he says – 'Look here, just hold her a minute, I have
to go downstairs and get some coffee.' And away he went. [*Laughter.*]
Well, instinct made me take the wheel – you musn't leave a steamer
to pilot herself. Then I looked around to see if I could make out where
we were … I recognised it as the worst place in the whole Mississippi
River … a place called the Grand Chain. Even an apprentice pilot,
who had been through it a few times, would never forget it in all his
life because the marks have to be so exactly followed. There is one
place where there is a crossing two miles long, and in the very midst
of it there are two rocks. Neither of them shows above water, but they
make a little break which you can hardly notice. Those deadly rocks
are only seventy feet apart, and a Mississippi steamboat is twenty-five
feet wide, so you must not diverge at all. If you hit one of those rocks
you would be in heaven in two minutes. [*Laughter.*] I recognised that
I was in the Grand Chain but I didn't know exactly what part of it. I
suspected, though, that I was in the part that passes between those
two rocks. However, I knew one thing – that that pilot would never
have put that wheel into my hands until he had satisfied himself that
the boat lay exactly in the right course. He knew that if I had any
sense at all I had sense enough to keep between the marks – which I
did most diligently. [*Laughter.*] We passed between the rocks, and I
saw those breaks, and I didn't do any harm. But I was very glad when
he came back. [*Laughter.*] Then he said – 'You go and play fictitious
names on people and try to get your fun out of them, but I knew your

damned drawl the minute you spoke to that boy.' [*Laughter.*] Well, of course we got to be friendly, then. [*Laughter.*] It turned out that just as I was leaving the river he had finished his apprenticeship, but he had struck a pretty bad snag, and he could only get one pilot to sign his application. He required to have two. He was looking round and he found me, and I signed his papers and saved him – made a pilot of him.

So we had a jolly good time. I was always on his watch – and the other fellow's watch too. I stood all the watches there were. [*Laughter.*] All the day long, no matter which pilot's turn it was, I took the wheel. I couldn't get enough of it … A jackass could pilot a steamboat in that part of the river if he had just enough wit to follow the shape of the river. So the pilots would leave me there the whole watch, and there in that sunny country I would stand at the wheel, and pilot along down, and ponder, and think, and dream, and dream over all that old vanished time on the river. It was delightful – full of pathos, full of poetry, full of the charm of unconsciousness of anything else in the world but that old past …

But I musn't stand here and talk all night of old reminiscences. I was going through all the texts of the chairman, but now I come to think of it – I had forgotten it for the minute – I am entertaining a carbuncle unawares. [*Laughter.*] I have got it on my port hind leg, and it reminds me of its company occasionally. I have a greater respect for it than for any other possession I have in the world. I take more care of it than I do of the family. [*Laughter.*] But before I sit down I just want to thank you once again for your kind and cordial reception of me tonight, and to assure you that I do most sincerely appreciate it and value it. [*Loud and continued cheers.*]

'What is light?'

William Bragg

'The lessons of radioactivity': Adelaide University

11 JANUARY 1909

Englishman William Bragg (1862–1942) migrated to Australia at
the age of twenty-three to take up an appointment as professor of
mathematics and experimental physics at Adelaide University.
Physics soon became his discipline of primary interest and he
began experimenting with the new technique of X-rays. Bragg
returned to Cambridge University in 1909 and three years later
began working with his son, Lawrence Bragg (1890–1971), on
crystal structure. Together they established the field of X-ray
crystallography and were awarded the 1915 Nobel Prize for physics
– the only parent and child to ever receive a Nobel Prize together.
The following address, given to the Australasian Association for
the Advancement of Science before Bragg returned to England,
foreshadowed the work that would win him science's highest
honour.

*

For ages men have asked themselves, 'What is light?' When the
ancient writer recorded as one of the great acts of creation the command of God, 'Let there be light!', he testified truly of its importance
to mankind, and bore witness to the extent to which the seers of his
day had grasped that importance. When men bowed to sun and
moon and stars, they did but recognise their debt to the radiation on
which their whole lives seemed to depend. And though we can now
look past these creatures of light and heat, yet still we recognise their
vast importance in the universal scheme. Not only are they necessary
to our life upon the earth, but they alone bring us intelligence from
the infinities of space, and help our thoughts to rise from the earth

and stretch themselves to worthier and greater comprehensions. It is no matter of surprise that the study of the character and properties of radiation has at all times filled the thoughts of men.

There are two sides of this study to which I would particularly call your attention. We examine the properties of radiation in order to discover on the one hand the nature of radiation itself, on the other the nature and constitution of the atoms and molecules which emit it. For such information as we can obtain of the nature of atoms is of the utmost value since it is one of the main purposes of science, having once recognised the atomic composition of all material substances, to seek how to account for the properties of bodies in bulk from a knowledge of the properties of the atoms of which these bodies are composed. We therefore try to judge the atom by that radiation which proceeds from it. We can never hope to see an atom in the sense in which we see objects generally; we must form our estimates by indirect means. Yet the direct and the indirect are not so entirely different as might at first appear. We draw our conclusions as to the form, colour and position of the objects which we see in this room by the aid of the radiation emitted by the artificial light. The radiation is reflected, scattered and modified by the surfaces on which it falls; and our seeing is really no more than the perception and interpretation of these effects. In fact, the objects in the room are emitting radiation, borrowed, it is true, and thereby we judge them. In this case our perceptions deal immediately with the objects themselves, not the atoms of which they are composed.

Can we ever perceive effects upon radiation due to individual atoms as apart from the effect due to their action in bulk? The answer is, of course, in the affirmative. We may pass a ray of white light through coloured glass or any substance which shows selective absorption, so that the rays of certain wavelengths are removed, and the rest pass on. The result is the sum of separate actions by the billions of atoms of which the body is composed, so that the light which emerges may be considered as representative of light proceeding from each atom after modification therein. Here, then, is a way by which we may hope to learn something of the individual atom. These absorption effects have indeed been closely studied, and have, as is well known, yielded results of the utmost importance not only to pure scientific research but also to commerce and industry. But, as regards the matter we are especially considering, they serve more to open our eyes to the complexity and richness of the inquiry than to yield us laws of any precision or generality.

In experiments of this kind we must make use of sources of radiation external to the atoms, and permit the atoms to modify the original rays. We can, however, force the atoms to become themselves the primary source of radiation; and, in doing so, we avail ourselves of a much more fruitful means of investigation. We may raise substances to incandescence by placing them in a flame, or subjecting them to the more intense heat of the electric arc or discharge; or we may turn our instruments to the heavens, where glowing suns form furnaces which far exceed in temperature anything we can find on earth. The atoms are now addressing themselves to us directly; each kind sends us radiation peculiar to its nature and condition. If we could but read the messages! But we are overwhelmed by the complexity and infinite variability of the effects which we observe. From a bewildering wealth of results we are able to disentangle a few fundamental truths, just enough to make us impatient of our ability to do more; the work required to elucidate one law successfully seems at the same time to add to the pile of facts yet unclassified and unexplained. The science of spectrum analysis grows year by year. It has taught us of the natures and motions of the stars, and revealed to us fundamental laws of physics; it has been a keen weapon of chemical research, and given powerful aid to industrial development. But, as to the constitution of the atom, it tells us too much at once; there is a roar of sound from which we can hardly disentangle separate sentences. Not only are the radiations emitted by each atom of exceeding complexity, but they vary, in a broad sense at least, with the conditions of the atom and with its electrical state, with the temperature and the pressure of the gas of which the atom forms part, and so forth. We are staggered by difficulties of interpretation, and crave for some simple method of attacking the great problem. Spectrum analysis speaks a language which we barely understand as yet.

Now you will understand the welcome which we give to a new science like radioactivity, which addresses us in simple phrases. We are here still concerned with radiations emitted by atoms, either directly or in a secondary sense; and still we try to gain from an examination of the radiations some knowledge of the atoms from which the radiations proceed. But we work under totally different conditions. Nothing marks the change more forcibly than the disappearance, complete or almost complete, of all dependence on physical and chemical conditions. The radioactive substances exercise their marvellous powers at a rate which cannot be hastened or delayed by any known agency, such as heat or cold or pressure; not even if they are made to form chemical compounds with other substances. And, again, when the radiations which they emit pass through material substances and are scattered or absorbed, as we find to be the case, the scattering and absorption are independent of the physical or chemical conditions of those substances. We have, as it were, gone below the foundations of physics and chemistry to the simpler primordial conditions on which the more complex sciences are built. There are radioactive phenomena which go so far as to take no account of those fundamental distinctions between atoms on which chemistry is based. The most penetrating gamma rays, in passing through substances, recognise no other property than that of mass; four atoms of aluminium affect them no more and no less than one atom of silver, because the former weigh as much as the latter, and the names 'silver' and 'aluminium' no longer convey a distinction.

It is clear that we are dealing with the most fundamental characteristics of the atoms, with the building material, and not with the structure: with the inner nature of the atom, and not its outside show; and it is this which differentiates radioactivity from the older sciences. You will remember how Jules Verne in one of his bold flights of imagination drives the submarine boat far down into the depths of the sea. The unrest of the surface, its winds and waves, are soon left behind; the boat passes through the teeming life below, down into regions where only a few strange and lonely creatures can stand the enormous pressure, and, diving still, reaches at last black depths where there is a vast and awful simplicity. Here, where no man 'hath come since the making of the world', the silent crew gazes on the huge cliffs which are the foundations and buttresses of the continents above …

In the history of every new country there is a phase – it has not yet passed away in Australia – when the prospector and the surveyor traverse the land through and through mapping its features, investigating its riches and its possibilities. Their labour is absolutely necessary, though they set out on their quest in ignorance of what they shall find. Just so the workers of science cover the new fields of research: they are prospectors who must do their part before the new country can be made to contribute to the enrichment of mankind. Now it is true that there are branches of scientific research which have a more or less obvious relation to Australasian progress. But we may also aspire to do work which does not appear to advantage our own country more than the world at large. Indeed, if we wish to take our place amongst the progressive peoples of the world, to gain the strength and inspiration which come from sharing in a common advance, and to shun the soul starvation which would follow on a selfish concentration on our own immediate advantage, we must play our part in this sense also, and play it enthusiastically and well …

'What are we singers but the silver-voiced messengers of the poet?'

Dame Nellie Melba

Speech to the students of Guildhall School of Music, London

19 MAY 1911

Australia's first and grandest prima donna, Dame Nellie Melba (1861–1931), reigned supreme in the golden age of opera. Born into a musical family and with a well-tuned childhood whistle and hum, Melba received her first singing tuition from Pietro Cecchi, who believed her voice would 'enthral the world'. Later, in Paris, Melba came under the tutelage of Mathilde Marchesi, who oversaw her rise to international fame. Melba enthralled her audiences wherever she went, singing before Tsar Alexander III in St Petersburg, Emperor Franz Joseph in Vienna and Kaiser Wilhelm II in Berlin. But it was the 'years of monotonous brilliance' at

Covent Garden – where she was the only artist to maintain a permanent dressing room – for which she is best remembered. Melba returned to Australia for several tours, where she was revered as a symbol of international glamour and success. In 1909 she purchased a cottage in Coldstream, Victoria, where she spent many of the remaining years of her life. Melba was an 'adept at elocution' from childhood and did not take kindly to abuse of the English language, the subject of her address to the students of Guildhall School of Music.

*

I should like to use this occasion to give expression to a few thoughts on the Art of Singing. The subject is as inexhaustible as it is fascinating, and it occurred to me when I was honoured with the request to address you today, that I should be more likely to be of interest and possible guidance to you if I confined the few remarks I can make on an occasion like this to one only of the many aspects of the art we all love. Every art is made up of a family of contributory arts. The art of singing, for example, includes among others in its composition, the arts of musical and temperamental expression; of the judicious employment of sensibility, and dramatic and poetic feeling; of tone colour; of phrasing and of diction. Of these, in England at least, the art of diction is the Cinderella of the family; and so, with your permission, I will employ the brief time at our disposal in considering the somewhat neglected art of English diction in singing.

In France, Germany and Italy there are certain more or less hard and fast rules governing the expression of each language. The right way to speak the words has been thought-out and formulated, and has been confirmed by tradition, and in case of dispute and misapprehension, reference can be made to irrefutable authorities, and the point at issue placed beyond doubt. Now in England, as far as I know, such felicitous conditions do not exist. The result is nothing short of lamentable. No two singers employ the same form, and it is doubtful if any two responsible teachers agree in regard to the pronunciation of every English word in song. To whom is the young singer, anxious for the right way and eager to excel, to refer on a nice point in diction, or even in respect to any of the most obvious stumbling blocks the language presents? Echo answers 'To whom?' The opinion is largely held that English is not a musical language, or at least, not a language which lends itself felicitously to expression in music. I rather think that, for a time, I held that opinion myself. My maturer judgement and experience tell me that I was wrong; that although the English language lends itself to expression in music less readily than the Italian, it is, in that respect, at least equal to the French, and certainly superior to the German; and that the reason why I held that opinion for a time, and why others hold it still, is that the art of English diction, whatever it may have been in other days, of which we have no direct knowledge, has been during our own time in a very uncultivated condition. It is true that there are exceptional instances to the contrary, and that occasionally we hear our native language spoken in song with distinction and clearness; but it is, alas! equally true that our ears are too frequently tortured by mispronunciations and verbal obscurities, and at times to such an extent that it is difficult to decide in which particular language the singer is delivering his message.

After all, what are we singers but the silver-voiced messengers of the poet and the musician? That is our call; that is our mission; and it would be well for us to keep it constantly and earnestly in our minds. What we should strive for is to attain as nearly to perfection as possible in the delivery of the message, sacrificing neither the musician for the poet nor the poet for the musician. If we sing a false tone or mispronounce one word, we are apt to awaken the critical faculty which, consciously or unconsciously, exists in every audience; to create a spirit of unrest, and destroy the burden of our message. A similar disastrous effect may, of course, be made by a miscalculation of breathing power, an inappropriate facial expression, or by any other inartistic happening on the singer's part.

I think it will be generally admitted as an ideal that the English language should be sung as it should be spoken, with just sufficient added distinctness, or one might even use the word 'exaggeration', to counteract the obscuring effect of the singer's voice and the piano or other musical accompaniment. You have observed that I have said 'as the English language should be spoken', and I am sure that the thought has occurred to you that the majority of people, singers and non-singers, do not habitually speak the language with justice, distinction and grace. How many persons do you know who could read aloud a verse of poetry, or of fine prose, in a manner to include the qualities mentioned? Not many, I fear. And yet I have a strong feeling that that is what the singer should be able to do before he or she enters seriously into the training of the singing voice. In a word, if verbal diction were early acquired, vocal diction would not be so serious a stumbling block to our singers.

> She dwelt among the untrodden ways
> Beside the springs of Dove,
> A maid whom there were none to praise
> And very few to love.

These words of Wordsworth are very simple, very beautiful and surely very singable; and yet I suppose I am not the only person present today who has heard them sadly mutilated in song. I have heard the word 'Dove' given as Doïve, the word 'whom' as 'oom', and the word 'love' – a particularly long-suffering word in song, by the way – given as 'loïve'. Suppose that a man – anxious to communicate to you the condition of his sentiments – were to say to you, 'I loïve you,' he would surely excite either your ridicule or your distrust. In any case the exhilarating message would be dreadfully discounted by its pre-posterous delivery. Perhaps if singers knew that audiences uncon-sciously made that discount every time the beautiful old Saxon word is mishandled in song, they would make some effort to sing the word as it is spoken.

For another example: would any man, with the possible exception of an Irishman, address you as 'darling', or draw your fugitive atten-tion to the emotions of his 'heart', as do singers in your concert rooms daily? In speaking 'darling' or 'heart', your tongue never curls up to touch the 'r'; then why should it in song? Consider for a moment the word 'garden'. Speak it aloud to yourself. It is a simple word of two syllables, in the pronunciation of which the tongue is practically unemployed. It is too simple a word, apparently, for a great many singers – a determined attack must be made on the offending 'r', and the result is a word of three syllables which sounds anything but English. The 'r' in garden is the third letter in a six-lettered word.

It occupies the same position in the word 'forest'; but if you will speak the word 'forest' to yourself, you will find that your tongue comes into active employment. I think, then, that it logically follows that when you sing 'garden' the 'r' should be passive, and that when you sing 'forest' the 'r' should be active; and I feel sure that in this, and in all that is implied in the passing examples I have ventured to give you, I shall have the approval of the eminent professors of elocution and singing who add so much lustre and efficiency to this splendid School of Music.

If you wish to sing beautifully – and you all do – you must love music; and the nearer you get to music, the more you will love it. If you wish to sing your native language beautifully – and you all should – you must love your native language; and the nearer you get to it, the more you will love it. Aim high. Let your ambition be ever on tiptoe. Fill your minds with Shakespeare's sonnets; Keats' 'Ode to a Grecian Urn'; Shelley's 'Ode to a Skylark'; Matthew Arnold's 'Forsaken Merman'; Swinburne's 'Spring Song' in 'Atlanta', and many other of the poetic ecstacies with which your beautiful language is so rich. Let them become the delightful companions of what might otherwise be sometimes lonely hours; learn to speak them aloud with distinction and understanding, and so enable yourselves to bring to your singing the added glory of a perfect diction.

'The beautiful ivy of friendship covers many ruins'

Rose Scott

Speech on the occasion of the unveiling of her portrait, New South Wales Art Gallery

22 SEPTEMBER 1922

Rose Scott (1847–1925) worked all her life to improve the status and conditions of Australian women, her causes including the extension of the franchise, the lot of female prisoners and prostitutes, and the age of consent for women (which she advocated raising to sixteen). A 'renowned beauty' and 'staunch opponent of competition and aggression', she was identified with a range of women's associations and societies, such as the Womanhood Suffrage League of NSW, the Women's Literary Society, the Prisoners' Aid Association, the Women's Political Educational League and the Peace Society. Scott was famous, too, for the salon of politicians, judges, philanthropists, writers and poets that she maintained on a Friday night in her Woolahra home. In response to the unveiling of her portrait by artist John Longstaff – now hanging in the Art Gallery of New South Wales – Scott reflected on the subject of friendship; not one of her usual themes of address, but at seventy-five years of age, it illustrated her gratitude and thoughts on a topic usually described in Australia as 'mateship'.

*

It is by no means an easy task to thank all those who have been so very good to me, and words will not be able to express one half of all I feel. ...

Long ago when I admired Henry Lawson's picture in the gallery, I used to say none should ever paint me but Mr Longstaff – little thinking that my wish would ever come true. And indeed I must pay a tribute to Mr Longstaff for all his patience and courtesy. For when I first went to him, I had been very ill. Then came summer with its glorious sunshine, bluebirds and dragonflies, and I most aggravatingly became ten years younger! At any rate he painted a Rose Scott that cannot make speeches, or argue upon every subject in heaven or earth – silence being an excellent gift in a woman – and *this* Rose Scott being a restless being, found it very hard to sit still – and so she moved the only thing she could move, and that was her tongue.

It has been said by a great writer 'That the end of life is a journey amongst ruins'! Well, my friends, we all have our Gethsemanes, our losses and our sorrows, and if our hearts embrace all humanity in our own dear country and in the world. The last few years have brought *many ruins*. But in my own case, and I am sure in many others, the beautiful ivy of friendship covers many ruins. What affection is there so deep, so lasting as friendship? Love without wings it has been called.

In all other relations of life, unless there is a spice of friendship, how insipid and often antagonistic they become. Make chums of your children, pals and mates of your husbands and wives, brothers and sisters, and those you employ, and at once we see this glowing opal entering into the common ore of life, and all relationships are transfigured.

We Australians are a great people for *liberty*, for wide spaces and deep silences, and friendship typifies all these.

So you will see how hard it is for me to thank you, as I would like to do, for this priceless gift of friendship which is the origin of any honors you have conferred upon me.

'We are still comparatively in the wilderness'

Herbert Gepp

'The real purpose of life': speech at the Melbourne Technical College

22 OCTOBER 1937

Herbert Gepp (1877–1954), a scientist, industrialist and public official who became one of Australia's ablest managers, believed in 'scientific solutions to industrial and economic problems'. He argued that people failed to apply the benefits of technical and scientific advancements 'in the best interests of man's happiness'. At the age of sixteen, Gepp was employed as a chemist in explosives manufacture and worked in Melbourne and Scotland until 1902. In order to study chemistry at Melbourne University, Gepp would cycle sixteen kilometres three times a week for lectures.

In 1905, Gepp joined the Collins House group, bringing new technology to metal refining and overseeing the establishment of the giant Electrolytic Zinc Company in Tasmania. As managing director of Australian Paper Manufacturers from 1936 to 1950, he was responsible for the company's investment in plantation forest that freed it of dependence on imported woodchip and wastepaper. Prominent in the scientific organisations that prefigured the CSIRO, Gepp also acted as a government consultant and chaired several royal commissions. Gepp discusses 'the real purpose of life' in the following address, delivered at a 'Jubilee Smoke Social' in 1937.

*

It has been truly said – I think by James Harvey Robinson, one of the finest historical brains which the United States of America has developed – that memory alone makes us sane and enables us to make terms with things as they are, and helps us to make improvements in all that concerns us. Again, it has been said by Bergson that the brain is an organ of forgetfulness. It certainly has to forget almost everything in order to remember anything, and its usefulness consists in recalling the right thing at the right moment.

Education is concerned with the training of memory, with the proper activation of the brain, with the development of faculties which enable us to select and appreciate in their right perspective the things in life which really matter. It has been excellently said: 'Education alone can conduct us to that enjoyment which is at once best in quality and infinite in quantity.'

And speaking tonight to the toast of this educational institution I suggest that we might commune for a few minutes upon the only really worthwhile purpose of life, and upon the extent to which we are directing our energies to enable mankind to achieve a higher and better existence.

It is a sad reflection upon us that we devote a great deal more scientific thought to the better feeding and breeding of domestic animals than we do to eliminating the words 'more or less' from the phrase '*homo* more or less *sapiens*'. The science and art of eugenics are still in the phase of rather disdainful wonderment so far as the majority of mankind is concerned. While in a few countries, such as the United

States of America, efforts are being made to determine intelligence and personality quotients, and other important personal characteristics, generally speaking such matters still constitute a vast unexplored region of which we have so far merely touched the fringes.

Problems of this type are particularly acute in the democratic countries, in which one of the greatest obstacles with which education is faced is to reconcile the requirements and wants of the individual with the broader needs of the community. It is not too much to say that democracy is in grave danger of extinction unless the individual citizens adjust their methods, and contribute jointly and severally towards the discussion and solution of the problem of living in harmony as a nation.

The day of the stark individualist is gone because unbalanced individualism has one interpretation only, and that is shortsighted personal selfishness. Individualism is the most valuable attribute of human beings, provided that this selfishness is adjusted and the driving force, innate in individualism, contributes to the necessary material extent, towards collective advancement and collective security. Surely we all must realise the responsibility resting upon those who have been given spiritual, mental and physical powers above the average.

There is urgent need for sustained cooperative effort between individuals, institutions and nations if we are to add materially to the useful sum of human knowledge. I fear it is correct to say that we are still comparatively in the wilderness so far as the directing of our innate human ability into the best channels is concerned.

The world is approaching the end of an era; and the people, even those who realise this fact, are only blindly groping in an endeavour to discover the basic facts which will command the new condition of things. Obviously, there will be no catastrophic change. The alteration of things is coming continuously, almost unrecognised; it is coming like a thief in the night, and the disturbances are not recognised in the morning because we have no proper system of registering the condition of affairs at frequent intervals.

Mankind has not yet appreciated that there is no longer any necessity to fight for the basic means of existence, because of its increased knowledge and power over the material means of production. It is still obsessed with the individual fear of the future. Until this fear is removed mankind will not support organisation, long-range thinking and planning, and the allocation of the right brains to this work.

We have not yet realised the new rapidity of change. But the fact is that no longer can any generation direct its plans upon a basis of stable conditions. And we have not had the courage and vision to endeavour by organisation and the utilisation of the appropriate brains, to forecast trends so that our plans for the future can have some chance of success.

So in common with all other sections of the community which are giving responsible service to the nation, the educationalists are called upon to do two things urgently; first, they must survey their own profession critically in an attitude of non-acceptance of past beliefs and practices; and second, they must confer with all cognate professions concerned with national and world progress and understanding, and try to recast the educational system and framework so as to produce from the nation's raw material instruments of the most value for the future.

I was trained as a chemical engineer and as a metallurgist. My mind turns to the interesting and rather wonderful developments pioneered by Australians at Broken Hill in the treatment of complex ores. Yet, these ores are simple in their make-up compared with the invariable variability of the human body and mind. ...

An institution such as this has a flow of different types of human raw materials passing through its treatment plant continuously. From the national standpoint, there is an urgent need for a selective process to be applied so that the potential ability of the students can be properly classified and thereafter directed. ...

I suggest, therefore, that our educational authorities should enlist the help of other sections of the community to emphasise the need for wider, broader and deeper education of the youth of the nation. Our old friend Diogenes, who lived in a tub, is reported to have said that the foundation of every state is its youth; and Lord Brougham is reported to have stated that education makes a people easy to lead but difficult to drive; easy to govern but impossible to enslave.

There are so many interests and activities in present-day life that emphatic methods are necessary to command public attention and create a public conscience in any direction. I make bold to say that the educationist in Australia is not yet educated in the methods of creating a public sense of the urgent, vital need for education in its broadest and widest sense. To do this we have got to begin with the young, because of the fact so succinctly stated by Joseph Chamberlain at the beginning of this century when he said 'You cannot teach old dogs new tricks' – and some of us are getting old.

'An obstinate adherence to heresies'

Sir Owen Dixon

'Two constitutions compared': address at the annual dinner of the American Bar Association, Detroit

26 AUGUST 1942

Lord Evershed, president of the British Court of Appeals, once described Owen Dixon (1886–1972) as 'the greatest judge and lawyer in the world', and Sir Robert Menzies thought him 'a legend in his own lifetime'. Dixon, who took silk in 1922, believed that to be a sound lawyer required an understanding of the history of institutions, the development of ideas and moral philosophy. Dixon was unsuccessful in one of his most challenging diplomatic roles – as a United Nations mediator in the 1950 Kashmir dispute between India and Pakistan – but his 'strict and complete legalism' as chief justice of the High Court between 1952 and 1964 helped raise the court's international status, and his 'absolute independence of thought' ensured his connections and personal beliefs never interfered in his judgements. During World War II, Dixon was appointed by Menzies as Australian minister to Washington, and it was during this time that he addressed the American Bar Association on the constitutions of Australia and the United States.

*

The purpose of inviting me to speak at this gathering was, I believe, to pay a compliment to the country which I have the honour to represent. The compliment is a high one and I wish at once, Mr President, gratefully to acknowledge it in my representative capacity. It is indeed true that I fill the office of Minister for the Commonwealth of Australia to the United States. But that I do so is merely one of the odd accidents for which the war must be blamed. My work in life is that of a member of the legal profession. I have undertaken the duties of my present office as a wartime interlude and in fact I still remain a member of the bench of the High Court of Australia. Notwithstanding, therefore, the character in which I come, it is as an Australian lawyer that I should like to speak to you.

To be allowed to do so is a great satisfaction. For it enables me to tell you how strong a community of interest between Australians and Americans is to be found in the systems by which they are governed. The very court to which I belong has been fashioned upon the model of the Supreme Court of the United States. It is true that it can muster at full strength only six justices. But a younger and less populous country may be permitted the privilege of seeking juristic wisdom, and perhaps the greater unanimity, in fewer legal minds. Notwithstanding its numbers it is esteemed to be a pillar of our constitution.

Whatever strains the war may impose upon legal pillars, my colleagues, though only five in number, must be prepared to undergo. Judges are always generous to one another, and they have readily acknowledged that no one need fear lest my absence should unduly weaken the court or increase the difficulty of withstanding whatever stresses the times may set up; a compliment to me the ambiguity of which can hardly be called latent.

Australia, as you know, is a common-law country. That simple statement carries with it prodigious consequences. I believe that the outlook of a people nurtured in and living under the Roman law tradition can never be the same as that of a people whose conceptions of government, of liberty, of justice and of right have been moulded by the common law. This fact explains some of the features of the present conflict.

There are many things that contribute to make Anglo-American culture a uniform thing, but lawyers who have looked at the two systems know how powerful a cause of this uniformity has been our fealty to the common law.

We all accept without question the Anglo-American conception of the rule of law. Deeply as it enters into our habits of thought about the relations of the individual to the state, we seldom reflect that this conception is foreign to the Roman system. It is a conception that belongs only to the common law, by which it has been preserved and transmitted. It is a conception without which the theory of a rigid constitution could never have grown, and that theory is indispensable to federalism as we know it. But great as is the unifying influence among Anglo-American people of the common law, Australia has brought even closer her community of legal interest with this country. For as you know she has adopted a federal system.

Australians have enjoyed a federal constitution of a rigid character for forty years. With the British constitution every Australian lawyer has some familiarity, and I may confess that the great adaptability and efficiency shown by that form of government has led some among us to doubt what is the place of federalism in the modern world. When the life of a nation is at stake it is no disadvantage to have a unitary form of government and a parliament supreme over the law. But the example of this country will, we hope, remove all misgivings as to the efficacy of federalism in war.

For good or ill, Australia at the beginning of the century became a federal Commonwealth. Till then she had consisted of six colonies, each of which was ruled by a parliament of two houses and by an executive formed according to the cabinet system. Union, like unity, is a thing that cannot easily be attained; and it was only after conventions and plebiscites spreading over the 1890s that the six colonies united in a federal Commonwealth and under a constitution framed after the pattern of that of the United States. The men who drew up the Australian constitution had the American document before them; they studied it with care; they even read the standard books of the day which undertook to expound it. They all lived, however, under a system of responsible government. That is to say, they knew and believed in the British system by which the ministers are responsible to the parliament and must go out of office whenever they lose the confidence of the legislature. They felt therefore impelled to make one great change in adapting the American constitution. Deeply as they respected your institutions, they found themselves unable to accept the principle by which the executive government is made independent of the legislature. Responsible government, that is, the system by which the executive is responsible to the legislature, was therefore introduced with all its necessary consequences.

In this country, men have come to regard formal guarantees of life, liberty and property against invasion by government as indispensable to a free constitution. Bred in this doctrine you may think it strange that in Australia, a democracy if ever there was one, the cherished American practice of placing in the fundamental law guarantees of personal liberty should prove unacceptable to our constitution makers. But so it was. The framers of the Australian constitution were not prepared to place fetters upon legislative action, except and in so far as it might be necessary for the purpose of distributing between the states and the central government the full content of legislative power. The history of their country had not taught them the need of provisions directed to the control of the legislature itself. The working of such provisions in this country was conscientiously studied, but, wonder as you may, it is a fact that the study fired no one with enthusiasm for the principle. With the probably unnecessary exception of the guarantee of religious freedom, our constitution makers refused to adopt any part of the Bill of Rights of 1791 and *a fortiori* they refused to adopt the Fourteenth Amendment. It may surprise you to learn that in Australia one view held was that these checks on legislative action were undemocratic, because to adopt them argued a want of confidence in the will of the people. Why, asked the Australian democrats, should doubt be thrown on the wisdom and safety of entrusting to the chosen representatives of the people sitting either in the federal parliament or in the state parliaments all legislative power, substantially without fetter or restriction?

In our steadfast faith in responsible government and in plenary legislative powers distributed, but not controlled, you as Americans may perceive nothing better than a wilful refusal to see the light and an obstinate adherence to heresies; but we remain impenitent. Yet, in most other respects our constitution makers followed with remarkable fidelity the model of the American instrument of government.

Indeed it may be said that, roughly speaking, the Australian constitution is a redraft of the American constitution of 1787, with modifications found suitable for the more characteristic British institutions and for Australian conditions. It included of course the establishment of federal courts. The supreme federal court was called the High Court of Australia, perhaps to avoid confusion with the Supreme Courts of the states.

The High Court of Australia was conceived as a federal court like the Supreme Court of the United States. But they made what you will think a strange innovation. The court was given appellate jurisdiction not confined to federal matters, but covering the whole field of state and federal law. That is to say, the High Court of Australia is an appellate tribunal to which an appeal lies from the Supreme Courts of the states, in state matters as well as in federal matters. It is a full appeal upon law and fact. The High Court has thus become a final court of appeal in Australia.

You may be sure that legal ideas in Australia have been profoundly influenced by the introduction of so great a part of the American structure of government, aided in no small measure by the establishment of a court of final resort fulfilling what to you must seem a dual function. But the dual function of the court and the combination in our constitution of principles characteristically British with American federalism have, I believe, given to Australian legal ideas a very special place.

For we naturally stand midway between the two great common-law systems, that of England and that of America. We study them both; we feel that, in some measure, we understand them both, and we seek guidance from them both.

'There is no beauty in the world like the beauty of a woman's hands'

Dame Enid Lyons

Mother's Day broadcast

CIRCA 1960

Dame Enid Lyons (1897–1981) was over-qualified to speak on the topic of Mother's Day. During a period in which the birthrate was declining she had raised twelve children with her husband, former prime minister Joseph Lyons, as well as embarking on her own successful political career. A devoted wife and mother, Lyons was no radical feminist; she celebrated the virtues of clotted cream and slippers by the fire, lamented Australia's slow population growth and abhorred the termination of the unborn. The manuscript of this speech is held at the National Library with Lyons' papers, in a folio marked 'non-political speeches', but does not specify the year or place of its broadcast. It was almost certainly written after her retirement from politics in 1951 when she turned her public attention more specifically to the promotion of family and women's issues, and was most likely delivered in the early 1960s. It is a revealing speech on the sentiments of a remarkable pioneer in Australian public life.

*

There is an amusing little sketch of Mother's Day by Stephen Leacock that has long been a standing joke in our family. Everyone was determined that the great day should be suitably celebrated. Everyone had decided views as to how it should be spent – except Mother; and somehow, every idea put forward involved Mother in extra work. Mother's place in the family was at length appreciated.

Whenever I wish to point a little lesson in filial duty without being too severe on the offender, I say 'Mother's Day'. Instantly, the small delinquent pushes forward a chair, or stands aside to make a passage for his mother with a smile of understanding.

It is a cheery, jolly sort of thing, this 'Mother's Day', that gives expression to a normal, healthy, respectful affection, somehow easily neglected in these hectic days. I like a 'dear old Mum' atmosphere about it, not sadly sentimental but full of a sense of happy comrade-ship and love and genuine understanding. A little teasing: 'Dad, how many girls did you love before you met Mum?' or 'You couldn't get into your wedding dress now, Mum.' The atmosphere of love and appreciation that marks this day brings a great deal of joy for mothers. But the real value of its observance lies not so much in its appeal to mothers as in the revival of thought on what motherhood and mother love represent.

I like the name of Mother to stand for happiness at home – cosy fires, and apple pie, and clotted cream, and choruses round the piano and good-night kisses, and prayers; and that is why sometimes I am unhappy in this rushing age. That is why I find my own life so diffi-cult, leaving only little intervals of time to create that pool of restful-ness and refreshment that alone makes home.

Perhaps that is why fewer families of even medium size are to be found than formerly. Perhaps women feel that they cannot keep up with the world and have their babies too. Perhaps they are beginning to think that there are pleasures in the world that will give them more lasting happiness than the love of children. Certain it is that there has overtaken our generation an unwillingness to reproduce itself, so that families have grown smaller and smaller, and, everywhere, civilised populations are threatened with an early arrival at a point where they must actually begin to diminish.

Many civilisations have preceded our own. Many causes have con-tributed to their downfall, but loss of racial vitality has characterised them all in the days of their decline. We, in Australia, have one of the lowest birthrates in the world. Are we then to assume that we, as a race, are losing our vitality? I cannot believe it; yet this reluctance to propagate has expressed itself not only in a falling birthrate. There has grown during the last thirty years a feeling that parents of large fami-lies were imposing, not only upon themselves, but upon the state, a burden too great to be borne. Mothers have lost that ready sympathy that had always brought them willing helpers in times of difficulty. Not only have they had to face physical distress, but psychological difficulties have beset them that mothers of an earlier generation never knew. The whole current of modern life has appeared to be set against them, and motherhood has been achieved almost in defiance of civilisation.

And yet interest in families and family life was never greater than today. It is everywhere displayed; in newspaper articles, in the pulpit, in scientific books, among social workers and by people in every grade of society.

It has given birth to Mother's Day!

Undoubtedly the institution of Mother's Day is a sentimental one, providing an opportunity for an expression of emotion and a revival of devotion to a persona and an ideal. But it is founded upon a sentiment rooted deep in racial instinct; an instinct that gives honour to woman as the vehicle of life, that alone can preserve the race from extinction.

It is based, too, upon a fundamental faith in human nature that in the relationship between mother and child is the nearest human image of the relationship between God and man. There is expected of a mother's love a quality of selflessness, a capacity for sacrifice, unsought in any other human attachment. It is a tribute to modern women that that expectation is not less now than at any former time, nor is it less justified. The great blot on the fame of this generation is the readiness of ever-increasing numbers of women to terminate the lives of the unborn. To all women whose sensibilities have not been blunted by unhealthy and unnatural modes of life and thought, the voluntary quenching of the precious fontanelle of life already throbbing beneath a mother's heart, is an act that produces only feelings of horror and shame. It is a stain that future generations will find it hard to overlook.

In a world adopting more and more a purely materialistic conception of life, it is not easy to preserve a true standard of human values. It is in the power of mothers to achieve it. The fierce and tender love of a mother for an afflicted child is a phenomenon everywhere recognised. The worth of that clouded life is not less to her than that of any other of her children. Instinctively she knows that human value is not to be measured in terms of physical health alone, nor in ability to take an active part in the work of the world. For who shall estimate the value of a flower, or set a price upon the colour of a robin's breast?

A desire for beauty is inherent in the human heart. It is expressed in many ways. Beauty of form, of colour and of sound is everywhere about us. Some see it and some do not, and those who do not are suffering a form of blindness. Beauty of spirit is less readily perceived and the number of those who are blind to it is great.

There is no beauty in the world like the beauty of a woman's hands. They may be rough and work-worn, with knotted fingers and hardened palms, but if they have performed the work that they were put into the world to do, if they have guided little feet along rough paths to manhood, and led the tripping feet of girlhood into the serenity of gracious womanhood, then they are beautiful with a beauty not of this earth at all.

And on 'Mother's Day' we think a little on these things and the world is a better place.

'What am I?'

Sir John Eccles

'Conscious experience': Boyer Lecture, broadcast nationally on ABC radio

6 NOVEMBER 1965

Sir John Eccles' (1903–1997) Boyer Lectures in 1965 called for a 'renewal of faith in the great mystery and dignity of human existence'. Eccles was fascinated with the relationship between body and mind, and focused his scientific research on the cerebellum – the part of the brain that controls posture and movement. An Oxford Rhodes Scholar, Eccles was elected as a Fellow of the Royal Society in 1962 and headed research teams at the universities of Otago and Chicago, the Australian National University and the State University of New York. In 1963 he was awarded the Nobel Prize for Medicine with British scientists Andrew Huxley and Alan Hodgkin for 'establishing the relationship between inhibition of nerve cells and repolarisation of a cell's membrane'. In his Nobel Prize banquet speech Eccles said that if it was asked of him what he would do if he were to begin his life's work now, he would reply, 'I would start where I left off.' In the following lecture he grapples with an abiding question from a scientist's point of view.

*

First of all, I am going to talk to you generally about the title for this lecture. And while I do this, I want each one of you to participate with me in an effort to grasp the meaning of what I am trying to say and to apply it to yourself. If you do this with me, we shall have a kind of dialogue in thought, so that my thoughts communicated in language will give you thoughts that parallel mine. You become then not my audience, but my collaborators in this conjoint effort to reach an understanding of what is central to our being.

The series of talks that I am giving will be an attempt to see how far we can answer the question: What am I? This is a question which each of us can ask ourselves and which is quite unashamedly a looking within ourselves – an attitude which is called subjective and introspective.

I am not alone in posing this question and attempting to answer it. For example, Schrodinger, the physicist who was awarded the Nobel Prize for his wave mechanics, wrote in his book *Science and Humanism*: 'Who are we? The answer to this question is not only one of the tasks, but the task of science.' This assessment would have been supported by Sherrington, the founder of modern neurophysiology, and many other scientists would be in agreement. I can mention Eugene Wigner, Hinshelwood and Michael Polanyi.

I have chosen to talk to you in the field of the philosophy of the person, because I wish to do all I can to restore to mankind the sense of wonder and mystery that arises from the attempt to face up to the reality of our very existence as conscious beings. Too often we have statements that a man is but a clever animal and entirely explicable materially. And again, we are often told that man is nothing but an extremely complex machine and that computers will soon be rivalling him for supremacy as the most complex machine in existence, and that they will have performances outstripping him in all that matters.

I want to discredit such dogmatic statements and bring you to realise how tremendous is the mystery of the existence of each one of us. It is beyond my competence to go further and deal with the way in which religion is related to this mystery of existence.

First of all, let us consider what I mean by 'conscious experience'. This is strangely difficult to define, but fortunately I do not think a definition is necessary. I hope that, as my talk develops, you will come to appreciate just what I am talking about when I refer to 'conscious experience' or 'mind' or 'mentality'; but I have chosen the expression 'conscious experience' in order to stress the experienced character of consciousness in all its aspects. It will comprise all of your experiences in waking life and also your dreams.

Some of you may have come under the influence of philosophers, such as Ryle and Ayer, who have attempted to discredit the usage of such a word as 'mind'. They assert that there is no significance or meaning in this word and that we should instead describe and study the behaviour of people and, in particular, their use of language, instead of introducing an assumption of mind as some spiritual existence underlying this behaviour or this use of language.

I hope that I shall be able to bring you to see how unjustified and illogical are the claims of such philosophers. In fact, their work has recently been very severely criticised by the psychologist John Beloff, in a book called *The Existence of Mind*, and also by the philosopher Kneale, who has re-established the philosophic status of mind in his book *On Having a Mind*. For example, Beloff begins his book by stating:

> The thesis of this book, if it can be stated in two words, is that Mind exists, or, to be more explicit, that minds, mental entities and mental phenomena, exist as ultimate constituents of the world in which we live.

And also:

> Those who take seriously the existence of Mind are often taunted with being worried by a 'ghost in the machine'; I suggest it is high time we refused to let our critical facilities be paralysed any longer in this pert gibe.

This counterattack is very encouraging to neurophysiologists and neurologists, for many of us, despite the philosophic criticisms, have continued to wrestle with the problem of brain and mind, and have come to regard it as the most difficult and fundamental problem concerning man. However, as far as possible, I am not going to employ such words as 'mind', 'mental' and 'mentality', because they have been used in a most confusing manner; for example, it has [been] frequently stated that even inorganic matter has some primitive quality of mind or mentality. To me such statements are quite meaningless, and to avoid confusion, I am going to use instead the term 'conscious experience'.

My approach to conscious experience is, in the first instance, based on my direct experience of my own self-consciousness. I believe this to be the only valid way in which I can begin to talk to you about this problem that lies central to our being. I want you to understand that this initial position of myself in regard to my own consciousness must also be adopted by each of you in regard to your own self-consciousness. I am aware that a philosophical position of this kind is often criticised, because it is alleged that it gives rise to the exclusive attention of each one of us to our own conscious experiences – an attitude which is called solipsism. However, for a start, I want each of you to face up to the problem discussed in this lecture in this way, and it will soon become apparent that we move from this restricted initial position into the wider field of vision, where we recognise the existence of other conscious selves or persons. That recognition provides, of course, the basis of social life, and it is the denial of solipsism.

So let me now start with this experience that each of us has as a kind of inner illumination. I am going to state quite categorically that this conscious experience is all that is given to me in my task of trying to understand myself, and similarly, this is true for each one of you. Further, I am going to state that only because of and through my conscious experience do I come to know of a world of things and events and so to embark on the attempt to understand it; as, for example, I do in my work as a scientist. This again is true for each one of you, and in all that you do in your own individual lives.

In developing the significance of this conscious experience, I would like to quote from a recent lecture, 'Two kinds of reality', by Eugene Wigner, Nobel laureate in physics in 1963. These quotations illustrate how important and urgent is the problem of consciousness to one of the most eminent theoretical physicists in the world today. I quote:

> There are two kinds of reality or existence – the existence of my consciousness and the reality or existence of everything else. This latter reality is not absolute, but only relative. Excepting immediate sensations, the content of my consciousness, everything is a construct; but some constructs are closer, some further, from the direct sensations.

You will see from this quotation that the whole of what we call the material world, that is, the constructs, is regarded by Wigner as having a second order of reality in contrast to the absolute reality of our conscious experiences, and he develops this theme in the course of his lecture. Wigner continues:

> As I said, our inability to describe our consciousness adequately, to give a satisfactory picture of it, is the greatest obstacle to our acquiring a rounded picture of the world.

I shall further reinforce this primacy of our conscious experiences by two quotations from recent lectures by eminent scientists. Sir Cyril Hinshelwood, in his lecture, 'The vision of nature', says:

> To deny the reality of the inner world is a flat negation of all that is immediate in existence: to minimise its significance is to depreciate the very purpose of living, and to explain it away as a produce of natural selection is a plain fallacy.

Julian Huxley, in his lecture 'Higher and lower organisations in evolution', states: 'To start with, let us recall that the only primary reality is the reality of our subjective experiences.'

Of course, reality, as used in these quotations, must not be confused with truth. Let me illustrate by such experiences as those reported of flying saucers. Recently, a lady wrote me a long documentary account about flying saucers and what they do. To her they were as real as ordinary saucers, but she did not convince me. They are real to her but not to me. You will appreciate that the question of their actual existence is not implied. I am merely stating my disbelief – not dogmatising on their non-existence!

You may think that, as a scientist, I have some privileged insight into truth. On the contrary, I am not able to claim to have made an absolutely true statement that has scientific value. The most I can say is that this scientific explanation or hypothesis is in accordance with all known facts as given in experiments, though probably it will not be reconcilable with further experimental investigations. The most that I can claim is that my scientific hypothesis is an approximation to truth. As St Paul says, 'We see as in a glass darkly.'

After this digression on reality and truth, let me return to the reality of conscious experiences.

I would now suggest to you that conscious experiences are of two kinds. One is what I call the inner experiences; and the other the perceptual experiences that are derived from the stimulation of some sense organ or other, with the consequence of an almost immediate sensory experience. Both of these experiences, of course, belong to our single unitary self that I will speak of in more detail later.

It is entirely from such perceptual experiences as vision, hearing and touch, for example, that I get to know the external world of things and events, which is a world other than my consciously experiencing self. You may be surprised to hear me say that a special part of this external world is, in fact, my own body, which I actually only come to know because of such senses as vision and touch; and in this same way I come to know of innumerable other human bodies that appear to belong to selves like my own self.

This is, of course, so self-evident that it may appear to you to be a trite statement. Nevertheless it is of great significance, in that it leads me to believe in the existence of other persons or selves like myself with bodies and conscious experiences. It leads to the rejection of solipsism. For example, Julian Huxley states:

We can only deduce that other human beings have subjective experiences like our own. This is not only scientifically legitimate and necessary; it is justified pragmatically and operationally: human existence would be impossible unless we did so.

From our earliest childhood days, we have learnt to exchange communication with other selves by all kinds of movements or signals. For example we do this in babyhood by gestures; and as we become progressively more educated, we use speech and writing; and of course, we learn to exploit still more sophisticated and subtle means of communication, as in the shared joy in aesthetic experience and imagination that even make words seem too crude.

This takes us into the world of communication by artistic creation and by shared appreciation. But no matter how intimate is our linkage with some dearly loved person, we still remain separated in a most heart-rending way. We are dependent on some movement that gives to the other a sensory experience. Never does there seem to be direct communication of one conscious self to the other. At least, I shall say that the direct thought transfer postulated in telepathy appears to be a very inefficient way of communicating between selves. I would not deny the possibility of telepathy, neither do I think it proved. We need further rigorous investigation in this most difficult scientific field.

Thus we come to believe that there is a world of selves, each with the experience of inhabiting a body that is in a material world comprising innumerable bodies of like nature and a tremendous variety of other living forms and an immensity of apparently non-living matter. I would agree with Wigner that this material or objective world has the status of a second-order or derivative reality.

Let me now talk about the other kind of conscious experience. Inner experiences, as I call them, are of a much more varied character than perceptual experiences. For example, experiences arising from a memory-recall have the character of some past sensory experience and are recognised as such. Thus we can remember, in what we appropriately call our 'mind's eye', some striking scene or happening, or we can remember a musical tune, and even tastes and smells, but much more important are the extremely complex memories that we have of other people, particularly of those dear to us.

You will recognise that, because of memory, each of us links his life together into some kind of continuity of inner experience, which is what we mean when we talk of a self or person. This involves a recognition of unity and identity through all past vicissitudes. Of course, we do not have a continuity of conscious experience. You will appreciate that the continuity is broken every time we go to sleep or lose consciousness in some more unpleasant way. But we wake up after each period of unconsciousness, recognising, because of memory, our continuity with the self of the preceding day, and we continue with its trains of experiences.

Is it not a curious experience that, when we wake up in the morning, we slowly come around to recognise that we are in just the same room as when we lost consciousness the night before? Thus we bridge the periods of unconsciousness and identify ourself in the morning with the person who went to sleep the night before. It is the same self that awakes to another stream of consciousness for another waiting day.

Moreover, by my inner experience, I do not mean just the recall of my past experiences in memory, but I also include in my inner experience the extraordinary texture of thoughts and ideas, the deliverances of imagination, emotional feelings, wishes, desires and volitions. In addition to all of these experiences of waking life, one also has such bizarre phenomena as dreams and hallucinations, about which I shall speak in a later lecture. All of this is part of our conscious experience, and the whole assemblage throughout our lives has contributed to the formation of ourselves, to each one of us as a person.

I want you to understand that there is a unity of the self through all these diverse conscious experiences, each of which is assimilated to the self; and this even occurs in dreams, as I think you will readily agree. For always in a dream we find ourselves as the agent central to the whole play of imagery; and this likewise occurs with hallucinations and the fantasies of waking life that we may call daydreams.

I want you to recognise that each of you can look back in memory through, as it were, the thread of the long years of accumulated experiences that make up your life, so that eventually you come to your earliest memories, where you have the amazing experience in retrospect of waking up in life in the very limited environment of a young child. Each of you has a personal identity from these earliest times, which is built up from remembered experiences.

I want further to suggest to you that in literature we have not just a description of the behaviours of people going through motions in some determined and stereotyped manner and observed always from the outside. But instead – central to literature – there are descriptions of inner experiences with thoughts and motives and the emotional feelings of the characters that the author, as it were, brings to life in this way.

You can yourself recollect all the range of emotional feelings of love and friendship and hate and antipathy, as well as your experiences of fear and terror and of delight in the beautiful. All of these contribute to the richness of your direct inner experiences.

This richness of our experiences is enormously developed, when we fuse, as it were, our immediate perceptual experiences with an imaginative range of inner experiences. This occurs particularly in aesthetic experiences. The artist attempts to express not some exact rendering of what he sees, but his vision, which has a creative enrichment given by his imagination. In great art this artistic creation has for the artist some compelling necessity. Unfortunately, much imitative work masquerades as art, though in itself it is only an artificial contrivance. Superficially, there is, of course, much resemblance between this imitative contrivance and true artistic creation. For this reason, we often need art critics and historians to guide and inform us – but not, let me add, to compel us.

I now return to perceptual influences by asking the question: How can my perceptual experiences in vision, hearing, touch and movement give me such an effective knowledge of the objective world that I can find my way round in it and even manipulate it with such success?

So effective is this practical operation that I am not conscious of this problem in my whole experience of practical living; my body and its environment appear to be directly known to me. This attitude towards perceptual experiences can be termed naive or direct realism; but this belief must be rejected, because it is based on a misunderstanding of the way in which we come to know of the external world by means of our sense organs and our brains.

In response to some sensory stimulation, I experience a private perceptual world which must be regarded, neurophysiologically, as an interpretation of specific events in my brain that we will be considering in more detail in a later talk. Hence I am confronted by the problem: How can these diverse cerebral patterns of activity give me valid pictures of the external world?

Usually this problem is discussed in relation to visual perception. There seems to be an extraordinary problem in explaining how information from my retinae, when relayed to and activating my cerebral cortex, gives me a picture of an external world with all its various objects in three-dimensional array and endowed with brightness and colour. This problem has led to much philosophical confusion when it has been discussed on the assumption that fully patterned visual perception is an inborn property of the nervous system. On the contrary, my visual perception is an interpretation of data provided by my eyes, that in a lifetime of experience I have learned to accomplish, particularly in association with sensory information provided by receptors in muscles, joints, skin and the special receptors for spatial orientation in my inner ear, and in addition, with the central experience of my willed effort.

Apart from trivial differences, such as colour blindness, we agree with one another about the external world, because we can point to things and talk about them, and others know what we are talking about. This is the world we call objective, because it can be tested, reported upon and agreed upon. And amongst sane people there is a tremendous measure of agreement.

As I shall suggest in a later talk, we have specific patterns of activity in our cerebral cortex for every detailed event we can remember and for every visual image that we can recollect. When we experience an object, we can see it and confirm its presence by touch. We can lift it, examine it and by virtue of complex reactions in our brains, we can give it secondary properties like colour, texture and weight. This all comes about because diverse sense organs are busy signalling to the central nervous system and so transmitting information. The richness of our sensory experience derives from the great diversity and wealth of interaction of all the information pathways into the brain.

Many philosophers will not agree with this, saying, for example, that the taste is in the apple, or the colour in the flower. The taste is not in the apple; certainly it is the result of chemical substances that are in the apple, which act on the tastebuds, stimulating specific pathways leading to the brain and evoking therein specific spatio-temporal patterns of activity; the result is a taste you can remember, report on, talk about and compare. But the taste itself is primarily the result of a specific cortical activity; and, of course, likewise with colour, where all that the observed object emits is a complex of spectral wavelengths that is transmitted in coded patterns to our cerebral cortex and there transmuted into the perception of colour.

In my next lecture, I shall be dealing particularly with the way in which we come to learn to interpret all the information that comes from our sense organs and to derive from it our experience of an external world in all its detailed variety and richness.

'Four rules for a modern ethic'

Sir Macfarlane Burnet

'The ethics of a biologist': Boyer Lecture, broadcast nationally on ABC radio

25 OCTOBER 1966

While Nobel laureates John Eccles, Howard Florey and William Bragg spent much of their professional careers overseas, Sir Macfarlane Burnet (1899–1985) based his working life in Australia. After graduating in medicine in 1922, Burnet was appointed resident pathologist at Royal Melbourne Hospital, where his research in bacterial viruses led him to the Walter and Eliza Hall Institute for Medical Research. After a period of study in London, he returned to Melbourne and began his work on the influenza virus, conducting vaccine experiments on soldiers in World War II.

In 1944 Burnet was appointed director of the Hall Institute, studying virology and immunology. When his hypothesis that inoculation against viruses could prevent the attack of antibodies was proven by English immunologist Peter Medawar, they shared the Nobel Prize for medicine and physiology. Turning down prestigious offers to work overseas, Burnet continued his research in Melbourne and was a prominent voice against the White Australia Policy and cigarette smoking. While his life's work was based in the extremely complex world of antibodies and the immune system, Burnet maintained a belief that 'the most precious truths of nature were essentially simple'.

*

As far back as men have written down their thoughts, they have dreamt of a world in which people could live together in amity and banish war and cruelty, poverty, hunger and disease, and death itself. The great religions arose in response to those dreams, to keep hope alive in the midst of any almost unbearable reality and to strengthen those aspects of social behaviour that made the life of human communities more tolerable.

In the last hundred years, the situation has changed in a fashion that would be wholly inconceivable to the great moralists and philosophers of the eighteenth century and earlier. Poverty, hunger and disease have virtually vanished in the affluent societies like our own. That is the work of science and invention. For the great majority of people for most of their lives, war, serious crime and death can all be half-forgotten. Yet war and crime and violence are all with us in increasing intensity, and our achievement of general health and prosperity has brought new social and medical problems, such as overpopulation and the mounting incidence of coronary disease.

To a scientist, there can never be final answers – truth in science is that complex of recorded observations, generalisations and theories which in the opinion of competent scholars have not yet been proved to be wrong. Equally, there can be no final statement as to what is good, and only too clearly can we recognise the changing nature of what is said to be beautiful.

In this talk, I want to discuss only the question of whether in the modern world our increasing knowledge of human biology can provide us with a working picture of what is 'good'.

I think I can indicate the sort of approach I will adopt by quoting a few lines from an American professor of anthropology (S.L. Washburn). He said:

> Throughout most of human evolution, man was adapted to ways of life radically different from those of today, and there has been neither the time nor the control of breeding to change human biology from what was adaptive in the past to what is adaptive now.

Washburn was concerned mainly with aggression and violence, but his remarks are equally applicable to many other aspects of human life.

The evolution of man seems to have taken about two million years, and, as far as can be gathered from skull and brain size, men physically similar to ourselves were in Europe 20,000 years ago, before there was any agriculture, domestic animals or any of the other precursors of civilisation. What has happened since then has been the development of new cultures and an always increasing amount of learned and transmitted technical know-how. The physical background of brain structure and the basic patterns of instinctive or easily learnt behaviour were developed over at least a half-million years, and civilisation is no more than a few thousand years old. In the eyes of the modern anthropologist, the problem of today is how to use the intelligence of a relatively small number of men and women to devise ways in which patterns of behaviour, laid down in a million years, can be modified, tricked and twisted if necessary, to allow a tolerable human existence in a crowded world. There are three imperatives: to reduce war to a minimum; to stabilise human population; and to prevent the progressive destruction of the earth's irreplaceable resources. At the present time, none of these seems possible, but it may be that, by thinking, writing, experimenting and observing, they will gradually become more nearly approachable.

I was trained as a physician, and though I have been a laboratory scientist for more than forty years, my approach to ethics is deeply influenced by the doctor's point of view. There can be all sorts of answers to the question of what is good, but no sane man or woman will deny that vigorous health, appropriate to an individual's age, is good and desirable. This universally accepted principle has, however, some important implications for human behaviour. It means education in the fundamentals of healthy living; it means baby health centres; immunisation of children; good water supply and sanitation; and dozens of other things that we take for granted. It means good hospitals and good doctors; and it calls for things which we haven't yet been able to develop. Far too many people are killed by accidents on the roads. Men who eat too much, smoke too much and take too little exercise are candidates for heart attacks. And although everyone nowadays knows that cigarette-smoking is wholly responsible for most lung cancer, deaths from that disease continue to rise steadily upward each year. One of the best things I know about doctors is that they are the only group of people who have mostly stopped smoking, and in England, they are the only group whose incidence of lung cancer is falling.

Can I now try to suggest and discuss four rules for a modern ethic? The first rule then would be this:

> To ensure for every individual the fullest measure of health that is allowed by his inheritance.

If physical health is desirable, so is mental health, and like physical health it can be assessed objectively. The intelligent, socially adaptive individual is recognisable as easily in Russia or China as in Australia or Japan, and in all countries it is now a clear objective that every child should be educated to the limit of his capacity and desire to learn. This again has immense implications for society. Once we begin to visualise and ponder on the distribution of ability amongst individuals, the nature of mental disease and the infinite gradations of mood, personality and behaviour that run from the normal to the insane, the problem seems infinite. Education can do much, but there are other possibilities. One day, we may know enough about the genetics of mind and brain to devise eugenic programs that will reduce the numbers of children born with substandard brains. And in quite a different approach, already well under way, drugs which can modify mood and emotion may make people socially adaptable who would otherwise have to be kept under institutional care.

For the great majority of sane individuals, with their range of intelligence and manipulative skills from genius to dullness and from the born artist or mathematician to the inept, education must be made available to bring out in each individual his best value to the community and to himself.

Now let me suggest the second rule for this modern ethic:

> To provide for every individual the opportunity to develop intellectual and manipulative skills to the limit of his inherited capacity.

Health and a trained mind are good in themselves, but there is a third aspect of human life that is equally acceptable to people of all sorts as good. This is that achievement and success should be recognised. There are so many thousands of different fields in which a man or a woman may exceed that there should be few individuals without the possibility of feeling a sense of achievement. One person's success may temporarily hurt his direct competitors, but by and large, people like seeing another's success in any of the thousand activities in which they are not competitors.

So I come to the third rule, with just the faintest reservation that it may not always be accepted as valid. It would be:

> To ensure to all, the opportunity for achievement, and the recognition of success.

All three of these rules are concerned simply with the individual, but still staying within the limitation of the doctor's outlook, we have to look at the future as well as the present. Darwin and Mendel, Galton, Malthus and Margaret Sanger have taught us to look at the implications of reproduction and inheritance, both in regard to quality and quantity. We have all suddenly become aware of the dangers of overpopulation and of the availability of the pill and of mechanical methods of birth control. There is no doubt about the desirability, for both affluent and underdeveloped countries, to attempt to stabilise their population by reducing the birthrate. Even if this were successful, it would still leave some very important long-term biological problems. As Darwin and his successors have so often pointed out, throughout the whole range of animals many more individuals are born or hatched than survive to reproduce themselves. Twentieth-century man is the only exception, and he may have to face the consequences. With medicine removing nature's method of maintaining genetic quality by selecting against harmful mutants, it is conceivable that in a few thousand generations more than half the people will carry what we now regard as severe genetic disabilities like haemophilia or diabetes. In quite a different direction, it seems entirely possible that one or other of the industrial wastes or specific chemicals that are beginning to poison air, earth or water, may have severe and unexpected effects on the health of this or future generations.

This regard for the future calls for a fourth rule. It is this:

To ensure that opportunity to attain bodily and mental health and to find satisfaction in achievement, will be available to all future generations in measure not inferior to what we now enjoy.

I believe that those four imperatives are sufficient to cover all those human objectives that can be regarded by all intelligent and knowledgeable men, irrespective of race and culture, as desirable, right and good. Taken together, they represent the humanist approach, by which human welfare is the sole measure of what is good.

There are, however, other matters quite closely related to the fourth point but expressible in non-human terms. They allow us to express what might be called the conservationist approach. This is, I think, self-evident enough for me to condense it into a few brief statements.

The resources of the Earth must be maintained for the use and enjoyment of future generations by ensuring four things:

First: That irreplaceable mineral resources shall not be exhausted before effective substitutes can be made from always-available materials.

Second: That energy from fossil fuels will be replaced in time by perpetually renewable sources of energy.

Third: That the environment shall not be poisoned by industrial and military wastes.

Fourth: That adequate areas shall be preserved, to allow the indefinite persistence of all significant forms of wildlife and many areas of natural beauty or special interest.

In principle, few would disagree with any of these aspirations: in practice, no one seems to regard them as of any significance whatever.

To express these things as an ethical basis for action, in terms that come naturally to a scientist with a medical-biological background, may be helpful to some and can do no harm to anyone.

To be a biologist or a medical man is to be a realist. May I quote two more short passages from Washburn? The first:

> Throughout most of human history, society has depended on young adult males to hunt, to fight and to maintain the social order with violence ... (using) aggressive action which was socially approved, learned in play and personally gratifying.

And the second:

> Evolution has equipped us with the ability to learn certain things easily: we learn to speak easily, we learn easily to use tools or to handle weapons ... These things have been built into us by evolution. It does not mean that they are inevitable but it does mean that they are probable.

Men carry the marks of their evolution and we have to recognise that capacity to exert dominance over one's fellows, aggressive courage in the face of danger and identification of one's own group with oneself were all absolutely necessary for survival, except in times and places where a well-policed and stable civilisation could develop. Those characteristics have been bred into every race of men, and the whole art of civilisation is to find ways by which the instinctive drives towards dominance and violence can be directed into relatively harmless channels, and the capacity for identification with one's group directed toward progressively larger groups.

So we come squarely against the central dilemma of our times: that, men being what they are, stability of social life is only possible by the constant availability of force to stamp out any antisocial violence with the more effective violence of an organised and disciplined police.

In a scientifically based civilisation, where the power of weapons has suddenly expanded to something which makes nonsense of biology, an effective police force at the world level is an obvious and urgent necessity. It is illuminating to see that the ostensible reason for military action nowadays is always to counter antisocial violence by the enemy. Perhaps a world police force may come into being in one way or another sooner than we think.

It is not the job of a biologist to solve major human problems, but it is his job to look at those problems from his own highly relevant point of view and to ask that men with the responsibilities of power should become aware of the lessons of human biology, as well as those of human history.

In the last fifteen or sixteen years, I have been fortunate to have travelled widely to nearly all those countries where active medical and biological research is going on. My interests have been in one of the fields of human knowledge that has always had a rather specially privileged place in the human mind – the prevention of infectious disease. I have been to a dozen or more specialised conferences on ways of preventing polio, and influenza, and twice I have acted as chairman of a full-international committee. What has impressed me about these experiences has been the relative ease with which agreement can be reached on matters which are based on science – on accurate knowledge obtained by methods which are the same in every country. And it is the almost universal experience that, if the language barrier can be overcome, people doing this sort of work together find that they like each other. Perhaps it is only a desperate hope to find some way of escape from the threat of extermination that hangs over us all, but this ease of intercourse amongst technically trained and intelligent men seems to give promise that, if we can only widen the understanding of human affairs at the scientific level, the possibility of escape may gradually increase.

Perhaps the position can be summarised in two propositions. The first is concerned with what favours aggression and violence; the second with the equally important factors that can prevent or minimise violence.

First then, we look at those inborn qualities that are needed for survival, which developed during human evolution. We can, if we like, call them instincts, but psychologists tend rather to speak of attitudes or actions that are specially easy to learn. There are three such qualities, all more evident in men than in women:

First: All human beings appreciate a chance to dominate or feel superior to other people.

Second: On the background of the group and territorial instincts of primitive man, they readily develop loyalty to much larger groupings.

Third: Most men find it relatively easy and gratifying to use weapons effectively.

But the other side is equally important, equally natural. The second proposition is that with the development of stable human communities, means have been developed over the centuries which can virtually eliminate overt violence. The use of intelligence and commonsense to see the implications of violence, plus group feeling and to some degree a broadening of family affection, see to that.

To a human biologist, the hope is that the second set of factors which do allow people to live together in communities as large as the USA or the USSR, can gradually be applied even more widely.

Two things interest me particularly: the first I have already mentioned. It is the ease with which scientific and technical discussions can be fruitful, effective and happy across any set of frontiers. Art and music are by tradition equally international, but science comes much closer to the realities of power, and interchanges at the scientific level are likely to be more helpful.

The second is the small, but growing, proportion of international and interracial marriages amongst scientists and scholars. In the last analysis we are unlikely to see 'one world' in any stable sense, unless the strong social taboos in nearly every community against marriage outside the accepted groups can be broken down. There is no sound biological reason against interracial marriage, and there is some evidence that, where many human stocks are blended, vigour and capacity for achievement may be increased. England and southern Germany are the classical examples. Sooner or later, race prejudice will be broken down, and what the anthropologists call mating groups, and the geneticists gene pools, will be enlarged to include essentially the whole human species. I think we begin to see the first steps in that direction, even if we fully realise the strong feeling against racial intermarriage which undoubtedly exists in most parts of the world.

All that I should like to leave with you is the feeling that the only way in which we can overcome the inborn instincts that have made war and conflict the pattern of history, is by the application of intelligence and commonsense – and the scientific approach is no more than systematised intelligence and commonsense. There are clear indications from human biology – from the scientific study of our own species – as to the aims that will allow the full achievement of human potentialities. I may be quite unduly optimistic, but I look to progressive education in human biology as the most likely agent to help us to move in the direction which we all desire; and in my last lecture, I shall touch on the problems and potentialities of education in human biology.

'That great deposit of human experience'

Manning Clark

'A talk to graduate students': Australian National University, Canberra

JANUARY 1967

The six-volume *History of Australia* that Manning Clark (1915–1991) composed in the upstairs study of his Canberra home has been described by admirers as 'a majestic blue gum' and detractors as 'gooey subjective pap'. Clark did not expect otherwise after such an acutely personal work. At the Sydney launch of volume six, Clark described it as 'the child of my heart. Every creator of such a child knows its flaws. But there is a wonderous moment after birth, before the straiteners and the whippers begin their attacks'.

Educated at Melbourne University and later at Oxford – where he returned in 1978 as a visiting professor – Clark worked from

1949 to 1975 at Canberra University College (later the ANU). At odds with the establishment for his 'unwillingness to denounce communism', he spoke publicly on many issues, including the 1975 sacking of the Whitlam government, claiming it was enacted by the 'forces of Mammon'. With his broad-brimmed hat and characteristic beard, Clark was easily recognisable – perhaps too recognisable for his scholarly reputation. But he did much to popularise the study of Australian history, as did his former students Geoffrey Blainey and Geoffrey Serle.

*

Today we are all like travellers who have gathered in a waiting room before setting out on a long journey of discovery. We can't all be great travellers like Herman Melville, that mariner and mystic who came back to tell people of the mystery at the heart of things, the beauty and the horror. But all of us are travellers, who will meet from time to time to report to each other on what we have found.

I take it we are all driven on by curiosity, by wonder about that mystery at the heart of things, by delight as well as by some sorrow, or regret that things are not different – the sense of the Aboriginal calamity, or man's errors, or his folly. And I take it that you belong to either of the two great groups of preyers on mankind: to those who have the *amor fati*, that love of things as they are, and therefore believe that truth is beauty; or to the groups with a drive to change things. These either believe they should and can be changed, or adopt the much harder position of saying that they should be changed but cannot. I take it that you are looking at history not for a sign, because no such sign will be given to you, but rather as the great deposit of human experience. I like to think of all of us in the way in which Goya saw us: the elephant – the dark cave – behind him the light. More laws for mankind. There is the essence of the human situation, and like all great work it does not give one simple instruction, but rather many answers, for what is seen in that great work depends on the eye of the beholder. Either men can see the light but they prefer the darkness, with all its insupportable burdens: their deeds are evil. Or a warning about the sources of human darkness, or an aristocratic elitist disdain for the surrender of the masses to their passions, etc.

So let me say simply that one of the objects of your search or your journey is to find something to say, of which there are many. History, that great deposit of human experience, is rather reminiscent of Anna Karenina's point about love – just as many hearts, just as many kinds of love: just as many minds and hearts, just as many views of history. You must hope that your view is a central one, that you are in the mainstream of life of your day and age. I would urge you to examine what you believe you have to say, to identify it, separate it out from the dross, the accretions, etc., and then study *how* to say it.

You will never find the final answer to the *how*. Part of it is in knowing, first, what you want to say, and second, to whom it is addressed. You can improve how you say it, first by reading about how other people who are good at it set about doing it. I recommend you to real La Nauze, *Presentation of Historical Theses* and P. Ryan, *The Preparation of Manuscripts*. I recommend you also to read books on how to write English, such as J. Middleton Murry, *The Problem of Style*, and A.T. Quiller-Couch, *The Writing of English*. Above all, you should have certain essential tools of the trade: a manual of punctuation; the *Shorter Oxford English Dictionary*; perhaps a magnifying glass. You may find it helpful to have another language, and to study economics, statistics, psychology as aids to your work, and for practise in that precision which historians so often lack, to their great damage.

I am not going to talk to you about how to write. That is a subject in itself. But I am going to urge you to practise and practise and practise until you acquire some mastery over the words with which you communicate what you have to say. Work at it. Recognise the magnitude of your task, which is twofold – to write sentences which are unambiguous, and to write memorably. It is the combination of these two which is so very, very difficult.

Every work must have a beginning, a development and a conclusion. Let me remind you of two which are connected with our own country – J.G. Frazer's *The Golden Bough* and Henry Handel Richardson's *The Fortunes of Richard Mahoney*.

Aim high. Above all, I hope you are all believers, whether you take a religious view of the world, or a materialist view or a not-knowing view. I hope you all believe in writing history, that all you do over the next year or so will strengthen that faith. I know it is fashionable in some intellectual circles to sneer at the historian, to ask whether there is such a subject, or to mock and deride and call history 'the anus of the human mind'. Do not be troubled. You are engaging in an activity which has gone on since time immemorial. If you want to write history as literature, I hope that you will have that 'soul's right of wonder'; that, as Emerson wrote to Carlyle, you will award your 'righteous praise and doom ... without cant', that you will indeed be that 'ungodliest divine man [who] cantest never' with 'not a dull word'. I hope that, if you analyse society and so belong to a great tradition which includes de Tocqueville and Marx, you will end, as Frazer did, with reverence and awe, that you will hail both Mary and Apollo, and Diana and Dionysus.

'Life is not meant to be easy'

Malcolm Fraser

'Towards 2000 – challenge to Australia': Alfred Deakin Lecture, Melbourne

20 JULY 1971

Malcolm Fraser (1930–), the Oxford University educated son of a wealthy pastoral family, left his family farm at the age of twenty-five to take up the federal seat of Wannon and remained on the parliamentary backbenches for ten years. Nicknamed 'the Prefect', he won the army portfolio in 1966, education and science in 1968 and defence in 1969. Fraser was directly involved in ending the leaderships of Bill Snedden, John Gorton and Gough Whitlam, being swept into prime ministerial office by the constitutional crisis of 1975. Since his retirement after defeat at the polls in 1983, he has devoted his attention to humanitarian issues, particularly the work of CARE International, openly criticising the party he once led on a range of economic and social issues.

The quotation 'life is not meant to be easy' stuck to Fraser, though it is as much a simplification and misinterpretation as 'the lucky country'. At a Liberal Party Federal Council address in 1981, Fraser remarked that, 'Over the years, a quotation about what life was or wasn't meant to be like has often been talked about. Some people have said it represents my philosophy. I think that now is the time to let you into a secret. Only half the quotation is ever quoted. In full, it says: "Life is not meant to be easy, my child; but take courage; it can be delightful."' The quote – from Bernard Shaw's play *Back to Methusaleh* – was first uttered by Fraser in his 1971 Deakin Lecture; the context, provided by the theories of the historian Arnold Toynbee, is clarified by the following introductory section of the speech.

*

Alfred Deakin knew that an Australia divided into separate and quarrelsome colonies could never become the great free land we now know. Therefore he devoted himself to the challenge of that time. He was significantly responsible for moves that led to federation. His mind and his heart lay in what Australia was to become.

In the seventy years since federation which Alfred Deakin worked so hard to achieve, Australia has experienced much. A rural agrarian economy, dependent largely on wool, meat and wheat, has become greatly diversified; our industrial strength has grown, and still expands. Our greatly expanded population has become housed largely in two great cities leading to a concentration of people which has not been equalled in other countries.

The development of our economic activity has advanced pragmatically. It is true, however, that our current economic policies have been influenced significantly by what Galbraith would call the 'conventional wisdom' of the time. We could not forestall the boom of the late 1920s, nor could we avert the Great Depression. Conventional economics made the Depression heavier and darker. Keynes had not yet written and been accepted and Theodore, who might have been an Australian prophet, left himself vulnerable. He could not shake the conventions and so Australia, like the world, lay in idleness and agony.

We have been involved in two world wars. We have participated in several minor wars. They have given us an Australian tradition and an Australian pride in the courage and fortitude of our people. They leave us with a sorrow that we remember.

These seventy years have seen good times, but they have been weighted by war and economic adversity.

Strong ties to Britain prevented the full assumption of independence until the century had nearly half gone. Policies of parent and child remained close, and continued so, despite the late understanding in the Second World War that it was the United States and not the United Kingdom that could save Australia from invasion.

Australia was to be given further years of comfort, comfort that stemmed from the knowledge that she had substantial interests in common with 'great and powerful friends', whose support would be unquestioned if the need arose. This was not an accident of history. It grew from an understanding of great power politics, of the tides then flowing, and of the Australian interest.

We stand now at the start of the last thirty years of this century. We look towards 2000. This paper will examine some problems that lie ahead. I will argue that the uncertainties, the challenges to be mastered will require greater responsibility and independence of decision from Australia, and that the wellbeing and security of our citizens will depend upon our response to the changing tide.

This changing attitude and approach is entirely consistent with the Liberal idea. Our philosophy of government is a vital living thing. We apply our basic ideas to the problems of the present and the challenge of the future.

Challenge to a nation can come from within, or from external sources. My theme will then be divided into two parts, but at the conclusion they will join, because while we could falter on either front, the kind of nation we build within ourselves will determine our capacity to respond to external challenge.

Arnold Toynbee once wrote twelve volumes to demonstrate and analyse the cause of the rise and fall of nations. His thesis can be condensed to a sentence, and is simply stated: that through history nations are confronted by a series of challenges, and whether they survive or whether they fall to the wayside depends on the manner and character of their response. Simple, and perhaps one of the few things that is self-evident. It involves a conclusion about the past that life has not been easy for people or for nations, and an assumption for the future that that condition will not alter. There is within me some part of the metaphysic, and thus I would add that life is not meant to be easy.

'Kevin, you're too slow to do all this finessin''

Tom Hafey

Address to the Richmond Football Club, preliminary final, VFL Park

20 SEPTEMBER 1975

The Richmond Football Club had not won a premiership for almost twenty-five years when Tom Hafey (1931–) was appointed coach in 1966. A tough, compact back-pocket player who had played seventy-seven games for his club between 1953 and 1958, Hafey brought a no-frills approach to the job. He was one of the first coaches to devote himself to his players' physical conditioning, having himself become a disciple of the athletics coach Percy Cerutty, and his personal integrity extracted great loyalty from senior players. He coached the 'Tigers' through a golden premiership era, including four premierships, then went on to coach at Collingwood, where he took the team from the bottom of the ladder to a grand final in twelve months.

After seasons at Geelong and Sydney, he finished his career having coached 522 games, but his influence outlived him, through the eighteen of his players who became VFL and AFL coaches in their own right. The most famous, Kevin Sheedy, played 251 games for Richmond between 1967 and 1979 before commencing his tenure at Essendon in 1981. Like Hafey, Sheedy was 'tough and totally fearless' – but not tough enough in the 1975 preliminary final against North Melbourne, when Hafey pleaded with his star defender to stop his 'finessin''. The straight-talking demands were not enough; Richmond lost by seventeen points to North Melbourne.

*

We're not runnin' straight at the ball. That's the cruel part about it, Tigers. Nothin' more Tigerish than a bloody Tiger, a wounded Tiger. Kevin, fair dinkum mate, you've got to put your boot into the ball, you're too slow to do all this finessin'. Bloody back pocket plumber, that's what I want. You see the bloody straight, get your boot to the damn thing headin' towards goals. Same with Michael, same with Balmy, we've gotta get a lift from you players. Surely you can see this, everybody's gotta get a lift. Kevvy Morris, where you been? Get in now, come on, in the front of your man, you know he's gunna run like mad. But the biggest problem, fellas: across the half forward line. David, I've given you a big job, a big job, centre half forward – but at the end of the day, at the end of that half, you were joggin' along, you were joggin' as though you were waiting for the bloody bell to come along. We've gotta remember that every time the ball comes to our area you've gotta fight like hell. Fight on your hands and knees, fight over for the mark, run over, and then when it does come to the ground, that's when Sheeds or Bruce Montieth …

And I told you Johnny Rantall's a great mark, well you oughta know better than anybody right now, because every time the ball's come up he's marked over ya Bruce, fair dinkum. I can't remember you once tryin' to knock the ball to the ground, can't remember you once doin' it.

'Fight for the ball'

John Kennedy

Half-time address at the Victorian Football League Grand Final,
Melbourne Cricket Ground

27 September 1975

Coming to Hawthorn Football Club from Teacher's College
in 1950, John Kennedy (1928–) played 165 games, fearless and
defiant at a time when the club was still struggling to make its
presence felt. But it was as a coach in thirteen seasons between
1960 and 1976 that he would make his impact, imposing a fitness
regime without precedent and driving 'Kennedy's Commandos' to
four flags with stirring, largely *ex tempore*, addresses. 'Not in the
habit of making speeches to football teams', his words were
instead 'a product of the circumstances – often desperate'. He
might prepare the gist of an address, but the notes were always discarded when the time came for delivery – Kennedy hoping 'the
trams and trains' would not let him down.

The 1975 grand final was an emotional time for his club. Their
champion captain, Peter Crimmins, was not selected to play in
the match in a dilemma 'unique in its sadness and difficulty': he
was suffering from cancer. North Melbourne took control of the
match early, and by half-time Hawthorn were down by twenty
points. Kennedy's speech is the sound of a coach in desperation,
exhorting and entreating his players to greater effort even as the
match and the season slip away. It wasn't enough, with North
Melbourne winning their first grand final flag by fifty-five points.
Crimmins died of cancer three days after the following year's
grand final – when Hawthorn had its revenge on North
Melbourne and won what will always be known as 'Crimmo's
flag'.

*

Not one of us just let it run on up the field. What a pathetic performance. Half the game over. We've been thrashed … One thing is to be beaten, another thing is to be beaten the way you blokes have been beaten. [*Pause.*] Nick, you're in the forward pocket this time … Now look, one bloke went out on the flank and battled against three, and I don't know what in the name of fortune you're doing, there's only one thing in football and that's to get in and fight for the ball. Fight for the ball! You're a disgrace to the name of Moncrieff, the way you're not fighting. All the year, if you fight for the ball you'll get a few. If you hope you won't. [*Pause.*] Bomber, a player can be beaten for half a game and come back in the second half. Now you've got to get your eye on the ball and use your tremendous ability to get the ball. At first when you get it you'll have to kick it because you haven't had many kicks. Get it and kick it and don't expect anything else. Get the ball and kick the ball and kick it long. [*Pause.*] How many times have North Melbourne kicked out, and the rover, or the ruck rover has been completely on his own? There's the indicator, there's the barometer of the way you're playing. Not enough puff to run there and stop the pass. And then you wonder why it goes bang, bang, bang, up the ground. No, throw it on to your team-mate further on. [*Pause.*] We're so far into the mess that we have to be desperate to get out of it. And we will not get out of it with kick-and-mark football. Knock the ball towards our goals and anybody who takes a mark, handball on, handball on, one handball and kick the cover off it. Have you got that? One handball and kick the cover off it. I wonder how many blokes are prepared to go totally with me and take the risk. It couldn't be worse than it is. It's disgraceful out there running along pushing blokes after they get rid of the ball, running over the, over the mark, on the, on the back line and giving them fifteen yards on the back line. Get the ball, if you take a mark, you've got the ball under control, we've been through it fifty times. Go back, have your kick. I've seen Matthews on his own over there, but naah, don't kick it to him, don't handpass it, run on and kick it, over the man on the mark, and give it to him if it's on. Better still if there's a man coming past give him the ball. If it goes wrong, it goes wrong, at least you're doing what I asked and at least I'm responsible. But I'm not responsible for the gutless, witless display that's going on out there. I don't know how you can, you can, face one another and carry on as you're carrying on out there.

Now positively, ruckman up and knock the ball with us, with us, all the time, right? Anybody who takes a mark take the risk and handpass, and players without the ball you must have the initiative to come past, but don't all come past and no one go in, that's half the trouble. There's a lot of blokes prepared to run past but not too many are prepared to go in. Go in, get the ball and blokes come past for the handball. Take the risk, if you make the mistake, if you do it and it doesn't come off, do it again. Do it again. And keep doing it. Keep doing it. That way, we'll either get beaten by twenty goals or we'll win. This way we can't win. We can't win this way. We can't win by doing what you blokes are doing. Play virile strong football, put your bodies in to get the ball. That's the first thing. If you're in the pack no messying about, no three votes, knock it towards our goal, that's the only, only, way to do. If you take a mark, and you hear the call, give him the ball. Give him the ball. If he gets into trouble, back him up, give him the ball and run after him like we do in training. That way we've got a chance. This way we've got none. You stay on the ball Bernie, put your body in all the time, down the back line, knock the ball out towards our goals, on the forward line over the back as I said before. [*Pause.*]

If you're feeling tired, if you're feeling tired just think of Crimmins. He's home, he's not here. He brought his insides up this morning, he's vomiting. He's not here. You weren't at the match committee on Thursday night as I was when we had a big argument as to whether he ought to be in or out and everybody spoke his mind and he finished up out. He's not happy, he wasn't happy about it, who would be? But I can't understand the mentality of blokes. And even the governor, Sir Henry Winneke, he has often said 'At least do something.' Do. Don't think, Mick, don't hope. Do. At least you can come off and say, 'I did this, I shepherded, I played on. At least I did something for the sake of the side.' Do. Act. Don't think, act. Eye on the ball. The contest is still the same. You must win the ball to win the match. And more than that, when you win the ball you must cooperate with fellas coming past. And you must be desperate enough to stick with me and do it. The crowd might laugh. It might go wrong. I'm game enough to tell you to do it. Are you game enough to back me up? Are you game enough, Scotty, to back me up on that? [*Growls of assent.*] Make the ball run our way, knock it a long way out in front of the bloke. In front of the player.

'Lap, Phar'

Barry Andrews

After-dinner speech at the first Sporting Traditions Conference, Coogee Bay Hotel, Sydney

JULY 1977

The inaugural Sporting Traditions Conference, hosted by the University of New South Wales, marked the beginning of inter-disciplinary sports scholarship in Australia. A friendly but serious affair, 'Sports 1' was groundbreaking for its time, preceding the present-day proliferation of sports history and sociology. The highlight of the conference was the after-dinner speech by Barry Andrews (1943–1987), author, editor and scholar in the English department at Duntroon Military College. Andrews was the second choice as speaker, the first invitee having been considered prohibitively expensive. Like the Coogee Bay Hotel, Andrews was cheap, available and at hand. With his 'wretched paper' delivered earlier in the day 'out of the way', Andrews wrote the speech at the bar before dinner was served. Composed as 'a gentle dig at academic pretensions and absurdities', 'Lap, Phar' follows the style and tone of an *Australian Dictionary of Biography* entry. The audience 'laughed until we could bear no more; the timing of the performer and the occasion was perfect'. The community of sports scholars who emerged from the conference credit Andrews with 'setting the tone' for Sporting Traditions with his after-dinner speech, which began with thanks to Frank Crowley, the Dean of Arts who had supplied the funds and support for the event.

*

Lap, Phar (1926–32), sporting personality, business associate of modest speculators and national hero, was born on 4 October 1926 at Timaru, New Zealand, the second of eight children of Night Raid and his wife Entreaty, née Prayer Wheel. The family had military connections, including Carbine and Musket (qq.v.), although Raid himself had emigrated to Australia during the First World War.

A spindly, unattractive youth with chestnut hair, Lap was educated privately at Timaru until January 1928, when he formed a liaison with the Sydney entertainment entrepreneur Harold Telford. With Telford, Lap moved to Sydney and established premises in the suburb of Randwick. A number of short-term (distant) ventures were unsuccessful, although after James E. Pike (q.v.) commenced employment and Telford became a silent partner, the business flourished. A small, dapper man who dressed flamboyantly in multicoloured coats and hats, Pike's nervousness caused him to lose weight before each speculation with Lap; yet their affiliation lasted for over two years and proved beneficial to hundreds of Australian investors.

The most successful years were between 1930 and 1932, when the business expanded into Victoria, South Australia and Mexico. Pike and Lap received numerous awards for services to the entertainment industry, including an MC in 1930; they shared with Telford a gross taxable income of over 50,000 pounds. This income was substantially increased, however, by generous donations from several Sydney publishers, including Ken Ranger and Jack Waterhouse (qq.v.).

Early in 1930 Lap journeyed to North America to strengthen his interests there; Telford, who disliked travelling, and Pike who had weighty problems to contend with, stayed behind. Tall and rangy, known affectionately as 'Bobby', 'The Red Terror' and occasionally as 'you mongrel', Lap died in mysterious circumstances in Atherton, California, on 5 April 1932, and was buried in California, Melbourne, Canberra and Wellington. A linguist as well as businessman, he popularised the phrase 'get stuffed!', although owing to an unfortunate accident in his youth he left no children.

'We are celebrating our freedoms by being here'

Michael Kirby

'The phallus and its functions': speech at the opening of an art
exhibition, Ivan Dougherty Gallery, Sydney

18 April 1992

Justice Michael Kirby (1939–) is one of Australia's most respected
jurists and most dedicated and outspoken human rights advocates. The youngest man appointed to federal judicial office in
Australia, Kirby was called to the New South Wales Bar in 1967,
appointed a judge of the Federal Court in 1983, and has served as
a justice of the High Court since 1996. Kirby has also served as
deputy president of the Australian Conciliation and Arbitration
Commission, president of the NSW Court of Appeal and chairman of the Australian Law Reform Commission.

Renowned for his long working hours, Kirby once remarked
that his idea of death was 'sitting on a beach and drinking gin and
tonic'. In addition to his legal work, he has devoted his energies to
a host of causes and bodies: he was a member of the International
Labour Organisation Commission mission to South Africa, the
World Health Organisation Global Commission on AIDS, the
AIDS Trust of Australia and president of the International Commission of Jurists in Geneva. His work was recognised in 1991
when he was awarded the Australian Human Rights Medal.

Both his vocation and his vision can be sensed from the following speech at the opening of an art exhibition, where, with
urbanity, wit and sympathy, Kirby reflects on the history of censorship in art, the relationship between freedom of expression
and the law, and the need to learn from past oppression.

*

As I came here my car seemed to be surrounded by police-wagons travelling up Oxford Street with us. Could it be, I asked myself? Could it really be a raid? Perhaps the police intend to raid the Dougherty Gallery and confiscate the phallic symbols collected in this exhibition. We should not laugh. It has happened. And in the lifetime of most of us here. ...

Be in no doubt that the law has played an important part in suppressing the representation of the phallus in art and in literature. When I saw the police cars apparently following me to this gallery my mind raced back to the case in which I was involved soon after my admission to the Bar. It is a reported decision so all who want to can see how far we have travelled in the past twenty-five years. They can read *Crowe v Graham*. My client had published two magazines with the provocative titles *Censor* and *Obscenity*. The titles they chose did not make it easier for their lawyers to assert that censorship had no place in their sights and that obscenity was the furthest thing from the minds of the publishers. A sensitive policeman purchased these two journals from a news vendor in Kings Cross. He was a Detective Sergeant of Police and was doubtless deeply offended by what he read. He could not get to the magistrate quickly enough to charge my client with publishing obscene and indecent material.

We won in the Court of Appeal – ever a liberal guardian of civic rights under the law. But our victory was short-lived. It was overturned in the High Court of Australia. In that Court, Justice Windeyer, a soldier, lawyer and historian, traced the history of obscenity in the common law of England. He referred to the old form of indictment for an obscene libel:

> This commenced by referring to the accused in opprobrious and perjorative terms as, for example – 'a person of most wicked, lewd, lascivious, depraved and abandoned mind and disposition and wholly lost to all sense of decency, chastity, morality and religion'. It then went on to allege, in language of which the following is an illustration, that he 'wickedly, devising, contriving and intending to vitiate and corrupt the morals as well as of youth as of divers other liege subjects of our lord the King and to stir up and excite in their minds filthy, lewd

and unchaste desires and inclinations did publish obscene, filthy and indecent prints.

The adjectives were taken to be synonymous. Other epithets such as 'bawdy', were sometimes thrown in to accompany 'obscene'. Doubtless each new epithet was designed to work the judicial recipient into a higher lather of anger and outrage.

At about the same time as the *Graham* case, the opponents of the use of law to suppress art in the name of obscenity were gathering strength in the United States of America for the assault which, in that country, was to prove largely successful. In the way stood, of all people, the Chief Justice of the United States who was later to become a symbol of the liberalism of that court – the 'Super Chief', Earl Warren. According to a recent analysis:

> Warren's biographers are agreed that from the day he joined the Court to the day he stepped down, the 'Super Chief' could not shed his conventional middle-American attitudes or his puritanism. 'If anyone showed that [dirty] book to my daughters, I'd have strangled him with my own hands,' he reputedly told a fellow justice. The otherwise humanistic Chief's defensiveness about sexual expression made rational decision-making and opinion-writing in this area of the Court's work difficult. Warren could not reconcile the disgust he felt for sexually oriented materials with the respect he professed for 'arts and sciences and freedom of communication generally'. He was puzzled by his inability to get anything out of 'modern' literature and art. To him 'smut peddlers' had no rights under the First Amendment, for what they peddled had nothing to do with literature and art, or even communication. Not only was their conduct an affront to Warren's personal sensibility, it also presented in his view, a peril to America's moral fiber.

The beginning of the end of this approach occurred under the intellectual leadership of Justice William J. Brennan Jr. He has said:

> Warren was a terrible prude, like my father was. If Warren was revolted by something, it was obscene. He would not read any

of the books. Or watch the movies. I'd read the book or see the movie and he'd go along with my views.

However, Warren did not, at least at first, surrender his conventional views or go along with Brennan on things sexual. The test came in the late 1960s and early 1970s with landmark cases involving Henry Miller's novel *Tropic of Cancer* and Louis Malle's film *The Lovers*. At last, the Supreme Court of the United States, invoking the First Amendment with its guarantee of freedom of speech, struck down state obscenity laws. It largely removed the threat of such laws in the United States to literature, film and art.

We, in Australia, followed. We did so not because of any First Amendment or Bill of Rights here – nor even because of the liberalism of the common law or the dedication of judges and magistrates to art in all of its forms. A far greater influence was the sheer volume of published material arriving from the United States – in film, print, picture and art form. This material began to flood the English-speaking world. In that sense, we were all the children of the United States constitution. We all became the beneficiaries of the First Amendment. And it should not be forgotten that that amendment was adopted in an age when the perceived threat was not simply to printed newspapers:

> The framers of the First Amendment ... must have had literature and art in mind, because our first national statement on the subject of 'freedom of the press', the 1774 address of the Continental Congress to the inhabitants of Quebec, declared: 'The importance of this [freedom of the press] consists, beside the advancement of truth, science, morality and arts in general, in its diffusion of liberal sentiments on the administration of government.

A hundred and sixty-five years later, President F.D. Roosevelt said:

> The arts cannot thrive except where men are free to be themselves and to be in charge of the discipline of their own energies and orders. The conditions for democracy and art are one and same. What we call liberty in politics results in freedom of the arts.

The symbols of the change could be seen most vividly in Australia as the 1960s turned into the 1970s. On 5 June 1969, at the Metro Theatre, Kings Cross, Sydney, the musical *Hair* first came to Australia. More than a million theatregoers saw that production. It shocked the country at the time, basking as we were in the afterglow of indolent imperialism and dutiful subservience to powerful allies. *Hair* shook the conservative complacency of Australia. It heralded an era of freedom and protest which was to change the face of this country forever. The famous nude scene at the end of *Hair* confronted the old-fashioned ideas of obscenity and indecency. No prosecution was launched.

Yet the censor was still about. In 1973 a poster of Michaelangelo's *David* was actually confiscated from the Myer department store in Melbourne on the ground that it was obscene! The increasing number of bathers at the proliferating nude beaches of Australia provoked the occasional arrest. But then, because of general acceptance in the field of art censorship, confiscation, police raids and the like became much more infrequent. The advent of AIDS consolidated these changes. Now there is direct talk, even to the young children at school, of the dangers of unprotected sex, the use of condoms, specifics of anal intercourse and things which once would never had been talked of in puritanical Australia.

Yet we should not think that the age of censorship is dead. By no means. The censor's blue pencil is ever-ready to do its work of controlling freedoms. For most censors it is as if nothing has been learned from the changes of the past few decades. …

We have no First Amendment to protect us here. There are indications that those who would censor and restrict freedom of communication are busily at work again after a period of relative quiescence.

The movie *Henry, Portrait of a Serial Killer* and others since were banned after they arrived in Australia. When certain portions of the film, deemed unacceptable, were removed it was reclassified and released in its expurgated form.

Derryn Hinch, hot from coverage of the 1991 'Strathfield Massacre', called for the banning of Brett Easton Ellis' book *American Psycho*.

Calls were vigorously made by some churchmen for banning the movies *Hail Mary* and *The Last Temptation of Christ*.

The office of the Film and Literature Classification has prohibited the distribution of a book on suicide techniques called *Final Exit*.

In Western Australia, the Minister for Health rejected the candid coverage of safe sex, declaring that it was part of the 'condom culture'. Instead, apparently motivated by his own moral beliefs (informed doubtless by St Paul), he promoted the campaign 'It's all right to say no'. Whilst chastity is certainly one option in the face of AIDS, available empirical data suggests that it is an option lacking universal appeal. It only takes one act of unsafe intercourse to transmit the HIV virus. The need for alternative messages is therefore plain. This is accepted by experts, including by the World Health Organisation. But not by the Minister of Health of Western Australia. Politicians have great responsibilities. When they descend into moral censorship in a field of public health as vital as HIV/AIDS, they may have the death of the infected upon their consciences. Censorship in the face of AIDS may have truly deathly results. A needless death from AIDS occasioned by ignorance or embarrassed fear to procure or use a condom in sex, is a truly awful obscenity.

Western Australia seems to be in the vanguard of Australia's censorship revival. It has been announced there that laws will ban the display of advertising of two of Australia's biggest selling magazines, *People* and *Picture*. The Western Australian Minister for the Arts, of all people, explaining the new restrictions, said that her office had found that people were much less offended by the nudity in *Penthouse* and *Playboy* than in the 'degrading and offensive' depiction of women in *People* and *Picture*. The criterion for public access now seems to be the moral sensibilities of the people in the office of the Minister for the Arts. How ironic that ministries established for this purpose become the censors: determining what 'arts' people may, and may not, receive. It is as if we have learned nothing from the history of legal regulation of literature and art in this century. If we impose the opinion of the censor about art, it soon takes on its own dynamic. Some of the most vigorous proponents of the obscenity laws of the United States were the postal and customs officials who policed such laws with heavy-handed efficiency and fearsome moral zeal.

We should learn from the oppression of the past. We should certainly keep the hands of the law off literature and art in all of its forms. It is important, not least at this time, for people to speak up for freedom of expression. Human rights for the popular majority is easy. They can generally look after themselves. Human rights matter most when minorities and their beliefs, opinions, actions and expressions are at risk.

That is why I was glad to be associated with this exhibition. Here we are, free citizens in a generally free country. We are celebrating our freedoms by being here. The police wagon with its siren passed by, attending to truly urgent dangers. We must ensure that our freedoms endure and flourish.

'A true university is (and has always been) anchored in values'

Pierre Ryckmans

'Learning': Boyer Lecture, broadcast on ABC Radio National

12 NOVEMBER 1996

Despite professing an 'innate and invincible indolence', the scholar and sinologist Professor Pierre Ryckmans (1935–) is one of this country's most fertile and free-ranging minds. He grew up in his native Belgium and, after a period teaching art history in Hong Kong, settled here at the age of thirty-five, becoming a lecturer in Chinese literature at the Australian National University, then serving as professor of Chinese studies at Sydney University from 1987 until 1993. Ryckmans published many of his fifteen books under the pen name of Simon Leys, including *The Death of Napoleon*, which won the Christina Stead Prize in 1991 and was later made into a feature film. Disinclined to follow the intellectual fashions of the day, he has been denounced by some for his conservatism. 'The cultivated public always follows the directives of a few propaganda commissars,' he has retorted. 'There is much more conformity among intellectuals than among plumbers or car-mechanics.' His 1996 Boyer Lectures, entitled 'The view from the bridge: aspects of culture', were a reflection of his disaffection for universities, which he contended could not be genuine when operating 'on the scale of a sausage factory'.

*

In the confessions of Jean-Jacques Rousseau, there is a passage which I have always found singularly affecting. (Well, actually, there are a great many passages in the *Confessions* that are singularly affecting. Whatever you may think and feel regarding Rousseau – some people have idolised him, while others loathe his continual floods of tears and his cumbersome self-pity – one thing is certain: among all the great writers of the eighteenth century, he specially strikes you by his modernity: he has a strange power to move us as if he were our *contemporary*. What is at times so touching, and at other times so disturbing, in what he says is that he is actually expressing some of our own experiences, innermost thoughts and feelings.) Anyhow, in the passage I had in mind, Rousseau is recalling how he was once summoned to appear before the council of his local church, which suspected him of heresy. Since the council was comprised of country bumpkins, Rousseau, who was already famous throughout Europe for his inspired and passionate eloquence, had good reason to feel complete confidence regarding the outcome of the confrontation. Things, however, turned out quite differently: to his own astonishment and dismay, once in front of his philistine judges, he found himself virtually speechless. Unable to improvise any effective reply to their bigoted accusations, he eventually had to leave the meeting, humiliated, confused and defeated. Later on, walking alone in the night on the long way home, he pondered over his disastrous performance, replaying in his mind the proceedings of the day. But now, suddenly, the inspiration that had failed him earlier in the day, returned with cruel vengeance. A flow of brilliant ideas surged in his mind – he thought of all the irrefutable arguments and witty retorts with which he could so easily have confounded his opponents. But the opportunity was lost forever ... He cried with frustration, and beat his own head with his fists.

Have you ever had a similar experience? I suspect that many people, when reading this episode, must have said to themselves: 'Oh yes! How well I know that feeling!' Life throws many challenges at us, and when we fail to live up to them, they leave burning memories of shame and loss, and an intense desire to be granted the impossible chance to re-enact the test in which we disgraced ourselves. Still, in our misfortune, we may perhaps derive some melancholy comfort from the thought that, in this respect at least, we have something in common with a genius ...

In my own case, I vividly remember an incident which occurred many years ago. You may find it small and trivial – and I myself still remain puzzled by a sense of disproportion between what seemed the trifling nature of the actual episode, and the imprint it left on my memory. Perhaps it is only now, as I am (in a certain way) re-enacting this ancient test which I so miserably failed, that I come to measure its full import and begin to understand its original meaning.

It was during a scholarly conference organised in one of our leading universities. A guest speaker had been invited from abroad to address the conference. He was a fairly distinguished elderly academic, already retired, who had come to Australia specially for the occasion. He was a rather frail and refined old gentleman, and he spoke with erudition and feeling on the topic which had occupied him for his entire life: Chinese literati painting. When the old professor finished his talk, a young local academic stood up, and instead of addressing questions to the lecturer, launched himself into a lengthy and passionate denunciation of the lecture that had just been delivered. In brief, his argument was that to attach such an exclusive value and importance to what China's feudal oppressors had deemed to be superior art, merely reflected the speaker's narrow bourgeois elitism – whereas the true art of China, which was produced by the broad working masses, was being systematically ignored or dismissed by the academic mandarins, etc.

The violence of the attack took the old gentleman by surprise, but he remained silent and impassive. The chairman of that particular session, a rather shy and ineffectual man, was visibly shaken, and appeared totally unable to resume control of the proceedings. One could feel widespread embarrassment and discomfort among the public; unfortunately the usual reaction of decent people who are being confronted with a gross indecency is to pretend studiously that nothing happened. A younger segment of the audience, however, had obviously come in the expectation of watching the fireworks of their local hero; his show was geared towards them, and they cheered loudly. (I was suddenly reminded of a similar scene in a novel by Saul Bellow; Bellow's image has remained engraved on my mind; in his story, a young mob was compared to a certain species of big ape – baboons, I seem to remember: whenever a trespasser ventures into their forest, the baboons frantically defecate in each other's hands and bombard the hapless visitor with their own excrement.)

The young academic talked nearly as long as the original speaker, interrupted only by the applause of his supporters. When he concluded at long last, there was no more time for discussion, and the entire session was hastily brought to an end.

For all its aggressive energy, the improvised speech by the spokesman for the baboons was in itself quite banal. It merely rehashed some slogans which, for a time, the Chinese 'Cultural Revolution' had made fashionable among smart academics in our universities. Its actual argument was trite, and could easily have been disposed of: after all, to state that an artist (or an art historian, for that matter) is a bourgeois (or a proletarian, or an aristocrat) is exactly as pertinent and as informative (no more, no less) as to observe that he has red hair or flat feet. No, the truly disturbing aspect of his intervention did not reside in what he said, but in the reaction of the audience – or rather, in the lack of reaction from the audience. This absence of reaction, in turn, reflected something ominous about the state of the university, and about ourselves as academics. It became suddenly evident to me that most of us *were dead*, and had been dead for many years already – and the stench made one gasp for air.

For the larger part, the audience was composed of scholars who, being educated and courteous, naturally deplored the poor manners displayed by their young colleague; but, as to the *content* of his intervention, even though some of them might have had reservations about what he said, *all* apparently believed that, in a so-called intellectual debate, every opinion should be granted a fair hearing. None of them, it seemed – and this is what truly frightened me – perceived that what they had just heard was *not* one opinion among many, but a statement which, if validly issued, certified the fully consummated demise of the university.

Indeed, what the young academic had proclaimed (without provoking any challenge) was the impossibility and intellectual illegitimacy of all value judgements. From his perspective, value judgements were necessarily a form of cultural arrogance; any attempt to assess objective qualities were doomed to remain a vain and subjective expression of social prejudice.

But such a view, in turn, must reduce all scholarly endeavour to a hollow comedy, and, in this regard, I am irresistibly reminded of an old cartoon by Michael Leunig, portraying a trendy modern cleric. The caption read: 'Reverend So-and-So does not believe in God, but needs the job.' For, clearly, to deny the existence of objective values is to deprive the university of its spiritual means of operation. Values are the prerequisite of any inquiry into art, letters and the humanities. For example, how can you study literature without passing literary judgement and making reference to literary *quality*? Without having recourse to aesthetic appreciation, what enables you to assess that Jane Austen truly pertains to your discipline – but not Barbara Cartland? Is such a discrimination truly a mere expression of subjectivity and intellectual arrogance? If, in the name of a spurious scientific objectivity, every bit of printed matter has an equal right to call upon the literary scholar's attention, on what basis should we exclude from his scrutiny lawnmower handbooks and Superman comics? The actual fact is that, nowadays, *he does not*. In these areas, the most grotesque imagination is always overtaken by stark reality, and I should not be surprised if I were to learn that, right now, in the English Literature departments of our vanguard universities (duly renamed departments of Human Communications and Socio-cultural Deconstruction), there are earnest candidates for the doctoral degree, hard at work 'deconstructing' the telephone directory.

A true university is (and has always been) anchored in values. Deprived of this holding ground, it can only drift at the caprice of all the winds and currents of fashion, and, in the end, is doomed to founder in the shallows of farce and incoherence.

In a private letter (posthumously published), Hannah Arendt provided a striking insight on the relation between truth and thought that could provide an illuminating paradigm for the dependence of any scholarly investigation upon a pre-existing concept of values. Arendt wrote:

> The chief fallacy is to believe that Truth is a result that comes at the end of a thought process. Truth, on the contrary, is always the beginning of thought ... *Thinking starts after an experience of Truth has struck one*, so to speak. The difference between philosophers and other people is that the former refuse to let go, but not that they are the only receptacles of Truth ... Truth, in other words, is not *in* thought, but ... it is the condition for the possibility of thinking. It is both beginning and *a priori*.

The view that Truth is not a conclusion, but a premise – and the very condition for any intellectual inquiry – is important and profound, but not as new as Arendt thought. Two thousand three hundred years ago, the Chinese philosopher Zhuang Zi (one of the greatest thinkers in the universal history of ideas, and a wonderful writer) expressed a similar idea in one of his rich and enigmatic parables, which could be paraphrased in English as follows: Zhuang Zi and his friend the logician Hui Zi were taking a stroll on the bridge over the River Hao. It was a beautiful day, and they stopped for a moment to watch the little fish below. Zhuang Zi said: 'Look at the fish: how free and easy they swim – that is their happiness!' But Hui Zi immediately objected: 'You are not a fish, whence do you know that the fish are happy?' 'You are not me,' replied Zhuang Zi, 'how can you possibly know that I do not know if the fish are happy?' Hui Zi said: 'We'll grant that I am not you, and therefore cannot know what you know. But you must grant that you are not a fish, and therefore cannot know whether the fish are happy or not.' Zhuang Zi replied: 'Let us return to the original question. When you asked me "Whence do you *know* that the fish are happy?" your very question showed that you knew that I knew. Still, if you insist on asking *whence* I know, I will tell you: I know it from this bridge.'

To make a minute exegesis of such a piece would ruin it – it would be as brutish as pulling off the wings of a butterfly. Still, I merely wish to underline one point. Hui Zi's attitude represents the fallacy of a certain cleverness. With his abstract logic, he attempts to erode Zhuang Zi's living grasp of reality. But Zhuang Zi, in turn, develops his unanswerable riposte in two movements, on two different levels. In a first move, he shows Hui Zi that he can beat him at his own game, countering logic with logic. Indeed, on a strictly formal level, a question of the type 'Whence do you know' does not put your knowledge into question – it takes it for granted, and merely queries the starting point of your inference. But Zhuang Zi does not stop there; to win a sterile contest of wits is unsatisfying. In his final move, with a pun, he breaks free from the fetters of empty intellectual games, and enters the realm of reality, which in the end, alone matters. Borrowing Hui Zi's original word *whence*, he transforms its meaning: whereas Hui Zi had used it in the abstract sense of logical deduction, Zhuang Zi now takes it in its literal sense – 'from which point in space' – and he answers it literally. But the literal answer proves also to be the most profound – more profound even than the truth, for any truth can only be *about* reality, whereas here we reach what truth is about: reality itself, which is irrefutable: I know it from this bridge. Here, one is reminded of Samuel Johnson's powerful retort to an interlocutor who had invoked Berkeley's idealism, questioning the reality of reality: without a word, he vigorously kicked a rock of good size, that was lying on the ground.

Looking from the bridge, to know that the fish are happy is ultimately an act of faith. The saying 'to see is to believe' must be reversed: *to believe is to see.*

He who believes in nothing, sees nothing. The trap of 'seeing *through*' things was best exposed by C.S. Lewis, at the conclusion of his memorable essay in defense of values, *The Abolition of Man*:

> The whole point of seeing through something is to see something through it. It is good that the window should be transparent, because the street or garden beyond it is opaque. How if you saw through the garden too? It is no use trying 'to see through' first principles. If you see through everything,

then everything is transparent. But a wholly transparent world is an invisible world. To see through all things is the same as not to see.

A recent episode in Australian politics did shed a revealing light upon our attitude towards education. Do not misunderstand me: I am *not* making a political comment here – I won't even name the protagonists of the incident. The leader of what was then the Opposition lost his post during an inner-party struggle. The new leader, for the sake of party unity, had to offer him some sort of position within the shadow cabinet – not too menial, and yet not genuinely influential either. In consequence, the former leader was offered the education portfolio, but he refused it, as he found that it was 'not important enough'. In our political context, he made the right decision, of course – any experienced politician would have done the same. But the objective reality illustrated by this incident is that, in this country, it is publicly accepted and universally perceived that *education does not greatly matter*.

Actually *nothing* should matter more for a modern nation.

Some of our neighbours realised this long ago, and we can see the benefits they have now reaped. At the risk of appearing lazy and pretentious in quoting my own words (normally, to quote one's own writings is a fatuous habit) I shall repeat once more what I formerly wrote in an introduction to *The Analects of Confucius* – and I shall continue to repeat it in the future, whenever the opportunity arises:

> It is often remarked that the most successful and dynamic societies of East and South-East Asia (Japan, Korea, Taiwan, Hong Kong and Singapore) share a common Confucian culture. Should one therefore conclude that the analects of Confucius might actually yield a secret formula that would make it possible elsewhere to inject energy into flagging economies, and to mobilise and motivate a slovenly citizenry? The prosperity of a modern state is a complex phenomenon that can hardly be ascribed to one single factor. Yet there is indeed one common feature that characterises the various 'Confucian' societies – but it should be observed that this same feature can also be found in other social or ethnic groups (for instance some Jewish

communities of the Western world) which are equally creative and prosperous, and yet do not present any connection with the Confucian tradition: and it is *the extraordinary importance which these societies all attach to education.* Any government, any community, or any family which would be willing to invest into education as considerable a proportion of its energy and resources, should be bound to reap cultural, social and economic benefits comparable to those which are currently achieved by the thriving 'Confucian' states of Asia, or by some dynamic migrant communities of the Western world.

If it is true that, nowadays, the state of the economy commands the entire political life of a country, one should not forget that, in turn, the economy itself is dependent upon the level of culture and education of the nation. On this point, leading economists and political scientists are now in agreement, and their scholarly conclusion confirms what commonsense already knew: 'Human resources – the talents of the people – will be far more crucial to the prosperity and competitiveness of a nation than any natural resources and capital.'

Although it would be difficult to conclude these reflections on education without making some reference to my own experience as a former academic, I still think I should refrain from making specific comments on the University. I chose to leave Academe before my time was up, but seeing my former colleagues still there, on the frontline, battling bravely in a hopeless struggle, I feel like a deserter; and since I cannot encourage them, it would be disgraceful for me – a man cosily sheltered away from the action – to aggravate their predicament with what might appear as heartless comments. Anyway, the situation has already reached a point that is probably beyond remedy. Huge and ancient institutions take a very long time to die; in human affairs the process of decay, transformation and regeneration is often slow, erratic and blind. The main problem is not so much that the University of Western civilisation [as we] knew it is now virtually dead, but that *its death has hardly registered in the consciousness of the public, and even of a majority of academics themselves.* In principle, I do not mind the idea of a reform in higher education, however drastic it might be; what I do mind is the intellectual muddle and confusion. We obstinately insist on calling 'universities' institutions that correspond less and less to what is normally meant by this name. In their intriguing lack of awareness, our education ministers, vice-chancellors and other senior academics resemble strangely the early leaders of the Protestant Reformation, as described in a recent scholarly work on the history of the Church:

> Melanchton and Calvin claimed to be 'Catholic' until the end of their lives – and all the while, they were attacking the followers of the old faith as 'papists'. The faithful long clung to Mass and to their saints, but the Church regulations introduced by Lutheran magistrates took over many Catholic customs – even processions and pilgrimages. *The bulk of the simple faithful never understood that the 'Reformation' was not a reform of the Church, but the construction of a new Church set up on a different basis.* In retrospect, one must therefore maintain: *the schism of the Church succeeded by nothing so much as by the illusion that it did not take place at all.*

How long can the illusion persist? The University increasingly resembles the cardboard theatrical props that were used on [the] Elizabethan stage, or in Peking opera, and on which was written in big characters: 'THIS IS A CASTLE' or 'THIS IS A FOREST' – it amounts to little more than a symbolic signboard: 'THIS IS A UNIVERSITY'. Can such a fiction retain credibility with the public? Malcolm Muggeridge once observed that the main reason why many people previously looked at universities with a certain feeling of awe and respect was that so few of them had actual access to it. But once everybody goes to the university, they will get another view of it. This healthy awakening has been accelerating lately, and it will be complete on the day – now not very distant – when we shall see Universities of Catering, Car Driving Instruction and Quilt Making.

Anyway, on this subject we probably need not get too worked up. After all, any intelligent young person will always happily survive mediocre or inept university teaching, whereas no one can escape unharmed from a mediocre or inept primary school education. *This* should be *the* issue of greatest concern. I can think of no news more ominous than a recent report on ABC television according to which it appears that one-fifth of all pupils finishing primary school are functionally illiterate. This information is most frightening for the future of the country – and by comparison, all the problems of higher education pale into insignificance.

'Go and pick on someone your own size, you greedy bastards'

Phillip Adams

Speech to teachers, Collingwood Football Club, Melbourne

6 AUGUST 1997

Writer, critic and broadcaster Phillip Adams (1939–) has been at the forefront of Australian cultural life for over three decades. A successful advertiser whose company originated the 'Life, be in it' campaign, he has also promoted ceaselessly those activities and causes he holds dear. Crucial to the development of the Australian film industry in the 1970s, Adams chaired the Film, Radio and Television Board from 1972 to 1975 and the Australian Film Commission between 1983 and 1990. His weekly columns, in the *Age* and the *Australian*, have riled, informed and uplifted for decades; he is famous, too, for his avidity as a collector of all things, from antiquities to abuse: 'Each week it arrives in indignant dribbles or frumious floods, and the grosser the insult the greater my joy.' Sometimes provocative in his scepticism – 'Let's not let a little thing like God come between us' – and incurably involved in the issues that concern him, Adams is now best-known as the host of Radio National's wide-ranging *Late Night Live*.

*

Children are, in a sense, obsolete. Yes, there are hundreds of millions of kids running about but they're not meant to be children anymore. This is not permitted. They are, instead, to be little economic units. Diminutive adults with fully-fledged appetites for junk. Junk food, junk films, junk ideas, junk toys and junk culture.

Perhaps we should think of children in the same category as we think of other small, fanciful critters like fairies, gnomes, elves and leprechauns. Or moving up the mythological scale, in the way we think of unicorns, bunyips, Big Feet, Yetis and Nessies – creatures that we speculate about for which little physical evidence is available. Or perhaps we should simply regard kids as an endangered species that, like so many others, ran out of time. Like the dodo, the rhino, the panda, the American Liberal.

British comic Spike Milligan, an absurdist as considerable as Samuel Beckett or Ionesco, said, years ago, that we'd destroyed childhood. At the time he seemed a tad alarmist. But it turns out that Spike was right on the money ...

Of course, history records many a terrible era for kids. Quite recently they were being sent down mines and shoved up chimneys. And we know they're still used as cheap labour in a host of countries, or sold into prostitution. Nonetheless there remain clearly identifiable traits that identify the child – involving curiosity, soaring imagination and restless physicality which set them apart from older members of the same species.

No, I'm not going to romanticise children. I remember being a child and vividly, painfully recall the savageries of the schoolyard, the pecking order in the playground, the racism, incipient fascism and bigotry that coexists with the innocence and openness of the child. Demagoguery is, of course, alive and well and living in the sandpit in the enduring form of the bully. Kids are authoritarian and, more significantly, kids are conformist.

But bad behaviour around the swings and slides doesn't justify making the child cannon fodder for commerce, with psychologists and market researchers and creative directors and film producers and highly paid marketing men in manufacturing companies and so-called service industries targeting them ruthlessly and relentlessly. No, we don't send kids up chimneys or down mines any more.

Now we send them into stores to buy, to consume, to coerce their parents. Their curiosity is turned to commercial advantage, their physical restlessness into profit.

There's a theory that old nursery rhymes aren't as innocent as they sound, that many contain coded references to unpopular monarchs whilst others hint at political subversion. One authority suggests that 'Ring-a-ring-a-rosy' refers to the first symptom of the Black Death, to a lesion on the skin that presaged the inevitable outcome of 'all fall down'. The pocketful of posy? The herbalists' attempt at warding off the Grim Reaper. The tishoo, the tishoo? Apparently the sneeze was another ominous symptom. Well, better the pocketful of posy than the nursery rhymes of the '90s, the black death of the advertising jingle. Those avaricious anthems that teach our children to sing of new plagues, like the dread pestilence of the fast-food franchise.

Jingles? That's what today's kiddies chorus. What children chirrup. And it isn't Jack and Jill going up the hill to fetch a pail of water but songs that urge the prepubescent consumer to head off for a Big Mac.

Just as the jingle is the nursery rhyme of our era, the television commercial is the fairy story. All those lurid, high-tech animations, designed for peak-time rather than bedtime, replacing the works of Christian Andersen and the Brothers Grimm. Instead of Rumpelstiltskin, the soft sell for Reebok. And, dammit, we take this for granted, surrendering our children to the battles of the big brand names for market share. Children aren't children anymore but another demographic with spending power, a means of accessing parental income.

I railed against advertising to kids during my years in advertising, seeing the vast budgets aimed at littlies as a cultural atrocity, advocating an age of consent for commerce just as there is for sex. No advertiser should be permitted to aim ads at kids under the age of (to pick a number) thirteen. Or ten. Or at the very least, eight. It was immoral to allow corporations the right to kidnap the young imagination, to see our kindergartens and playgrounds as the appropriate targets for manipulative marketing exercises.

Time and the courts will tell whether or not Michael Jackson is/was a child molester. Meanwhile, Jackson, obviously a tragic child himself, is used for purposes of mass-molestation by the mighty companies who hire him for ad campaigns. Companies employ the likes of Jackson as turbo-charged Pied Pipers to lure vast hordes of kids away, turning them into addicts for these shoes, that soft drink, this brand of video game. This is molestation on an immense scale, corporate paedophilia, backed by a global culture of breathtaking crassness and banality.

We tell kids they shouldn't talk to strangers, that they most certainly shouldn't accept rides in strange vehicles. Yet we allow them to be taken for a ride by total strangers over and over again. And it's amazing how far a kid can travel in twenty seconds, thirty seconds or sixty seconds of extensively researched, expensively produced advertising …

There's a lot of talk about censoring television to protect children from violent imagery. But what about protecting kids from all those cute, ruthless, exploitative ads? This is something that does real violence to children. I remember the West murmuring pieties about communist propaganda, at the stuff shoved at Chinese kids by Chairman Mao or at Russian kids by the heirs of Stalin. Yet the same people happily accept capitalist propaganda, every bit as ideologically driven, forced on kids by all-powerful companies. And there's a question of equity here, given that the barrage of buy, buy, buy blandishments, the endless inventory of things that simply must be bought, impacts on the children of the disadvantaged and the unemployed just as it does on the children of the affluent. Indeed, it would clearly impact on them more …

For years I've been remounting this foundered hobby horse, knowing that nothing can be done about it, or will be done about it. Like everyone else, children have to be subjected to those sacrosanct free-market forces. Like parents everywhere, Australians have delivered their kids to the brand names, seeing no way to escape their strategy. Meanwhile the fast food and the soft drinks are welcomed into the playgrounds and the classrooms by education departments actively seeking brand-name sponsorships for school activities. From Mousketeers to marketeers, the whole ghastly process has taken just a few decades. Now Australian kids have adopted the body language – of the Dream Machine. And as the Infobahn moves ever closer, these trends will exaggerate, accelerate, until any notion of preserving national identity will be regarded as quaint and anachronistic.

Pop-cultural theorists insist that a text is a text is a text, that an advertising jingle can be as worthy as a piece of poetry. Or a fairy story. Far from being criticised, pop culture is celebrated, praised to the heavens. The heavens, where, 'tis said, we'll soon see the moon being used as a screen for laser-projected logos.

We are proud of Australia as a multicultural society. Aah, if only it were true. Thanks to the diet of cartoons and commercials we feed our kids, they're destined to become irredeemably monocultural. That's unless you think multiculturalism is giving kids a choice between Coke and Pepsi.

What I'm describing is, of course, a form of paedophilia. Australia is currently convulsed by a moral panic on the issue. In a society all but inured to shock, the paedophile is still shocking. Yet for every such predator who tries to seduce a child or a dozen children, there's a major corporation that successfully seduces a million. For every individual who molests a child there's a corporation that molests childhood.

A few months back, New York's Calvin Klein got into the trouble he was undoubtedly seeking thanks to an ad campaign emphasising pubescent sexuality. Boys bare to the waist, lounging provocatively against walls. A girl who looked twelve, thirteen, gazing into the lens with soulful eyes, revealing inner thighs. A succession of crotch shots. 'He's gone too far,' huffed competitors in the fashion industry. What they really meant was that Calvin had gone just a little further than the rest of them.

For years fashion models have been getting younger and younger. It's been cradle-snatching on a major scale. The poshest, most upmarket mags, looking for fresher faces and softer skins, have been recruiting schoolgirls, touching up their hair, eyes, lips, bodies. On every other page, another Lolita. Innocents repackaged as *femme fatales* have been standard issue. If anything, Klein was just more honest. He did a Nabokov, what Louis Malle did with Brooke Shields in *Pretty Baby*. Except that Klein did it on poster sites all over Manhattan. He did it in thirty-second spots. He did it in the road.

And the other people who'd been doing it were outraged, because it demonstrated how they'd been sexualising children, telling the world that, these days, you can be a sexual object at ten or twelve.

Most of the time this activity is regarded as harmless, even charming. After all, Lewis Carroll did it in Victoria's England – when he wasn't telling of Alice's adventures in Wonderland he was persuading proud parents to let him photograph their prepubescent daughters in the nude. More recently, we had Johnny Young's *Young Talent Time*, where pouting children like Tina Arena were put into micro-minis and encouraged to sing 'My heart belongs to Daddy'. Prancing before countless thousands of voyeurs. Chorus lines of virgins encouraged to vamp, pout and thrust their pelvises. Paedophilic fantasies masquerading as middlebrow, middle-class, mass entertainment.

This is the century when we became all too aware of infant sexuality. We've Sigmund Freud to thank for it, though he couldn't seem to make up his mind what exactly was going on. In the beginning Freud was convinced that his patients' neuroses derived from sexual molestation as children, usually at the hands of their parents. Later he'd argue that such seductions were fantasies, that it was the children who dreamed of seducing Mum or Dad. His unveiling of the Oedipus complex sent a shudder through society and parent–child relationships would never be quite the same again.

Now the pendulum is swinging back as therapists outdo each other with lurid accounts of 'repressed memories', conjuring horror stories out of the minds of unhappy patients, convincing them that they were molested, raped or sodomised by their parents.

Yet Freud and his illegitimate professional progeny notwithstanding, the thought of kids being sexually active or responsive remains an affront to wider society. A wider society that, nonetheless, is only too willing to destroy the innocence of the child by turning him or her into an economic unit, into a consumer, into a mini-adult, at an ever-decreasing age.

Big business prostitutes children as surely as the paedophiles named in the Wood Royal Commission. Whilst demonising Phillip Bell, society gives marketing awards and accolades to the business geniuses who turn kids into customers for carbonated drinks, fast foods and crappy toys …

Mass marketing to kids is mendacious and what is marketed is invariably meretricious, worthless, violent, shabby. Visit a toy shop and you'll see an armoury of weapons. Watch the video games –

they're cacophonous with destruction. So much so that the word 'game' is now analogous to carnage. While little girls are taught to compete with their big sisters, to see themselves as sexual beings, their brothers are recruited to be soldiers, killers, exterminators.

Go and pick on someone your own size, you greedy bastards ...

Suffer the little children. In this century kids have truly suffered. The softest of soft targets, they've been rounded up, bombed, napalmed, butchered, massacred, experimented on, shoved into gas chambers, starved to death. They've had to contend with everything from the grim prospect of nuclear war to the ongoing social crime of youth unemployment. They've been witness to unimaginable horror, and victims of it. We've grown bored with images of their emaciated bodies and their despairing faces. In the richest countries kids have been entertained with endless murders on television, encouraged to kill on computer screens and have been the principal targets of hundred-million-dollar movies that mow down and blow up human beings in increasingly graphic and inventive ways. Little wonder that in the world's wealthiest country, children form gangs to prowl the street with automatic weapons, selling and using narcotics, pimping and prostituting. We got used to old-faced children filling the streets of Saigon and Belfast. Now there are countless thousands of them in the war zones of Los Angeles.

Whilst education has reached out for kids, whilst medicine has sought to save them, whilst laws have been passed to guarantee their rights, whilst UN declarations have been signed to protect them, the brutalities go on. If it isn't famine, disease or war it's the corruption of children in the name of commerce – with the myriad Pied Pipers of drugs, movies and music luring them away from helpless, incompetent parents ...

'The city as we know it is an artefact'

David Malouf

'The city as artefact': address to the first Brisbane Institute
Annual Dinner

24 MARCH 2000

The recipient of numerous literary honours including the Miles Franklin Award, the Pascall Prize and the Commonwealth Prize for Fiction, Queenslander David Malouf (1934–) left Australia at the age of twenty-four to teach English in London and Birkenhead, and remained abroad for nine years. In 1968 Malouf returned to teach at the University of Sydney and now divides his time between Australia and Tuscany. His voluminous work encompasses novels, autobiography, short stories, opera librettos and poetry, often drawing on his Lebanese and English heritage and his childhood in Brisbane. In the following inaugural Brisbane Institute address, Malouf takes Beethoven's Ninth Symphony as his prompt to reflect on the modern city.

*

A couple of weeks ago, at a performance of the Beethoven Ninth at the Sydney Opera House, I was struck by something that crystallised at last my rather vague thoughts on the subject of tonight's talk, the notion – the reality too – of the modern city. What I was struck by was the largeness and complexity of the art forms our culture tends towards.

This isn't always the case. Some high cultures discover their essence in the small-scale and exquisite, Haiku, for instance, and Indian or Persian miniatures, and of course there are times when we do that too. But faced, say, with St Peter's Square, Michelangelo's *Last Judgement* or Leonardo's *Last Supper*, the European nineteenth century novel, or what happens when we settle in our seats and an orchestra of some hundred players, plus chorus and soloists, gets to work to produce for us the experience we call the Beethoven Ninth, we do recognise something distinctive, something representative of the way we do things.

The Ninth, as well as being the product of great individual genius, is also the end-product of a long cultural process. Think of the perfecting over centuries of the various instruments – horns, woodwind, percussion, strings, and the development of a technique of playing that makes it possible for a horn-player, for example, to deal with the difficulties Beethoven sets up. Think of the development, in the west, of a theory and practice of harmony, the adoption of particular scales, the exploitation of key relationships and the establishment, through the work of composers like Haydn and Clementi and Mozart, of a form for the symphony – the four movements, then Beethoven's astonishing extension of all that in creating a new sort of finale, a choral movement, longer than some whole symphonies of an earlier period, that is a complete musical drama in itself and a great summing up of the musical possibilities, recitative, chorale, sonata-form development, Turkish march, fugue. This coming together of so many forces, this gathering up of so many strands of development, this pushing of the form towards largeness and ever increasing complexity, this education too, of an audience in the appreciation of it all, seems to me to be very typical of our culture, which is in every way additive and inclusive, always appropriating and assimilating influences from elsewhere, as in the inclusion here, in a work of high culture, of peasant dances and a Turkish military band.

The Ninth seems to me to be very useful for pondering what is unique in the structures we make, and in our way of making them; and since I want to use music as an analogy for what I have to say tonight about the City, I'll just go on a little about the way the development of music offers itself as a mirror for ideas as well, about society, the way musical forms themselves become models for what is possible, and ideally perfect, in the social sphere.

Orchestral pieces in the Baroque period – Bach's Brandenburg Concertos for instance – are ideal conversations, in which each individual voice speaks and is heard; and yet the voices together are in perfect harmony. Bach's great contemporary, the philosopher Leibnitz, used such music as an image for the way he saw reality itself. His atoms, or monads – little closed off entities, each going its own way separate and independent of the others – are, he tells us, like musicians closed off in separate rooms, each playing his own line of melody but producing, when it is heard by a larger intelligence, God, a music that is harmonious because it is part of a plan. It was an image, too, of what the enlightened society might be, or at least aspire to.

But the Romantic view, both of society and of music, was very different. What it saw when it looked at the social world was not an ideal conversation of many voices in harmony but a field of forces in competition and conflict, and the aim of musical form, as Beethoven and later Romantics conceived it, was to allow these forces play, to create a drama that in working itself towards resolution would allow the listener to enter the drama and experience a personal catharsis.

What I want to suggest is not that the Romantic symphony provides a useful image for the modern city – though that might well be argued – or even a useful model of how the modern city works; but that the city as we know it is an artefact just as a symphony is; an expression of the same sort of thinking and making, the same vision. Cultures tend to express themselves in diverse forms, from door-knockers to dresses, from poems to palaces, but in the same style, and the modern city is an artefact, an expression of our culture like any other.

But I should say at once what I mean by 'the modern city'.

I do not mean those vast agglomerations of people that have developed over these last years – mostly in third world countries – where village workers have crowded into a metropolis to make centres of eleven or fifteen or twenty million souls, many of them living from hand to mouth on the streets, most of them without work, and the city itself unable to provide anything but the most rudimentary infrastructure; a place where people, in order to survive at all, need to preserve their village or family loyalties, and where there is as yet no concept of vital citizenship on which civil order can be based. These vast aggregations have become a feature of our age, and they are, frankly, frightening. But humans being what they are – that is, endlessly enterprising and adaptable – they do get by in such places, though at the cost of a good deal of disorder and violence and much suffering. The sort of city I have in mind is very different.

It too is a modern phenomenon, that is, it is post nineteenth century. Earlier cities, sixteenth-century London or Paris, or Imperial Peking, or the largest of them all, Edo, old Tokyo, were by comparison small, both in population and area. They were also homogenous to this extent, that the population, even if it was divided – as it certainly was in Paris and London – by religious difference and political faction, was for the most part ethnically uniform; people did speak the same language.

Only one period in the past offers the example of large cities with mixed population like modern New York, or London or our own; economically sophisticated, technologically advanced communities with populations that were made up of various ethnic groups, many of them new arrivals – immigrant workers or entrepreneurs; urban centres with a highly developed infrastructure that provided their citizens with security, order and amenities of every sort but also demanded a high sense of citizenship.

Late classical cities like Imperial Rome and Hellenistic Alexandria were highly organised urban places, with a population that spoke many languages but had a *lingua franca* of Latin or demotic Greek, and were of different origins, but shared a common citizenship. They worshipped a wide range of gods but respected the state in the form of the emperor and shared a common public culture, living, in an orderly way, as citizens of a place that extended to them the rights of citizens and demanded citizenly obligations in return. These two great cities seem modern, in our sense, because large as they were, they were both orderly and well managed, affording their citizens all the benefits of a sophisticated and managed economy and the fruits of an advanced technology: multi-storied apartment blocks, efficient plumbing and waste disposal, and for the exercise of the mind, universities and academies, schools of rhetoric, galleries, gymnasia, arenas, spaces whose architecture, as in our own cities, was meant to reinforce a sense of citizenship by providing the opportunities for interaction of a citizenly kind, and creating a theatre in which it might be acted out; not least of all, in play.

The cultural life of these cities was extraordinarily complex. Roman Alexandria, for example, was at once the centre of Greek culture, of neo-Platonic philosophy and applied science, but also of Jewish learning – the Septuagint, the Greek version of the Old Testament, was produced there. It was the home of Plotinus, the Greek Platonist, but also of the Jewish Platonist, Philo. Greek and Jewish cultures, however different they might seem, were in close communication there; and later, of course, it was home to some of the most important of the Church fathers. It must have been very much like a modern multi-ethnic city – New York or London or Paris or our own cities – in the opportunity it offered for a mingling of voices and forms of investigation and learning, in the forms of its applied technology (we know there were slot-machines in some of the temples for the dispensing of holy water) – and the high level of order and social integration it achieved.

Nineteenth-century historians, with their prejudice in favour of nationalism, that is their preference for a society that is ethnically and culturally 'pure', tended to characterise these great cities as decadent, precisely because they were mixed and because of the variety of worship and behaviour they permitted. Imperial Rome, in the popular mind, has been characterised by the brutality of some of its entertainments, the arena and gladiatorial shows for example, rather than by its sophistication and complexity as a social artefact: the managerial culture of its emperors or the way citizen rights were extended beyond the narrow circle of high-born Romans, the *gens*, to all men whatever their origin – it was, I'm afraid, only men – all, in fact, who were prepared to accept those rights and to take on citizenly obligations in return. It has always seemed extraordinary to me that all these extensions of citizenship and guarantees of liberty – what we would call civil rights – have generally been interpreted by historians, pretty much in the manner of some of our Asian neighbours, as evidence of decline.

So what is it like, this modern city I am speaking of?

We know because we live in such places, here in Australia. Then there are the American cities; and big cities these days, in Europe, Paris, London, Berlin, Geneva, are also cities made up of people of differing ethnic groups, differing faiths and cultural backgrounds, differing interests – most of all different temperaments and psychologies, who have decided, for one reason or another, to live together in a complex social unit – strangers, that is, who have come together as fellow citizens and neighbours. And this notion of neighbourliness, of shared interest and concern, mutual respect and tolerance, is the personal form of those more public things – res publica – that we intend when we speak of citizenliness.

These are men and women who have decided to add to tribal or family loyalty the larger loyalty of those who share with them all that belongs to the public sphere – to the shared life in the city. Now this area, shared as it must be, is not one of universally accepted laws, rights, obligations, because these things – given the way individuals see the world, the way religious or political or even temperamental forces exert an influence on the way we see the world – can never be universal or universally accepted. The area of *res publica* – public things – is an area of argument, even of conflict, but one in which conflict can, and in the end must be resolved, by argument, negotiation, compromise, in a neighbourly way.

We judge a society and its forms and institutions by the means it has set up for allowing conflicting arguments and views to be stated and then negotiated, resolved – resolved and re-negotiated; but without violence, and in the acceptance that others will bring to the public place different ideas of what is right and good, that at first sight seem irreconcilable but for which a compromise can be found; places where it is essential to the richness of the society that views should differ, that the argument should take place. A place, I mean, where no single voice prevails but none either is extinguished.

Beyond that shared life in the realm of public things, res publica, I mean our individual acceptance of the laws, and of other people's rights and our obligation to others – and rights means precisely the right not to be interfered with by your fellow citizens as well as by the law – beyond that, in our private life in such cities, we are free as individuals to be whatever we please and to be as different as we please; in our religious beliefs and observances, in our domestic customs, our sexual orientation, in the magazines and books we read, the sort of music we listen to, the way we spend our leisure, even the language we speak. And this does not result in chaos. What it produces is a sophisticated diversity in which what belongs to our duty as citizens and as neighbours is sharply distinguished from what we owe only to ourselves. A hard line exists between the public life and all those areas of our private being which we are free to express with no cost to the other, and for which we are accountable only to ourselves.

The truth is that we can expect such a city, such a society, to be socially cohesive – a willingness to act like a citizen, to become a good neighbour, is the price of entry to it. What we cannot expect it to be is culturally cohesive, except to this extent: that our understanding of what such a city is, our education into the use of the city's facilities, its transport and communications systems, its libraries, galleries, etc., is itself a form of culture, and is thus one of the cultures we all take on when we agree to share our lives as citizens.

I am not making a plea here for that vague thing called multi-culturalism. What I am pleading for is a recognition of the simple fact that in being individually different – by having different interests, in belonging to different age groups, different sexes, different religions or political affiliations, by choosing to follow this or that form of football, drinking beer or wine, reading this newspaper rather than another, playing bridge or going to the opera or to dance parties, or to clubs, gay or straight, in making individual choices of this sort – we each make up our own version of the available culture, feeling free to mix and move between its various elements. Because one of the features of the modern city is that it offers so many different possibilities. Along with a highly organised transport system and high-tech communications, it also offers its citizens a variety of pleasures, ways of expressing themselves and exploring their needs. In fact, it is the complex provision of all these facilities of a rich and varied existence, but also of a comfortable and secure one, that attracts us to the city in the first place.

To evoke something of that complexity, I'd just ask you to hold in your head for a moment what you might think of as the map of the road system and all its network of signs, intersections, highways, one-way streets, traffic lights, traffic signs, parking facilities; or the postal system; or the means of distribution of food and other goods to super-markets and stores. And then I would suggest a similar complexity in the way we ourselves, each one of us, use these facilities and move between these many possibilities. Think of the map of your own day, your own week; the way we dip, according to our needs and interests, into the pool, the way by changing what we find useful in the cultural mix, we change our personal culture, or extend it by adding new interests to the old, opera or chamber music, for instance, to an older interest in pop or jazz. That interaction with the various elements of what the city offers is for any one of us, I'd suggest, every bit as complex as the transport system, as we would see if we had some means of laying side by side the two diagrams or maps. And that sort of complexity, that sort of cultural diversity, is worth defending, because it is often attacked: as being somehow impure; as being merely eclectic; as being a trivial form of culture for which the true model is the supermarket, with all its associations of instant appeal and glitter, and ultimate disposability.

What we are sometimes offered as an alternative is a society that existed somewhere in the past, a society whose culture was uniform and single, the product of a golden age when men and women shared the same values, all of them undisputed, and the national culture was just itself, uncontaminated by outside influences or contradiction or conflict. But that surely is wishful thinking. There never was such a society in our past, and the nostalgia for it, the desire to restore what in fact never existed is a dangerous one.

The model for this – the nineteenth century was especially fond of it – is medieval Christendom, with the great cathedrals – the work of so many anonymous hands – its living symbol. But such a view of Christendom is itself a dream. We know this from the number of outsiders and dissidents – heretics of every kind, witches, philosophers and scientists, homosexuals, Jews – who had to be silenced and suppressed, forced to recant and then punished with extinction, to prove that it was uniform and ensure that it was pure. Just this week the Pope has apologised for all that. We know it too because members of Christendom – England and France, or the Italian city states of Genoa and Pisa and Siena and Florence and Venice – were continually at one another's throats; and of course what the records tell us – poems, plays, folk tales, as well as village records like the one the French historian Le Roy Ladourie used in his brilliant book, *Montaillou* – is that a large number of ordinary men and women, at village and household level, believed in nothing much at all.

Their adherence to the Church and to Christianity and its values was the merest lip-service. And this holds equally for the great political mono-culture of communism and the religious mono-culture of modern Islam. There is no such thing as a society with a uniform and universally accepted set of values, a universally shared culture. There are only oppressive tyrannies in which every voice of dissent has to be murderously suppressed. Or there are societies like our own, the great modern cities where, at their best, every voice, even dissident ones, are heard; and where the culture constantly revitalises itself, discovers new energies and new ideas by opening itself to influence, by an endless process of appropriation, and adaption and mixing, which is just what the City provides for and thrives on.

One of the signs of the modern city I have been describing, one of the signs that a city now aspires to be such a place and has recognised what it must do to become one, is the creation of public spaces that are designed, in their very architectural form, to encourage a sense of shared social life, of active citizenship, that may be exhibited as clearly in play as in other more serious ways. And I would just point out here the difference between the spaces I am thinking of, as they appear in modern cities, and the monumental spaces of, say, seventeenth-century Paris, which are meant to intimidate the king's subjects and re-enforce the image of his authority, or those nineteenth-century spaces that were opened up in the same city by Baron Haussmann, so that access to the heart of the city by revolutionary citizens could, if necessary, be prevented. The spaces I am thinking of are democratic, and in the provision they make for access, and for activity of every kind, are meant, in a way I'll explain in just moment, to be both useful and educative.

The South Bank here in Brisbane is such a space. One that provides for a diversity of interests, open-air swimming, eating and drinking; but also offers museums, a library, galleries, a concert hall, theatres – all this very much in the style of classical Rome or Alexandria – gardens, walks, an arena for large-scale pop concerts and pageants. It is the sort of architectural complex or precinct that by allowing all these various activities and interests to exist in the same place, suggests – but subtly – that the many 'levels' of culture they represent are related but also compatible, and may be part of the one complex culture. Such a site not only presents a notion of culture as open and continuous, but by example educates us into an acceptance of that, and of one another. It encourages flexibility and variety of response and a tolerance of where others find their interest; of the many ways in which we may fulfil ourselves in play.

Then there is that modern big-city phenomenon, the mall – both the street mall and the closed shopping mall.

We hear a good deal about malls and what they have done to our social life, most of it, I think, nonsense. That what they really represent is nothing more than the interests of developers and big business; that they are examples of an invasive Americanism; that they are dehumanising in that they have displaced the more neighbourly phenomenon of the corner shop; that they encourage people, especially the young, to 'congregate'.

These criticisms seem to me to misread their real purpose. The mall is a big-city phenomenon that is precisely fitted to what the big city I have been describing demands. That is a place where the complex needs of citizens are catered for in a single space and where we are encouraged to appreciate, and exercise the sort of neighbourliness that belongs to the city of large numbers rather than to the small town or village; a place where we feel at home with numbers, that is, strangers, and learn how to act well towards them; to deal with many people in complex social situations, rather than in the one-to-one way of the village shop. These spaces are sites of education, of re-education through experience, as well as convenient places for shopping, having coffee, going to a movie or just hanging out.

As for the question of congregating – isn't that exactly what the street mall and the shopping mall are designed to promote? To provide a space, like the Roman *agora*, for meeting, for social exchange, for play, and for learning to do these things in a civil way among strangers as well as among family or friends. If this produces more noise, more byplay and interaction, than some of us feel comfortable with, it may be because we have not yet got used to the sight and sound of informal congregations without also feeling a sense of threat; that is, that we have not yet been fully educated ourselves into the social modes of the big city, and see disorder or menace where there is only the energy created by crowds. We need to distinguish between lawlessness – real antisocial behaviour – and the sort of energetic high spirits that may belong to public spaces and for which we may need, as citizens, to develop a higher level of tolerance than we are used to in a small-town or village environment.

But the question of lawlessness is an important one. Vital to the secure and orderly life of the great city is the unsigned contract we enter into with our fellow citizens, the essence of which is that we respect one another's person and property, that our own security is guaranteed, our ability to move around the city or sit at home without fear of attack or interference, by respecting the integrity of others; that we accept our life in the city as being dependent upon a network of engagements, exchanges, with people we do not know and to whom we have none of the personal loyalty that binds us to family or friends or clan, but whom we agree to treat as if they were not strangers, as if our own shared life as citizens linked us to each one of them in bonds of mutual respect and concern. The contract is implicit in our becoming citizens. In becoming a citizen we become fellow citizens of others; but the contract is unsigned. What we need to do is convince people that their best interests are served by keeping the contract; that they have a stake in the preservation of it; that their security depends on their respecting the security of others. In fact the worst crime a citizen can commit, as citizen, is to break the contract, because that undermines the whole set of assumptions on which civil life in the city depends.

We sometimes hear people speak of property crimes as petty, and we tend to make a hierarchy of such crimes according to the value of what is stolen. But if someone's bag is snatched, if they are mugged in the street or knocked down at an automatic teller, or robbed behind a counter or at a petrol bowser, or if their house is broken into, the real crime has less to do with the amount stolen than with the absolute blow that has been dealt to the victim's sense of security, his or her faith in the contract and the goodwill of all strangers, which may take a very long time to heal; the blow that has been struck to a sense that the city is a safe place to move around in; that walking out into a crowd of strangers is not a fearful thing because those strangers

506 • *Well May We Say*

have re-defined themselves as neighbours. To take away from someone that right to security, that trust in their fellow citizens, is to strike a blow at the very fabric of things. To steal even twenty cents with violence from an old person in the street is, in the strictly civic sense in which I am speaking, a worse crime than to embezzle half a million from a big corporation. Though I should just add here that jail seems to me to be the very last response we should make to such a crime. What we need is some way of convincing these recalcitrant fellow citizens that they are just that: fellow citizens we are concerned for; convincing them if possible, by seeking to understand why, in them, the process of integration has failed, and by education, that they too have a stake in this joint business of living together in a way that leaves each of us secure.

It is easy to assume, looking around at cities where things mostly go well, and especially at Australian cities where, at big public events like New Year's Eve or the Bicentennial celebrations or the Mardi Gras in Sydney, no more than a handful of arrests are made and the police presence is light, that all this is easily achieved. It is not. It is achieved, like that resolution in the Beethoven, by overcoming great difficulty – and it is precarious. The miracle is that in the many millions of little interactions between people that each day constitute the life of the city, it works at all. But one of the things that is essential to its working is that every citizen should feel that he has, or she has, an equal stake in the civil enterprise, that his life is richer for being part of it; that his power over his own destiny is not diminished; that his future is better ensured. If every citizen does not feel this, then the whole enterprise is weakened; a source of resentment and potential disorder is let in.

And the truth is, not every group or individual in the city does feel included. There are some for whom the police presence, for example, is not felt as light, who do not feel enlarged or enriched. Things will be different from city to city according to the history of each place and the means by which groups and individuals enter the mix. For us the question arises in the way Indigenous people enter the mix and how they feel about their place in it, and the whole business of reconciliation is bound up – at the daily level, the level where people meet and face one another and arguments have to be resolved and bonds forged – with the questions of how far Aboriginal people do feel included;

do feel that the strangers they move among in the city really are neighbours and see *them* as neighbours; most of all in the extent to which they feel that to become citizens of a city is an increase in their lives; that they can become fully participant in the City without at the same time giving up as the price of it, their culture.

I go back to my original description of how we are all related to the city.

We have two lives there, a public life in which we adhere to citizenly values and requirements and which we share with others both in the public space of res publica and in real spaces where we move among strangers as if they were neighbours and feel secure in doing so. How we behave there is other people's business as well as our own. But only there. The other life, the personal, the private life, is entirely our own. There we are free to believe what we please, to hold our own views, follow our own gods and customs, live inside our own culture, even an eclectic one of our own making. The play between the two, public and private, may require delicate negotiations with ourself. But as we see in the case of orthodox Jews for example, or Pentecostals, or Muslims or Buddhists – there are many examples of groups who live apart in one sense and fully among us in another – it is perfectly possible to be integrated without being assimilated, to live richly inside a culture or religion, follow its customs, keep its rules, and still be an active participant in the society at large.

The interior negotiation may be delicate and even difficult; it may take time. But my feeling is that Indigenous people will in the end – and this too is part of reconciliation – work out ways of being Aboriginal, of being filled with the richness of their culture and empowered by it as Jews and others are, with no conflict of interest between that and what belongs to what I have called res publica. In fact what they bring with them to res publica will be energised by what comes from their culture; and what it adds, in the way of feeling and thinking, will be their particular gift.

Finally I want to point to this occasion tonight – not quite the Beethoven Ninth, I'm afraid – as a high example of much that I have been attempting to evoke, the complexity of what a big modern city like this one can provide: the variety of private worlds you bring to this very public occasion; the degree of attention you have committed yourself to; the interest, the citizenly curiosity and seriousness; the mixture of talk and of listening, of exchanging news and opinions over food and wine; the dedication of the Institute, our host tonight, to the business of allowing voices to be heard and arguments to flourish. All that is the essence of what I mean by the achievements of the city, and you sit here, and I thank you, as a fine embodiment of it. We can't expect to get the Ninth every night.

'Australia's equanimity is a mystery'

John Carroll

'The blessed country: Australian Dreaming 1901–2001': Deakin Lecture, Capitol Theatre, Melbourne

12 May 2001

One of Australia's most independent thinkers, Professor John Carroll (1944–) has been articulating the achievements and failures of Western culture for over thirty years. According to Carroll, we live amidst the 'colossal wreck' of Humanism, 'a flat expanse of rubble' – a culture that has lost its way and its sense of Dreaming. As an antidote he suggests a re-engagement with the archetypal stories that are central to the search for meaning in modern culture. Born in England and migrating to Australia as a young boy, Carroll completed a degree in mathematics at Melbourne University before undertaking his doctoral studies in sociology under the supervision of George Steiner at Cambridge University. Since 1972 he has taught at La Trobe University in Melbourne. A regular contributor to newspapers and forums outside the academy, Carroll recently chaired the National Museum of Australia review. In the following Deakin Lecture, Carroll brings the themes that have dominated his work for the past decade to bear on Australian culture, offering his perspective on Australian Dreaming.

*

This country is obscure. It was hard on its explorers, as if signalling its hostility to being mapped. Tracing its social contours has proved correspondingly tough, producing no more than a largely defunct legend of identity – that of the bushman and his ethos of egalitarian mateship – and a couple of summary phrases like the 'lucky country'. Perhaps a feature of this country is rather its resistance to interpretation.

The easy part is the question. What has enabled the new inhabitants of the Great South Land – *Terra Australis* – to start to feel at home in an alien land as far from their roots as they could have travelled? The land which looms as their 'Never Never', as merely 'Down Under', threatens them, whether consciously or not, as nowhere, other, without identity, of no significance.

The clue, I want to suggest, lies in the people themselves. What is notable, and admirable, about the Australian nation is the distinctive character of its people. They have their own constellation of virtues. It was on show during the Sydney Olympics – and if the first century opens with Federation, it ends with the millennium Olympic Games. *The Guardian* represented British, American and French reporting when it concluded that the Games had not only been the best ever, but Games no other country could possibly equal. As the London newspaper phrased it: 'The mixture of efficiency, friendliness and boundless enthusiasm is uniquely Australian.'

Throughout the West there has been rhetoric about a Third Way, one that might combine the efficiency of American capitalism with a broader, more compassionate social perspective, capitalism with a human face. A number of visitors observed that it actually exists, and is called 'Australia'. In a century in which Western philosophy focused on *being*, Australia has been less preoccupied than America with *doing*. It has struck a better balance. Recently the Victorian Government changed the words on its car numberplates to: 'Victoria – The Place to Be'.

To open in sociological terms: the people have built their own distinctive form of democracy. Australia has developed the three checks on power stressed by Tocqueville as essential to democracy: a flourishing culture of free associations – that is clubs, unions and societies – an independent judiciary and a free press. Then it has added a fourth. The main check on capitalism here, on its inherent tendency to favour the ruthless self-interest of those with economic and political clout, has been the people.

There was, for instance, the major role played at the Sydney Olympics by volunteers. They came from all corners of the country and helped to cast a temper of friendly informality over an event that shrewd observers had predicted would be remembered as the last global mega-circus, disintegrating in media sparks and scandal.

The Sydney mood was reflected in crowds that responded to Eric the Eel, as he was warmly nicknamed, an African swimmer floundering last in the pool, with no more ability than those watching. It was underscored by Roy and HG's nightly television show *The Dream* becoming the great hit of the Games, overshadowing the national triumphalism of gold-medal ceremonies. When the IOC attempted to ban athletes appearing on the medal dais with replicas of Roy and HG's star creation, Fatso the Wombat, rather than the officially credited mascots, it was public opinion that made it retreat in embarrassment.

The people led during the Olympics, the media followed – megaphone rather than opinion setter. Under the surface the same is true for politics. The attention politicians now pay to talkback radio is to hear what the people are thinking. To take a recent example, the public made their views clear when the Federal Minister for Workplace Relations, Peter Reith, was found to have defrauded the taxpayer of fifty thousand dollars. In terms of levels of corruption – here probably unwitting – this case was trivial. What the people did not like was the way the Minister handled the scandal. He refused initially to accept responsibility, scurried for cover, all the time attempting to shift blame to others – and he the Minister who had been the loudest to harangue against trade union rorts. With his character on trial he was judged guilty of not being worthy of high public office.

The example is commonplace, and not new. The ABC television series *Calypso Summer* documented the extraordinarily successful visit of the West Indian cricket team in the summer of '60–'61 – a team farewelled by half a million people crowding the streets of Melbourne. To select one incident. Richie Benaud, the Australian captain at the time, reports how during the Second Test in Melbourne he appealed when the cap of West Indian batsman Joe Solomon fell on his stumps, dislodging a bail. The umpire had no option but to give Solomon out.

Benaud recounts with wry, self-deprecating amusement how among the 70,000 present at the MCG that day there were only eleven who did not boo him. So much for one-eyed jingoistic crowds! It was the people who had educated their captain, defending the spirit of the game, its code of good sportsmanship. They were expressing their native hostility to letter-of-the-law bureaucratic controls. The older Benaud had also ingested the culture's distaste for bragging, posturing and pride.

A singular theme in the nation's history has been care taken to avoid conflict. John Hirst has outlined a range of cases in which institutions were planned in their foundation – government schools to name one – so as to minimise the sectarian strife between Protestants and Catholics that had plagued Britain. Australia, in its first decade as a nation, exhibited the same impulse when it set up a government-run industrial arbitration system, unique in the world, which successfully helped to limit conflict between workers and employers.

In the last half-century, the vast immigration of peoples from hundreds of different backgrounds has been overwhelmingly successful. The host society has, as human societies go, been welcoming and exceptionally tolerant of diversity. It has made it clear to 'New Australians' from wherever they came that they would be treated as equals, free to practise their traditional customs, as long as they left their ethnic conflicts behind them.

There is a manner in Australia, different to that met, say, in Britain or the United States. It may justly be called a democratic manner. Not only at the Sydney Olympics, but inside the local suburban ballet school on Saturday mornings, the tennis club, in pubs and restaurants, shops, even passing through Customs on arrival in the country, there is typically an openness, a willingness to engage the stranger. Going into shops, even on the street, the elemental human interaction is less governed by ritual predictability, or the platitudes of formality. There is some likelihood of an ironic twist, certainly a personal exchange in which the outcome is unclear, even testing. An effort is made.

Here we experience a type of public vitality, of warmth and interest in the nuances of everyday life, of making the most of them.

These themes are present at the MCG during a packed one-day cricket match, when the Mexican wave gets going, circling the ground. As it reaches the Members segment it stops, giving way to booing, before taking up again, in rhythm, on the far side. The booing is good-natured, even affectionate, a way of saying we know there is some sort of social hierarchy in this country – differences of wealth, position and status – but don't imagine that you are better. We are all here together, unified by the match, the experience, and being Australian. On display once again is the talent of the people for inclusiveness.

I have now reached the second stage in my argument. A people, to feel free to let their character virtues speak unimpeded, must be at ease in themselves. One of the leading symptoms of insecurity is a tendency to extremism, to fanaticism or fundamentalism. Peoples, like individuals, take flight into ideology, dogmatism and ranting when they feel under inner threat. It is a leading mark of Australia as a political culture to have always and without exception been sceptical of idealism, hostile to extremists, innately drawn to the moderate, the sensible, the unassuming. This parallels an openness to existential questioning. It points to a fundamental security of being.

Australia's equanimity is a mystery. Here, I suggest, is the central question about this country.

The political philosopher Hannah Arendt put the question for the United States. She asked how the new society had managed to find belief in itself – legitimacy – after breaking free from England. In answer she posited that Americans turned the act of foundation itself into their anchoring authority. The Declaration of Independence and the Constitution became the sacred texts. The 'founding fathers' as they were grandly called – Washington, Jefferson and later Lincoln – had special powers attributed to them, those of immortal ancestors. Arendt argues that without this monumental act of higher self-justification the United States would have, like most other new societies, foundered in instability. Australia has not sought a creation myth.

Nor has Australia followed another American tactic in what sociologist Robert Bellah has termed 'civil religion'. That is to cast itself as God's chosen people, selected for its virtue and set a divine mission.

America, furthermore, has been far more persuaded by the Enlightenment belief in progress. Much of its energy has been directed by hope that confident free individuals, through intelligent planning and hard work, may build a material civilisation that will sustain human virtue and happiness. Australians have been far more sceptical. Whatever their deeper view of the human condition, it is not this.

From where then has security of being come? I can claim no more than tentative moves, in proposing a minor and a major dynamic.

Let me simply note the minor dynamic, and then move on to the major one. Every culture, to follow the German philosopher, Nietzsche, depends on a 'fixed and sacred primordial site'. The Australian Aborigines amplify a similar view in their notion of the Dreaming. The implication is that all cultures are – like their own – centred on a body of myths or archetypal stories.

So what then is the Australian Dreaming? It must derive largely from the Western *mythos*. And there is one of the formative Western stories that is writ everywhere in Australia through the last century. It is that of the hero. Homer founded the archetype, in the figure of the great warrior, Achilles – his story told in *The Iliad*.

Here, there is Anzac and its enduring legend, and there is the pre-eminent role of sport in national life – exemplified in Don Bradman. Both domains project the hero archetype.

What is noteworthy, however, concerning Dreaming *mythos* is that the hero figure stands virtually alone. Its pervasiveness signals how one-dimensional a legacy it represents in the Australian imagination. Where are the other stories of tragic suffering, of the metamorphosis out of fallen worldliness, of love, of the gaining of poise of spirit? Where are the mothers, where are other trajectories of vocation, of fate, even stories of evil? There is not nearly enough authoritative *mythos* here to explain security of being.

Now to the major dynamic. Most of the people who have journeyed to Australia have found it the place to be because, I venture to propose, of a strange something in the air – both elusive and welcoming. Is there any better way of putting it than that this is a *blessed country*?

When the first generations of convicts, once freed, were given a choice of returning home to Britain, only a fraction accepted – in 1826, for which there are figures, it was a mere seven per cent. The rest decided that this country was not, to use Robert Hughes' term, a 'fatal shore'.

It will be countered that material factors provide sufficient explanation, as they have for successful migration ever since. Australia has been more prosperous, more comfortable, its suburban nuclear family way of life freer. Donald Horne took this line when he coined the phrase: 'the lucky country'.

Horne's phrase stuck, partly because of lack of alternatives. But it is essentially false. Geoffrey Blainey, in his histories of Australian mining, has shown how much success has depended on inspiration, initiative and resourcefulness, followed by gruelling and unremitting work usually in harsh environments. Gold nuggets did not fall out of the sky; nor did iron ore, nickel, diamonds and alumina. The same has been true for farming.

Nor were the Sydney Olympics merely the product of fortune – given what they represent in terms of a society's capacity for organisation, starting with well-designed and efficient infrastructure. Nor was the Bradman phenomenon. Indeed, the parameters for the right way of going about human business in this country were put in one of the Don's innings, as described by Neville Cardus: 'It was never uninteresting; he simply abstained from vanity or rhetoric.' C.E.W. Bean might have written the same, in graver tones, of the Anzacs. Indeed, the nation's motto could read: 'Never uninteresting – abstaining from vanity and rhetoric.'

In Arthur Streeton's painting of *The Land of the Golden Fleece*, blending into a parched landscape are a flock of sheep, a few cattle, a stockman on horseback and a man chopping wood – no more distinctive than dry grass and eucalypt. There is a sparse beauty here, the Grampians in the background, resonant with the bluish transcendent glow of some beyond. Diminishing the humans and their enterprises, a grander stillness pervades the land.

If the gods are present, though, their domain does not permit explicit human tracery. This mountain is not Mt Sinai – no God will appear to present the stone tablets of the Law to the people. And, as the nation's stories suggest, led by Burke and Wills and Patrick White's *Voss*, the country will rebuff those who rise above themselves. Would-be prophets and leaders who try to usurp the primacy of the place will fail in it.

The instruction and the warning are not just against excess and superfluity. The men in the Streeton scene are, like the great majority who populate the land – they in their cities – fringe dwellers. Patrick White, in his masterpiece, *Riders in the Chariot*, embraces this reality as nothing but well and fair. The sanest of his chosen ones, Mrs Godbold, lives in a dilapidated shed with her many children. It is there, as, once upon a time in a Bethlehem cattle shed, that the fundamental event takes place.

At issue are *proper-ties*. Property is the profane starting point. Just what do we possess? Are we merely occupying space? European Australians are becoming more self-conscious about the possibility that there could be a spirit to the land. It may project its own aura. It may even preside. They are intrigued by the Aboriginal mode of engagement. As different, even alien, as the way of the original inhabitants may be, perhaps it does hold some secret. Above all, there is the stress that proper ties oblige those who pitch camp to become faithful servants of place – they belong to it, rather than any bit of it belonging to them.

The furthest we fringe dwellers usually go in practice are Romantic, tamed encounters with the Bush – our Pearl Bays, surfing between the flags, native gardens and caravan tours round the coastal rim. The suburban home partly stands as fenced-in defence against infinitude of landscape, the boundlessness reverberating through laconic sprawling cities. Occupation remains a troubled category, and will continue so until the newcomers take in the Aboriginal lesson about how to dwell in order to belong. Theirs is a lesson about being.

Patrick White reads the country as receptive to wayward vision. It is there in the biggest film hit of the last decade, *The Castle*. Set in another shed, in another fringe suburb, this time on lead-contaminated soil, under power pylons next to an airport, the scene is Melbourne wasteland – at least as judged by prevailing standards of charm, taste and comfort. Yet to the father's eye it is his little corner of paradise. The love and energy with which he puts his vision of home into practice nurtures a very happy family. The film flirts with the quixotic ludicrousness of this man, as did Roy and HG's *Dream* with sports stars, and can do so because of that intangible Australian security of being which is not prickly about prestige and dignity. Such security is antipode to the 'cultural cringe' felt by sections of the intelligentsia – for whom uprootedness seems to be a life condition. There are traces in *The Castle* of many a suburban backyard – a blessed little corner. Just ask the children who grew up in them!

Special warmth has grown for kangaroo, koala, platypus and echidna that is more than of the cuddly toy sort. The marsupials set a tone, in their way of being. In part it is their lack of aggression – except when cornered. The quiet way they go about negotiating their habitat has affinity with the way the people respond to bureaucratic controls. Calm resistance, except when cornered, has met the Australia Card, Byzantine new tax systems and grand attempts to tidy up the constitution.

The kookaburra reminds humans, prone to taking themselves seriously, that they are easy to laugh at – and don't we recognise its cadences in the raucous vulgar zest of Sir Les Patterson? Then there was the wombat star of the Sydney Games. And how many Australians who travel overseas feel reassured when they first spot the Qantas kangaroo? The totemism of Aboriginal tribal culture seems to be colonising the colonisers.

But what about shark, crocodile and snake? During the Olympics it was as if the land put on its own show, with two fatal shark attacks, letting visitors who cared to notice know where they were. Here is a fruitful ambiguity. There is a dark strain in high Australian art, from Barbara Baynton to *Mad Max*, warning what happens when the blessing's off. Their 'heart of darkness' – its source in human evil – rises as counterweight to the Romantic idylls of the Heidelberg School painters. Patrick White negotiates a middle way, one that is, I think, more instructive.

Riders in the Chariot is set in a fringe suburb. There are the unchosen, those for whom the blessing was never on – Australia has had its own cruel practices and bad institutions. One of them is a Mrs Jolley – who clings to her decent morality, with grown-up daughters who don't want much to do with her. Mean not jolly, she represents the city Never Never. While working as housekeeper for an eccentric spinster, Mary Hare, she comes across a snake in the backyard and kills it with a spade. Miss Hare, who is one of the chosen, mourns: 'You killed it! I used to put out milk and it would drink and sometimes allow me to stand by, but I never quite succeeded in winning its confidence.' Mrs Jolley defends herself 'That is not killing. That is ridding the world of something bad.'

Never quite winning its confidence! Our country is resistant to liberties. Take care with the snake! Today we stand on the threshold of a century in which the land may repulse much of the first two hundred years of occupation. Already there are doubts about that triumph of 1950s nation building, of Enlightenment progress – the Snowy Mountains Hydro-electric Scheme. In the Hebrew Bible it is Lot's wife who, on disobeying God's law, turns to salt.

This country in refusing the great leader archetype – from Moses to Abraham Lincoln – invited the people themselves to preside. The choice was not for lack of candidates of stature, starting with the political visionary in whose honour these lectures are named.

Nevertheless, the people at times need authoritative direction. Governments in Canberra for the last two decades, steered by their mandarin bureaucrats, have neglected the Deakinite foundation – which had set up the institutions that turned the ethos of inclusiveness and a 'fair go' into practical reality. They have administered a growing divide between city and bush, a failure to prepare youth for adult responsibility, and a far-reaching rise in inequality as segments of the society are left to run down. The people have reacted with bewildered disenchantment to the behaviour of their leaders.

The death of Bradman, this year, was followed by a sustained, comprehensive outpouring of homage such as modern Australia has never experienced. Was this a means for the people to refocus on their character ideals, with a silent head-bowed lament about their scant presence in contemporary elites? Here is Australia's civil religion. The year 2001 is more likely to be remembered for the death of the Don than the first centenary of federation.

The Don reflected in his memoirs fifty years ago that the future of cricket would depend on the spirit in which it is played. What he had learnt, and what he passes on, is to forget about vanity and rhetoric – the spirit is everything. It depends on character, and a blessing. The people taught Richie Benaud the same lesson, as they do their politicians, as they do us all.

Terra Australis resists mapping. Yet in its own way it indicates to its new inhabitants that they will be favoured once they find their right relationship to it. In this slow process it has so far allowed them a pretty loose rein. At work, play or in everyday reverie those who dwell here might then come to find themselves supported, as by a benign presence. The country provides the human individual with a place, simply, to *be*. It offers its blessing.

'Punching above one's weight'

Owen Harries

'Punching above our weight': Boyer Lecture, broadcast on ABC Radio National

21 DECEMBER 2003

Once described as 'a man who enjoys talk the way others enjoy football', Owen Harries (1930–) has been a leading advisor on Australian foreign policy since the 1970s. Born and educated in Wales and later graduating at Oxford University, Harries taught at the University of Sydney and the University of New South Wales before being appointed senior advisor to the shadow foreign affairs minister, Andrew Peacock, in 1974. In the late 1970s he became the head of policy planning in the Department of Foreign Affairs, and later, the senior advisor to prime minister Malcolm Fraser. From 1982 to 1983 Harries was Australia's ambassador to UNESCO in Paris.

Expertly attuned to American foreign policy, Harries was the founding editor of the influential Washington-based *The National Interest*, a foreign policy quarterly established in 1985. He has published hundreds of articles in leading newspapers and journals around the world, including *The New York Times, The Spectator, The Wall Street Journal* and *The Times*. Harries returned to Australia in 2001 to take a position as Senior Fellow at the Centre for Independent Studies, and contributes regularly to *The Bulletin, Quadrant* and Australian newspapers. His 2003 Boyer Lectures were titled *Benign or Imperial? Reflections on American Hegemony*.

*

A couple of years ago, Walter Russell Mead, a Fellow of the Council on Foreign Relations in New York, wrote a book identifying four traditions of American foreign policy, each one represented by a leading American statesman.

The Hamiltonian tradition consists of a combination of commercialism and realism.

The Jeffersonian tradition is apprehensive of the corrupting influence of the outside world and therefore sceptical about international commitments and what Thomas Jefferson referred to as 'entangling alliances'.

The Jacksonian tradition is populist, patriotic, pugnacious and ultra-sensitive concerning any slight to the country's honour.

And last there is the Wilsonian tradition of crusading liberal internationalism.

Throughout this country's history, Mead maintains, these four traditions have interacted: sometimes mutually supporting each other, sometimes competing and conflicting, always overlapping, the mix changing as both domestic and international circumstance change.

Reading Mead's book encourages reflection as to what a similar exercise concerning Australia's foreign policy traditions would yield. It seems to me that here there have been three main traditions.

First, there is the Menzies tradition. This is a thoroughly realist, power-and-interest-based tradition, though in Menzies own case it was sometimes obscured by his taste for sentimental declarations of attachment to Britain and the Queen, which misled some into thinking that he was merely a romantic loyalist.

As a realist and a conservative, Menzies was sceptical of abstract, general schemes. He looked to interest rather than principle as the motive for action; to history and experience rather than abstract reasoning for the basis of sound judgement.

Menzies' central assumption was that in an international environment that was inherently dangerous – and which in his day contained predators like Nazi Germany, a militarised Japan and later the Soviet Union – it was vital for a large, sparsely populated and geographically isolated Western country like Australia that the global balance of power should favour the leading democratic powers. And it was also vital that Australia should have close, friendly relations with those powers.

In order to ensure that state of affairs, Australia must be prepared to support the United States and Britain politically and, when necessary, militarily. Such support was our insurance policy.

It was also highly congenial to Menzies personally, since it was a policy which enabled Australia – and Menzies himself – to be wired in to the main game of global power politics in a way that was otherwise impossible.

National interest and personal ambition, then, were both served by such a policy. But inherent in it was the risk of losing sight of a distinctive Australian identity and of exaggerating the cohesion and solidarity represented by the larger concept, whether it be the British Commonwealth, 'the West' or 'the Free World'.

The Menzies tradition is sceptical of most international institutions, including the United Nations, which it claims should be seen not as an alternative to power politics, but as power politics with a different facade – a different way for sovereign states to play essentially the same game. The Security Council is in reality no more than a kind of permanent conference of the great powers, where important and contentious issues can be discussed. Every member votes according to how it sees its own interests. To think otherwise, Menzies once argued, was to see the organisation as a 'house fully constructed which in due course, by some miracle, would be able to build its own foundations'. The United Nations reflects the realities of international politics, but it does not and cannot change them significantly. The United Nations had no particular moral authority, and to make one's response to a course of action depend on whether or not it is sanctioned by the UN is more a way of evading than of making a moral choice.

The Menzies tradition, is, of course, strongest on the conservative side of politics, though it has its representatives across the spectrum. John Howard is probably the tradition's purest representative since Menzies himself.

The second tradition is, I think, best identified as the Evatt tradition. It is both strongly nationalist and internationalist. No contradiction is involved here, since internationalism is favoured, not only on principle, but because international organisations are regarded as the most congenial and effective forums for a middle power like Australia to register its presence and extend its influence.

This tradition is assertive and energetic. It is concerned to give Australia a high profile as a country capable of making a distinctive contribution to international affairs. Sometimes it leads to hyperactivity and attention-seeking. At the Paris Peace Conference of 1946, to take an extreme example, Dr Evatt, as leader of the Australian delegation, managed to table no fewer than 400 amendments. Sadly, only one of them was adopted.

The Evatt tradition is concerned to establish Australia's independence, is sensitive to slights and is concerned with status. It is suspicious of great powers, and will go out of its way to assert its independence of them, both in order to preserve its freedom of action and to strengthen its own sense of identity. It is inclined to believe that lesser powers like itself, being more detached, are better able than great powers to assess the morality and justice of an issue objectively. Power politics tends to be seen as a chosen mode of behaviour, rather than something inherent in a system of sovereign states and necessary for survival.

One of Evatt's favourite words was 'machinery', by which he meant organisational and institutional frameworks, procedures and rules. In his view, getting the machinery right was the secret of progress, for he believed that, to a great extent, form determines substance. Those of this persuasion tend to subscribe to the dictum 'build and they will come'.

They also attach great importance to international law. Thus in

Evatt's first ministerial statement to parliament, only a few days before Pearl Harbor and in an atmosphere of impending crisis, he found time to express concern that Australia was not legally at war with Finland, Hungary and Romania, explaining that if this was not rectified the consequences 'might well be disastrous to Russian morale'. In somewhat the same spirit, three decades later, another eminent representative of the tradition, Gough Whitlam, was to feel compelled to recognise formally the incorporation of the Baltic States into the Soviet Union, in order to clarify the legal situation. Realists, on the other hand, tend to be sceptical about the claims made for a system of law that lacks any coercive power to enforce itself.

Unlike the Menzies tradition, the Evatt tradition draws a sharp distinction between power politics and the United Nations, seeing the latter as laying a foundation for an entirely different international order and norms of behaviour. Action that is sanctioned by the UN has a legitimacy and moral quality that is otherwise lacking. For, whatever its shortcomings, the organisation represents an ideal to be strived for. A typical realist reaction to the stress on machinery and forms is that of Nicholas Mansergh in his magisterial *Survey of Commonwealth Affairs*: 'Dr Evatt did not appear to understand ... that no elaboration of machinery could sensibly modify a relationship determined by relative power.'

This is a tradition represented mostly clearly on the Labor side of politics and, as well as Evatt himself, Gough Whitlam and Gareth Evans have embodied much of what it stands for.

The distinguishing mark of the third tradition – call it the Spender-Casey tradition, or if you prefer, the Keating tradition – is the importance it attaches to regional affairs. The nature and content of that concern has varied over the decades: strategic and security matters during and immediately after World War II; support for Indonesian independence by the Chifley government in the late 1940s; the Colombo Plan and other aid to the newly independent states of the region in the 1950s; concern over the increasing instability, violence and radicalisation of the region in the 1960s, leading to military involvement in Malaya and Vietnam; and, increasingly from then on, a concern to develop relations, and to integrate with a region that had become economically dynamic and significant.

As Ministers for External Affairs, both Percy Spender and Richard Gardiner Casey represented this tradition early on, creating and extending the Colombo Plan and developing diplomatic relations with the region's new states. All this in the face of considerable indifference on Menzies' part. According to Spender, Menzies viewed his preoccupation with the region as a 'hobby horse' and was given to saying patronisingly, 'Come on Percy, let's have your thesis about South-East Asia.'

Menzies' power-centred outlook made him a big-picture man, inclined to play down a regional approach. 'Regionalism,' he once reflected, 'is open to the view that it may involve nothing more than a slightly enlarged form of isolationism – a collective form of isolationalism, if I may use a curious phrase.' He tended to regard the parochial affairs of weak, inexperienced regional states as low on the agenda. Like many conservative realists, he was slow to identify, and to react to, significant forces of change. As time passed, such an attitude toward the region became increasingly unsustainable. By the 1990s, Paul Keating was giving priority to regional relationships.

In contemplating these three traditions, the question is not which one of them is the right one for Australia to adopt in perpetuity, but what balance or mix of them is appropriate at any given time, as circumstances, and the priorities of our interests, change.

Against this background, what can be said about the policy of the Howard government since 2002? That has been a policy of unhesitating, unqualified and – given the attitude of many other states – conspicuous support for the United States in its wars against terrorism and against Iraq. As such, it is a policy that can be and has been defended both on Menzian grounds – that is, protecting one's own security and paying one's insurance premium to a great and powerful friend – and in terms of our values, given that it was tyranny and terror that were being combated.

Many people whom I respect have found this combination of arguments a compelling one, demanding support for the policy of the Howard government. I would like to explain why, on realist grounds, I have not.

First, a bit of self-protective ground-clearing. As things have not exactly gone according to plan in Iraq since Saddam Hussein was overthrown, and as a favourable outcome seems less than certain, it might seem that I'm simply being wise after the event and second-guessing the government. This isn't so. As it happens, I published a relevant piece on Australian–US relations in the *Australian Financial Review* on the 10 September 2001: that is, precisely one day *before* the terrorist attack on New York and Washington. In it, I argued that:

> Australia should proceed carefully and without illusion in dealing with its powerful ally. For one thing, post Cold War American foreign policy is still, in some respects, a work in progress, and those who get too close to it run the risk that a piece of scaffolding might fall off and hit them ...
>
> Even more important, while the United States is by historical standards a benevolent hegemon, a hegemon is what it is. Not only is its power vast, but it is concerned to use that power ... to create a world in its own image with institutions and rules determined by Washington ...
>
> While such a world would have many attractions, the attempt to bring it into being will inevitably generate serious opposition and a great deal of strife and conflict. It would be inappropriate and dangerous for a country of Australia's limited means and interests to associate itself closely with such an enterprise.

I went on to maintain that 'however sweet the rhetoric and however warm the hugging, the priorities of the two countries are likely to differ at least as often as they coincide'.

I believe that, while these arguments had validity before September 11 and the Iraq War, they, and some additional ones, have even more validity today. Let me enumerate.

First, concerning terrorism, the first and overriding responsibility of an Australian government is not to combat global terrorism generally, but to protect this country from terrorism. The two ends are not necessarily identical. By being an early, unqualified and high-profile supporter of American policy, when so many others – including long-standing allies of the United States and some of our neighbours – were expressing serious reservations about both the legitimacy and the effectiveness of that policy, Australia may well have increased rather than decreased its chances of becoming a terrorist target.

Second, the course Australia has followed since September 11 is open to the charge that it has got the balance between alliance policy and regional policy wrong. We are living in the same region as the most populous Muslim state in the world, a state that is less than a model of stability and order, and which is a breeding ground for terror. As well, we are in close proximity to some failed or failing states which are potential hosts for terrorists.

Looking ahead, by the year 2050 – that is, by the time someone born now will be entering middle age – the population of the nine countries extending from Pakistan to China will have increased by something in the order of 1.4 billion. That of Indonesia alone is projected to increase by 120 million in that period.

While all this does not mean that the region is inevitably going to be more unstable or threatening than it is now, it does suggest that its importance is going to loom larger rather than smaller in our strategic calculations, and that anything that can justify distracting our attention and resources from it must be of a compelling nature.

But, third, the case made by the British administration for the Iraq War was not compelling. Indeed, it was inconsistent and surprisingly incompetent, with dubious and shifting rationales being offered: one day, weapons of mass destruction; the next day, links with al Qaeda; after that, the cruelty of the regime and the liberation of the Iraqi people; and then Saddam's alleged reckless, unpredictable nature, which, it was claimed, ruled out deterrence and required pre-emption. As well as all that, the case for overthrowing Saddam Hussein was made against the background of a proclaimed new strategic doctrine aimed at nothing less than remaking the world in America's image.

Given all this, restraint, some deep reflection and a request for clarification, rather than eager and unqualified support, would have been an appropriate Australian response; appropriate not only in terms of Australia's own interests but that of its greatest ally. And it could have been accompanied by a clear statement of our need to give priority to dealing with terror where it was most likely to impinge on us, that is, not in the Middle East but in South-East Asia.

Supporters of the policy might respond to such criticism by saying that, however things turn out in Iraq, Australia has built up a lot of credit in Washington and with the American people, and that this on its own justifies the policy followed by Prime Minister Howard. Perhaps so. But – and this is my fourth point – in international politics, expectations of gratitude rest on shaky foundations. As Charles de Gaulle once remarked, great powers are 'cold monsters', and gratitude is not one of their strongest motivators. When, in 1848, Tsarist Russia intervened to put down an insurrection in Hungary, thus saving the Hapsburg Empire, which was then in deep trouble, the Hapsburg prime minister commented that, 'We shall astonish the world with our ingratitude.' Sure enough, half a dozen years later when Britain and France went to war with Russia in the Crimea, the Hapsburgs studiously stayed on the sidelines. But the world was not very astonished.

Now you may think that this example, like de Gaulle's remark, represents the cynicism of Old Europe. However, it was not de Gaulle but George Washington who observed that 'no nation can be entrusted further than it is bound by its interests' and that 'there can be no greater error than to expect or calculate on real favours from nation to nation'.

Fifth, these words of Washington's are just as relevant and carry just as much weight when considering another assumption that many Australians, including John Howard, make concerning our American connection, which is that a great deal of weight should be attached to cultural affinity. Listen to Mr Howard in a radio interview, expressing a conviction about Australian–US relations that he has repeated many times: ' ... they do have a lot of values and attitudes that we share, and I'm a great believer that you should have close relations with the countries whose way of life is closest to your own.'

Mr Howard is not alone in this belief. In recent years there has been renewed support for an old idea – that English-speaking nations with cultural affinities should draw together and form some kind of political and economic union, what has been termed an 'Anglosphere'.

The whole notion that cultural affinity can be the solid foundation of a relationship needs to be treated very warily. Consider this: Great Britain and the United States fought World War II together in an extraordinarily close alliance. One million American soldiers were stationed in Britain before D-Day. British soldiers fought under

American generals, and American soldiers under British generals. President Roosevelt and Prime Minister Churchill were in constant touch and there was extraordinary intimacy between the top people on both sides. The American establishment at the time was very Anglophile and much more WASP (White, Anglo-Saxon, Protestant) than it is now.

Yet as soon as the war was over, the United States cut off Lend-Lease aid to a virtually bankrupt Britain and imposed very harsh terms on the loan it negotiated with the Attlee government.

And only a decade after that close relationship, when Dwight D. Eisenhower and Anthony Eden, two wartime colleagues, were leading their respective governments, the United States publicly humiliated their British and French allies at the time of the Suez Crisis, forcing them to climb down and leave the Canal in Egyptian President Nasser's hands. From this episode the British and the French drew opposite conclusions: the British, that they should never again cross the United States; the French, that they should never again depend on the United States.

Coming nearer home, all Australian prime ministers should bear in mind the American handling of the Dutch New Guinea question in the early 1960s. Despite the ANZUS alliance, and despite the fact that Robert Menzies was a great 'Western values' man whose standing in Washington was high, the Kennedy administration chose to try to placate a radical, anti-Western Sukarno over the issue, rather than support either Australia or America's NATO ally, the Netherlands.

None of this is meant as a criticism of the United States, which just behaved as great powers normally behave – quite properly putting their own interests ahead of everything else, and giving less weight to those whose support can be taken for granted than to those whose support they wish to gain.

Most people who follow international politics are familiar with a version of Lord Palmerston's dictum: 'We have no eternal allies, and we have no eternal enemies. Our interests are eternal and perpetual, and those interests it is our duty to follow.' But again, George Washington had said it more crisply fifty years earlier: 'Permanent, inveterate antipathies against particular nations and passionate attachments to others, should be avoided.'

Sixth, for the internationalists of the Evatt tradition, one of the drawbacks of this policy followed by the Australian Government is that is has weakened Australia's position in the UN, by associating conspicuously with a course of action that, in the eyes of most members, lacked UN authority. Normally, this would be a matter of little concern to realists, but at a time when much of the serious diplomatic power game is likely to be played in the UN, as the other permanent members of the Security Council use it to try to restrain the United States, this has more significance than it would normally have.

My seventh and last point concerns ends and means. Australia is a large continent to defend. It exists in a region characterised by a great deal of turbulence. As by far the most populous, powerful and wealthy country in the south-west Pacific, it properly assumes responsibility for stability in some of the smaller countries of the region which have serious problems.

To meet these commitments, Australia spends two per cent of its gross national product on defence. It has an army of only 25,000 personnel. In these circumstances, for it to engage in serious military campaigns beyond its region as well, and to do so pre-emptively and when it is not directly threatened, is to leave itself open to a charge of being a cheap hawk, which is a dangerous and irresponsible thing to be. Punching above one's weight may be a source of pride, but it is also hazardous and a form of activity best avoided.

Back in the 1940s, Walter Lippmann wrote a sentence which has a claim to be one of the most important ever written about foreign policy. It reads as follows:

> Without the controlling principle that the nation must maintain its objectives and its power in equilibrium, its purpose within its means and its means equal to its purposes, its commitments related to its resources and its resources adequate to its commitments, it is impossible to think at all about foreign affairs.

Those responsible for Australian foreign policy could do worse than have that sentence framed and hung prominently on their office walls.

OPENINGS AND COMMENCEMENTS

'It therefore behoves us to be very careful'

Captain James Cook

Orders to men on board the *Resolution*

26 NOVEMBER 1778

Captain James Cook (1728–1779), in initiating British colonisation of the Pacific, probably gave the first reported speech on Australian soil. Cook recorded the claiming of 'New Holland' in his journal, noting his sunset proclamation on 22 August 1770: 'Notwithstanding I had in the Name of His Majesty taken possession of several places along this coast, I now once more hoisted English Colours and in the Name of His Majesty King George the Third took possession of the whole Eastern Coast ...'

Although Cook would have given many addresses, orders and proclamations on and about his three voyages to the Pacific, few were recorded in the first person. An exception were the following orders to his men on board the *Resolution*, given on Cook's third and ill-fated voyage to the Pacific, where he 'discovered' the islands of Hawaii. The speech, while not directly concerning Australia, illustrates the challenges that beset naval commanders of his time – not only those of navigation, but those involving the discipline and command of men.

*

Whereas it is of the last importance to procure a supply of Provisions from the Inhabitants of Sandwich Islands, or any other Islands we may happen to fall in with in this Sea; it therefore behoves us to be very careful in keeping up the prices of such few Articles as we have left, and they most value, as it is for such Articles only we can expect to draw from them the Supplies we are in want of. And whereas it is obvious, from past circumstances, this cannot be done, if every person is allowed to trade in his own way, and for what [he] pleases; it is therefore hereby ordered and directed that no Officer or other person in or belonging to the Ships, not authorised by me or Captain Clerke, shall Trade or make Exchanges with the Inhabitants of the Islands aforesaid, and that no Curiosities or other Articles whatever but Provisions and Refreshments shall be bartered for until farther Order, or leave first obtained by me.

And whereas it has frequently happened that by Officers and others travelling in the Country with Fire-Arms and other Weapons, in order to obtain which, the Natives have committed thefts and outrages, they otherwise would not have attempted; it is therefore Ordered that no Officer or other person (not sent on duty) shall carry with him out of the Ships, or into the Country, any Fire-Arms whatever, and great care is to be taken to keep the Natives ignorant of the method of charging such as we may be under a necessity to make use of.

And whereas there are Venereal complaints remaining onboard the Ships, and in order to prevent as much as possible the communicating this fatal disease to a set of innocent people, it is hereby ordered that no Woman on any pretence whatever be admitted onboard the *Resolution* without my permission, nor onboard the *Discovery* but by permission of Captain Clerke. And whoever brings a woman into the Ships, or suffers her to come in of her own accord contrary to this Order shall be punished; and if any person having, or suspected of having the Venereal disease or any Symptoms thereof, shall lie with any Woman, he shall also be severely punished, and no such suspected persons, (of whom a List is to be kept on the Quarter Deck) shall be suffered to go onshore on any pretence whatever. Given under my hand Onboard His Majesty's Sloop the *Resolution* at Sea this 26th of November 1778.

'A plan has been formed, by my direction'

King George III

'His Majesty's most gracious speech': opening of the imperial
parliament, London

23 JANUARY 1787

The reasons for Australian settlement by the British, lost in time, have been extensively debated by historians. Arguments have been advanced based on geopolitical, economic and military objectives. The precise regal *fiat* by King George III (1738–1820) at the opening of the imperial parliament in 1787 articulates the old view that Australia was looked upon as a depository for convicts after the loss of Britain's American colonies. That this was no small matter, however, is indicated by the fact that the king chose to issue the pronouncement himself, and was offered 'humble thanks' by the House of Lords for delivering his 'most gracious speech'; the regal speeches were usually delivered by proxy. Impetuous and unstable, a monarch who 'gloried in the name of Britain' and thought Shakespeare 'sad stuff', George III was prone to 'outbursts of overwhelming nervous excitement', spoke rapidly and was often difficult to understand.

*

My Lords and Gentlemen,

I have particular satisfaction in acquainting you, that since I last met you in Parliament, the tranquillity of Europe has remained uninterrupted, and that all foreign powers continue to express their friendly disposition to this country ...

A plan has been formed, by my direction, for transporting a number of convicts, in order to remove the inconvenience which arose from the crowded state of the gaols in different parts of the Kingdom;

and you will, I doubt not, take such further measures as may be necessary for this purpose.

I trust you will be able, in this session, to carry into effect regulations for the ease of merchants, and for simplifying the public accounts in the various branches of the revenue; and I rely upon the uniform continuance of your exertions in pursuit of such objects as may tend still further to improve the national resources, and to promote and confirm the welfare and happiness of my people.

'Those men are all we have to depend upon'

Arthur Phillip

Orders to men on the First Fleet

MAY 1787

The commodore of the First Fleet and New South Wales' inaugural governor, Arthur Phillip (1738–1814), spent nearly five years establishing Australia's first colony. It was a challenge merely to keep his people from starvation in conditions of extreme deprivation and isolation. A friend of Phillip's said of him in 1791: 'Upon my soul ... I do think God Almighty made Phillips [*sic*] on purpose for the place, for never did man better know what to do, or with more determination to see it was done.'

Phillip's poise in circumstances that always bordered on chaos emerged early on the First Fleet's journey. Of the 1500 people aboard its eleven vessels, about half were convicts and the remainder volunteer sailors, marines, officers and civilians. When Phillip was informed of the flogging of sailors not maintaining their watch on deck he ordered every officer on board into the cabin and gave the following speech, recorded by an American volunteer, Jacob Nagle.

*

Those men are all we have to depend upon, and if we abuse those men that we have to trust, the convicts will rise and massacre us all. Those men are our support. We have a long and severe station to go through in settling this colony, at least we cannot expect to return in less than five years.

This ship and her crew is to protect and support the country, and if they are ill-treated by their own officers, what support can you expect of them? They will be all dead, before the voyage is half out, and who is to bring us back again?

'No expedition has ever started under such favourable circumstances'

Robert O'Hara Burke

Speech on commencement of the expedition of Burke and Wills, Royal Park, Melbourne

20 AUGUST 1860

Several thousand people turned out in Melbourne to wish Robert O'Hara Burke (1821–1861) and his party 'God speed' on their journey to cross the Australian continent. The Anglo-Irish police inspector set off on his little grey horse 'Billy' at the head of a column comprising twenty-seven camels, twenty-three horses and twenty-one tons of equipment, including sixty gallons of rum for the camels. The mayor of Melbourne wished the party well on behalf of the citizens of the colony and called for 'three cheers for Mr Burke'. Burke replied in a 'clear, earnest voice that was heard all over the crowd' with sentiments of a grandiosity that, in hindsight, almost invited disaster. What one writer has described as 'a comic-opera cavalcade' would end in calamity around nine months later with the deaths of Burke, William Wills and Charles Gray at Cooper's Creek – a subsequent royal commission would condemn Burke's leadership.

*

Mr Mayor,

On behalf of myself and the expedition I beg to return to you my most sincere thanks. No expedition has ever started under such favourable circumstances as this. The people, the government, the committee – all have done heartily what they could do. It is now our turn; and we shall never do well until we entirely justify what you have done in showing what we can do. [*Cheers.*]

'There is much stuff on these shelves that wants reverent handling'

Lord Chelmsford

Speech at the opening of the Mitchell Library, Sydney

8 MARCH 1910

Lord Chelmsford, third Baron (1868–1933), was a London lawyer appointed as governor of Queensland in 1905. A capable cricketer who captained Oxford University and a gifted cellist, Chelmsford retained the confidence of the British government despite a series of political blunders in the Queensland parliament, and in 1909 became governor of New South Wales. Returning to England in 1913, he was unexpectedly promoted to viceroy of India three years later and helped introduce the Montague–Chelmsford reforms, setting India on the path to 'responsible government'.

The preservation of books, manuscripts, newspapers and other historical materials is a job held in trust by the libraries of Australia. The Mitchell Library was created in honour of David Scott Mitchell, a Sydney bibliophile, who bequeathed his unique private collection of Australian publications and manuscripts, and a considerable endowment, to the State Library of New South

Wales. Chelmsford used the occasion of the Mitchell Library's opening to speak about the need for reverence in the use of its collection.

*

There are records here which are not mere records of history, but which are history in themselves. You could touch and handle things here which, if they did not exist – well, Australian history might have been written in a different way. But while you may regard these things here today as dry and without form, I feel sure some man some day will come along who will touch with the pencil of genius those dry bones and make them live ...

As I have pleaded for reverence in the valuing of this library, so also would I plead for reverence in the using of it. I would always make that plea in any such case. It may seem unnecessary to make it, but consider if it is not. There is much stuff on these shelves that wants reverent handling; and there is much stuff there that would furnish very fine copy for the gentleman whose remuneration, I understand, is a penny a line. I hope the trustees of the library will take all precautions against improper and irreverent use of it.

And may I hope that those who are going to mine this quarry will do so in the scientific search of truth. It may seem superfluous to caution this – but is it? Supposing any one of you were going in to consult a library, would you go in merely to find out what was the truth? I believe ninety-nine out of a hundred of us that go into a library go there not to find out what is the truth, but to find out something that is going to support our preconceived ideas and notions. In this matter we must be students in the school of science, and science has no greater claim to admiration than this, that it pursues truth regardless of prepossessions, and regardless of established theories.

'That word "lonely" will be eliminated from Australian life'

Earle Page

Speech at the opening of the Wireless and Electrical Exhibition, Sydney

12 DECEMBER 1923

Australians were already busy users of the telegraph when radio broadcasting began in the 1920s, opening new avenues of commercial, political and social communication. The first Australian radio service was inaugurated in Sydney by 2SB (later 2BL) on 23 November 1923, and listeners were able to tune in to programs by paid subscription. By 1924, Class B stations were able to offer free-to-air broadcasts through advertising. Listeners were reassured that they did not need to keep their windows open, for this new and mysterious technology was able to penetrate solid walls.

Earle Page (1880–1961), a surgeon from Grafton and leader of the federal Country Party, entered parliament in 1919 and remained there for forty-two years, during which he served as acting prime minister for nineteen days, in April 1939. While the advent of the television was lamented by his conservative contemporary Robert Menzies, Page understood the importance of the radio, particularly in a land of such vast distances.

*

The discovery and utilisation of wireless is probably the most remarkable achievement of the last one hundred years. It was a remarkable thing to have enabled us to girdle the earth in one-seventh of a second, and it gives promise of becoming more universal in its effects and consequences than any other single discovery. It has already revolutionised communication and is really the crowning triumph of a series of electrical developments since the discovery of electricity ...

Wireless is of immense importance to Australia, first by reason of our geographical isolation; by the immense distances from other parts of the Empire, and the fact that Australia is a huge island reached only by sea, and secondly, because of her own vast spaces and their present sparse population.

In dealing with the isolation of Australia it must be remembered that wireless has already, to a great extent, annihilated distance. Take the cause of *trans-ocean wireless*. One of the greatest benefits that radio communication can offer to Australia is the provision of direct telegraphic communication between Australia and all the other important world centres. Australia needs additional avenues of communication, faster routes and cheaper rates with the heart of the Empire, and also more effective communication with other important world centres such as North America, South America and the Far East. This offers further great possibilities and advantages to the commercial and social life of the Commonwealth. It will place our primary producers on a better footing than in the past in comparison with such an important competitor as the Argentine Republic. It will encourage migration by keeping us in closer touch with the people of the Old World, and it will be invaluable for defence ...

Radio communication is specially important in removing Australia's isolation from other parts of the Empire, and its further development, by assuring continuous connection with other parts of the Empire – and especially with England – will be of great assistance to us in discussing Empire problems and in maintaining a definite, coherent and connected Empire policy.

In regard to broadcasting, the Commonwealth Government desires to encourage this phase of wireless to the fullest possible extent, particularly because of its value to outback settlers. If sufficiently powerful stations can be erected at the principal cities to broadcast to the remotest settlement, very great benefits will be derived by all sections of the community. The man who lives in the outback and produces our primary wealth could receive from those stations weather forecasts and general meteorological information within a few minutes of its being produced by the meteorological department. He could get valuable information about the city and overseas markets – not a week old as in some cases at the present day – but as promptly as if he were living in the heart of the city itself. Every morning he would get the same world's news as the city man, and again in the evening, during his spare moments, that lack of contact with his fellow men would be overcome by wireless. He could listen to the operas, concerts, orchestras and the popular addresses in the city as they actually take place …

The 'lonely bush' has long been a phrase that Australians have not liked. Hence, where we find that by wireless 'the music, song and story' of our city can be spread to the most remote of country homes, that word 'lonely' will be eliminated from Australian life, and all who love Australia will welcome the day of the medium, wireless. [*Applause.*]

'Whereas I have it in command from His Majesty'

Sir Douglas Mawson

Proclamation of the Territory of King George V Land, Antarctica

5 JANUARY 1931

'We really have in him an Australian Nansen, of infinite resource, splendid physique, astonishing indifference to frost.' Thus spoke Professor Edgeworth David of his protégé Douglas Mawson (1882–1958) after their first foray to the Antarctic in 1908. Mawson was also a man of intensely patriotic sentiment; his subsequent expeditions in 1911–1914 and 1929–1931 would result in Australia laying claim to forty per cent of the southern continent. His final BANZARE (British, Australian and New Zealand Antarctic Research Expedition) aboard the ship *Discovery* provided the accurate geographic data establishing the extent of the Australian Antarctic Territory, and included the following proclamation for King George V Land. A flag was hoisted on a rocky point and Mawson spoke from a written script. Placed in a cylinder made from food tins and buried under a cairn, the document was not retrieved until 1976, when it was dug up by members of the Department of Science Antarctic Division and taken to the National Library in Canberra for conservation.

*

In the name of His Majesty George the Fifth King of Great Britain, Ireland and the British dominions beyond the seas, Emperor of India. By Sir Douglas Mawson.

Whereas I have it in command from His Majesty King George the Fifth to assert the sovereign rights of His Majesty over British land discoveries met with in Antarctica.

Now, therefore, I, Sir Douglas Mawson, do hereby proclaim and declare to all men that, from and after the date of these presents, the full sovereignty of the Territory of King George V Land and its extension under the name of Oates Land situated between longitudes 142 and 160 degrees east of Greenwich and between latitude 66 degrees south and the South Pole. Included herein are the following islands: Curzon Archipelago: Way Archipelago: Dixson Island: Mackellar Islets: Hodgeman Islets, vests in His Majesty King George the Fifth, his heirs and successors, for ever.

'I now declare this bridge open'

Captain Francis de Groot

Opening of the Sydney Harbour Bridge

19 MARCH 1932

The opening ceremony of 'the mighty link' was attended by more than 75,000 people on a beautiful sunny Sydney day. A *Herald* reporter described the waiting crowds 'scattered in colourful masses and groups and patches like vast handfuls of confetti dropped by a giant from the skies'. The dignitaries in attendance included the governor-general, the prime minister, the chief justice, the state governor and the premier of New South Wales. All was going to schedule 'but for a slight contretemps which failed to mar the enjoyment of the proceedings, and certainly added considerable excitement to them'. After premier Jack Lang had delivered his speech, but before he had cut the ribbon, Captain Francis de Groot (1888–1969) of the eccentric paramilitary group the New Guard – an imposter in the official party – strode up on horseback and slashed the ribbon in two with his sword, declaring the bridge to be open. The ribbon was held together and cut again while de Groot was dragged away for interrogation by the police. De Groot was an antique dealer who had joined the New Guard – an organisation loyal to the British crown – and was protesting against premier Lang, rather than the governor-general, performing the opening ceremony. An initial charge of insanity was dropped and de Groot was later fined for bad behaviour.

*

On behalf of the decent and loyal citizens of New South Wales, I now declare this bridge open.

'*I want to tell you all how happy I am to be amongst you*'

Queen Elizabeth II

First speech in Australia, Farm Cove, Sydney

3 February 1954

Australia had been settled by Europeans for 166 years before a ruling monarch set foot on its soil. Between six and seven million people are estimated to have lined the streets of towns and cities throughout the country to catch a glimpse of the young Queen Elizabeth II (1926–) on her royal tour. It is still the best-attended event in Australian history.

The image of the royal yacht *Gothic* arriving at Sydney Harbour was the first feature-length local film to be shot in 35 mm colour in Australia, and was shown all over the world. The Queen and the Duke of Edinburgh were welcomed ashore by the lord mayor of Sydney, Alderman Hills, who said, 'We humbly pray that Divine Providence may be pleased to safeguard Your Majesty and His Royal Highness in your journeyings in these distant parts, and that you may be granted the blessing of good health at all times' – perhaps an allusion to the attempted assassination of the first royal visitor to Australia, Queen Victoria's son, the then Duke of Edinburgh, in 1868. The Queen replied, speaking 'clearly and firmly', from the dais at Farm Cove.

*

I thank you and your aldermen most sincerely for the welcome you have given me and my husband on behalf of the citizens of Sydney. I would like to take this opportunity of telling you how delighted we both were by the spectacular greeting given to us this morning by the yachtsmen in the harbour and by the citizens on shore.

I have always looked forward to my first visit to this country, but now there is the added satisfaction for me that I am able to meet my Australian people as their Queen.

So, this morning, as the *Gothic* moved up the great expanse of this magnificent harbour, and I saw before me the city of Sydney, I was filled with a sense of pride and expectation. Only 166 years ago the first settlement was made not far from where we stand by Captain Phillip and his small band of Englishmen, and now there stands a fine city that has become famous throughout the world.

In the same short space of time we have seen the rise of Australia as a great nation, taking her full share in the counsels of the British Commonwealth and of the world.

I am proud indeed to be at the head of a nation that has achieved so much. Standing at last on Australian soil, on this spot that is the birthplace of the nation, I want to tell you all how happy I am to be amongst you, and how much I look forward to my journey through Australia.

'In the hushed stillness of this huge amphitheatre the youth of the world stand ready'

Sir Wilfred Kent Hughes

Speech at the Opening Ceremony of the XVI Olympiad,
Melbourne Cricket Ground

22 NOVEMBER 1956

Wilfred Kent Hughes (1895–1970) was a controversial figure in Australian politics from the time he entered the Victorian state parliament in 1927 until his death as a federal backbencher in 1970. Energetic and ambitious, Kent Hughes served in both World Wars, receiving a Military Cross for his service in the Light Horse Brigade in World War I, and surviving as a prisoner of war at Changi in World War II. He studied as a Rhodes scholar at Oxford University and represented Australia in athletics at the 1920 Olympic Games in Antwerp.

Mercurial, sometimes intemperate, he described himself as 'a fascist without a shirt'. Despite being dismissed from a Menzies ministry 'reshuffle' in January 1956, Kent Hughes retained his position as the organising chair of the Melbourne Olympics, and so had the honour of speaking at the Opening Ceremony. It was also Kent Hughes who, two weeks later, convinced the president of the International Olympic Committee to allow the athletes to mingle together beyond national groups in the Closing Ceremony – a tradition that has continued ever since. Kent Hughes died with a knighthood 'and five Olympic circles under each eye'.

*

Here in the land of the Southern Cross in the colourful city of Melbourne, we await the arrival of the Olympic flame, the symbolic emblem of true sportsmanship. Our fervent desire is that it may kindle in the hearts and minds, not only of those of us gathered together in this vast multitude, but also of all peoples in all countries – kindle a warm enthusiasm and a burning desire to uphold and strengthen the true ideals and the high standard of the Olympic Games.

In the hushed stillness of this huge amphitheatre the youth of the world stand ready to play their part in these inspiring ceremonies. From the plains of Olympia in Greece, one of the oldest civilisations in history, the torch has been borne aloft by human hands and by the modern wings of Daedelus. Through the ancient city of Athens, over mountains and plains, over rivers and oceans, through many lands and acclaimed by many peoples, the torch has come at last to one of the youngest nations and youngest cities of our present era.

This is a proud period in the short history of Australia and a memorable moment in the history of the Games. This is the first occasion on which the honour of the Olympic site has been granted to the southern hemisphere or to any city outside Europe or the United States of America. In 1896 and to every Olympic Games during the intervening sixty years, young Australian sportsmen and women have set out across the highways of the world to take part in the Games. Today, Australia greets their counterpart on her own home soil. From sixty-eight nations you have travelled the highways, the skyways and the seaways of the world. Across the northern polar icecaps, over equatorial jungles and over many lands and seas you have winged your way to be here with us in Melbourne. To one and all – welcome and warm greetings.

Your Royal Highness, you have travelled halfway around the world to honour the Olympics in the city of Melbourne by graciously accepting our invitation. On behalf of all amateur sportsmen and women I tender to you, Sir, our very humble gratitude. We would ask you to convey to our Patron of the Games, Her Gracious Majesty, the Queen, the warmest of all greetings from every man, woman and child present at this feast of sport and festival of international goodwill. Your presence here today is indicative of the high place the Olympics hold in the hearts of many millions of men and women, wherever they may live and whatever language they may speak.

To you, Mr President, and members of the International Olympic Committee, we give grateful thanks for your guardianship of the high ideals of the Olympics. It is no easy task to translate that trust into the rules and regulations which control the conduct of the Games. And so, today, in the Olympic story begins a new chapter full of promise. We are all inheritors of a noble and magnificent tradition. In Melbourne, we make our contribution with both pride and humility not only as heirs of a splendid past but also, we trust, as builders for a still more splendid future. May the 1956 Olympic Games give increased strength and renewed hope to all mankind in their struggle for a closer understanding between all men.

'I did but see her passing by'

Sir Robert Menzies

Speech welcoming Queen Elizabeth, Canberra

18 February 1963

As a boy of fifteen, Sir Robert Menzies (1894–1978) had received a leather-bound copy of *The Poetical Works of Wordsworth* and marked the following passage:

> I traveled among unknown men,
> In lands beyond the sea;
> Nor England! did I know till then
> What love I bore to thee.

Menzies did not travel to England until 1935, aged forty, but the journey fulfilled all the promise of his imagination. His life-long attachment to the country was not uncommon for someone of his age and background; his public displays of affection were more unusual. In an address at the official welcome for the

Queen and the Duke of Edinburgh on their 1963 Australian tour, Menzies expressed both his imperial allegiance and his lifelong love of poetry, culminating in a couplet by the poet Thomas Ford (1580–1648). Detractors saw the object of his rapture as a 'ludicrous anachronism'; the faithful remained reassured with his good manners and aplomb.

*

Ma'am, there are a lot of interesting people in the world who like to attack the monarchy. There are clever people in the world, at least, so I understand, who have suggested all sorts of things ought to be done to democratise the monarchy. We are proud to say that ours is the most democratic monarchy in the whole, wide world. [*Applause.*] We pay no attention to that. When we see you, we see you as our Queen. We see you as our Sovereign Lady. We see you as the successor of monarchs who, in this very century, by their own standards and their own conscience helped to preserve our monarchy in a world in which crowns have tumbled and disasters have beset mankind. We are proud to think that so far from abrogating any of our liberties because we are your subjects, we know that we add to our liberty because we are your subjects.

It is a proud thought for us to have you here, to remind ourselves that in this great structure of government which has evolved, you, if I may use the expression, are the living and lovely centre of our enduring allegiance. [*Applause.*]

You have today begun a journey around Australia. It is a journey you have made before. You will be seen in the next few weeks by hundreds of thousands, and I hope by millions, of Australian subjects. This must be to you now something that is almost a task.

All I ask you to remember in this country of yours is that every man, woman and child who even sees you with a passing glimpse as you go by will remember it, remember it with joy, remember it in the words of the old seventeenth-century poet who wrote those famous words: 'I did but see her passing by but yet I love her till I die.'

'One version is that it meant a meeting place'

Bob Hawke

Speech at the opening ceremony of the new Parliament House, Canberra

9 May 1988

It took sixty-one years for the sturdy and simple 'temporary' Parliament House in Canberra to be replaced by the 'new and permanent' building that now crowns Capital Hill. Designed by Mitchell, Giurgola and Thorpe, the new Parliament House completes the precinct that is Australia's political centre of gravity.

In the bicentennial year of 1988, Bob Hawke (1929–) was into a record third term as a Labor prime minister. A hard-living, heavy-drinking, bare-knuckled union official, he had successfully reinvented himself as a political populist. Queen Elizabeth unlocked the front doors of the new building with a ceremonial key and the dignitaries gathered in the Great Hall. Sir John Kerr and former prime ministers Gough Whitlam and Malcolm Fraser were seated together in the second row. Outside, a large contingent of Aboriginal protesters waved their red, black and gold flags.

*

Your Majesty, Your Royal Highness, Excellencies, Ladies and Gentlemen.

At a time like this each one of us will have some thoughts of the ghosts, or spirits, of the past.

At the most remote level, we are reminded by the historians and archeologists that this region has nurtured human habitation for at least 21,000 years. The Aboriginal civilisation and culture that developed from those earliest times was so quickly disrupted after the arrival of European settlers that we do not even know with precision what they meant by their word 'Canberra'. Certainly, one version is that it meant a meeting place. So it seems that this place, by its geography and the actions of its inhabitants, has been a natural meeting place for countless generations.

But we think too of more recent settings. We think of those in the first abode of the parliament of the Commonwealth – the first twenty-seven years in Melbourne's Legislative Council building – so many of them the giants of the federation conventions which gave birth to our nation.

We think then of those who over the next sixty-one years have graced what surely must be one of the more durable 'temporary' Parliament Houses in the history of democracy. The names are too legion to mention. But they are certainly not for us all ghosts or spirits, as the robust presence today of Whitlam, Gorton, Daly, Killen and Anthony so well testify.

I do, however, mention one who for so long dominated our long-time temporary residence. I believe the spirit of Sir Robert Menzies, whose commitment to the concept of Canberra as a truly great national capital should be respected across the political spectrum, would be smiling with approval today.

These intimations of our mortality and the presence of the Treasurer remind us of the paradoxical truth that in life the only certainties are death and taxes.

And so it is true that just as we have looked with some wonderment at Tom Roberts' remarkable painting of the guests and members in the first parliament in Melbourne, so future generations will look at photographs and films of today, remark on the quaintness of our style and costume, and ask – of us – 'What was in their minds on that momentous occasion?'

And what will our answer be?

I hope it would be something like this:

- That we have a feeling of deep gratitude to all who are responsible for this great and imaginative building – to those who conceived and designed it, to all who by the labour of their mind and body have made it the remarkable reality it is.

- That we do feel a sense of history and indebtedness to those who have fought in war, and in peace, to ensure the survival and the enlargement of the democratic principle.
- That we understand the danger of taking for granted the continuing survival of this principle in a world where so many people have succumbed or been subjected to despots to whom the concept of a parliament of the people is anathema.
- That we therefore understand the awesome obligation that is upon us. For those in the new parliament this will be an obligation to recognise always in the conduct of debate that whatever their views, their ideology, their party, they are part of something bigger – an institution which must endure long after the divisive issues of the day have been fought and resolved.
- That because we know we will discharge that obligation this building will become for our nation both the forum for our differences and the instrument of our unity – a building for all Australians, a parliament reflecting the diversity of our entire society and responding to the needs of the whole community.

Your Majesty, Your Royal Highness, Excellencies, Ladies and Gentlemen.

If these things are indeed in our minds today, then it will be a worthy answer to that question that may be asked about us when we are all long gone. For none of us can now foretell with any precision all the issues which will confront the parliament of Australia in its new home in the centuries ahead.

We face rapid, dramatic change in all areas of our national life and in the wider world. The challenge of adaptation will be great, the problems often complex, the decisions difficult.

But we do know this to be true. This new meeting place, this parliament, like the old, represents that principle of government – indeed the only principle of government – capable of meeting, and mastering, that challenge.

'We are part of nine hundred years of parliamentary tradition'

John Howard

Speech at the opening ceremony of the new Parliament House, Canberra

9 May 1988

John Howard (1939–) is the great 'survivor and pragmatist' of Australian politics. The solicitor from suburban Sydney won the seat of Bennelong in 1974 and has weathered every attempt at his removal – from both sides of politics – ever since. The opening of the new Parliament House found him during one of several spells as leader of the Opposition, with his own premiership still eight years ahead.

The opening ceremony took place eighty-seven years to the day after the first federal parliament met in 1901. On that occasion the honours were performed by the Queen's grandfather. It was also the sixty-first anniversary of the opening of the 'temporary' Parliament House, performed by the Queen's father on 9 May 1927.

*

Your Majesty, Your Royal Highness, Prime Minister, Excellencies, my Parliamentary Colleagues – current and past, Distinguished Guests, Ladies and Gentlemen.

I am very happy indeed on behalf of the Liberal and National Parties to support the warm words of welcome from the Prime Minister.

This is a very special occasion. It's an Australian occasion. It celebrates so much of what we have achieved. It offers hope about the future. It reminds us of the parliamentary giants of the past. And it reminds us of the uniqueness of the Australian achievement.

Two hundred years of tolerance and progress is brought together in a gathering such as today, which is such a blend of the old and the new. It's a day tinged with nostalgia as many of us look down at that great building which has witnessed so much of our history since 1927. We are reminded as we look beyond it to the War Memorial of the blood and the sacrifice of those that have kept this country free. And we look from this building with hope to the future.

It is also, Ma'am, an occasion to celebrate our membership of a wider being and existence, and that is the great world-wide institution of parliamentary democracy. We are part of nine hundred years of parliamentary tradition. Whatever may now be the diversity of this country and the enrichment of it through that diversity, we owe a great debt to the genius of British parliamentary democracy and the contribution that democracy has made to the moulding of this country and to so many other countries.

Part of that tradition is to be generous about the contribution of all strands of opinion. It's representative of that that today's parliament is opened in the presence of you, the leader of the Australian Labor Party. The decision to build this parliament was made under the prime ministership of Malcolm Fraser, who is present with us today. I trust and I know that I speak on behalf of everyone in this gathering and throughout Australia in expressing the hope that this building will fulfil the aspirations of all people for good, honest, fair and progressive government.

Finally, through your own presence, Ma'am, as with your father and your grandfather successively present at Melbourne and in Canberra in 1927, you with your presence remind us of the integral role that the Crown has played in the development of our parliamentary system of democracy. Through that nine hundred years your ancestors, some of them quite vigorously, have tangled with the struggling emergence of the parliamentary system. It is with a real delight that we have you here today.

Thirty-five years have now passed since you came to the throne. That period of time has seen astonishing change not only in Australia but throughout the world. The decades of the 1960s and 1970s have been probably the most cynical and sceptical of modern times. Yet through all of that your institution and you yourself as a person have retained the respect and the admiration of millions of people throughout the world.

You are here today as a friend, you are here today as the pinnacle of our democratic system of government and you are here today as an integral and enduring part of the great parliamentary tradition that we all celebrate today.

'There will be no U-turns'

Michael Kirby

Speech at the Opening Ceremony of the Gay Games VI at Aussie Stadium, Sydney

2 NOVEMBER 2002

An ecstatic crowd of 38,000 welcomed 11,000 athletes representing more than seventy countries at the Opening Ceremony of the 2002 Gay Games in Sydney – the first to be held in the southern hemisphere, and the sixth since their conception by Dr Tom Waddell in 1982 to 'bring a global community together in friendship, to experience participation, to elevate consciousness and self-esteem and to achieve a form of cultural and intellectual synergy'.

The keynote speech of the ceremony was delivered by Michael Kirby (1939–), Australia's most prominent openly gay man. When the High Court Justice included his partner of over thirty years, Johan van Vloten, in his entry for the 1998 *Who's Who in Australia*, he accepted the inevitable backlash as a necessity of 'bringing home the truth', saying: 'If the choice is between silence and upsetting nobody, or honesty and candour and upsetting a few who had demons in their minds, then I'm afraid people like me have to accept the latter …' His speech at the opening ceremony was received with tremendous applause and the Games began.

*

Under different stars, at the beginning of a new millennium, in an old land and a young nation, we join together in the hope and conviction that the future will be kinder and more just than the past.

At a time when there is so much fear and danger, anger and destruction, this event represents an alternative vision struggling for the soul of humanity. Acceptance. Diversity. Inclusiveness. Participation. Tolerance and joy. Ours is the world of love, questing to find the common links that bind all people. We are here because, whatever our sexuality, we believe that the days of exclusion are numbered. In our world, everyone can find their place, where their human rights and human dignity will be upheld.

This is a great night for Australia because we are a nation in the process of reinventing ourselves. We began our modern history by denying the existence of our Indigenous peoples and their rights. We embraced White Australia. Women could play little part in public life: their place was in the kitchen. And as for gays, lesbians and other sexual minorities, they were an abomination. Lock them up. Throw away the key.

We have not corrected all these wrongs. But we are surely on the road to enlightenment. There will be no U-turns.

Little did my partner Johan and I think, thirty years ago, as we danced the night away at the Purple Onion, less than a mile from this place, that we would be at the opening of a Gay Games with the Queen's representative and all of you to bear witness to such a social revolution. Never did we think we would be dancing together in a football stadium. And with the Governor. And that the Governor would be a woman! True, we rubbed shoulders on the dance floor with Knights of the Realm, such as Sir Robert Helpmann and with a future premier, such as Don Dunstan. But if an angel had tapped us on our youthful shoulders and told us of tonight we would have said 'Impossible'. Well, nothing is impossible to the human spirit. Scientific truth always ultimately prevails. So here we are tonight, men and women, indigenous and newcomers, black and white, Australians and visitors, religious and atheist, young and not so young, straight and gay – together.

It is put best by Corey Czok, an Australian basketballer in these Games: 'It's good to be able to throw out the stereotypes –

we're not all sissies, we don't all look the same and we're not all pretty!'

His last comment may be disputed. Real beauty lies in the fact that we are united not in the negatives of hate and exclusion, so common today, but in the positives of love and inclusion.

The changes over thirty years would not have happened if it had not been for people of courage who rejected the common ignorance about sexuality. Who taught that variations are a normal and universal aspect of the human species. That they are not going away. That they are no big deal. And that, between consenting adults, we all just have to get used to it and get on with life.

The people of courage certainly include Oscar Wilde. His suffering, his interpretation of it and the ordeal of many others have bought the changes for us. I would include Alfred Kinsey. In the midst of the McCarthyist era in the United States he, and those who followed him, dared to investigate the real facts about human sexual diversity. In Australia, I would also include, as heroes, politicians of every major party, most of them heterosexual. Over thirty years, they have dismantled many of the unequal laws. But the first of them was Don Dunstan. He proved, once again, the astonishing fact that good things sometimes occur when the dancing stops.

I would also add Rodney Croome and Nick Toonen. They took Australia to the United Nations to get rid of the last criminal laws against gay men in Tasmania. Now the decision in their case stands for the whole world. I would include Neal Blewett who led Australia's first battles against AIDS. Robyn Archer, Kerryn Phelps, Ian Roberts and many, many others.

But this is not just an Australian story. In every land a previously frightened and oppressed minority is awakening from a long sleep to assert its human dignity. We should honour those who looked into themselves and spoke the truth. Now they are legion. It is the truth that makes us free.

- I think of Tom Waddell, the inspired founder of the Gay Games. His last words in this life were: 'This should be interesting.' Look around. What an understatement.
- I think of Greg Louganis, twice Olympic gold medallist, who

came out as gay and HIV positive and said that it was the Gay Games that emboldened him to tell it as it was.

- I think of Mark Bingham, a rowdy rugby player. He would have been with us tonight. But he lost his life in one of the planes downed on 11 September 2001, struggling to save the lives of others. He was a real hero.
- Je pense à Bertrand Delanoé, le maire ouvertement gay de Paris, poignardé à l'Hôtel de Ville au course de la Nuit Blanche. Il a fait preuve d'un très grand courage – et il est un homme exceptionnel. When the gay Mayor of Paris was stabbed by a homophobe he commanded the party, at which it happened, to 'dance till dawn'. Do that in his honour tonight. And in honour of the Cairo 52; the Sister movement in Namibia; Al Fatiha – the organisation for Gay Muslims and many others struggling for their human rights.
- And I think of all of you who come together on this magical night to affirm the fundamental unity of all human beings. To reject ignorance, hatred and error. And to embrace love, which is the ultimate foundation of all human rights.

Let the word go out from Sydney and the Gay Games of 2002 that the movement for equality is unstoppable. Its message will eventually reach the four corners of the world. These Games will be another catalyst to help make that happen. Be sure that, in the end, inclusion will replace exclusion. For the sake of the planet and of humanity it must be so.

Amusez-vous bien. Et par l'exemple de nos vies défendons les droits de l'humanité pour tous. Non seulement pour les gays. Pour tout le monde.

Enjoy yourselves. And by our lives let us be an example of respect for human rights. Not just for gays. For everyone.

LAST WORDS
AND FAREWELLS

'An offence of this kind is of no ordinary character'

Sir Redmond Barry

The sentencing of Ned Kelly, Supreme Court, Melbourne

29 OCTOBER 1880

Sir Redmond Barry (1813–1880), the man who sentenced to death Australia's most infamous police killer, was probably the greatest single benefactor of any Australian city. An Irishman who emigrated to Australia at the age of twenty-six, Barry devoted himself to the cultivation of Melbourne institutions, founding the University of Melbourne, the State Library and the Art Gallery. He thought Victoria ill-developed, and 'threw in his lot with the destiny of the Province when it was a weak struggling settlement ...' Although known as a harsh and conservative judge, Justice Barry did lend his considerable energy and support to schemes assisting prisoners who had escaped a death penalty and completed their prison time, and did much *pro bono* work with Aboriginals.

Sir Redmond's 'invincible politeness and unfailing, if elaborate and old-fashioned, courtesy' are evident in the following speech – despite frequent interjections from the prisoner – as is his perception of Victoria at the time as a frontier land. Kelly's 'curse' at the completion of his sentencing – 'I will see you there, where I go' – is one of the great moments of Australian oratorical prophecy: the two great Irish Australians of their generation, one sentencing the other to death, and both in the grave within a month. Redmond Barry died after a very sudden illness, just twelve days after Kelly hanged.

*

The facts are so numerous, and so convincing, not only as regards the original offence with which you are charged, but with respect to a long series of transactions covering a period of eighteen months, that no rational person would hesitate to arrive at any other conclusion but that the verdict of the jury is irresistible, and that it is right. I have no desire whatever to inflict upon you any personal remarks. It is not becoming that I should endeavour to aggravate the sufferings with which your mind must be sincerely agitated. ...

An offence of this kind is of no ordinary character. Murders have been discovered which had been committed under circumstances of great atrocity. They proceeded from motives other than that which actuated you. They have had their origin in many sources. Some have been committed from a sordid desire to take from others the property they had acquired, some from jealousy, some from a desire for revenge, but yours is a more aggravated crime, and one of larger proportions, for with a party of men you took up arms against society, organised as it is for mutual protection and for respect of law. ...

In new communities, when the bonds of society are not so well linked together as in older countries, there is unfortunately a class which disregards the evil consequences of crime. Foolish, inconsiderate, ill-conducted, unprincipled youth unfortunately abound, and unless they are made to consider the consequences of crime, they are led to imitate notorious felons whom they regard as self-made heroes. It is right therefore that they should be asked to consider and reflect upon what the life of a felon is. A felon who has cut himself off from all decencies, all the affections, charities and all the obligations of society is as helpless and degraded as a wild beast of the field. He has nowhere to lay his head, he has no one to prepare for him the comforts of life, he suspects his friends, he dreads his enemies, he is on constant alarm lest his pursuers should reach him, and his only hope is that he might use his life in what he considers a glorious struggle for existence. That is the life of the outlaw or felon, and it would be well for those young men who are so foolish as to consider that it is brave of a man to sacrifice the lives of his fellow creatures in carrying out his own wild ideas to see that it is a life to be avoided by every possible means, and to reflect that the unfortunate termination of your life is a miserable death. New South Wales joined with Victoria in providing ample inducement to persons to assist in having you and your companions apprehended, but by some spell which I cannot understand – a spell which exists in all lawless communities more or less – which may be attributed either to a sympathy for the outlaws, or dread of the consequences which would result from the perform-ance of their duty – no persons were found who would be tempted by the reward. The love of country, the love of order, the love of obedience to law, have been set aside for reasons difficult to explain, and there is something extremely wrong in a country where a lawless band of men are able to live for eighteen months disturbing society. During your short life you have stolen, according to your own state-ments, over 200 horses. ...

You are self-accused. The statement was made voluntarily by yourself. Then you and your companions committed attacks on two banks and appropriated therefrom large sums of money, amounting to several thousands of pound. Further, I cannot conceal from myself the fact that an expenditure of £50,000 has been necessary in conse-quence of the acts with which you and your party have been con-nected. We have had samples of felons and their careers, such as those of Bradley and O'Connor, Clark, Gardiner, Melville, Morgan, Scott and Smith, all of whom have come to ignominious deaths; still the effect expected from their punishment has not been produced. This is much to be deplored. When such examples as these are so often repeated society must be reorganised, or it must soon be seriously affected. Your unfortunate and miserable companions have died a death which probably you might rather envy, but you are not afforded the opportunity. ...

In your case the law will be carried out by its officers. The gentle-men of the jury have done their duty. My duty will be to forward to the proper quarter the notes of your trial and to lay, as I am required to do, before the Executive any circumstances connected with your trial that may be required. I can hold out to you no hope. I do not see that I can entertain the slightest reason for saying you can expect anything. I desire to spare you any more pain, and I absolve myself from anything said willingly in any of my utterances that may have unnecessarily increased the agitation of your mind. I have now to pronounce your sentence.

You will be taken from here to the place from whence you came, and thence on a day appointed by the Executive Council to a place of execution, and there you will be hanged by the neck until you be dead. May the Lord have mercy on your soul.

[Kelly: I will go further than that, and say I will see you there, where I go!]

'It is not that I fear death; I fear it as little as to drink a cup of tea'

Ned Kelly

Statement to the court on sentencing, Supreme Court, Melbourne

29 OCTOBER 1880

The jury at the trial of Ned Kelly (1855–1880) took thirty minutes to reach a guilty verdict. It had taken Victorian police more than six months to capture the bushranger, who was sentenced to death for the murder of constable Thomas Lonigan at Stringybark Creek. Upon his detention, Kelly told a reporter he had 'outlived the care that curries public favour or dreads the public frown'. Yet Australia has not outlived its fascination with Kelly, turning his story into one of its most sophisticated and abiding myths. He has been called both our 'only folk hero', and 'one of the most cold-blooded, egotistical, and utterly self-centred criminals who ever decorated the end of a rope ...' Part of Kelly's legend derives from the *sang froid* with which he received Justice Redmond Barry's death sentence. Kelly was twenty-five years old at his execution, his last words witnessed by Alfred Deakin: 'Ah, well, I suppose it had to come to this.'

*

Well, it is rather too late for me to speak now. I thought of speaking this morning and all day, but there was little use, and there is little use blaming any one now. Nobody knew about my case except myself, and I wish I had insisted on being allowed to examine the witnesses myself. If I had examined them, I am confident I would have thrown a different light on the case. It is not that I fear death; I fear it as little as to drink a cup of tea. On the evidence that has been given, no juryman could have given any other verdict. That is my opinion. But as I say, if I had examined the witnesses I would have shown matters in a different light, because no man understands the case as I do myself. I do not blame anybody – neither Mr Bindon [Kelly's lawyer] nor Mr Gaunson [the Crown Prosecutor]; but Mr Bindon knew nothing about my case. I lay blame on myself that I did not get up yesterday and examine the witnesses, but I thought that if I did so it would look like bravado and flashness.

'To beard the kangaroo in his den'

Ivo Bligh

Speech at the farewell dinner for the English cricket team in the Pavilion at the Melbourne Cricket Club

13 MARCH 1883

The Honourable Ivo Bligh (1859–1927), a stylish right-handed batsman who had learned his cricket at Eton, was only twenty-three years old when he departed England in 1882 to reclaim his country's sporting honour, following the English team's unexpected loss to Australia at The Oval. It was this Test match that had prompted the famous mock obituary notice in the *Sporting Times*:

In Affectionate Remembrance of English Cricket
Which died at The Oval
on 29th August, 1882
Deeply lamented by a large circle of sorrowing friends
and acquaintances
R.I.P.
N.B. – The body will be cremated and the ashes taken
to Australia

So began the contest for the mythical 'Ashes of English cricket'. Dubbed 'St Ivo' by London *Punch*, Bligh made the sentiment of the obituary into a motif of the tour. The official three-Test series was won two to one by England, although a fourth unofficial Test won by Australia levelled the series overall. The Melbourne Cricket Club's farewell dinner to the touring side took place on Bligh's twenty-fourth birthday. He remains the youngest captain in Anglo-Australian Test history.

*

I and the other members of the team feel deeply the very hearty reception which the toast has accorded.

I remember exceedingly well the last occasion on which I had to make a speech in this pavilion, and for two reasons – first because I cannot forget the slight feeling of awe which we all felt at being in the assemblage of members of the far-famed Melbourne Club, and second because I also remember distinctly that the meal then partaken of was the fourth of four plentiful ones the English team had partaken of in two hours. [*Laughter.*]

I said at the time that the team was an unlucky one, but I did not then know how unlucky we were to be. We had actually been going through the whole of our tour with a man who had a broken rib without its being known. That was an extraordinary piece of bad luck, and all would agree in saying how much the team regretted such an accident to that best of bowlers, Morley – [*applause*] – and how much we admired his pluck, which we have only just begun to appreciate, in going through the whole tour with such a wound as he received. [*Loud applause.*] I also had the audacity to say on one occasion that the team had come to beard the kangaroo in his den. Now that four months have passed, I am afraid that the kangaroo still hops as jauntily as ever. [*Laughter.*] I am afraid that it must be confessed also, with regard to those 'ashes' referred to by the chairman, that the team cannot take them back to England. The best thing to do with them would be for their respected friend Mac to bury them in some corner of the ground. [*Loud laughter and applause.*] There is only one thing I have to request, and that is that all present see to it that none of Murdoch's eleven touch them, because they really have no right to them. [*Laughter and applause.*] The English team have not much to say about the last match. [*Laughter.*]

Now that the tour is over, I am happy to say that the team can look back upon it as having been a happy time. It is hardly possible to play a long succession of matches without some little unpleasantness, but if there had been any during the recent season they are not worth mentioning. The English team will look back upon the trip with unmixed feelings of pleasure. The matches have been among the hardest we have ever played or will play, and there is only one thing the team were badly treated in, and that was after coming 16,000 miles to meet Spofforth on a dry wicket, we failed to get one. As dry wickets as were got here in Australia can be got even in England, but I suppose the seasons might improve.

On looking back at the tour, I feel compelled to thank the press for its treatment of the team. On the whole it has been fair and impartial. [*Applause.*] Of course pressmen are mortal, like other people, and of course one always imagines that the shower falling on the wicket of his side is heavier than that which falls on the wicket of the adversary. But these little things cannot be helped. [*Laughter.*] I have also to thank the people for their kind reception of the team. They have always been most impartial – as impartial as similar assemblages are in England; and it shows at any rate that the principle of a fair field and no favour holds sway here. [*Applause.*]

I do not know how soon another Australian team might be seen in England again. A great deal is said about these cricket tours being overdone, but I am of the opinion that as long as truly representative teams can be got together there is no danger of 'overdoing' the sport. I hope that when the next Australian team come home that it will play more than one representative match. [*Applause.*] The present English team have been rash enough to offer to play five matches against Australian teams; but in my opinion, the proper number to be played is three. I must express my most heartfelt thanks to the members of the club for the kindness they have invariably shown towards the English Eleven. They have been so kind to us as to make us feel perfectly at home in the pavilion – I might say for myself that though I felt not at all at home in the middle of the ground, I feel quite so in that building. [*Laughter.*] Where so many members of the committee have discharged their onerous duties so well, it would be invidious to make distinctions, but I feel that the thanks of the team are due to our manager, whose well-known suavity of manner did so much to smooth over many little difficulties. [He alluded to Mr Alexander.] [*Applause.*] I join with the chairman in regretting the absence of Sir W. Clarke, whose judicious and generous use of his power and position has made him one of the most popular men in Victoria. [*Applause.*] Sir W. Clarke has in many ways endeared himself to the English team.

Of course there is a certain pang in having to say 'goodbye', but one or two members of the team, including myself, will remain a little after the others have departed. [*Loud cheers.*] In the hope that we might meet again I will not say 'farewell', but *'au revoir'*. The pretty badges which the team have received will always serve to remind us of the kindness of the club, whose public spiritedness has enabled us to make the present trip. I can only conclude by proposing the toast of 'The Melbourne Club'.

'*Dreadful! Dreadful!*'

Sir Frederick Holder

Last words, House of Representatives, Canberra

23 JULY 1909

A former journalist who became South Australia's premier, Sir Frederick Holder (1850–1909) was elected first Speaker of the House of Representatives in the 1901 federal elections, then re-elected without contest in 1903 and 1906. Holder eschewed party politics and won universal favour, although he once admitted 'an almost overwhelming desire to step out of the chair and tear off the gag'. His death is perhaps the most dramatic in Australian political history. At 5.06 a.m. on 23 July 1909, following a turbulent all-night sitting on the Old-Age Pensions Appropriation Bill, Holder fell from his Speaker's chair exclaiming his last words, before collapsing insensible to the floor. Assuming Holder would recover, Alfred Deakin resumed the session at 5.47 a.m., expressing 'profound regret that the Speaker, whom we all prize and value for his devotion to duty and great ability, has evidently over-taxed his strength'. The bells of the House were ordered off so as not to disturb the gravely ill Holder, but he never regained consciousness and later in the day became the only member of either House to die in the Australian parliament.

*

Dreadful! Dreadful!

'*I am sorry my personal contribution has been so small*'

Sir Donald Bradman

Speech on the occasion of his final Test match, the Oval, England

18 August 1948

Few professional sportsmen or women are granted the good fortune to choose the moment of their retirement; injury, poor form, greed and the politics of administration can all unhinge the best-laid plans. And although Sir Donald Bradman (1908–2001) chose propitious circumstances for his farewell, the result was a classic illustration of sport's uncertainty.

Bradman's Australian team of 1948 was 'entitled to the description *great*' and were perhaps the strongest to leave these shores: they became the first team to proceed unbeaten through an English tour. Eight of the team averaged more than forty wickets, seven exceeded fifty, seventeen matches were won by an innings, and four of the five Tests were won in comfort. Bradman himself hit eleven hundreds in thirty-one innings, averaging ninety. Everywhere he went, the English crowds responded with warmth and gratitude. As English cricket writer R.C. Robertson-Glasgow put it: 'We want him to do well. We feel we have a share in him. He is more than Australian. He is a world batsman.'

The only interruption to this pageant of success came in the Fifth Test at The Oval where, needing four runs to finish his career with an average of one hundred, Bradman was bowled second ball for nought. About this, he was not best pleased; as he said later, 'No, I don't laugh much about it, because I'm very sorry that I made a duck, and I would have been glad if I had made those four runs so I could finish with an average of a hundred.' But he showed the good grace to make the following generous speech after Australia's comfortable victory.

*

No matter what you may read to the contrary, this is definitely my last Test match ever. I am sorry my personal contribution has been so small. There are two reasons for that. One was the generosity of the reception I received and, secondly, the very fine ball bowled to me. It has been a great pleasure for me to come on this tour and I would like you all to know how much I have appreciated it. Our most important matches are over. We have played against a very lovable opposing skipper. He has been kind to us in every way and it is a great pleasure for us to have him captain England against us. The captain of the losing side has a very difficult job. Yardley had the misfortune to run against one of the strongest Australian teams ever. It will not be my pleasure to play ever again on this oval but I hope it will not be the last time I come to England.

'Secondly, you can have my neck'

Frank Worrell and Richie Benaud

Speeches on the balcony at the Melbourne Cricket Ground

15 FEBRUARY 1961

At a time when cricket seemed to be in the doldrums, the 1960–61 series between Australia and the West Indies produced some of the most memorable and breathtaking play in the history of the game. After winning a game apiece, playing a thrilling tie and desperate draw, the countries came to Melbourne for the Fifth Test with all to play for: a world-record 90,800 people turned up to watch the second day's play on Saturday 11 February. The Australians finally prevailed, in a heart-stopping finish, by two wickets.

Comradely feeling between the teams had been obvious from the start – on and off the field. Frank Worrell (1924–1967), the captain of the West Indies team, was thirty-six years old and the first black man to lead the West Indies on a tour. A Manchester University graduate with honours in social sciences who was later elected a senator in the Jamaican parliament, Worrell was intelligent, urbane and charismatic, his captaincy radiating 'a monumental calm'. The Australian crowds were smitten with his team – tens of thousands turning up to a farewell ticker-tape parade up Collins Street in Melbourne.

Australia's captain, Richie Benaud (1930–), the journalist son of a school teacher, was not merely a fine all-rounder – the first to combine 2000 runs with 200 wickets in Tests – but was also a lateral thinker and keen promoter of the game. Cricket writer Ray Robinson called him 'the spectator's best friend', a leader with a knack for 'snap decisions that did not snap back'. He had in 1960, with the BBC, already begun the broadcasting career that continues to this day.

At the conclusion of the 1960–61 series, the Australian Board of Control for International Cricket, chaired by Sir Donald Bradman, created a perpetual trophy for competition between the teams in order to commemorate the wonderful series. From the balcony of the Melbourne Cricket Ground, Bradman announced to the crowd that, 'in honour of a very brilliant cricketer, who unfortunately has now played his last Test match in Australia … we should call it the Frank Worrell Trophy.' Worrell, deeply moved, responded by presenting his cap, his tie and his shirt to Benaud, who accepted them graciously and responded.

*

Frank Worrell

I've got two duties to perform. I've got to present this trophy to Richie and to congratulate him and his men for the wonderful cricket. And secondly, I've got a little token which I should like to present him also. And firstly, Richie, congratulations to you and the boys. [*Applause.*] And finally, ladies and gentlemen, we've got a symbol here of a scalp [*laughter and cheers*]. Secondly, you can have my neck [*laughter*]. And you can have the upper half of my body [*laughter and prolonged applause*]. I shall refrain from offering the lower half of my body because the knees wouldn't stand him in any stead.

Richie Benaud

Sir Donald Bradman, Frank, ladies and gentlemen,

Frank was kind enough to say that he was offering me the scalp and his neck, and the upper half of his body, but I'm quite certain that you will all agree with me, that he himself will remain in the hearts of cricket lovers in this country for many a long day.

[*With the crowd*] For he's a jolly good fellow ... and so say all of us!

'I therefore take total responsibility for the defeat of the Liberal Party'

Malcolm Fraser

Resignation speech, Southern Cross Hotel, Melbourne

6 MARCH 1983

It took the pain of defeat for ousted prime minister Malcolm Fraser (1930–) to finally break his stern political facade. Fraser had called a snap election on 3 February 1983 to capitalise on Labor Party leadership divisions, but was trumped when Opposition leader Bill Hayden stood down the same day to make way for the popular and charismatic trade union leader Bob Hawke. One month later, Fraser was a beaten man, conceding defeat at one o'clock in the morning at the Southern Cross Hotel in front of shattered party members, Young Liberal supporters and television cameras, struggling through this short address only with the support of his wife Tamie.

*

Ladies and gentlemen, I have a short statement that I would like to make. Firstly, I would like to congratulate Mr Hawke and the Australian Labor Party for winning this election. I hope they can achieve what they intend for the people of Australia. They have set a high ambition and I hope they can achieve it because if they can it will advantage this country. I want to say that from this moment I resign from the leadership of the Liberal Party. I will not contest the leadership of the Liberal Party ... I want to make it plain that I take full responsibility for the timing of the federal election. I take total responsibility for the conduct of that election. I therefore take total responsibility for the defeat of the Liberal Party. I would like to thank all my colleagues and the Liberal Party right around Australia for the support they have given me, not just over recent weeks, but for the past seven years ... There really has been magnificent support in very difficult times. There are many wonderful people who believed in what the government was doing and I thank them for that.

'It is still winter at home. But the golden wattles are coming into bloom'

Sir William Deane

Address at ecumenical service, Interlaken, Switzerland

5 AUGUST 1999

Sir William Deane (1931–) was one of the most affectionately regarded men to have held high public office in Australia. During his term as Australia's twenty-second governor-general from 1996 to 2001, his compassion and humanity became a rallying point for those disaffected by politics. An outstanding law student – he was awarded the Diploma of The Hague Academy of International Law before being called to the bar in 1957 – who became a successful barrister and Queen's Counsel, Deane served on the bench of the NSW Supreme Court. Between 1982 and 1996, he was a justice of the High Court.

It was Deane's duty on numerous occasions to represent Australia in times of sadness and tragedy; he spoke at the dedication of the Port Arthur memorial garden, at the memorial service for the victims of the Childer's Palace backpacker hostel fire, and delivered the eulogy at Sir Donald Bradman's funeral. When fourteen Australians died in a canyoning tragedy in Interlaken, Switzerland, the governor-general provided a genuine and simple expression of national sorrow.

*

We are gathered in great sadness to mourn the deaths of the twenty-one young people who were killed in the canyoning accident near here, last week. They came from five nations – Switzerland, the United Kingdom, South Africa, New Zealand and Australia. Their loss is a profound tragedy for their families and friends who are in the thoughts and the prayers of all of us at this service today. We pray with them for their loved ones who have died. And we also pray that, in the words of our Lord (Matthew Ch.5, v.4), they will truly be comforted.

Fourteen of the victims of the tragedy came from Australia. Collectively, their deaths represent probably the greatest single peace-time loss of young Australians outside our own country. That loss affects not only their families and friends, dreadful though that is. It also deeply affects our nation as a whole and all of its people.

I have, as Governor-General of Australia, with Senator John Herron of our government, come here on behalf of Australia and of all Australians, to mourn them, to be with and to sympathise with their family members and friends who are here, and to demonstrate how important they were to their homeland. For us, the tragedy is somehow made worse by the fact that they died so far away from the homes, the families, the friends and the land they loved so well.

Australia and Switzerland are on opposite sides of the globe. Yet, in this age of modern telecommunications, one effect of the disaster has been to bring our two countries closer together. On every night since the accident, Switzerland has been in every Australian home that has been tuned into the television news, as well as on the radio, in all our newspapers and other media outlets. Conversely, the fact that two-thirds of those who died came from Australia has given rise to an increased awareness here in Switzerland of my country and its people.

Switzerland has, of course, itself experienced the shock of overseas tragedy in the past. Perhaps that has heightened the sympathy and understanding which it has shown in recent days. I have already had the privilege of meeting with you, Madam President, and with Vice-President Ogi and exchanging condolences. I would, on this solemn occasion, like to express to the Swiss authorities and to the people of Switzerland, particularly the people of Wilderswil and Interlaken regions, our abiding gratitude for all the help and assistance they have provided in the aftermath of the tragedy. In particular, I pay tribute to the bravery of all those who worked in the rescue efforts. We thank them for their skill and dedication. I also particularly mention the competence, the compassion and the kindness of all who have helped to look after the survivors and the relatives who have come here.

The young people – certainly the young Australians – who have been killed all shared the spirit of adventure, the joy of living, the exuberance and the delight of youth. That spirit inspired their lives, and lit the lives of all who knew them, until the end. We remember that and so many other wonderful things about them as we mourn them and grieve for young lives cut so tragically short. And all of us feel and share in their collective loss. For these twenty-one young men and women were part – a shining part – of our humanity. As John Donne wrote, 'No man is an island.' Anyone's 'death diminishes' us all because we are all 'involved in mankind'.

Yesterday, my wife and I, together with family members and friends of the Australian victims, visited the canyon where the accident occurred. There, in memory of each of the fourteen young people who came from our homeland, we cast into the Saxetenbach fourteen sprigs of wattle, our national floral emblem, which we had brought with us from Government House in Canberra. Somehow, we felt that was bringing a little of Australia to them.

It was also, in a symbolic way, helping to bring them home to our country. This is not to suggest that their spirit and their memory will not linger forever, here in Switzerland, at the place where they died. Rather, it is to suggest that a little part of Switzerland has become, and will always be, to some extent, part of Australia. As it will also be part of the other countries outside Switzerland – New Zealand, South Africa and the United Kingdom – where whence they came.

It is still winter at home. But the golden wattles are coming into bloom. Just as these young men and women were in the flower of their youth. And when we are back in Australia we will remember how the flowers and the perfume and the pollen of their and our homeland were carried down the river where they died to Lake Brienz in this beautiful country on the far side of the world.

May they all rest with God.

'I'll hang the boots up as of tonight'

Jason McCartney

Retirement address, Telstra Dome

6 JUNE 2003

After surviving the Bali bombings and spending eight months in intensive recovery, Kangaroos footballer Jason McCartney (1974–) rejoined his team-mates on the field in a game against Richmond at the Telstra Dome midway through the Australian Football League 2003 season. McCartney – a 182-game AFL veteran – had suffered agonising burns to fifty per cent of his body and shrapnel wounds to his legs while drinking in Paddy's Bar on an end-of-season Bali trip on 12 October 2002; many doubted he would play top-level football again. McCartney kicked a goal of his own in the last quarter and set up the winning goal in the final minutes of the match before announcing to the crowd after the siren that his comeback game would be his last. His determination to play again was 'a symbol of recovery', inspiring and uplifting other burns survivors, but it had taken its toll. Prime Minister John Howard expressed what many felt: that 'millions of people admire your guts'.

*

It's what dreams are made of. I can't thank the Kangaroo boys enough. The Richmond guys were sensational. It's just a great win …

I think I've used up every inch of my determination through my fitness and mental effort, and I find it fitting now that I'll hang the boots up as of tonight and go out on a great note. I'm spent, it's been a tough time, but that's enough for me, mate.

Once I got selected I knew I didn't have much more in me. It's been a huge mental battle to get where I am today. Look, my body's still healing and it needs a rest, and mentally, it's been hard carrying the hopes of a nation, I can tell you, so I'm going to enjoy a couple of beers tonight with my family and friends. I love these guys, they've been great to me – what a way to go out.

Sources

MS 8086 Box 544/14-15, State Library of Victoria, Melbourne

P. 91   Blamey, Thomas, radio broadcast, Blamey papers, 3DRL/6643 series 7/1 Box 59, Australian War Memorial Archives, Canberra

P. 93   Menzies, Robert, *The Age*, 4 September 1939

p. 100 Curtin, John, *Voices of History: speeches and papers delivered during 1941 to 1945–46*, Grameroy Publishing Company, New York, 1946

P. 101 McLeod, A.L., *Australia Speaks: an anthology of Australian speeches*, Wentworth Press, Sydney, 1969

P. 107 MacArthur, Douglas, *The Sydney Morning Herald*, 28 March 1942

p. 108 Rischbieth, Bessie, radio broadcast, Rischbieth papers, NLA MS 2004/2/121, National Library of Australia, Canberra

P. 114 Burt, Fred, speech to the Returned Services League, NAA: A5954/69,532/14, National Archives of Australia, Canberra

P. 117 Calwell, Arthur *Commonwealth Parliamentary Debates, H of R*, 4 May 1965

P. 123 Holt, Harold, *The Australian*, 1 July 1966

P. 125 Johnson, L.B., *The Australian*, 22 October 1966

P. 128 White, Patrick, *Patrick White Speaks*, Primavera Press, Sydney, 1989

P. 134 James, Clive, *Even As We Speak: new essays 1993–2001*, Picador, London, 2001

P. 137 Howard, John, from the Prime Minister's website (www.pm.gov.au/news/speeches)

Politics

P. 141 Deakin, Alfred, *Commonwealth Parliamentary Debates, H of R*, 18 March 1902

P. 146 Deakin, Alfred, *The Argus*, 2 February 1904

P. 148 Brett, Judith, *Robert Menzies' Forgotten People*, Macmillan, Chippendale, 1992

P. 157 Lyons, Enid, *Commonwealth Parliamentary Debates, H of R*, 29 September 1943

P. 164 Evatt, H.V., *Australia in World Affairs*, Halstead Press, Sydney, 1946

p. 167 Chifley, Joseph, from Australian Politics website (www.australian politics.com/parties/alp/chifley-light-on-hill.html)

P. 169 Menzies, Robert, *Commonwealth Parliamentary Debates, H of R*, 3 April 1963

P. 176 Whitlam, Gough, *Commonwealth Parliamentary Debates, H of R*, 10 October 1972

P. 177 Freudenberg, Graham, *A Certain Grandeur: Gough Whitlam in politics*, Penguin, Ringwood, 1987

P. 179 Daly, Fred, *Commonwealth Parliamentary Debates, H of R*, 28 October 1975

P. 182 Ryan, Susan, *Trust the Women: Women in Parliament*, Papers on Parliament, No.17, Department of the Senate, Canberra, September 1992

P. 190 Keating, Paul, *The Australian*, 15 March 1993

p. 194 Keating, Paul, unpublished, transcript supplied by author

Great Debates

P. 205 Headon, D. & Perkins, E. *Our First Republicans*, The Federation Press, NSW, 1998
P. 216 Deakin, Alfred, *Commonwealth Parliamentary Debates, H of R*, 12 September1901
P. 227 Australian Labor Party, *Manifesto and speeches on the national referendum: presenting the case for the reinforcement of the Australian armies in France by the national vote of the Australian people, by W.M. Hughes,* National Referendum Council, Melbourne, 1916
P. 235 Bryan, Cyril, *Archbishop Mannix: A Champion of Australian Democracy*, Advocate Press, Melbourne, 1918
P. 239 Street, Jessie, radio broadcast, NLA, MS 2683/3/655, Street papers, National Library of Australia, Canberra
P. 243 Roper, David, *The Sydney Morning Herald,* 9 November 1944
P. 244 Calwell, Arthur, *Commonwealth Parliamentary Debates, H of R*, 2 December 1947
P. 246 Tangney, Dorothy, radio broadcast, NLA, MS 7564/3/2, Tangney papers, National Library of Australia, Canberra
P. 249 Menzies, Robert, *Commonwealth Parliamentary Debates, H of R*, 27 April 1950
P. 254 Evatt, H.V., *Commonwealth Parliamentary Debates, H of R*, 19 October 1955
P. 261 Altman, Dennis, *Coming Out in the Seventies*, Wild & Woolley, 1979
P. 267 Blainey, Geoffrey, *In Our Time: The Issues and the People of Our Century*, Information Australia, Melbourne, 1999
P. 279 Garner, Helen, *The Sydney Papers,* the Sydney Institute, Spring 1995
P. 290 Hanson, Pauline, *Commonwealth Parliamentary Debates, H of R*, 10 September 1996
P. 297 Jones, Barry, unpublished, transcript supplied by author
P. 301 Mackay, Hugh, from the Australian Republican Movement's website (www.republic.org.au)

Indigenous Affairs

P. 311 Reynolds, Henry, *This Whispering in Our Hearts*, Allen and Unwin, St Leonards, 1998
P. 314 Saunders, John, *The Colonist*, 17, 20 and 23 October 1838
P. 319 Inglis, K.S., *Men and Women of Australia: speech making as history*, Dept. of English, University College, University of New South Wales, Australian Defence Force Academy in association with the Barry Andrews Trust, 1993
P. 320 Neville, A.O., *Aboriginal Welfare: Initial Conference of Commonwealth and State Aboriginal Authorities*, Commonwealth Government Printer, Canberra, 1937

p. 324 Stanner, W.E.H., *After the Dreaming: The 1968 Boyer Lectures*, Australian Broadcasting Commission, NSW, 1969

p. 335 Bonner, Neville, *Commonwealth Parliamentary Debates, Senate*, 8 September 1971

p. 341 Whitlam, Gough, *The Whitlam Government*, Penguin, Ringwood, 1985

p. 341 Hercus, L., & Sutton, P., *This is what happened: historical narrative by Aborigines*, Australian Institute of Aboriginal Studies, Canberra, 1986

p. 344 Goonan, M., *The Pope in Australia*, St Paul's Publications, Sydney, 1986

p. 351 Ryan, Mark (ed), *Advancing Australia: The Speeches of Paul Keating*, Big Picture Publications, Sydney, 1995

p. 357 Craven, Peter (ed), *The Best Australian Essays 2000*, Black Inc., Melbourne

p. 359 Pearson, Noel, *The Age*, 12 May 2002

Attacks, Scandals and Controversies

p. 365 McLeod, A.L., *Australia Speaks: an anthology of Australian speeches*, Wentworth Press, Sydney, 1969

p. 371 Inglis, K.S., *Men and Women of Australia: speech making as history*, Dept. of English, University College, University of NSW, Australian Defence Force Academy in association with the Barry Andrews Trust, Sydney, 1993

p. 372 Hughes, W.M., *Commonwealth Parliamentary Debates, H of R*, 28 May 1909

p. 379 Mahon, Hugh, *The Tribune*, 11 November 1920

p. 382 Page, Earle, *Commonwealth Parliamentary Debates, H of R*, 16 June 1939

p. 386 Santamaria, B.A., *The Movement of Ideas in Australia* pamphlet in printed books catalogue, Mitchell Library, Sydney

p. 396 Kerr, John, from the Whitlam Dismissal website (www.whitlam dismissal.com)

p. 399 Whitlam, Gough, Australian Broadcasting Commission Radio Broadcast, 11 November 1975

p. 400 Kerr, John, Australia Day Address 1976, NLA, MS 9524/9, Kerr speeches, National Library of Australia, Canberra

p. 402 Murdoch, Rupert, *The Times*, London, 2 September 1993

Ideas and Inspiration

p. 411 Twain, Mark, *The Australasian*, 5 October 1895

p. 418 Shirley, John, *Report of the Twelfth Meeting of the Australasian Association for the Advancement of Science*, AAAS, Brisbane, 1910

p. 422 Melba, Nellie, Address at Guildhall School of Music, May 1911, NLA, MS 2647, Mathilde Marchesi papers, National Library of Australia, Canberra

p. 426 Scott, Rose, speech on the unveiling of her portrait, September 1922, Scott papers, ML MS 38/27, Mitchell Library

p. 428 Gepp, Herbert, *Democracy's Danger: Addresses on Various Occasions*, Angus & Robertson, Sydney,1939

p. 432 Dixon, Owen, *Jesting Pilate and other Paper and Addresses,* Law Book Company, Sydney, 1965

p. 437 Lyons, Enid, Mother's Day address, NLA, MS 4852, Lyons papers, National Library of Australia, Canberra

p. 440 *The Boyer Collection: Highlights of the Boyer Lectures 1959-2000,* selected and introduced by Donald McDonald, Australian Broadcasting Corporation, Sydney, 2001

p. 450 *The Boyer Collection: Highlights of the Boyer Lectures 1959-2000,* selected and introduced by Donald McDonald, Australian Broadcasting Corporation, Sydney, 2001

p. 459 Clark, Manning, *Speaking Out of Turn: Lectures and Speeches (1940–1991)*, Melbourne University Press, Carlton, 1997

p. 462 Fraser, Malcolm, The 1971 Alfred Deakin Lecture *Towards 2000: Challenge to Australia,* Alfred Deakin Lecture Trust, 1971

p. 465 Hafey, Tom, previously unpublished. Audio courtesy of the Australian Football League

p. 467 Kennedy, John, previously unpublished. Audio courtesy of the Australian Football League

p. 470 Headon, D. (ed), *The Best Ever Australian Sports Writing,* Black Inc., Melbourne, 2001

p. 472 Kirby, Michael, unpublished, manuscript supplied by the author

p. 478 Boyer Lecture, *The View from the Bridge: Aspects of Culture,* Australian Broadcasting Corporation, Sydney, 1996

p. 488 Adams, Phillip, unpublished, manuscript supplied by the author

p. 495 Malouf, David, The Brisbane Institute Transcripts: (www.brisinst.org.au)

p. 508 Carroll, John, Alfred Deakin Lectures, Radio National, 12 May 2001

p. 518 Harries, O., *Benign or Imperial? Reflections on American Hegemony,* Australian Broadcasting Corporation, Sydney, 2004

Openings and Commencements

p. 531 Beaglehole, J.C. (ed), *The Journals of Captain James Cook on his voyages of discovery,* Cambridge University Press, Cambridge, 1968

p. 533 King George III, *Parliamentary Papers*, Great Britain Parliament, London, 1797

p. 534 Dann, John (ed), *The Nagle Journal: a diary in the life of Jacob Nagle, sailor, from the year 1775 to 1841,* Weidenfeld & Nicholson, New York, 1988

p. 535 Henry, William, *The Shimmering Waste: The Life and Times of Robert O'Hara Burke,* W. Henry, Ireland, 1997

p. 536 Crowley, F.K., *Modern Australia in Documents, Vol. 1, 1901–1939,* Wren, Melbourne, 1973

P. 538   Crowley, F.K., *Modern Australia in Documents, Vol. 1, 1901–1939,* Wren, Melbourne

P. 540   Mawson, Douglas, proclamation, January 1931, NLA, MS 5970, National Library of Australia, Canberra

P. 541   Ellyard, David, *The Proud Arch: the story of the Sydney Harbour Bridge,* Bay Books, Sydney, 1982

P. 542   Queen Elizabeth II, *The Age,* 5 February 1954

P. 544   *The Official Report of the Organising Committee for the Games of the XVI Olympiad,* Melbourne, 1956

P. 546   Sir Robert Menzies Memorial Foundation Limited: (www.menziesvirtualmuseum.org.au)

P. 548   Hawke, Bob, transcript available from the Prime Minister's Office, Parliament House, Canberra

P. 551   Howard, John, transcript available from the Prime Minister's Office, Parliament House, Canberra

P. 553   Kirby, Michael, unpublished, manuscript supplied by author

Last Words and Farewells

P. 559   Barry, Redmond, *The Argus,* 30 October 1880

P. 562   Kelly, Ned, *The Argus,* 30 October 1880

P. 563   Bligh, Ivo, *The Australasian,* 17 March 1883

P. 567   Nairn, B. & Serle, G. (eds) *The Australian Dictionary of Biography,* Vol. 9, Melbourne University Press, Melbourne, 1983

P. 568   Fingleton, J., *Brightly Fades the Don,* Collins, London, 1949

p. 569   *More Cricket Flashbacks,* ABC audio cassette, 1989

P. 571   Hindhaugh, Christina, *It wasn't meant to be easy: Tamie Fraser in Canberra,* Lothian Publishing, Melbourne, 1986

P. 572   Deane, William, from the website of the Governor-General (www.gg.gov.au/speeches)

P. 575   McCartney, Jason, *After Bali,* Lothian Books, Melbourne, 2003

Chronological Index

King O'Malley *Cold climates have produced the greatest geniuses* 8 October 1903 P. 21

Alfred Deakin *Cricket... if there were three elevens in the field* 1 February 1904 P. 146

William Bragg *What is light?* 11 January 1909 P. 418

William 'Billy' Hughes *I do not agree with that; it is not fair to Judas* 28 May 1909 P. 372

Sir Frederick Holder *Dreadful! Dreadful!* 23 July 1909 P. 567

Lord Chelmsford *There is much stuff on these shelves that wants reverent handling* 8 March 1910 P. 536

Dame Nellie Melba *What are we singers but the silver-voiced messengers of the poet?* 19 May 1911 P. 422

Andrew Fisher *Our last man and our last shilling* 31 July 1914 P. 73

William 'Billy' Hughes *We turned our backs on the purifying waters of self-sacrifice* 17 March 1916 P. 74

William 'Billy' Hughes *If the Allies are defeated, we go down* 18 September 1916 P. 227

Archbishop Daniel Mannix *Wait and see what they have ready for you* October 1917 P. 235

Hugh Mahon *If there is a just God in heaven, those sobs will reach Him* 7 November 1920 P. 379

Rose Scott *The beautiful ivy of friendship covers many ruins* 22 September 1922 P. 426

Earle Page *That word 'lonely' will be eliminated from Australian life* 12 December 1923 P. 538

Sir John Monash *Feed your troops on Victory* 30 March 1926 P. 81

Sir John Monash *It is an occasion for elevating the public spirit* 26 April 1930 P. 90

Sir Douglas Mawson *Whereas I have it in command from His Majesty* 5 January 1931 P. 540

Captain Francis de Groot *I now declare this bridge open* 19 March 1932 P. 541

Miles Franklin *The hardy pioneer in Australian literature* 12 April 1935 P. 24

A.O. Neville *No matter what we do, they will die out* 21 April 1937 P. 320

Herbert Gepp *We are still comparatively in the wilderness* 22 October 1937 P. 428

Sir Thomas Blamey *It is in this outlook that danger lies for Europe* 1 May 1938 P. 91

Earle Page *I was compelled to consider the qualifications of the new leader* 20 April 1939 P. 382

Sir Robert Menzies *It is my melancholy duty to inform you* 3 September 1939 P. 93

John Curtin *The hands of the democracies are clean* 8 December 1941 P. 100

John Curtin *We are fighting mad* 20 March 1942 P. 101

General Douglas MacArthur *We shall win, or we shall die* 26 March 1942 P. 107

ACKNOWLEDGEMENTS

The compilation of an anthology inevitably incurs a host of debts, material, intellectual and personal. I am, of course, primarily grateful to those who granted permission for the reproduction of their speeches in *Well May We Say*: I hope I have honoured their work.

A good deal of the time spent researching the speeches might well have been wasted and valuable opportunities missed had it not been for the counsel of many people. Geoffrey Blainey, John Hirst, Marilyn Lake and Robert Manne were especially generous with their wisdom and encouragement. For advice on tracing people and sources I am grateful to Dennis Altman, Anna Blainey, Judith Brett, Jack Carmody, John Jenkin, Barry Jones, Paul Keating, Lyn Martin, Henry Reynolds, June Senyard and Dennis White. Friends who helped directly with this book, in ways too numerous to mention, include Phillip Adams, Ginger Briggs, John Carroll, Stephen Crittenden, Tony Jarvis, Tim Lane, Chris Middendorp, Patrice Newell, Peter Phipps, David Studham, John Waterhouse and my brother, Gideon Warhaft. For their patience and flexibility, I am indebted to the Globalism Institute at RMIT.

One of the most enjoyable phases of this project was working in the manuscript rooms at the National Archives of Australia, the Australian War Memorial, the National Library of Australia, the Mitchell Library in Sydney and the State Library of Victoria. Thanks to all of the staff for many happy weeks spent there. And to Black Inc. – Morry Schwartz, Rebecca Arnold, Eugenie Baulch, Thomas Deverall, Chris Feik, Roisin FitzGerald, Meredith Kelly, Sophy Williams and Caitlin Yates, who all combined immense capabilities with unfailing goodness.

In their own ways Uri Auerbach, Marcus Corn, Nigel Cooper, Martin Perkins, Allison Pye and Joshua, David and Baiba Warhaft have each offered me sustenance and kindness. I am grateful to each of them. And, as always, to my mother Joyce Warhaft. In every way, my partner Gideon Haigh has given his unstinting care and forbearance. He was my editor of first and last resort, chief librarian and greatest support. This book is for Gideon.